W9-CDT-809

Criminal Procedure

Massachusetts Police Manual 2022

**The Massachusetts Police Reference
for Criminal Procedure**

Current up to February 21, 2022

Print date July 18, 2022

John Sofis Scheft, Esq.

with **Lisa A. Sofis**

Law Enforcement Dimensions, LLC
7 Central Street, Suite 100
Arlington, Massachusetts 02476
781-646-4377
Fax 781-646-1776
www.ledimensions.com

Goodway Group of Massachusetts
16 A Street, Burlington, MA 01803

ISBN 978-1-944630-56-0

Part No: 14141

John Sofis Scheft, Esq.

About the Author

John Sofis Scheft has been providing specialized legal training and promotional examination seminars for over twenty-five years, with a record unmatched in Massachusetts. Among the many topics addressed: criminal law, narcotics offenses, domestic violence, stop & frisk, searches with and without warrants, interrogations and identifications, court testimony and report writing, sexual assault investigation, and juvenile law and procedure.

Aside from legal preparation, John Scheft performs consulting services for police agencies concerning management. He has also developed programs in community policing, problem solving and street mediation.

Scheft has taught extensively for the Drug Enforcement Administration (DEA), Massachusetts State Police, Boston Police, Massachusetts Juvenile Police Officers Association, Massachusetts Criminal Justice Training Council, Maine District Attorney's Association, New England Community Police Partnership, and police academies and departments throughout the Commonwealth.

From 1993 to 1995, Scheft served as Director of the Attorney General's Elderly Protection Project, which provided multi-disciplinary training to police officers on community policing issues affecting the elderly. Funded through a national grant, the Project received a 1994 innovation award from the U.S. Department of Justice.

Prior to serving with the Attorney General, Scheft worked as an Assistant District Attorney in Middlesex County, Massachusetts, where he became a specialist in child abuse and hard core juvenile offender cases. A graduate of Harvard University and Northeastern University School of Law, John Scheft lives with his wife and two children in Arlington, Massachusetts.

Quick Find for Key Topics

A

Arrest
- booking 10-1, 18-1
- jurisdiction 8-2
- probable cause 2-3
- right of 7-6
- warrant 7-1

Automatic License Plate Reader 20-14

B

Body-worn cameras (BWC) 20-10

C

Cell Phone Searches 17-10, 20-1
Comm Caretaker 2-22, 4-30
Complaint 7-10
Computer Recs 13-1, 14-8, 20-7
Consent Search 15-1, 15-8 (mv), 15-6 (homes)
Controlled Buy 3-21

D

De-escalation 6-2
Detention (see Investigative Detention)
Domestic Violence, entry 16-9
Duty to Intervene 6-8

E

E-911 16-13
Emergency Aid 16-13, 20-15
Encounter 2-2, 4-5, 5-1
Exculpatory Evidence 1-10
Execute Warrant 8-9, 14-1
Exigent Circumstances 16-1
- domestic violence 16-9
- factors home entry 16-19
- fires 16-18
- homes 16-7
  - hot pursuit 16-7
  - house parties 16-11
Exit Orders 4-21
Eyewitness Evidence 25-10

F

Fire Scene 16-18
Flashlight use 4-18, 11-12
Force, use of 6-1
Foreign National 10-6
Fresh Pursuit 8-3
Frisks 5-1
- packages 5-12
- person 5-9
- vehicle 5-13

G

GPS Tracking 20-18
Gun Possession 3-15

H

Handcuffing, pre-arrest 4-15
House Parties 16-11

I

Identifications 24-1, 25-19
- field views 25-10
- lineups 25-12
- showups 25-5
Incident to Arrest, search 17-1
- packages 17-14
- person 17-7
- vehicle 17-14
Informants
- basis of knowledge 3-7
- corroboration 3-11
- veracity or reliability 3-4
Interrogation (see Miranda)
Inventory 18-1 (book), 18-4 (mv)
Investigative detention 4-1
- duration 4-16
- activities 4-16
- movement 4-18

J

Jurisdiction, for arrests 8-1

K

K-9 4-31
Knock & Announce 14-3

L

Lineups 25-12

M

Mental Health Emergency 9-8
Miranda 22-1
- custody 22-2
- interrogation 22-10
- juveniles 22-20
- mandatory recording 22-23
- public safety exception 22-15
- waiver 22-17
Motor Vehicle Exception 16-1
Motor Vehicle Stops
- dealing with driver 4-19
- dealing with passengers 4-20, 4-23 & 4-31
- exit orders 4-22
- inventory 18-1
- search incident 17-14
Mutual Aid 8-4

N

Names
- field ID checks 4-16
- vehicle stops 4-21 & 4-27

O

One-Party Wire/Blood 20-27

P

Phone Call, right to 10-1
Plain Feel 5-11
Plain View 12-1
Pole Cameras 20-12
Probable Cause 2-3
Protective Custody 9-1
Protective Sweep 17-11

R

Racial Profiling 2-15
Reasonable Expect Privacy 11-4
Reasonable Suspicion 2-3
Rental Vehicles 18-9

S

Seizure, definition of 4-5
Strip Search 17-3
Suicide 10-3

T

Threshold Inquiry (see Investigative Detention)
Traffic Stop (see MV Stop)

U

Use of Force (UOF) 6-1

W

Warrants
- arrest 7-1
- execution of 14-1
- search 13-1
Wiretaps 20-21

Q, V, X, Y, Z (no entries)

Key Changes for 2022 Criminal Procedure

✓ Definition of untruthfulness that POST applies to police officers under 6E, § 1. Pg. 1-8.

✓ A roadside community caretaking encounter did not justify a traffic stop when the car drove away. *Comm. v. Aulston*, 2021 WL 1889757 (Appeals Court). Pg. 2-23.

✓ A community caretaking encounter may transform into the detention of a possibly impaired driver. *Comm. v. Sargsyan*, 99 Mass. App. Ct. 114 (2021). Pg. 2-23.

✓ Example of rejected roadside investigation during traffic stop. *Comm. v. Soriana-Lara*, 99 Mass. App. Ct. 525 (2021). Pg. 4-19.

✓ Suggesting the driver open the glovebox to find the registration is not a search. *Comm. v. Gervet*, 2021 WL 4805267 (Appeals Court). Pg. 4-26.

✓ Furnishing marijuana applies to under 21 year old occupants in vehicle. *Comm. v. Ellis*, 2021 WL 162599 (Appeals Court). Pg. 4-27.

✓ Inconsistently nervous behavior of known citizen is very relevant. *Comm. v. Hem*, 2021 WL 684237 (Appeals Court). Pg. 5-4.

✓ Example of experience leading to valid stop of young woman for illegal gun possession. *Comm. v. Karen K.*, 99 Mass. App. Ct. 216 (2021). Pg. 5-6.

✓ New chapter on de-escalation and use of force (UOF) under police reform. 6E, §§ 1, 14, 15, and 555 CMR 6.0. Pg. 6-1.

✓ Massachusetts police officers must be certified by the Peace Officer Standards and Training (POST) Commission. 6E, §§ 1, 4. Pg. 8-1.

✓ No expectation of privacy for suspect patient in intensive care unit (ICU). *Comm. v. Welch*, 487 Mass. 425 (2021). Pg. 11-15.

✓ Automatic standing does not apply to unlawful possession at an earlier time. *Comm. v DeJesus*, 99 Mass. App. Ct. 275 (2021). Pg. 11-19.

✓ When outside activity is involved, there must be multiple sales in order for police to have probable cause to search the dealer's residence. *Comm. v. Defrancesco*, 99 Mass. App. Ct. 208 (2021). Pg. 13-4.

✓ Unlike a felony, misdemeanors may be quite minor. This is why hot pursuit into a home is not always permitted. *Lange v. California*, 141 S.Ct 2011 (2021). Pg. 16-7.

✓ Police may not delay their impoundment decision pending the results of their inventory. *Comm. v. Lek*, 99 Mass. App. Ct. 199 (2021). Pg. 18-5.

✓ Inventory proper even if driver allowed to leave in the tow truck. *U.S. v. Rivera*, 988 F.3d 579 (1st Cir. 2021). Pg. 18-5.

✓ A warrant affidavit for an electronic device should state a date range for the relevant events, which will limit the time period to explore for relevant information. *Comm. v. Snow,* 486 Mass. 582 (2021). Pgs. 20-5 and 20-3 (facts of case).

✓ Good example of "confirming circumstances" showing texts came from the defendant in violation of 209A order. *Comm. v. Gonsalves*, 99 Mass. App. Ct. 638 (2021). Pg. 20-8.

✓ When done for a new investigation, police must get a search warrant to review bodycam footage from inside a home. SJC approved warrantless review of bodycam for reports and resolving citizen complaints. *Comm. v. Yusuf,* 488 Mass. 379 (2021). Pg. 20-10.

✓ 6, § 220 authorizes the police use of facial recognition undertaken by the State Police, FBI, or registry, if supported by written, reasonable suspicion. Pg. 20-13.

✓ No warrant required for limited search of CharlieCard data and accompanying video surveillance. *Comm. v. Henley,* 488 Mass. 95 (2021). Pg. 20-15.

✓ A police request to a company for CSLI may not take the place of a search warrant. *Comm. v. Gumkowski,* 487 Mass. 314 (2021). Pg. 20-15.

✓ GPS movement data requires expert testimony to prove its accuracy. *Comm. v. Davis,* 487 Mass. 488 (2021). Pg. 20-19.

✓ *Miranda* warnings must be conveyed in a language the defendant understands. *Comm. v. Rosario*, 2021 WL 1263892 (Appeals Court). Pg. 22-18.

Procedure Contents

PART I: CONTEXT

Chapter 1. The Constitution & Law Enforcement

The Legacy of the Revolution: A Constitutional System 1-1
  Intrusive Activities Regulated 1-1
  Policing Under Federal & State Constitutions 1-1
  The United States Constitution 1-2
  The Massachusetts Constitution 1-3
Making Rights Mean Something: The Exclusionary Rule 1-3
  "Fruit of the Poisonous Tree" 1-4
  Exceptions to the Exclusionary Rule 1-4
    Attenuation 1-4
    Independent source 1-5
    Inevitable discovery 1-6
    Collateral proceedings 1-6
The Legacy of the Constitution: Ethical Police Officers 1-7
  Truthful Reports & Testimony 1-8
  Adequate Investigation 1-9
  Exculpatory Evidence 1-10

Chapter 2. Police Information: Officer Observations

The Need for Information: Official Duties 2-1
Constitutional Activities & Levels of Information 2-1
  The 3 Levels 2-2
  Comparing Reasonable Suspicion & Probable Cause 2-3
    The differences 2-3
    The similarities 2-4
    Collective knowledge doctrine 2-5
Officer Observations & Investigation 2-6
Environment 2-6
Suspicious Behavior & Background 2-7
  Unusual Activity 2-7
  Violation of Ordinance or Bylaw 2-7
  Recovering Evidence or Contraband 2-8
  Concealing or Transferring Possible Contraband 2-8
  Apprehension or Flight 2-10

Record, Reputation, & Association 2-12
Evasive or Implausible Responses 2-12
Admission or Confession 2-13
Identification 2-13
Investigation Techniques 2-14
Motor Vehicle Stops 2-14
Traffic Infraction 2-14
Parking Violation 2-20
Marijuana Odor 2-20
Information from Motor Vehicle Databases 2-21
Community Caretaking 2-22
Criminal Activity 2-24

Chapter 3. Police Information: Secondary Sources

SOURCES 3-1
Identified Citizens 3-1
Identifiable Citizens 3-1
Spontaneous street report 3-1
911 call 3-2
CAD sheet 3-3
Confidential Informants 3-3
Purpose of confidentiality 3-3
Disclosure of identity 3-3
Disclosure of surveillance location 3-4
Anonymous Informants 3-4
Test for Reliability 3-4
Veracity 3-4
Identified or Identifiable Citizen 3-4
Track Record 3-5
Confirmed arrest or conviction 3-5
Confirmed information 3-5
Track record endures 3-6
Admission of Criminal Conduct 3-6
Payment or Promises 3-7
Basis of Knowledge 3-7
When Basis of Knowledge Must be Satisfied 3-7
All informants 3-7
Police channels 3-7
Police K-9 3-8
How to Prove Basis of Knowledge 3-8
Explain the source 3-8
Provide a high level of detail 3-9
Informant's informant 3-9
Best practice — Convey source & details of tip 3-10

Corroboration 3-11
    Suspect or Vehicle Near Recent Crime Scene 3-13
    Report of Impaired Operator 3-14
    Report of Gun Possession 3-15
        Report of gun, by itself, insufficient 3-15
        Plus factors 3-16
        Adequate description of person with gun 3-19
        Authority to demand license 3-19
    Future Event Predicted 3-20
    Multiple Sources 3-20
    Controlled Buy 3-21
    Undercover Buy 3-22
    Trash Inspection 3-22
    Surveillance 3-22
    Innocent Details 3-23
    Records 3-23

Entrapment or Agency 3-23

PART II: ENCOUNTERS, INVESTIGATIVE DETENTIONS, & FRISKS

Chapter 4. Encounters & Investigative Detentions

Origin & Overview 4-1
    Detention & Frisk Overview Chart 4-3
Difference Between Encounter & Detention 4-5
  Introduction 4-5
  Restraint 4-5
  Pursuit 4-6
    Pursuit: Obvious Intent to Detain 4-6
    Surveillance: No Show of Authority 4-7
        Suspects on foot 4-8
        Suspects in a stationary vehicle 4-9
        Suspects in a moving vehicle 4-9
        Checking plate number of vehicle 4-9
  Command 4-10
    Normal Interaction 4-10
    Nonintrusive, Protective Measures 4-11
    Authoritative Communication 4-12
    Checking Identification 4-12
    Activating Cruiser Lights 4-12
Investigative Detention 4-13
  Initiation 4-13

Scope 4-15
  Length 4-15
  Investigative Activities 4-15
    Check identity and warrants 4-15
    Take photograph and/or prints 4-16
    Interview suspect and witnesses 4-16
    Conduct identification procedure 4-17
  Avoid Moving Suspect 4-17
Traffic Stops 4-18
  Initial Interaction 4-18
    Driver 4-18
    Passengers 4-20
  Exit Orders 4-21
    Officer Safety 4-21
    Investigation 4-25
      Operator without license or proper registration 4-25
      Operator possibly under the influence of alcohol (OUI) 4-26
      Operator possibly under the influence or distributing marijuana . . 4-27
      Occupants possibly involved in any crime 4-29
    Police Function 4-30
    Community Caretaking 4-30
  K-9 Use 4-31
    Drug Investigation 4-31
    Firearms Investigation 4-32
Checkpoints & Roadblocks 4-33
  Administrative Checkpoint 4-33
  Sobriety Checkpoint 4-33
  Crime Control Roadblock 4-33
  Public Information Checkpoint 4-34
  Fleeing Felon Roadblock 4-34

Chapter 5. Frisks

Frisk Foundation 5-1
Basis & Method 5-1
  Frisk Factors 5-1
    Crime Under Investigation 5-1
    Environment & Time 5-2
    Advance Information 5-2
    Suspect's Background 5-3
    Suspect's Behavior 5-4
      Acting nervous 5-4
      Evading police 5-4
      Observing possible weapon 5-5

Reaching toward possible weapon 5-5
Failing to obey reasonable commands 5-7
Acknowledging possession of a weapon 5-7
Collateral Individuals 5-7
Companion of suspect 5-7
Individual provided with police transport 5-8

Timing 5-8

Scope 5-9
Persons 5-9
Removing object that might be a weapon 5-9
Plain feel doctrine 5-11
Possessions 5-12
Vehicles 5-13

Chapter 6. Police De-escalation & Use of Force

Proper Use Of Force (UOF) 6-1
Police UOF in Context 6-1
Non-deadly Force 6-2
Reasons 6-2
De-escalation 6-2
Proportionate force 6-3
Requirements after non-deadly UOF 6-4
Mass demonstrations 6-5
Deadly Force 6-6
Permissible & Impermissible Reasons 6-6
Additional Requirements After Deadly UOF 6-6
Chokeholds 6-7
Shooting at Vehicles 6-7
Duty to Intervene 6-8

Improper UOF 6-8
Three Potential Consequences 6-8
POST Process 6-9

PART III: ARRESTS

Chapter 7. Charging Offenders with Crimes

Introduction: Three Methods to Charge 7-1

Warrant 7-1
Obtaining an Arrest Warrant 7-1
Written probable cause 7-1
Warrant management system 7-2
Authority Under Arrest Warrant 7-2

Arrest 7-3
   Introduction 7-3
      Arrest Defined 7-3
      Authority, Discretion, & Timing 7-4
      Release of Arrestee. 7-5
   Police Right of Arrest for Massachusetts Offenders 7-6
      Felonies 7-6
      Misdemeanors 7-6
         Statutory right of arrest for a past misdemeanor . . . 7-6
         Statutory right of arrest in officer's presence 7-6
         Breach of peace in officer's presence 7-6
         Municipal laws 7-7
   Right of Arrest for Out-of-State Offenders 7-8
      Fugitive from Justice 7-8
         Warrantless arrest. 7-8
         Fugitive warrant 7-8
         Interstate rendition 7-8
   Probation Officer's Right of Arrest 7-9
   Citizen's Right of Arrest 7-9

Complaint 7-10
      Introduction 7-10
      Four Police Paths 7-10
      One Citizen Path. 7-11
      Application for Criminal Complaint 7-13

Chapter 8. Arrest Jurisdiction & Execution

Jurisdiction from Appointing Authority 8-1
Arrest Warrants: Statewide Enforcement 8-2
Warrantless Arrests 8-2
   Officers Outside of Their Jurisdiction 8-2
      Introduction 8-2
      Outside Jurisdiction: Felonies 8-3
         In Massachusetts: Citizen's arrest. 8-3
         Outside Massachusetts: Fresh pursuit of felon . . . 8-3
         Citizen's stop 8-3
      Outside Jurisdiction: Misdemeanors 8-3
         Mutual aid agreement — 40, § 8G. 8-4
         Fresh pursuit — 41, § 98A 8-5
         Requisition of officers — 41, § 99 8-6
         Transferred authority — 268, § 24. 8-6
         Other grounds. 8-7

Outside Offenders in Officers' Jurisdiction 8-7
    Initiate Investigation 8-7
    Assess Arrest Authority 8-7
    Misdemeanor Rules 8-8
        Statutory right of arrest 8-8
        Continuing breach in presence 8-8
        Complaint 8-9
    Booking Process 8-9

Execution of the Arrest 8-9
  Proper Use of Force 8-9
  Location of Arrest 8-9
    Public Place: Warrantless Arrests Allowed 8-9
    Private Home: Need Warrant, Consent, or Exigent Circumstances . . . 8-10
        Accused inside his home 8-11
        Accused outside his home 8-12
        Accused inside another person's home 8-12
        Exceptions to warrant requirement 8-13

Chapter 9. Protective Custody

Incapacitation with Alcohol or Drugs 9-1
  Alcohol Incapacitation — 111B, § 8 9-1
    Incapacitation 9-1
    Procedures 9-1
        In the field 9-1
        In the station 9-2
        Civil liability 9-3
  Drug Incapacitation — 111E, § 9A 9-4
    Incapacitation 9-4
    Procedures 9-4
        In the field 9-4
        Transport & treatment 9-5
        Narcan protocol 9-5
        Civil liability 9-6
  Juvenile Exposed to Drugs — 94C, § 36 9-7

Medical Emergency 9-7

Mental Health Issues 9-8
  De-escalation & Understanding 9-8
  Mental Health Emergency — 123, § 12 9-10
    Reason for Involuntary Commitment 9-10
    Involuntary Commitment Categories 9-10
    Police Procedures 9-11
    Authority to Transport & Restrain 9-12

Other Interventions 9-12
  Commitment from Police Detention — 123, § 18. 9-12
  Commitment of Alcoholic or Substance Abuser — 123, § 35 9-12
  Longer-Term Hospitalization. 9-13
  Missing Mental Health Patients 9-13
Juvenile Issues 9-13
  Juvenile Runaway — 119, § 39H. 9-13
    Standard for Protective Custody. 9-13
    Proper Procedure 9-14
      Take child into custody. 9-14
      Transport & place child 9-15
  Abandoned or At-Risk Child — 119, § 24. 9-15
    Police Request DCF Assistance. 9-15
    DCF Requests Police Assistance 9-16
Animal Protection. 9-17

Chapter 10. Post-Arrest Procedures

Proper Booking Procedures 10-1
  Reason for Arrest 10-1
  Telephone Access 10-1
  Safe Custody 10-2
    Examine for injury 10-2
    Prevent suicide 10-3
    Prevent sexual abuse 10-3
  Mental Health Treatment Options 10-3
  6 Hour Rule 10-4
  24 Hour Probable Cause Hearing 10-4
  Admission to Bail 10-4
Special Booking Issues 10-4
  OUI Arrestees 10-4
  Juveniles 10-5
    Secure detention: Delinquents 14, 15, 16, & 17 years old 10-5
    Non-secure detention: Delinquents age 12 and 13 10-6
    No detention: All CRA children under age 18 10-6
  Foreign Nationals & Diplomats 10-6
  Federal Immigration Detainers. 10-7

PART IV: SEARCHES

Chapter 11. The Constitutional Definition of a Search

Fundamental Principles 11-1
State Action 11-1
  Law Enforcement Personnel. 11-1

Agents 11-2
   Private Citizens 11-2
   Medical Personnel 11-2
   Private Security Officers 11-3
Government Employees 11-3
   Government Employee Not Involved in Enforcement 11-3
   Public School Administrators 11-3

Reasonable Expectation of Privacy 11-4
Principle Defined 11-4
Persons 11-5
   Citizens in the Community 11-5
   Citizens in Areas of Heightened Security 11-5
   Prisoners & Probationers 11-6
Homes 11-7
   The Curtilage 11-7
   Open Fields 11-9
   Police Activities at the Edge of the Curtilage 11-11
      Overhearing conversations 11-11
      Knocking at door 11-11
      Shining flashlight in window 11-12
      Using binoculars 11-12
      Flying overhead 11-13
      Trying key in door lock 11-13
      K-9 drug detection sniff 11-13
   Technological Intrusion 11-14
Businesses 11-14
Possessions 11-15
   Expectation of Privacy for Possessions 11-15
   Limits of Privacy in Possessions 11-15
      Abandoned property 11-15
      Sniffing by trained dog vs. squeezing by officer 11-17
      Inspecting and testing impounded crash vehicle 11-18

Standing 11-18
Federal Standard: Reasonable Expectation of Privacy . . . 11-18
Massachusetts Rule: Automatic Standing for Possession . . 11-18
   Application of Automatic Standing 11-19
   Information Obtained Unlawfully from Third Parties 11-19

Chapter 12. Plain View

Justification 12-1
Lawful Presence 12-1
   Valid Reasons to be in Private Areas 12-1

Inadvertence 12-2

Apparent Evidence 12-2

    Contraband, Fruits, or Instrumentalities 12-2

    Other Possible Evidence 12-3

Chapter 13. Obtaining Search Warrants

Authority to Issue Search Warrants 13-1

The Affidavit 13-1

  Probable Cause to Search 13-1

    Magistrate Considerations 13-1

    Public Nature of Affidavit 13-2

  Connection Between Evidence & the Place to be Searched . . . 13-2

    Staleness 13-5

    Anticipatory Warrant 13-6

  Particularity of Places, Things, & Persons 13-6

    Particularity as to Places 13-6

    Particularity as to Things 13-8

      Proper descriptions 13-8

      Special rules: Marijuana cultivation 13-8

      Special rules: Alcoholic beverages 13-9

      Third party search warrants 13-10

      Partially defective warrant 13-10

    Particularity as to Persons 13-10

      Named individuals 13-10

      Body cavity searches 13-10

      All persons present 13-11

  Fatal Defects with Affidavits 13-11

Chapter 14. Executing Search Warrants

  Securing an Area Pending Receipt of Warrant 14-1

    Dwellings 14-1

    Persons, Possessions, & Vehicles 14-2

  Timing of Execution 14-2

  Manner of Entry 14-3

    Knock and Announce Rule 14-3

    Knock and Trick 14-3

    No-Knock 14-4

  Post-Entry Conduct 14-5

    Police Interaction with Occupants at the Scene . . . 14-5

      Detaining occupants 14-5

      Frisking & handcuffing occupants 14-5

      Searching occupants 14-6

    Actual Search Process 14-6

Scope of Search 14-7
    General principles 14-7
    Cellars, gardens, and cars 14-7
    Computers, cell phones, and other devices 14-8
Return of Warrant 14-9
Preservation of Evidence 14-9

Chapter 15. Consent

Justification 15-1

Requirements 15-1

Voluntary 15-1
   Standard 15-1
   Police Behavior 15-2
     No force 15-2
     Written consent not required 15-2
     Informed consent not required 15-2
     Pressure to consent 15-3
     Promise of leniency 15-3
   Suspect Characteristics 15-4
     Education, emotions, & substance abuse . . . 15-4
     Reaction to authorities 15-4
     Custody 15-4
   Clear Communication 15-5

Lawful Presence 15-6
   Home or Other Private Building 15-6
     Improper police authority 15-6
     Surreptitious police entry 15-7
     Scope of consent 15-7
     Scientific testing 15-8
   Vehicles 15-8
     Lawful stop 15-8
     Proper request 15-8
     Scope 15-10

Authority 15-11
   Person in Sole Possession 15-11
   Third Party: Joint Access & Control 15-11
     Family relationships 15-13
     Property relationships 15-14
   Apparent Authority 15-16

Chapter 16. Exigent Circumstances

Motor Vehicle Exception 16-1
   Justification 16-1

Requirements 16-1
   Probable Cause. 16-2
      Probable cause <u>after</u> stop 16-2
      Probable cause <u>before</u> stop 16-3
   Location of Search 16-5
   Scope of Search. 16-6

Home Exigency 16-7
  Hot Pursuit 16-7
  Potential Crime Scene 16-9
  Domestic Violence 16-9
    Reasons for Entry 16-9
      Serve restraining order 16-9
      Determine whether abuse occurring 16-9
      Reasonable belief subject of order present . . 16-10
    Limit on Entry 16-10
  Disturbance 16-11
    Loud Party 16-11
    Underage Drinking or Marijuana Use 16-12
  Emergency Aid 16-13
    E-911 hang up 16-13
    Injury Risk 16-14
    Suicide Risk 16-15
    Gas Leak 16-16
    Animal Safety 16-17
    Scope of Emergency Aid 16-17
  Fire Scene 16-18
    Warrantless Entry 16-18
    Administrative Warrant 16-19
    Search Warrant 16-19
  Danger of Violence, Destruction of Evidence, or Escape . . . 16-19
    Improper to Create Exigency 16-20
    Violent Crime 16-21
    Awareness of Police 16-21
    Unanticipated Offender Behavior 16-22
    Destruction or Loss of Evidence 16-22

Chapter 17. Search Incident to Arrest

Incident to Probable Cause or the Actual Arrest 17-1
  At Time of Probable Cause 17-1
  Situations Where Search Incident to Arrest Delayed . . . 17-2
    Searches at the station 17-2
    Strip searches 17-3

Scope of Search Incident to Arrest 17-6
   276, § 1 Restrictions 17-6
   People 17-7
      Body of the arrestee 17-7
      "Grabbing area" even when handcuffed 17-7
      Minimal impact of 276, § 1 17-7
      Keys 17-9
      Cell phones 17-10
      Moving arrestee and securing area 17-11
   Protective Sweep 17-11
      Automatic sweep of immediate area 17-11
      Beyond immediate area, reasonable suspicion of danger 17-11
   Motor Vehicles 17-14
      Passenger compartment & containers 17-14
      Impact of 276, § 1 17-14
   Search of Luggage or Other Containers 17-15

Chapter 18. Inventories

Booking Inventory 18-1
  Justification 18-1
  Requirements 18-1
   Detainee Lawfully in Police Custody 18-1
   Standard Policy 18-2
      Locked containers 18-2
      Medication 18-2
   Scope of Booking Inventory 18-3
   Third-Party Claims to Property 18-4
Inventory of Motor Vehicles 18-4
  Justification 18-4
  Requirements 18-4
   Vehicle Lawfully Impounded 18-4
   Reasonable Alternatives 18-6
      Alternative operator 18-6
      Lawfully parked 18-7
      Authorized impoundment 18-8
      Rental vehicles 18-9
   Scope of Vehicle Inventory 18-9
      Location 18-9
      Conform to policy 18-10
      No pretext for investigative search 18-11

Chapter 19. Administrative Inspections & Searches

Justification 19-1

Application to Massachusetts Businesses 19-2

    Dealers in Controlled Substances 19-2

    Motor Vehicle Dealers 19-3

    Commercial Vehicle Operators 19-3

    Dealers in Firearms 19-3

    Innkeepers 19-4

    Pawnbrokers 19-4

Chapter 20. Electronic Evidence

Digital Devices 20-1

  Cell Phones 20-1

    Intercepting Calls 20-1

    Abandoned or Lost Phones 20-1

    Phones Seized by Police 20-1

        Check for weapon 20-1

        View phone exterior 20-2

        Answer or search if exigent circumstances 20-2

        Secure if probable cause 20-3

        Obtain consent or a warrant 20-3

    Warrant Issues 20-5

    Court Order for Access 20-6

  Digital Cameras 20-6

  Phone & Computer Records 20-7

  Computers 20-7

  Miscellaneous Issues with Electronic Evidence 20-8

    Linking Communication to Defendant 20-8

    Social Media Investigations 20-9

    Third-Party Evidence 20-9

Video Surveillance 20-10

  Police Body Worn Cameras (BWC) 20-10

  Non-Targeted Surveillance 20-12

  Targeted Surveillance 20-12

  Facial Recognition 20-13

Location Monitoring 20-14

  Automated License Plate Reader (ALPR) 20-14

  Public Transportation Records 20-15

Cell Phone Location 20-15
   Search Warrant Required for CSLI 20-15
   Pinging Cell Phone in Emergency 20-16
   Using Cell Phone App to Track 20-17
GPS Tracking Device 20-18
   Police-Initiated Investigation 20-18
   Police Access to Probation GPS Records 20-18
   Private-Initiated Investigation 20-19
Mosaic Analysis 20-20
Secret Recording 20-21
  Purpose of Wiretap Statute 20-21
  Types of Secret Interceptions 20-21
  Other Exceptions to Ban on Secret Recording 20-23
  Nonconsensual Interception by Law Enforcement 20-24
  Pen Registers & Cross Frame Traps 20-26
  One-Party Interception by Law Enforcement 20-26
   Inside Dwelling: *Blood* Warrant 20-27
   Four Exceptions to *Blood* Warrant 20-27
   Consequences of Unlawful Interceptions 20-28

PART V: INTERROGATIONS

Chapter 21. Voluntary Statements Under the Fourteenth Amendment

Introduction 21-1
   Overview of Interrogation Issues 21-2
Fourteenth Amendment Requires Voluntary Statements 21-3
  Rational Speaker 21-3
  Lack of Coercion 21-3
   Police Behavior 21-4
    Physical coercion 21-4
    Threats 21-4
    Withholding or promising medical or mental health treatment . . . 21-5
    Tricks, tactics, & misrepresentations 21-5
    Promises and pressure 21-8
    Legal advice 21-8
    Setting & style of interrogation 21-10

Suspect's Characteristics 21-11
    Age 21-11
    Education 21-11
    Intelligence 21-11
    Mental illness 21-11
    Disability 21-12
    Language proficiency 21-12
    Experience with justice system 21-12
    Self-protection 21-12
    Physical condition 21-13
All Statements Against Accused Must be Voluntary 21-13

Chapter 22. Custodial Interrogation Under the Fifth Amendment & *Miranda*

The *Miranda* Warnings 22-1
When Must the *Miranda* Warnings be Given? 22-1
  Custody 22-2
    Arrest 22-2
    Significant Detention 22-2
      Location of the interrogation 22-2
      Interview style 22-5
      Focus of investigation 22-6
      Freedom to leave 22-6
    Noncustody Situations Where *Miranda* not Required . . . 22-7
      General on-scene questions 22-7
      Investigative detentions 22-7
      Traffic stops, accidents, & sobriety tests 22-8
      Telephone conversations 22-9
      Undercover work 22-9
  Interrogation 22-10
    Questioning 22-10
      Express questions 22-10
      Functional equivalent 22-10
    Testimonial Evidence 22-12
      Physical nontestimonial evidence 22-12
      Verbal nontestimonial evidence 22-14
  Public Safety Exception to Miranda 22-15
  Other Government Officials & Miranda 22-16

How Must *Miranda* Warnings be Waived? 22-17

   Elements of a Valid Waiver 22-17

      Proper Communication of Warnings 22-17

      Voluntary & Knowing Waiver 22-18

      Special Protections for Juveniles 22-20

         Parent or interested adult 22-20

         Mandated interaction 22-21

      Willing to Speak 22-22

         Length of time waiver lasts 22-22

         Polygraph 22-22

   Other Safeguards 22-22

      6 Hour Rule 22-22

      Mandatory Recording 22-23

How Suspects Invoke Their Rights & Officers Must Respond 22-25

   Invocation of Rights 22-25

      Right to Remain Silent 22-25

      Right to Counsel 22-27

         Pre-custodial request 22-27

         Post-custodial request 22-28

         Police response to attorney contact 22-30

   Proper Response to Invocation of Rights 22-32

   Potential to Resume Questioning 22-32

      Right to Silence 22-32

      Right to Counsel 22-33

Consequences of a *Miranda* Violation 22-34

   Adult Miranda Form 22-36

   Juvenile Miranda Form 22-37

   Right of Prompt Arraignment Form 22-38

Chapter 23. Right to Counsel Under Article 12

Right to Counsel Exists upon Indictment or Arraignment 23-1

Scope of Right to Counsel 23-1

   State Action 23-1

   Offense Specific 23-1

Potential Violations of the Right to Counsel 23-2

   Improper Police Conduct 23-2

      Direct communication 23-2

      Use of an informant 23-3

   Proper Police Conduct 23-3

   Improper Conduct by Other Officials 23-4

PART VI: IDENTIFICATIONS

Chapter 24. State Action & Right to Counsel

Principles 24-1

State Action 24-1

Right to Counsel 24-2

    Noncorporeal Procedures: No Right to Counsel 24-2

    Corporeal Procedures: Upon Indictment or Arraignment 24-3

Chapter 25. Fundamental Fairness

Introductory Concepts 25-1

Field Investigation 25-1

    Interviews 25-1

    Corroboration 25-3

Types of Eyewitness Evidence 25-4

Procedures 25-5

Showups 25-5

    Benefits 25-5

    Steps in the Field. 25-5

Field Views 25-10

    Benefits 25-10

    Steps in the Field. 25-11

Photo & Live Lineups 25-12

    Composing Lineups 25-12

    Conducting Sequential Lineups 25-13

    Special Issues. 25-15

Use of Single Photo in the Field. 25-16

Voice Identifications 25-18

Digital Imaging Systems ("Mug Books") 25-18

Composite Sketches 25-19

Identifying Objects 25-19

Documenting Identification Procedures. 25-20

SUBJECT INDEX   S-1

Part I

CONTEXT

Chapters 1 – 3

"In a government of laws, the existence of government will be imperiled if it fails to observe the law scrupulously. Our government is the potent, the omnipresent teacher. For good or for ill, it teaches the whole person by its example. Crime is contagious. If the government becomes a lawbreaker, it breeds contempt for law, it invites every man to become a law unto himself, it invites anarchy. To declare that in the administration of the criminal law, the end justifies the means . . . would bring terrible retribution."

Justice Louis Brandeis
Olmstead v. U.S., 277 U.S. 438 (1928)

The Constitution & Law Enforcement

This book is written for the police officer, supervisor, and commander. It defines and describes essential law enforcement activities that are regulated and shaped by a set of principles contained within our federal and state constitutions.

THE LEGACY OF THE REVOLUTION: A CONSTITUTIONAL SYSTEM

Prior to the Revolution, the British authorities relied extensively on "general warrants and writs of assistance." These warrants allowed British officials to almost indiscriminately violate the privacy of the colonists in support of the crown's efforts to discover wrongdoing. This practice was so hated by the colonists that, after the Revolution, the Bill of Rights was adopted containing the Fourth Amendment (prohibiting illegal searches and seizures), the Fifth Amendment (prohibiting illegal interrogations), and the Sixth Amendment (providing the right to counsel in court). *Comm. v. Cundriff*, 382 Mass. 137 (1980).

Our Constitution stood for the radical proposition that laws are more important than the government officials who enforce them. The Constitution tried to minimize the potential of those who govern to abuse their power.

INTRUSIVE ACTIVITIES REGULATED

Police officers, as societal agents of law and order, are limited when they engage in activities that intrude on the privacy of citizens. When all is said and done, the most intrusive authority that officers have is the power to search, seize, interrogate, and identify. That is why the Constitution limits these fundamental activities. The Constitution tells officers that if they are going to perform these functions, they need a good reason.

POLICING UNDER FEDERAL & STATE CONSTITUTIONS

Officers are governed by the federal constitution <u>and</u> by the Massachusetts Declaration of Rights. In particular, two important state provisions impact police behavior in Massachusetts: Article 14 (which is the Commonwealth's version of the Fourth Amendment) and Article 12 (which is similar to the Fifth and Sixth Amendments).

Our state constitution may never hold officers to a lesser standard than the federal constitution, but it may be more restrictive in how they must investigate. This is sometimes the case in Massachusetts. Federal standards are the floor, while our state standards are the ceiling. This is why, when there is a difference, officers are <u>directed to follow the Massachusetts rule</u> so their conduct is proper within the Commonwealth. See, e.g., *Comm. v. Upton*, 394 Mass. 363 (1985) (Massachusetts has stricter test for establishing an informant's credibility). *Comm. v. Gonsalves*, 429 Mass. 658 (1999) (no automatic exit orders during Massachusetts traffic stop). *Comm. v. Gonzalez*, 426 Mass. 313 (1997) (electronic surveillance issues).

THE UNITED STATES CONSTITUTION
Principles that lie at the heart of policing in a democratic society.
The following portions from the Bill of Rights most directly influence policing in America.

First Amendment

Congress shall make no law respecting an establishment of religion, or prohibiting the free exercise thereof; or abridging the freedom of speech, or of the press; or the right of the people peaceably to assemble, and to petition the Government for a redress of grievances.

Fourth Amendment

The right of the people to be secure in their persons, houses, papers, and effects, against unreasonable searches and seizures, shall not be violated, and no Warrants shall issue, but upon probable cause, supported by Oath or affirmation, and particularly describing the place to be searched, and the persons or things to be seized.

Fifth Amendment

(1) No person shall be held to answer for a capital, or otherwise infamous crime, unless on a presentment or indictment of a Grand Jury, except in cases arising in the land or naval forces, or in the Militia, when in actual service in time of War or public danger; (2) nor shall any person be subject for the same offence to be twice put in jeopardy of life or limb; (3) nor shall he be compelled in any criminal case to be a witness against himself; (4) nor be deprived of life, liberty, or property, without due process of law; (5) nor shall private property be taken for public use without just compensation.

Sixth Amendment

In all criminal prosecutions, (1) the accused shall enjoy the right to a speedy and (2) public trial, (3) by an impartial jury (4) of the State and district wherein the crime shall have been committed, which district shall have been previously ascertained by law, and (5) to be informed of the nature and cause of the accusation, (6) to be confronted with the witnesses against him, (7) to have compulsory process for obtaining witnesses in his favor, and (8) to have the assistance of defense counsel.

Eighth Amendment

Excessive bail shall not be required, nor excessive fines imposed, nor cruel and unusual punishments inflicted.

Fourteenth Amendment

All persons born or naturalized in the United States, and subject to the jurisdiction thereof, are citizens of the United States and of the State wherein they reside. No State shall make or enforce any law which shall abridge the privileges or immunities of citizens of the United States; nor shall any State deprive any person of life, liberty, or property, without due process of law; nor deny to any person within its jurisdiction the equal protection of the laws.

THE MASSACHUSETTS CONSTITUTION
The following portions of the Massachusetts Declaration of Rights are the constitutional principles that directly influence policing in the Commonwealth.

Article 12

No subject shall be held to answer for any crimes or offense, until the same is fully and plainly, substantially and formally, described to him; or be compelled to accuse, or furnish evidence against himself. And every subject shall have a right to produce all proofs that may be favorable to him; to meet the witnesses against him face-to-face, and to be fully heard in his defense by himself, or his counsel, at his election. And no subject shall be arrested, imprisoned, despoiled, or deprived of his property, immunities, or privileges, put out of the protection of the law, exiled, or deprived of his life, liberty, or estate, but by the judgment of his peers, or the law of the land. And the legislature shall not make any law that shall subject any person to a capital or infamous punishment, excepting for the government of the army and navy, without trial by jury.[1]

Article 14

Every subject has a right to be secure from all unreasonable searches, and seizures, of his person, his houses, his papers, and all his possessions. All warrants, therefore, are contrary to this right, if the cause or foundation of them be not previously supported by oath or affirmation; and if the order in the warrant to a civil officer, to make search in suspected places, or to arrest one or more suspected persons, or to seize their property, be not accompanied with a special designation of the persons or objects of search, arrest, or seizure; and no warrant ought to be issued but in cases, and with the formalities prescribed by the law.

MAKING RIGHTS MEAN SOMETHING: THE EXCLUSIONARY RULE

It was not until 1961, in the case of Mapp v. Ohio, that the Supreme Court made the exclusionary rule binding on state law enforcement.[2] Until that decision, officers were told not to violate the Constitution, yet no legal consequences occurred when they did. Declaring that rights were meaningless without some level of enforcement, the U.S. Supreme Court decided in *Mapp* that evidence obtained by unlawful police conduct should be excluded from criminal trials. In announcing its ruling, the court declared:

---

1 Article 12 evolved from a sense of disapproval of the inquisitorial methods of the Star Chamber and ecclesiastical courts in England. *The Colonial and Constitutional History of the Privilege Against Self-Incrimination in America,* 21 Virginia L. Rev. 763 (1935).
2 The facts in *Mapp,* 367 U.S. 643, were particularly egregious. Cleveland police arrived at the home of "Dolly" Mapp, expecting to enter and search for a suspect wanted in connection with an arson/bombing. Mapp refused to let them in and called her attorney. Other officers arrived. They unlocked the back door by breaking a window next to it, and they kicked open the front door. Officers also refused to let Mapp talk with her attorney when he came to the scene. Mapp demanded to see their warrant. When an officer held up a piece of paper, Mapp grabbed it and placed it in her bra. An officer retrieved the paper and arrested Mapp for belligerent conduct. Officers then ransacked her entire home, finally discovering several small pamphlets in a trunk in the basement. The pamphlets had nude sketches, so Mapp was also charged with possession of lewd and lascivious material.

"Our decision, founded on reason and truth, gives to the individual no more than that which the Constitution guarantees him, to the police officer no less than that to which honest law enforcement is entitled, and, to the courts, that judicial integrity so necessary in the true administration of justice."

The exclusionary rule remains controversial. Advocates say that it deters police misconduct while opponents insist that it allows the guilty to go free. Defenders of the rule point to its higher purpose:

"Letting the guilty at times go free is the price our society has agreed to pay in order to put privacy and the integrity of the home beyond the reach of unwarranted police intrusions. The community that fails to insist on scrupulous observance of high standards by its police and prosecutors has lost track of its fundamental purposes, and courts that approve well-meaning but unconstitutional conduct by law enforcement officers, even in the case of undoubtedly guilty defendants, deal the administration of justice and the integrity of the legal process a greater blow than when they permit a particular criminal to delay, or sometimes even wholly to escape, due punishment . . ." *Comm. v. DiGeronimo*, 38 Mass. App. Ct. 714 (1995).

The fact that an officer's conduct produces evidence may never, by itself, justify an improper search or seizure. This is why learning criminal procedure is the foundation of positive outcomes in court.

"FRUIT OF THE POISONOUS TREE"

The exclusionary rule is particularly unforgiving because, with few exceptions, it bars evidence obtained after the <u>initial</u> mistake. For example, even if officers do everything perfectly following a threshold inquiry based on a hunch, that initial, improper detention nullifies any police action that follows. The metaphor, "fruit of the poisonous tree," means that the roots of the poisonous tree (the initial police misconduct) can only produce tainted fruit (whatever evidence is obtained as a result of that misconduct). And that "fruit" is barred from the trial. *Wong Sun v. U.S.*, 371 U.S. 471 (1963). *Comm. v. Reyes*, 38 Mass. App. Ct. 483 (1995).

EXCEPTIONS TO THE EXCLUSIONARY RULE

There are four situations where the exclusionary rule does not apply. They are: (1) the attenuation doctrine; (2) the independent source rule; (3) inevitable discovery; and (4) collateral proceedings.

Attenuation

The attenuation doctrine applies when a court decides that police obtained evidence as an <u>indirect result</u> of their illegal detention or arrest. In other words, the discovery of evidence was "attenuated" or separated from the initial, improper police action. Consider:

- **Time delay.** *Comm. v. Fielding*, 371 Mass. 97 (1976): The SJC found the defendant's confession admissible even though he made it after his arrest on an invalid warrant unsupported by probable cause. The circumstances indicated that the confession was unconnected to the defective warrant: The defendant validly waived his *Miranda* rights a full three hours after his arrest, and the police allowed him to use the telephone to try to call a lawyer before they talked with him. The SJC was reluctant to punish the police in a situation where officers had taken the time to obtain a warrant, and the magistrate had improperly issued it.

  Compare *Comm. v. Yehudi Y., a juvenile*, 56 Mass. App. Ct. 812 (2002): No attenuation when a police officer obtained consent to search the house immediately after he entered the home illegally. His consent search exploited his improper entry.

- **Separate location**. When police improperly engage in a warrantless arrest of a suspect in his home, statements made *inside* his home are inadmissible. However, statements acquired *outside* his home are admissible if the underlying arrest was supported by probable cause. Since police would have been authorized to arrest the suspect when he came outside anyway, their later acquisition of statements is unconnected to the improper entry. *New York v. Harris*, 495 U.S. 14 (1990). *Comm. v. Marquez*, 434 Mass. 370 (2001).

  On the other hand, physical evidence *will* be suppressed whether obtained inside or outside the home. Unlike statements, the court views evidence possessed by the defendant at the time of arrest as the product of the improper arrest even if the police collected it outside the home. *Comm. v. Tyree*, 455 Mass. 676 (2010) (improper police entry tainted eventual acquisition of shoes worn by the defendant during a robbery; fact that they were later removed at the station was irrelevant).

- **Intervening event.** This will sometimes eliminate the taint of an illegal stop or arrest. *Comm. v. Maldonado*, 55 Mass. App. 450 (2002): Maldonado was the passenger in the car Lt. Hussey stopped, hoping to obtain information about a shooting. Hussey lacked reasonable suspicion, so the stop was unlawful. He did discover that the license of the driver, Arnaldo Burgos, had been suspended. Burgos was arrested. The car was registered to Maldonado's wife, but his license was also suspended. After Lt. Hussey told him that he would be released and the car towed, Maldonado asked if he could call his wife to pick up the vehicle. Hussey told him to use a nearby pay phone. Instead of calling his wife, Maldonado returned to the car. Another officer saw him get in and, on closer inspection, observed a gun on his lap. Maldonado was arrested for unlawful possession of a firearm.

  The gun was *not* suppressed because it was not really related to the initial stop. Lt. Hussey told Maldonado that he was free to call his wife and leave. His decision to return to the car was a voluntary act — attenuated from the initial stop — and caused police to discover his illegal weapon. Also see *Comm. v. Suters*, 90 Mass. App. Ct. 449 (2016).

Independent source

The independent source rule recognizes that officers should not be penalized for unconstitutional activity when the evidence also came from another, legitimate source. *Comm. v. Frodyma*, 393 Mass. 438 (1984) involved a state investigator who properly learned about a pharmacist who was illegally dealing drugs. Before the investigator could apply for a warrant, federal agents obtained an invalid warrant for the same pharmacy. Since the state investigator did not "exploit" the illegal federal conduct in any way, the SJC said it did not make sense to exclude the evidence that he lawfully acquired. *Comm. v. Pearson*, 486 Mass. 809 (2021).

Inevitable discovery

Under inevitable discovery, the issue is whether unlawfully found evidence would have eventually been discovered lawfully. To decide this issue, courts focus on:

- *Whether the evidence would, as a practical matter, have been found legally,* and

- *The character of the police misconduct that uncovered it in the first place.*

- **Successful case.** In *Comm. v. O'Connor*, 406 Mass. 112 (1989), the inevitable discovery exception applied to evidence seized from O'Connor, an incapacitated defendant being placed into protective custody. Although the officer improperly seized drugs from O'Connor during an initial frisk for weapons, there was no question the drugs would have been found during his booking inventory at the station. Also see *Comm. v. Ubilez*, 88 Mass. App. Ct. 814 (2016).

- **Unsuccessful case.** *Comm. v. Perrot*, 407 Mass. 539 (1990): The rape victim's pocketbook, which police found only after obtaining a statement from the defendant *in violation* of his right to counsel, would not have been inevitably discovered by lawful means. As a result, it was inadmissible in his prosecution for aggravated rape. The pocketbook had not been found in the ten days since the rape so its eventual discovery was uncertain, and the violation of the defendant's right to counsel was obvious.

Evidence seized in violation of the search warrant requirement will not be admitted even if its later discovery was inevitable. The SJC views the warrant requirement as too important to disolve on this basis. *Comm. v. Benoit*, 382 Mass. 210 (1981).

Collateral proceedings

The exclusionary rule prevents police from using illegally obtained evidence to prove their case at trial, but it does not eliminate using the evidence for all purposes. Here is a list of permissible "collateral" uses for suppressed evidence:

- **Impeach a defendant's false testimony.** When a lawyer challenges the credibility of a witness by presenting evidence that the witness previously told a different story, this cross examination strategy is called "impeachment." *Comm. v. Harris*, 364 Mass. 236 (1973) held that statements obtained in violation of a defendant's *Miranda* rights are still admissible to impeach his inconsistent trial testimony.

- **Revoke a defendant's probation or parole.** *Comm. v. Vincente*, 405 Mass. 278 (1989).

- **Remove children from the custody of their unfit parent(s).** *Care and Protection of Frank*, 409 Mass. 492 (1991).

- **Discharge or discipline a public employee.** *Kelly v. Civil Service Commission*, 427 Mass. 75 (1998) (Holyoke police arrested a Chicopee firefighter for an expired license and discovered cocaine; while evidence was suppressed in his criminal case, it was properly admitted in his Chicopee discharge hearing).

However, evidence may not be used when the investigators are employed by the same municipality as the disciplined employee. *Selectmen of Framingham v. BMC*, 373 Mass. 783 (1977) (Framingham officers illegally entered the home of an officer who had been shot; their entry allowed them to determine that he had lied about the way he was wounded, but the court would not allow the town to terminate its employee with improperly obtained evidence from its own police officers).

- **Prove a civil case.** *Carey v. Zayre of Beverly, Inc.*, 367 Mass. 125 (1975) (illegally seized evidence by police still admissible in civil action between two private parties). *U.S. v. Janis*, 428 U.S. 433 (1976) (illegally obtained evidence by state officers held admissible in a civil action for the collection of federal taxes).

  One exception to this rule: Suppressed evidence in a criminal drug prosecution is excluded from any civil forfeiture action. *Comm. v. One 1985 Ford*, 416 Mass. 603 (1993).

While there are certain exceptions to the exclusionary rule, police officers should not plan their investigative tactics around them. The best police work is undertaken with a working knowledge of constitutional principles, then the exclusionary rule does not become an issue.

Of course, many variables affect how a court will view investigative actions in a given case — the law's clarity or lack of clarity, the competence of the judge and attorneys, the local customs and attitudes toward the case under review, the experience and skill of the officers, and so forth. The fact that a court approves of officer conduct is no guarantee that it was performed properly. By the same token, the fact that a court disapproves is no absolute indicator that officers performed incorrectly. In short, the results are not always the best guide.

The only thing we can say for certain: Officers should always do their best to comply with the legal standards that govern their street performance. This author's hope is that this book helps the police meet their constitutional commitments in a way that fosters their safety, investigative effectiveness, and community standing.

THE LEGACY OF THE CONSTITUTION: ETHICAL POLICE OFFICERS

Police officers swear an oath to uphold the Constitution. It is a solemn promise that officers, throughout their career, will:

- Treat all citizens fairly and without discrimination;

- Only infringe on citizens' freedom for good cause;

- Use reasonable methods to conduct seizures and searches;

- Identify offenders fairly and accurately;

- Seek voluntary and accurate statements from accused citizens;

- **Protect citizen privacy from unreasonable physical and technological intrusions;**

- **Write reports and testify truthfully; and**

- **Disclose exculpatory evidence.**

Staying true to constitutional principles is easier said than done. Police officers get tempted to cut corners and rush to judgment but, in public safety, the end does not justify the means.

Although investigating crime is a competitive undertaking, officers must always remain objective and fair. This is why officers have three basic ethical obligations: (1) write and testify truthfully; (2) investigate adequately; and (3) disclose exculpatory evidence.[3]

TRUTHFUL REPORTS & TESTIMONY

The integrity of our criminal justice system depends on honest police officers. For this reason, it is a crime for officers to lie in a report or at court. 268, § 6A (false written report by public officer). 268, § 13B (lying to obstruct an investigation). 268, § 1A (perjury).[4] See, e.g., *Comm. v. Garvey*, 99 Mass. App. Ct. 139 (2021): Officer Garvey's report contained false statements, including that the victim bumped the officer several times. This lie, in particular, was designed to justify Garvey's use of OC spray and her baton. Her conviction for filing a false report (268, § 6A) was upheld.

The Peace Officer Standards & Training (POST) Commission regulates police behavior and may punish untruthful officers. Under 6E, § 1, untruthful officers:

- **Knowingly;**

- **Either:**

  - *Make an untruthful statement* about a material (i.e., important) fact; or

  - *Omit a material fact* from their statement; and

- **Their communication or failure to communicate occurs:**

  - In *any criminal justice record* (e.g., a police report, CAD entry, etc.); or

  - While *testifying* under oath; or

  - To the *POST Commission* or a POST employee; or

  - During an *Internal Affairs* (IA) investigation, or *administrative* investigation, or *disciplinary process.*

---

3 This discussion deals with the obvious ethical duties incumbent on every law enforcement professional. Of course, policing involves other, more complex ethical decisions, where the right or wrong action is not easy to determine. Navigating these situations is a more involved conversation. An excellent book for this purpose is Dr. Jeff Green's *Decision Point: Real-life Ethical Dilemmas in Law Enforcement* (2nd ed., Glocal Press).
4 For a breakdown of all of these crimes, see *LED's Criminal Law, Chapter 35.*

Because honesty is so integral to constitutional law enforcement, police departments may terminate dishonest officers. In *City of Boston v. Boston Police Patrolman's Association,* 443 Mass. 813 (2005), Officer DiSciullo got into an altercation with a man and his girlfriend. Both were sitting in a double-parked car. The situation got extremely heated. DiSciullo called the woman "a bitch," then arrested her and her boyfriend.

DiSciullo filed a report alleging disorderly conduct and resisting arrest. He claimed that he was repeatedly assaulted and suffered pain in his arm and right shoulder. None of that happened.

DiSciullo continued to lie in disciplinary hearings. The arbitrator decided to suspend DiSciullo for one year. On appeal, the SJC allowed the city to fire him, declaring: "Police legitimacy [is] damaged severely by . . . employ[ing] a police officer who ha[s] illegally abused his power and repeatedly lied about it under oath." Also see *City of Pittsfield v. Local 447 IBPO,* 480 Mass. 634 (2018).

Even minor falsehoods may lead to termination because of their impact on an officer's ability to be a credible witness. *Kinnas v. Town of Shrewsbury,* 24 MCSR 67 (2011) (when asked if he had accessed and posted on another person's open Facebook account in the police station, the officer said "no"; this lie allowed the police chief to see the officer as "damaged goods" whose untruthfulness might require disclosure to every defendant in future cases; his termination was upheld).

Officers may not justify filing a false report or lying on the grounds that they were following orders. *Comm. v. Luna,* 418 Mass. 749 (1994) (detective invented informants in his search warrant affidavits and blamed it on pressure from his drug unit supervisors; the SJC rejected his defense saying, even if true, it was no excuse).

ADEQUATE INVESTIGATION

Fairness demands that officers properly investigate. This means officers must interview witnesses, collect and preserve evidence, and follow up on reasonable leads. Consider *White v. Town of Marblehead,* 989 F.Supp. 345 (D. Mass. 1997): One evening officers were dispatched to a bar. Sandee Muxica said she had been assaulted by her boyfriend Dr. William White. The officers did not interview anyone else at the bar. They went to White's apartment, but he was not home. They took Muxica to the station and got her a 209A order.

The next day, another officer served White with the order. White denied pushing Muxica. He told the officer that, during dinner, Muxica had informed him she was not a law student (which she had led him to believe), but a stripper. She began to perform at the table, removing her clothes and exposing her breast to the bartender. (The bartender later corroborated this version.) White left the bar in disgust. The officer did not relay this information to the lieutenant in charge of the investigation, who then arrested White the next day. The charges were dismissed and White sued the police. Also see *Comm. v. Bowden,* 379 Mass. 472 (1980) (defendant may present evidence that the police investigation was incompetent).

EXCULPATORY EVIDENCE

Officers must disclose exculpatory evidence to the prosecutor, who then must turn it over to defense counsel. *Brady v. Maryland*, 373 U.S. 83 (1963). *Giglio v. U.S.*, 405 U.S. 150 (1972).

Exculpatory evidence includes information:

- **Consistent with the defendant's innocence** — e.g., a witness who fails to identify the suspect; or DNA results that do not match; or surveillance video showing a different person leaving the crime scene. Even if officers believe that exculpatory evidence fails to outweigh evidence of their suspect's guilt, they *must* still document it and give it to the prosecutor. If exculpatory evidence is a physical item, officers must preserve it in the evidence room.

  Consider *Comm. v. Green*, 72 Mass. App. Ct. 903 (2008): Derrick Green was arrested for possessing cocaine with intent to distribute. One of the central pieces of evidence against him was $1,950, found neatly folded in his pocket. At trial, Green offered the testimony of his friend, Precious Butler, who said the money was hers and she had called police to claim it. Two police officers contradicted her testimony. They had checked the log and found no evidence to support her claim. However, there was evidence that Butler made six telephone calls to police the day Green was arrested! Two recorded calls demonstrated that Butler demanded the money exactly as she reported. This information should have been included in the investigating officer's report and turned over to the prosecutor.

- **About a witness' past dishonesty.** *Comm. v. McMillan*, 98 Mass. App. Ct. 409 (2020): Law enforcement officers assigned to a federal task force observed a controlled buy in which their confidential informant (CI) used federal money to purchase heroin from the defendant. By the time of trial, however, their CI had been federally charged with theft of government money because, on five occasions, he had hidden some of the buy money in his shoe, stealing at least $685. Defense counsel should have received this information.

- **About a police officer's past dishonesty, bias, or criminal conduct.** *Matter of a Grand Jury Investigation*, 485 Mass. 641 (2020): A District Attorney received a video of an officer striking an arrestee who was not resisting. This officer had filed resisting arrest charges and lied in his report about what happened. He was prosecuted and lost his job.

Two other officers, who were there, presented the same dishonest version in their reports. They were granted immunity before the grand jury, but terminated afterwards for lying to conceal police brutality. In approving these results, the SJC:

- *Authorized prosecutors to inform a police chief about misconduct,* even if learned during secret grand jury testimony, because it complicates future investigations and prosecutions involving the identified officers. A chief needs to make personnel decisions — including termination — to ensure the integrity of the department.

- *Required that prosecutors keep a "Brady list"* of officers who have a prior history of criminal conduct, official dishonesty, on-duty bias, or falsified evidence. Prosecutors must notify all future defendants when officers on their *Brady* list might be a witness. While prosecutors must disclose *Brady* information, the trial judge ultimately decides whether the information is relevant to the trial.

Police Information: Officer Observations

THE NEED FOR INFORMATION: OFFICIAL DUTIES
CONSTITUTIONAL ACTIVITIES & LEVELS OF INFORMATION

The constitution regulates four physical intrusions performed by officers:[1]

- **Threshold inquiries:** Brief detentions to determine whether citizens are engaging in criminal conduct.

- **Frisks:** Pat downs of citizens' clothing, possessions, and/or vehicles to determine whether they are armed.

- **Arrests:** Taking citizens into formal custody because they have committed a crime.

- **Searches:** Intrusions into private areas to look for evidence of crime.

Officers must have sufficient information to justify their intrusive activity. The more invasive the conduct, the more information police must possess. If officers want to detain a citizen and/or perform a limited frisk to check for weapons, they need reasonable suspicion. But if they arrest the person and/or search him, they must have a higher degree of information — probable cause. Once the case goes to court, officers, assisted by prosecuting attorneys, must provide proof to the highest degree — beyond a reasonable doubt — to gain a conviction.

Officers typically develop information along a continuum. They may start with a hunch, gradually move to reasonable suspicion, then develop probable cause. It is critical that officers understand the amount of information that must be gathered in order to justify each investigative activity.

---

1 The other two constitutionally significant activities undertaken by police are: (1) identifying perpetrators; and (2) interrogating suspects — discussed in *Chapters 21, 22, 23* (interrogation) and *24, 25* (identifications).

THE 3 LEVELS

Constitutional Principle: The more trustworthy the information, the more intrusive the police conduct.

Level of Information	Definition	Permissible Police Conduct
Hunch	**Intuition** A hunch is an intuitive or "gut feeling" about something. Often described by officers as "instinct."	**Field Encounter** Officers observe and speak with a subject. However, officers cannot compel the subject to stay or even interact with them.
Reasonable Suspicion	**Explanation** Reasonable suspicion is more concrete than a hunch and involves specific facts that lead an objective police officer to suspect: (1) criminal activity has, is, or will occur; and sometimes (2) the suspect may be armed and dangerous.	**Threshold Inquiry *and/or* Frisk** • If a crime suspected, then conduct a <u>threshold inquiry</u>; • If crime and danger suspected, then <u>frisk</u>.
Probable Cause	**More Likely Than Not** Probable cause leads an officer to believe it is more likely than not that: (1) the suspect has committed or is committing a crime; and/or (2) evidence will be found in a particular place.	**Charge *and/or* Search** • <u>Charge a crime</u> by warrant, arrest, or complaint. • <u>Search for evidence</u> with or without a warrant.
When the case goes to trial . . .		
Proof Beyond A Reasonable Doubt	**To a Moral Certainty** Evidence convinces, to a moral certainty, the jury or judge (sitting without a jury) of the guilt of the accused beyond a reasonable doubt — not beyond all possible doubt, but to a high degree of certainty.	**Court Imposed Punishment & Conditions** Punishment depends on the type of crime and may include incarceration, fines, probation, and mandated programs (e.g., substance abuse, anger management, victim restitution).

Comparison of
REASONABLE SUSPICION
& PROBABLE CAUSE

Reasonable Suspicion	Probable Cause
• **Trustworthy.** There are trustworthy;	• **Trustworthy.** There are trustworthy;
• **Facts & inferences.** Facts and inferences;	• **Facts & inferences.** Facts and inferences;
• **Reasonable person.** That would lead a reasonable person to believe;	• **Reasonable person.** That would lead a reasonable person to believe;
• **Concretely possible.** There is a concrete possibility;	• **More likely than not.** It is more likely than not;
• **Crime and/or danger.** That:	• **Charge and/or search.** That:
• **A crime was, is, or will be committed;** and sometimes	• **A specific crime was or is being committed;** and/or
• **The suspect is armed and dangerous.**	• **Evidence of crime is in a particular place.**

COMPARING REASONABLE SUSPICION & PROBABLE CAUSE

The differences

Degree of certainty. The major difference between reasonable suspicion and probable cause is the amount of information — the degree of certainty — that the officer in the field possesses. For reasonable suspicion, the officer must be "concretely suspicious."[2] Probable cause requires proof that the accused is "more likely than not" the actual perpetrator, or that the location to be searched is "more likely than not" where evidence is located.[3] *Comm. v. Tarver*, 369 Mass. 302 (1975) (probable cause to arrest or search is essentially the same concept).

---

2 *Terry v. Ohio*, 392 U.S. 1 (1968) also referred to reasonable suspicion as "articulable suspicion." Articulate means, "to put into words." Bottom line: Officers must be able to describe why they thought their suspect might be committing or preparing to commit a crime.
3 In fact, probable cause is, technically, defined as less than "more likely than not" — so officers can confidently justify applying this standard to their probable cause determinations in the field. *Comm. v. Preston P.*, 483 Mass. 759 (2020).

Permissible conduct. The second difference is the authorized activity. Reasonable suspicion is the least amount of information that officers must possess to lawfully detain citizens and sometimes frisk them for weapons. For charging suspects with a crime, or searching them, officers must have probable cause.

The similarities

Trustworthy. The Constitution insists that officers rely on trustworthy information. Whenever officers establish a reasonable suspicion or probable cause, they basically use two types of information:

- **Their personal observations;** and/or

- **Information provided by other people (secondary sources).**

This chapter deals with officer observations in the field. *Chapter 3* outlines how officers must demonstrate that information from other people is trustworthy. This is more involved because secondhand information is subject to greater distortion.

Facts and inferences. Officers must deal in facts, not assumptions and innuendo. At the same time, officers may make inferences — reasonable deductions — from the facts they learn. Inferences must be reasonable, not inescapable. Let's say that officers see a known drug dealer cross the street and exchange a small item with a motorist who drives off. They may infer that a drug deal just took place. While it is *possible* that the offender gave the motorist a stick of gum, officers do not have to eliminate all innocent possibilities from a given situation before they can investigate.

Another name for an inference is *circumstantial evidence*. Circumstantial evidence may always be used to build a reasonable suspicion, probable cause, or even proof beyond a reasonable doubt. While no definitive number of facts must be present, it is usually necessary to rely on more than one to develop reasonable suspicion or probable cause. *Comm. v. Chavis*, 41 Mass. App. Ct. 912 (1996).

Reasonable person standard. Probable cause and reasonable suspicion are "concerned with probabilities . . . the factual and practical considerations of everyday life on which reasonable [people], who are not legal technicians, act." *Comm. v. Gentile*, 437 Mass. 569 (2002). The court is obligated to look at situations from the perspective of a reasonable person — not the biased perspective of an officer eager to make a case or a person antagonistic to law enforcement.

The test is objective. So an officer's belief about the legal basis for his authority is *irrelevant* — the circumstances must justify the action he took. *Comm. v. Peters*, 48 Mass. App. Ct. 15 (1999) ("[C]itizens . . . whom the police . . . protect . . . should not be bound or limited by the officer's choice of words [concerning] the active execution of his duties"). *Comm. v. Spagnolo*, 17 Mass. App. Ct. 516 (1984) (officer testified he only "suspected" he would find evidence, but facts revealed probable cause to search; therefore, search was lawful).

Officers do not have to show that the information they rely on in the field will be admissible at trial. Police should consider *all* of the reliable information they have. Officers should not limit themselves based on their perceptions about what evidence may be admissible in court. *Comm. v. Kotlyarevskiy*, 59 Mass. App. Ct. 240 (2003).

Collective knowledge doctrine

The collective knowledge of officers investigating a case is evaluated to determine if a reasonable suspicion or probable cause exists. In *Comm. v. Lanoue*, 356 Mass. 337 (1970), information provided to a police sergeant by a reliable person served as the basis for an arrest. The sergeant radioed a patrol officer with the defendant's description and directed him to be on the lookout. When the officer observed the defendant, he placed him under arrest. In upholding the arrest, the court made the now famous statement:

> "[I]t is unnecessary for the detaining officer to know all of the information pertaining to the incident [because] the knowledge of one [officer is] the knowledge of all."

This is true even if officers do not share their information with each other. It is *not* necessary for officers to actually trade information. The knowledge of one officer may be attributed to another as they work together to establish reasonable suspicion or probable cause.

- *Comm. v. Quinn*, 68 Mass. App. Ct. 476 (2007): On a snowy night two men broke into a gas station. Officer Harvey found fresh footprints between the gas station and the street. The footprints led to fresh tire tracks heading toward Route 18.

  Officer Donahue was informed of the break-in but not of the footprints or tire tracks. Only five minutes after the initial dispatch, he saw a vehicle on the road past the gas station. Donahue activated his blue lights and made a stop. He observed shards of glass, an aluminum bat, and a fresh cut on the hand of the motorist.

  Although Harvey had not shared his knowledge with Donahue, the stop was proper under the "collective knowledge doctrine." A combination of the officers' information created a reasonable suspicion based on:

  - Tire tracks suggesting the perpetrators left the crime scene in a car;
  - The defendants' car was the only vehicle on the road late at night; and
  - The car was near the gas station approximately five minutes after the initial dispatch.

- *Comm. v. Rivet*, 30 Mass. App. Ct. 973 (1991): Defendant Rivet rammed into an automobile driven by Jose DosAnjos. The crash severely injured DosAnjos and killed his wife and son. Officers Koyle and Dawes of the North Attleboro police responded. Koyle arrived at the scene and spoke with Rivet for approximately 25 minutes. Rivet told the officer that he had one beer at his grandmother's. Koyle noticed that Rivet's eyes were glassy. Because Rivet seemed to be in pain from injuries to his mouth and left leg, Koyle did not subject him to field sobriety tests. He did, however, place him under arrest.

  Meanwhile, Officer Dawes arrived. Dawes spoke to witnesses who reported seeing Rivet stagger from a convenience store and speed away in his truck at 60 mph just before the impact. Although the officers did not share their information before the arrest, the court found that Dawes' information could be used to bolster Koyle's arrest.

Collective knowledge includes information obtained by civilian dispatchers. In *Comm. v. Bell*, 78 Mass. App. Ct. 135 (2010), after a daytime shooting, three witnesses called 911 and described the suspect's hair style, clothing, and vehicle. Two callers also saw a "U.S." license plate — with one reporting the number as "6808" and another saying "1608." The radio broadcast that precipitated the stop did not include the plate numbers, but that information was still "factored into the calculus of reasonable suspicion" under the collective knowledge doctrine. This was helpful for the prosecution because the plate on the defendant's vehicle was actually US A608. Officers should routinely check with dispatch before writing their report to see whether the call-taker received additional information that did not get broadcast.

If so, the reporting officer should include it in a separate paragraph beginning, "Dispatch also knew from the caller that . . . " This documents the "collective knowledge" that did not get broadcast but was obtained by the dispatcher.

OFFICER OBSERVATIONS & INVESTIGATION

Officers frequently rely on what they see, hear, and smell. They might observe a drug deal in progress, smell gasoline at an arson scene, or hear a domestic violence victim screaming as they approach the door. *Comm. v. Monterosso*, 33 Mass. App. Ct. 765 (1992).

Officers may use their training and experience to interpret what they sense. For example, officers attach significance to repeated pedestrian traffic at a home because experience tells them it indicates possible drug sales. Or they may be suspicious of a person in possession of a "dent puller" in a parking lot at night, because they know this tool is typically employed by car thieves. *Comm. v. Blatz*, 9 Mass. App. Ct. 603 (1980).

ENVIRONMENT

Officers may take into account past criminal conduct in an area. *Comm. v. Freeman*, 87 Mass. App. Ct. 451 (2015).

The "high crime" nature of the area is only relevant if directly connected to the location and activity being investigated. In *Comm. v. Evelyn*, 485 Mass. 691 (2020), the officers testified to an ongoing feud between gangs, but their report lacked specific dates or descriptions about past incidents. Without evidence of a direct connection to their suspect or to the shooting, the high crime nature of the overall area could <u>not</u> be considered.

The history of a location is never, by itself, justification to stop someone. *Comm. v. Phillips*, 413 Mass. 50 (1992) rejected a police commander's "search on sight" gang policy. The SJC declared that it did not want law enforcement officials in a high crime area to feel they could sweep the neighborhood — stopping individuals who happened to live there, hoping to apprehend a suspect. "The problems that may face [this neighborhood] or any other single 'high crime area' will not be resolved any more readily by excluding the individuals who live there from the protections afforded by our Constitution."

SUSPICIOUS BEHAVIOR & BACKGROUND

UNUSUAL ACTIVITY

When activity is "out of character" with a particular location, officers may develop a reasonable suspicion to investigate.

- *Comm. v. Patti*, 31 Mass. App. Ct. 440 (1991): At 3:15 a.m., an officer observed the defendant working on an automobile with the hood up in a poorly lit motel parking lot. The location had experienced several car thefts and vehicle break-ins. The individual working on the car was unlikely to be a motel employee, since a shift change had not occurred recently. The very late hour also made it unlikely that he was a motel guest. The officer appropriately conducted a threshold inquiry.

- *Comm. v. Nickerson*, 79 Mass. App. Ct. 642 (2011): Shortly after midnight, a victim told police that her purse, containing a cell phone and other items, had been stolen. The perpetrator had entered her home through a rear window. A quarter mile from the scene, Sergeant Kelly saw Robert Nickerson emerge from a side yard carrying a flashlight and a 12-pack of beer. Upon seeing Kelly, Nickerson walked in the opposite direction, attempting to conceal his flashlight.

  Kelly told Nickerson to stop. Nickerson appeared nervous and said, "I'm just walkin' and drinkin'." Sergeant Kelly frisked Nickerson and found a cell phone. Nickerson identified himself and Kelly immediately linked his name to several past burglaries.

  Nickerson asked to call his girlfriend, at which point Kelly asked him who owned the cell phone. Nickerson said that it belonged to his friend, but could not provide a name. When Kelly asked if Nickerson had anything else, he responded, "No, go ahead, search me." The search revealed women's jewelry. Nickerson claimed that it belonged to his girlfriend but, when called by police, she denied owning the jewelry. Police then linked the items to the earlier break-in, and Nickerson was arrested.

Insufficiently suspicious activity provides no basis for detention. *Comm. v. O'Laughlin*, 25 Mass. App. Ct. 998 (1988): Officers observed one of the last passengers deplane in Boston. He was carrying only a cloth jacket, walking rapidly through the terminal and looking back at two, unidentified plainclothes officers following him. He ran to his car before officers stopped and detained him. These actions created no more than a hunch that this individual was up to some mischief. The Appeals Court noted that the defendant's actions did not set him apart from the majority of innocent travelers, particularly when he might have thought the plainclothes officers were a threat to his safety.

VIOLATION OF ORDINANCE OR BYLAW

May justify threshold inquiry.

- *Comm. v. Pierre P.*, 53 Mass. App. Ct. 215 (2001) reminds us that officers may detain a person based on a reasonable suspicion that he is violating an ordinance or bylaw. Ironically, *Pierre P.* involved an officer who fell short in articulating his reasonable suspicion. He relied on a Springfield loitering ordinance to detain a group of five youths, in gang colors, in a high crime area at 11:00 p.m. However, the officer did not testify that any of the youths were obstructing, hindering, or preventing others from passing — which is the standard set forth in the ordinance. This faulty foundation could not support his later decision to frisk one of the youths. The knife he discovered was suppressed.

- *Comm. v. Bones*, 93 Mass App. Ct. 681 (2018): Responding to a call for service, Chelsea Officer Brian Dunn recognized Leonides Bones, who was drinking a "nip" bottle of alcohol — an arrestable violation of a Chelsea ordinance. Bones said: "I'm sorry, I didn't see you. I'll dump it out." Dunn did not say anything to Bones about the alcohol but detained him to check for warrants. After determining that Bones had an active warrant, Dunn arrested him. Bones had $209 and heroin packaged for sale. This case was handled well from start to finish. Also see *Comm. v. Dyette*, 87 Mass. App. Ct. 548 (2015) (fact that lights were off gave police reasonable suspicion that the defendant, who was standing on a basketball court late at night, was trespassing).

May justify arrest. *Comm. v. Rushin*, 56 Mass. App. Ct. 515 (2002): Shortly after midnight, a Boston police officer drove his cruiser into a school parking lot, which was the site of numerous vehicle break-ins. He saw a vehicle with two men inside. The defendant was in the passenger seat drinking a can of beer. He was arrested for violating Boston's public drinking ordinance. During the search incident to his arrest, a loaded handgun was found.

RECOVERING EVIDENCE OR CONTRABAND

Officers may detain or arrest a suspect found in possession of evidence or contraband. *Comm. v. Mojica*, 59 Mass. App. Ct. 925 (2003): In Fitchburg, Officer Lake pulled his cruiser to the curb when he saw the defendant and another person bent over looking for something. The officer got out and noticed a white substance in a plastic bag on the sidewalk between the defendant's legs. The defendant stood up quickly and began to walk away. Officer Lake asked the defendant what he was doing. He replied that he was looking for a gold chain that had fallen from his neck. Lake looked unsuccessfully with his flashlight for a gold chain. Lake then arrested the defendant, who was wearing a silver chain. The bag of white powder appeared to be cocaine.

CONCEALING OR TRANSFERRING POSSIBLE CONTRABAND

Concealing an item or transferring it to another may indicate criminal conduct. *Comm. v. Montoya*, 464 Mass. 566 (2013). In *Comm. v. Timothy T.*, 2017 WL 445494 (Appeals Court), Methuen Police Officer Hardy was in a marked police car when he encountered two men in a disabled car in front of a gas station. He offered the men assistance, but they declined, saying they were waiting for a friend. Hardy became suspicious and checked for criminal records. One of them had a prior drug arrest.

Hardy notified the narcotics unit, and plainclothes officers joined him in surveilling the men. They watched one of the men approach a juvenile. The man and the juvenile engaged in a quick hand-to-hand exchange without speaking to each other, then parted ways. The entire "silent movie" — viewed through the eyes of an experienced narcotics officer — established probable cause:

- The two men rejected Hardy's offer of assistance because they claimed to be waiting for a friend, but then abandoned their car and walked to meet a juvenile;

- The brief exchange (it lasted three to five seconds and involved no conversation);
- The location of the encounter (Hardy had made 15–20 drug arrests there);
- One man had a prior arrest for illegal possession of drugs; and
- Hardy's experience (for 18 years he dealt with this area and its drug activity).

Officers are not required to see the object exchanged. In *Comm. v. Coronel*, 70 Mass. App. Ct. 906 (2007), a Lynn officer observed a female exit a blue Chevrolet van to make a brief call. She had been waiting in the van with co-defendant Eaton. Soon after, a white Toyota, driven by Oscar Coronel, slowly passed them. The van followed the Toyota around a corner. Eaton jumped out of the van and into the Toyota for 10 seconds. When he emerged, he was stuffing something into his front pocket. The officer recognized Coronel and his Toyota from an earlier drug arrest. He concluded a narcotics deal had just taken place.

The court agreed: "[It] would critically handicap law enforcement to require in every circumstance that an officer not only witness an apparent exchange, but also see what object was exchanged, before making a search incident to arrest." Bear in mind:

- **Suspect's drug history is a critical factor.** *Comm. v. Sanders*, 90 Mass. App. Ct. 660 (2016) (officer had arrested Emery Sanders before for cocaine distribution).

- **A public exchange is not automatically suspicious.** *Comm. v. Clark*, 65 Mass. App. Ct. 39 (2005): Officer Bisnette stopped the defendant in his SUV because he had been standing by his vehicle near the "French Connection" bar at 11:30 p.m. He had given an item to another man, who the officer recognized as a bartender from a nearby establishment. The defendant counted cash and drove away. While the incident occurred in a high drug location, the officer did not know either of these men to be drug dealers or users. There were no unusual movements by the defendant or anyone else, including the passengers in his SUV. Compare *Comm. v. Hernandez*, 448 Mass. 711 (2007) (officer saw defendant remove an item from his shoe and give it to a companion).

- **There must be proof an exchange took place — especially with multiple people present.** *Comm. v. Stewart*, 469 Mass. 257 (2014): Police saw Paul Stewart lead three people down a one-way street. The officers were familiar with Stewart from a previous arrest for cocaine distribution. One of the people following Stewart was counting money. The group briefly huddled together in a doorway and separated.

  Believing they had witnessed a drug transaction, the officers approached Stewart and asked him what just happened. Stewart's answers contradicted what officers had seen.

  Officer Dwan searched Stewart's bag and found drugs. The court held that he lacked probable cause. Dwan saw Stewart and three companions huddled in a doorway, but his view was limited to their upper torso area. He did not see any hand movements or see an object pass between Stewart and his companions.

  Also, when there are more than two people present during an exchange, the officer has to be clear who is involved. Here, Dwan did not identify how Stewart participated. The evidence was sufficient for reasonable suspicion, but fell short of probable cause. Stewart's false denial was not enough to turn reasonable suspicion into probable cause in this case.

- **Presence of object in mouth not enough.** *Comm. v. Evans*, 87 Mass. App. Ct. 687 (2015): Two officers observed Johnny Evans walking alone at 2:00 a.m. They followed him and asked where he was going. He nervously said he was going home. One of the officers believed Evans had something in his mouth based on the way he was speaking. He asked Evans what was in his mouth. Evans said "nothing" and opened his mouth. The officer used his flashlight to examine the inside of Evans' mouth, and saw a bag of crack cocaine wedged between his tongue and cheek. The officers did not have reasonable suspicion for this seizure. Nervousness was insufficient, so was the belief Evans had something in his mouth. It could have been food, gum, tobacco, or even a speech impediment.

APPREHENSION OR FLIGHT

The fact that a person is visibly nervous, flees, or hides may contribute to reasonable suspicion.

- *Comm. v. Mendez*, 476 Mass. 512 (2017): A witness called 911 to report that a man had been shot in his car and that the individuals involved had fled. A trooper in an unmarked cruiser responded to the scene and saw Charles Mendez "make a beeline" to a white Honda Civic that was stopped at the curb with its engine running. The car pulled away quickly, before Mendez had fully entered or closed the door. Because of the unusual absence of people in the area and the vehicle's quick departure, the trooper followed it as it meandered in a "serpentine route" through city streets.

  The trooper ran the plate and learned that an individual associated with the address of the vehicle's owner had a violent criminal history. The Civic stopped at a residence and the two backseat passengers got out and faced the trooper with their hands in their pockets. The trooper showed his badge and said, "Police. Don't move." The men fled in different directions. Mendez jumped back in the vehicle, ordering the driver to "take off." However, the driver complied with the trooper's order to turn off the motor. Mendez had a gun in his waistband. He was ultimately convicted of the murder.

  The trooper had a reasonable suspicion to justify the stop. There had been a shooting in the housing complex less than 10 minutes before he saw Mendez rush to the vehicle. He followed the car around the city, without an apparent destination, for eight minutes. The license plate was associated with a person with a violent criminal history.

- *Comm. v. Williams*, 422 Mass. 111 (1996): Officers had a reasonable suspicion to detain the defendant when they saw him sprinting down a busy street in broad daylight. He was sweating, had a strained expression on his face, and discarded his t-shirt without breaking stride. Officers followed in their car and observed him running through backyards and scaling chain link fences. Once captured, he was linked to a murder nearby.

- *Comm. v. Marrero*, 33 Mass. App. Ct. 440 (1992): While patrolling an area where a break-in had occurred in an abandoned building, officers stopped to talk with a group. They saw the defendant sneak from an alley adjacent to the building. He did a "double take" upon spotting the uniformed officers. When they asked to speak with him, he ran.

A companion's flight may support reasonable suspicion. *U.S. v. Cotton*, 782 F.3d 392 (2015): Officers were on patrol at an apartment complex when they saw a person throw a set of keys off a third-floor balcony to two men on the ground. Officers knew the property manager had instructed the residents not to throw their keys off the balcony for security reasons. The officers told the men on the ground not to pick up the keys. One man ignored police, picked up the keys, and hurried toward the back door of the complex. The other man, Marquis Cotton, stood still with a nervous look on his face. As an officer walked toward him, Cotton reached for his waistband. The officer grabbed his arm, and handcuffed and frisked him. He recovered a pistol.

While Cotton did comply with their initial order, the officers still had reasonable suspicion. Cotton was present in an area known for violence and drugs, his companion fled, and the manager's policy had been violated. Even though Cotton claimed he did not know the other man, officers were justified in believing that he did.

Flight cannot be the major factor for reasonable suspicion. There are reasons other than guilt why residents, especially minority groups, might want to avoid police contact. *Comm. v. Warren*, 475 Mass. 530 (2016): Boston Police Officer Anjos received a radio report of a breaking and entering in progress in Roxbury. Anjos went to the scene. The teenage victim told him a black male wearing a red hoodie had jumped out of his bedroom window with his computer, backpack, and other belongings. The man then joined two other black males, one in dark clothing and one in a black hoodie, as they ran down the street.

Officer Anjos drove around for 20 minutes, but saw no one. As he headed back to the station, he saw two black males in dark clothing walking near a park. Anjos rolled down his cruiser window and yelled: "Hey guys, wait a minute." The two men made eye contact, turned around, and jogged down a path to the park.

Anjos radioed dispatch that men fitting the description of the suspects were traveling through the park toward Dale Street. Officer Carr responded to Dale Street and saw the two men come out of the park. He approached on foot and said: "Hey fellas." One of the men, Jimmy Warren, turned and ran up a hill back into the park.

Carr ordered him to stop. He saw Warren clutch the right side of his pants as if he were carrying a gun. Carr chased Warren and commanded him to get down. After a brief struggle, Carr arrested and searched Warren. He had no weapons, but a firearm was found nearby.

The SJC decided that the officer lacked reasonable suspicion when he detained Jimmy Warren. Here's why:

- **Description of suspects.** The victim gave a general description of the thief and his accomplices. Police only knew that there were three black males, two wearing "dark clothing" and one in a "red hoodie." There was no information about facial features, hairstyles, skin tone, height, or weight that would distinguish the suspects from any other black male wearing dark clothes or a hoodie in Roxbury. With such a vague description, the police could not reasonably target Warren. He was one of two men, not three; he was not wearing a red hoodie; and neither he nor his companion carried a backpack. Officer Anjos had nothing more than a hunch that Warren had been involved in the crime.

- **Proximity.** Proximity to the crime scene has more value when the distance is short and the timing is close. Warren was stopped one mile from the scene. Dale Street was in the opposite direction from the broadcast direction of the perpetrators' flight. Most important, the perpetrators would have reached Dale Street long before Anjos encountered them there, 25 minutes after the crime.

- **No pedestrians.** It did not help that the suspects were the only people walking in the area. The crime occurred 25 minutes earlier. Warren's presence a mile from the crime, within a time frame inconsistent with having recently fled there, did not contribute to reasonable suspicion.

- **Flight.** Finally, Warren's flight from police could not make up for other deficiencies in the case. Warren was under no obligation to stop and speak with Officer Anjos. Unless an officer already has reasonable suspicion to detain, the suspect has a right to walk away and avoid police contact. According to the SJC, citizens, especially in high crime areas, may have disproportionate contact with police, and may want to avoid contact for reasons other than guilt.

RECORD, REPUTATION, & ASSOCIATION

A person's criminal record, reputation, or association with criminals may help create reasonable suspicion or probable cause. *Comm. v. McGrath,* 365 Mass. 631 (1974) (known felon observed leaving crowd of teenagers and concealing something).

Limitations on use of prior record. A prior record will not, by itself, justify police detention. Furthermore, any prior offense must be sufficiently recent and similar to the crime under investigation. *Comm. v. Monterosso,* 33 Mass. App. Ct. 765 (1992) (defendant's three convictions for drug distribution within two years contributed to probable cause to search).

Compare *Comm. v. Melendez,* 407 Mass. 53 (1990) (guilty plea to cocaine possession irrelevant; suspect's prior conviction for drug *possession* entitled to no weight in formulating probable cause for narcotics *distribution*); *Comm. v. Allen,* 406 Mass. 575 (1990) (four year old conviction for drug possession too old).

EVASIVE OR IMPLAUSIBLE RESPONSES

Evasive or implausible answers, coupled with other information, may provide reasonable suspicion or probable cause. *Comm. v. Rosado,* 43 Mass. App. Ct. 381 (1997) (defendant, who was found crouching next to a ground-floor stairwell, claimed he had three screwdrivers tucked into his pants because he had fixed his sister's stereo earlier that day).

- **Inconsistent statements by companions.** *Comm. v. Wardsworth,* 482 Mass. 454 (2019) (inconsistent statements by two suspects about their whereabouts during a recent murder contributed to probable cause). *Comm. v. Watson,* 430 Mass. 725 (2000) (car stop based on reasonable suspicion of drug dealing; Watson, the driver, said that the luggage belonged to passenger Smith, which Smith denied; police properly searched the luggage).

- **Knowing undisclosed facts about the crime.** *Comm. v. Charley,* 91 Mass. App. Ct. 223 (2017): Following a radio report of a robbery and shooting at a convenience store, Officer Quinonez observed Jarris Charley walking from the general direction of the store, sweating profusely on a cool night. He fit the description in the broadcast. Quinonez confirmed her suspicion by viewing the convenience store's surveillance video. When officers spoke to Charley an hour after the incident, he asked, "What did I do? Why are you stopping me?" An officer said there had been "an incident up the street." Charley said, "I had nothing to do with the shooting." Charley's reference to a shooting — when no one else had mentioned it — contributed to probable cause.

Comm. v. Sorenson, 98 Mass. App. Ct. 789 (2020)(Sorenson said he was not at the scene of a stabbing on Saturday but, at the time he volunteered this information, the officer had not told him on what day of the week the crime occurred).

• **Lack of cooperation with investigation.** *Comm. v. Scott*, 57 Mass. App. Ct. 36 (2003) (fact that defendant would not participate in an identification procedure helped establish probable cause that he was the rapist in two incidents).[4]

ADMISSION OR CONFESSION

Of course, an incriminating statement may create reasonable suspicion or probable cause. *Comm. v. Cromwell*, 53 Mass. App. Ct. 662 (2002) (when officers confronted the defendant about his possession of stolen property, he said, "You got me, just take me in"). Proper interview procedures are the subject of *Chapters 21, 22,* and *23*.

IDENTIFICATION

If a suspect resembles the description of a perpetrator, officers may detain him. A closer match results in probable cause. Field identification methods are discussed in *Chapter 25*.

Avoid generic, ethnic-based descriptions. The dispatcher in *Comm. v. Cheek,* 413 Mass. 492 (1992) described the assailant as "a young black male wearing a black parka." Such a vague description could not serve as the basis for stopping Zan Cheek one mile from the crime scene in a predominantly African-American section of Boston. Also see *Comm. v. Scott,* 440 Mass. 642 (2004) (court concluded that the officer based his stop simply on the fact that a black man was in the area of two rapes).

Demographic data cannot be used to connect a defendant to a crime. *Comm. v. Hilaire,* 92 Mass. App. Ct. 784 (2018): Police responded to a report of an armed home invasion with shots fired in East Bridgewater. The suspects were described as several young black males in "regular clothes." Two were carrying backpacks.

Shortly after the home invasion, about 100 yards from the scene, three black men fled from a Toyota Camry and ran into the woods. An officer stood by the abandoned Toyota while others searched. That officer observed a black Acura driving up and down the street. The officer stopped the car, and the driver, Ashley Smith, said she was lost and trying to get back to Brockton. Two hours later, Officer Andre stopped Smith in the same area and she repeated her story about being lost. When he returned to the station, Andre learned of Smith's earlier encounter with the other officer.

An hour later, Andre saw Smith again, talking on a cell phone. Andre stopped the vehicle and asked Smith why she had returned from Brockton and who she was speaking with. Smith denied talking on the phone, but consented when Andre asked to look at it. A recent text read, "Did you pick him up yet?" Smith claimed she knew nothing about the message.

An hour later, Andre saw James Hilaire walking down the street half a mile from the crime scene. He was wearing a backpack and talking on a cell phone. Andre asked if he could look in the backpack. Hilaire said "yes." Inside were large amounts of money and jewelry.

---

4 The SJC later reversed this case on other grounds. *Comm. v. Scott*, 440 Mass. 642 (2004).

- **Census data may never create reasonable suspicion.** A judge determined that the police had reasonable suspicion to seize Hilaire despite the fact that the description of the suspects was general and lacking detail. The judge specifically noted that the African-American population of East Bridgewater was less than 1% according to the U.S. Census Bureau. The Appeals Court rejected this kind of calculation.

- **Reasonable suspicion still existed.** While the description of the suspects as young black males in regular clothes, two with backpacks, was not enough for reasonable suspicion, this vague description was enhanced when Hilaire was found near the location of the crime. While six hours had passed, Ashley Smith's statements and behavior suggested that she was in phone communication with an offender who was still in the area.

INVESTIGATION TECHNIQUES

Investigative techniques may support reasonable suspicion or probable cause. Some are sophisticated. *Comm. v. Baptista*, 32 Mass. App. Ct. 910 (1992) (defendant's fingerprint found inside locked vending machine that had been vandalized). Some are simple. *Comm. v. Willard*, 53 Mass. App. Ct. 650 (2002) (officer followed suspect's footprints in newly fallen snow from the scene of a break-in).

MOTOR VEHICLE STOPS

TRAFFIC INFRACTION

Traffic stop may be based on a reasonable suspicion of a civil infraction. Most traffic stops are triggered when officers observe an obvious moving violation (e.g., the motorist fails to stop at a red light) or equipment violation (e.g., a headlight does not work), but the standard is reasonable suspicion.

- *Comm. v. Baez*, 47 Mass. App. Ct. 115 (1999) (trooper properly stopped the defendant's vehicle because his training and experience gave him reasonable suspicion that the windows were illegally tinted; the stop and later discovery of a firearm were valid).

- *Comm. v. Rivas*, 77 Mass. App. Ct. 210 (2010) (red rejection sticker on windshield gave officer reasonable suspicion that defendant was driving an unsafe vehicle).

- *U.S. v. Jenkins*, 680 F.3d 101 (2012) (officer reasonably believed that a reflective blue disc behind windshield was an illegal blue light; he properly stopped the van to check).

Traffic stop may not be based on an anticipated violation. *Comm. v. Whitehead*, 49 Mass. App. Ct. 905 (2000): State Police troopers noticed a car with four occupants idling in an unlit restaurant parking lot. The troopers did not know they were restaurant employees. The troopers heard a loud exhaust and saw the vehicle, with its lights out, back out of a parking space. They considered these circumstances suspicious and believed the driver would travel onto the public road so they prepared to follow. When the vehicle pulled back into its parking space, the troopers decided to make the stop anyway and activated their blue lights. They noticed the front seat passenger, Tahir Whitehead, reach under his buttocks. Whitehead was ordered out. A gun appeared on his seat. The initial stop was invalid. A driver may have his headlights off and a loud engine while warming up on a winter evening in a parking lot. The gun had to be suppressed.

Police may not stop a vehicle to serve a civil abuse prevention order. *Comm. v. Sanborn*, 477 Mass. 393 (2017): A police sergeant was parked outside a local bar. In the course of randomly checking the registration status of parked vehicles, he discovered that a 209A restraining order had not been served on vehicle owner Richard Sanborn. When Sanborn exited the bar and drove away, the sergeant stopped him and arrested him for OUI.

The stop was invalid. Chapter 209A does not independently authorize stops. Officers needed a warrant; reasonable suspicion of criminal activity; a civil traffic infraction; or an emergency. None of these applied, so the officer had to use an ordinary method for service (i.e., home delivery or mail).

Legitimate investigatory motives do not invalidate a civil infraction stop. *Comm. v. Buckley*, 478 Mass. 861 (2018): Detectives Bombadier and Campbell of the Whitman Police Department were conducting surveillance of an apartment building. At 10:50 p.m., the officers saw a parked car and watched its two occupants enter the building, re-emerge a few minutes later, and drive away without their headlights on. Detectives instructed Officer Nelson to stop the car for suspected drug activity. The officer did so a few minutes later, after seeing the car traveling above the speed limit.

The detectives arrived and Bombadier noticed a strong odor of marijuana emanating from the car. He asked the driver if she had any marijuana. The driver said she didn't think so and that he could check. The ensuing consent search revealed a firearm under the front passenger seat. The detectives properly arrested the driver and passenger.

The belief that vehicle occupants may be engaging in other illegal activity, like drug dealing, does not prevent a stop for traffic enforcement. The SJC remarked that rejecting these stops would yield the illogical result of allowing stops of non-suspect drivers who violate motor vehicle laws, but forbidding stops of suspected criminals who violate motor vehicle laws!

While legitimate investigatory motives do not invalidate a civil infraction stop, <u>police bias absolutely will</u>. *Comm. v. Long,* 485 Mass. 711 (2020) established a two-step procedure to deal with allegations of police bias.

- **Step 1: Defendant raises a reasonable inference.** In a written motion, defense counsel must raise a reasonable inference that bias played a role in the stop. Counsel may address:

    - *The specific agency policies and procedures regarding traffic stops.* Police departments are expected to provide these policies during discovery.

    - *The officer's regular assignment* — e.g., Does the officer engage in general traffic patrol where repeated stops for all sorts of vehicle offenses might be expected? Or is the officer in a drug or gang unit where traffic stops are not the primary function?

    - *The officer's enforcement patterns.* Citation or other data may be presented for this purpose, but statistical proof is not required. In any case, the SJC expects that police departments will provide relevant data during the discovery process.

- *The sequence of events prior to the stop* — e.g., Could the officer see the operator (and thus be aware of his or her race or ethnicity) before the stop? Did the officer follow the suspect vehicle for a long period of time?

- *The way the officer conducted the stop* — e.g., What did the officer say? What was his tone of voice? Were there exit orders, frisks, consent requests, evidentiary searches, and what was their basis?

- *The public safety interests at stake in enforcing the violation* — e.g., dangerous or impaired operation is less dependent on officer discretion than a technical equipment defect.

- **Step 2: Burden on prosecutor to rebut reasonable inference.** If the prosecutor fails, the judge will typically suppress the evidence. It is legally *insufficient* to simply assert that an actual traffic violation occurred.

Police testimony is key to disproving bias. Testify to the same factors listed above — with some additional points of emphasis — to <u>disprove</u> the allegations. This approach makes sense because judges tend to organize their findings based on the framework provided by the SJC.

- **Agency policy.** All police policies on bias say the same basic thing, and you should be able to articulate these principles in court:

  - Actual *or* perceived discrimination in policing is an ineffective and unconstitutional law enforcement strategy; it hurts the department's relationship with the community; and it is harmful and unfair.

  - Your agency requires that officers receive training so they can understand the nature of bias and avoid having it adversely affect their dealings with the public. Supervisors monitor officers and intervene in situations where bias policing may be intentionally or unintentionally occurring.

  - Officers who engage in this behavior are subject to discipline, including termination.

- **Personal commitment.** It is not enough to know department policy. You must be prepared to firmly state your personal and professional commitment to impartial policing[5] — e.g., "Counsel, I am personally and professionally committed to treating people fairly. I'm not naïve. I recognize there are some officers who do not, but that's not me. From my training, experience, and core values, I understand that biased policing is wrong." You do not have to say these exact words, but you need to communicate authentically.

- **Assignment.** If you are assigned to patrol, emphasize the public safety nature of traffic enforcement, and make sure you are consistent about stopping all motorists for the same type of violations.

  In *Long*, the SJC was assessing a traffic stop by officers from a specialized unit (the Youth Violence Strike Force) in an unmarked car. The SJC implied that traffic stops by

---

5 Obviously, you must do more than memorize the words. You have to embrace this mindset and continually reflect on whether you are performing your duties impartially to the best of your ability.

specialized units are more prone to abuse. There are two responses to this point of view depending on the circumstances:

- First, it is untrue that specialized units do not engage in general traffic enforcement. Explain if your unit members are assigned to specific areas and expected to engage in traffic enforcement as part of their public safety responsibilities — i.e., that you and your colleagues do make many violation-based stops as a part of your agency's overall strategy. It makes sense, in the wake of *Long,* for departments to adopt a policy which spells out these independent traffic enforcement responsibilities.[6]

- Second, there is <u>nothing wrong</u> with having an investigatory interest in stopping a motorist who *also* commits a traffic violation. It is *only* wrong if your investigatory interest stems from the racial and ethnic background of the people in the vehicle. See previous discussion of *Comm. v. Buckley, supra.*

  In these cases, explain the suspicious behavior that you observed that was separate from the traffic violation that also supported your stop. For example, a gang unit detective in Springfield stopped a vehicle that he and his partner saw idling near a "vigil" for a deceased gang member. As his cruiser approached, the driver conspicuously looked back twice and immediately pulled away from the curb. The driver committed a stop sign violation and, seeing the blue lights, made two quick turns before pulling over. This traffic stop resulted in the arrest of rival gang members carrying guns!

  A defense attorney might argue, under *Long,* that these specialized investigators made a minor traffic stop, which they normally would not worry about, because they saw young black men in a vehicle.

  The prosecutor, through the testimony of this knowledgeable detective, would argue the stop had nothing to do with the driver's race or ethnicity and everything to do with the risk of deadly assaults at gang vigils. The sudden departure of the vehicle added to the detective's concern so, yes, any legitimate traffic violation would be and should be used as a lawful reason to stop the vehicle and its occupants. Be up front about this strategy and explain the context and "neutral behavior clues" that supported your concerns.

  "Neutral behavior clues" is a good phrase to describe factors — unconnected to a suspect's race or ethnicity — that officers rely on for reasonable suspicion or probable cause (e.g., jiggling the door knob of a closed business; backing into a parking space to facilitate a quick getaway with the headlights off; the "meaningless ride" associated with drug deals).

- **Past patterns.** Attorneys will seek citation data to try to build a case that you have been biased in your enforcement patterns. In evaluating data, a court must be fair and consider the demographic makeup of the "driving population" on the road where the stop happened. *Comm. v. Lora,* 451 Mass. 425 (2008).[7]

---

6 In fact, *Long* pointed out that a defendant could argue that a stop in violation of a department's policy suggested bias, and the example the SJC gave was a traffic stop initiated by officers in an unmarked cruiser.
7 Given the likelihood of more motions to suppress on this issue, it may be cost-effective for police agencies to gather their own data regarding the racial composition of their motoring population.

Make it a habit to document all traffic stops with a citation. You still can and should exercise discretion about whether to impose money fines or warnings. The point is, by documenting <u>all</u> your stops, you exhibit a transparent approach to public safety. Testify about your practice — e.g., "Counsel, every vehicle stop I make is documented on a citation or in an incident report. Sometimes both. I do it to be completely transparent about when, where, why, and how I conduct any stop with a member of the public. In most cases, my citation is written within minutes of my interaction with the motorist."

- **Events prior to stop.** This is critical information that prosecutors and officers must present. Consider these issues:

  - *Vantage point prior to the stop.* It is virtually impossible for bias to affect officers when they cannot see the driver or passengers before the stop. Most stops begin with officers driving behind the offending motorist's vehicle, unable to see more than the back of the driver's head. Many stops occur at night. *Comm. v. Caudle*, 2019 WL 5092608 (Appeals Court) (the bicyclist's race was irrelevant because the trooper credibly testified that he could not see the race or ethnicity of the cyclist before this nighttime stop).

  - *Running plates.* Officers may check the status of registrations at any time, as long as they are not motivated by racial or ethnic bias. *Comm. v. Starr*, 55 Mass. App. Ct. 590 (2002). Testify about this legitimate, proactive strategy: "Your Honor, my department encourages us to constantly check registrations for public safety purposes. We discover unlicensed drivers, unregistered and uninsured vehicles, unsafe vehicles with invalid or expired inspection stickers, stolen vehicles, and motorists with outstanding arrest or default warrants."

    When challenged, see if your department can issue you a "run list" from the particular shift where you stopped the defendant or, also persuasive, from other shifts. If the run list shows that you check multiple plates during a shift on vehicles with occupants from different demographics, you rebut the inference that you ran the defendant's plate for a discriminatory reason.

  - *Nature of the violation. Long* emphasized that the more obvious the public safety risk, the less likely a court will be to draw an inference of officer bias. In other words, a stop for driving on the sidewalk is different from one for a defective plate cover.

    Anticipate a defense tactic of skepticism regarding whether the motor vehicle violation actually occurred. Add to your report any independent proof of the violation (e.g., another witness saw it; a photo of the equipment violation or improper sticker; the RMV printout from the stop, which includes the date and time it was run).

    Explain the public safety basis for the violation — e.g., "Your Honor, I have responded to a lot of crashes caused by following too closely," or "I could not read the unlit license plate. That means another driver could not either if the car were involved in a crash," or "We've had two pedestrian accidents involving drivers who illegally turned right on red at this location."

- *Following.* Most minority motorists convincingly provide accounts of times they were followed and improperly stopped by an officer — so this can be a "red flag" to a reviewing court. It goes without saying that officers should not consciously engage in this behavior. They should also reflect on whether they could be unconsciously falling into this pattern so they can stop it. (See "implicit bias" discussion below.)

  Of course, a motorist may sincerely believe they are being followed when, in reality, it is the farthest thing from the officer's mind. It is hard to change a driver's perception. Still, officers can avoid this issue by routinely initiating their stops as soon as they can after seeing a violation.

- **During the stop.** Naturally, a reviewing court will consider your behavior during the traffic stop. Biased comments have no place in professional policing. See, e.g., *Comm. v. Palacios*, 66 Mass. App. Ct. 13 (2006) (after defendant was arrested, officer alleged to have stated to female passenger: "What's a nice girl like you doing with a Spanish kid?").

  Officers must even avoid comments likely to be *perceived* as biased. For example, asking a minority motorist, "Do you know why I stopped you?" will often seem biased because, in the past, it was used as a cover for discriminatory enforcement.

  A good approach with all motorists, but especially those from minority groups, is for officers to identify themselves fully and explain the exact nature of the violation at the beginning of the stop — e.g., "Good evening. I am Officer John Maxwell of the Waltham Police. I stopped you because I saw your car make a turn onto Prospect Street without signalling." Clear identification of the officer and violation have been found to go a long way toward diffusing suspicion.

  Officers will also need to communicate appropriately when the nature of the stop changes — e.g., exit orders become necessary, or frisks, or consent requests, or motor vehicle exception searches, or pre-tow inventories.

- **Implicit bias.** The *Long* case opened the door for defense attorneys to challenge police stops on the basis that they were motivated by "implicit bias." It is important for officers to be trained in implicit bias and to understand how they can work to overcome it.

  - *Definition.* According to the Kirwan Institute at Ohio State University, "implicit bias" refers to the attitudes or stereotypes that affect our actions and decisions in an unconscious manner. These biases, which encompass both favorable and unfavorable assessments, are activated without an individual's awareness or intentional control. They cause us to have feelings and attitudes about other people based on characteristics such as race, ethnicity, age, and appearance. These associations develop over the course of a lifetime beginning at a very early age through exposure to direct and indirect messages.

    - Implicit biases are pervasive. Everyone possesses them.

    - The implicit associations we hold do not necessarily align with our declared beliefs.

- We generally tend to hold implicit biases that favor our own ingroup, though research has shown that we can still hold implicit biases against our ingroup.

- Implicit biases can be modified. Our brains are incredibly complex, and the implicit associations that we have formed can be gradually unlearned through a variety of techniques.[8]

- *Street test.* Given that implicit bias is a psychological phenomenon, it is probably unrealistic to think that officers, or any other human being, can overcome it through some technique. However, there is a practical, on-street mindset that will help officers counteract the influence of implicit bias.[9]

  When engaging in any law enforcement function — whether it is a traffic stop, detention, frisk, consent request, etc. — ask yourself one question: "Would I be doing this if this person were not _____ [fill in the perceived race, ethnicity, religion, sexual orientation, etc.]?" If, in your mind, the answer is "no" or "I'm not sure," then stop, because there is a good chance that bias is pulling you in the wrong direction.

  On the other hand, if your answer is "absolutely yes," then continue. A "yes" answer should mean you can to point to "neutral behavior clues" that justify the police action. This simple test, honestly applied, is a practical way for officers to screen against unconscious bias, in the moment, on the street.[10]

  The SJC in the *Long* decision did not provide a definition of implicit bias or give instructions on how trial judges are to apply this concept, which is why prosecutors and police officers must *proactively* address the issue!

PARKING VIOLATION

Traffic stop may follow a parking violation. *U.S. v. Shields*, 789 F.3D 733 (2015): An officer saw a parked SUV partially blocking a crosswalk. He approached Ernest Shields, who was sitting in the driver's seat, and asked for his license. After handing it over, Shields got out and ran.

While chasing him, the officer saw Shields pull out a gun and arrested him. The officer initially had reasonable suspicion to investigate the parking offense. Shields' flight interfered with that investigation. Once he saw the gun, the officer had probable cause to arrest.

MARIJUANA ODOR

Traffic stop may be based on marijuana odor, smoke, or visible use. Under 94G, § 13(d), drivers and/or passengers are assessed a $500 civil motor vehicle infraction (CMVI) for possessing an "open container"of marijuana. This law recognizes that road safety is compromised whenever marijuana is accessible to vehicle occupants. Clearly, officers have

---

8 The information in this definition section is an edited excerpt from kirwaninstitute.osu.edu/article/understanding-implicit-bias/.
9 I began teaching this "street test" to officers in 2007 when Law Enforcement Dimensions was contracted by the Executive Office of Public Safety and Security (EOPSS) to educate supervisors about bias policing.
10 Another way to overcome implicit bias is to have positive interactions with members of historically targeted groups. That is why community policing has been so important in the evolution of officer attitudes towards groups served by their department.

a reasonable suspicion to stop a vehicle for "open container" when they smell the odor of marijuana coming from a passing vehicle, or observe smoke, or see an occupant engaged in likely consumption (e.g., holding a bong or joint).[11]

INFORMATION FROM MOTOR VEHICLE DATABASES

Officers may check the status of vehicles and their owners by accessing a motor vehicle database. Officers frequently radio dispatch or use their mobile data terminal (MDT) to run random checks on vehicle license plates. They may watch traffic and enter several plates at a time or "run a plate" when their attention is drawn to a vehicle. *Comm. v. Starr*, 55 Mass. App. Ct. 590 (2002) (officer learned from dispatch that the vehicle she was following had the wrong plate, which allowed her to conduct a traffic stop; this led to the driver's arrest for operating after suspension).

When asked about the practice by members of the public, it is better for officers to respond: "We are encouraged to check the current status of registrations for public safety purposes," rather than, "We can run plates whenever we want."

While police have wide latitude, checking a registration is unacceptable in two situations.

- **Biased agenda.** Officers violate Article 14 if they check the status of a vehicle based on the race or ethnicity of an occupant. *Comm. v. Starr, supra.*

- **Personal agenda.** Officers should not check a vehicle for a non-law enforcement purpose (e.g., to learn the identity of an attractive motorist, to research a celebrity out of curiosity, or to identify someone for a friend).

Police may assume unlicensed vehicle owner is driving. *Comm. v. Puac-Cuc*, 97 Mass. App. Ct. 590 (2020): Sergeant Hutton checked the registration of a Chevy SUV in Framingham. Though properly registered, the vehicle was owned by a man who did not have a driver's license. Without knowing anything further, Sergeant Hutton stopped the SUV for the sole reason that he suspected the unlicensed owner was driving.[12] The driver turned out to be the owner's brother, Mario Puac-Cuc, who also did not have a valid license and was OUI. Hatton arrested him.

The stop was supported by reasonable suspicion. Without information to the contrary, police may assume the owner is driving. This is common sense. The fact that people sometimes drive vehicles belonging to others does not negate reasonable suspicion. *Glover v. Kansas,* 140 S.Ct. 1183 (2020).

On the other hand, officers must immediately release a motorist once they realize he is not the registered owner they were looking for. *Comm. v. Francis*, 2019 WL 994152 (Appeals Court): An officer in Arlington performed a random RMV check of a license plate number. The officer learned that the car's registered owner was Denis Leary, a 70 year old man. Leary's

---

11 94G, § 13(d) essentially overruled *Comm. v. Rodriguez,* 472 Mass. 767 (2015), an earlier case that prohibited traffic stops based solely on marijuana odor.
12 The RMV once used "X" numbers to identify vehicle owners who had no Massachusetts driver's license. The RMV now uses only "S" or "SA" identification numbers that are assigned to everyone — licensed drivers, unlicensed car owners, and out-of-state drivers who get a citation.

license had been revoked. The officer pulled the vehicle over and quickly observed the driver was too young to be Leary. He was actually Gerard Francis, whose license showed he was 28.

Francis was nervous and shaking as he reached into the glove compartment for the registration. As the officer ran an RMV check of Francis' license, he saw Francis place an object into the center console. An ensuing frisk led to the discovery of drugs and a gun.

Unfortunately, the officer unlawfully seized Francis when he detained him to check his license. Reasonable suspicion ended once the officer discovered the driver was obviously not Leary. Francis' nervousness did not provide a new basis to detain him.

Under an approach approved in *Comm. v. Garden*, 451 Mass. 43 (2008), the officer should have immediately ended the stop: "I now see that you are not the vehicle owner, who I needed to talk with. You're free to go. Sorry for the inconvenience."

Finally, officers may rely on database information that is _later_ determined to be incorrect. *Comm. v. Wilkerson*, 436 Mass. 137 (2002) (officers on the street cannot be held responsible for the accuracy of database entries in CJIS; the motorist was properly stopped and arrested based on information, which later turned out to be incorrect, that his license was suspended; the arrest resulted in the discovery of a rifle in the vehicle).

COMMUNITY CARETAKING

"Community caretaking" is a legitimate reason to stop a vehicle if a driver or passenger may be at risk. *Cady v. Dombrowski*, 413 U.S. 433 (1973).

- **Sufficient basis.** *Comm. v. Cordeiro*, 2012 WL 1933756 (Appeals Court): At 2:00 a.m., William Cordeiro, driving 20 mph on a highway with a speed limit of 50, turned into an unmanned fire station and circled around it. When he appeared to be traveling around a second time, an officer blew her horn. When Cordeiro did not respond, the officer turned on her blue lights because she believed that Cordeiro might be ill or having some other kind of difficulty. Her decision led to his arrest for OUI. Also see *State v. Fuller*, 556 A.2d 224 (Maine 1989) (blinking headlights caused officer to believe driver needed help). *Wright v. Texas*, 7 S.W.3d 148 (1999) (passenger vomited out window at 4:00 a.m.).

- **Insufficient basis — lost motorist.** *Comm. v. Canavan*, 40 Mass. App. Ct. 642 (1996): The defendant had not committed any traffic violation when the officer pulled him over around 1:00 a.m., thinking he was lost. The officer had seen the defendant stop his vehicle for nearly three minutes at the entrance to a confusing rotary, then enter and circle back toward a closed gas station. The officer pulled him over with lights and siren. He detected a strong odor of alcohol and observed an empty case of beer. An OUI arrest followed.

  Although this officer was motivated by a desire to help, his justification was inadequate under our constitution, which minimizes intrusions on citizen privacy. The Appeals Court was also concerned that officers might routinely fall back on the justification, "Your Honor, I thought he was lost."[13]

---

13 A well-being check directed toward a stationary vehicle is treated differently. Its occupants do not have the same expectation of privacy. *Comm. v. Leonard*, 422 Mass. 504 (1996) (trooper's concern about a woman parked in the breakdown lane at 1:00 a.m. allowed him to tap on her window; OUI arrest proper when she exhibited obvious signs of intoxication). See *Chapter 4* for more on this issue.

A roadside community caretaking encounter did not justify a traffic stop when the car drove away. Comm. v. Aulston, 2021 WL 1889757 (Appeals Court): Lakeville Police Officer Sederquist saw a vehicle parked ten feet onto the grass at the side of Route 140 at 2:30 a.m. The car's parking lights and brake lights were illuminated. He pulled in behind the vehicle with his blue lights on to check on the operator's well-being. The vehicle operator, Alex Aulston, immediately pulled out onto the highway and headed south.

Officer Sederquist followed with his blue lights still illuminated. The vehicle accelerated to the speed limit of 65 miles per hour and the officer turned on the siren. After a pursuit of two miles, Aulston was stopped by police and charged with OUI 5th offense.

Officer Sederquist properly started a community caretaking inquiry by pulling in behind Aulston's car with blue lights. However, once the defendant drove onto the highway, there was no reason to continue the caretaking inquiry and stop the car. At most, Officer Sederquist could have followed Aulston with his blue lights off to see if any other concerns arose.

A community caretaking encounter may transform into the detention of a possibly impaired driver. Comm. v. Sargsyan, 99 Mass. App. Ct. 114 (2021): On a cold January night in Newton, Officer Bergdorf was dispatched to a dead-end street to check on the well-being of a motorist who was sitting behind the wheel of a running vehicle for some time. Arriving around 8:00 p.m., Officer Bergdorf saw a man asleep in the driver's seat. Knocking on the window many times failed to get the attention of Sergey Sargsyan. Officer Bergdorf knocked harder. Sargsyan put up his hand and waved the officer away.

Officer Bergdorf knocked again and asked Sargsyan to lower the window, which he did. The officer asked for Sargsyan's license. He was slow to get his license and offered credit cards first. Sargsyan was confused. His speech was slurred. He could not say where he was going or where he came from. His eyes were bloodshot, but the officer smelled no alcohol.

After getting a license, the officer asked for the registration. When Sargsyan leaned over to retrieve this document, Officer Bergdorf saw the handle of a knife tucked inside the waistband of his jeans. An exit order followed. Sargsyan said he did not have a weapon when asked. Officer Bergdorf handcuffed and frisked him, recovering the knife. Officer Bergdorf also saw a syringe and heroin in the car.

Although Sargsyan waved the officer off, there were reasons to continue the inquiry into his well-being. The officer was concerned that Sargsyan might not be fit to drive. When he opened his window at the officer's request, the officer asked for his license and registration, which was a "minimal intrusion." This allowed the officer to see the knife, which properly triggered an exit order and the discovery of drug evidence.

Community caretaking also justifies stopping a vehicle for a condition that would cause the driver to fail a safety inspection. 540 CMR 4.04 lists all the safety defects that would cause a vehicle to fail an annual safety inspection. *Comm. v. Elwell*, 2015 WL 4633768 (Appeals Court) (officer properly stopped vehicle for muffler dragging on roadway; regardless of the technical possibility of issuing a citation, this type of safety stop is always justified).

CRIMINAL ACTIVITY

Reasonable suspicion of minor crime justifies traffic stop.

- **Trespassing.** *Comm. v. Petrillo,* 399 Mass. 487 (1987): Although trespassing in a car was not always enforced at the high school, officers decided to arrest Petrillo. Their traffic stop was valid even though it was mainly motivated by Petrillo's reputation as a drug dealer.

- **Littering.** *Comm. v. Sabetti,* 411 Mass. 770 (1992): A trooper saw the driver tossing trash onto the ground of a Burger King parking lot — a violation of 270, § 16. This alone was adequate grounds for the trooper to investigate.

- **Underage drinking.** *Comm. v. Saint Louis,* 59 Mass. App. Ct. 928 (2003): Officer Simmons of the Bridgewater State University police was on patrol at 1:00 a.m. He noticed a Toyota with four people. When the front seat passenger saw the officer, he seemed alarmed. Simmons was called away to assist another officer. He returned 15 minutes later to find no one in the vehicle. Using his flashlight, he saw a bottle of rum; wires hanging from where a radio should have been; the back seat armrest ripped out, and a cloth covering the hole. A license plate check revealed that the owner, Jose Casillas, was 19 years old and on parole.

  Officer Simmons waited until four males came back and drove away. He did not know whether they were the same people he had seen earlier. All of them appeared to be under 21. Simmons activated his blue lights and pulled the car over. Casillas produced his license and registration. The other occupants handed over two bottles of alcohol. Simmons arrested Casillas for being a minor in possession. Two other officers searched the passenger compartment. They found two guns. The stop and search were proper.

Reasonable suspicion may develop based on the time, place, and type of activity.

- **"Meaningless ride."** *Comm. v. Levy,* 459 Mass. 1010 (2011): At 10:00 p.m. Detective Khoury saw a green Ford occupied by a male and two females. The male placed a 20 second phone call, drove to a residential area, and turned off his headlights.

  A few minutes later, a Pontiac with three occupants appeared. The driver from the Ford ran to the Pontiac and got into the backseat. The Pontiac traveled approximately 200 yards and stopped. The driver of the Ford got out and walked back to his car.

  Khoury checked the Pontiac's plate and learned that the registered owner had a suspended license. Other officers stopped the Pontiac nearby. The occupants were searched, and officers recovered $350 and 28 bags of crack cocaine in Levy's boot.

  The SJC agreed that the detective's observation of the "meaningless ride" amounted to a reasonable suspicion of drug dealing. However, the court felt probable cause to search Levy's boot was lacking. The missing ingredient that would have supplied probable cause: (1) observation of an exchange; or (2) a more in-depth field interview with Levy; or (3) knowledge that Levy or other occupants had a prior record of drug dealing or possession.

- **"Do you mind if I play through?"** *Comm. v. Miller,* 2014 WL 1758209 (Appeals Court): After a break-in at a country club's pro shop, Officer Berger and Mark Miller's vehicles met head-on in a narrow driveway leading from a nearby conservation area. Miller was wearing golf gloves and sweating profusely on a cool March night. He looked "stunned" and kept looking around as he backed out of Berger's way. Berger had a reasonable suspicion that Miller was involved in the break based on: (1) the seclusion of the conservation area, and its proximity to the break and likely use as a staging area or escape route; (2) the conservation area being closed for normal activities; and (3) the obvious connection between the break and the golf gloves Miller was wearing.

While separate actions may appear innocent, they may combine to match a legitimate, behavior-based profile. Consider *Comm. v. Watson,* 430 Mass. 725 (2000): Troopers at Logan Airport with special training in drug interdiction knew that dealers often arrived from certain "source states" (California, Arizona, Texas), stayed in hotels at the airport with no reservations, paid cash, talked on cell phones, and carried "hard-sided" luggage. In this case, defendants matched the profile After arriving in Boston, they met a man at their motel and emerged quickly with two suitcases that they had not brought on their trip. Further suspicion developed when the suspects drove evasively after leaving the motel parking lot. Troopers reasonably stopped their vehicle.

Insufficiently suspicious activity does not justify a stop. Officers must be able to explain how the activity suggested criminal wrongdoing. *Comm. v. Bacon,* 381 Mass. 642 (1980): Officers stopped two men operating an expensive car in the early morning. The basis for the officers' action was the youthful appearance of the men and the attempt by the passenger, upon seeing the cruiser, to obscure his face from view. Standing alone, these factors did not provide a reasonable suspicion to justify the stop. *Comm. v. Thibeau,* 384 Mass. 762 (1981).

Stop must immediately end once reasonable suspicion evaporates. *Comm. v. Tavares,* 482 Mass. 694 (2019): The officer stopped a Chevy Malibu believing that a passenger was a wanted person, Jose Correia. As he approached the car, the officer realized the passenger was not Correia. The officer then asked the driver for his license and rental agreement. When the officer realized that none of the occupants was listed on the agreement, he impounded the vehicle.[14]

The initial stop was proper based on the officer's belief that Correia was a passenger, but it should have stopped when the officer knew Correia was not in the car. There was no reason to continue. The officer did not have a reasonable suspicion of any other crime. The fact that the Malibu was rented was not enough to prolong the stop and check the driver's license.

Under an approach approved in *Comm. v. Garden,* 451 Mass. 43 (2008), the officer should have simply said: "I thought I saw a person I needed to talk to in your car, but I was wrong. You're free to go. Sorry for the inconvenience."

---

14 This led to the identification of the vehicle and discovery of evidence implicating the defendant in a drive-by shooting. Luckily, the Commonwealth had other admissible evidence proving the defendant participated in this murder.

Police Information: Secondary Sources

SOURCES

Officers must assess their sources and decide whether their information is reliable enough to justify police action. A longstanding legal test helps. Named after two Supreme Court cases,[1] this *Aguilar-Spinelli* test has two parts. Officers must prove their source's:

- **Veracity** — meaning the person is generally worthy of belief; and
- **Basis of Knowledge** — meaning the information provided is most likely accurate.

There are 4 types of sources — identified citizen, identifiable citizen, confidential and anonymous. The classification affects how officers must prove a source's reliability.

IDENTIFIED CITIZENS

These individuals, including police officers, are willing to have their name associated with the information they provide. Identified citizens have automatic "veracity" because they know they face consequences if they lie. They are liable in criminal and civil court. *Comm. v. Cavitt*, 460 Mass. 617 (2011). Their revealed identity makes them accountable. This is true even if they act out of spite, a desire for revenge, or disclose the information only after police inquiry. *Comm. v. Stack*, 49 Mass. App. Ct. 227 (2000) (initially a confidential informant, a former Latin Queens gang member agreed to let police use her name in order to "put a stop to gang violence in the community").

IDENTIFIABLE CITIZENS

Sometimes officers do not learn or reveal a source's name, but provide enough information to allow that person to be identified. These "identifiable" sources are also worthy of belief because they "place their anonymity at risk" by revealing enough information about themselves to be brought into court in the event they lie. Consider the following situations in which unnamed, but identifiable citizens give crucial information:

Spontaneous street report

By making an <u>in-person</u>, spontaneous report to police, a citizen knows that he is identifiable and, as a result, accountable. *Comm. v. McDevitt*, 57 Mass. App. Ct. 733 (2003).

- *Comm. v. Vazquez*, 426 Mass. 99 (1997): An officer saw several people on the street wave him over. They told him that a Hispanic man in a brown jacket was chasing another man down the street with a gun. Such an immediate report is usually authentic.

---

1 *Aguilar v. Texas*, 378 U.S. 108 (1964) and *Spinelli v. U.S.*, 393 U.S. 410 (1969).

- *Comm. v. Love*, 56 Mass. App. Ct. 229 (2002): A man stopped at a State Police barracks and reported that a maroon Grand Prix was traveling in excess of 80 mph chasing a laundry truck. Faced with an urgent situation, the desk officer neglected to record the man's name, but saw the man's car in the parking lot and noted its plate number. The court concluded that any tip justifies police investigation if it comes from a citizen who presents himself in person to report an urgent situation and is identifiable (here, by tracing the license plate number).

Veracity is also assured when an unnamed citizen is unaware that she is speaking with a police officer. In *Comm. v. Simpson*, 442 Mass. 1009 (2004), an undercover officer was approached by a woman outside a bar. She told the officer that she could get cocaine from a black male playing pool inside. The officer gave her marked money. She entered and returned with cocaine. Two uniformed officers then arrested the defendant, who possessed cocaine and the marked money. The woman's statement about her source was reliable because it was given to someone who she thought was a customer. She had no motive to fabricate her report.

911 call

Unnamed callers have veracity if they know their call is recorded <u>and</u> there is other identifying information — such as a confirmed call back number, presence at the scene, or employment information. Calling 911 does not, by itself, indicate veracity. *Comm. v. Depiero*, 473 Mass. 450 (2016).

- *Comm. v. Costa*, 448 Mass. 510 (2006): At 7:30 p.m., a Cambridge 911 operator told a woman that her call was being recorded and asked her to describe the emergency. The caller said that she was at a basketball game and saw a teenager with a pistol. The teenager was wearing dungarees with red trim, a black shirt and a blue baseball hat with red trim. She said that he was standing behind a car "on the corner of Columbia and Washington right now as I am talking to you, so when y'all roll up he'll know that I'm the one who called — okay." The caller could not identify the type of gun. The dispatcher immediately directed two units to respond.

  Officer Michael Regal knew the area had a history of drug activity and shootings. Once on scene, Regal observed three black males at the corner of the park. One appeared to be much younger than the others (approximately 18 years old) and his clothing matched the broadcast. There were other people in the area, including families with children. Regal told the young man, Nilton Costa, "Don't move!" His frisk located a handgun with a defaced serial number. The officer who transported Costa found cash and cocaine in the police van afterwards.

  In this case, the citizen's cell phone number was identified by the E-911 system and repeated out loud while she was on the line. The caller placed her "anonymity at risk" because her cell phone number could have been traced.[2] The caller was also standing near the defendant, meaning that police could have questioned those nearby had they wished to identify her.

---

2 Even if the caller had borrowed the cell phone, she was potentially traceable through its owner.

- *Comm. v. Rodriguez*, 70 Mass. App. Ct. 904 (2007): A taxi driver called 911 to report that someone had just hit his car. He gave the dispatcher the description and license plate number of the offender's vehicle and identified himself as a driver for Community Taxi. He hung up without giving his name. The dispatcher relayed the information to an officer nearby, who stopped the vehicle and arrested the driver for operating under the influence.

  Although he did not give his name, the taxi driver provided the name of his employer. There is little difference between a caller who identifies himself by name and one who identifies himself by his employer.

Having a recording of the call is significant for two reasons:

- **It eliminates the possibility of police fabrication,** a major concern in assessing the validity of anonymous tips. *Comm. v. Costa, supra.*; and

- **It is the best evidence of what dispatch knew.** For this reason, courts recommend that prosecutors play the 911 recording. *Comm. v. Perez*, 80 Mass. App. Ct. 271 (2011).

CAD sheet

CAD sheet may establish caller's reliability. *Comm. v. Marinez*, 2016 WL 2755861 (Appeals Court): Officers stopped and arrested four suspects who met the description provided to 911 by the victim of a home invasion at 514 Talbot Avenue. The Computer-Aided Dispatch (CAD) sheet attributed the call to apartment 1 at 514 Talbot Avenue, and identified the specific phone number and its owner as "Rodney Davis." It also tracked statements made by the female victim to the police operator, including her description of the suspects. Even though the victim and Rodney Davis were not the same person, the source of the information lived at the premises. If necessary, police could have identified her through Davis.

CONFIDENTIAL INFORMANTS

Purpose of confidentiality

Investigators do not reveal their confidential sources to protect them and ensure they are available for future operations. The privilege to withhold an informant's identity prevents the release of the informant's name *and* any other details that would identify him. *Comm. v. John*, 36 Mass. App. Ct. 702 (1994).

Disclosure of identity

The informant privilege is not absolute. In determining whether a court should order disclosure of an informant's identity, the public interest in protecting the flow of information to law enforcement must be balanced against the individual's right to prepare a defense.

Disclosure is usually required when the informant is an active participant at the time of arrest. Police should carefully consider whether to use a "buy-bust" strategy with an informant for this reason. In *Comm. v. Healis*, 31 Mass. App. Ct. 527 (1991), an informant known as "Orlando" had to be disclosed because he arranged the meeting where the defendant was arrested. The defendant claimed that he was "set up" when Orlando threw a bag of cocaine into his car before the arrest. To resolve the different versions, it was necessary for the police to produce Orlando in court.

On the other hand, the government usually does not have to reveal an informant who was absent when the target was arrested. *Comm. v. Youngworth*, 55 Mass. App. Ct. 30 (2002) (informant told detective that he delivered a stolen Chevy van to the defendant one week prior).

Disclosure is also required if the defendant claims entrapment or points out significant inconsistencies in the government's case. *Comm. v. Dias*, 451 Mass. 463 (2008): The police informant implicated a female drug dealer. The female then told police that she was subletting her apartment to Dias, who was the real dealer. The prosecutor was going to have this woman testify against Dias, but Dias' attorney successfully argued that the government should have to reveal its confidential informant. It was the only way to resolve the glaring discrepancy between the informant's version, which had the female as the major dealer, and the government's version, which presented her as an innocent bystander.

Disclosure of a federal informant may be ordered in a state case. *Comm. v. Bonnett*, 472 Mass. 827 (2015).

If court orders disclosure, prosecutor may dismiss the case rather than reveal the informant. This is often recommended. Effective recruitment is impossible once an investigator gets a reputation for "burning" informants. *Comm. v. Nelson*, 26 Mass. App. Ct. 794 (1989).

Disclosure of surveillance location

The right to withhold the location of an observation post is similar to the informant privilege. In *Comm. v. Hernandez*, 421 Mass. 272 (1995), the police saw the defendant selling drugs from a surveillance post overlooking a playground. The defendant argued that he needed to know the surveillance location so that he could check whether it had been possible for the officers to observe what they claimed to see. The judge ordered disclosure. The police refused to do so on the grounds that it would jeopardize an ongoing investigation into gang-related violence. Consequently, the case was dismissed.

ANONYMOUS INFORMANTS

Anonymous informants are more difficult to rely on because their identities and backgrounds are unknown to police. *Comm. v. Anderson*, 366 Mass. 394 (1974).

TEST FOR RELIABILITY
VERACITY

Veracity refers to an informant's overall credibility. It can be demonstrated in four ways: (1) identified/identifiable citizen; (2) track record; (3) admission of crime; or (4) corroboration.

IDENTIFIED OR IDENTIFIABLE CITIZEN

Once classified as "identified" or "identifiable" the source automatically has veracity. *Comm. v. Costa*, 448 Mass. 510 (2006).

TRACK RECORD

Veracity may be shown by past instances when the informant supplied correct information.

Confirmed arrest or conviction

The fact that a confidential informant previously gave information leading to a person's conviction demonstrates his veracity. *Comm. v. Amral*, 407 Mass. 511 (1990).

A confirmed arrest also demonstrates veracity. Officers must provide details about the arrest that *confirms* the accuracy of the previous tip.

- **Evidence discovered.** In *Comm. v. Lapine*, 410 Mass. 38 (1991), the warrant affidavit established the informant's veracity by pointing out that the tipster had supplied information leading to previous arrests, and by mentioning that the informant had correctly described the target's house and predicted the presence and amount of drugs inside.[3]

- **Indictment.** In *Comm. v. Soto*, 35 Mass. App. Ct. 340 (1993), police used a confidential informant whose prior tip had led to an arrest *and* Superior Court indictment. The validity of an arrest that results in indictment is significantly more assured than a mere arrest.[4]

- **Unconfirmed.** The SJC has held that a "naked assertion" by officers that an informant's tip led to an arrest (or even multiple arrests) does *not* show veracity. In *Comm. v. Mejia*, 411 Mass. 108 (1991), the warrant affidavit stated that the confidential informant had previously provided information leading to three separate arrests for narcotics violations, within one month, in the same city. Still, the warrant was invalid because there was no additional information about these past arrests.

Must disclose name or docket number of prior case, or explain failure to do so. When relying on a past conviction or arrest to prove an informant's veracity, a police affiant must include the defendant's name or "docket number" from the past case — unless the affiant explains the risk of providing this information. This rule also applies when an officer is presenting his informant's track record to justify a warrantless seizure or search. *Comm. v. Rodriguez*, 75 Mass. App. Ct. 290 (2009).

Confirmed information

The fact that police verified an informant's past information demonstrates veracity. This is true even if the prior information did not lead to a conviction or arrest. *Comm. v. Farinon*, 29 Mass. App. Ct. 945 (1990) (informant previously identified area where detective located narcotics). *Comm. v. Vynorius*, 369 Mass. 17 (1975) (informant helped recover stolen property).

---

3 The issue is whether the informant proved to be factually accurate in a past investigation that culminated in an arrest. If that is the case, it becomes part of the informant's track record. It is irrelevant that the prosecution, which resulted from the investigation, ultimately ended in the defendant's favor. *Comm. v. Gonzalez*, 90 Mass. App. Ct. 100 (2016).
4 Although the *Soto* court did not specifically address the issue, the same finding of reliability would likely apply to an arrest that was followed by a successful district court probable cause hearing.

Track record endures

Once established, an informant's track record applies to future investigations. In *Comm. v. DiPietro*, 35 Mass. App. Ct. 638 (1993), the court credited the informant's track record, even though it was ten years old!

Past instances of dishonesty must be disclosed and overcome. The police must disclose information that shows their confidential informant was unreliable. *Comm. v. McMillan*, 98 Mass. App. Ct. 409 (2020) (informant stole money from his police handlers).

Once disclosed, officers must show why, in spite of their informant's past difficulties, he is reliable in the present case. If they cannot meet this burden, their informant will be (and should be!) disqualified by a reviewing court.

ADMISSION OF CRIMINAL CONDUCT

If the informant admits to participating in a crime, it helps establish his veracity. The theory is that anyone who willingly admits criminal conduct to the police must be conveying truthful information. These admissions of criminal conduct are also referred to as "declarations against penal interest." *Comm. v. Parapar*, 404 Mass. 319 (1989).

Reasonable fear of prosecution. For a statement to be credited, the informant must have had a *reasonable fear of prosecution* at the time that he told police. *Comm. v. Melendez*, 407 Mass. 53 (1990) talked about the reason for this standard. There, a confidential informant with no track record met with the police on numerous occasions to help them obtain a search warrant. The informant admitted to criminal acts, claiming to have recently purchased cocaine. The SJC was troubled by the police/informant relationship. It appeared that the informant had little or no fear in giving false information because he expected no consequences would result from his own crimes.

Showing reasonable fear. Officers may show an informant's reasonable fear by indicating:

- **Identity.** They know the identity of the informant. Remember, anonymous informants have no fear of being prosecuted because police have no way of identifying them. This is why police can *never* rely on an admission of crime by an anonymous informant to show veracity. *Comm. v. Allen*, 406 Mass. 575 (1990).

- **Contact information.** They have the ability to contact the informant. *Comm. v. Alvarez*, 422 Mass. 198 (1996) (fifteen year old informant provided a legitimate admission of crime when he gave investigators his home address and phone number, and told them that he had been selling drugs for a particular dealer).

- **Incriminating connection.** Officers should report if an informant's comments were made *after* he was confronted with evidence of his criminal activity. In *Comm. v. Muse*, 45 Mass. App. Ct. 813 (1998), Charles Willett admitted that he had stolen his grandmother's jewelry to buy cocaine. Willett told the detective where he had purchased the cocaine and provided descriptions of the dealers. Willett had a reasonable fear of prosecution. He knew that his confession, and the recovery of stolen jewelry at his dealers' home, would cement a larceny case against him.

- **Warning.** It is persuasive (but not required) for officers to warn an informant that he can be prosecuted for past and/or future crimes.

PAYMENT OR PROMISES

Informants may receive compensation, but not a contingent fee. According to *Comm. v. Gratereaux*, 49 Mass. App. Ct. 1 (2000), paying informants is a reasonable investigative practice. However, a *contingent fee* is prohibited because it requires a conviction in order for the informant to get paid. Such an arrangement creates too much temptation for the informant to lie.

In all cases, police must properly monitor their informant's activities. Any payments to an informant should be agreed to in advance and properly documented.[5]

At the same time, the fact that an informant did not receive any payment or promises should be noted, because it helps demonstrate veracity. *Comm. v. Muse*, 45 Mass. App. Ct. 813 (1998).

BASIS OF KNOWLEDGE

There are 3 ways to demonstrate basis of knowledge: (1) explain the source of the tip; (2) provide details; or (3) engage in police corroboration. Ideally, officers do all three.

WHEN BASIS OF KNOWLEDGE MUST BE SATISFIED

All informants

All informants, even other officers, must satisfy this second part of the reliability test — so that officers act on good information. "It is especially important that the tip describe the accused's criminal activity in sufficient detail so the [police know they are] relying on something more substantial than a casual rumor circulating in the underworld or an accusation based merely on an individual's general reputation." *Comm. v. Robinson*, 403 Mass. 163 (1988).

Police channels

Officers may act on information obtained through police channels without knowing its original source. However, the tip's legal validity must be demonstrated later in court. *Comm. v. Keene*, 89 Mass. App. Ct. 902 (2016): Ten minutes after Stoughton police saw two men run out of a nightclub and get into a Nissan Altima, there was a shooting outside the club. Stoughton police issued a "be on the lookout" (BOLO) for the Altima even though it had left the scene before the shooting. Boston police saw the Altima and stopped it based solely on the BOLO. The officers found two guns in the car. While Boston understandably relied on the BOLO, the guns still had to be suppressed because the source of the BOLO, the Stoughton police, had lacked a reasonable suspicion for the stop.

---

5 *LED's Drug Cases* has detailed information, including forms and policy, about the proper way to monitor and compensate informants.

Radio broadcasts. When reasonable suspicion or probable cause depends on a radio message, officers must, at some point, learn the factual basis behind the transmission. *Comm. v. White*, 422 Mass. 487 (1996): The initial radio broadcast was based on police interviews with witnesses at the scene of a home invasion, so officers were justified in stopping a car with a distinctive antenna and New York plates. This enabled them to observe the green and black jackets that had also been described by witnesses. The officers even telephoned a Malden police lieutenant who had investigated the home invasion to confirm the descriptions of the assailants. As the SJC remarked: "There can be no doubt that such thorough police work provided probable cause for the subsequent search of the automobile for weapons."

Roll call reports. Officers should learn the source of roll call information when it results in an investigative detention that leads to an arrest or search. *Comm. v. Dottin*, 353 Mass. 439 (1968) (roll call briefing mentioned several housebreaks in the area that involved perpetrators in a taxi; an investigative stop was proper when an officer later observed a taxi pulling away from a house with a television set on the front seat and three men in the rear).

Wanted posters. Wanted posters are treated in the same way as radio bulletins and roll call reports. Officers may rely on them, but a court will later decide whether the poster had an adequate factual basis for publication. *U.S. v. Hensley*, 469 U.S. 221 (1985).

Police K-9

Since a police dog implicates criminals with its sense of smell, the handler has to be able to explain how the dog signals its discovery and why it is reliable. *Comm. v. LaPlante*, 416 Mass. 433 (1993) (handler must state his and the dog's qualifications and training).

HOW TO PROVE BASIS OF KNOWLEDGE

Explain the source

Key inquiry: How does the informant know what he claims to know? The answer to this simple question enables officers to assess whether their informant has a basis of knowledge. The informant's answer will reveal the *source* of his information and convey why police should trust his tip.

Most often, the informant has seen or heard what he describes. If so, basis of knowledge is established. *Comm. v. Toledo*, 66 Mass. App. Ct. 688 (2006) (informant described the defendant and said he saw the illegal guns). *Comm. v. Lapine*, 410 Mass. 38 (1991) (informant overheard three accomplices discussing how they burglarized a Rockport home and hid their stolen goods on a fishing boat). *Comm. v. Tapia*, 463 Mass. 721 (2013).

A spontaneous report about an event demonstrates veracity and basis of knowledge. The reason is the report occurs before the speaker has time to fabricate. *Comm. v. Baldwin*, 476 Mass. 1041 (2017) (defendant's six year old son told 911 dispatcher, "My dad just choked my mom"). *Comm. v. Lauture*, 2013 WL 5707877 (Appeals Court) (unidentified caller's panicked tone of voice described a suspect with "long dreads . . . right there . . . going to shoot someone!" The caller's frantic tone of voice indicated an immediate threat and firsthand observation).

Provide a high level of detail

Details show an informant's basis of knowledge, even though he does not reveal the source of his information. *Comm. v. Kiley*, 11 Mass. App. Ct. 939 (1981) (detailed description of Kiley's dwelling and hiding place for his drugs showed the personal knowledge of the informant). *Comm. v. Parapar*, 404 Mass. 319 (1989).

On the other hand, details never show veracity. *Comm. v. Oliveira*, 35 Mass. App. Ct. 645 (1993): A police informant spoke with Oliveira, who said he was getting two kilos of cocaine, which he planned to store at 60 Middle Road in Acushnet. He had customers already lined up for New Year's Eve, and he described how the cocaine would be transported from Florida.

The affidavit noted that, in the past, this informant had provided information leading to the arrest of a cocaine distributor. The magistrate issued the warrant. Police discovered over 200 grams of cocaine, yet the Appeals Court reversed based on the faulty affidavit.

- **Basis of knowledge clearly existed** since the informant had direct contact with Oliveira and learned firsthand about his cocaine operation.

- **Veracity was the problem.** The affidavit said that the informant had assisted in one prior arrest, but gave no confirming details. The affiant did not engage in any independent police activity to corroborate the tip either.

  Despite these flaws, the government asserted that the affidavit was so detailed that it satisfied both basis of knowledge and veracity. In rejecting this argument, the Appeals Court held that, unlike basis of knowledge, the level of detail does not demonstrate veracity. In the court's opinion: "If the informant were concocting a story out of whole cloth, he could fabricate in fine detail as easily as with rough brush strokes. Minute detail tells us nothing about veracity . . . . Uncorroborated detail of any amount hardly supports an inference that the informer is trustworthy." For this reason, detail only helps to show basis of knowledge.

Informant's informant

Sometimes the police informant obtains information from his own informant. When police rely on this "totem pole" tip, they must be sure that the informant *and* the informant's informant satisfy the test for veracity and basis of knowledge. *Comm. v. Zorn*, 66 Mass. App. Ct. 228 (2006): Robert Zorn was convicted of indecent assault and battery on his 8 year old granddaughter. The victim's parents found the address of a pornographic website written on a piece of paper in their older daughter's pocket. The daughter said her sister, the victim, had gotten the address from Zorn the night they slept over his house. The victim confirmed this, and added that when she and Zorn were alone in the basement looking at the sites, he "touched my private spot under my panties, rubbing me with one of his fingers." Afterwards, Zorn told her not to tell anyone. According to the victim's therapist, she provided the same account.

The police relied solely on the statement provided by the DCF investigator to obtain a warrant to search Zorn's home (where they found evidence on his computer). The DCF statement was "totem pole" hearsay because it was based on the mother's report of what the victim told her. The mother was credible because she voluntarily went to DCF and provided her name. Her account was consistent with the therapist, who also spoke directly with the child. Since the information came from reliable sources, probable cause existed for the warrant.

Best practice — Convey source & details of tip

When possible, officers should present <u>both</u> the source of the informant's knowledge and the details of his account. *Comm. v. Atchue,* 393 Mass. 343 (1984).

If informant's tip contributed to reasonable suspicion or probable cause, the police and prosecutor should present this information to the court — unless there is a compelling reason not to. *Comm. v. Barreto,* 483 Mass. 716 (2019). Boston Police received information from an informant that a green Volvo station wagon containing a "large" amount of drugs would be at a certain intersection. Officers waiting at the intersection observed a green Volvo enter without using its turn signal and park near a residential building. The operator reached toward the floor of the passenger side with both hands. A few minutes later, a man approached the driver's window from an adjacent building and interacted with the driver for 30 seconds. The pedestrian leaned toward the car as if he were "reaching inside the Volvo," but officers did not see the two make an exchange.

The vehicle drove away and was stopped for failure to signal. One of the officers ordered the driver out of the car. As the driver stepped got out, the officer saw a roll of cash in a clear plastic bag on the inside of the door. A drug-sniffing dog was called, which led to discovery of over $11,000 in cash and over 200 grams of cocaine.

- **The tip was not considered.** Because no evidence was introduced regarding the veracity or basis of knowledge of the informant, or the corroboration by officers on scene, the contents of the tip was not considered in determining whether officers had reasonable suspicion to order the driver to exit.

- **What the officers saw at the scene — divorced from the underlying tip — did not provide reasonable suspicion for an exit order.**[6] The police did not observe any hand-to-hand exchange, they had no independent knowledge that the driver or pedestrian were involved with drugs in the past, and the area was a quiet residential street not known for drug activity. While the event might have been a drug exchange, it was also consistent with a number of innocent events, such as a driver asking directions or dropping off an object to a friend. Officer observations created, at most, a hunch.

  Even though police had probable cause to search once they saw the cash in the car, that discovery never would have happened without their invalid exit order. The evidence had to be suppressed.

- **Commentary.** In this case, the prosecutor did not offer the contents of the tip into evidence so that officers would not be cross examined about it. This was a poor strategy because it resulted in insufficient facts during the motion hearing. Through better officer preparation, this prosecutor could have protected the confidential source and presented the full story.

---

6 Exit orders are more fully discussed in *Chapter 4.*

CORROBORATION

Corroboration is independent police verification. In establishing reasonable suspicion or probable cause, corroboration compensates for deficiencies in an informant's veracity *and/or* basis of knowledge. *Comm. v. Cast*, 407 Mass. 891 (1990).

Corroboration rescues a deficient tip. *Comm. v. Brea*, 2018 WL 1095780 (Appeals Court): A confidential informant told Officer Smith that his former cell mate, Bernardo Brea, brought him to unit E39 at Uncle Bob's Self Storage facility on December 6th and showed him three stolen dirt bikes for sale. On December 12th, Officer Smith went to Uncle Bob's, where the manager said Brea had recently vacated unit E39. Smith entered the unit and observed multiple sets of tire tracks consistent with dirt bike patterns. The manager provided a document indicating Brea vacated unit E39 on November 29th and moved to unit C03. Smith obtained a search warrant for C03 and found the dirt bikes.

The discrepancy between the informant's statement that he visited the unit on December 6th and the document revealing that Brea moved out on November 29th reduced the informant's veracity. However, even if he did not visit the unit on that date, his knowledge of the unit number strongly suggests he visited at some point since Brea started renting it in October. The bike tracks in E39 corroborated the informant's statements that he had seen dirt bikes there recently. Police had the informant's contact information, which also bolstered his veracity.

Corroboration is <u>essential</u> if police rely on an anonymous informant. Because police lack any knowledge of an anonymous informant's background, officers must engage in independent investigation. Then, the anonymous tip does not stand alone — it is supported by information confirmed by police.

- *Comm. v. Montanez*, 55 Mass. App. 132 (2002) started with an anonymous telephone tip about a fight on the third floor of a Holyoke apartment building. Within two minutes of the call, officers arrived at the building. They observed two men hurriedly leaving. One of the men had a swollen red face and looked like he had been in a fight. The officers were justified in making an investigatory stop.

- *Comm. v. Anderson*, 461 Mass. 616 (2012): Eight minutes after a family market was robbed, an anonymous citizen called the community service line at the police station. The caller had seen two black males hop into a silver or gold Toyota Camry. The caller said the license plate number, the direction of the car, and that a woman was driving.

  Police checked the plate number and found no record of any vehicle. However, when they changed one of the letters from "O" to "D," they found a Toyota Camry registered to a woman. Then, within 40 minutes of the robbery, officers stopped this Toyota 1½ miles from the market. A woman was driving with two male passengers. The three occupants were removed and the vehicle searched. A gun was found.

Corroboration is important if police rely on a "first time" confidential informant.

- **Sufficient corroboration.** *Comm. v. Voris*, 38 Mass. App. Ct. 377 (1995): A first time informant described the suspect as a musician who was selling large quantities of marijuana from a house in Watertown. Police verified the description of the defendant and that he owned the home at the particular address. In addition, they observed more than 25 people entering for a short time. Two visitors had criminal records for drugs. A detective also stopped an individual in front of the defendant's home who "reeked" of marijuana and had $2,500 in his pocket. This level of corroboration compensated for the informant's lack of a track record.

- **Insufficient corroboration.** *Comm. v. Paris*, 97 Mass. App. Ct. 785 (2020): Detective Dacunha was at dinner with four other New Bedford gang unit detectives when a previously untested confidential informant (CI) provided a tip. Two members of the West End gang, Shazan Gilmette and a dark skinned male in a white t-shirt, were at a restaurant in the South End gang's territory, and one of them had a gun. As the detectives were driving, their CI called in a second tip. These two men had left the restaurant and were heading south on Acushnet Avenue in a gray Kia.

  Detective Dacunha in one cruiser headed to the restaurant, while other detectives drove to Acushnet Avenue. That second cruiser shortly came across a gray Kia parked near a housing complex in West End gang territory. The detectives pulled behind the Kia and turned on their blue lights. They observed that the car was running and two doors were slightly ajar. Shazan Gilmette stood on the sidewalk next to the car near two known gang members who were not wearing t-shirts. A dark-skinned man in a white t-shirt, the defendant, was five feet from the rest of the men walking away. One detective frisked Gilmette and found nothing, while another followed the defendant and brought him back.

  The group was asked who the car belonged to. The defendant said it was his grandmother's. As this was happening, a detective searched the car and found a revolver in the center console. Detective Dacunha then arrived with further information from his CI: the dark-skinned male in the white t-shirt had pointed a firearm from the Kia at people standing near the restaurant. The defendant was arrested.

  Though the CI knew the full name of one gang member, the CI did not provide the name of the male in the white t-shirt, or mention who had the gun, or describe the gun, or even say that the CI had personally seen the gun. Summed up, the CI said that two affiliates of a gang had been in one place, had left (according to the second tip) without incident, and were driving south. The detectives corroborated only obvious details. This was insufficient proof of either basis of knowledge or veracity — even for the lower standard of reasonable suspicion to make the stop.[7]

Sometimes informant information is considered reliable without corroboration. *Comm. v. Sabanero*, 2018 WL 4395005 (Appeals Court): The affidavit filed with the warrant established probable cause of Roy Sabanero's drug dealing from his residence. The informant had a basis of knowledge as a participant in the defendant's drug dealing. He provided a clear description of Sabanero and identified him from a booking photo. The informant satisfied the veracity test by providing past information leading to an arrest and seizure of drugs.[8]

---

7 Not addressed in the decision was the timing of Detective Dacunha's discovery that people had been threatened with a gun and whether this was collective knowledge justifying the search of the Kia by the other detectives. See *Chapter 2*.
8 Interestingly, the court noted that the affiant did corroborate his informant's tip although, strictly speaking, it was not legally required.

SUSPECT OR VEHICLE NEAR RECENT CRIME SCENE

Most common corroboration: Officers see a person or vehicle near the scene of a recent crime matching a witness' description. *Comm. v. McKoy,* 83 Mass. App. Ct. 309 (2013).

For example, in *Comm. v. Molina,* 2021 WL 48604 (Appeals Court), Detective Casallas was assigned to investigate an assault committed near the Brandywine Housing Development. An identified caller had reported to 911 that he witnessed the assault and saw one perpetrator enter a sedan bearing Massachusetts registration 4TF-148. The victim's grandfather voiced his concern that the offender had a gun.

Four days after the crime, Detective Casallas was near the scene when he saw Jamal Molina carrying his food out of the Royal Roast Beef restaurant. When Molina saw the detective's cruiser, he put his head down and walked briskly to a black sedan parked in the lot. The vehicle's number tag was bent slightly up so it was hard to read. Detective Casallas decided to follow the vehicle after it left the lot. Once he was able to read the plate, he saw it was 4TF-148. Detective Casallas stopped the car.

Molina reached under his seat and turned his back to the approaching detective. He emotionally said he "wanted to go home." The detective frisked the floor where Molina had reached and found a gun.

Four days was not too long a time gap between the crime and the investigatory stop. Reasonable suspicion relied on Molina's evasive behavior, the bent license plate, and the matching plate all observed close to the scene of the original attack.

Minor discrepancies between tip and corroboration do not defeat reasonable suspicion. *Comm. v. Ancrum,* 65 Mass. App. Ct. 647 (2006): A double shooting occurred at 9:00 p.m. in Fitchburg. Dispatch described a newer model red Cadillac, with a tan top and long tail lights. Two males — 5'8", 170 pounds, wearing "do rags" on their heads — ran from the scene.

Thirty minutes later, two troopers saw a 1995 green Cadillac, with long tail lights and a tan roof. It was registered to a woman in Chelsea and had not been reported stolen. The Cadillac was committing no traffic violations.

As troopers pulled alongside, they illuminated its interior by using their "alley light." Dougherty saw four males and noticed that the driver and right rear passenger were wearing "do rags." He pulled the vehicle over for a "felony stop." Troopers ordered the defendants to exit the car separately, handcuffed and frisked them.

Dougherty frisked the Cadillac and noticed that the rear passenger seat was loose and a Burger King bag on the seat was warm. There were two Burger Kings in the area, one in Fitchburg and one in Leominster. Dougherty asked the driver, Tony Ancrum, where he had come from. He gave the first name of a friend, but was unable to state her last name, phone number, address, or route he traveled. Dougherty asked if he had gone to a Burger King that day. Ancrum said no, but thought he had gone to one the day before.

Dougherty next talked to Giovanni Rivera, the front seat passenger, who also said he came from a friend's house. He, too, was unable to provide her last name or other information. He stated that they had gone to a Burger King just before getting on the highway.

Meanwhile, the dispatcher ran record checks on each occupant. Among the four men, there were numerous charges involving firearms and drugs. Trooper Cullen arrived and conducted a more thorough search of the back seat — finding two handguns and cocaine. Troopers later obtained a search warrant and discovered a third gun in the engine compartment. The court approved the fine work of these law enforcement professionals.

- **Radio broadcast.** The police corroborated significant details of the original broadcast: (1) a short period of time had elapsed; (2) the vehicle had 2-toned coloring; (3) it was a Cadillac with long tail lights; (4) two of the vehicle's occupants wore "do rags;" and (5) the Cadillac was registered to a woman in Chelsea, but there was no woman in the car.

- **Discrepancies do not nullify reasonable suspicion.** The defendants argued that differences between information in the radio dispatch and the troopers' observations negated reasonable suspicion. Specifically, the radio broadcast described a newer model red car with two passengers, and troopers stopped a 1995 green car with four passengers. These differences were insignificant. The court noted: "Reasonable suspicion may exist absent a full match-up of all parts of a description. Police must be allowed to take into account the possibility that some descriptive facts supplied by victims or witnesses may be in error." To his credit, Dougherty testified that, from his training and experience, he knew witnesses sometimes mistake vehicle colors, especially at night.

- **Exit orders & frisks.** Here, police reasonably believed the occupants had been involved in a shooting. The fact that the driver took several minutes to respond to police commands and that passengers looked out the rear window and ducked down, further supported the exit orders and frisks for weapons.

- **Search of vehicle.** The search of the Cadillac was permissible under the motor vehicle exception. When Trooper Cullen searched, he clearly had probable cause.[9]

REPORT OF IMPAIRED OPERATOR

A detailed tip concerning recent, erratic operation provides reasonable suspicion of impaired driving. *Comm. v. Depiero*, 473 Mass. 450 (2016): An unidentified man reported to 911 that a "drunk driver" was "swerving all over the road." He gave the location, as well as the color, make, and plate number of the vehicle. Dispatch determined that the vehicle owner was on probation for drunk driving. Trooper Dwyer did not observe any erratic driving as the suspect vehicle turned onto a private driveway, but the broadcast justified the stop anyway. Dwyer arrested the drunk driver, who almost fell getting out of his car.

Deficient vehicle description may derail the case. In *Comm. v. Miranda*, 2011 WL 4088322 (Appeals Court), an officer received a report of an erratic driver on Rt. 88 in Westport. The callers reported a large, red Ford truck traveling at mile marker 5. The officer drove to mile marker 7 and waited. He saw a truck matching the description. He did not see an infraction. He pulled the truck over and arrested the driver for OUI.

---

9 The motor vehicle exception is discussed in *Chapter 16*.

In this case, the callers did not provide any distinctive features of this common vehicle (e.g., year, condition, age, decals, bumper stickers, etc.), or a license plate number. Since the road had at least one entrance ramp between markers 5 and 7, the officer may have stopped a different truck than the one seen by the callers.

Field recommendations. Officers should:

- **Rely on reports from citizens with firsthand knowledge** — especially when they are calling on their cell phones. Dispatch should learn specific details about the "erratic operation" and the vehicle (e.g., bumper stickers, plate number).

- **View the possibility of an impaired driver as an imminent danger to the public.** The quicker officers can spot the suspect vehicle, the more likely a court will approve the intervention.

- **Look for moving or equipment infractions upon seeing the suspect vehicle.** A civil infraction provides an additional reason to conduct a traffic stop.

- **Always stop the vehicle immediately. Don't follow in order to see if the operator engages in erratic driving.** This risks the possibility of a collision and may, ironically, cause reasonable suspicion to evaporate if the officer observes good driving.

- **Check with the dispatcher for collective knowledge before writing an incident report.** Oftentimes, a dispatcher will alert patrol units with available information while remaining on the phone with the caller. Information collected after the initial broadcast, even if it does not reach the airwaves, is still part of the reasonable suspicion calculation under the collective knowledge doctrine. See discussion in *Chapter 2*. Officers should include *all* of the information the caller furnished to dispatch in their incident report.

REPORT OF GUN POSSESSION

Report of gun, by itself, insufficient

A report that a person is carrying a firearm does not, without more, provide reasonable suspicion of unlawful possession. *Comm. v. Couture*, 407 Mass. 178 (1990) first articulated this rule. Since then, numerous cases have affirmed it. *Comm. v. Barros*, 435 Mass. 171 (2001). *Comm. v. Devoe*, 95 Mass. App. Ct. 1107 (2019) (fact that firearms sniffing K-9 alerted to defendant's blue bag was not, by itself, proof that she unlawfully possessed the gun; she was an adult and there were no other indicators that she was unlicensed to carry).

Need "plus factor." Since knowledge that someone possesses a gun is, by itself, insufficient to justify an investigative detention, officers must have at least one additional reason why the suspect might possess the gun unlawfully. The necessary information is referred to as a plus factor — since an officer needs possession "plus" something else.[10]

---

10 While it can be argued that it is statistically probable that a citizen carrying a concealed firearm is unlicensed, the SJC has rejected this argument. *Comm. v. Alvarado*, 423 Mass. 266 (1996).

Plus factors

Most obvious — suspect appears to be under 21. In Massachusetts, it is almost always unlawful for a person under 21 to possess a firearm.[11] Thus, a tip indicating that a suspect is *probably* underage provides reasonable suspicion to detain. *Comm. v. Powell*, 2014 WL 1315013 (Appeals Court) (officer could reasonably suspect the defendant was illegally carrying a firearm because he appeared to be under 21, was incredibly nervous, was driving a car recently involved in a gang-related shooting, violently punched the dashboard when he was pulled over, and had a rigid bulge in his pocket).

Gun history.

- **Past arrest with gun.** *U.S. v. Belin*, 863 F.3d 13 (1st Cir. 2017): Two officers responded to a report of a fight. The site was known for recent firearm incidents. They saw five men walking down the sidewalk. One of the men, King Belin, hurried across the street. Officer Bissonnette had previously arrested him for having a firearm without a license and knew he belonged to a local gang. Belin was wearing a heavy hooded sweatshirt even though it was 70 degrees. Bissonnette caught up with Belin and asked if he had anything on him. Belin became unusually nervous and looked around as if searching for a means of escape. Bissonnette had a reasonable suspicion that Belin had a gun, which was discovered during a frisk.

- **Ineligible for license to carry (LTC).** *Comm. v. Rivas*, 466 Mass. 184 (2013) (using binoculars, an officer saw Angel Rivas remove a firearm from his jacket and show it to a man; the officer was familiar with Rivas' record and had arrested him for drug offenses; he knew Rivas was ineligible to obtain an LTC).

Firing. *Comm. v. Edwards*, 71 Mass. App. Ct. 716 (2008): Officers received a call for shots fired at 106 Lincoln Street in Springfield. When they arrived, witnesses told them that a light-skinned black male with glasses had fired a handgun into the air, then fled in a gold Toyota. A person who wished to remain anonymous said the man's name was Jamal, that he lived at 192 Pearl Street and his girlfriend lived at 106 Lincoln.

Officer Kakley drove by 192 Pearl and saw the gold vehicle. He ran the plate and learned that it was registered to Jamal Edwards. At the station, Kakley saw Edwards' record and photograph.

The next night, Kakley saw the gold Toyota near Lincoln Street. He pulled it over and recognized Edwards. There was a partially visible handgun under his seat. Edwards did not have an LTC and was arrested. The fact that the police did not search for Edwards after locating his vehicle on the night of the incident did not affect their ability to stop him 18 hours later.

Pointing. *Comm. v. Manha*, 479 Mass. 44 (2018): A woman called 911 to report a road rage incident. She said an aggressive driver had pointed a gun at her after she cut him off. She provided a detailed description of the driver and his vehicle. A State Police trooper located the vehicle and pulled it over. He and two other troopers approached with weapons drawn, and ordered the driver out. The driver was arrested and police searched the vehicle. A gun was found inside a black case.

---

11 See 140, §§ 121 and 131.

Selling. *Comm. v. Rupp*, 57 Mass. App. Ct. 377 (2003) (caller identified two men in a high crime area of Boston, at night, engaging in a possible gun sale).

Loading. *Comm. v. Haskell*, 438 Mass. 790 (2003): In Pittsfield shortly before 2:00 a.m., a bartender saw the defendant in his car loading a handgun. The defendant drove away. The bartender reported this to police. Less than a minute later, Officer Barber stopped the defendant's car. Barber saw the defendant reach down. He drew his gun and ordered him to get out. A search led to the discovery of a loaded .45 under the driver's seat. The SJC remarked: "While a licensed gun owner might . . . carry a handgun for protection . . ., the act of publicly loading a handgun is an event that creates a reasonable suspicion that a crime may be about to take place."

Brandishing or provocatively carrying.

- **A report that a suspect brandished a gun is more serious than simple possession.** *Comm. v. Germaine*, 2012 WL 751678 (Appeals Court): A Boston officer was off-duty at a bar when he saw Gontrand Germaine "flash" a firearm. The officer called the station to report. Officer Lynch entered the bar and saw Germaine standing by the jukebox. He noticed a bulge in his waistband. Lynch grabbed Germaine's arm and removed the handgun. While mere possession of a gun does not provide a basis to believe someone is engaging in criminal activity, Germaine "flashed" the gun in a public drinking establishment at 1:25 in the morning.

  Compare *Comm. v. Rosado*, 2017 WL 445495 (Appeals Court): A 911 caller reported that, as he was driving, he saw another driver with a gun inside his car. The caller recorded the driver's plate number because he was "really scared." The caller made no prediction that criminal activity was about to occur, and the officer observed no suspicious behavior. A tip that an individual is carrying a firearm does not, without more, establish reasonable suspicion. The stop was not justified.

- **While "open carry" has not been prohibited in Massachusetts and other states, police are still authorized to respond to provocative displays.** *Deffert v. Moe*, 111 F.Supp.3d 797 (2015): Police were not liable for handcuffing, frisking and detaining Johann Deffert for 13 minutes. Even though Deffert was within his rights to carry, officers reasonably believed that he could be a danger to himself or others. A 911 caller saw Deffert walking in a residential neighborhood across the street from a church on Sunday. He was wearing camouflage and loudly singing a Disney song. He had a pistol in a leg holster, with a tactical light and laser mounted on it.

Concealing. While merely carrying a gun does not create reasonable suspicion, *attempting to conceal one does*. *Comm. v. Colon*, 87 Mass. App. Ct. 398 (2015).

- *Comm. v. Matta*, 483 Mass 357 (2019): Sent to an anonymous call for a gun in a car in an area known for shootings, the officer saw the defendant leave the car when he arrived. The defendant reached with both hands to one side and adjusted his waistband and then walked off the sidewalk towards the bushes. He fled when the officer asked to speak with him, holding his waistband as he ran. The officer testified that, in his experience, people not licensed to carry firearms often carry them inside their waistband.

- *Comm. v. Pannell*, 2017 WL 5894209 (Appeals Court): A woman on the street flagged down Officer Pietrucci. She was with a man who was bleeding from the head. She pointed to Reyshawn Pannell, who was walking away while carrying a small child, a backpack, and a diaper bag. The woman said Pannell had a gun in the diaper bag. Officer Pietrucci relayed the information to Officer Hiney, who ordered Pannell to stop. Pannell ignored him and continued walking. When he finally stopped, Officer Pietrucci took the baby and handed her to another officer. He then removed the backpack and diaper bag from Pannell's shoulder. As he did so, he noticed the bag was unusually heavy and felt a hard object that was not consistent with diapers or baby wipes. When he placed the bag on the ground, he saw the barrel of a handgun. Pannell did not respond when asked if he had a license to carry. Officer Pietrucci seized the firearm and arrested Pannell. A report of a gun in a diaper bag provided a reasonable suspicion.

No holster. *Comm. v. Edwards*, 476 Mass. 341 (2017): Officer Lanteigne responded to a 911 report of a man standing in the street holding a gun. The caller did not see the man threaten anyone. As Lanteigne approached, the 911 caller ran outside and pointed at a dark car, yelling: "That's the guy. He's about to drive away." A stop of the vehicle was justified by a combination of factors. While not required by law, licensed owners typically carry their firearm in a holster. The defendant also possessed the handgun in an area known for gun violence at 1:30 a.m., and had driven in circles before sitting in an unlit car.

Possessing during crime. Police may check people who possess a gun in criminal circumstances. *Comm. v. Anderson*, 366 Mass. 394 (1974): The police appropriately seized a handgun from an individual who had been identified in an anonymous, handwritten note that said: "New York to Boston. Please get Boston Police. Bus terminal Boston Greyhound. Man Armed & Dangerous. Blue hat. Brown Paper Bag. Important! Has Narcotics. This is no joke." That someone took the time to write the tip gave it an extra degree of authenticity, and the placement of the gun next to narcotics indicated illegal activity.

Weapon typically connected with crime. In *Comm. v. Alvarado*, 427 Mass. 277 (1998), a citizen told officers that he had just seen someone in a car with a sawed-off shotgun. Although, at the time, it was possible to legally possess a sawed-off shotgun (the law has since changed), its "lethal character" led the SJC to conclude that officers properly conducted an immediate stop. It turned out that the defendant did not possess a shotgun, but he did have a handgun without a license, resulting in his arrest and conviction.

Other weapons and attachments might justify police investigation based on their "lethal character" — large capacity firearms, rifles, shotguns, assault weapons, feeding devices, and machine guns. See 140, § 121 for definitions of these devices.

Impaired. Even someone with a license to carry may not ever possess a gun in public while under the influence of alcohol or drugs. It is a crime under 269, § 10H.

Public safety risk. When the tip describes a person who appears out of control or unconscious, police must deal with the public safety threat. *Comm. v. Johnson*, 36 Mass. App. Ct. 336 (1994) (citizen told officer that woman down the street was carrying a handgun in her purse; officer observed defendant in the street shouting obscenities; she refused to calm down; officer patted down her handbag and retrieved her gun). *Comm. v. Souza*, 2013 WL 1919112 (Appeals Court) (citizen reported unconscious man in a parked vehicle with a silver handgun in his waistband; the officer gently lifted the defendant's shirt and seized the gun without waking him; officer did not want to risk that the defendant would wake up in a confused and belligerent state; the defendant's car was parked in a busy shopping center where anyone could have reached in and grabbed the weapon; the officer secured the gun before assessing the defendant's condition).

Adequate description of person with gun

A tip will not provide a basis for action unless it adequately describes the person in possession. Consider *Comm. v. Berment*, 39 Mass. App. Ct. 552 (1995), where officers received a radio call about "a man waving a gun" at a particular address. When officers arrived, they saw three men, one woman, and a motor vehicle in a parking lot adjacent to the address. Frisking one of the men, they uncovered a hand gun with a defaced serial number. The officers based their frisk on four factors: (1) the encounter was at 3:00 in the morning; (2) in a high crime area where six previous drug arrests had occurred; (3) the radio call reported a man waving a gun; and (4) upon arrival, the officers observed the four individuals.

The Appeals Court was not persuaded. There was no evidence regarding the time of the 911 call, the caller's identity, or the description of the man waving a gun. The fact that four people were gathered at 3:00 a.m. "just talking" did not point to criminal activity, or to the particular defendant who was frisked. *Comm. v. Grinkley*, 44 Mass. App. Ct. 62 (1997).

Authority to demand license

140, § 129C requires a citizen to produce his license on demand. This statute declares: "Any person who, while not being within the limits of his own property or residence, or such person whose property or residence is under lawful search . . . shall on demand of a police officer, exhibit his license to carry firearms, or his firearm identification card . . . [or explain his exempt status] . . . Upon failure to do so such person may be required to surrender [his gun to the officer, which shall be] . . . returned forthwith upon presentation within thirty days of [the proper license] . . . ."

No Miranda necessary when officer _orders_ a citizen to produce his license. *Comm. v. Haskell*, 438 Mass. 790 (2003) held that *Miranda* warnings are not required before an officer demands, pursuant to 140, § 129C, that a suspect produce his license. The SJC reasoned that it serves no purpose to advise a suspect of the right to remain silent when the police are only demanding the production of physical evidence — a proper gun license — that the suspect may not withhold anyway.

However, once officers locate a gun, they may run afoul of *Miranda* if they ask the suspect whether he has a license.[12] To avoid a legal mishap, use this language in the field:

> Sir, I now have your gun. Listen carefully and don't move. Just tell me where your license to carry is located so I can get it myself. [The suspect should indicate where it is or, more likely, admit that he does not have a license.]

This practice is less risky for officers. Asking a suspect to physically produce his license could invite him to reach into his pocket or elsewhere to retrieve a weapon.

---

12 This is based on a technical legal distinction. A demand for evidence is *nontestimonial* and need not be preceded by *Miranda* warnings. A question about the suspect's knowledge, on the other hand, calls for *testimonial* evidence, which is protected by *Miranda*. For more on the difference between testimonial and nontestimonial evidence, see *Chapter 22*.

FUTURE EVENT PREDICTED

When a future event develops precisely as the informant predicted, this establishes his reliability. *Comm. v. Welch*, 420 Mass. 646 (1995). *Draper v. U.S.*, 358 U.S. 307 (1959).

- **Sufficient corroboration.** *Comm. v. Shoulders,* 2012 WL 2196397 (Appeals Court): A confidential informant told police that at 1:00 p.m., a black male named Anthony would arrive at the South Shore Plaza driving a black Dodge Charger or a Mitsubishi Galant. He said Anthony would have two ounces of crack cocaine for sale and would park directly in front of Joe's American Bar and Grill. The informant had purchased cocaine from Anthony on at least ten prior occasions. He described Anthony as 30 years old, 6' tall, weighing 200 pounds, with scars on his neck. He provided Anthony's cell phone number. At 12:45 p.m., the informant reported that Anthony would be driving the Mitsubishi Galant and that another man would be with him. Police conducted surveillance and the scenario played out exactly as predicted.

- **Insufficient corroboration.** In *Comm. v. Lyons,* 409 Mass. 16 (1990), an anonymous caller telephoned police at 1:15 a.m. with the following information: Two white males, one named "Wayne," had just bought cocaine in Chelsea and would be heading for Bridgton, Maine, in a silver Hyundai with Maine registration 440-44T. After seeing the exact car at 2:00 a.m., with two male occupants, traveling north on the interstate toward Maine, Trooper Manzi pulled the vehicle over by activating his blue lights. The driver provided a license identifying him as "Wayne Lyons." Manzi observed a cocaine straw and residue on the floor, which led him to search and uncover more cocaine.

  The SJC found this tip and accompanying corroboration insufficient for an investigatory stop — although the justices admitted that it was a "close call." The tip did not indicate the tipster's basis of knowledge — how did he know about the two suspects? — or his veracity. Corroboration had to make up for these deficiencies, yet the trooper could only verify the description of the car, the general direction it was headed, and the race and gender of the occupants.

MULTIPLE SOURCES

Multiple tips corroborate one another because facts reported by individuals not acting together are likely true. *Comm. v. Barbosa*, 463 Mass. 116 (2012): After a shooting at a party in Boston, police applied for a warrant for Manuel Barbosa's apartment. The affidavit contained information from three confidential informants, each of whom reported being at the party.

- Informant No. 1 observed two Cape Verdean men known as "Fausto" and "Fish" at the party. The informant described "Fish" as dark-skinned, wearing black jeans, a red shirt and a black hooded sweatshirt. The informant also witnessed the victim arrive with a man known as "Sandy," who later got into a fist-fight with "Fausto" in the living room.

- Informant No. 2 reported that during the fight, a 5'6" Cape Verdean man, wearing a red t-shirt, emerged from a staircase with a silver semi-automatic handgun and fired one shot into the living room. The informant did not see the shooter's face.

- Informant No. 3 recognized "Sandy" and "Fausto" as the individuals fighting in the living room. The informant observed "Fish" standing in the stairway, where he pulled a semi-automatic handgun from his jacket pocket, held it with his left hand, and gestured it toward the fight. The informant followed "Fish" up the stairs and heard a gunshot coming from the doorway.

The basis of knowledge prong was satisfied because each informant provided a detailed account. The affidavit also included statements by Barbosa, confirming that he was at the party and is known as "Fish."

The veracity prong was satisfied too. The detailed statements of the unnamed informants corroborated each other. Informant Nos. 1 and 3 each placed "Fish" at the party. Informant No. 1's description of "Fish" matched Informant No. 2's description of the shooter. Informant No. 2's statement that the shooter stood by the staircase with a semi-automatic handgun in his left hand corroborated No. 3's observations of "Fish." Taken together, the three informants provided probable cause to issue a search warrant for evidence related to the homicide.

CONTROLLED BUY

An operation that __confirms__ a suspect's criminal activity has obvious value. The SJC declared that a "controlled purchase of narcotics provides probable cause to issue a search warrant." *Comm. v. Cruz,* 430 Mass. 838 (2000). This tactic is not mandatory. *Comm. v. Russell,* 46 Mass. App. Ct. 513 (1999) (controlled purchase is helpful but not required).

A valid controlled buy involves a minimum of 4 steps. *Comm. v. Desper,* 419 Mass. 163 (1994).

- **Meet.** A police officer meets the informant at a location other than the location where it is suspected that criminal activity is occurring.

- **Search.** The officer searches the informant to ensure that he has no drugs on his person and furnishes the informant with money to purchase drugs.

- **Escort.** The officer escorts the informant to where the illegal activity is occurring. Ideally, police observe the informant enter the target's dwelling, but this is not required if it will risk disclosure. When a multi-unit building is involved, officers must monitor a controlled buy more closely because of the risk that the informant might "set up" the target by purchasing drugs at someone else's apartment. To prevent this type of subterfuge, officers should do what they can to observe the buy — e.g., ride in elevator with the informant to the floor where the target lives.

- **Retrieve.** The informant turns over the substance he purchased to his police handler.

A controlled buy in a multi-unit apartment building requires either close monitoring or an explanation. *Comm. v. Ponte*, 97 Mass. App. Ct. 78 (2020): New Bedford police detective Barbosa used a confidential informant (CI) to make a controlled buy of narcotics. The CI bought cocaine by visiting Joseph Ponte's apartment building, pressing the button in the vestibule, and getting buzzed into the building. The CI would go by elevator to the second floor, turn left to get to apartment 2F, and complete the purchase inside the apartment.

The CI provided a description of Ponte and it matched a police photo. The building manager told officers that Joseph Ponte rented apartment 2F. The search warrant yielded 109 grams of cocaine and $3,866 in cash.

The CI's basis of knowledge was clear but, with no track record, the CI's veracity relied entirely on the controlled buy.

- **This controlled buy did not provide probable cause.** Unlike controlled buys in smaller buildings with 3 or 4 units, there was a much greater chance the CI could obtain cocaine from somewhere besides Ponte in this six-story building. Without watching the CI enter Ponte's apartment — or proof that closer monitoring was impossible — the controlled buy in a multi-unit apartment building did not establish probable cause for the warrant.

- **Whether probable cause exists from a controlled buy at the target's apartment depends on:**
  - Number of apartments and building size and layout;
  - Description of the inside of the target's apartment;
  - Where the drugs were stored inside; and
  - Whether police saw the CI enter the target's apartment, or why it was not feasible to watch that closely.

Intermediary may conduct buy. *Comm. v. Villella*, 39 Mass. App. Ct. 426 (1995): Police searched their informant and gave him marked money. They watched him meet "an intermediary" and followed them to the defendant's home. They observed the intermediary enter the house and, a short time later, leave with a package. The intermediary entered and exited the informant's car. The informant immediately provided a bag of drugs to police. This provided probable cause for a search warrant directed to the defendant's house.

UNDERCOVER BUY

Since law enforcement personnel directly obtain the evidence during an undercover buy, this tactic is much less regulated than a controlled buy. *Comm. v. Watson*, 36 Mass. App. Ct. 252 (1994) (officer who performs undercover buy only has to report what happened; credibility presumed).

TRASH INSPECTION

Police may corroborate a suspect's location and illegal activity by finding evidence in his trash. *Comm. v. Matias*, 440 Mass. 787 (2004) affirmed the usefulness of this investigative tactic. Officers must link discarded evidence with the particular suspect. In *Matias*, investigators found personal papers indicating that the defendant lived in a particular apartment in the same trash as drug packaging. Thus the drugs originated in the defendant's apartment, not another tenant's home. This information corroborated the informant's underlying tip and justified the issuance of a search warrant.

SURVEILLANCE

Police surveillance may corroborate an informant. *Comm. v. O'Day*, 440 Mass. 296 (2003): Brief visits by a number of people arriving in cars on two separate evenings corroborated that the defendant sold drugs. The fact that there may have been other explanations for this activity did not negate the opinion of the experienced investigator. For the court to credit this evidence, police must relate the number of visitors and length of their visits.

INNOCENT DETAILS

Corroboration of nonobvious, "innocent details" contributes to reasonable suspicion or probable cause. Some of the most effective police corroboration concerns innocent details known by an "inside player." *Comm. v. Powers*, 39 Mass. App. Ct. 911 (1995).

- *Comm. v. Cast*, 407 Mass. 891 (1990): State and federal agents confirmed every detail of the informant's tip regarding the defendant's personal life — the origin of his name and citizenship status, his appearance and phone number, his truck, and his business practices. This level of corroboration helped establish probable cause to search the defendant's vehicle.

- *Comm. v. Santos,* 94 Mass. App. Ct. 696 (2019): Officers received information about a concealed firearm from their confidential informant. They corroborated a nonobvious detail in the tip — the connection between the vehicle and the defendant, even though the car had been parked in a separate lot and deliberately registered under a female family member's name. The warrant authorized officers to search the parked vehicle and recover the illegal gun.

RECORDS

Referring to records can be a potent form of corroboration. The most prominent example is acquiring a suspect's criminal record indicating activity similar to that described by the informant. *Comm. v. Washington*, 39 Mass. App. Ct. 195 (1995).

Numerous other sources of data and records may confirm a tip. The Registry of Motor Vehicles can look up what kind of car the suspect owns or whether his license is active. The gas and phone companies can confirm whether the target of an investigation lives at a particular address. These are just a few examples of officers seeking information to confirm a suspect's background, location, employment, lifestyle, or criminal conduct.

ENTRAPMENT OR AGENCY

Entrapment forbids the police from "implanting criminal ideas in innocent minds . . . [and] bringing about offenses that otherwise would never have been perpetrated." *Sorrells v. U.S.*, 287 U.S. 435 (1932).

This requires that police do much more than simply present an opportunity to commit a crime. *U.S. v. Tran*, 226 F.Supp.3d 58 (2016) (government did not entrap defendant by seizing a child pornography website and keeping it open to catch users).

- *Comm. v. Doyle*, 67 Mass. App. Ct. 846 (2006): State Trooper Thomas Nartowicz went undercover as a member of the Longriders Motorcycle Club to investigate narcotics sales. A paid informant, William Donais, introduced Trooper Nartowicz to James Doyle, who was a former president of the club.

  Trooper Nartowicz attempted to make a purchase from Doyle, but Doyle was unable to obtain cocaine at that time. He took Trooper Nartowicz alone into a bathroom and told him that he was not given enough time to get the cocaine, that he did not do business over the phone, and that he could probably get him something later.

A month later, Trooper Nartowicz met Doyle at the clubhouse to buy cocaine. Trooper Nartowicz complained that the price had gone up, and Doyle explained that he was "getting it from a different guy now," because the "other guy" was in jail. Trooper Nartowicz made the purchase, and Doyle told him they could make the purchase a "weekly thing." When Trooper Nartowicz attempted to negotiate a lower price for a weekly purchase, Doyle would not budge.

Doyle raised the entrapment defense by testifying that Donais, the government agent, had induced him to sell drugs to Trooper Nartowicz. Donais was large and intimidating, and Doyle claimed Donais re-addicted him to cocaine after he became clean. Doyle said he reluctantly agreed to sell cocaine after Donais persistently asked him.

Here, Doyle's ability to obtain drugs showed that he was not an innocent party. His refusal to reduce the price showed that he was looking to make a profit and not acting out of pressure from Donais to sell to Trooper Nartowicz.

- *Comm. v. Shuman*, 391 Mass. 345 (1984): Undercover troopers pretended to be involved in a motor vehicle accident, then sought out a crooked doctor and lawyer who recommended they file a false insurance claim. These "professionals" coached the troopers — explaining that this was the way to "play the game" — then created medical bills for nonexistent services. Although the undercover officers had staged the accident and drafted false accident reports and fictitious insurance policies, this did not come close to entrapping the doctor and lawyer, who were eager to commit insurance fraud.

Overreaching conduct by police constitutes entrapment. Indicators that the police went too far include: (1) aggressive persuasion; (2) lengthy negotiations; (3) appeals to sympathy or some other emotion; or (4) significanct logistical support.

- *U.S. v. Barta*, 776 F.3d 931 (2015): As part of a sting operation, government officials played on Barta's sympathies by pressing him to make a deal that would benefit one of his less fortunate friends.

- *U.S. v. Borum*, 584 F.2d 424 (D.C. Cir. 1978): Undercover agents solicited guns from the defendant and only received them after twenty requests.

- *U.S. v. Twigg*, 588 F.2d 373 (3rd Cir. 1978): Police suggested the criminal activity, provided essential ingredients and a location for an illegal drug laboratory, supervised the manufacturing process, and furnished expertise the defendant lacked.

- *Comm. v. Harding*, 53 Mass. App. Ct. 378 (2001): Encouraging a known addict to purchase and sell drugs may constitute entrapment depending on how blatant the police solicitation is.

Because the purpose behind the entrapment defense is so fundamental, a defendant may raise the issue at any time during trial. Once a defendant argues entrapment, the burden shifts to the government to prove, beyond a reasonable doubt, that the defendant was predisposed to commit the crime. *Comm. v. Penta*, 32 Mass. App. Ct. 36 (1992).

Police must adequately monitor their informants or agents. In *Comm. v. Podgurski,* 81 Mass. App. Ct. 175 (2012), the defendant admitted that he had purchased Vicodin from the detective's informant, George Dukakis, in the past. He had seen Dukakis carry guns and knew he was in a motorcycle gang. He testified that, when undercover detective Robert Morrissey and Dukakis came to buy drugs, he and Dukakis talked while Morrissey was out of the room. Dukakis threatened that he would stop providing Vicodin unless he agreed to sell to Morrissey. Dukakis amplified the threat by saying that he knew exactly where the defendant's family lived. The defendant sold drugs to Morrissey because he was afraid.

Interestingly, the *Podgurski* case did not decide whether entrapment occurred. We present it as a good example of how the issue is typically raised.

Defense of agency. The defense of agency comes into play when a defendant claims that he honestly believed he was working for the government. It is typically raised by a defendant accused of trafficking in narcotics. In *Comm. v. LeBlanc,* 30 Mass. App. Ct. 1 (1991), two State Police troopers testified that, while conducting an undercover investigation in Chelsea, they purchased cocaine from the defendant on January 12 (28 grams) and on February 12 (200 grams). At the scene of the second sale, the troopers disclosed their true identities and arrested LeBlanc and his supplier.

Testifying on his own behalf, LeBlanc claimed that the troopers revealed themselves to him after he had agreed to arrange the first sale in January. Rather than arresting him, they promised that they would try to "work something out" if he would cooperate and serve up his supplier. The defendant stated that he arranged the sales with the troopers' approval. He emphasized that he would never have arranged the kilogram sale on February 12 without police assurances that he would get off. Ultimately, the jury disbelieved LeBlanc and he was convicted.

Difference between entrapment and agency. Entrapment means that the defendant claims he was induced to commit the crime by a law enforcement official or someone acting at that official's direction. Agency, on the other hand, means the defendant is claiming that his criminal activity was specifically approved by a known law enforcement official.

Investigators must anticipate entrapment or agency defenses. Deal with any ethical issues as they surface. The best prevention strategy is to always document investigative steps and closely monitor informants and undercover officers.

Part II

ENCOUNTERS, INVESTIGATIVE DETENTIONS, & FRISKS

Chapters 4 – 6

<table>
<tr><td>

4

</td><td>

Encounters & Investigative Detentions

</td></tr>
</table>

ORIGIN & OVERVIEW

Terry v. Ohio, 392 U.S. 1, is the classic 1968 case that established investigative detentions and frisks. This case featured a 39-year veteran, Officer McFadden, who was working a plainclothes detail in downtown Cleveland. He saw two men "that didn't look right . . ." His interest was based on "routine habits of observation" developed over years of "watch[ing] people at many intervals of the day."

McFadden noticed that the two men were pacing in front of a store and looking in the window. They each did this about 12 times, and spoke to each other repeatedly. A third man joined the conference. Believing that they were "casing . . . a stick up," McFadden approached the group and asked some basic questions. Hearing their mumbled responses, McFadden grabbed one of the men, John Terry, placing Terry between himself and the other two suspects. A quick pat frisk of Terry's outer coat produced a revolver, and another handgun was discovered on a second suspect, Chilton. The third man was unarmed.

Notice how Officer McFadden used his knowledge of the downtown area and his experience with people in the neighborhood as the basis for focusing on the two men. McFadden did not rush to judgment, however, and waited until he had observed additional suspicious behavior.

Just seeing the two men looking in a store window gave McFadden a "hunch" that something might happen. When he added their measured pacing and conferences, he had enough to justify a brief intrusion. In fact, as the Supreme Court noted, "It would have been poor police work indeed for an officer . . . to have failed to investigate further."

How the suspects responded — not providing names, surprised looks, mumbled responses — added to McFadden's well-founded suspicion and deepened his concern that the men might be armed. His natural response: a frisk to neutralize the risk.

The key message: Officers must be able to articulate their reasons for stopping and seizing a citizen. For this reason, *Chapters 2* and *3* talked about the various factors that may establish an officer's reasonable suspicion to investigate (and also his probable cause to arrest and search). This chapter continues the discussion by outlining the types of police conduct that result in the seizure of a person, and how officers must conduct their investigative detentions. *Chapter 5* discusses the factors that justify a frisk and the proper scope of that procedure.

An officer's decision to detain and/or frisk is subject to review by a judge. As the Supreme Court said in *Terry:* "Anything less would invite intrusions upon constitutionally guaranteed rights based on nothing more substantial than inarticulate hunches." The demand for specific reasons to justify an officer's intrusion into a citizen's privacy is "the central teaching of . . . [the] Fourth Amendment . . ."

Statutory authority to detain and frisk. Beyond its constitutional roots, the authority to detain and frisk in Massachusetts stems from a statute. 41, § 98 states: "[Police officers] may examine all persons abroad whom they have reason to suspect of unlawful design, and may demand of them their business abroad and [where] they are going . . . If a police officer stops a person for questioning pursuant to this section and reasonably suspects that he is in danger of life or limb, he may search such person for a dangerous weapon. If he finds such weapon or any other thing the possession of which may constitute a crime, he may take and keep it until the completion of the questioning, at which time he shall return it, if lawfully possessed, or he shall arrest such person."

During an investigative detention, the suspect is not free to leave. Since a detention is brief, it does not need to be based on probable cause like an arrest. However, it still must be based on something more substantial than a "hunch." The middle ground between hunch and probable cause is "reasonable suspicion."

Reasonable suspicion to detain does not automatically entitle officers to frisk. The purpose of a detention — find out whether the suspect is involved in crime — is different from the purpose of a frisk — learn whether the suspect is armed. There are times when an officer will have a reasonable suspicion of crime (e.g., a person might be trespassing), but lack a reasonable suspicion to frisk (e.g., the possible trespasser immediately complies with the officer's command to keep his hands in plain sight).

DETENTION & FRISK OVERVIEW

Issue	Investigative Detention	Frisk
Standard	<u>Reasonable suspicion</u> that suspect was, is, or will be committing crime.	<u>Reasonable suspicion</u> that suspect is armed and dangerous while committing crime.
Seizure	Police <u>show of authority</u> by restraint, pursuit, or command (i.e., verbal order or activation of blue lights/siren).	
Factors **Think EASE!**	<u>**E**nvironment</u> (character of the area). **<u>A</u>dvance Information** Dispatch report of crime. Officer develops crime tip. **<u>S</u>uspect Behavior & Background** Near scene of recent crime. Matches description of offender. Flight or nervousness. Record, reputation, & association. Evasive or implausible responses. Unusual activity (consider time of day). Traffic observations: • Vehicle infraction (unless based on bias). • Vehicle status (e.g., revoked reg.). • Motorist public safety. Ordinance/by-law violation. Evidence/contraband: • Recovered at scene (including prints, blood, clothing, etc.). • Possibly exchanged or concealed. Admissions or confession. Investigative corroboration: • Predicted crime event. • Surveillance. • Controlled/UC buy, trash pull, etc. **<u>E</u>xpertise & Experience of Officer**	<u>**E**nvironment</u> (character of the area). **<u>A</u>dvance Information** Dispatch report of crime. Tip mentions possible weapon. **<u>S</u>uspect Behavior & Background** Near scene of dangerous crime. Matches description of offender. Flight or nervousness. Record, reputation, & association. Evasive or implausible responses. Quick, dangerous movements. Potential weapon (e.g., hip bulge). Refusal to obey officer commands. Traffic stop observations: • Failure to stop. • Quick move to get out. • Dangerous movement (e.g., duck under dashboard, reach to floor). • Visible weapon (e.g., baton, knife). Admits possessing weapon. **<u>E</u>xpertise & Experience of Officer**

Issue	Investigative Detention	Frisk
Initiation	**Reasonable force** & communication style under the circumstances (including pre-arrest handcuffing when necessary).	
Scope	<u>Duration</u> No exact time limit; take reasonable amount of time to confirm or dispel suspicion. <u>Activities</u> *At __any__ investigative detention:* Identify suspect (but no general requirement for citizen to ID himself). Check for warrants. Seek evidence (e.g., look for B&E entry point, drugs on ground, gun in bush, stolen property nearby, etc.). Photograph/fingerprint. Conduct ID procedure. *Do not* move unless: • Bring-back to witness for ID. • Emergency because scene unsafe. • Very, very voluntary desire to accompany police to station. *During a traffic stop:* Check license/registration status. • Only request ID from passenger if necessary for protection, MV issue, or community caretaking. If reasonable suspicion of crime exists: • Exit order to driver/passengers to prevent collaboration. • K-9 detection sniff of vehicle. • Consent search may be requested.	<u>Timing</u> At the time officers become aware of the potential danger. *Non-tactical* delay defeats need to frisk. <u>Object of Concern</u> *Person* Pat outer clothing. • Remove possible weapons. • Remove evidence/contraband if "plain feel." *Container* Depends on size and texture. • Small and pliable: pat down. • Heavy and pliable: open and look. • Large and pliable: open and look. • Hard-sided: open and look. *Vehicle* Exit order for officer safety. Frisk the "realistic reach area" where occupants had, have or *will* have access to weapon. • Locked glove box. • Passenger compartment (including under seats, console, etc.). • *Not* trunk, unless easy access from passenger compartment. Only open containers that may *reasonably* contain a weapon.

DIFFERENCE BETWEEN ENCOUNTER & DETENTION
INTRODUCTION

Prior to the moment they <u>detain</u> a citizen, officers are free to approach and talk with anyone. These voluntary interactions are called "field encounters," and they are a highly valuable police strategy. On the other hand, when officers seize, detain, or stop[1] a citizen, they must have a reasonable suspicion. This is why officers need to understand when their actions amount to a detention.

A detention or seizure occurs when a police officer engages in a <u>show of authority</u>. This means the officer's words or conduct will communicate to a reasonable person that he will be forced to stay. A show of authority includes police restraint, pursuit, or command. *Comm. v. Matta*, 483 Mass. 357 (2019).

"Obviously, not all personal intercourse between policemen and citizens involve 'seizures' of persons. Only when the officer, by means of [a] . . . show of authority, has in some way restrained the liberty of the citizen may we conclude that a 'seizure' [or detention] has occurred." *Terry* v. *Ohio*, 392 U.S. 1 (1968).

RESTRAINT

The most obvious detention occurs when officers physically restrain a person. *Comm. v. Stoute*, 422 Mass. 782 (1996).

Incidental touching is not a detention. *Comm. v. Polignone*, 2019 WL 7171337 (Appeals Court): In a train station entrance, a lone plainclothes officer asked to talk to Gary Polignone. Polignone agreed and the officer briefly placed a gentle hand on his shoulder while gesturing toward a corner for a private talk. This did not create any sort of seizure.

Blocking the path of a suspect on foot is a detention. *U.S. v. Camacho*, 661 F.3d 718 (2011): Police responded to reports of a gang fight. Three members of the New Bedford Police Gang Unit arrived in an unmarked car. They were wearing raid jackets marked with "police."

Several people scattered from the brawl. Officers recognized some as members of the Latin Kings. Officers Sousa and Conceiaco followed two men they did not recognize in their cruiser as they walked around a corner. They pulled ahead of them into a driveway, partially blocking their path. Officer Sousa stepped out and approached Angel Camacho, while Officer Conceiaco ordered Louis Osario-Melendez to put his hands on the hood of the car. Neither officer had reason to believe these men were Latin Kings.

Camacho was ordered to take his hands out of his pockets, which he did slowly — clasping them in front of his waistband. Officer Sousa tapped Camacho's waist with his open palm. He immediately felt the butt of a gun.

---

1 These are all terms used to describe the same police activity.

- **Point of seizure.** The officers intentionally blocked Camacho's path with their vehicle. Osario-Melendez had to place his hands on the hood. A reasonable person would not have felt free to leave.

- **The officers lacked reasonable suspicion.** They did not recognize Camacho or Osario-Melendez, or believe they were gang members. No one had identified them, or men fitting their description, as participants in the fight. They were just walking down the street and did not appear nervous when officers approached. Being seen in a high crime area walking away from a possible fight is not reasonable suspicion. The discovery of the gun was tainted by the invalid stop. It had to be suppressed.

Officers also detain a citizen when they block his vehicle.

- **Seizure, but insufficient justification.** *Comm. v. Badore*, 47 Mass. App. Ct. 600 (1999): Police received a complaint about a "loud automobile." Initially, an officer found no vehicle in the area. Following a second phone call, police arrived but heard no disturbance. They did see a parked vehicle that had not been in the neighborhood, but there was nothing to indicate that it was the source of the earlier complaints — yet officers blocked this car with their cruisers. They approached and observed a rifle between the driver and his passenger. The gun was later suppressed as the product of a stop conducted *without* reasonable suspicion.

- **Seizure with sufficient justification.** *Comm. v. Campbell*, 69 Mass. App. Ct. 212 (2007): Brockton police received phone calls reporting that: (1) a man in a black coat had a gun; (2) he drove away in a black car with a specific plate number; and (3) gunshots were heard nearby. Detectives Almeida and Delahoy saw a black Grand Prix with the reported license number at a stop light. Delahoy pulled his cruiser so close to the Grand Prix that its driver's door could not open. Almeida made eye contact with Daryl Campbell, a passenger, who opened the door and dropped an object that made a metallic thud. Almeida drew his gun and ordered everyone to stay in the car and show their hands. There was a gun lying on the street by Campbell's door. He was arrested. Police were justified in blocking the Grand Prix.

PURSUIT

PURSUIT: OBVIOUS INTENT TO DETAIN

Under Article 14, officers seize citizens when they initiate <u>pursuit</u> with the intent to detain them for questioning.[2] The "stop starts when pursuit begins" because the citizen is the object of police authority. At that moment, police must possess a reasonable suspicion. *Comm. v. Stoute*, 422 Mass. 782 (1996) ("Were the rule otherwise, the police could turn a hunch into a reasonable suspicion by inducing [flight]").

Under Article 14, police must consider a suspect's age in deciding whether he is detained. *Comm. v. Evelyn*, 485 Mass. 691 (2020): Following a shooting, Boston officers Abasciano and

---

2 Under the Fourth Amendment, *California v. Hodari D.*, 499 U.S. 621 (1991) announced that a person is seized *only* when a police officer actually manages to detain him. This means that a police officer may commence a pursuit of the suspect and use the fact of his flight, and any other information obtained during the pursuit, to justify the initial decision to detain.

Garney looked for potential suspects. No description had been provided. One-half mile from the shooting and 13 minutes afterward, the officers saw Tykorie Evelyn, a 17 year old juvenile, walking on Dewitt Street.

It was cold and the officers had seen no other pedestrians. Evelyn walked with his hands in his jacket pockets and seemed to be holding an object about the size of a firearm in his right pocket. Evelyn turned his body away from the officers in a manner that blocked their view of the object. The officers drove alongside and asked if they could talk with him. Evelyn answered, "For what?" and quickened his pace. When Officer Abasciano told Evelyn that something had happened nearby, Evelyn's reply was mumbled. He did not stop or look at the police, but was looking around in general.

After driving next to Evelyn for about 100 yards, Officer Garney opened his door. Evelyn then ran with his hands still in his pockets. Eventually Officer Abasciano ordered him to stop at gunpoint. A firearm was found nearby along the route Evelyn ran.

- **The officers showed they intended to stop the suspect.** The officers followed Evelyn for 100 yards in their cruiser, trying to get him to talk with them. When an officer got out of the cruiser, the police demonstrated they were going to talk with Evelyn whether or not he wanted to. Evelyn was detained at that moment.

- **The nearby shooting, the absence of other pedestrians, and a person under 21 seeming to hide a firearm justified the stop.** The case was close, but the officers' credible testimony about their observations were enough to show reasonable suspicion by the time Officer Garney got out of the cruiser.

- **Officers must anticipate juveniles will react differently from adults to police authority.** When known, the age of a child should affect officers' understanding of whether they have compelled the juvenile to stop. Juveniles view police communication as more coercive than adults. This rule did not apply here, because officers could not tell that Evelyn, who is six feet tall and 17 years old, was a juvenile.

- **Nervous behavior by an African-American during a police encounter may have little connection to a guilty conscience.** An innocent black citizen may have the same motivation to avoid the "danger and indignity" of a police encounter as a guilty person — so evidence of nervousness and evasion by a black person has limited weight in the reasonable suspicion analysis.

SURVEILLANCE: NO SHOW OF AUTHORITY

In contrast to pursuit, surveillance is not a detention because there is no assertion of authority. As eloquently stated by the Supreme Court in *Michigan v. Chesternut*, 486 U.S. 567 (1988): "Observation without activation of siren or flashers, without command to halt, without display of weapons, and without operation of [the police cruiser] in an aggressive manner to block [a citizen's] course or otherwise control the direction or speed of his movement, is not pursuit."

Suspects on foot

Officers may approach or follow suspects on foot in public. In *Comm. v. Laureano*, 411 Mass. 708 (1992), no seizure took place when a detective merely followed Laureano into the men's room at a public bar. The detective did not engage in any show of authority, so he was free to observe Laureano and recover drugs that Laureano discarded in a urinal before trying to leave.

Officers do not seize a person just because they run after him — unless they engage in a show of authority. *Comm. v. Shane S.*, 92 Mass. App. Ct. 314 (2017): Police responded to a radio broadcast that Dion Ruiz, who was on conditional release from a pending criminal charge, was in a GPS exclusion zone. When Officer Merner located Ruiz, he observed a juvenile, Shane, jogging toward him. Shane had both of his hands in front of his waist and his elbows tucked into his sides as he ran. Shane met Ruiz and walked with him down the street. Merner called for a patrol car to stop Ruiz.

Officer Crabbe responded and walked toward Shane and Ruiz. He said, "Hey guys, can I talk to you for a sec?" Shane took off running past Crabbe. His right arm was held against his body and his left arm was swinging. Crabbe watched him run for a bit, then chased after Shane but did not order him to stop. He observed Shane stop and bend over two grills at the side of a building, then resume running with both arms swinging freely. Crabbe lost sight of Shane, but he and Merner encountered him walking nearby shortly after. They had a brief conversation before Crabbe placed his hand on Shane's chest and felt his heart beating quickly. Shane was placed in handcuffs. Crabbe retraced his flight path and found a loaded firearm by the grills.

- **Surveillance was not a detention.** The officers did not seize Shane by watching him jog toward Ruiz while holding his waist.

- **Questioning was not a detention.** Crabbe did not seize Shane by approaching and asking, "Hey guys, can I talk to you for a sec?"

- **Following was not a detention.** Crabbe did not call out for Shane to stop, and there was no evidence Shane even knew he was being pursued. Crabbe's conduct would not communicate to a reasonable person in Shane's position that police were making an effort to capture him.

- **The moment of seizure occurred when Crabbe put his hand on Shane's chest.** At that point, the officers' observations provided reasonable suspicion of his unlawful possession of a firearm.

Officers may also approach or follow suspects in their cruiser. *Comm. v. Franklin*, 456 Mass. 818 (2010): Officers were on patrol in an unmarked Crown Victoria, typically recognized by neighborhood residents as a police vehicle. As the cruiser approached two unknown men on the sidewalk, the defendant immediately stopped talking and looked around. The cruiser stopped, and the defendant took off running. The officers jumped out and followed, observing the defendant clutching his waist. The defendant ran toward a six foot high fence. Both officers saw him make a throwing motion, then heard a "metallic thud." They were able to pull the defendant down from the fence and handcuff him. One officer saw a handgun on the sidewalk.

While the defendant argued that he was detained when the officers stopped their cruiser, the court disagreed. The defendant ran before the police did or said anything. He was not seized until he tried to go over the fence. Officers had good reason to stop him then.

Suspects in a stationary vehicle

Approaching a <u>stationary</u> vehicle to check on its occupants is typically not a detention. A stationary vehicle is treated differently from a moving one because its occupants have less of an expectation of privacy. They know that an officer, like any other citizen, may simply walk up to their parked vehicle. *Comm. v. Murdough*, 428 Mass. 760 (1999) ("[An officer] may . . . knock on any vehicle window without having to explain why").

- *Comm. v. McHugh*, 41 Mass. App. Ct. 906 (1996): An officer observed the defendant's car stopped in the traffic lane. He pulled alongside and asked if he could be of assistance. The defendant's response was unclear, leading the officer to have further conversation and arrest him for OUI. The court rejected the defendant's argument that the officer's approach from the opposite direction amounted to an investigatory stop because he did not feel free to leave. Here, the officer took no action, such as blocking the vehicle, to prevent the defendant from leaving.

- Compare *Comm. v. Dodson*, 2017 WL 2274617 (Appeals Court): Police observed two men sitting inside a lawfully parked car in a garage. The driver was smoking marijuana. The officers approached from each side of the car, "straddling the vehicle in a more aggressive than nonaggressive manner." They announced "Boston PD" and displayed their badges. They asked if they had more marijuana. The officers ordered the driver out. A frisk revealed cocaine, pills, and marijuana.

  The men were confined inside the car when officers approached aggressively. Yet, the officers did not have a reasonable suspicion at that point. The men were parked lawfully and were not recognized by police from prior incidents. The driver's possession of a single marijuana cigar did not provide reasonable suspicion of criminal activity.[3]

Suspects in a moving vehicle

Following a moving vehicle is not a seizure. *Comm. v. Groves*, 25 Mass. App. Ct. 933 (1988): A marked cruiser followed the defendant's car for a quarter mile. As it arrived at an intersection, two more cruisers approached from different side streets based on a report that the occupants might have committed an armed robbery. No seizure occurred at that time because the police did not block or signal the defendant's vehicle.

Checking plate number of vehicle

Checking the status of a stationary or moving vehicle is not a seizure. Operators have no expectation of privacy in the information provided by their number plates, which must be displayed conspicuously by law. *Comm. v. Starr*, 55 Mass. App. Ct. 590 (2002).

---

3 Even if the officers had probable cause to issue the driver a civil citation for marijuana, they could detain him for that purpose, but no more.

COMMAND

NORMAL INTERACTION

Police do not detain an individual when they identify themselves and ask questions in a normal tone of voice — even though the average citizen does not feel free to walk away without responding. The fact that a citizen feels "inhibited" is not enough. A detention occurs only when an officer speaks in an authoritative manner.

- *Comm. v. Lopez*, 451 Mass. 608 (2008): Victor Lopez was riding a bicycle over a bridge. In uniform and a marked cruiser, Sergeant David Strycharz followed him. Strycharz stopped, motioned for Lopez to come over, and asked: "Can I speak with you?" Officer Romanovich then pulled up in another cruiser. There was no evidence the officers physically blocked Lopez from leaving. Lopez placed his bicycle on the sidewalk and walked over. Romanovich saw Lopez drop something. She found crack cocaine on the ground.

  The question — "Can I speak with you?" — was an inquiry, not an order. An order demands obedience. Strycharz's tone was calm. Since no detention took place, officers did not need a reasonable suspicion to interact with Lopez.

- Compare *Comm. v. Matta*, 483 Mass. 357 (2019). A Holyoke officer arrived in response to an anonymous report of a gun in a car. When he pulled up behind a vehicle without activating his blue lights or siren, the officer saw both occupants get out. The defendant reached with both hands to one side of his body and adjusted his waistband and then walked away. The officer said, "Hey, come here for a second." This was not a command.

  The defendant turned, locked eyes with the officer, and began to run while holding his waistband. The officer yelled, "Stop!" This was a command, so the officer needed, at that moment, a reasonable suspicion. He had it based on the initial broadcast and defendant's reaction. The defendant threw heroin packets over a fence before being tackled.

An officer's unspoken decision to detain is irrelevant in deciding whether a citizen has been seized. The sole issue is how the officer *outwardly* communicates.

- *Comm. v. Caldwell*, 36 Mass. App. Ct. 570 (1994): Two officers approached the defendant because he closely fit the description of an assailant in a rape case. During their conversation, the defendant identified himself. One officer pretended that he wanted a cigarette, which induced the defendant to offer one of his "Newport Lights." This was the brand the victims said their assailant had smoked. This voluntary interaction did not constitute a seizure, despite the officers' ulterior motive for the conversation.

- *Comm. v. Thomas*, 429 Mass. 403 (1999): After receiving information from an undercover officer, a uniformed officer approached and asked the defendant his name and whether he had any money. The defendant produced two marked bills that the undercover officer had previously given him for drugs. This was not a detention. The officer approached the defendant on a public street and calmly asked him whether he had money. The officer did not order him to turn over money. The defendant voluntarily handed over his cash.

- *Comm. v. Cook*, 419 Mass. 192 (1994): The officer's request that Cook have a seat in the stationhouse lobby was not a detention. Nor were his follow-up questions about Cook's identity and whereabouts. Cook had entered and asked whether he could post bail for his friends. The officer became suspicious when Cook lied about receiving a call from his friends (neither of them had been allowed to use a telephone at that point). The officer later testified that he would not have allowed Cook to leave the station, *but* he never said that to Cook because Cook sat there patiently until investigators appeared and placed him under arrest for the murder involving his friends.

Requesting to take someone's photograph is not a detention if he is free to refuse. *Comm. v. Cao*, 419 Mass. 383 (1995).

NONINTRUSIVE, PROTECTIVE MEASURES

Officers may calmly ask a person to show his hands. The request is not so intimidating that it converts an encounter into a detention requiring reasonable suspicion. Consider *Comm. v. Pinckney*, 93 Mass. App. Ct. 1114 (2018): At 4:00 a.m., an officer in a marked cruiser saw two males on a motorized scooter, neither of whom was wearing a helmet. The officer recognized the driver, Claudio Lopes; he did not know the scooter's passenger, the defendant. At a red light the officer and Lopes began conversing. During this conversation the officer noticed that the defendant was leaning forward with his hands pressed against his abdomen, a posture the officer recognized as a threat to his safety. He asked the defendant where he was from. The defendant gave an address that the officer knew to be involved in firearms incidents. The officer then said to the defendant, "I'd feel more comfortable if you put your hands away from your waist." The defendant complied. The officer saw what he thought was the butt end of a firearm in the defendant's waistband. Up to this point there was no detention requiring reasonable suspicion. Requesting that the defendant move his hands, without more, did not sufficiently change this encounter into a detention.

The officer then asked Lopes to pull over to discuss the lack of helmets. Lopes sped off. The officer drove after the scooter and activated his lights. At that point, there was a detention, but by then the officer had a reasonable suspicion the defendant was illegally carrying a firearm.

Officers may also confiscate a visible weapon during their interaction with a citizen. *Comm. v. Greenberg*, 34 Mass. App. Ct. 197 (1993) (when the defendant answered the door, police confiscated a knife visibly protruding from his shirt pocket; the officers told him he would get it back after the interview). Also see 41, § 98.

No detention when a suspect voluntarily searches herself. *Comm. v. Romero*, 2017 WL 2793901 (Appeals Court): Two officers walked into an open nail salon and approached Melady Romero. They asked for her name and whether she had received money from a "white girl who had just entered the salon." Romero said she had. The officers asked her whether she had any drugs, and Romero began to pat down her own body, reaching into her pockets. As she did so, a small plastic bag of heroin dropped on the floor. The encounter was not a detention. The officers did not issue any commands or use a hostile tone. Instead, she voluntarily patted down her clothing and turned over the bag after it fell.

AUTHORITATIVE COMMUNICATION

*A detention does occur when a police comment makes a person believe he **must** stay.* *Comm. v. Matta*, 483 Mass. 357 (2019). *Comm. v. Chin-Clarke*, 97 Mass. App. Ct. 604 (2020) (telling suspect, "Go stand against the wall," was an unconstitutional seizure because the officer, at that point, did not have reasonable suspicion of shoplifting).

CHECKING IDENTIFICATION

Checking a person's identification results in a detention. *Comm. v. Lyles*, 453 Mass. 811 (2009): Officers were on patrol. They had received complaints about drug activity in the area. Officers saw Oscar Lyles walking on the sidewalk. They did not know him. They exited their unmarked vehicle, displayed their badges, and asked his name. One officer requested to see Lyles' ID and then took it to run a warrant check. When an outstanding warrant appeared, Lyles was arrested and searched. He possessed heroin.

In *Lyles,* the officers' initial approach was a field encounter. By taking Lyles' ID, the officers transformed their encounter into a detention (before they had a reasonable suspicion). Identification is a necessary part of everyday life, and no person will walk away while an officer is holding his license; this has the same effect as ordering him to remain at the scene.

Two ways to avoid a seizure in this type of interaction.

- **Citizen offers his identification without being asked for it.** In *Comm. v. DePeiza*, 449 Mass. 367 (2007), the defendant was walking alone shortly past midnight when officers approached him. Without being asked, the defendant gave them his student ID and license.

- **Officer conducts a warrant check without asking for identification.** An officer may also ask a person his name and date of birth. Conducting a warrant check afterwards would not be a seizure. Also see *Comm. v. Mathis*, 76 Mass. App. Ct. 366 (2010).

ACTIVATING CRUISER LIGHTS

*The most obvious seizure involves **blue lights** directed at a moving vehicle.* This is the classic police command to pull over! *Comm. v. Smigliano*, 427 Mass. 490 (1998).

***Blue lights** directed at a stationary vehicle is not a seizure when necessary for safety.* *Comm. v. Evans*, 50 Mass. App. Ct. 846 (2001): A trooper saw a vehicle parked in the breakdown lane. Since police routinely offer motorist assistance, the trooper parked behind the vehicle and activated his blue lights.

He noticed that the driver, Willie Evans, was alone and reclining with his eyes closed. The keys were in the ignition. Evans rolled down the window. The trooper asked for his license and registration. Evans replied that he did not have a license. The trooper also learned about an outstanding warrant. It was proper for the trooper to activate his blue lights for public safety — alerting passing motorists to vehicles in the breakdown lane.

***White light** is not a seizure.* Artificial light allows officers to see at night what they typically see during the day. Unlike blue light, it is not a signal of police authority.

- **Directed toward vehicle.** *Comm. v. Briand*, 71 Mass. App. Ct. 160 (2008): Sergeant Ziemba of the Environmental Police saw a truck with two occupants parked near a boat ramp late at night. He activated his white "take down" lights and approached on foot. He noticed the driver quickly throw something out the window. As Ziemba got closer, he smelled marijuana and saw a pistol on the floor. Arrests followed.

- **Directed toward a pedestrian.** *Comm. v. Grandison*, 433 Mass. 135 (2001): Two Springfield officers were on patrol when they observed Kenneth Grandison on foot. Grandison saw the cruiser and did an immediate "about face," which made the officers suspicious. They followed Grandison and he reversed direction again. The officers turned on their cruiser high beams and followed Grandison into an alley. They added their "alley lights" in time to see him spit out a small projectile. Officers arrested Grandison when they saw a cocaine packet near his feet. The use of headlights and alley lights did not amount to a seizure.

INVESTIGATIVE DETENTION
INITIATION

Aside from being based on a reasonable suspicion, an investigative detention must be initiated with reasonable force. What is reasonable depends on the reason for the detention. 6E, § 14 (if de-escalation fails or is not feasible, proportionate force may be used to conduct a lawful detention). See *Chapter 6* for more on reasonable force guidelines.

Approaching with gun drawn is only permitted when there is serious potential danger. *Comm. v. Santiago*, 93 Mass. App. Ct. 792 (2018) reminds officers to testify about their realistic fears and safety concerns, such as:

- **Specific information suggesting their suspect would be armed;**

- **Any relevant criminal history or prior incidents;**

- **Their tactics and training.** For example, a drawn firearm down by their side with their finger off the trigger (i.e., the "ready position") is very different from actually pointing a weapon at a suspect.

Consider *Comm. v. Miller*, 2014 WL 1758209 (Appeals Court): An officer stopped Miller at night near the scene of a break-in at a country club pro shop. He properly drew his weapon. The officer was alone in a secluded, unlit conservation area parking lot. He was investigating a crime in which the fruits of the crime, golf clubs, could easily be used as weapons.

Reasonable force may include pre-arrest handcuffing. Officers should *not* routinely handcuff suspects during investigative detentions. It is proper if at least one of the following factors apply:

- **Possibly armed.** *Comm. v. Pandolfino*, 33 Mass. App. Ct. 96 (1992) (even though it was daytime, police were detaining a possible masked carjacker; pre-arrest cuffing made sense).

- **Flight.** *Comm. v. Williams*, 422 Mass. 111 (1996) (suspect with a bloody shirt took police on a crazy sprint that ended with the suspect on the ground in handcuffs).

- **Precarious location.** *Comm. v. Harkness*, 35 Mass. App. Ct. 626 (1993) (at 3:00 a.m., officer ran into a building after Harkness, who had a record of drug and gun sales; Harkness went onto the roof; because the officer was alone, he properly ordered Harkness into a "prone position" at gunpoint and cuffed him).

- **One-on-one or officer outnumbered.** *Comm. v. Harkness, supra.*

- **Nighttime interaction.** *Comm. v. Harkness, supra.*

- **Struggle with officer.** *Comm. v. Gordon*, 47 Mass. App. Ct. 825 (1999) (female suspect was compliant at first, but then struggled with officers when she realized they were detaining her for a recent store robbery; handcuffs were appropriate at that point).

Particularly when outnumbered, officers may place uncuffed individuals in the back of their cruiser. *Comm. v. Scott*, 57 Mass. App. Ct. 36 (2003): A rape suspect was placed in the cruiser for questioning. Although he argued that his confinement was unjustified, the court disagreed. The officer had learned that the suspect's middle name matched the one reported by a victim. The stop occurred in an open area near a highway, and the suspect had no ID.

Acts of restraint become improper in less dangerous situations. *Comm. v. Borges*, 395 Mass. 788 (1985): Officers had enough information to detain Borges for possible heroin possession, but they insisted that he remove his shoes so he would not run away. The SJC viewed this extra act of restraint as unnecessary for officer safety. The officers had turned a detention into an arrest *before* they had probable cause. The court suppressed the heroin.

Blocking a vehicle may be proper, or it may be excessive and transform the detention into an arrest.

- **Blocking necessary.** *Comm. v. Vesna Sam*, 63 Mass. App. Ct. 189 (2005): At 1:00 a.m., Roland Souza and his wife were awakened by voices in their kitchen. They called the Fall River Police, who arrived within two minutes. Mr. Souza told officers that he had just seen a male wearing a red football jersey and jeans running down the street. His kitchen had been ransacked. A neighbor reported that he had seen a black van circling earlier.

  Within 30 minutes, Sergeant O'Connell located a black van and a man matching the intruder's description two miles away. As O'Connell radioed for backup, the van pulled into a driveway. O'Connell maneuvered to block the van, and arriving officers frisked it for weapons. They saw a meat cleaver and a Sony remote control on the rear seat. The Souzas arrived and identified the remote as theirs. The defendant and another occupant were arrested.

- **Blocking deemed excessive.** *Comm. v. Stawarz*, 405 Mass. 387 (1993): Two officers in an unmarked cruiser were informed that a blue Ford LTD was stolen. An hour later, the officers saw a car fitting the general description near the location of the theft. The driver and occupant were looking around suspiciously. One marked cruiser stopped the LTD by cutting off its path. Several other cruisers converged on the car which, up to this point, had been operating lawfully. Eight officers "swarmed" the vehicle; one immediately saw that the ignition was missing. The defendants were pulled out and arrested.

On appeal, the defendants acknowledged officers had reasonable suspicion to stop their car. However, they insisted, and the SJC agreed, that forcing their vehicle to the curb was excessive considering there had been no dangerous driving or other indication of potential violence before the stop.

SCOPE

An investigative detention is limited by time, activity, and location. If officers exceed its proper scope, they transform the detention into an invalid arrest lacking probable cause.

LENGTH

There is no set rule for the length of a detention, but it must take no longer than necessary to investigate the circumstances giving rise to the officer's suspicions. Typically, a warning bell should go off in the officer's mind when the detention begins to exceed *15 minutes*. But it can certainly last longer if there is a reason to extend the inquiry. In *U.S. v. Ramdihall*, 859 F.3d 80 (1st Cir. 2017), police approached a car in a 7-Eleven parking lot identified by an employee as belonging to people who bought thousands of dollars worth of gift cards. Boxes of electronic devices were on the floor, and the occupants gave conflicting responses to the officers' questions. The 82-minute detention was lengthy, but reasonable to investigate potential fraud.

INVESTIGATIVE ACTIVITIES

Check identity and warrants

Officers who have a reasonable suspicion may demand a suspect's ID and check for outstanding warrants. *Comm. v. Pagan*, 440 Mass. 62 (2003) (police investigating a possible break-in asked the defendant for ID to confirm his address, because all suspicion would dissolve if he lived there).

At the same time, citizens do not have a general, legal obligation to identify themselves, and may not be detained indefinitely. Officers may prolong the detention if their suspect refuses to provide his name or identification, but they must eventually let him go if they lack probable cause to arrest. *Comm. v. Obiora*, 83 Mass. App. Ct. 55 (2013).

There are times, however, when officers may take enforcement action if a citizen refuses to identify himself or provides false information about his identity. Here are specific laws:

- **Vehicle operator.** The most common example is 90, § 25, which permits the arrest of a driver who refuses to provide his license or registration or provides false information. Passengers have no general obligation to identify themselves. *Comm. v. Alvarez*, 44 Mass. App. Ct. 531 (1998).[4]

---

4 A detailed description of this law appears in *LED's Motor Vehicle Law, Chapter 2.*

- **Citizen in possession of gun.** 140, § 129C requires that a citizen in possession of a gun provide his license on demand to a police officer who is lawfully present. The failure to do so enables the officer to confiscate the gun and wait for proof that it is legally possessed. *Comm. v. Haskell*, 438 Mass. 790 (2003).[5]

- **Bicyclist.** If a bicyclist refuses to identify himself to an officer issuing him a citation, the bicyclist may be arrested under 85, § 11E.[6]

- **Littering.** If a person litters in violation of a local ordinance or bylaw, and refuses to properly dispose of the trash upon police request, he may be arrested under 272, § 60 if he refuses to identify himself. Section 60 requires that police release the citizen *the moment* they learn his true identity.[7]

- **False information post-arrest.** 268, § 34A authorizes a separate criminal charge against a person who provides false information about his identity to a police official *after* his arrest. *Comm. v. Clark*, 446 Mass. 620 (2006).

- **False name with intent to impede or delay investigation.** 268, § 13B is a felony that, among other things, prohibits misleading a police officer with the intent to obstruct, delay or "otherwise interfere" with a criminal investigation. In more serious matters, officers may arrest a suspect who furnishes a false name during their investigation.[8] However, simply refusing to provide one's name, or denying one's guilt, is *not* misleading an officer under § 13B. *Comm. v. Morse*, 468 Mass. 360 (2014).

Take photograph and/or prints

Taking a suspect's photo and/or prints during an investigative detention is permissible. *Hayes v. Florida*, 470 U.S. 811 (1985) criticized police for transporting their rape suspect from his home to the station for prints. The Supreme Court did permit fingerprinting a suspect in the field, provided that officers: (1) have a reasonable suspicion that the suspect committed the crime; (2) have a reasonable basis "for believing that fingerprinting will establish or negate the suspect's connection with that crime"; and (3) carry out the procedure quickly.[9]

Interview suspect and witnesses

A good field interview is the most common way that officers elevate from reasonable suspicion to probable cause.

- **Suspect provides implausible or false responses.** *Comm. v. Chaisson*, 358 Mass. 587 (1971): Police saw the defendant get into a truck and signal other accomplices in a warehouse with the headlights. When officers asked the defendant about the truck, he responded, "What truck?" *Comm. v. Duarte*, 2012 WL 4896204 (Appeals Court) (nervous defendant claimed that he had been on vacation in New York during the past week, but unwittingly gave

---

5 See earlier discussion in *Chapter 3* of this manual.
6 For more on bicycle law, see *LED's Motor Vehicle Law, Chapter 14.*
7 This is discussed in *LED's Criminal Law, Chapter 23.*
8 See *LED's Criminal Law, Chapter 35.*
9 Of course, "neither reasonable suspicion nor probable cause [will allow] officers to make a warrantless entry into a person's house for the purpose of obtaining fingerprint identification." A warrant is required for that. *Hayes v. Florida*, 470 U.S. 811 (1985).

the officer a receipt that placed him in Leominster). *Comm. v. Valentin*, 2015 WL 2260144 (Appeals Court) (defendant claimed his girlfriend owned the car and lived at a certain address, but that address did not exist).

- **Another source furnishes incriminating information.** *Comm. v. Latney*, 44 Mass. App. Ct. 423 (1998): Circumstantial evidence linked the defendant to a break at a nearby house. He was caught with a lawnmower, jewelry and cold beer. The homeowner was brought to the scene and identified the property. Finally, the cold beer nullified the defendant's claim that he had stumbled on these items and not been the one who stole them from the house.

Conduct identification procedure

Police may conduct a showup identification during a detention.[10] *Comm. v. Phillips*, 452 Mass. 617 (2008).

AVOID MOVING SUSPECT

Moving a suspect usually transforms a detention into an arrest. Consider the landmark case of *Florida v. Royer*, 460 U.S. 491 (1983): Federal agents stopped Royer in the airport terminal and moved him to a room 40 feet away to conduct their investigation in private. While the agents argued they moved Royer to spare him public embarrassment, they could not claim that he consented since they had his license, plane ticket, and luggage at the time. Stating that the move was not necessary for officer safety, the court held the agents exceeded the permissible limits of an investigative detention. Since the detention became an arrest before agents developed probable cause, the evidence from Royer was suppressed.

Three exceptions to this rule: (1) identification; (2) safety; and (3) clear consent.

- **Identification.** Officers may move a suspect in order to conduct a showup at another location nearby. *Comm. v. Crowley*, 29 Mass. App. Ct. 1 (1990).

- **Safety.** *People v. Courtney*, 11 Cal. App. 34d 1185 (1970) (angry crowd threatened safety of officers and suspect; moving him to a safe area for questioning was proper). *Comm. v. Mays*, 2012 WL 1080409 (Appeals Court) (directing the defendant to operate his vehicle a short distance to a safer location did not amount to an arrest; the stop took place in a construction area and was altering the flow of traffic).

- **Clear consent.** A suspect is not considered to be under arrest if he *voluntarily* accompanies officers to the station. Be careful. Courts will find an arrest occurred if officers: (1) spoke or acted in a way that compelled the suspect to come; or (2) said they would restrain him if he did not come; or (3) controlled him physically; or (4) tried to keep it a secret that the suspect was going to the station.

  Comm. v. Melo, 472 Mass. 278 (2015): After speaking with Melo at the hospital, the detective told him: "We're going back to the station and finish this interview." The detective ordered an officer to drive Melo to the station. This was an arrest without probable cause, so Melo's statement had to be suppressed.

---

10 How to conduct proper field identification procedures is the subject of *Chapter 25*.

Compare *Comm. v. Gallett*, 481 Mass. 662 (2019): The officer informed Gallett that he was not under arrest and free to leave, then asked him to come to the station to speak with detectives. Gallett agreed, but was concerned about a friend who was crying. The officer told him that they would give the friend a ride. Gallett rode in an unmarked vehicle to the station and was not handcuffed. *U.S. v. Swan*, 842 F.3d 28 (1ˢᵗ Cir. 2016) (allowing suspect to drive his car to station for an interview is a good way to avoid a premature arrest).

TRAFFIC STOPS
INITIAL INTERACTION

DRIVER

Officers should tell a motorist the reason for the stop during the initial approach. Complaints, especially over perceived racial bias, are often avoided by taking this basic step.[11]

Officers may shine their light into a vehicle. The flashlight is viewed as an extension of the eyes. *Comm. v. Oreto*, 20 Mass. App. Ct. 581 (1985). However, if officers insert their head or flashlight into the vehicle, it is considered a search. *Comm. v. Podgurski*, 386 Mass. 385 (1982).

Request to roll down window proper. *Comm. v. O'Brien*, 2013 WL 708877 (Appeals Court): After observing Kaitlyn O'Brien's vehicle repeatedly cross onto the "rumble strip" of the highway, a trooper pulled her car over. The trooper asked O'Brien, whose window was only partially open, to roll it down completely. When she did, he smelled alcohol. The trooper's request was minimally intrusive. He had to obtain her license and registration, so he had the right to avoid the barrier of a partially closed window.

Officers may insist on seeing a motorist's license and registration. The *refusal* to produce these documents subjects the motorist to arrest. 90, § 25. If a Massachusetts motorist is willing to produce her license and registration — but simply does not have them with her in the car — she may only receive a $40 civil citation under 90, § 11.[12]

Officers may also engage in brief conversation with the driver — ideally <u>before</u> checking the status of the license and registration. Massachusetts does not limit officers to robotically asking for license and registration when they pull a car over. Brief conversation with drivers serves multiple purposes. It builds community connections and "humanizes" the police; educates motorists about the reason for the stop; and, at times, reveals possible illegal conduct.

- **Proper conversation.** *Comm. v. Rosario-Santiago*, 96 Mass. App. Ct. 166 (2019): Trooper Reynolds stopped the defendant for "following too closely" on a highway. The trooper engaged in a two-minute conversation, asking where the defendant was coming from and where he was going. This is standard police dialogue. The defendant's slow and incomplete answers were suspicious. When asked, the defendant acknowledged having a

---

11 Weitzer, et al. *Criminology* 40, no. 2 (2002). Also see articles at <u>aclu.org</u>.
12 For a detailed discussion of these laws, see *LED's Motor Vehicle Law, Chapters* 2 and 4.

criminal history involving drug distribution.[13] It turned out his license was suspended, so the trooper arrested him. This brief conversation, combined with the trooper's observation of a possible hidden compartment and drug packaging, led to probable cause. The ensuing search[14] uncovered a lot of Oxycodone pills and cash.

- **Improper conversation.** *Comm. v. Cordero*, 477 Mass. 237 (2017): The license and registration had already checked out, and the trooper could have simply issued Cordero a citation for his civil motor vehicle infractions. Instead, he improperly extended the stop and asked about Cordero's travel activities without a reasonable suspicion of crime. At that point, he should have allowed Cordero to leave.

  Comm. v. Soriana-Lara, 99 Mass. App. Ct. 525 (2021): Trooper Farrell stopped a Massachusetts-registered Volvo operated by Johan Soriana-Lara on Route 1A in Lynn after he failed to signal a lane change. Soriana-Lara handed the trooper a Rhode Island driver's license that gave a Cranston address. Trooper Farrell asked Soriana-Lara where he lived, and got the answer, "Providence." The driver and passenger were nervous and breathing heavily.

  After Trooper Farrell had determined that the license was valid and returned to the car, he asked where Soriana-Lara was coming from. Soriana-Lara said a friend had just fixed his brakes — though he could not provide the name of the shop, its location, or his friend's name. When the trooper looked, it was obvious that the dust-covered wheels had not been off the Volvo recently for a brake job.

  Now the trooper asked the driver, again, where he lived. The driver answered, "Cranston." Soriana-Lara could not name any streets near his alleged Cranston address, which the trooper had looked up in his cruiser.

  The trooper now noticed evidence of a "drug hide" near the center console and ordered the driver to exit. The secret compartment was searched, which revealed illegal drugs.

  This stop was impermissibly extended by the trooper's drug investigation. While the trooper had a reason to investigate the driver's identity so that he could properly issue a citation, the court objected to his further investigatory questions about where he had been earlier. Since these extended questions contributed to probable cause to search Soriana-Lara's vehicle, the court suppressed the discovery of the drugs.

Officers may routinely observe the Vehicle Identification Number (VIN). The VIN is part of a regulatory system designed to prevent automobile theft and facilitate compulsory insurance. For this reason, *whenever* officers lawfully stop a vehicle, they may see the VIN. Officers must use the least intrusive means to view it. First, they must see if the VIN is visible from outside the vehicle. They may enter if the VIN is obscured and the occupant is unavailable to remove whatever is blocking it. Their right to look at the VIN does not allow them to inspect inside the vehicle. *Comm. v. Hason*, 387 Mass. 169 (1982). *New York v. Class*, 475 U.S. 106 (1986).

---

13 The Appeals Court did not object to the trooper's inquiry about criminal history.
14 This search for evidence was legal under the motor vehicle exception. See *Chapter 16*.

PASSENGERS

Officers may <u>not</u> detain a passenger during a stop based solely on the driver's civil motor vehicle infraction. In the rare instance that a passenger gets out and walks away, officers should let him if it is safe (e.g., not on a highway). *Comm. v. Perkins*, 465 Mass. 600 (2013). Officers may insist that a passenger either leave the area *or* remain in the car and follow orders. There is no middle ground. Noncompliance may justify an arrest for "disorderly" or "interfering with a police officer."[15]

Officers may <u>not</u> routinely request a passenger's identification. *Comm. v. Alvarez*, 44 Mass. App. Ct. 531 (1998) disapproved of an officer's "routine practice" of asking passengers for identification at night: "[T]his sort of dragnet . . . is uncomfortably associated with authoritarian societies."[16]

At the same time, officers may detain a passenger and request ID for a legitimate purpose. This includes passengers that officers have a reasonable suspicion:

- **Pose a safety risk;** or

- **Committed a civil infraction** (e.g., not wearing a seat belt); or

- **Can help resolve the violation** (e.g., sitting next to a learner's permit operator); or

- **Are involved in criminal conduct;** or

- **Are involved in unsafe/improper conduct** (e.g., underage and impaired by alcohol, truant or a runaway); or

- **Are a witness to crime** (e.g., driver under arrest for OUI or operating to endanger).

See *Comm. v. Pacheco*, 51 Mass. App. Ct. 736 (2001) (officer stopped a car with an expired inspection sticker; driver told officer that his passenger's father owned the car; the officer was justified in asking the passenger for identification).

Officers may prolong stop to resolve a passenger's name discrepancy. *Comm. v. Obiora*, 83 Mass. App. Ct. 55 (2013): Trooper Mansi stopped a vehicle for speeding. When she approached the car, she observed that none of the three occupants were wearing seat belts. She asked them for identification, which only the driver provided. Trooper Mansi then asked Obiora, who was in the front passenger seat, to write his name and date of birth on a piece of paper, along with the name of the rear passenger. Obiora wrote "Antoine" for the rear passenger, and passed him the paper. "Antoine" wrote his name as "Samuel Jean." Mansi asked Jean to exit the vehicle.

Although she had asked the other two occupants to keep their hands on the dashboard, Obiora lowered his hands to the floor and shuffled as if he were trying to move something. Mansi ordered Obiora and the driver out too. She found a gun under the seat near Obiora.

---

15 Both crimes are described in *LED's Criminal Law, Chapters 5* and *23*.

16 Even though 85, § 16 requires that any vehicle occupant provide "his true name and address" to a police officer at night, the Appeals Court insisted that this statute is nullified by Article 14.

The fact that none of the occupants were wearing seat belts entitled Mansi to prolong the stop to issue them citations. Once Jean provided a different name from what the defendant gave, Mansi was justified in investigating further to resolve the discrepancy. After all, a passenger who lies about his name may be trying to avoid an outstanding warrant.

Officers must deal with safety and investigative concerns relating to passengers before concluding the traffic stop. *Comm. v. Ellsworth*, 41 Mass. App. Ct. 555 (1996): There was no dispute that the initial stop for erratic driving was proper, and there was no doubt that the passenger's "ducking movement" allowed the officer to get him out of the car and frisk him. The problem was that the officer did not deal with the passenger until *after* he had concluded his interaction with the driver and returned her paperwork. At that point, there was no longer any reason to detain the occupants.

EXIT ORDERS

Article 14 prohibits automatically ordering a driver or passenger to get out.[17] In *Comm. v. Gonsalves*, 429 Mass. 658 (1999), the SJC declared: "Citizens do not expect that police officers handling a routine traffic violation will engage, in the absence of justification, in . . . strained conversation or unjustified exit orders . . . in the hope that, sooner or later, the stop might yield up some evidence of an arrestable crime. That a small percentage of routine traffic stops may result in the detection of more serious crime is no reason to subject the vast majority of citizens to orders to get out of their vehicles."

There are <u>four reasons</u> for an exit order: (1) officer safety; (2) investigation; (3) police function; and (4) community caretaking.

OFFICER SAFETY

Taking driver's keys acceptable when officer outnumbered during suspicious traffic inquiry. In *Comm. v. Moses*, 408 Mass. 136 (1990), an officer on patrol noticed four men leaning into the passenger window of a car idling at a bus stop. The men jogged quickly into a nearby building as soon as they noticed the cruiser. As the officer drove by, he saw the passenger duck underneath the dashboard. The officer parked and approached. He directed the driver to turn off the engine and give him the keys. With backup, he ordered the occupants to exit, one at a time. As the front seat passenger got out, cocaine was visible on the seat. A frisk underneath produced a gun. A search of the trunk exposed more cocaine and another gun.

The SJC approved. The initial behavior in the vehicle provided a reasonable suspicion its occupants were drug dealers. The officer knew he was outnumbered. Having the driver turn off the engine and surrender the keys was a limited protective step that ensured these suspects would not drive away.

For safety, officers may rely on a source with unknown reliability. *Comm. v. Bryan*, 98 Mass. App. Ct. 238 (2020): Boston Police Officer Daniely saw a vehicle turn left from a side street near a nightclub. The minivan's headlights were not on, it moved slowly, it swerved from

---

17 Under the Fourth Amendment, automatic driver and passenger exit orders are allowed. *Maryland v. Wilson*, 519 U.S. 408 (1997).

one lane to another, and then made a U-turn before the officer stopped it. Officer Daniely saw the driver staring at him through the side-view mirror. The passengers were not wearing seat belts. The officer collected identification from the three men in the minivan and learned the front seat passenger had a firearms conviction. Nightclub security guards came over to tell the officer that these men had been kicked out of the club, and that a patron had informed the guards that one of the men entered the minivan with a gun. Joined by two other officers, Daniely decided to order the men out for frisks.

When the back seat passenger got up, an officer saw a gun on the seat. Arrests followed. Here, the seizure of the gun was the product of a lawful exit order. The officer had no obligation to check into the reliability of the person who talked to the security guards before acting on their information.

While an exit order may occur on <u>less</u> than reasonable suspicion, officers <u>must have</u> <u>reasonable suspicion to frisk</u> occupant(s) and vehicle. Heightened vigilance is warranted given the number of officers killed and assaulted each year during traffic stops in the United States. In *Comm. v. Torres-Pagan*, 484 Mass. 34 (2020),[18] two Springfield police officers saw Manuel Torres-Pagan operating a vehicle with a cracked windshield and an expired inspection sticker. The officers signaled for the car to pull over. Torres-Pagan drove a short distance and parked in a driveway. The officers left their cruiser. Torres-Pagan stepped out without receiving instructions to do so. His hands were visible. Torres-Pagan repeatedly looked back at the inside of his car.

The officers handcuffed him and conducted a frisk, finding a knife in his pocket. They asked if he had other weapons in his car. He said "yes." Officers recovered a pistol in the car.

- **Though surprised that Torres-Pagan left his vehicle, the officers had an insufficient basis to find his conduct suspicious.** He stepped out into full view. He was not visibly hiding or reaching for anything. His other conduct — turning to look toward his front seat — suggested only that Torres-Pagan had "something of interest in his vehicle."

  According to the SJC, Torres-Pagan's behavior did not give officers a reasonable suspicion to believe that he was "armed and dangerous" — the standard long required to conduct a frisk. Once the SJC found the frisk improper, they suppressed the firearm.

- **An exit order is designed to resolve a safety concern related to the car itself** — without having to engage in the greater intrusion of putting hands on the suspect to check his or her body for weapons.

  This distinction makes sense. Once an officer issues an exit order and removes occupants, their access to hidden weapons and the vehicle-as-weapon is eliminated. Officers are free to give an exit order when they see abnormal movement inside a car, or notice a driver scanning his surroundings or leaving it in "drive" suggesting possible flight.

- **At the same time, officers must decide whether what they saw and/or learned about an occupant adds up to a reasonable suspicion that he is armed and dangerous.** That separate assessment is necessary to perform a frisk.

---

18 This case overruled *Comm. v. Torres*, 433 Mass. 669 (2001) which, for almost twenty years, had allowed officers to automatically frisk an occupant once they ordered him to get out because he posed a safety risk.

- **There are certain actions that officers can <u>always</u> take to help resolve their safety concerns.** Let's consider these approaches in the context of *Torres-Pagan*:

  - *Ask questions.* Officers could have asked Torres-Pagan to explain his suspicious conduct — e.g., "What are you looking at?" If Torres-Pagan did not respond, officers would then have reasonable suspicion to frisk. If Torres-Pagan mentioned a child or dog in the car, officers could have taken a quick look. If that was accurate, the police could have simply continued their traffic stop outside the vehicle. If untrue, police could have frisked.

  - *Direct suspect to move.* Once he got out, officers could have told Torres-Pagan: "Shut the door and move to the back of your car." This basic direction would have improved their safety if Torres-Pagan complied. If he did not, officers would have elevated to reasonable suspicion and taken the extra precaution of a frisk.

  - *Move to a better position.* Once Torres-Pagan looked repeatedly toward the vehicle, nothing prevented one of the officers from moving over to the car, shining his light inside, and looking for anything dangerous or suspicious. This intermediate action would have lessened their safety concerns or justified a follow-up frisk (or even probable cause search if a gun or other evidence came into view).

- **Do not lump exit orders, handcuffs, and frisks together based on any safety concern.**

  - *Exit order and intermediate steps.* Get people out based on any concrete safety concern. If appropriate, take other intermediate, non-intrusive safety steps (like asking questions, directing the suspect to move, and looking in the vehicle yourself).

  - *Frisk.* Only take the extra step of frisking an occupant and vehicle based on a reasonable suspicion that the occupant is armed and dangerous.[19]

  - *Handcuffing.* Finally, just because a frisk is justified does not mean that pre-arrest handcuffing automatically follows. Officers must have a reason why the extra restraint provided by "cuffs" is necessary.

Key factors contributing to an exit order and a reasonable suspicion of danger during a traffic stop:

- **Initial failure to stop.** *Comm. v. Santana*, 420 Mass. 205 (1995) (defendants continued driving for 1½ miles after troopers activated their blue lights).

- **Officers outnumbered.** This factor alone is insufficient. *Comm. v. Depina*, 2017 WL 2297579 (Appeals Court).

---

19 The high court did not address whether, if the frisk of an occupant is justified by reasonable suspicion, officers may automatically frisk the vehicle before placing the occupant back inside. In the author's opinion, this longstanding rule survives until further notice. The historical reason — for allowing officers who frisk the body to automatically frisk the vehicle — is the right of officers to know that the suspect will not gain easy access to a weapon at the time he is allowed to re-enter the vehicle. This reason still makes sense. See *Comm. v. Santiago*, 53 Mass. App. Ct. 567 (2002) and discussion in *Chapter 5*.

- **Removal of seat belts.** This suggests that occupants may be preparing to flee on foot. *Comm. v. Depina, supra.*

- **Quick move to get out.** In *Comm. v. Riche,* 50 Mass. App. Ct. 830 (2001), Trooper Lopes observed a speeding vehicle with a broken plate light. When the car pulled over, the driver abruptly jumped out and admitted his license was suspended. A quick pat down revealed no weapon. The driver said that the car belonged to the mother of the young woman in the front seat. The driver asked repeatedly whether he was going to be arrested. Backup arrived, and the female passenger was ordered out. She clutched her jacket, but 61 grams of crack fell onto the sidewalk. The driver's questions suggested that he wanted to be arrested to separate himself from any shady activity in the car.

- **Dangerous object in vehicle.** *Comm. v. Mitchell,* 2014 WL 7343820 (Appeals Court) (black military-style knife near feet of rear passenger, who refused to make eye contact with officers). *Comm. v. Rivera,* 67 Mass. App. Ct. 362 (2006) (police baton visible).

- **Dangerous movement.**

  - *By driver. Comm. v. Galarza,* 93 Mass. App. Ct. 740 (2018): State Police Trooper Matthew Stone was on patrol at 1:50 a.m. in Springfield. He saw a speeding pickup truck with no plate light and a cracked driver's side mirror. Trooper Stone stopped the truck and, as he approached, the driver: (1) ducked down; (2) ignored Stone's command to end his cell phone call multiple times; (3) appeared nervous; (4) refused to open the center console despite saying his registration was inside; and (5) put his hand over the center console. Trooper Stone ordered the driver out and handcuffed him. Stone opened the center console and saw a gun. Also see *Comm. v. Fernandes,* 95 Mass. App. Ct. 1116 (2019).

  - *By passenger. Comm. v. Douglas,* 472 Mass. 439 (2015): Police watched as members of a gang gathered at a restaurant. They saw Jason Douglas leave the restaurant appearing agitated, walking with Wayne Sneed. The men got into a vehicle, which failed to signal when turning; Officer Hawkins stopped it. There were four people inside. Hawkins knew that Douglas and another occupant, Shakeem Johnson, had lengthy records for violence and drugs. Johnson turned with one arm stretched across his torso by his waist. An officer ordered Johnson out and frisked him, but found nothing. The officer realized Johnson was drunk and had only been removing his seat belt. (Notice the honest testimony! This enhances credibility when you distinguish between threats that remain and those that dissipate.)

    Sneed appeared to be clutching something in his front pocket while avoiding eye contact. A frisk found nothing there. Officer Hawkins was familiar with Jason Douglas. Typically calm, Douglas was nervous and got out, without being asked, to complain. Ordered to get back in the car, he did — but then attempted to shift from "park" to "drive." This caused officers to take him out again.[20] Officer Hawkins saw a revolver under the seat. Douglas' conduct (especially attempting to put the car in gear) justified his exit order, and body and vehicle frisk.

---

20 Officers did not frisk the female driver because no female officers were present, and her clothing did not suggest that she had a weapon.

- **Movement and false ID.** *Comm. v. Goewey*, 452 Mass. 399 (2008): Trooper O'Neill pulled a car over for an expired inspection sticker. Noticing that all four occupants were not wearing seat belts, he asked for ID so he could issue tickets. Thomas Goewey, a passenger, produced an expired license with a picture that did not look like him. Trooper Hamilton noticed that Goewey's hands were shaking and that he continuously turned to look at the officers. Hamilton saw Goewey reach "either into his coat, around his body, or down below his seat." Goewey was smoking a cigarette when Hamilton asked him to get out. During the frisk, Goewey admitted to having illegal drugs taped to his calf.

  While a passenger's inability to produce identification is not suspicious, offering a false ID is. Goewey's fake license, nervousness, and repeated turning justified the exit order. The fact that Goewey retrieved a cigarette did not negate the safety risk. It was possible that he obtained a weapon along with the cigarette. Officers are not expected, in the words of the court, "to bet their lives on possible explanations."

- **Advance knowledge of dangerous situation.** *Comm. v. Widener*, 91 Mass. App. Ct. 696 (2017): Police knew Widener was transporting drugs and firearms from Florida to Massachusetts, and that he would be accompanied by Tobin, who had been present during Widener's illegal purchases. The officer reasonably believed there were firearms in the vehicle. Taking Tobin out of the car at gunpoint when she refused to show her hands was reasonable.

INVESTIGATION

Operator without license or proper registration

No license or registration, in suspicious circumstances, justifies an exit order. *Comm. v. Wright*, 85 Mass. App. Ct. 380 (2014): Trooper Shugrue pulled over a gray Nissan for following another vehicle too closely. When he approached, he smelled a strong odor of air freshener. He asked the driver, Christopher Wright, for his license. Wright produced a New York license and said they were traveling to Vermont to visit his niece. The passenger, Mitchell Degroat, said he owned the vehicle, but the registration showed the car was leased from New Jersey. When Shugrue asked Degroat for identification, he produced an expired, faceless New York driver's permit. Degroat did not make eye contact.

Shugrue called for backup and conducted a warrant check. Both occupants had lengthy criminal histories. Wright had recently been released from prison in Vermont.

Shugrue called in a K-9, "Dash," who arrived within 20 minutes. Shugrue asked Wright to exit the vehicle. Dash alerted to a black bag on the back seat. Another trooper opened the bag and discovered cocaine. Wright and Degroat were arrested.

Shugrue had a reasonable suspicion to prolong the stop, call for the dog, and order the men out. Degroat, a New York resident, had produced a faceless New York permit and New Jersey registration listing a third-party owner.

Wright had drug and gun convictions and was traveling to a place where he was probably on parole. In addition, there was a strong odor of air freshener and their leased vehicle was registered in a state where neither of them lived.

On the other hand, police may not overreact when operator fails to produce documents.
Comm. v. Santos, 65 Mass. App. Ct. 122 (2005): During the day, a Taunton officer stopped Antonio Santos for a stop sign violation. As the officer approached, he saw Santos sit upright from a reclined position and lean forward. Santos identified himself, but was unable to produce a license or registration. He said he had an active license and gave his date of birth.

After telling Santos that he was not under arrest, the officer handcuffed him and secured him in the rear of his cruiser. The officer then approached the empty vehicle "to attempt to identify the owner." He believed that paperwork might be in the glove box or door pockets. The officer saw a gun and arrested Santos. At the station, he learned that Santos had a valid license and the car belonged to his mother.

- **Aside from the defendant's failure to produce documents, this was an "unremarkable traffic stop."** The defendant's movement — sitting up and leaning forward — added little to the officer's concerns. The court remarked: "A citizen is not required to sit absolutely motionless in a stopped vehicle."

  It is true that failing to produce a license or registration may indicate other offenses, but here no additional evidence of a stolen car or crime surfaced. Nothing prevented the officer from checking on Santos' identity — yet ordinary checks were not performed until after the exit order, handcuffing, and vehicle search.

- **This was an impermissible search for evidence.**[21] Antonio Santos was a driver without a license or registration. To allow handcuffs and a search for papers in these situations would invite, in the words of the Appeals Court, "unequal treatment of minority motorists."

Police may suggest that the driver open the glovebox to find the registration. *Comm. v. Gervet*, 2021 WL 4805267 (Appeals Court): A vehicle driver opened the center console and a blue folder inside, then tapped his legs and arms before announcing he could not find the registration. The trooper said the driver had not looked in the glovebox, and asked if the registration might be there. When the driver failed to put the key in the glovebox lock to open it, the trooper pointed this out as well. A gun became visible when the driver opened the glovebox. The trooper did not order the driver to open it, so this was not a search requiring probable cause.[22]

Operator possibly under the influence of alcohol (OUI)

Reasonable suspicion supports exit order to investigate and administer field sobriety tests. *Comm. v. Eckert*, 431 Mass. 591 (2000): A trooper approached the defendant's vehicle at a roadside rest area. The trooper woke him up and asked if he was "ok." Eckert said that he was, but the trooper noticed his bloodshot eyes and odor of alcohol. Directed to exit for tests, Eckert performed poorly and was arrested. The SJC held that an officer may require sobriety testing based on a reasonable suspicion.[23]

---

21 See discussion of *Comm. v. Blevines*, 438 Mass. 604 (2003) in *Chapter 17.*
22 The trooper was not required to tell the driver he had the right to refuse to open the glovebox.
23 The trooper did not need reasonable suspicion to approach Eckert's stationary vehicle. See earlier discussion of *Comm. v. Murdough*, 428 Mass. 760 (1999).

Driver's red and glassy eyes, slurred speech, and odor of alcohol create probable cause to arrest. These factors alone, even without sobriety testing, justify an OUI arrest. *Comm. v. Blais*, 428 Mass. 294 (1999) also held that a motorist has *no* right to refuse to perform field sobriety tests following a lawful stop. While a driver is legally obligated, officers may never physically force a citizen to perform these tests.[24]

Operator possibly under the influence or distributing marijuana

Marijuana legalization makes traffic stops more complicated. Officers should apply the following principles. *Comm. v. Cruz*, 459 Mass. 459 (2011). Not all of them apply to every stop.[25]

Principle 1 — Traffic stop may be based on marijuana odor, smoke, or visible use. Clearly, any of these signs provide officers with reasonable suspicion to stop a vehicle for "open container" under 94G, § 13(d).

Principle 2 — Like any stop, frisk occupants if they pose a safety risk. However, a protection concern must be based on more than marijuana odor and nervousness. *Comm. v. Daniel*, 464 Mass. 746 (2013) (valid basis to frisk during stop: officer smelled a strong odor of marijuana, but also saw the passenger duck under the dashboard, quickly empty his pockets when not requested to do so, and place a small knife on the dashboard).

Principle 3 — Investigate OUI based on odor alone.

- **While the odor of marijuana is not probable cause to search, it usually provides reasonable suspicion that the driver may be OUI.** Investigate the driver's possible impairment with an exit order and sobriety testing. *Comm. v. Davis*, 481 Mass. 210 (2019).

- **If there is probable cause to arrest the driver for OUI, there is also probable cause to search the passenger compartment for evidence.** *Comm. v. Davis, supra.*

Principle 4 — Investigate furnishing marijuana if occupants under 21. *Comm. v. Ellis*, 2021 WL 162599 (Appeals Court): Following a lawful traffic stop, Malden Officer Manolian recognized the two passengers as gang members, and suspected the driver was too. The officer had a casual conversation with the occupants for a few minutes. He smelled marijuana in the car and saw baggies on the floor. All three occupants were under 21.

Officer Manolian asked for and received permission to search two unzipped backpacks he saw in the car. One contained a Mason jar with a small quantity of marijuana. Officer Manolian then made a license and warrant check on the driver. He decided to give the driver an oral warning for the inspection violation and window tint, but wanted to do so privately. He asked the driver to get out.

Though the driver questioned the officer as to why, he complied. Outside the car, the driver adjusted his waistband in such a way that Officer Manolian suspected he had a firearm. His frisk located a gun.

---

24 The most detailed discussion of OUI enforcement is found in *LED's Motor Vehicle Law, Chapter 10.*
25 The best reference for marijuana laws — what activity is legal, what draws a civil fine, and what results in criminal consequences — appears in *LED's Criminal Law, Chapter 21.*

With other officers present, Officer Manolian removed the other men. He asked Victor Ellis if he had a weapon. Ellis said he did. He recovered a firearm in Ellis' pants pocket.

- **This stop was justified by civil infractions.** The officer's initial, casual conversation with the car's three occupants "did not measurably extend the traffic stop beyond what was necessary." Manolian did not impermissibly prolong the stop when he returned to the car and, rather than issue a citation to the driver, sought to discuss a more lenient disposition.

- **The ensuing exit order was justified based on a reasonable suspicion of criminal activity in the car — furnishing marijuana to a person under 21.** Under 94G, § 13(i), since all of the occupants were under 21, it was a crime to give marijuana to any of them. At the same time, being under 21 did not prevent these men from being charged with furnishing marijuana. See *Comm. v. Knerman*, 63 Mass. App. Ct. 371 (2005) (19 year old "furnished" to other minors).[26]

  Here, the court assumed that a motor vehicle qualifies as "property" for the crime of furnishing, which must occur "on premises or property owned or controlled" by the defendant. Thus, a vehicle is now a location to furnish marijuana and alcohol. As a result, officers properly ordered the occupants to exit to investigate furnishing and, based on other indicators, to frisk for weapons.

Principle 5 — Investigate drug distribution in appropriate situations.

- **Officers need more than odor or "social sharing" to search for evidence of distribution.** *Comm. v. Jackson*, 464 Mass. 758 (2013) (three people passing a joint in a public park were not "distributing" marijuana to each other; the act only justified a civil ticket; police could not search the individuals and their backpack for evidence of criminal distribution). *Comm. v. Pacheco*, 464 Mass. 768 (2013) (social sharing did not justify searching a vehicle either).

- **Officers should also take into account that adults may legally give away up to 1 ounce of marijuana to another adult.** 94G, 7(a)(4). The person transferring marijuana may not be compensated, and the exchange may not be advertised or publicly promoted.

- **Federal law is not a reason to search for marijuana.** *Comm. v. Craan*, 469 Mass. 24 (2014) (illegality under federal law does not affect Massachusetts traffic stop procedures).

- **K-9 alert not helpful.** A dog's detection is not helpful because a K-9 cannot tell whether the *amount* of marijuana is legal or over two ounces.[27]

- **Even the blatant odor of marijuana is still not probable cause to search without other indicators.** *Comm. v. Locke*, 89 Mass. App. Ct. 497 (2016) (odor from 159 pounds of raw marijuana was found insufficient, by itself, to provide probable cause to search a minivan). In addition to smell, these factors create probable cause that vehicle occupants are distributing marijuana:

---

26 In *Knerman* the court ruled on the almost identical statutory language of 138, § 34, prohibiting "furnishing" alcohol to persons under the age of 21.

27 Adults 21 and over may legally possess up to 1 ounce in public (with no more than 5 grams being concentrate). Possession by an adult of over 2 ounces is a crime. See 94G, §§ 7(a)(1), 13(e).

- *Report of sales. Comm. v. Sprague,* 2012 WL 1470298 (Appeals Court) (a detective stopped a vehicle after observing occupants purchase drugs; these suspects admitted to buying a "dime bag" from the defendant; detective then found the defendant's car, searched it and arrested him for dealing marijuana).

- *Dealer behavior. Comm. v. Alcantara,* 2016 WL 702018 (Appeals Court) (odor of marijuana, cash, and defendant's "meaningless ride" created probable cause).

- *Observable paraphernalia* — e.g., packaging, scale, notations of sales, air fresheners, multiple cell phones, substantial cash. *Comm. v. Duncan D.,* 2012 WL 3627501 (Appeals Court).

- *Cash and after-market alteration. Comm. v. Fontaine,* 84 Mass. App. Ct. 699 (2014): "overwhelming" odor in vehicle with open windows on a cold night coupled with additional information amounted to probable cause — (1) no smoking implements; (2) three bundles of cash; (3) excess wiring for a "hide"; (4) inconsistency between strength of odor and small amount visible; and (5) occupants' prior drug convictions.

- *Prior criminal record for drug distribution* (however, a normal odor of marijuana and this factor, by themselves, do not amount to probable cause to search). *Comm. v. Keefner,* 461 Mass. 507 (2012).

Principle 6 — Pursue applicable civil infractions.

- **While police may not search for evidence of a civil infraction, they may: (1) ask for consent to search; or (2) demand that suspects turn over marijuana for forfeiture.** Either strategy can be effective at the outset of a traffic stop or street encounter. *Comm. v. Sheridan,* 470 Mass. 752 (2015): When officers saw a small amount of marijuana that was subject to civil forfeiture in Sheridan's SUV, they should not have entered his vehicle to retrieve it. Instead, according to the SJC, they should have either obtained his consent to retrieve it, or demanded that Sheridan turn the marijuana over to them. If Sheridan had refused, the only recourse for officers was to issue him a civil citation and allow him to leave.

- **Issue applicable civil tickets.** Although officers may be tempted to reject this lesser sanction, it should be used.[28]

Occupants possibly involved in any crime

Reasonable suspicion of any crime justifies ordering the driver to exit so he will not try to escape. *Comm. v. Bostock,* 450 Mass. 616 (2008): Quincy Officer Donald Allison received a dispatch about a vehicle break-in. A security guard told him that the male suspect was wearing a light colored shirt and blue jeans, and carrying a duffel bag. The guard saw the suspect jogging toward Bracket Street.

There, Richard Richu hailed Officer Allison. Richu said that he observed a white male in a light colored shirt and jeans walking away from his van. Several items were missing, including a radar detector and Nextel cell phone.

---

28 For detailed information about marijuana civil violations, see *LED's Criminal Law, Chapter 21.*

Meanwhile, another officer reported he found a person matching the suspect's description in a pickup truck nearby. Identified as William Bostock, he was ordered to exit. Bostock gave his name and explained that it was too late for him to get a bed at a homeless shelter. Inside the vehicle, Officer Allison noticed a Nextel phone and three bags. Bostock denied owning these items. The security guard and Richu identified Bostock at the scene. He was arrested.

Bostock argued that, even with a reasonable suspicion, officers could not order him out of his vehicle unless they feared for their safety. The SJC disagreed. When police have a reasonable suspicion of crime — *any crime* — the motorist should expect that police will be more intrusive than on a stop for a civil infraction. After all, a motorist suspected of *any crime* might try to flee. The exit order protects officers and the public from the danger of high-speed pursuit.[29]

When reasonable suspicion of _any crime_ leads police to focus on a car with multiple occupants, exit orders prevent suspects from collaborating. *Comm. v. Riche*, 50 Mass. App. Ct. 830 (2001) (exit orders have the "practical purpose of separating those in a stopped car to [prevent] . . . collaboration among them").

Reasonable suspicion that a passenger lied about his identity justifies an exit order too. *Comm. v. Obiora*, 83 Mass. App. Ct. 55 (2013) (officer outnumbered at night; she also reasonably believed that a passenger might have lied about his identity to avoid being caught for something, perhaps an outstanding warrant).

POLICE FUNCTION

Removing all occupants is necessary before officers use a K-9, search for evidence, or conduct an inventory. This approach protects occupants and officers during a legitimate police function. *Comm. v. Cruz*, 459 Mass. 459 (2011). *Comm. v. Griffin*, 79 Mass. App. Ct. 124 (2011) (passenger properly ordered to exit a car about to be searched).

COMMUNITY CARETAKING

Exit order enables an officer learn whether an occupant needs help. When functioning as "community caretakers," officers are looking out for the well-being of citizens.[30] *U.S. v. Cintron*, 592 F.Supp.2d 198 (D. Mass. 2008) (passenger lying on back seat during traffic stop; trooper properly opened door to check on his well-being and have him exit car).

In *Comm. v. Fisher*, 86 Mass. App. Ct. 48 (2014), it was 1:25 a.m. when Northampton police responded to a report that a person in a car might be having a seizure. They asked Cyrus Fisher if he needed medical attention. He said "no," but his speech was slurred, his eyes were half closed, and he was nodding his head. There was no odor of alcohol.

An officer shined his flashlight on Fisher's pants and saw a baggie with white powder sticking out of his pocket. He asked Fisher to remove the object. Fisher did, but the officer still

---

29 The SJC found the search of the bags proper under the motor vehicle exception. See *Chapter 16*. After all, the officer was aware that a phone had been stolen just minutes before he saw it in the truck. Bostock also denied ownership of the bags.
30 Community caretaking is a reason to make a traffic stop in the first place. See *Chapter 2*. It is referred to as "emergency aid" when used as the reason for entering a home without a warrant. See *Chapter 16*.

could not see what it was. He ordered Fisher out and searched the passenger compartment. Fisher possessed crack cocaine and PCP.

This officer's decision was not invalid simply because it uncovered criminal activity. Sometimes community caretaking transforms into a criminal investigation. Here, officers would have been neglecting their duty if they had not tried to find out the cause of Fisher's impairment.

Asking for license and registration permitted during community caretaking interaction. *Comm. v. Evans*, 436 Mass. 369 (2002): Trooper Lenti saw a car parked in the breakdown lane of Route 20 at 11:30 p.m. As part of his community caretaking duties, the trooper pulled behind the car with his blue lights on. He found Willie Evans asleep in a reclined driver's seat. Trooper Lenti's knocking on the window woke Evans. When Lenti asked what Evans was doing, he replied, "Nothing."

Lenti then learned that Evans was unlicensed. He arrested him and, during the ensuing search, found illegal drugs.

Several reasons justified Trooper Lenti's request for Evans' license and registration:

- **Officers often must make reports of contacts with citizens;**

- **Officers must know whom they are assisting in the event of a citizen's complaint;** and

- **Even seemingly innocent activity may turn out to be criminal,** such as refueling a car on the roadside in an effort to steal it.

K-9 USE

DRUG INVESTIGATION

Reasonable suspicion of drug activity allows detention of vehicle for K-9 sniff. *Comm. v. Feyenord*, 445 Mass. 72 (2005): Trooper Pinkes noticed a car behind him with a headlight out. Kenton Feyenord could not produce his license or a registration in his name, claiming the car belonged to his aunt. He was nervous and his hands were shaking. Pinkes ordered him to exit the vehicle so he could question him away from the passenger. Feyenord gave his name and birth date, but stumbled when asked for his age. He claimed the passenger was his brother-in-law.

Pinkes then spoke with the passenger, who said Feyenord had been his friend for three years but could not come up with his last name. The men also gave conflicting information about their destination. Pinkes summoned a K-9 and it "alerted" at the trunk. A search revealed cocaine.

- **Under Article 14, a dog sniff is not a search requiring probable cause** because the dog visibly reacts only to narcotics. Citizens do not have an expectation of privacy concerning the odor of contraband emanating from their vehicles.

- **Still, conducting a dog sniff detains the motorist — an intrusion that requires reasonable suspicion.** Given Feyenord's inability to produce a license and his inconsistent story, the trooper reasonably concluded that he and his passenger were engaged in criminal activity — perhaps automobile theft, fugitive flight, or the transportation of contraband. It was entirely reasonable to call in a dog to confirm or dispel the possibility of illegal drugs.

- **Waiting up to 1 hour for a K-9 acceptable.** The wait was 30 minutes in *Feyenord*.

- **Dog alert is probable cause to search the vehicle.**[31]

After-market alteration of vehicle provides reasonable suspicion for K-9 sniff. *Comm. v. Sinforoso*, 434 Mass. 320 (2001): Following a traffic stop for speeding, the officer saw knives on the floor. The officer ordered the nervous driver and passenger to get out. While retrieving the weapons, the officer noticed, under the dashboard, a switch that did not seem factory-installed. Inspecting the vehicle exterior, the officer saw the gas tank had been lowered, suggesting the vehicle had been modified to create a secret compartment. The officer requested a K-9. The dog alerted. A vehicle search revealed cash and cocaine.

The SJC commented: "The conduct of this stop and search was a measured response to an evolving set of facts that, at each step, justified the officer's concerns for his safety and ultimately his suspicion that there was contraband hidden in a secret compartment."

Reasonable suspicion of <u>drug-impaired</u> operation allows K-9 sniff. *Comm. v. Perry*, 2019 WL 4047599 (Appeals Court): A state trooper received a report about an erratic driver and saw the defendant weaving between lanes. The trooper noticed that the defendant's speech was slurred and accelerated, but he did not smell alcohol. The defendant explained that his poor night vision caused him to weave. He passed four sobriety tests, yet exhibited an accelerated perception of time, which the trooper believed indicated drug impairment. The trooper requested a K-9 unit, which arrived 10 minutes later. The dog alerted to drugs in a backpack.

Here, the trooper did not exceed the permissible scope of the stop when he called for a K-9. The trooper had a reasonable suspicion that the defendant may have been under the influence of narcotics.

A drug dog should never be deployed during a routine stop. In *Feyenord*, Justice Marshall wrote that a K-9 sends a clear signal, not only to the motorist, but to all others passing by, that a drug investigation is underway: "For these reasons, the use of a narcotics detection dog is intimidating and upsetting to the innocent motorist."

FIREARMS INVESTIGATION

Use of firearm sniffing dog requires, at least, a reasonable suspicion of <u>illegal firearms</u> possession. The problem, identified in *Comm. v. Devoe*, 95 Mass. App. Ct. 1107 (2019), was that an alert by a firearms sniffing K-9 showed that Devoe had a gun in a bag in a park, but not that the gun was illegally possessed. Unlike a sniff that reveals only illegal narcotics, a firearms dog sniff reveals potentially noncriminal activity, since there are legal ways for citizens to possess firearms in public. This is why police should deploy a firearms dog when:

---

31 This is true even if the dog is later shown to be mistaken. *Comm. v. Pinto*, 45 Mass. App. Ct. 790 (1998).

(1) there is a blanket prohibition of gun possession, so that any alert would trigger a search (e.g. courthouse, stadium, prison, etc.); or (2) police have information about the object of the search that would make gun possession illegal (e.g., under age 21, prior criminal record, improper storage), so that the use of the dog would be the final component of probable cause.[32]

CHECKPOINTS & ROADBLOCKS

Detentions not based on individualized suspicion are authorized only in special situations. These administrative searches are tolerated because they serve "special needs beyond the normal need for law enforcement." *U.S. v. Costilla-Alfano*, 726 F.Supp. 327 (D. Mass. 1989).

ADMINISTRATIVE CHECKPOINT

Administrative inspections permitted if prior notice provided to citizens. While inspections at vulnerable locations (e.g., airports and courthouses) are allowed, the intrusiveness of these screening procedures must be minimized. Conspicuously posted signs warn persons that they will be subject to search if they proceed past a certain point. Advance warning allows visitors to bypass a search by electing not to enter the area. *Comm. v. Carkhuff*, 441 Mass. 122 (2004).

SOBRIETY CHECKPOINT

A sobriety checkpoint is a limited intrusion justified by compelling need. The public interest in reducing highway fatalities justifies this relatively minor intrusion on personal liberty. *Comm. v. Shields*, 402 Mass. 162 (1988).

A checkpoint must satisfy five requirements. Comm. v. McGeoghegan, 389 Mass. 137 (1983) requires that: (1) the selection of the location must be based on recent and reliable crash and arrest data; (2) the selection of motor vehicles must not be arbitrary; (3) the checkpoint must be configured in a way that ensures public safety; (4) it must be conducted in a way that minimizes public inconvenience; and (5) officers must operate the checkpoint in strict conformity with a written plan devised by supervisors. A motorist should be greeted by an officer and, if the officer observes any sign of impairment or contraband, the motorist must be referred to a secondary area for sobriety screening. *Comm. v. Emerton*, 94 Mass. App. Ct. 365 (2018). The SJC *recommends* that police departments provide advance notice of the date of the checkpoint to reduce public surprise and inconvenience. *Comm. v. Aivano*, 81 Mass. App. Ct. 247 (2012).

CRIME CONTROL ROADBLOCK

The Supreme Court and SJC have ruled that a roadblock to facilitate general crime control is unconstitutional. In *Comm. v. Rodriguez* 430 Mass. 577 (2000), police established a roadblock in a high crime neighborhood to deter narcotics abuse. Fifty-eight vehicles were stopped and 25% were directed to a secondary area for questioning. The police made three arrests. The desire to prevent drug use in a neighborhood does not warrant methods "beyond the normal need [for] law enforcement." *City of Indianapolis v. Edmond*, 531 U.S. 532 (2000).

---

32 For more on the "plus" factors that suggest that gun possession is illegal, see *Chapter 3*.

PUBLIC INFORMATION CHECKPOINT

A checkpoint to solicit information from the public about a recent, serious crime is permissible. In *Illinois v. Lidster*, 540 U.S. 419 (2004), a hit and run driver struck and killed a 70 year old bicyclist. A week later, police set up a late night checkpoint at the scene. Police cruisers partially blocked eastbound lanes of the highway. An officer stopped each vehicle for 10 to 15 seconds to ask occupants if they had seen anything the previous week and to hand out flyers that might lead to identifying the driver.

Robert Lidster swerved his minivan as he came toward the checkpoint. Lidster was directed to a side street where he failed sobriety tests and was arrested for OUI. Lidster argued unsuccessfully that the checkpoint was unconstitutional.

Its purpose was to ask members of the public for help. Police ordinarily are permitted to seek the voluntary cooperation of the public in investigating crimes.

On the other hand, stopping a motorist is still a seizure that must be reasonable. In this case, the public concern was grave due to the homicide. The checkpoint was temporary and, most important, its interference with motorists was brief.

FLEEING FELON ROADBLOCK

In a swiftly developing situation, a roadblock to apprehend a dangerous, fleeing felon is appropriate. In *Comm. v. Grant*, 57 Mass. App. Ct. 334 (2003), there was a shooting incident at Chestnut Circle in Randolph at 3:40 a.m. Lieutenant Arthur Sullivan investigated and found several empty shell casings. He ordered officers to stop all vehicles leaving the scene and question occupants. Officer Michael Tuitt positioned his cruiser approximately one quarter mile from Chestnut Circle. He stopped ten vehicles, including one in which the defendant was a back seat passenger. Officer Tuitt asked the driver to exit and proceeded to question him. He then asked the front seat passenger to exit. Officer Tuitt could now see the butt end of a handgun beneath the front passenger seat. The two back seat passengers were then ordered out. All four were arrested.

The Appeals Court balanced the minimal intrusion of a roadblock against the strong public interest in apprehending dangerous, fleeing suspects while they are still nearby.

5   *Frisks*

FRISK FOUNDATION

A frisk must be based on a reasonable suspicion that the suspect is engaged in criminal activity <u>and</u> is armed and dangerous. Officers cannot approach citizens for an encounter and automatically frisk just because the citizen refuses to answer questions or take his hands out of his pockets. The fundamental question remains: "Officer, what crime did you think he might be committing when you felt the need to frisk?"

In the words of *Comm. v. Narcisse*, 454 Mass. 1 (2010): "[P]olice officers may not escalate a consensual encounter into a protective frisk absent a reasonable suspicion that an individual has committed, is committing, or is about to commit a criminal offense and is armed and dangerous . . . However, this is not to say that such suspicions must arise sequentially; it is clear that they may occur simultaneously." See *Comm. v. Jones-Pannell*, 472 Mass. 429 (2015).

At the same time, having a reasonable suspicion of crime does <u>not</u> mean officers may automatically frisk. *Comm. v. Nichols*, 2016 WL 4395369 (Appeals Court) (cooperative defendant was properly detained on suspicion of drug dealing, but improperly frisked; there was no indication he was armed).

BASIS & METHOD
FRISK FACTORS

Officers must explain their frisk decision. *Terry v. Ohio*, 392 U.S. 1 (1968) declared: "A frisk is [a] serious intrusion upon the sanctity of the person, which may inflict great indignity and arouse strong resentment, and it is not to be undertaken lightly."

Conclusory statements about being "in fear for my safety" will not work. In reality, police officers need not be afraid. They must be <u>aware of specific facts</u> that create a *reasonable* belief of danger. Indeed, when officers automatically say they were afraid, judges become skeptical. Some frisk situations are truly scary (and should be described that way), but the majority are not as highly charged. Officers should focus on the facts — e.g., "Your Honor, I was very concerned that Mr. Smith might have a weapon because he reached under his coat"; or "Your Honor, I felt at risk because there were two large men in the alley and backup had not yet arrived."

CRIME UNDER INVESTIGATION

In deciding whether to frisk, the <u>most important factor</u> is the crime under investigation. *Comm. v. Heughan*, 40 Mass. App. Ct. 102 (1996) (police investigating gun shots).

The facts of the particular offense control, not the category of offense. *Comm. v. Laskoski*, 74 Mass. App. Ct. 858 (2009) (officer's decision to frisk could not be based solely on the fact that a domestic dispute had taken place). *Comm. v. Levy*, 2014 WL 183893 (Appeals Court) (bar fight, in which no weapons were used, could not be the dominant reason to frisk this calm suspect with no prior criminal history).

ENVIRONMENT & TIME

The environment and time of day. Does the officer face the suspect at night or during the day? Is the location known for violent episodes? Are the suspects in a motor vehicle or on foot? Are they located in a building, on the street, or in a secluded area? Such considerations are essential. *Comm. v. Sumerlin*, 393 Mass. 127 (1984). *U.S. v. Martinez*, 762 F.3d 127 (2014) (police on alert following an emotional funeral in an area where two gang members had been shot to death).

Past criminal incidents in an area are relevant. However, *Comm. v. Gomes*, 453 Mass. 506 (2009) reminded officers that "many honest, law-abiding citizens live and work in high crime areas." A general statement about a high crime area is entitled to no weight. Only specific information about the particular times, locations, and types of past crimes merit consideration. *Comm. v. Evelyn*, 485 Mass. 691 (2020).

ADVANCE INFORMATION

Prior information about a suspect may justify a frisk.

- **Immediate response.** *Comm. v. Vazquez*, 426 Mass. 99 (1997): A police officer observed a number of people on the street. They told him that a Hispanic man in a brown jacket was chasing another man down the street with a gun. At least two people pointed at Vazquez standing next to a Mazda automobile. The officer pulled his cruiser behind the vehicle and frisked Vazquez, but found no weapon. The officer told the female driver and passenger to put their hands on the dashboard. There were two children in the back seat. The officer ordered the passenger to step out, then looked under her seat and found a handgun. She was arrested. Vazquez admitted the gun was his.

  Citizen reports gave the officer a reasonable suspicion that Vazquez was armed. Once Vazquez no longer possessed a gun, the officer wisely concluded it might be in the car.

- *Comm. v. Famania*, 79 Mass. App. Ct. 365 (2011): Springfield police received an anonymous tip that a tall black man — wearing blue jeans and a black shirt — was walking from the bus station on Liberty Street with a handgun in his backpack. Two officers spotted someone fitting that description on Liberty Street. They approached Jose Famania and asked if they could talk to him.

  Famania seemed hesitant, his eyes were wide, and he started looking over his shoulder. Officers believed Famania was going to run. Then he started reaching toward the shoulder straps of his backpack. One officer grabbed the backpack. It was made of soft leather. The officer felt a gun. Having no license to carry, Famania was arrested.

An anonymous tip that describes someone with a gun does *not*, without more, amount to a reasonable suspicion to stop and frisk. Here, officers properly approached Famania and only frisked when he started to access the location where the gun was supposed to be. While officers could have simply asked Famania to stop removing his backpack, the court refused to second guess because "officers are not required to gamble with their personal safety."

- **Delayed response.** *Comm. v. Varnum,* 39 Mass. App. Ct. 571 (1996) involved a Massachusetts officer receiving a report from the Vermont State Police about a white Pontiac Firebird (Mass. plate PUCK 22), which had been spotted at the scene of a Vermont burglary with three white males. The report specified that the car might contain stolen property, including a shotgun. Several hours later, the officer saw the car and signaled it to pull over even though there was a white male and woman inside. Minor discrepancies between the report and this officer's later observations did not eliminate reasonable suspicion and the need for safety measures. The stop and frisk was approved.

SUSPECT'S BACKGROUND

A suspect's prior record for weapons possession or other dangerous conduct is a key factor. *Comm. v. Rivas*, 466 Mass. 184 (2013).

Membership in dangerous group. Officers may not frisk an individual *only* because he belongs to a particular group, but it may be a significant factor. *Comm. v. Stephen*, 2014 WL 683757 (Appeals Court): Officer Higgins approached Kashawn Stephen, who was observed riding his bicycle in circles at 3:00 a.m. in the middle of the street. He was wearing a baseball hat with the letter "W" on it. He acknowledged that the "W" stood for Wheatland Avenue. Officer Higgins knew that Wheatland Avenue was associated with a nearby gang whose members had recently been arrested for robberies, firearms possession, and other crimes. When Higgins asked Stephen if he had any weapons, Stephen tensed his body and looked around. A frisk revealed a gun.

Here, several factors supported the frisk: (1) Stephen's odd circling behavior at 3:00 a.m.; (2) his affiliation with a gang whose members had been previously arrested for violent offenses; and (3) his reaction to the question whether he had any weapons. See *Comm. v. Heon*, 44 Mass. App. Ct. 254 (1998) (motorcycle rider wearing "Hell's Angels" colors — a group known for violence and weapons possession).

Reputation. A suspect's dangerous reputation is also relevant. *Comm. v. Andrews*, 403 Mass. 441 (1988): Police were called by the defendant's girlfriend, who said that he had threatened to kill her and her children "just like he killed two men in Plymouth." When officers found the defendant sleeping in a parked vehicle, they properly ordered him out and frisked him. They recovered an illegal knife.

SUSPECT'S BEHAVIOR

Acting nervous

A suspect's nervous movement, demeanor, and speaking style have an impact on the frisk decision. *Comm. v. Hawkes*, 362 Mass. 786 (1973) (defendant "looked scared").

Nervousness of unknown citizen may <u>not</u> be the primary factor. *Comm. v. Brown*, 75 Mass. App. Ct. 528 (2009): A trooper stopped a taxi in Brockton after he observed it traveling too close to the left hand side of a two-way street. He saw two occupants not wearing seatbelts. He asked for their IDs. At first, the passengers refused to provide them. Then they said they did not have IDs, but verbally gave their information to the trooper.

A moment later, a Brockton police officer arrived. The trooper asked him to standby because he believed the passengers were "tense" and had "nervous looks on their faces." The trooper informed the Brockton officer that he wanted to remove the passengers and frisk them. He found a gun in the defendant's pocket. Here, nervousness was not enough to justify an exit order and frisk.

Inconsistently nervous behavior of <u>known</u> citizen is very relevant. *Comm. v. Hem*, 2021 WL 684237 (Appeals Court): One night at the Las Vegas restaurant in Revere, a man identified as Timmy Hem raised his shirt to display a firearm tucked in his waistband. A still image of this act was distributed by Revere Police to its officers.

Officer Trifkovic knew Hem, a self-admitted gang member with a criminal record that included possession of ammunition. Hem had always been willing to talk with Officer Trifkovic on the street.

Two weeks after the Las Vegas incident, Officer Trifkovic saw Hem walking on the street with others. The officer attempted to get Hem's attention, but Hem purposely looked away.

Officer Trifkovic approached Hem and asked if he had a minute. In a nervous, troubled voice, Hem responded, "Yeah, what's up?" Officer Trifkovic found Hem's demeanor unusual as Hem normally was very relaxed. The officer told Hem that he understood there had been some issues in the neighborhood involving a firearm. Hem became more nervous, stepped back, and took a "bladed" position. Hem also was pulling up his pants as though they were weighed down.

Based on his training and experience, Officer Trifkovic testified that blading and the adjustment of the pants — an assurance check — are consistent with a person carrying a firearm. Concerned that Hem was armed, Officer Trifkovic frisked and pulled a firearm from Hem's waistband.

Evading police

Evasive behavior contributes to reasonable suspicion. *U.S. v. Adair*, 925 F.3d 931 (7th Cir. 2019): A 911 caller reported a group drinking alcohol outside her apartment. The caller mentioned a short, black male wearing a hoodie with a gun in his front pocket.

Officer Squires arrived quickly and saw Adair, who he knew did not live in the apartment complex. Adair was the only person who resembled the caller's description. He had a large bulge in his front pocket, and he tried to evade Officer Squires by moving and weaving throughout the group. Squires stopped and frisked Adair, finding a gun.

Evasive behavior by unknown minority citizen less significant. *Comm. v. Evelyn*, 485 Mass. 691 (2020) (in calculating reasonable suspicion, an officer should significantly discount evasive behavior by an unknown African-American suspect — because even an innocent black person may seek to evade the "danger and indignity" of a police stop).

Observing possible weapon

The risk is obvious when a potential weapon or ammunition becomes visible.

- *Comm. v. Rosado*, 84 Mass. App. Ct. 208 (2013): At 1:55 a.m., Trooper Pinkham stopped a vehicle for a civil infraction. As the driver, Jesus Rosado, reached toward the glove box to get his registration, Pinkham noticed a wooden or leather handle in the area between the driver's door and seat. Thinking it could be nunchucks (an illegal weapon), Pinkham ordered Rosado to put his hands on the steering wheel, then opened the door and retrieved the object. It turned out to be a "bullwhip." Rosado moved his right hand toward his hip. Now Pinkham got Rosado out for a pat down — which revealed a stash of 80 heroin packets.

  Pinkham was not required to ask about the item before removing it. He did not have to be certain that it was nunchucks either. The standard is reasonable suspicion. Discovering that it was a bullwhip, not nunchucks, did not end Pinkham's safety concerns. A bullwhip is an unusual item to have.

- *Comm. v. Whitehead*, 85 Mass. App. Ct. 134 (2014): Officers saw ammunition and a hunting knife inside a locked Jeep in a parking lot. The Jeep had decals that read: "Kill 'Em All Let God Sort it Out," and "Sniper, No Need to Run — You'll Only Die Tired." Jason Whitehead, a student, walked toward the vehicle. He was wearing Army camouflage and a backpack. Officer Donovan asked if he was the owner. Whitehead "aggressively approached" and said he was. Donovan frisked him and found a valid FID card, permitting him to carry ammunition but not a firearm in public.

  Donovan told Whitehead he was going to place him in his cruiser while he frisked the backpack. Whitehead said, "Wait, there's a loaded gun inside." Whitehead was arrested for unlawful possession of a firearm. Clearly, the initial frisk of Whitehead *and* his backpack were necessary safety precautions.

A bulge in the suspect's clothing may indicate a weapon. *Comm. v. Colon*, 87 Mass. App. Ct. 398 (2015) (officer saw a bulge on Colon's right hip under his shirt that was consistent with a firearm in both size and location).

Reaching toward possible weapon

A suspect's quick movement may indicate that he is grabbing, concealing, or checking a weapon. *Comm. v. Fisher*, 54 Mass. App. Ct. 41 (2002) (defendant suddenly moved his left hand toward his waist after looking at officers; while such a gesture could be innocent, it could also be a "reflex action" to draw *or* check a concealed weapon; given the potential danger, police must "immediately resolve the ambiguity").

Describe the suspect's actions clearly. "Furtive movement" is a term sometimes used in police reports and testimony. Avoid it. The phrase tells the judge nothing about what the suspect did. Instead, explain how the suspect moved and why it suggested a possible weapon — e.g., "Your Honor, the defendant quickly reached his right hand toward his waist. I thought he might be grabbing or checking a weapon since this is the most common place a person keeps a knife or gun." See *Comm. v. Isaiah I.*, 450 Mass. 818 (2008) (excellent testimony).

Rely on training and experience.

• *Comm. v. DePeiza*, 449 Mass. 367 (2007): Around midnight, Boston Officers Conway and Bickerton were in an unmarked vehicle in an area known for gun offenses. These officers had received training concerning how individuals carry firearms — including "the straight arm method," which employs "an arm pressed against the concealed weapon." Three or four of their gun arrests in the previous eight months involved this method.

The officers saw the defendant walking on the sidewalk, talking on his cell phone and holding his right arm rigid and pressed against his side. They displayed their badges and noticed the defendant shielding his right side. They noticed that his right, jacket pocket tilted as if it held an object "heavier than a cell phone, wallet, or pack of cigarettes." He avoided eye contact, looked left and right, and shifted his weight from side to side. Bickerton grabbed the defendant's pocket and felt a gun.

While there may have been an innocent explanation for the way the defendant walked, that possibility did not nullify the officers' assessment. These officers wisely relied on their training and testified *fully* about what caused them to act:

- After midnight;
- Area had experienced many firearms incidents;
- Walk suggested the suspect was carrying a firearm;
- Suspect nervous;
- Suspect hid his right side from view, a move known as "blading," to shield a weapon (SJC felt this was the most persuasive factor); and
- He possessed a heavy object in his pocket.

• *Comm. v. Karen K.*, 99 Mass. App. Ct. 216 (2021): Officer Lopes went to a public housing project in response to a report by an unnamed citizen that young people were loitering and displaying a firearm.

Officer Lopes had made multiple firearms arrests at the complex in the past, and knew that shots had been fired there the day before. When he arrived, Officer Lopes focused on two persons in particular, one of whom was the female juvenile, Karen K. While Karen walked, she continuously looked back over her shoulder. She then changed her direction, adjusted her waistband, and turned part of her body away from view.

Karen and her companion moved to the left, away from Officer Lopes, but towards other officers. Once Karen saw those officers, she turned around, leaving her companion, and walked towards Officer Lopes. She tried to walk around, but he grabbed hold of her arm. Karen responded, "I'm a female. You can't search me." When a female officer arrived, her frisk uncovered three cell phones and a handgun in Karen's waistband.

Failing to obey reasonable commands

Keeping hands in pockets may justify frisk in close cases. *Comm. v. Johnson*, 454 Mass. 159 (2009): Springfield police officers Edward Van Zandt and Justin Walter were on uniformed patrol in a neighborhood known for drugs, guns and property crimes. As they approached an apartment complex, officers noticed six young people standing under a tree. One male was known to both officers because he had received a trespass notice for that location. Both officers arrested the man.

Another person in the group, Anthony Johnson, was separately approached by Officer Walter — who had seen him digging into the front pockets of his sweatshirt and jeans as if looking for something. Johnson was told to remove his hands from his pockets. He briefly complied, then put them back. Walter patted Johnson down, discovering an object in his pocket which felt like the butt of a gun. Walter removed the item, which turned out to be a glass jar. He recognized crack cocaine inside. Neither officer had met Johnson prior to this interaction. The whole case turned on whether Officer Walter's frisk was justified.

- **The officers legitimately approached the group because one of the young men was trespassing.**

- **On balance, the SJC found that Officer Walter had good reason to frisk Anthony Johnson:** "The officer's command to the defendant to take his hands out of his pockets presumably was intended to avoid the need for any frisk. When the defendant disregarded the directive, from the officer's perspective, the need arose."

- **Practically speaking, if an officer asks a suspect to take his hands out of his pockets, and he complies, then the need to frisk evaporates** — unless other information indicates a possible weapon.

Acknowledging possession of a weapon

Officers should routinely ask a suspect if he has anything dangerous. An affirmative response clearly supports their frisk decision. *Comm. v. Robinson*, 83 Mass. App. Ct. 419 (2013) (officer ordered defendant to exit vehicle and asked if he had any weapons; defendant said he had a small knife on his necklace).

COLLATERAL INDIVIDUALS

Companion of suspect

Police may not automatically frisk the companion of a person under arrest. Under Article 14,[1] officers must have a reasonable suspicion that a companion might be armed and dangerous. In deciding whether to frisk, officers may consider the *nature of the crime* and *the relationship* of the arrestee to his companion.

- *Comm. v. Calderon*, 43 Mass. App. Ct. 228 (1997): While executing an arrest warrant for drug offenses, police officers acted reasonably in ordering the two companions walking

---

1 The SJC has rejected the federal "automatic companion" rule, which allows police to automatically frisk the companion of someone being arrested. *Comm. v. Ng*, 420 Mass. 236 (1995).

with their target to step aside. When the companions challenged the officers ("Hey, why are you always hassling us . . . ?"), a round of frisks made sense. This was especially true because officers knew the companions had criminal records involving drug offenses and burglaries. The court approved the officers' discovery of a weapon and stolen jewelry.

- *Comm. v. Ramirez*, 92 Mass. App. Ct. 742 (2018): Police obtained an arrest warrant for Joshua Perez for his role in a shooting. They saw Perez walking down the street with William Ramirez. An officer stepped out of his cruiser, identified himself, and said to the two men, "Come here, I want to talk to you." Perez walked over to the cruiser, but Ramirez walked away, adjusting his waistband as he did so. The officer ordered him to come back and he complied. A frisk revealed a knife and firearm.

  While police are not permitted to automatically seize a suspect's companions any time they have an arrest warrant for him, officers must "exercise unquestioned command at the scene." Here they reasonably believed Ramirez was armed and dangerous. He defied a valid police order to stop and tugged at his waistband.

Individual provided with police transport

Accepting a ride is not consent to frisk. *Comm. v. Mejias*, 96 Mass. App. Ct. 1103 (2019): Mejias was stumbling along a dark road in East Brookfield when Officer Ramos and his partner pulled alongside and asked where he was headed. Mejias said he had argued with his girlfriend and was walking to the store for cigarettes. He had been drinking, and he asked for a ride to the store.

Officer Ramos offered a ride home instead, which Mejias accepted. The officer got out and performed a frisk, finding a pistol on his ankle. Mejias was arrested.

Officer Ramos testified that he recognized Mejias from an earlier call for assistance at his home where he had learned about his long criminal history. Other than this, Ramos had no particular safety concerns at the time and did not feel that Mejias' condition qualified him for protective custody. As a result, the frisk was improper.

However, officers may insist that a person consent to a frisk in exchange for being given a ride in a police cruiser. The problem in *Mejias* was he never had the chance to decide whether he would consent to a frisk for a ride.

TIMING

A frisk should typically occur at the time officers develop reasonable suspicion. If officers wait, their opportunity may evaporate. For example, in *Comm. v. Gutierrez*, 26 Mass. App. Ct. 42 (1988), the court questioned whether police were really concerned for their safety. Officers viewed the suspect's crotch area during a five minute conversation, yet did not frisk him despite their claim that they noticed a weapons-type bulge in that area.

At the same time, a frisk may be delayed for a legitimate tactical reason. *Comm. v. Silvelo*, 486 Mass. 13 (2020): Trooper Schumaker asked for identification to write the passenger, Silvelo, a seat belt citation. As Silvelo retrieved his ID from his cargo pants pocket, a black object —

that Schumaker believed was a handgun — fell into the gap between the seat and console. In the car with Silvelo were his mother, another adult, a teenager, and two children. Concerned about their safety, Trooper Schumaker decided not to address, or even acknowledge, the weapon. He returned to his cruiser, radioed for backup, and checked Silvelo's record.

He found a warrant for Silvelo. Fifteen minutes later, when enough help was on hand, Trooper Schumaker ordered Silvelo to exit and arrested him on the warrant. Once Silvelo was cuffed and in the back of his cruiser, Schumaker frisked the area under the defendant's seat and found a revolver.

At trial, defense counsel sought to discredit Schumaker's testimony by arguing that a trooper would never leave a suspect in a vehicle if he actually saw a weapon. The judge and jury had no problem believing the trooper wisely chose this tactic for the safety of the children in the car.[2]

SCOPE

A frisk extends to those areas where the suspect might realistically gain access to a weapon. Frisks typically involve a suspect's body, possessions, and vehicle.

As a rule, frisk suspects first since they can access a weapon on their person most easily. *Comm. v. Saywahn,* 2019 WL 6605512 (Appeals Court) (Worcester officer saw Benjamin Saywahn, the front seat passenger, look back at the officer twice, reach to the left side of his waistband, lean forward, and quickly shut the glove box door; the officer wisely frisked Saywahn's body first and, finding nothing, then checked the glove box; there was a gun inside).

PERSONS

Removing object that might be a weapon

With reasonable suspicion that a suspect may be armed and dangerous, officers should pat the outer clothing and remove any item that might be a weapon. Officers are not expected to "gamble with their personal safety" by making fine distinctions about what does and does not feel like a weapon. In *Comm. v. Johnson,* 413 Mass. 598 (1992), an Alfa-Romeo operated by Johnson crossed a Boston street and almost collided with an unmarked police cruiser. The officers chased the defendant for five minutes at speeds of up to 50 mph. After the stop, Officer Flynn saw Johnson "place something inside the waistband of his pants." Flynn drew his weapon and told Johnson to "freeze." Officer McGill frisked Johnson's waist and withdrew a bag containing cocaine and a pouch with three bullets.

Johnson argued that the officer improperly removed the cocaine because he could not have thought it felt like a weapon. The court disagreed, pointing out the need for "swift measures to neutralize the threat." Also see *U.S. v. El-Gabrowny,* 825 F.Supp. 38 (S.D.N.Y. 1983) (officers frisked a suspect near the scene of an explosion in a building; they felt a rectangular object, which they thought could be plastic explosives; they properly removed the object, which turned out to be narcotics).

---

2 The defense attorney's attack on Trooper Schumaker's credibility was discussed in the Appeals Court decision. *Comm. v. Silvelo,* 96 Mass. App. Ct. 85 (2019).

Police must pat down their suspect first, not lift his clothing. *Comm. v. Flemming*, 76 Mass. App. Ct. 632 (2010): Boston officers were in an area where shots had been fired. They knew the defendant, Robert Flemming, lived nearby and that he had been shot at two months prior. The officers saw Flemming an hour later. Flemming knew about the earlier shooting "but did not want to be a snitch." He claimed to be on his way to get a slice of pizza. One officer noticed a bulge beneath Flemming's t-shirt. He told Flemming to put his hands in the air, then lifted the shirt to reveal a large revolver in his waistband. Flemming was arrested.

- **Decision to frisk.** Clearly, officers had a reasonable suspicion to frisk Flemming:

  - They received a report of shots fired in the area;
  - Flemming's mother informed them that he had been fired upon recently;
  - Flemming corroborated his mother's report when he told officers that he knew who was involved, but did not want to tell; and
  - There was a bulge in an area where offenders commonly carry firearms.

- **Scope of frisk.** The problem in this case was *how* the officer conducted the frisk. He deviated from the standard practice of patting down the suspect.

- **Exceptions.** The Appeals Court recognized only two instances when officers may dispense with the pat down:

  - *The police have specific information about the location of a weapon.* **U.S. v. Hill,** 545 F.2d 1191 (9th Cir. 1976) (since bank teller had seen the suspect lift his shirt to display a gun in his waistband, it was reasonable for the police to immediately reach there when they found the suspect a short time later).

  - *The suspect may be reaching for a weapon when encountered by police.* *People v. Superior Court,* 15 Cal. App. 3d 806 (1975) (responding to a report of shots fired, officers permissibly reached directly into the defendant's pocket after seeing him do so as they approached).

During a frisk, officer dialogue may justify removing an object that is either a weapon or evidence. *U.S. v. Brake,* 666 F.3d 800 (2011): Police received a 911 call reporting a man with a gun making threats in a residence. Police arrived and saw two men walking away from the house in bulky, hooded sweatshirts. They watched the men walk toward a parked minivan. One man slid open the side door and the other leaned inside. They quickly slammed it shut and walked away.

Two officers ran after them, shouting: "Hey!" When the men did not respond, the officers ordered them to stop. The officers informed the men about the complaint and told them they would be "patted down for weapons."

While performing a frisk, one officer felt a "squishy" object in the front pocket of Adam Brake's sweatshirt. Aware that it was not a weapon, the officer asked Brake what he had.

Brake explained that it was a plastic bag he found in the bushes. The officer asked him whether he was curious about what was inside. Brake responded by opening the bag. He looked inside and threw it on the ground, exclaiming: "Those aren't mine!" The officer picked it up and saw several hundred pills.

This was excellent police work. The suspects' baggy clothing could have hidden a handgun, and the suspects might have been getting weapons from the van. The fact that Brake was cooperative did not negate the officer's need to frisk him. Realizing that he was not touching a weapon, the officer wisely asked Brake for an explanation about the package and persuaded him to open it.

Plain feel doctrine

Under Article 14,[3] *"plain feel" occurs when an officer immediately recognizes evidence during a frisk. Comm. v. Wilson*, 441 Mass. 390 (2004). Here is an effective way to describe plain feel: "When I frisked the suspect's [describe area specifically — e.g., left front pants pocket, or right windbreaker patch pocket, etc.], I felt an object which I immediately knew was not a weapon. In fact, its size, shape and texture immediately felt like [describe what it felt like — e.g., a vial of crack cocaine, several bundles of heroin, etc.]."

Verbal comments, and even reaching into a pocket, does not nullify plain feel. Comm. v. Cullen, 62 Mass. App. Ct. 390 (2004): At about 2:00 a.m., a perpetrator kicked in the door to an elderly woman's house. The burglar repeatedly hit her, demanding that she tell him where the money was. She grabbed the maroon cap from his head and saw that he was a white man, bald on top with hair on the sides. Within moments of the burglar's flight from her house, a passing motorist encountered a black, hatchback automobile "barreling" out of the intersection near the scene. At the traffic light, the witness caught up to the car and observed a black male driving and a white male passenger. A short time later, the witness noticed police at the elder's house and related his encounter with the black car.

At 3:00 a.m., Sergeant Elliot spotted the black hatchback and saw that the driver matched the woman's description of her attacker. Elliot now activated blue lights and siren. Driver and passenger were ordered out. Another officer frisked Robert Cullen and felt a hard mass in his coat pocket, hearing a jingling sound as the objects moved. The officer asked Cullen what he had. He replied, "Keys." Based on the physical qualities of these objects, the officer knew Cullen was lying. The officer thrust his hands into the pocket and felt coins. He retrieved almost a dozen half-dollars, which Cullen said his wife had given him earlier. In fact, the coins came from the elder's home.

- **Reasonable suspicion to stop vehicle:** (1) the black hatchback described by the witness; (2) the number, gender, and race of its occupants; (3) the incident involving the black car happened within minutes of the burglary and close to a known staging area used in previous burglaries in the area; (4) the reckless manner in which the car was operated, as if making a getaway; and (5) the driver matched the description of the burglar.

- **Plain feel of coins.** The exit order and frisk were proper. Once the officer felt metal objects, his reach inside the defendant's pocket was "minimally necessary" to determine whether the objects were dangerous. The defendant forcefully argued that the coins could not be immediately recognized as evidence under the plain feel doctrine because the officer lacked direct knowledge that coins had been taken during the burglary. However, plain feel extends to contraband *and* the fruits of crime. The incriminating nature of evidence may be inferred. Here, the sheer number of coins (which was greater than a person would

---

3 Under the Fourth Amendment, the U.S. Supreme Court first recognized that an officer may seize nonthreatening contraband detected through the sense of touch. *Minnesota v. Dickerson*, 508 U.S. 366 (1993).

ordinarily carry); Cullen's initially false story about keys; and the fact that the perpetrator had demanded money while beating the elder — all led to the officer's sensible conclusion that "the coins in the defendant's pockets were among the swag from the home burglary."

Touching item a second time does not nullify plain feel. *Comm. v. Osborne*, 62 Mass. App. Ct. 445 (2004): Acting on a reliable informant's tip that the defendant was selling cocaine, Sergeant Murphy stopped Osborne in Boston. During the course of a frisk, Murphy removed from Osborne's jacket pocket a wooden-handled folding knife. Continuing the frisk, Murphy felt, through Osborne's clothing, a hard object located between his buttocks. Murphy again felt this area and decided that Osborne was hiding cocaine. When Osborne did not permit officers to take the plastic bag protruding from his buttocks during the booking process, Murphy obtained a warrant and the packet was removed at the hospital.

Agreeing that his detention and frisk were valid, Osborne argued that the officer's need to touch his buttocks twice meant that the contraband was not "immediately apparent." The court responded: "It is clear that the officer immediately recognized the item, from its size, hardness and location, as contraband. That he . . . touched it a second time before proceeding does not remove the encounter from the category of a plain feel seizure."

POSSESSIONS

Proper method for frisking a suspect's container depends on the type of container. The officer must do what is minimally necessary to discover whether it contains a weapon.

- **Specific information container holds weapon — should open.** If officers already have specific information that a particular container holds a weapon, it would be redundant to require that they perform a frisk before opening it. *People v. Ritter*, 54 Cal. App.4th 274 (1997) (where officer observed outline of handgun in outer compartment of suspect's "fanny pack," officer could search compartment without pat down).

- **Hard container — should open.** When the container has a hard exterior, a frisk will provide no useful information about its contents. It is pointless, for example, to frisk a cardboard box or a hard-sided suitcase. *U.S. v. McClinnhan*, 660 F.2d 500 (D.C. Cir. 1981) (hard briefcase containing sawed-off shotgun was properly opened by agents conducting a frisk).

- **Heavy, pliable container — should open.** Frisking the outside of a heavy, pliable container will not reveal anything beyond what officers already know — that it contains a hard, heavy object that might be a weapon. As a result, officers will have to open the container anyway. *Comm. v. Pagan*, 440 Mass. 62 (2003) (during break-in investigation, defendant's heavy backpack had to be opened to ensure objects inside were not weapons).

- **Small, pliable container — should frisk.** A small container made of soft, pliable material should be patted down because that action is enough to reveal any possible weapon inside. *Comm. v. Sumerlin*, 393 Mass. 127 (1984).

- **Large, pliable container — should open.** The fact that a particular container is made of soft material does *not* always mean that a frisk will provide useful information about the presence of a weapon. For example, frisking a full duffel bag will reveal a weapon located near the outer surface, but not one packed in the middle. The bag must be opened to determine whether a weapon is hidden deeper inside.

The presence of several officers holding a suspect's container does <u>not</u> eliminate the need to frisk it. Equally important, "no matter how many officers are present, the police cannot safely allow a detained suspect to reach inside a container that they reasonably fear may contain a weapon." *Comm. v. Pagan, supra.*

VEHICLES

The frisk of a vehicle extends to areas where the suspect <u>realistically</u> had, has, or will have access to a weapon. The right to frisk does not end when the suspect is removed from the vehicle. *Comm. v. Santiago,* 53 Mass. App. Ct. 567 (2002) explains why: "[Vehicle stops] frequently terminate with the release of the suspect . . . [A police officer is] not required to risk becoming a victim upon the suspect's reentry into the vehicle."

Police are not authorized to frisk every area that a suspect can possibly reach without any evidence that he actually did so. *Comm. v. Meneide,* 89 Mass. App. Ct. 448 (2016): Police observed a car take a right turn from a left-turn only lane. The driver, Jerry Meneide, was driving very slowly while talking on his cell phone and looking around. The officers followed the car and observed him take a right turn on red without coming to a complete stop.

When they pulled the car over, the troopers saw Meneide lift his buttocks six inches and appear to put his hand underneath. The troopers smelled an overwhelming odor of unburnt marijuana and air fresheners. Meneide acknowledged that he had "a little weed." The troopers asked him to exit the car for a frisk. He nervously complied. The troopers found a packet of marijuana in his jacket pocket and a smaller one in the pocket of his pants. Together, the packets weighed less than an ounce.

The troopers then frisked the car. They found nothing in the front seat area, but when they pulled down the back center armrest, they discovered a gun.

- **The exit order, frisk, and search of immediate area.** Meneide's unusual action of lifting himself off the seat by six inches in a manner consistent with concealing something was sufficient to justify the exit order and frisk. While the odor of marijuana suggested he could have been concealing drugs, he just as well could have been concealing a weapon.

- **Search of armrest.** At the same time, pulling down the back armrest exceeded the scope of the frisk for safety. Police are not authorized to search every area that a suspect can possibly reach without any evidence that he actually did so. Although the car was small, and the armrest was within Meneide's reach from the driver seat, he had made no movement toward the backseat, and there was no other evidence to suggest a weapon might be concealed there. Meneide was cooperative and produced his license.

- **Recommendation: When officers testify, they should explain how they focus on the <u>realistic reach area</u>.** Weapons can be hidden and quickly accessed in a vehicle, so officers must check the entire area toward which an occupant reached.

Opening locked glove box. *Comm. v. Graham,* 78 Mass. App. Ct. 127 (2010): Boston officers were speaking with a group on the sidewalk in an area known for shootings. As a car drove onto the street, the individuals retreated toward the cover of a nearby building. Concerned by this reaction, officers decided to follow the vehicle. Its license plate was not properly illuminated, and several turns were made without directional signals.

Having stopped the car, officers recognized that three passengers were associated with a local gang. The driver, Robert Kines, was seen locking the glove compartment after retrieving his registration. Kines continued to reach down between the seats after one of the officers told him to keep his hands in plain sight.

Exit orders followed. Kines expressed concern about leaving his keys behind. His frisk revealed a knife. The frisk of William Graham, who had been in the front seat, exposed a knife in a sheath. The rear seat passengers were "clean."

The vehicle interior was inspected for weapons, including the glove box. It was opened with the key Kines had left in the car. Police found a revolver. Frisking this locked area was proper because it was easily accessible and large enough to hold a weapon.

Do not open containers that probably do not hold a weapon. *Comm. v. Cruz-Rivera*, 76 Mass. App. Ct. 21 (2009) agreed that officers had grounds to frisk the center console of the defendant's car when he abruptly reached toward that area after a motor vehicle stop for dangerous driving. However, once officers found no weapons on the defendant or underneath the seats, they could not justify opening a small, vitamin pill bottle inside the console. The fact that the pill bottle could theoretically hold a razor blade or "pen gun" was not a good enough reason. There was no evidence that tiny weapons had been spreading in the community or that this defendant had a history of using tiny weapons. With no protective reason to look inside the bottle, the cocaine found inside had to be suppressed.

Checking trunk usually forbidden. It is hard to claim that a vehicle occupant may quickly access a weapon in the trunk, which is why frisks of this area are typically forbidden.

However, some vehicles come equipped with a seat-back or panel that folds down to allow trunk access. Although Massachusetts appellate courts have yet to rule on this issue, it does make sense for an officer to frisk the part of the trunk that is directly accessible to passengers. If the officer frisks this way, he must testify about the location of the passengers and how they were reaching near the particular portal into the trunk.[4]

---

4 In an analogous situation, *Comm. v. Bongarzone*, 390 Mass. 326 (1983) held that the rear portion of a Ford Bronco behind the last passenger seat was part of the passenger compartment, not the trunk. A search incident to arrest revealing drugs was approved because the passengers had access to this area.

6 Police De-escalation & Use of Force

PROPER USE OF FORCE (UOF)
POLICE UOF IN CONTEXT

61.5 million people over the age of 16 in the United States had police contact in 2018. Yet, only 2% experienced a situation in which an officer used force or threatened to use force.[1] In the same year, officers shot and killed 990 people throughout the United States.

Although it is a remarkable success that UOF occurs in a tiny fraction of police contacts, it remains a major public concern. The reasons are: (1) police are the only officials in our society formally authorized to use force — so officers are naturally the object of scrutiny; (2) there is evidence that, historically, some police UOF decisions have been affected by bias towards disfavored groups; and (3) increased media exposure of the worst incidents of excessive force have galvanized public sentiment, resulting in greater civilian oversight of police training and decision-making.

In the United States, police UOF must be objectively reasonable to comply with the Fourth Amendment. This command appears in the legendary case of *Graham v. Connor* 490 US 386 (1989). In the words of the Supreme Court, police officers "are often forced to make split-second judgments — in circumstances that are tense, uncertain, and rapidly evolving — about the amount of force that is necessary in a particular situation." That is why UOF "must be judged from the perspective of a reasonable officer on the scene, rather than with the 20/20 vision of hindsight."

Deciding what is objectively reasonable requires "careful attention to the facts and circumstances of each particular case, including the severity of the crime at issue, whether the suspect poses an immediate threat to the safety of the officers or others, and whether he is actively resisting arrest or attempting to evade arrest by flight." It is, above all, a practical standard — "Not every push or shove, even if it may later seem unnecessary in the peace of a judge's chambers, [amounts to excessive force]."

In Massachusetts, the constitutional mandate of reasonableness is supplemented by statutes and regulations containing more specific guidelines. Beyond *Graham's* objective reasonableness, Massachusetts officers must abide by Chapter 6E and 555 CMR 6.00. which present joint regulations from the Municipal Police Training Committee (MPTC) and Peace Officer Standards & Training Commission (POST).

---

1 "Contacts Between Police and the Public, 2018 — Statistical Tables," December 2020, NCJ 255730, Bureau of Justice Assistance.

NON-DEADLY FORCE

REASONS

Under 6E, § 14(a), when de-escalation is not feasible or has failed, officers may use proportionate and necessary force to:

- Conduct a lawful arrest or detention;

- Prevent an escape from custody;

- Defend themselves;[2],[3] or

- **Prevent imminent harm to another** (e.g., break up a fight; stop a suicide attempt; take someone into protective custody; intervene during a medical or mental health emergency). See, e.g., *Lachance v. Town of Charlton*, 990 F.3d 14 (1st Cir. 2021) (delusional and injured, William Lachance tried to push past medics and officers, who had been dispatched to his house at the request of his wife; it was reasonable for officers to try to restrain him before he went out the front door onto an ice-covered stairway in the middle of the night).

Imminent means "about to happen." It describes an immediate concern.[4]

DE-ESCALATION

Under 6E, § 1, de-escalation involves proactive approaches to stabilize a law enforcement situation so that more time, options, and resources are available to gain voluntary compliance and reduce or eliminate the need for force. These approaches include:

- Verbal persuasion,

- Warnings,

- Slowing down the pace of an incident,

- Waiting out a person,

- Creating distance between the officer and a threat, and

- **Requesting additional resources to resolve the incident** (e.g., calling mental health professionals).

None of these tactics are new to professional police officers.

---

2 An officer may "defend against an individual who initiates force against an officer." 555 CMR 6.04(1)(d).
3 One issue that may come up more frequently during department and/or POST investigations is known as "officer-created jeopardy." In some civil rights lawsuits, courts have been willing to examine an officer's conduct in the minutes prior to a use of force to determine if the officer unreasonably placed himself in a dangerous situation from which he could only rescue himself through force. It then becomes an open question whether the proper application of policy, de-escalation tactics, and UOF tactics would have prevented the incident, at the outset, from escalating into a dangerous one for the officer. The classic example is the officer who deliberately stands in front of the vehicle of a suspect fleeing a minor crime, and then explains he had to shoot the driver in self-defense. See generally *Young v. City of Providence*, 404 F.3d 4, (1st Cir, 2005).
4 See dictionary.com.

De-escalation tactics must be feasible. The term "feasible" is not defined by 6E, § 1, but it means "capable of being used successfully."[5] In short, de-escalation must be realistic under the circumstances.

• **When an officer is confronted with a danger of *imminent* harm to himself or another, de-escalation may not be feasible.**

• **There are competing values in deciding whether de-escalation continues to be feasible.** For example, at 3:00 a.m. the subject is drunk and screaming on the front porch of a stranger's house and insisting that he has arrived home. It may be *possible* to "wait the person out" in the hopes that he will fall asleep or sober up, but is it *socially acceptable* to inflict more fear and sleeplessness on the home's occupants in order to wait for voluntary compliance? Officers must make commonsense and realistic judgments.

• **The incident report is the most important tool for officers to explain how de-escalation succeeded or failed, or why it was not feasible to begin with.** These are the only three legal possibilities — either de-escalation worked, failed, or was not attempted. Remember, citizens are less likely to be hypercritical of police departments who insist that their officers rigorously document all the times they successfully de-escalate encounters, as well as those times when de-escalation failed and force became necessary.

PROPORTIONATE FORCE

Non-deadly force is defined as "physical effort, however slight, to compel compliance by an unwilling person." 555 CMR 6.03. This includes:

• **Pointing a weapon.** Pointing a firearm, electronic control weapon (ECW), or a chemical weapon (CW) at a person is a UOF. 6.04(3). This definition does *not* include those times when an officer removes her firearm or ECW from its holster (i.e., the "ready position") but does not end up pointing it at a citizen.

• **OC spray is not a CW.** Therefore, only spraying OC at a person is a UOF. 6.04(3).

Escort or handcuffs <u>not</u> force. Physically escorting or handcuffing a person "with minimal or no resistance" is not a UOF. 6.04(3).

While the term "proportionate" is not defined in Chapter 6E, its traditional meaning is "balanced."[6] Thus, a proportionate UOF is a balanced response by an officer.

In particular, the "UOF Continuum" is proportionate because officer tactics are influenced by the amount and intensity of a suspect's resistance. *Jennings v. Jones*, 499 F.3d 2 (1st Cir., 2007) (court talks about how force continuum is a guide to proportionate police responses).[7]

---

5 See dictionary.com.
6 See dictionary.com.
7 The MPTC and other training authorities in Massachusetts have been teaching officers to apply the use of force continuum for decades. To learn more and see the UOF continuum model, go to https://medfordpolice.com/m-p-t-c-use-of-force-continuum/

A basic premise of the continuum is that force should be adjusted as the threat increases or decreases. *Jennings v. Jones, supra.*: Adam Jennings initially resisted arrest, which justified Detective Jones employing an "ankle turn control technique." Even though this move caused Jennings to immediately stop resisting, Detective Jones, rather than maintaining or reducing his hold, increased pressure and broke Jennings' ankle. This was not proportionate force.

Two force situations call for heightened awareness:

- **Passive resistance.** When a person is non-compliant with officer commands, but is completely non-violent (e.g., a protester who simply sits on the ground), officers shall *only* use the force necessary to make the arrest or conduct the investigative detention. In appropriate cases, officers may choose to simply apply for a criminal complaint instead of making an arrest. 555 CMR 6.03, 6.04(2).

- **Pressure on a person's chest, neck, or spine.** Except to <u>temporarily</u> gain, regain, or maintain control of a person, or to apply handcuffs, an officer shall not intentionally sit, kneel, or stand on a person's chest, neck, or spine, and shall not force a person to lie on their stomach. After being handcuffed on his stomach, a person should be moved into a recovery or seated position as soon as practicable. 6.04(7).

Finally, force is only proportionate and necessary when applied to an actual threat. Consider *Armstrong v. Village of Pinehurst*, 810 F.3d 892 (4th Cir. 2016): Ronald Armstrong fled the hospital where he was being admitted as a psychiatric patient for "poking holes in my skin to let the air out." He willingly stopped to talk with an officer outside the hospital. When a doctor signed a commitment paper, however, Armstrong resisted the efforts of three officers to get him to return to the hospital by sitting on the ground and wrapping his arms and legs around a post. After briefly trying to pull Armstrong off the post, officers deployed an ECW in drive stun mode five times within two minutes. In his position, Armstrong posed no threat of violence to anyone, including himself. The court concluded: "Immediately tasing a non-criminal, mentally ill individual, who seconds before had been conversational, was not a proportionate response."

REQUIREMENTS AFTER NON-DEADLY UOF

Medical treatment. Following a use of non-deadly force, officers shall provide the appropriate medical response to a person <u>exhibiting or complaining of injury or illness</u> when safe and tactically feasible. 555 CMR 6.04(4).

Separate UOF report. Officers must complete a UOF report on a standard form approved by MPTC and POST. <u>All</u> UOF must be reported [6.07(1)], and these reports are subject to discovery and access as public records [6.07(8)]. Finally, officers who lie or fail to disclose important information in a UOF report are subject to discipline or decertification. 6.07(5).

In addition to receiving all UOF reports, POST must <u>investigate</u> any report concerning an officer-involved injury or death. 6E, § 8(c)(1). The term, "officer-involved injury or death," is defined by 6E, § 1 to cover the following actions when they result in injury or death to another person:

- Discharging a firearm;
- Discharging a stun gun (aka ECW, taser);

- Using a chokehold;
- Using tear gas or other chemical weapon;
- Shooting rubber pellets;
- Deploying a K-9;
- Using deadly force;
- Failing to intervene; or
- Engaging in a physical altercation, but only if the person sustains serious bodily injury or requests or receives medical care.

MASS DEMONSTRATIONS

6E, § 14(e) creates additional requirements to reduce the potential for violence at a "planned mass demonstration." While the term, planned mass demonstration, is undefined in the law, § 14(e) does mandate that police departments:[8]

- **Engage in a good faith effort to communicate with organizers** and discuss logistical plans, strategies to avoid conflict, and communications between police and participants at the planned demonstration; and

- **Appoint an officer in charge of developing de-escalation plans** and communicating them throughout the department.

No officer on scene shall use or order any of the following types of force unless de-escalation is not feasible or has failed *and* the measures used are necessary to prevent imminent harm *and* are proportionate to the threat:

- **Tear gas or any other chemical weapon,**[9]

- **Rubber pellets,**[10]

- **Electronic Control Weapon (ECW),**[11] or

- **A dog to influence or control a person's behavior.** While a dog should not be used for crowd control, restraint, or management of peaceful demonstrations, it may be deployed in isolated circumstances related to bomb detection, pursuit of suspects in buildings, and related situations. A dog is not being "used" when kept in close proximity to its handler on a short lead well behind the line of contact with civilians. 555 CMR 6.08(5).

If police use any of these specific types of force, the agency must explain why in a separate report to POST.

---

8 269, § 1 defines an unlawful assembly as ten or more people "riotously assembled," or five or more people who are armed with dangerous weapons. For more, see *LED's Criminal Law, Chapter 23.* With respect to 6E, § 14(e), the clear intent is to push police departments to proactively engage with demonstration organizers before an event to prevent or mitigate violent behavior.
9 "Tear gas or other chemical weapon" is defined as " [a]ny weapon that contains chemical compounds that temporarily make people unable to function by causing irritation to the eyes, mouth, throat, lungs, and skin, or that otherwise restrain a person by causing pain." OC spray is not included in this definition. 555 CMR 6.03.
10 "Rubber pellets" are not defined. The obvious intent was to cover rubber bullets and all other "less lethal" projectiles used for crowd control.
11 The reporting requirement for ECW use appears in 555 CMR 6.08(4), but not in 6E, § 14(e).

Finally, a tactic known as "kettling" is prohibited. 555 CMR 6.08(6). Kettling is defined as "confinement or corralling by law enforcement of a group of demonstrators or protesters in a small area without any means of egress as a method of crowd control, management, or restraint." 6.03. In short, police must always maintain a safe exit for crowd members.

DEADLY FORCE

PERMISSIBLE & IMPERMISSIBLE REASONS

Under 6E, § 1, force becomes "deadly" if it is expected to cause death or serious injury.

Under 6E, § 14(b) and 555 CMR 6.05, deadly force is <u>authorized</u> when:

- **De-escalation.**[12] The officer attempts as many de-escalation tactics as are feasible under the circumstances, including using barriers; and

- **Warning.** When feasible, the officer identifies himself and issues a warning before using deadly force; and

- **Proportionate & necessary.** Deadly force is proportionate and necessary to prevent an imminent and current risk of death or serious bodily injury to the officer or another person.[13]

Deadly force is <u>prohibited</u> when a person poses a danger only to themselves. 555 CMR 6.05(3). Officers may not employ deadly force when the only risk is the subject's suicide.

ADDITIONAL REQUIREMENTS AFTER DEADLY UOF

Medical treatment. Following a use of deadly force, officers shall always provide the appropriate medical response when safe and tactically feasible. 555 CMR 6.05(7).

Beyond regular UOF reporting, agencies must perform the following in response to a use of deadly force <u>or</u> to any UOF that results in death or serious injury:

- **Immediate notice to agency head.** The officer in charge (OIC) shall immediately notify the agency head or their designee when force causes death or serious bodily injury. The agency shall conduct an investigation. 555 CMR 6.09.

- **Secure the weapon used.** The agency head or designee shall secure any weapon used for examination and maintain its chain of custody. 6.09.

- **National UOF Database.** A report to this database is required any time: (1) an officer's actions result in death or serious bodily injury to any person; or (2) a firearm was discharged at or in the direction of a person, even if no death or injury resulted. 6.07(2).

---

12 See earlier discussion of de-escalation under 6E, § 1. The same principles apply to deadly force, although the circumstances may be markedly different.
13 The regulations emphasize that deadly force cannot be justified by the fact that there was a sufficient threat at an earlier point in time. In other words, officers cannot assume that a prior threat automatically carries over in the future. See 555 CMR 6.05(5).

Training or the destruction of an animal does <u>not</u> require a UOF report. 6.07(3).

CHOKEHOLDS

Under 6E, § 14(c), officers shall not use a chokehold. Officers must not be trained to use chokeholds, regardless of what the technique is called.

Definition of chokehold. 6E, § 1 defines a chokehold as "the use of a lateral vascular neck restraint, carotid restraint or other action that involves the placement of any part of a law enforcement officer's body on or around a person's neck in a manner that limits the person's breathing or blood flow with the intent of or the result of causing bodily injury, unconsciousness, or death."

Regulations further prohibit any restriction of breathing or circulation. Regardless of their physical position, officers "shall not obstruct the airway or limit the breathing of any individual, nor . . . restrict oxygen or blood flow to an individual's head or neck." 555 CMR 6.04(7) and 6.05(2).

SHOOTING AT VEHICLES

Under 6E, § 14(d), officers may not shoot at or into a fleeing motor vehicle unless shooting is necessary to prevent imminent harm and is proportionate to the threat. This happens when:

- **The operation of the vehicle is deliberately intended to strike a person**, and all other options — including moving out of the path of the oncoming vehicle — have been exhausted or are not practical; <u>and/or</u>

- **An occupant is threatening to use deadly force, other than the vehicle itself.** In other words, officers may not later justify shooting at a vehicle by claiming that the vehicle itself was the equivalent of a gun being pointed at them. 555 CMR 6.05(4)(a).

Important tactical requirements:

- **Officers must not intentionally position themselves to create a likelihood of being struck by the vehicle.** 6.05(4)(b).

- **Officers must not shoot strictly to disable the vehicle.** The goal of discharging their weapons must be to stop the threat by striking the driver, and there must be a high probability of stopping or striking the intended target. 6.05(4)(c) and (4)(d)].

DUTY TO INTERVENE

Officers must act to prevent excessive force. 6E, § 15(a) states: "An officer present and observing another officer using physical force, including deadly force, beyond that which is necessary or objectively reasonable . . . shall intervene to prevent the use of unreasonable force unless intervening would result in imminent harm to the officer or another identifiable individual."

This duty to intervene has existed for decades in Massachusetts. The SJC recognized this constitutional and statutory duty (see 12, § 11H) in *Comm. v. Adams*, 416 Mass. 558 (1993). *Adams* began near Fenway Park at sunrise. John L. Smith had just snorted cocaine in his car when he drew the attention of Boston officers in a marked cruiser. Smith drove through a red light and the pursuit was on. After swerving at cruisers and evading a partial roadblock, Smith's engine died on a Brookline side street. Eight cruisers converged with thirteen officers — and not supervisor in sight.

Although Smith sat motionless in his unlocked car, several officers smashed his windows and dragged him out. They threw him on the pavement and piled on top. Other officers later put their foot on Smith's head and back while he lay on the street in handcuffs. No officer sought treatment for Smith or reported his injuries. The SJC classified all officers on scene as accomplices because they either applied excessive force or witnessed and approved this misconduct. The high court's concern was magnified by the fact that the officers provided false testimony and displayed no awareness or concern about their misconduct.

Intervene regardless of rank. The duty to intervene exists regardless of the rank of the officer who is observed using excessive force. 555 CMR 6.06.

Aside from the duty to intervene, there is a duty to report. Officers must also report excessive force that they witness to their department. 6E, § 15(b).

- **Report as soon as possible to the appropriate supervisor,** but no later than the end of the reporting officer's shift. This is classified as a UOF report. 555 CMR 6.07(4).

- **Report without retaliation.** Agencies must protect all agency employees, sworn or non-sworn, against retaliation or the fear of retaliation. 6.07(6). In fact, decertification is authorized for any officer who harasses, intimidates, or retaliates against any officer who intervened, or reported, or was required to report excessive force. 6.07(7).

IMPROPER UOF

THREE POTENTIAL CONSEQUENCES

Criminal charges. Police officers may be charged with assault and battery (A&B) or other crimes related to their use of excessive force. The prosecutor must prove any criminal charge beyond a reasonable doubt. *Comm. v. Garvey*, 99 Mass. App. Ct. 139 (2021) (upset officer pushed, used her baton, and OC-sprayed a civilian onlooker during the officer's interaction with a drunk person; video surveillance showed that the officer also lied in her incident report about what happened; she was convicted of these crimes).

Civil lawsuit. Citizens may file a civil lawsuit under federal and/or state law based on allegations of excessive force. The burden of proof in civil court is a preponderance of the evidence. Most federal lawsuits are based on 42 U.S.C. § 1983, a statute that imposes money damages and attorneys fees for police violations of a citizen's constitutional rights. See, e.g., *Bastein v. Goddard*, 279 F.3d 10 (1st Cir. 2002) (excessive force). *Harrington v. City of Nashua*, 610 F.3d 24 (1st Cir. 2010) (malicious prosecution).

Professional decertification or suspension. When allegations are proven by "clear and convincing evidence" to the Peace Officer Standards & Training Commission (POST), a police officer may be decertified or have his certification suspended for engaging in excessive force, failing to intervene, or providing untruthful information about an incident. Based on a lesser finding of "substantial evidence," POST may order a police officer to undergo remedial training.

POST PROCESS

POST's Division of Police Standards (DS) conducts preliminary investigations. 6E, § 8(g). The DS must notify an officer, the head of the officer's collective bargaining unit, and the head of the appointing agency of the general allegation within 30 days of commencing an inquiry. 6E, § 8(c).

The appointing agency has the opportunity to investigate allegations against its officers before POST holds a final hearing. Under 6E, § 10(h), prior to its final decertification or suspension hearing, POST give the officer's appointing agency up to 1 year to reach its own final disposition. Section 10(h) also allows:

- **Investigation delay.** For good cause, POST may extend the time for an agency to complete its investigation.

- **Arbitration delay for 1 year.** An officer may suspend a hearing pending an appeal or arbitration for a maximum of 1 year following notification to POST.[14]

- **Criminal proceedings.** If an officer requests, POST must postpone a hearing while criminal charges are pending, provided the officer's certification is suspended during the delay.

- **Interim suspension unaffected.** Delays of final suspension or decertification hearings do not affect POST's interim suspensions, which are based on a preponderance of the evidence. An officer may appeal an interim suspension to a POST commissioner within 15 days. If not overturned, the interim suspension continues until a final decision by POST. 6E, § 9.

The agency must report to POST when an officer resigns during an investigation. The agency head must make a recommendation for action by POST. 6E, § 8(b).

Mandatory decertification occurs when POST finds *by clear and convincing evidence* any of the following [6E, § 10(a)(i)–(xvi)]:

- The officer was **convicted** of a felony;[15]

---

14 In a confusingly written section, the law seems to allow continuances of up to 6 months within the overall maximum delay period of 1 year. 6E, § 10(h).
15 Conviction carries a special definition, found in 6E, § 1, and includes all dispositions of a case other than straight dismissal or a not guilty verdict!

- The officer's **certification was issued in error**, was obtained through misrepresentation or fraud, or was issued or renewed based upon an officer's falsified documents;

- The officer's certification was **revoked in another jurisdiction;**

- The officer knowingly filed a **false police report**, committed perjury (268, § 1), or was convicted of submitting false time sheets (231, § 85BB);

- The officer **tampered with a record** to be used in an official proceeding (268, § 13E);

- The officer engaged in the **intimidation of a witness** (268, § 13B) or engaged in conduct that would constitute a **hate crime** as defined in 22C, § 32;

- The officer **used force in violation of 6E, § 14**, used a chokehold, or used excessive force resulting in death or serious bodily injury;

- The officer **failed to intervene** to prevent another officer from engaging in prohibited conduct, including excessive force, in violation of 6E, § 15;

- The officer is **terminated by the appointing agency** (and any appeal is completed) because the officer's intentional conduct resulted in:

  - Obtaining a *false confession*;
  - Making a *false arrest*;
  - Creating or using *falsified evidence*;
  - Engaging in a *hate crime*; or
  - Receiving a reward, gift, or *gratuity on account of official services*.

- When the officer is not fit for duty and is **dangerous to the public.**

***Non-mandatory* decertification or suspension** if POST finds *clear and convincing evidence* that [6E, § 10(b)]:

- The officer was **convicted of a misdemeanor;**

- The officer's conduct "was **biased** on the basis of race, ethnicity, sex, gender identity, sexual orientation, religion, mental or physical disability, immigration status or socioeconomic or professional level";

- Was **suspended or terminated by their appointing agency** for disciplinary reasons (and any appeal has been completed); or

- Has **repeated and sustained internal affairs complaints** for the same or different offenses;

- Has a **pattern of unprofessional police conduct** that POST believes may escalate.

At the end of the suspension period, POST may reinstate the officer if its conditions (such as retraining) have been completed. However, retraining is not an option when decertification is mandatory. 6E, § 10(c).

Part III

ARRESTS

Chapters 7 – 10

Charging Offenders with Crimes

INTRODUCTION: THREE METHODS TO CHARGE

This chapter outlines the methods that officers may use, once they develop probable cause,[1] to charge an offender and bring him before the court. There are three options:

- Warrant.
- Arrest.
- Complaint.

Felony or misdemeanor. An officer's decision to pursue a warrant, arrest, or complaint depends on whether the offender committed a felony or misdemeanor. Under 274, § 1, a felony is defined as any crime for which the offender may be sentenced to state prison. All other crimes are misdemeanors.

WARRANT

A court is more likely to uphold the validity of an arrest made under a warrant. "Law enforcement officers may find it wise to seek arrest warrants [because] their judgments about probable cause may be more readily accepted [when] backed by a warrant issued by a magistrate." *U.S. v. Watson*, 423 U.S. 411 (1976).

OBTAINING AN ARREST WARRANT

Venue. Under 218, § 32, an officer may seek an arrest warrant from the district court that has jurisdiction over the location of the crime *or* where the offender may be found.[2]

Written probable cause

Application and incident report. Under Rule 3(g) of the *Massachusetts Rules of Criminal Procedure*, to obtain a warrant, a police officer must submit a written application *and* statement of probable cause to a magistrate.

- The application requires completion of the standard form. See *page 7-13*.

---

1 Probable cause consists of trustworthy facts and inferences which would lead a reasonable person to believe that it is more likely than not that the offender committed or is committing a crime. The type of evidence that creates probable cause was discussed in *Chapters 2* and *3*.
2 Judges of the Supreme Judicial Court, superior court or district court, or clerks or assistant clerks of the district court may issue arrest warrants. Most officers find it more convenient and expeditious to apply to a clerk or assistant clerk in their local district court. 218, § 33. 276, § 21.

- The statement of probable cause is typically satisfied when the officer submits his incident report. It is also acceptable (although rare) for an officer to verbally describe the facts that support probable cause and have his statement recorded *or* written down by the magistrate.

Proper description. An arrest warrant must contain the name of the offender. If the correct name is unknown, an officer may use "any name or description by which [the offender] can be identified with reasonable certainty." In *Comm. v. Baldassini*, 357 Mass. 670 (1970), the court upheld a "John Doe" warrant which described the defendant as: "John Doe, also known as 'Baldi' and Baldassini, a white male between 50 and 55 years of age, 5'8", 170–180 pounds, with dark hair, of Quincy, Massachusetts."

Warrant management system

276, § 23A establishes a Warrant Management System (WMS). The best feature of WMS is instant access through a computer network known as the Criminal Justice Information System (CJIS). A printout of a WMS warrant is considered "a true copy" and may be served immediately.

Civil liability protection. Section 23A also states: "No law enforcement officer, who in the performance of his duties relies in good faith on [a] warrant appearing in [WMS], shall be liable in any criminal prosecution or civil action alleging false arrest, false imprisonment, or malicious prosecution."

Check WMS again before arresting on a warrant. *Comm. v. Maingrette*, 86 Mass. App. Ct. 691 (2015): Boston police officers received information that Brian Maingrette was involved in a gun-related, domestic incident the night before. Officer Burrows checked WMS at 1:00 p.m. He saw that a default warrant for Maingrette's arrest after he failed to appear in court.

Officers went to Maingrette's mother's apartment at 2:40 p.m. No one answered the door. At 4:15 p.m., detectives conducting surveillance saw Maingrette enter the apartment. He left at 5:00 p.m. They stopped his vehicle and arrested him. They found a loaded gun too.

During booking, officers discovered that Maingrette had reported to court. The warrant had been recalled at 3:00 p.m.! Because his arrest was illegal, the gun had to be suppressed. The SJC held that, if possible, officers must check WMS before they make an arrest. In this case, officers had plenty of time to do that.

AUTHORITY UNDER ARREST WARRANT

Arrest power. Any official authorized to serve criminal process in any county may execute an arrest warrant. Authorized officials include municipal officers, state troopers, constables and deputy sheriffs. A warrant may not be served by a private citizen. 276, § 23. 218, § 37. *Comm. v. Foster*, 1 Mass. 488 (1805).

Statewide jurisdiction. An arrest warrant may be executed anywhere in the Commonwealth, regardless of the court that issued it. Officers may travel outside their territorial jurisdiction to apprehend a person named in a warrant. They may enter a suspect's home and apprehend him inside. 276, § 23. 218, § 37. *Payton v. New York*, 445 U.S. 573 (1980). This is discussed extensively in *Chapter 8.*

Need not possess warrant at time of arrest. Officers must have "actual knowledge" of a warrant, but need not physically possess it. However, they do have to show the warrant to an arrestee if he requests to see it. Officers should print out a copy from WMS during booking. 276, § 28. Mass. R. Crim. P. 6(c)(3).

Police may execute a warrant to take a person into custody who is suspected of other crimes. *Comm. v. Sullivan*, 354 Mass. 598 (1968): The police suspected the defendant of armed robbery, but lacked probable cause to arrest. An officer did arrest him on a warrant for unrelated charges. The SJC upheld the arrest, noting that the police had obtained the warrant before the robbery and had not unreasonably delayed its execution.

At the same time, police may not obtain a warrant for the sole purpose of conducting a search. *Taglavore v. U.S.*, 291 F.2d 262 (9th Cir. 1961): Officers obtained an arrest warrant charging the defendant with two minor traffic violations. They then delayed serving the warrant until they thought the defendant would be carrying illegal drugs. The court rejected this "deliberate scheme to evade the requirements of the Fourth Amendment by using a traffic arrest warrant to search for narcotics."

All warrants must be served without "unreasonable delay." 268, § 32. If the unsuccessful efforts to serve a warrant are documented, an arrest made years later will be upheld. *Comm. v. Jones*, 360 Mass. 498 (1971). Delay only results in a case being dismissed if it causes "substantial prejudice" to a defendant's ability to mount a legal defense, or if it is the result of deliberate police misconduct. *Comm. v. Anderson*, 9 Mass. App. Ct. 699 (1980).

State agency support. To aid in the apprehension of individuals with outstanding warrants, 22C, § 36A mandates that *any* Commonwealth agency provide state troopers and municipal officers with "identifying information including, but not limited to, name, date of birth, all pertinent addresses, telephone numbers and social security numbers." This statute only applies to locating people named in warrants.

ARREST

INTRODUCTION

ARREST DEFINED

An arrest occurs when a person is taken into custody and significantly deprived of his freedom. *Massachusetts General Hospital v. Revere*, 385 Mass. 772 (1982). The test is whether a reasonable person would have understood that he was under arrest. Typically, officers tell a person, "You are under arrest," but an arrest may be initiated nonverbally. *Comm. v. Sanderson*, 398 Mass. 761 (1986) (suspect was held on the side of a road for too long; his detention became an arrest even though officers did not intend this result).

The point of arrest is significant because probable cause must exist and rights must be honored. If police lack probable cause at the time of arrest, they lose any evidence discovered during the post-arrest search or booking process.[3] *Comm. v. Street*, 56 Mass. App. Ct. 301 (2002).

---

3 These related topics are fully explored in *Chapters 10* (post-arrest procedures), *17* (search incident to arrest), *18* (booking inventory), and *22* (post-arrest interrogation and *Miranda*).

AUTHORITY, DISCRETION, & TIMING

Officers must have the legal authority — the "right of arrest" — to arrest without a warrant for a particular crime. *Comm. v. Murphy*, 353 Mass. 433 (1968).

At the same time, officers may exercise discretion. Just because officers have the "right of arrest" does not mean that they must arrest. There are times when it may be best to obtain a warrant, apply for a complaint, or warn the offender. Officers should consider:

- **Severity of the crime.**

- **Prior criminal history and background of the offender.**

- **Vulnerability of the victim and loss suffered.**

- **Offender's willingness to engage in a positive response** (e.g., pay restitution for the theft; clean up and repair the damage; apologize to the victim).

- **Police department and community enforcement priorities.**

There are two situations where arrest is mandatory. Officers must arrest any offender who violates a domestic violence restraining order (209A, § 6) or harassment prevention order (258E, § 8).

Police may not arrest to "teach a lesson." *Scott v. City of San Bernadino*, 903 F.3d 943 (2018): A middle school principal in California asked a School Resource Officer (SRO) to counsel a group of girls who had been involved in ongoing incidents of bullying and fighting. Once the officer concluded that the girls were not listening, he told them he was going to arrest them for unlawful fighting to "teach them a lesson." He said he did not care who was at fault. The girls' parents successfully sued. First, there was only evidence of bickering, not unlawful fighting. Second, the arrests were a response to perceived disrespect, not the commission of a crime.

Mental health issues do <u>not</u> nullify probable cause to arrest. *Comm. v. Newton N.*, 478 Mass. 747 (2018) (while youth had obvious mental health problems, this did not affect the authority of police to arrest him for breaking and entering).

For a legitimate reason, an arrest may be delayed after probable cause is first formed.

- **Investigative judgment.** The police may wish to build a stronger case or catch the suspect committing a more serious crime. *Comm. v. Celestino*, 47 Mass. App. Ct. 916 (1999) (although he had probable cause to arrest the defendant for drug distribution on Wednesday, the investigator waited until Friday because his informant said the defendant would be carrying a greater quantity of narcotics). *Comm. v. Garcia*, 421 Mass. 686 (1996).

- **Discretion at the scene.** After deciding to release an offender, an officer may change his mind — provided that he has a "right of arrest." *Comm. v. Suggs*, 70 Mass. App. Ct. 1104 (2007): A random check indicated that Michael Suggs' vehicle was unregistered and uninsured. During the stop, Officer Kmiec learned that Suggs' license was suspended. Instead of arresting Suggs, which he had the authority to do, Kmiec issued him a citation and called for a tow truck.

Suggs asked if he could stay with his vehicle so he could learn where to recover it later. Kmiec agreed, provided that Suggs and his passenger remained in the car. Driving by the scene, Sergeant Vail recognized the passenger, Maurice Bennett, and radioed Officer Kmiec about Bennett's history of carrying handguns. In response, Kmiec decided against merely issuing a citation and arrested Suggs — locating an illegal pistol during the search.

In upholding the officer's action, the Appeals Court made two important rulings: (1) the issuance of a citation does not eliminate an officer's arrest authority; and (2) probable cause to arrest, once formed, continues to exist for the indefinite future.[4]

- **Release and recapture.** A classic case, *Comm. v. Hastings*, 9 Met 259 (1845), is still good law in the Commonwealth. In *Hastings*, a police officer, Grant Learned, encountered an extremely inebriated man named Davis near a theater. Davis was causing a ruckus, and Officer Learned arrested him for disorderly conduct. On the way to the station, Learned released Davis because he promised to go home and sober up. Shortly thereafter, Learned watched Davis walk into a tavern! Learned took him back into custody — a move the SJC approved on appeal.[5]

Hastings reminds officers that they have "a right of recapture" when a previously detained or arrested subject fails to abide by the conditions of his release (e.g., "If you walk home with your brother and don't cause any more trouble, I'll release you now").[6]

RELEASE OF ARRESTEE

A magistrate should typically decide whether to release an arrestee. In *Brady v. Dill*, 187 F.3d 104 (1st Cir. 1999), William Brady was held by the State Police on an outstanding default warrant in connection with an OUI in Middleboro. Brady repeatedly claimed that he had never been arrested in Middleboro, and the troopers became aware of facts supporting his claim (e.g., Brady had none of the tattoos noted in the OUI report).

In an effort to help him, the troopers persuaded a bail commissioner to come to the barracks. The commissioner offered to release Brady on personal recognizance, but he refused to sign the agreement. The next day troopers took him to court, where he was arraigned and released. The OUI charge was eventually dismissed.

Sued by Brady, the troopers were not liable for their refusal to release him after they had begun to suspect they had the wrong man. This was the magistrate's responsibility.

Only when officers are absolutely certain that they lack probable cause should they release an arrestee on their own. These facts should be documented in a report. *Thompson v. Olson*, 798 F.2d 522 (1st Cir. 1986).

---

4 The court went so far as to say: "Indeed, having probable cause to arrest, the police presumably could have pursued the defendant even had he left the scene."

5 It was at this point that a man named William Hastings got involved and assaulted the officer. His conviction on that charge served as the basis for his unsuccessful appeal.

6 In the words of the *Hastings* court: "We think the authority of the police officer was not gone, when he permitted his prisoner to go from him, on his promise to go directly home, and be guilty of no more disorderly conduct . . . When therefore, being still in sight of the officer, in violation of his engagement to leave the scene of disorder, he entered a bar room, where he was likely to aggravate his offence . . ., the officer was well justified in arresting him."

POLICE RIGHT OF ARREST FOR MASSACHUSETTS OFFENDERS

FELONIES

An officer may conduct a warrantless arrest in public for any felony.[7] *U.S. v. Watson*, 423 U.S. 411 (1976).

MISDEMEANORS

Four types of misdemeanors determine the authority of an officer to make a warrantless arrest. Absent proper authority, an officer may not arrest a misdemeanor offender and must, instead, apply for an arrest warrant or a criminal complaint. Here are the four types:

Statutory right of arrest for a past misdemeanor

Officers may make a warrantless arrest for a past misdemeanor based on probable cause if specifically authorized by statute. A complete list of misdemeanors that fall into this category appears on the inside front cover of *LED's Criminal Law*. Common examples are: A&B during domestic violence, 209, § 6; shoplifting, 266, § 30A; possession of ammunition, 269, § 10(h); operating under the influence, 90, § 24.

Statutory right of arrest in officer's presence

Officers may make a warrantless arrest for a misdemeanor committed in their presence if specifically authorized by statute. A complete list of these misdemeanors also appears on the inside cover of *LED's Criminal Law*. Common examples are: larceny or attempted larceny, 276, § 28; minor in possession of alcohol, 138, § 34C; trespassing, 266, § 120.

In presence defined. For the purpose of an arrest, "in presence" means officers are able to see the offense as it is occurring. *Comm. v. Conway*, 2 Mass. App. Ct. 547 (1974): Officers should not have arrested the defendant for his unauthorized use of a motor vehicle. While 90, § 21 enables officers to arrest for this "in presence" violation, the officers arrived fifteen minutes after the vehicle had been used. They did not observe the defendant in the car.

On the other hand, if officers see the suspect committing the offense, they have a right of arrest. The fact that they delay their arrest decision, or even change their mind at the scene, is permissible. *Comm. v. Suggs*, 70 Mass. App. Ct. 1104 (2007) (officer initially decided to issue a citation, then changed his mind and arrested the defendant).

Breach of peace in officer's presence

Even without statutory authority, officers may make a warrantless arrest for any misdemeanor involving a breach of peace in their presence. *Comm. v. Ceria*, 13 Mass. App. Ct. 230 (1982) (no statute provides a right of arrest for operating to endanger; however, since this is an obvious breach of peace, an officer may arrest a motorist who he observes driving dangerously).

---

7 The officer usually needs a warrant to conduct an arrest in the offender's home. The warrant requirement honors the heightened expectation of privacy that any citizen has in his dwelling. The rules surrounding the execution of a criminal arrest are discussed in *Chapter 8*.

Breach of peace. To be a breach of peace, "an act must at least threaten to have some disturbing effect on the public." *Comm. v. Ubilez,* 88 Mass. App. Ct. 814 (2016) (revoked registration not a breach of peace). *Comm. v. Dias,* 349 Mass. 583 (1965) (most gambling offenses do not involve a breach of peace). *Comm. v. Tobin,* 108 Mass. 426 (1871) (a fight or assault is a typical breach of peace).

The breach of peace may be anticipated: "An officer, who sees a person committing a misdemeanor [where] a breach of the peace is likely to follow . . . need not delay an arrest until the harm has been done." *Comm. v. Gorman,* 288 Mass. 294 (1934).[8]

Municipal laws

Officers may <u>not</u> arrest for most violations of municipal law. The term "municipal law" encompasses "ordinances," which are enacted by city governments, and "bylaws," which are enacted by towns. Most local laws are enforced by a civil fine. See 40, § 21D.

Officers may arrest adults for certain violations under 272, § 59. This statute enables officers to arrest a person within their jurisdiction seen violating an ordinance or bylaw that deals with three types of behavior:

- **Possessing or drinking an alcoholic beverage in public.** *Comm. v. Dessources,* 74 Mass. App. Ct. 232 (2009) (defendant subject to arrest when an officer observed him drinking a beer on a public bench, which violated a Cambridge ordinance).

- **Remaining in a public place in willful violation of a local law.** *Comm. v. Petrillo,* 399 Mass. 487 (1987) (officers appropriately arrested the defendant for violating a Saugus ordinance prohibiting trespassing on school property). *Diaz v. City of Fitchburg,* 176 F.3d 560 (1st Cir. 1999) (police justified in arresting six people for their willful violation of the Fitchburg ordinance prohibiting "obstructing a public passageway").

- **Accosting another person in public with obscene language.**

Juveniles may not be arrested for violating an ordinance or bylaw. 119, § 52.

Must prove content of ordinance or bylaw. The preferred method is to provide the judge with a copy in court. *Comm. v. Bones,* 93 Mass. App. Ct. 681 (2018). For simple local laws, the arresting officer's testimony is sufficient. *Comm. v. Rushin,* 56 Mass. App. Ct. 515 (2002) (coverage of public drinking ordinance basic). Compare *Comm. v. Pierre P.,* 53 Mass. App. Ct. 215 (2001) (officer's testimony about what the Springfield loitering ordinance prohibited was inadequate; its actual language was necessary to resolve the legal issue in the case).

---

8 Interestingly, *Gorman* found that the offense of operating under the influence constituted a breach of the peace because of the *potential* danger to the public. The court noted that "even [a] milder degree of alcoholic effect is likely to make [a vehicle] operator a public menace." (The arrest had to be justified in this fashion because in 1934, OUI was not yet arrestable.) Thus, an important concept emerged from *Gorman*: Officers may arrest based on an "anticipated" breach of peace. The *Gorman* court refused to define a breach of peace, saying that it depended on the circumstances.

RIGHT OF ARREST FOR OUT-OF-STATE OFFENDERS

Sometimes Massachusetts officers encounter a fugitive from another state. The law allows officers to perform a warrantless arrest or obtain a "fugitive warrant." A separate legal process — known as "rendition" — returns a fugitive to his home jurisdiction.

FUGITIVE FROM JUSTICE

Warrantless arrest

276, § 20B authorizes a Massachusetts officer to arrest a fugitive based on "reasonable information that the accused stands charged in another state with a crime . . . punishable by imprisonment for a term exceeding one year."

- **Charged in another state.** The statute does not define the term "charged." Cases from Massachusetts and other states require: (1) an arrest warrant from the original jurisdiction; (2) an indictment or criminal complaint; or (3) written information from a law enforcement source that the person is wanted for a crime. *In re Whitehouse*, 18 Mass. App. Ct. 455 (1984).

- **Punishable by more than 1 year.** This threshold ensures that minor offenders will not be held. For example, if Massachusetts officers learn that an out-of-state offender has been charged with something minor like disorderly conduct, they will not have the right to arrest the fugitive. Instead, the officers should direct the offender to return to his home state and clear up the matter. If needing a stronger response, the officers may obtain a fugitive warrant (since that covers *any* crime).

- **Post-arrest.** Once in custody, the fugitive should be brought to the next session of the Massachusetts district court in the place where the arrest occurred.

Fugitive warrant

276, § 20A allows any person to apply for a warrant concerning a person from another state who is in the Commonwealth and has committed any crime, violated probation or parole, or escaped from custody. The judge may issue a warrant authorizing any Massachusetts officer to arrest the individual.

Out-of-state bail bondsman. Comm. v. Wilkinson, 415 Mass. 402 (1993): Out-of-state bail bondsmen must comply with the Uniform Criminal Extradition Act (276, §§ 11-20R). They have two options. The bondsman may appear before a Massachusetts court and have an arrest warrant issued for the person, or may ask police to arrest the fugitive. Once taken into custody by a Massachusetts officer, the fugitive must be brought to a local court, informed of his right to counsel, and given the opportunity to challenge the legality of his arrest. The SJC believes this is "a far more civilized process."

Interstate rendition

The authority for interstate rendition is found in Article IV of the United States Constitution. The Uniform Extradition Act was adopted by 48 states to carry out Article IV.

- **The demanding state seeks rendition by preparing an application for the requisition of the individual.** The governor of the demanding state sends it to the governor of the asylum state, which has custody of the offender.

- **The governor of the asylum state then issues a Governor's Warrant.** This authorizes personnel from the demanding state to retrieve the prisoner. Before transport, the accused may challenge his transfer in what is called a *habeas corpus* proceeding. 276, §§ 16, 19, 20K and *In re Ierardi*, 366 Mass. 640 (1975).

PROBATION OFFICER'S RIGHT OF ARREST

Police officers should forge relationships with probation officers. Probation officers perform a vital function in the criminal justice system by monitoring offenders and providing them with services. They are key allies of law enforcement because they have the ability to enforce a broad array of terms and conditions that their probationers are bound to follow — e.g., curfews, mandatory employment, drug and substance abuse counseling, anger management counseling, travel restrictions, etc. Sometimes a police officer may not be able to mount a criminal case against an offender who is acting out in the community. Probation often has the ability to intervene in that offender's life. Constant collaboration between police and probation is essential.

Massachusetts probation officers have significant arrest authority. 279, § 3 provides a probation officer with the authority to:

- **Arrest an individual without a warrant for violating a term or condition of his probation.** Or the officer may seek an arrest warrant. The court will then hold a "surrender hearing" and may impose new conditions (including incarceration).

- **Arrest a defendant with a pending case, who has violated a condition of his pre-trial release.** Or the officer may issue a warrant to hold the probationer for up to 72 hours.[9]

CITIZEN'S RIGHT OF ARREST

A Massachusetts citizen may arrest a person who has "in fact" committed a felony. The "in fact" requirement is stricter than probable cause "to prevent 'the dangers of uncontrolled vigilantism' . . . [and] deter private citizens from [taking] irresponsible action." *Comm. v. Colitz*, 13 Mass. App. Ct. 215 (1982).

Bail surety and his agents have the lawful authority to apprehend and deliver a principal to court — provided they use reasonable force. The person who posts the required bail is called the "surety" while the "principal" is the person who has been arrested and released pending his court appearance. The surety must warn the principal before resorting to force. Also, a surety's authority to use force is not the same as a police officer's. The surety has only a financial interest while officers protect public safety. *Comm. v. Cabral*, 433 Mass. 171 (2005).

---

9 Interestingly, this warrant is issued without any judicial review or supervision.

COMPLAINT

INTRODUCTION

Complaint application avoids arrest. Instead of obtaining a warrant or conducting a warrantless arrest, an officer may apply for a criminal complaint. Massachusetts law expresses a preference for this process because it does not infringe on an accused citizen's liberty. Officers should consider a complaint when the offender is likely to appear in court and does not pose a risk to public safety. 276, § 24.

In a complaint application, an officer may select one of four paths to court depending on whether the offender is accused of a felony or misdemeanor. The offender will be notified by a "summons," which is sent by mail or delivered to his residence. A summons is a written notice that directs an individual to appear in court as a defendant.[10]

FOUR POLICE PATHS

1st path: If the offender is accused of a misdemeanor and not under arrest, the officer must typically afford him a hearing. 218, § 35A requires that the court clerk conduct a "show cause" hearing if requested by the accused. This brief, informal hearing tests whether probable cause exists for the crime(s) alleged. "The implicit purpose of the 35A hearing is to enable the court clerk to screen a variety of minor criminal . . . matters out of the justice system through a combination of counseling, discussion, or threat of prosecution." *Gordon v. Fay,* 382 Mass. 64 (1980).

At the conclusion of the hearing, the clerk may find probable cause and send the defendant to court for arraignment.[11] Or the clerk may decide that probable cause is lacking, in which case the defendant is discharged and his case ends.

2nd path: The misdemeanor offender may be denied a hearing if he fails to request one, or if he presents a safety or flight risk. Section 35A allows a complaint to issue without a show cause hearing when the allegations involve "an imminent threat" of violence, the commission of another crime, or flight from the Commonwealth. To determine whether a serious threat exists, the clerk takes into account the facts of the case, the accused's criminal record, and any history of domestic violence. *Comm. v. Tripolone,* 44 Mass. App. Ct. 23 (1997).

The accused also forfeits his right to a hearing if he fails to request it, and probable cause is documented in the police report. *Comm. v. Irick,* 58 Mass. App. Ct. 129 (2003). In misdemeanor cases where no hearing occurs, the defendant receives a summons to appear in court for his arraignment.

3rd path: The officer decides whether to grant a hearing for a felony. Section 35A authorizes a show cause hearing for a felony *only if* it is requested by the police officer who applied for the complaint. An officer might choose this approach in a marginal felony case where he believes the clerk's input at a hearing might help resolve the matter and prevent future problems.

---

10 When the legal document orders a witness or officer to appear in court to testify, it is called a "subpoena." A witness who has been subpoenaed and fails to attend may be arrested (233, § 6); held in contempt (233, § 5); and/or held on bail until he testifies (276, §§ 47, 49).
11 An arraignment is the initial formal appearance in court for a defendant who is going to be prosecuted.

***4th* path: The officer requests that the clerk issue a felony complaint.** The clerk has no discretion to grant a hearing, and the defendant receives a summons to appear for his arraignment.

ONE CITIZEN PATH

A citizen may apply for a criminal complaint. When a citizen feels that he has been the victim of a crime, he can apply for a criminal complaint in the district court. Sometimes an officer may, when faced with a marginal case, recommend that a citizen pursue his own complaint.[12]

The clerk may evaluate the basis of the citizen's claim and schedule a show cause hearing for a misdemeanor or felony complaint. In the case of a felony, the clerk may decide to issue the complaint without a hearing. 218, § 35A.

Unlike an application submitted by a police officer, a citizen's application may be rejected by the clerk without a hearing. *Taylor v. Newton District Court*, 416 Mass. 1006 (1993).

Even if a hearing is granted and probable cause exists, the clerk may decline to refer the case for prosecution. *Victory Distributors, Inc. v. Ayer District Court*, 435 Mass. 136 (2001) (a judge or clerk has final authority; "there are complex factors beyond the determination of probable cause that affect the decision whether to grant or deny a criminal complaint").

No delay in ruling permitted at the hearing over the objection of the police or citizen complainant. In *Comm. v. Clerk of the Boston Juvenile Court*, 432 Mass 693 (2000), a detective sought four misdemeanor civil rights complaints on behalf of four Jewish men who were harassed by the defendant and his friends while walking to temple. The magistrate, at the conclusion of the show cause hearing, declined to grant or deny the complaint. Instead, he decided to hold the applications "open" and dismiss them in the future if the defendant complied with certain conditions. While a magistrate has the power to grant or deny a criminal complaint application, he lacks the authority to keep an application open. Once the hearing begins, he may only order an informal resolution if the police or citizen complainant agrees. See *District Court Complaint Standard* 3:08. *Comm. v. Bior*, 88 Mass. App. Ct. 150 (2015).

A criminal complaint against a police officer does not have to be heard outside the officer's jurisdiction. *Matter of Application for Criminal Complaint*, 477 Mass 1010 (2017) (procedural safeguards are adequate to protect against bias).

Requests for specific show cause hearing records. *Boston Globe v. Chief Justice of Trial Court*, 483 Mass. 80 (2019): Show cause hearing records are not usually public. However, any member of the public may request records of a hearing where probable cause was found, but the clerk did not issue a criminal complaint.

A request must state why the interests of justice will be served by making these normally private documents available to the public. In considering a request, the clerk must balance the interests of transparency, accountability, and public confidence against the risk that disclosure will unfairly affect the accused.

---

12 This referral strategy is not permitted in cases of domestic violence. The officer is responsible for making an arrest or seeking a complaint. See *LED's Criminal Law, Chapter 13*.

In any case, all show cause hearings must now electronically record the following information: (1) the judicial officer presiding; (2) court where hearing occurs; (3) date when complaint was filed and hearing took place; (4) whether the complainant is a law enforcement officer or private citizen; (5) gender and race of the accused and of any private citizen complainant; (6) whether the accused or a private complainant is represented by an attorney; (7) the names of any attorneys; (8) the offense(s) alleged; and (9) the disposition of the show cause hearing.

Once the clerk–magistrate finds probable cause and issues a complaint, it may not be dismissed until after the defendant's arraignment. *Comm. v. Moore*, 93 Mass. App. Ct. 73 (2018): Though a judge may act on a motion to dismiss for lack of probable cause *after* the defendant has been arraigned, a dismissal *before* arraignment for that reason (or others) is not permitted without the prosecution's consent. Only a juvenile court judge may consider a motion to dismiss before arraignment. *Comm. v. Humberto H.*, 466 Mass. 562 (2012).

APPLICATION FOR CRIMINAL COMPLAINT	APPLICATION NO. (COURT USE ONLY)	PAGE ____ of ____	Trial Court of Massachusetts District Court Department

I, the undersigned complainant, request that a criminal complaint issue against the accused charging the offense(s) listed below. If the accused **HAS NOT BEEN ARRESTED** and the charges involve:

☐ ONLY MISDEMEANOR(S), I request a hearing ☐ **WITHOUT NOTICE** because of an imminent threat of ☐ BODILY INJURY ☐ COMMISSION OF A CRIME ☐ FLIGHT ☐ **WITH NOTICE** to accused.
☐ ONE OR MORE FELONIES, I request a hearing ☐ **WITHOUT NOTICE** ☐ **WITH NOTICE** to accused.

☐ WARRANT is requested because prosecutor represents that accused may not appear unless arrested.

ARREST STATUS OF ACCUSED
☐ HAS   ☐ HAS NOT been arrested

INFORMATION ABOUT ACCUSED

NAME (FIRST MI LAST) AND ADDRESS	BIRTH DATE	SOCIAL SECURITY NUMBER
	PCF NO.	MARITAL STATUS
	DRIVERS LICENSE NO.	STATE
	GENDER / HEIGHT / WEIGHT	EYES

HAIR	RACE	COMPLEXION	SCARS/MARKS/TATTOOS	INTERPRETER NEEDED (language)	BIRTH STATE OR COUNTRY	DAY PHONE

EMPLOYER/SCHOOL	MOTHER'S MAIDEN NAME (FIRST MI LAST)	FATHER'S NAME (FIRST MI LAST)

CASE INFORMATION

COMPLAINANT NAME (FIRST MI LAST)	COMPLAINANT TYPE ☐ POLICE ☐ CITIZEN ☐ OTHER	PD
ADDRESS	PLACE OF OFFENSE	
	INCIDENT REPORT NO.	OBTN
	CITATION NO(S).	

1	OFFENSE CODE	DESCRIPTION	OFFENSE DATE
	VARIABLES (e.g. victim name, controlled substance, type and value of property, other variable information; see Complaint Language Manual)		

2	OFFENSE CODE	DESCRIPTION	OFFENSE DATE
	VARIABLES		

3	OFFENSE CODE	DESCRIPTION	OFFENSE DATE
	VARIABLES		

REMARKS	COMPLAINANT'S SIGNATURE X	DATE FILED

COURT USE ONLY →	A HEARING UPON THIS COMPLAINT APPLICATION WILL BE HELD AT THE ABOVE COURT ADDRESS ON }	DATE OF HEARING	TIME OF HEARING AT	← COURT USE ONLY

DATE	PROCESSING OF NON-ARREST APPLICATION (COURT USE ONLY)	CLERK/JUDGE
	NOTICE SENT OF CLERK'S HEARING SCHEDULED ON:	
	NOTICE SENT OF JUDGE'S HEARING SCHEDULED ON:	
	HEARING CONTINUED TO:	
	APPLICATION DECIDED WITHOUT NOTICE TO ACCUSED BECAUSE: ☐ IMMINENT THREAT OF ☐ BODILY INJURY ☐ CRIME ☐ FLIGHT BY ACCUSED ☐ FELONY CHARGED AND POLICE DO NOT REQUEST NOTICE ☐ FELONY CHARGED BY CIVILIAN; NO NOTICE AT CLERK'S DISCRETION	

DATE	COMPLAINT TO ISSUE	COMPLAINT DENIED	CLERK/JUDGE
	☐ PROBABLE CAUSE FOUND FOR ABOVE OFFENSE(S) NO(S). ☐ 1. ☐ 2. ☐ 3. BASED ON ☐ FACTS SET FORTH IN ATTACHED STATEMENT(S) ☐ TESTIMONY RECORDED: TAPE NO._____ START NO._____ END NO._____ ☐ WARRANT ☐ SUMMONS TO ISSUE SCHEDULED ARRAIGNMENT DATE:	☐ NO PROBABLE CAUSE FOUND ☐ REQUEST OF COMPLAINANT ☐ FAILURE TO PROSECUTE ☐ AGREEMENT OF BOTH PARTIES ☐ OTHER: COMMENT	

DCCR-2 (07/11)   COURT COPY   www.mass.gov/courts/districtcourt

JURISDICTION FROM APPOINTING AUTHORITY

Massachusetts police officers must be certified by the Peace Officer Standards and Training (POST) Commission. 6E, §§ 1, 4. Officers generally serve in one of the following agencies:

- **Municipal police.** Municipal police officers have full law enforcement authority within the borders of the city or town that appointed them. 41, § 98.

- **State police.** State police officers or "troopers" have full law enforcement authority within the borders of the Commonwealth. 22C, § 10.

- **Environmental police.** Environmental officers have the same enforcement authority as State troopers, but their specialized duties are more focused on the laws and regulations that protect natural resources and wildlife. 21A, § 10A.

- **Transit police.** Transit officers are authorized to enforce the law on any Massachusetts Bay Transportation Authority (MBTA) property. They also have full law enforcement authority within the 175 cities and towns served by or containing MBTA facilities. Chapter 664 of the Acts of 1968. *Comm. v. Mottola*, 10 Mass. App. Ct. 775 (1980).

- **College and university police.** These "campus" officers are appointed by public and private colleges and universities. For the most part,[1] campus officers are appointed as Special State Police Officers (SSPOs) under 22C, § 63, which empowers them to make arrests for *any* crime committed on property owned, used or occupied by their institution.

  The term "used" includes public ways that connect campus facilities. This enables all SSPOs to enforce vehicle crimes like operating to endanger or OUI. *Comm. v. Smeaton*, 465 Mass. 752 (2013). Civil enforcement is more complicated. Basically, public college and university officers may issue citations for vehicle infractions, while those employed by private educational institutions may not.[2]

  Finally, the authority of SSPOs extends to the area surrounding their campus when they are dealing with an incident involving students, staff or other people connected with their institution. *Young v. Boston University*, 64 Mass. App. Ct. 586 (2005) (Boston University police officer had the authority to arrest an individual on a street near the campus because he had recently violated a restraining order obtained by a student).

---

1 The University of Massachusetts derives its powers under 75, § 32A, and other state colleges and universities are granted similar authority under 15A, § 22 and 73, § 18.
2 See 90C, §§ 1, 2A. *Comm. v. Mullen*, 40 Mass. App. Ct. 404 (1996).

- **Deputy sheriffs.** Elected county sheriffs acknowledge that their primary function is the care and custody of pre-trial detainees and post-conviction inmates, along with the service of civil process. However, sheriffs and their deputies may exercise law enforcement authority within their counties if certified by POST. 6E, § 1.

ARREST WARRANTS: STATEWIDE ENFORCEMENT

An important benefit of an arrest warrant is that it may be served anywhere in the Commonwealth. Arrest is authorized if probable cause exists that a warrant is in effect, *and* that the suspect being detained is the "wanted" person. 276, § 23A (good faith reliance on any warrant in WMS prevents liability for arresting officers). See *Comm. v. Hernandez*, 456 Mass. 528 (2010) (one exception: campus police officers may not execute an arrest warrant off-campus — unless it is connected to a crime on campus or involves a member of the campus community).

WARRANTLESS ARRESTS

OFFICERS OUTSIDE OF THEIR JURISDICTION

INTRODUCTION

Within their jurisdiction, officers may conduct warrantless arrests for felonies and misdemeanors for which they have the right of arrest. *Comm. v. Grise*, 398 Mass. 247 (1986).

Officers may rely on visible boundary markers to decide the extent of their jurisdiction. *Comm. v. Coburn*, 62 Mass. App. Ct. 314 (2004).

Officers may always go outside their jurisdiction to investigate, as long as they do not detain, search, or arrest a suspect.

- *Comm. v. Albert*, 51 Mass. App. Ct. 377 (2001) involved Boston drug officers conducting surveillance of a blue truck in the city. The driver and his female passenger led police into Revere, where a standard on-street drug transaction unfolded. Officers followed the blue truck back to Boston, where they stopped it. When the female passenger got out, officers noticed a suspicious bulge in "the top portion of her chest." Eighty bags of crack were nestled in her bra. It was entirely proper for these officers to wait and stop the defendant in Boston, where they had jurisdiction.

- Compare *Comm. v. Luna*, 92 Mass. App. Ct. 523 (2017): Springfield Police were told by a confidential informant that an individual named "Gio" would be making a large delivery of heroin at a Springfield intersection at noon. When he did, Gio was properly arrested in Springfield. His three cell phones began ringing. Concerned that the delay in his arrival would compromise their investigation, Springfield officers went to a Chicopee address and searched Gio's Honda in the driveway. They seized several bricks of heroin and a firearm. The warrantless search of the vehicle in Chicopee was unlawful. The search happened outside of Springfield. While Chicopee police were called for assistance, they were not present during the search.

OUTSIDE JURISDICTION: FELONIES

In Massachusetts: Citizen's arrest

"Citizen's arrest" authority for officers. As previously discussed in *Chapter 7*, any citizen has the legal authority — anywhere in the Commonwealth — to arrest a felon who might otherwise escape. *Comm. v. Harris*, 11 Mass. App. Ct. 165 (1981).

The same rule applies to police officers. *Comm. v. Timothy T.*, 2017 WL 445494 (Appeals Court): Methuen Police Officer Hardy watched a heroin sale occur just over the town line in Lawrence. Because distributing Class A heroin is a felony, Hardy had jurisdiction to make a citizen's arrest in Lawrence, even though he was a Methuen officer.

Outside Massachusetts: Fresh pursuit of felon

A Massachusetts police officer in "fresh pursuit" of someone who has committed a felony may continue into a border state to make an arrest. This authority appears in 276, §§ 10A–10D. New York, Rhode Island, Connecticut, Vermont, and New Hampshire have enacted similar statutes, which give their officers the right to pursue felons into Massachusetts. After an out-of-state arrest, the offender must be brought before a court within the county where the arrest took place. *Comm. v. Gullick*, 386 Mass. 278 (1982).

Citizen's stop

An attempt to stop that ends outside the officer's jurisdiction, when made with lights and siren alone, is permitted as a citizen's investigatory stop. *Comm. v. Lariviere*, 94 Mass. App. Ct. 440 (2020): Officer Henderson of the Seabrook, N.H., Police Department saw Donald Lariviere's vehicle traveling south on Route 1A. It crossed into the oncoming traffic lane, after which it weaved within its travel lane. Officer Henderson activated the cruiser's blue lights and, when Lariviere crossed into Massachusetts, he turned on the siren. Lariviere pulled over.

Officer Henderson remained in his cruiser and immediately contacted Salisbury Police for assistance. Officer Kelley from that department arrested Lariviere for OUI after he failed field sobriety tests.

Officer Henderson's actions outside of his jurisdiction did not constitute a misdemeanor arrest, which he lacked the authority to make as an officer or citizen. Though he used his lights and siren, Officer Henderson made no contact with Lariviere, instead calling Salisbury Police and waiting in his cruiser. The court classified Officer Henderson's behavior as a "reasonable investigatory stop by a citizen."

OUTSIDE JURISDICTION: MISDEMEANORS

In order to stop a misdemeanor suspect outside their jurisdiction, officers must have legal authority. There are four major reasons: mutual aid, fresh pursuit, requisition, or transferred authority.[3]

---

3 It is unclear whether POST will continue to authorize the longstanding practice of police officers being "sworn special officers" in multiple communities. See 41, § 99 and *Comm. v. Callahan*, 428 Mass. 335 (1998). For this reason, the authors recommend that agencies avoid this designation until POST specifically approves. See 6E, § 1.

Mutual aid agreement — 40, § 8G

Agreements between separate municipalities are the <u>best way</u> to avoid challenges to police jurisdiction. 40, § 8G empowers a city or town to enter into an agreement with one or more cities or towns "to provide mutual aid programs for [their] police departments to increase the capability of such departments."[4]

- **Responding officers have arrest powers.** When providing mutual aid, police officers have their full arrest powers.

- **Municipalities in neighboring states eligible.** Massachusetts cities and towns may have mutual aid agreements with cities and towns from border states.

- **Essential for small municipalities.** The SJC recognizes that mutual aid agreements are especially important for small police departments, given "the frequently fleeting and emergency nature of many situations that confront police officers, even in bucolic communities." *Comm. v. McCrohan*, 34 Mass. App. Ct. 277 (1993).

Effective use of mutual aid. Comm. v. Bartlett, 465 Mass. 112 (2013): Merrimac police officer Charles Sciacca was on patrol when he crossed the town line into Amesbury to go to a convenience store. On his way back, he saw a Chrysler sedan cross the double yellow line, return to the travel lane, then cross the "fog line" on the side of the road.

Sciacca followed the Chrysler for a half mile. He observed the Chrysler weave several times more before it abruptly stopped and pulled into a restaurant parking lot. Sciacca blocked the Chrysler with his cruiser. He radioed Amesbury police that he had initiated a stop. Amesbury police arrived within one minute. Their officer administered field sobriety tests and arrested the defendant for his 5th OUI.

Amesbury and Merrimac are "mutual aid" partners. Their agreement provides that on-duty officers from each municipality may exercise "full police powers . . . when circumstances [dictate] an immediate response . . . [for] public safety."

Here, the vehicle veered into the oncoming traffic lane several times, giving Sciacca a reasonable suspicion that the motorist presented an immediate danger. The mutual aid agreement granted the authority for the stop, and Officer Sciacca radioed Amesbury immediately after, which satisfied the other requirement that he "notify the host community as soon as practically possible."[5]

Present agreement in court and method of activation. When justifying police action under a mutual aid agreement, be sure to bring the document to court and testify how it was activated. *Comm. v. Sullivan*, 2017 WL 3611680 (Appeals Court).

---

4 § 8G explicitly states that a mutual aid agreement may provide for "methods of activation" and address issues such as "pay and benefits for officers, insurance, indemnification, injury compensation, and other operational matters related to police services."
5 Notice how Officer Sciacca's stop could *not* be justified by "transferred authority" because he stopped the defendant *before* he received permission from the Amesbury police. See discussion next page.

Fresh pursuit — 41, § 98A

Officers may engage in "fresh and continuous pursuit" to stop an offender for any arrestable offense committed in their presence within their jurisdiction. 41, § 98A. Pursuit may consist of following and does not have to involve lights or siren. It may also begin in another jurisdiction, as long as the suspect travels through the officer's home jurisdiction before the stop. In *Comm. v. Magazu,* 48 Mass. App. Ct. 466 (2000), a Whitman officer drove over the town line into neighboring East Bridgewater. He observed the defendant crossing the center line and accelerating and decelerating his speed. The officer believed that the defendant was OUI as he followed him back into Whitman, and he had fresh pursuit authority when the defendant suddenly pulled his vehicle into a driveway that was situated just over the town line in neighboring Hanson!

Officers need not have probable cause when they leave their jurisdiction, but they must have reasonable suspicion the offender is committing an arrestable offense.

- *Comm. v. LeBlanc,* 407 Mass. 70 (1990): A Natick officer had no reason to suspect that the defendant was committing an arrestable offense when he drove through a red light and traveled into Framingham. The officer improperly followed the defendant into this neighboring town when he pulled him over and discovered he was OUI. The stop and arrest were invalid.

- Compare *Comm. v. Riedel,* 76 Mass. App. Ct. 911 (2010): In Orleans, Officer Davis observed a vehicle traveling at a high rate of speed at night. The vehicle crossed the double-yellow line twice, and then crossed the fog line on the side of the road. Davis activated his emergency lights. When the vehicle pulled over, it had entered the neighboring town of Brewster. Officer Davis arrested Mark Riedel for OUI.

  Although Riedel had only committed civil infractions in Orleans, the nature of these infractions — significant erratic driving — gave Officer Davis reasonable suspicion that Riedel was committing the arrestable offense of OUI.

  Interestingly, Officer Davis testified that he did not believe, at the time of the stop, that the defendant had committed an arrestable offense. The court reminded officers that their "subjective beliefs" are irrelevant: "[T]he circumstances are to be viewed objectively. The issue is whether the facts . . . warranted the officer's belief and pursuit, not whether the officer's 'feeling' warranted his belief and pursuit." Davis did the right thing.

Outstanding warrant constitutes an arrestable offense for fresh pursuit. *Comm. v. Owens,* 414 Mass. 595 (1993) (owner of a Cadillac was wanted under a warrant, which justified the detective's decision to follow the vehicle into a neighboring city and stop it there).

Fresh pursuit may be a cooperative effort. *Comm. v. Zirpolo,* 37 Mass. App. Ct. 307 (1994): A Framingham police officer ordered an intoxicated defendant to stop his vehicle in the parking lot of a tavern after he struck a parked vehicle. The defendant did not stop, turned off his headlights, and pulled onto Route 9 at a high rate of speed. Another Framingham officer pursued the vehicle into a neighboring town and arrested him. Both Framingham officers properly joined forces to apprehend the defendant.

Requisition of officers — 41, § 99

No written agreement necessary (unlike mutual aid). This authority is granted to the OIC in each community. Enacted in 1880, 41, § 99 authorizes the officer in charge (OIC) of a police department in one town to request that the OIC in another town send officers. Once the request is approved, the responding officers have full police authority when they arrive in the requesting community.

Transferred authority — 268, § 24

Transferred authority applies to a breach of the peace. *Comm. v. Morrissey*, 422 Mass. 1 (1996): After assisting Officer Stillings in West Boylston, Officer McArthur was returning to his own town of Sterling. McArthur observed the defendant engage in extremely hazardous driving (running a stop sign, veering between lanes, just missing a telephone pole). He radioed Officer Stillings, who requested that McArthur stop the vehicle even though he was still in West Boylston. Stillings arrived and arrested the defendant for OUI.

In *Morrissey*, the SJC pointed out that Officer McArthur had a legal obligation under 268, § 24 — just like any other citizen — to assist the local officer "in the preservation of the peace or in the apprehension . . . of a person for a breach of the peace." In other words, Officer Stillings could "transfer his authority" to a citizen who, in this case, happened to be Officer McArthur!

Transferred authority is allowed for civil infractions that threaten public safety. *Comm. v. Twombly*, 435 Mass. 440 (2001) involved the defendant traveling in Salisbury at 55 mph on an off-ramp with a posted limit of 25 mph. He continued speeding on the adjacent roadway. While he did stop at a red light, the defendant abruptly continued through the green light and illegally passed a vehicle, gunning his engine. The observing Amesbury police officer entered Salisbury. Over the radio, a Salisbury officer granted the Amesbury officer's request to stop the defendant. The Salisbury officer arrived and arrested the defendant for OUI.

Here, the actions of the motorist did not amount to a breach of the peace, but the stop was still valid. A local officer may ask for assistance under 268, § 24 to preserve the peace. The court insisted that stopping this motorist preserved the peace by protecting the public from a dangerous driver.

Out-of-state officers. In *Comm. v. Savage*, 430 Mass. 341 (1999), a Vermont state trooper received a report from a motorist with a cell phone about an erratically driven vehicle heading toward Massachusetts. The Vermont trooper called the Massachusetts State Police and learned that no cruiser was available. He entered the Commonwealth, saw the vehicle, pulled it over, and observed the driver's inebriated condition. Ten minutes later, a Massachusetts trooper arrived to make the OUI arrest.

The stop could not be justified as interstate fresh pursuit because no felony was alleged.[6] Transferred authority did not apply either, because the Massachusetts trooper never explicitly requested that the Vermont trooper stop the vehicle. Interestingly, the SJC said it might approve a clear request for interstate transferred authority in the future.

---

6 For the same reason, the Vermont trooper could not claim "citizen's arrest" power.

Other grounds

An officer outside his jurisdiction, who is involved in a vehicle accident, may detain the driver pending the arrival of local police. *Comm. v. Limone*, 460 Mass. 834 (2011): Somerville Officer Robert Kelleher was driving home from work, still in uniform, in his private vehicle. While stopped at a red light in Woburn, his vehicle was rear-ended. Kelleher got out of his car and approached Joseph Limone's car. Limone apologized repeatedly.

Kelleher took the keys from the ignition so that Limone would not leave, but did not ask for his license and registration or attempt to investigate. Instead, Kelleher told Limone to get back in his car, then called the Woburn police. The two waited in separate cars. A Woburn officer arrived and arrested Limone after he failed sobriety tests. This was Limone's 7th OUI!

Kelleher did not demand a license and registration, collect evidence, touch Limone, or order him to perform sobriety tests. He simply removed the keys and contacted the Woburn police. The fact that an officer happens to be in uniform does not convert an interaction into an arrest — *as long as* the officer: (1) takes only reasonable safety measures; and (2) does not take advantage of his uniform by attempting to collect evidence that a private citizen would not be able to gather.

As a last resort, a lack of jurisdiction may be overcome by the "inevitable discovery" rule. *Comm. v. Lahey*, 80 Mass. App. Ct. 606 (2011) (while out-of-town officer had no legal basis to pull the defendant over, the court found that the local police would have inevitably made a legal stop because they had been notified and arrived quickly).[7]

OUTSIDE OFFENDERS IN OFFICERS' JURISDICTION

Offenders from other jurisdictions. How do officers from one municipality handle offenders from another municipality when they come to town? Consider the following steps:

INITIATE INVESTIGATION

Once they have a reasonable suspicion, officers may detain a suspect in their community — even one whose original crime occurred in another municipality. Officers may ask the suspect questions to determine his identity and develop probable cause for the original crime. They may check for warrants. 41, § 98.[8] The preferred identification method is to have officers from the original jurisdiction transport the witness to the new location for a showup. As an alternative, officers may bring the suspect back to the original jurisdiction for a showup.

ASSESS ARREST AUTHORITY

When they have detained an offender from another community, officers should determine whether they may arrest him. Their arrest authority may be based on: (1) the existence of a warrant; (2) commission of a felony; or (3) commission of a misdemeanor for which there is a right of arrest.

---

7 See discussion of inevitable discovery in *Chapter 1*.
8 This authority is so well established that no Massachusetts case even raises the issue.

Complaint application. Otherwise, police from the original jurisdiction[9] (where the crime took place) should apply for a complaint based on information about the offender's identity furnished by officers who conducted the stop outside the original jurisdiction.

MISDEMEANOR RULES

In general, officers in their own jurisdiction may not make a warrantless arrest for a misdemeanor that occurred outside their jurisdiction. This is true *even though* officers from the original jurisdiction communicate their probable cause and request that they do so.[10]

Two exceptions. The *only* exceptions to this general rule are: (1) a statute permits arrest outside the jurisdiction where the misdemeanor originally occurred; or (2) the misdemeanor involves a breach of the peace and is continuing in the officer's presence. *Comm. v. Grise*, 398 Mass. 247 (1986).

Statutory right of arrest

Warrantless arrest may be authorized under the terms of a mutual aid agreement between municipalities. 40, § 8G. *Comm. v. Twombly*, 50 Mass. App. Ct. (2001).

Warrantless arrest is authorized by 276, § 28 for certain domestic violence crimes.

- **Violation of a protective order anywhere in Massachusetts.** The order must be authorized under Chapter 209A (by far the most common), or Chapters 208, 209, and 209C (these orders are similar to 209A but issued by the probate court in conjunction with divorce, child support and paternity proceedings). *Note:* 258E, the Harassment Prevention Order, is *not* covered by this statute.

- **Domestic assault or A&B anywhere in Massachusetts.** Even without a protective order in effect, officers may arrest a suspect in their jurisdiction who has committed an assault or A&B against a "family or household member" in any Massachusetts community.

Continuing breach in presence

Warrantless arrest authorized for a misdemeanor still continuing in the new jurisdiction. An officer "may arrest without a warrant for a misdemeanor which (1) involves a breach of the peace, (2) is committed in the presence or view of the officer . . . , and (3) is still continuing at the time of the arrest or only interrupted, so that the offense and the arrest form parts of one transaction." *Comm. v. Conway*, 2 Mass. App. Ct. 547 (1974).

Without statutory authority, any clear break in time or place will render an arrest improper for a misdemeanor that occurred in another jurisdiction.[11]

---

9 An officer from outside the jurisdiction could also apply for a complaint. A complaint application must be supported by probable cause; it does not have to be signed by an officer within the jurisdiction of the court, so long as the underlying offense itself occurred within the territorial jurisdiction of the court.

10 Officers in the neighboring town may *not* receive transferred authority from officers in the original town where the crime occurred. The original officers may only transfer their authority within their *own* appointing jurisdiction. *Comm. v. Morrissey*, 422 Mass. 1 (1996).

11 "Fresh pursuit" does not apply to the delayed discovery of a misdemeanor offender outside the original jurisdiction. *Comm v. Conway*, 2 Mass. App. Ct. 547 (1974).

Officers who rely on this legal authority should charge the offender in the new jurisdiction — since the offender was still committing the crime at the time he was stopped — and use the officers from the original jurisdiction as witnesses in the underlying case. Otherwise, release the offender and apply for a complaint.

Complaint

If warrantless arrest is not permitted, the best course of action is for officers from the original jurisdiction to apply for a criminal complaint.

BOOKING PROCESS

"Courtesy booking" recognized but not required. A courtesy booking happens when the offender is booked by the jurisdiction making the arrest and then transferred to the original department. Massachusetts courts recognize this practice but do not require or even recommend it. *Comm. v. Williams,* 456 Mass. 857 (2010).

After an arrest, the prisoner can be brought to the station, examined for injuries, booked, and then transferred to the original jurisdiction for re-booking, bail and court processing. On the other hand, if the arrest occurs near the original jurisdiction, it may make sense to transport the arrestee directly there. Whatever option is used, it should be documented.

EXECUTION OF THE ARREST

PROPER USE OF FORCE

If de-escalation fails or is not feasible, officers may use reasonable force to effect a lawful arrest. 6E, § 14. This is discussed extensively in *Chapter 6.*

Unless the police use excessive force, a citizen may <u>not</u> forcibly resist even an unlawful entry into his home or an unlawful arrest by police. A citizen may file a complaint alleging police misconduct with the officer's agency and/or the Peace Officer Standards & Training (POST) Commission. 6E, § 8. A citizen may also file a civil lawsuit. But the citizen may <u>not</u> take matters into his own hands and resist. *Comm. v Moreira,* 388 Mass. 596 (1983). *Comm. v. Gomes,* 59 Mass. App. Ct. 332 (2003).

LOCATION OF ARREST

PUBLIC PLACE: WARRANTLESS ARRESTS ALLOWED

Warrantless arrests are authorized in public even if there is ample time to obtain a warrant. U.S. v. Watson, 423 U.S. 411 (1976). This is true even if the police successfully persuade occupants to come outside. *U.S. v. Rengifo,* 858 F.2d 800 (1st Cir. 1988) (warrantless arrest of hotel room guests was proper when police used a telephone call to induce them to leave their room; court noted that this strategy was a "creative investigative effort"). *Comm. v. Sorenson,* 98 Mass. App. Ct. 789 (2020) (defendant voluntarily left his apartment).

Avoid making arrests at courthouse. *Comm. v. Richardson*, 2017 WL 4542933 (Superior Court): Armed with a warrant,[12] police arrested the defendant in the public area of a courthouse as he waited in line to go through security screening. This occurred in front of jurors who had already sat for 14 days at his trial. The judge had to declare a mistrial. The police had other options — they could have contacted the Assistant District Attorney, court officers, or probation officers and alerted them about the arrest. At a minimum, the police should have thought twice about the potential waste of judicial resources associated with arresting a defendant on trial in the courthouse.

PRIVATE HOME: NEED WARRANT, CONSENT, OR EXIGENT CIRCUMSTANCES

Residents have a high expectation of privacy in their homes. That is why police must have a warrant, consent, or exigent circumstances in order to enter and arrest them there. *Payton v. New York*, 445 U.S. 573 (1980). The entire curtilage is covered by this rule. *Comm. v. Jubrey*, 2017 WL 1731148 (Appeals Court) (defendant's arrest occurred in an enclosed yard; police should have had an arrest warrant in this area).

Common areas and hallways of a multi-unit dwelling are considered a public area. *Comm. v. Boswell*, 374 Mass. 263 (1978). The same is true for an open shelter. *Comm. v. Mott*, 2013 WL 2247758 (Appeals Court) (defendant had no expectation of privacy when police arrested him at a homeless shelter; residents shared sleeping quarters in an open dormitory room; they were not given keys).

This rule covers overnight guests, but not visitors. *Minnesota v. Olson*, 495 U.S. 91 (1990) held: "We will all be hosts and we will all be guests many times in our lives. From either perspective, we think that society recognizes that a houseguest has a legitimate expectation of privacy in his host's home." A visitor is not entitled to the same protection. *Minnesota v. Carter*, 119 S.Ct. 469 (1998) (the defendants were present at someone's home for several hours; these visitors had no right to expect that police would get warrants for them).

Massachusetts does not recognize out-of-state warrants for this purpose. *Comm. v. DeRosia*, 402 Mass. 284 (1988): Leo DeRosia was wanted on New Hampshire warrants for weapons and drug offenses. A Keene, New Hampshire police officer requested that a Gardner, Massachusetts officer arrest DeRosia. The Gardner officer confirmed DeRosia's warrants through NCIC, then arrested him at his mother's house with a gun in his waistband. The SJC viewed the entry as an unexcused warrantless arrest.

To be safe, officers should obtain a Massachusetts fugitive warrant under 276, § 20A or, an even easier strategy, wait until the fugitive leaves the dwelling and arrest him without a warrant pursuant to 276, § 20B. This would have worked for DeRosia. See discussion of fugitive arrests in *Chapter 7*.

The suspect is considered inside his home when he answers the door. In *Comm. v. Marquez*, 434 Mass. 370 (2001), the defendant was identified by the victim of a home invasion several days after the crime. Sergeant Murray, accompanied by two detectives, went to his apartment. Murray knocked and the defendant opened the door, remaining inside his apartment. Murray asked, "Are you Victor Marquez?" The defendant said, "Yes." He was arrested. A stolen bike was seized.

---

12 There was no emergency. This was a misdemeanor warrant.

Officers had probable cause to arrest Marquez. The problem was they did not have a warrant, consent, or exigent circumstances to make the arrest in his home.

- **Suspect is not in public just because he opens the door.** The fact that Marquez spoke with officers "at the threshold" did not place him in public. Compare *Comm. v. Sorenson*, 98 Mass. App. Ct. 789 (2020): An officer went to Sorenson's apartment. When the door opened, the officer saw Sorenson inside and asked him to step out into the common hallway. When Sorenson was entirely out of his apartment, beyond his doorway, the officer arrested him for a felony assault. This was a legitimate "public" arrest.

- **Suspect does not consent to entry just because he opens the door.** Officers argued that Marquez, by opening his door, consented to their entry. However, valid consent requires that an occupant *clearly invite* officers to enter. That did not happen.[13]

- **Best practice — get warrant.** In *Marquez*, the SJC said that officers can avoid litigation on this issue if they simply get a warrant when they intend to go to a home to make an arrest.

Officers must knock and announce their presence and purpose prior to entering a home.[14] The two exceptions to this constitutional command are: (1) when officers engage in a trick that causes someone to voluntarily open the door in the suspect's home; or (2) when the situation requires that officers dispense with the "knock and announce rule" because they fear violence.

Accused inside his home

Before executing an arrest warrant, the police must have reasonable suspicion that the defendant is present. Comm. v. Gentile, 466 Mass. 817 (2014): Trooper David Napolitano and three Leominster police officers went to Conan Gentile's address at 9:30 a.m. on a workday to execute an arrest warrant. A teenage girl answered, followed by her mother, Maura. Napolitano informed Maura that he was looking for Gentile and had a warrant. Maura appeared nervous. She said Gentile was not there, but looked toward a nearby bedroom. Napolitano heard movement. He told Maura he did not believe her and entered. He opened the bedroom door and found Gentile.

Trooper Napolitano lacked reasonable suspicion that Gentile was home.

- **Before knocking.** While there was sufficient evidence that Gentile lived at the apartment, there was no information indicating he was home at that time. No physical surveillance was conducted, no third party had informed police he was home, and no evidence linked him to any vehicle parked at the residence.

  If the officers had entered earlier in the morning, the early hour alone would have provided reasonable suspicion that he was present. *Comm. v. Webster,* 75 Mass. App. Ct. 247 (2009). *Comm. v. York,* 2020 WL 6708672 (Appeals Court) (Montague officers and the State Police STOP team arrived at the residence at 5:45 a.m.). However, at 9:30 a.m. there was no evidence that Gentile was unemployed or had a daily routine that led officers to believe he would be home.

---

13 Consent to enter and search is fully discussed in *Chapter 15.*
14 This procedure is fully discussed in *Chapter 14.*

- **After** knocking. The evidence that Maura was lying was not compelling — it is normal to be nervous when an officer shows up with an arrest warrant, and there are many reasons she could have been looking toward the bedroom during her conversation.

  According to the SJC, studies show that officers are more confident "in their ability to ascertain whether someone is lying than is [legitimately] warranted by the [statistical] evidence." The high court actually referenced five separate studies in support of its conclusion. Here, Napolitano did not question Maura enough to show support for his hunch. For example, he did not ask her where Gentile was and then ask follow-up questions to test her credibility — as he told the court he normally did. He simply found her assertion implausible.

  The fact that Napolitano heard movement was not enough either. Napolitano did not know whether other people lived there, and he did not ask Maura whether anyone else was home.

Compare *Comm. v. Silva*, 440 Mass. 772 (2004): The building manager told Holyoke officers that the man listed in their warrant was his tenant. The apartment door was ajar and officers could see a man inside. It turned out that this person, Reinald Silva, was selling drugs but was not the one listed in the warrant. Since officers had reasonable suspicion, the SJC approved the entry and arrest.

Police may enter a home based on any resident's arrest warrant. *U.S. v. Hamilton*, 819 F.3d 503 (2016): Police believed that Anthony Hamilton lived in a particular home. While they had ample probable cause that Hamilton committed a felony, officers did not have enough information linking him to that address for a warrant. Still, they were able to legally enter the house because another inhabitant, Tommy Smith — whose residency they *could* prove — had an outstanding arrest warrant. When they executed Smith's warrant, they found Hamilton and arrested him.

Accused outside his home

An arrest warrant does not automatically allow officers to enter a home if the arrest occurred outside. In *Comm. v. Gonzalez*, 60 Mass. App. Ct. 903 (2003), Rosa Ortiz was arrested in the hallway outside her apartment, so an entry incident to that arrest was initially unnecessary. That changed when Ortiz agreed to retrieve a coat and her ID, which was required for bail. Since the officer was trying to help her, the court approved his following Ortiz inside for this limited purpose.

Accused inside another person's home

The police must have an arrest warrant for an overnight guest and a search warrant, consent, or exigent circumstances to justify entering the home of a third party to get him. The search warrant requirement is designed to protect the privacy rights of the homeowner. It prevents the police from searching numerous homes under the guise of looking for a wanted fugitive. *Lankford v. Gelston*, 364 F.2d 197 (4th Cir. 1966) (police used an arrest warrant for two fugitives to justify their warrantless entry of 300 homes).

- *Stegald v. U.S.*, 451 U.S. 204 (1981): Federal agents received information that a particular fugitive could be found at the home of another party in Atlanta. Armed with an arrest warrant for the fugitive, agents forcibly entered the home of Gary Stegald. The search did not produce the fugitive, but it did uncover 43 pounds of cocaine. The Supreme Court suppressed the cocaine because agents needed a search warrant, consent, or exigent circumstances to enter Stegald's house in the first place.

- Compare *Comm. v. Jackmon*, 63 Mass. App. Ct. 47 (2005): Kevin Jackmon and an accomplice robbed a McDonald's restaurant at gunpoint. Jackmon fled with two hostages. Two months later, after his photograph appeared on "America's Most Wanted," authorities received a tip that he was located in North Carolina. Local officers obtained a search warrant. The warrant affidavit relied on a confidential informant who had seen Jackmon and knew the name and address of the person with whom he was staying. Officers entered with the search warrant and took Jackmon into custody. Well done.

The person named in the arrest warrant may not challenge the absence or validity of a search warrant. Remember, the search warrant protects the *owner's* privacy, not the fugitive's. *Comm. v. Allen*, 28 Mass. App. Ct. 589 (1990) (a guest should not be able to require that the police obtain a search warrant before entering to arrest him; this would give a person greater privacy rights in someone else's home than he has in his own). *Comm. v. Tatum*, 465 Mass. 45 (2013).

Exceptions to warrant requirement

Consent to enter must be voluntary.[15] In *U.S. v. Bey*, 52 F.Supp.3d 299 (2014), police had multiple arrest warrants for Paul Bey. They learned that he may be staying with Clarissa Summons. They knocked on Summons' door, informed her of the warrants, and asked if Bey was inside. Summons became nervous. She placed her finger to her lips and repeated the question out loud: "Is Paul in the house?" She looked toward her bedroom, keeping her finger at her lips, and said: "I don't think he's here." She then slowly backed away, her finger still on her lips. The police entered and arrested Bey in the bedroom. While Summons did not explicitly invite police in, her intent was obvious. *Comm. v. Voisine*, 414 Mass. 772 (1993).

Exigent circumstances call for immediate police entry.[16] *Comm. v. Dejarnette*, 75 Mass. App. Ct. 88 (2009) is a good example of police possessing an arrest warrant, but lacking a search warrant for a third-party dwelling. This was excused because they had exigent circumstances. It began when Nickolas Dejarnette and his brother Brandon shot their mother's landlord. Police obtained arrest warrants for both men. Two weeks later, police learned that the brothers were staying at a particular Worcester address. Surveillance revealed Nickolas getting into a car. When police stopped the vehicle, Nickolas was lying on the back seat.

After establishing a perimeter, officers knocked loudly and announced their presence. Brandon Dejarnette was arrested after he jumped from a second-floor window. Exigent circumstances existed. Police were concerned that Brandon might escape because Nickolas' arrest had attracted a lot of attention — increasing the likelihood that a bystander might notify Brandon.

---

15 The law of consent is discussed in detail in *Chapter 15*.
16 This topic receives in-depth treatment in *Chapter 16*.

9 | *Protective Custody*

INCAPACITATION WITH ALCOHOL OR DRUGS
ALCOHOL INCAPACITATION — 111B, § 8

INCAPACITATION

111B, § 3 definition. A person is incapacitated if he drank alcohol and is either: (1) unconscious; (2) in need of medical attention; (3) likely to cause physical harm or damage property; or (4) disorderly. *Comm. v. Tomes,* 400 Mass. 23 (1987).

Disorderly for protective custody (PC) is the same standard as the criminal charge. *Veiga v. McGee,* 26 F.3d 1206 (1994)(Veiga was drunk and "ranting and raving," so police took him into PC; he sued the officers and city for seizing him without justification; while "disorderly" is not defined in the PC statute, it is applied the same way as the crime).

PROCEDURES

In the field

Officer has specific facts to believe adult or juvenile is incapacitated due to alcohol. *Comm. v. O'Connor,* 406 Mass. 112 (1989).

Intoxication is not incapacitation. *Alfano v. Lynch,* 847 F.3d 71 (2017) (defendant drank six to eight beers over four to six hours; he was denied admission to an Xfinity Center concert but had already arranged for bus transportation home; protective custody was not warranted).

Reasonable suspicion of incapacitation triggers sobriety testing. *Comm. v. McCaffery,* 49 Mass. App. Ct. 713 (2000).

PC may be used to remove someone from his or her home. *Lally v. Carmichael,* 56 Mass. App. Ct. 1103 (2002): While highly intoxicated, Susan Lally made hostile telephone calls to her daughter and former husband. Walpole officers went to her apartment and asked her to stop. She then made belligerent calls to 911! The officers returned and pleaded with her to stop, but she refused. They placed her into PC. Lally later sued. The court ruled in favor of the officers, noting their attempts to pacify her and their good use of discretion.

Reasonable force authorized during PC. Handcuffing is advised. If subject resists, consider A&B on Police Officer (265, § 13D) or Interfering with Police Officer (Common Law).[1]

---

1 Both offenses described in detail in *LED's Criminal Law, Chapter 5.*

Officer may search subject and immediate surroundings for weapons. 111B, § 8.

> **Good Samaritan immunity.** 138, § 34E. A person under 21 years of age who, in good faith, seeks medical assistance for someone experiencing alcohol-related incapacitation, or seeks assistance for himself, or is the subject of a request for assistance, shall not be charged under 138, §§ 34 (furnishing, "social host"), 34A (procurement or attempted procurement of alcohol) or 34C (minor in possession) if the evidence was gained as a result of seeking medical assistance.
>
> Immunity does *not* apply to adults 21 and over who host an underage party or, in some other fashion, engage in illegal conduct with minors.

With or without consent, the officer may transport the individual:

- **Home.** Be careful: Do not leave subject at home unless another person, who officers believe can control him or her, takes responsibility.

- **Hospital.** A "treatment facility" for protective custody is defined in 111B, § 3 as "any private or public place . . . providing services especially designed for the detoxification of intoxicated persons."

- **Station.** The subject may be brought to the police station.

When in doubt, officers should summon emergency medical services (EMS) to transport the subject for evaluation and treatment. Sometimes EMS will refuse to transport if an adult states that they do not want to go. However, the right to refuse transport and treatment does not apply to a police PC decision. Officers should say to the EMS crew: "This person is in police protective custody; they do not have a choice. Don't worry, you are not responsible or liable for a police decision to transport and evaluate."

In the station

Immediately inform the subject of his or her right to a phone call and allow phone use.

Notify parent or guardian of a minor under 18 as soon as possible. 111B, § 10.

Determine if treatment available. This should be documented *every* time a person is brought to the station. *Lucia v. City of Peabody*, 2013 WL 394870 (U.S. District Court).

Provide breathalyzer (BT) option. Under 111B, § 8, a BT of .10 or above establishes incapacitation (*not* like .08 for OUI). A BT of .06, .07, .08, and .09 authorizes sobriety testing. An officer must then decide whether to release or hold the subject. Finally, .05 or below entitles the subject to *immediate release. However*, if a minor registers *any* BT reading, insist on releasing him to a parent, guardian, or other responsible adult.

Use of the preliminary or portable breath test (PBT) permissible. For protective custody purposes, officers may use their station breathalyzer (BT) *or* their PBT. The reason they have this option is that the breathalyzer test authorized by 111B is not restricted in the same way as the one for OUI. See 90, § 24K (valid test for OUI consequences must be performed by a certified operator on an infrared breath-testing device). If they have a choice, officers should use the station BT, which is more technologically advanced and has a setting for "protective custody." At the same time, if officers are dealing with people in the field and looking for a quick way to "triage" a potential PC subject (which often happens at youth parties), the PBT is an invaluable tool.

Inventory the subject's personal possessions.

Duty to release or transfer:

- **For adults 18 and over:**

    - *1ˢᵗ Priority: Treatment.* If suitable treatment available, transport subject to the facility; or

    - *2ⁿᵈ Priority: Hold in cell until sober or no longer than 12 hours.* Officers should not hold those in PC longer than 12 hours without at least: (1) considering whether they may be safely released; (2) considering whether to transport them home; or (3) re-booking them for another period of confinement. *Ringuette v. Fall River,* 888 F.Supp. 258 (D. Mass. 1995).

- **For minor under 18:**

    - *1ˢᵗ Priority: Release minor upon request of parent or guardian.* However, hold the child and call DCF if the parent/guardian arrives incapacitated or unable to act responsibly.

    - *2ⁿᵈ Priority: If treatment available, transport minor to facility.*

    - *3ʳᵈ Priority: If treatment unavailable, hold minor in <u>non-secure</u> detention. Never* place in a cell; keep in an unlocked area under continuous visual supervision; and try to get a parent, guardian, or responsible person to remove the child from the station as soon as possible.

Recordkeeping: § 8 states that, while PC is not considered an arrest or crime, police may write an incident report for their records. The best practice is to write a report explaining the subject's behavior that led the officer to believe he or she was incapacitated. The report should also state who was willing to take custody of the subject if he or she was left at home or brought to a hospital.

Civil liability

Officer protection. Under 111B, § 13, "[p]olice officers, facility administrators or other persons acting in a reasonable manner . . . shall not be held criminally or civilly liable." However, failure to act may result in liability. *Comm. v. O'Connor,* 406 Mass. 112 (1989).

Court will not second-guess an officer's reasonable decision that did not work out. *Tremblay v. McClellan,* 350 F. 3d 195 (2003): Police picked up 16 year old Jason and his friend after they were found walking at 2:00 a.m. smelling of alcohol. At the station, Jason denied drinking, and the police could only pinpoint an odor coming from his friend. Believing he did not have enough to keep Jason in custody, the officer tried to contact an adult to take him home. Jason told the officer his parents were not home and he did not know how to reach them. The officer called Jason's friend's mother, as well as the mother of another friend, and neither agreed to be responsible for him. Unable to locate an adult, the officer drove Jason home at 3:00 a.m., making him promise that he would stay home. Jason took his parents' car, picked up two friends, and drove to another state. At 5:00 a.m., he was speeding and hit a tree, paralyzing himself. The officer was not liable because a reasonable officer would have done exactly what he did.

DRUG INCAPACITATION — 111E, § 9A

INCAPACITATION

111E, § 9A definition. Incapacitated refers to a person who consumed a controlled substance, toxic vapor, or substance *other than alcohol* and is either: (1) unconscious; or (2) in need of medical attention; or (3) likely to cause physical harm or damage property; or (4) disorderly.

PROCEDURES

In the field

Officer has specific facts to believe adult or juvenile is incapacitated due to drugs, inhalants, or some other substance. The decision may be based on field sobriety tests or other information or observations.

Reasonable force may be used to take person into custody. Handcuffing is permissible and advised. If the subject resists, consider A&B on Police Officer (265, § 13D) or Interfering with a Police Officer (Common Law).

Officer may search the person and immediate surroundings to discover weapons. Any item taken must be inventoried and, except for contraband or other illegal items, returned.

- **Officer may search to facilitate on-scene treatment.** *Comm. v. McCarthy*, 71 Mass. App. Ct. 591 (2008): Officer McGinnis responded to a report of an unconscious woman at a restaurant. He found Linda McCarthy thrashing about on the floor. He called for EMTs, who told McGinnis they believed McCarthy was suffering from an overdose. They asked McGinnis if he knew what she had taken. McGinnis searched her handbag to assist the EMTs. He found cocaine.

  While McGinnis lacked probable, the purpose of his search was to assist the EMTs in treating McCarthy. After all, he did not search the handbag until the EMTs told him McCarthy may be suffering an overdose.

- **Good Samaritan immunity.** While police may criminally charge a person for illegal items, under 94C, § 34A, a person cannot be charged with drug possession (§ 34) if he seeks medical assistance (in good faith) because he believes he or another person is overdosing. The person who overdosed also cannot be charged.

This law does <u>not</u> prevent prosecution for distribution, possession with the intent to distribute, trafficking, or any other crime (e.g., OUI). It also does not prevent prosecuting a drug user if the police discover the overdose without the user or someone else requesting medical assistance.[2]

With or without consent, the officer may assist the individual to an emergency medical facility.

When minor under 18 taken into PC, officer must notify parent or guardian as soon as possible.

Transport & treatment

Custody may last through transport <u>and</u> emergency treatment. The subject may be held against his will in order to immediately transport him to an emergency facility. At a minimum, officers may insist that a subject be evaluated by medical staff before release. See 111, § 51½ (overdose patient must be examined by physician before release or physician must explain, in writing, why evaluation did not occur).

Best practice — use EMS transport and accompany ambulance to treatment facility. § 9A does not define the method of transport. It is recommended that an officer call EMS and, ideally, follow the ambulance to the treatment facility and make sure that the subject is checked in and evaluated.

- **Only the officer has the legal authority to place the subject into PC.** That authority cannot be delegated to EMS personnel or health care clinicians.

- **Sometimes EMS will refuse to transport if an adult states that they do not want to go.** However, the right to refuse transport and treatment does not apply to a police PC decision. Officers should say to the EMS crew: "This person is in police protective custody; they do not have a choice. Don't worry, you are not responsible or liable for a police decision to transport and evaluate."

Unlike an alcohol PC, transport to the police station or to the subject's home is <u>never</u> an option for a drug PC.

Recordkeeping. § 9A states that, while PC is not considered an arrest or crime, police must write "an entry of custody" indicating the date, time, location, and the name of the "assisting officer" and OIC. The best practice is for police to write an incident report outlining the behavior that led the officer to believe the subject was incapacitated.

Narcan protocol

Naloxone is an opioid antagonist known by its brand name Narcan. When administered quickly, it can reverse the effects of an opiate overdose. The Massachusetts Department of Public Health (DPH) is providing Narcan to addicts and their families. 94C, § 34A(e). The

---

2 The basis for this law was research by the Department of Public Health (DPH) showing that many drug users failed to call 911 when they or a friend were experiencing an overdose because they feared criminal prosecution.

DPH has also instituted a law enforcement program that allows properly trained officers to carry and administer nasal Narcan. 105 CMR 171.000.

Anyone who receives Narcan for an overdose should be placed into protective custody if they refuse transport to a hospital. According to Dr. Daniel Muse, Medical Advisor to the Municipal Police Training Committee (MPTC), a person who has received Narcan may appear normal and refuse transport. However, medical evaluation is mandated — either voluntarily or pursuant to PC under 111E — because:

- **A near fatal overdose is evidence that the person is incapacitated** and warrants an evaluation now offered in all Massachusetts emergency departments. 111, § 51½.

- **The effects of Narcan may only be temporary.** The use of potent opioids, such as fentanyl, may cause a delayed relapse. Secondary medical complications from the overdose may exist.

- **Using Narcan causes withdrawal and often makes a person reuse opioids**.

- **Releasing the person is a public safety risk** because he or she may attempt to drive a car, which could result in injury or death.

Civil liability

The realistic sources of liability are failing to act in an obvious case or using excessive force.

- **Fail to act.** *Esmaili v. State of California,* 2014 WL 6907545 (Court of Appeal): 17 year old Sophia attended a house party where drugs and alcohol were furnished to guests. She became disoriented and, at midnight, left the party without her cell phone and attempted to walk home. At 12:30 a.m., Sophia approached two California Highway Patrol (CHP) officers in a convenience store parking lot. She was visibly distraught and lost. She was clearly underage and alone on the streets. Sophia asked the officers for help returning home, but instead of rendering assistance themselves, they procured a cab for her. Sophia refused to get in the cab, and the officers allowed her to leave alone in the dark. They watched Sophia walk in the opposite direction from the home address she had given them. Shortly after leaving, Sophia walked onto a state highway and was killed by a motorist.

- **Excessive force.** *McCue v. City of Bangor,* 838 F.3d 55 (1st Cir. 2016): Officers sought to take Michael McCue into protective custody due to his erratic behavior believed to be caused by "bath salts." In an attempt to restrain McCue, who initially resisted, the officers placed him face down in a prone position with their weight on his back and shoulders. McCue was declared dead shortly after. An expert attributed the cause of death to "prolonged restraint under the weight of multiple officers [while in a] state of excited delirium."

JUVENILE EXPOSED TO DRUGS — 94C, § 36

Under 94C, § 36, officers must:

Reasonably believe a child under 18 has knowledge of and is present with a controlled substance in Class A, B, or C (not D). Notice that this statute only applies when the juvenile is present with Classes A, B, and C, *but not* D, which excludes marijuana.

Hold the child in protective custody no longer than 4 hours. *Never* place the child in a juvenile cell; instead keep the minor in an unlocked area under continuous visual supervision.

Make every effort to notify the child's parent or guardian. The child should be released as soon as possible to the parent or guardian but, in any event, should not be held for over 4 hours at the station. Consider filing a 51A report with DCF if appropriate.

MEDICAL EMERGENCY

Generally, a person has the right to refuse medical treatment. 111, § 70E(h). "Unless there is an emergency . . . , medical treatment of a competent patient without his consent is [A&B]." *Matter of Spring*, 380 Mass. 629 (1980). Officers must respect this restriction when they encounter injured citizens in the field.

Emergency exception. There is an exception to the general requirement of consent. As *Shine v. Vega*, 429 Mass. 456 (1999) notes:

- **Unconscious or incompetent.** The patient must be unconscious or incompetent to decide, and no one is available to legally act for the patient;

- **Time is of the essence.** Delay to gain consent risks death or serious bodily injury; and

- **Treatment reasonable.** Under the circumstances, a reasonable person would want treatment.

Use of force must be reasonable in relation to the subject's medical condition. *Hill v. Miracle*, 853 F.3d 306 (6th Cir. 2017): Corey Hill suffered a diabetic emergency in his home. Paramedics found Hill disoriented and combative. They inserted a catheter to intravenously administer dextrose to raise Hill's blood sugar. Deputy Miracle arrived just as Hill ripped the catheter from his arm, causing blood to spray. Hill kicked, swung, and swore as paramedics tried to restrain him. Miracle had attended more than a dozen diabetic emergencies.

He deployed his Taser in drive-stun mode on Hill's thigh, distracting Hill long enough for paramedics to secure the catheter and administer dextrose. Hill "became an angel" and was "very apologetic" after the dextrose took effect. Paramedics took him to the hospital. Later, however, Hill sued. He claimed his diabetes worsened and he suffered contact burns as a result of the Taser. The court held that Deputy Miracle used reasonable force so that lifesaving medicine could be administered.

To insist on transport for medical treatment, the police do not have to be dealing with an unconscious citizen. *Comm. v. St. Hilaire*, 43 Mass. App. Ct. 743 (1997) (the defendant's protest against treatment was properly overruled by police because he was highly intoxicated, had been involved in a head-on car crash, and might be seriously injured).

MENTAL HEALTH ISSUES
DE-ESCALATION & UNDERSTANDING

Mental illness can affect anyone. It is not a result of weak character or lack of intelligence. Many well-known and accomplished people have mental health problems. Mental illness may interfere with perception, judgment, behavior, and the ability to relate to others. Many individuals have episodic illnesses, meaning they have good and bad days.

When extreme behaviors occur, do not assume that the Emotionally Disturbed Person (EDP) is a criminal. Consider the possibility of a mental health disorder.[3]

Most people with mental health needs are no more violent than the general population. In fact, many are withdrawn and uncomfortable. If they become aggressive, it is usually because they feel frightened, confused, or hopeless. Maintaining safety may be especially challenging when a person has stopped taking prescribed medication or has a dual diagnosis — that is, a major mental health disorder and a substance abuse problem.

Consult individuals on scene who know the EDP. They often provide the best information. A person on scene (e.g., a parent, family member, friend, or coworker) often has information about the person's illness and behaviors, which will alert officers about ways to calm the EDP instead of provoking a "fight-or-flight" response. Always ask about medication. Many people with mental health needs do not take prescribed medications.

If knowledgeable people are unavailable, look for clues of a mental health episode:

- Emotionless facial expression and body language.
- Incoherent statements.
- Inability to focus.
- Bizarre appearance, movements, or behaviors.
- Delusions about personal importance or identity.
- Hallucinations.
- Agitation, often without clear reason.
- Pronounced feelings of hopelessness, sadness, or guilt.

Overall goal: Least intrusive intervention consistent with public, EDP, and officer safety.

- **Referral.** Many non-dangerous calls involving an EDP are best handled by supporting the parent's or mentally impaired adult's wishes and encouraging professional intervention.

- **Mental health detention for evaluation.** If the EDP is a danger to himself or to others, officers may initiate a mental health evaluation under 123, § 12.

- **Arrest for crime.** While officers are free to use their discretion and not pursue charges, they should arrest a mentally ill person when necessary.

---

3 It is estimated that 40% of emotionally disturbed persons are, at some point in their lives, arrested by police. Swanson, *Police Administration* (Pearson Education, Inc.; 9th Ed.) at page 487.

A mental health condition does <u>not</u> nullify probable cause to arrest or charge. This is important for police to understand. While officers *may* take into account an offender's mental condition in their charging decision, they do not have to. In situations involving more serious crime, police should arrest, or at least charge, a mentally ill offender *and* get help for him. Keeping charges before the court in serious cases helps ensure public safety in the event the defendant fails to comply with treatment or gets released prematurely.

Consider *Comm. v. Newton N.*, 478 Mass. 747 (2018): The police arrested a 12 year old boy who broke into an apartment at 1:30 a.m. and stole a handgun and rifles. They brought him to the hospital for evaluation when he began screaming in a deranged fashion at the scene. The prosecutor and police properly opposed the judge, who dismissed the boy's case on the basis of his mental condition. The SJC ruled: As long as police have probable cause, the prosecutor must be allowed to go forward. A defendant's mental status will be addressed post-arraignment as part of the trial process.

Sometimes the best way to help an EDP is to suggest voluntary commitment. A family may be more inclined to push for an inpatient stay if they know it will persuade the police to avoid a § 12 commitment. This approach may also work with an EDP who is rational enough to acknowledge a need for treatment. Under 123, § 10, voluntary commitment may be sought by: (1) a person at least 16 years old; (2) a parent or guardian on behalf of a person under 18; or (3) a court-appointed guardian on behalf of a person under his care (no age limitation).

The facility may discharge a patient,[4] or an adult patient may choose to leave, or a parent or guardian may withdraw his child. As a safeguard, facility staff may insist on three days' written notice and restrict departure to normal business hours. In extreme cases, a patient may be held beyond three days if the facility files a petition for involuntary commitment.

Police presence does not automatically waive a person's psychotherapist privilege. *Comm. v. Waweru*, 480 Mass. 173 (2018): Patrick Waweru stabbed the mother of his child to death. A police arrest quickly followed, and Waweru was brought to a hospital when he acknowledged taking pills to kill himself. Because of his potential for violence, police officers stayed in his hospital room when a psychiatrist came in to evaluate him. Officers heard Waweru make statements implicating himself in the murder.

A patient may request a private consultation. At the same time, the police are not required to leave a hospital room so a defendant can speak with the psychotherapist alone. Psychotherapists should not have to put their safety at risk in order to treat a dangerous patient.

As a result, if officers are present during an evaluation, the defendant's statements are typically inadmissible unless the court later rules that "the interests of justice [require] that the communication be disclosed."

---

4 If the patient is a child, the facility must provide a parent or guardian with 14-days' notice.

MENTAL HEALTH EMERGENCY — 123, § 12

REASON FOR INVOLUNTARY COMMITMENT

Involuntary commitment must be based on a "likelihood of serious harm" due to mental illness.[5] 123, § 1 defines this as:

- **Danger to self.** The EDP presents a substantial risk of physical harm to himself (e.g., a suicidal threat or attempt, or self-abuse); or

- **Danger to others.** The EDP presents a substantial risk of physical harm to other persons; or

- **Inability to protect self.** The EDP presents a *very* substantial risk of injury to himself based on evidence that the EDP's judgment "is so affected that he is unable to protect himself in the community." See *In the Matter of D.K.*, 95 Mass. App. Ct. 95 (2019) (D.K. believed she was being persecuted, and she was refusing psychiatric treatment and not bathing or changing her clothes).

INVOLUNTARY COMMITMENT CATEGORIES

Under 123, § 12, four categories of commitment are recognized. *Ahern v. O'Donnell*, 109 F.3d 809 (1997). Any § 12 commitment is for a maximum of three days.

- **Category 1 — Clinician issues a commitment order based on examination.** Following a personal examination of an EDP, a qualified mental health clinician[6] may sign a commitment order if he or she has reason to believe that the EDP poses a likelihood of serious harm.

- **Category 2 — Clinician issues an order in an emergency.** Even if the EDP refuses examination, a qualified clinician may still issue an order based on facts that show the EDP poses a likelihood of serious harm.

- **Category 3 — Officer restrains EDP.** In an emergency situation, officers may restrain an EDP who they believe poses a likelihood of serious harm.

- **Category 4 — Judge issues Warrant of Apprehension.** At any time, *any person* may apply to a district or juvenile court for a commitment order. After hearing, a judge may issue a warrant for the apprehension of an EDP who poses a likelihood of serious harm.

---

5 The likelihood of serious harm must be the result of mental illness, which the Department of Mental Health (DMH) defines as "a substantial disorder of thought, mood, perception, orientation, or memory that grossly impairs judgment, behavior, capacity to recognize reality or ability to meet the ordinary demands of life, but shall not include alcoholism or substance abuse." 104 CMR 27.05.
6 A clinician for this purpose is a physician, psychiatric nurse, psychologist, or licensed social worker.

POLICE PROCEDURES

Categories 1, 2, and 4

- **Since the commitment order is issued by a clinician and/or a judge, officers may enter private homes to place the EDP into protective custody.** Categories 1, 2, and 4 are, in effect, arrest warrants for mental health detention. *McCabe v. Lifeline Ambulance & City of Lynn*, 77 F.3d 540 (1996).

- **Since EDPs constitute a diverse and, at times, unpredictable group of people, officers should obtain information from the court, clinician, and/or family.** When asked to execute a commitment order or warrant of apprehension, officers should get some preliminary information from those familiar with the EDP. For example, is the EDP paranoid? Would it be better to have plainclothes personnel handle the situation? Should a family member be present during police entry?

  Considering potential difficulties *before* the police enter and detain the EDP may avert a tragic result. *McCabe v. Lifeline Ambulance, supra.* (64 year old Holocaust survivor died at her home during a traumatic effort by police to execute a commitment order).

- **Transport EDP to appropriate local facility (Categories 1 and 2) or to the court that issued the warrant (Category 4).** Officers should either use their own cruiser or have an ambulance assigned for transport. Officers should follow or ride in the ambulance to ensure that the EDP arrives safely. Officers may take reasonable precautions, including the use of handcuffs, but should avoid unnecessary restraint.

Category 3

- **Since street officers make the decision to take the EDP into custody, they must have probable cause that the EDP poses a likelihood of serious harm.** This is a commonsense determination. *Ahern v. O'Donnell*, 109 F.3d 809 (1997) (messages left by EDP revealed a deeply disturbed and depressed individual).

- **Entry into a home to take an EDP into custody under Category 3:**

  - *If there is time to consult with a clinician who can issue a Category 2, police have independent support for their entry.*

  - *If exigent circumstances make consulting with a clinician impractical, officers should seek consent from an occupant to enter and, if that fails, force entry.* If possible, seek supervisory approval prior to forced entry. *McCabe v. Lifeline Ambulance, supra.* ("The potential consequences attending a delayed commitment — both to the mentally ill subject and others — may be extremely serious . . . including death or bodily injury"). Compare *Comm. v. Allen*, 54 Mass. App. Ct. 719 (2002) (police sergeant had insufficient evidence that a disabled person was in need of immediate assistance; therefore, his warrantless entry into the apartment was invalid).

- **Transport EDP and file the application for evaluation.** An officer should fill out the 12(a) application form at the hospital to initiate the clinical evaluation.

AUTHORITY TO TRANSPORT & RESTRAIN

Officers are given explicit authority to transport and restrain patients. 123, § 21 (restraints may be used on an adult for up to 2 hours prior to examination; for a minor, up to 1 hour).

Officers who act in good faith are immune. 123, § 22 declares that officers are "immune from civil suits . . . for restraining, transporting, . . . or admitting any person to a facility."

At the same time, use of force decisions must take into account the subject's mental condition. *McKenney v. Mangino*, 873 F.3d 75 (1st Cir. 2017) (essentially without warning, police officer shot subject who he knew was suicidal).

OTHER INTERVENTIONS

COMMITMENT FROM POLICE DETENTION — 123, § 18

§ 18 covers serious mental health situations in police lockups and correctional facilities. The OIC may initiate an involuntary or voluntary transfer of the prisoner to a mental health facility. See discussion in *Chapter 10* concerning post-arrest procedures.

COMMITMENT OF ALCOHOLIC OR SUBSTANCE ABUSER — 123, § 35

Petition to district court. Under § 35, if a police officer, physician, spouse, blood relative, guardian, or court official reasonably believes that a person is a "chronic" alcoholic or substance abuser (including inhalants), he or she may petition the district or juvenile court to commit the person. Similar to the § 12 warrant of apprehension, a benefit of § 35 is that it gives officers the choice of taking matters into their own hands or calling upon another party to initiate the process.

A § 35 commitment must be based on clear and convincing evidence that: (1) the person is unable to protect himself in the community from physical harm; and (2) there is a substantial risk that, without treatment, harm will happen reasonably quickly (days or weeks rather than months). *In the Matter of G.P.*, 473 Mass. 112 (2015). *In the Matter of N.F.*, 93 Mass. App. Ct. 1115 (2018) (texts showed mother's son was a heroin addict and suicidal).

§ 35 warrant remains active for 5 consecutive days (excluding days when the court is closed). It must be executed by police within this time period.

Home entry is justified under warrant. *Hill v. Walsh*, 884 F.3d 16 (2018): 28 year old Matthew Hill, who struggled with opioid addiction, was taken to the hospital. The next day, his sister filed a § 35 petition to have him committed. The court issued a warrant of apprehension with his parents' home address. Officers arrived and thought they saw someone. They reasonably believed it was Matthew and properly entered.

With a § 35 warrant, the subject must be presented immediately before a judge. This requirement rules out seizing the subject after hours unless the police independently use alcohol or drug protective custody.

Commitment for up to 90 days. The person is evaluated at court and, after a hearing in which he is represented by counsel, he may be committed for up to 90 days. The person is housed separately from convicted criminals and may be released by the superintendent prior to the end of 90 days.

LONGER-TERM HOSPITALIZATION

All of the previously discussed mental health options are short-term approaches. Persons committed pursuant to § 12 may be held for up to three days. If voluntarily committed under § 10, persons are typically held without their consent for three days.

For longer hospitalization, the facility superintendent must petition the court. Under 123, § 8, the court holds a hearing to decide whether the person is mentally ill and whether his discharge will create a likelihood of serious harm. If the court decides to hold the person, he stays initially for another six months. His commitment is reviewed annually after that. For longer-term hospitalization, the standard is proof beyond a reasonable doubt. *Guardianship of Roe*, 383 Mass. 415 (1981).

MISSING MENTAL HEALTH PATIENTS

From a Massachusetts facility — length of absence and reason for commitment dictate action. According to 123, § 30, when a patient is absent without authorization, the facility superintendent must notify state and local police, the district attorney, and the patient's next of kin. If the patient is absent for less than six months, the patient should be returned to the facility by officers. Patients absent beyond six months should not automatically go back to the facility. Facility staff should obtain judicial review before the patient's re-commitment. A patient must always be returned if he had been committed after being found incompetent to stand trial or not guilty by reason of insanity.

From out-of-state facility. Chapter 123 also permits officers to detain a person who has escaped from an out-of-state mental health facility and may be dangerous. Officers should hold the person and alert the district attorney's office to begin *rendition* proceedings under 123, § 20. They are identical to those used for out-of-state fugitives.[7]

JUVENILE ISSUES
JUVENILE RUNAWAY — 119, § 39H

STANDARD FOR PROTECTIVE CUSTODY

First, police officers may place a child age 6 to under 18 into protective custody (PC) for running away from his or her legal custodian. The term "legal custodian" refers to a parent, guardian, or agency (such as DCF) who is responsible for the child's welfare.

- Officers must have probable cause that a child has run away and will not respond to a summons.

---

7 See discussion in *Chapter 7.*

- **A prior episode of running away is not required.** Police must simply believe that the child is likely to run away again without their intervention. *In the Matter of Odetta*, 68 Mass. App. Ct. 862 (2007).

Second, officers must PC a child named in a Warrant of Protective Custody (WPC) if they can deliver the child to juvenile court no later than 4:30 p.m. The WPC is sent by the court to the police department in the community where the child lives. It *never* appears in the Warrant Management System (WMS). The 4:30 p.m. deadline appears on the face of the WPC.

Important note: If officers find a child named in a WPC after hours, they may: (1) inform the child (and parent or guardian) about the WPC and direct them to go to court the next day; or (2) place the child into PC as a runaway (if applicable) and execute the WPC the next day.

Police may not PC a child for failing to obey a legal custodian, failing to obey school regulations, truancy, or violating a local curfew. *Comm. v. Weston W.*, 455 Mass. 24 (2009).

PROPER PROCEDURE

Take child into custody

Be as understanding as possible. These are young kids who often do not think they have done anything wrong. Many come from difficult home situations. If they sense that officers are nonjudgmental, they are more likely to cooperate.

Explain why you are taking them into custody. Children find it easier to accept a decision that is motivated by the officer's concern for their welfare *and* is legally justified. Listen with empathy, but avoid debating the merits of their case.

Never use handcuffs. 119, § 39H clearly states that "a child may not be confined in shackles or similar restraints."

Always take other safety precautions. Although handcuffing is not permitted, officers should: (1) search a child for weapons and/or contraband prior to placing him or her into PC; and (2) transport the child in the secure back-seat area of the cruiser. *Comm. v. Chism*, 2015 WL 924236 (Superior Court) (officer properly searched runaway youth and unexpectedly discovered evidence linking him to a murder).

It is best if an officer of the same sex conducts the search and transport. If not possible, radio to dispatch the destination, exact departure and arrival times, and mileage traveled.

Charge youth, but only as a last resort. For the child who is significantly noncompliant during the PC process, officers may consider charging interfering with a police officer or A&B on a public employee. *Comm. v. Lacey L*, 2013 WL 4835158 (Appeals Court) (the juvenile, who was a runaway, was stopped by police in the backseat of a cab; she began screaming at her mother, who was standing nearby; when officers took her into custody, she yelled, "Take your hands off me, pig," and refused to get into the cruiser; she kicked an officer). Depending on the circumstances, other offenses may be committed by runaways at the time they encounter police — e.g., disorderly conduct, disturbing the peace, or trespass.

Transport & place child

Officer executes Warrant of Protective Custody (WPC). Transport child to the court that issued the warrant, but no later than 4:30 p.m. File a return of service in the clerk's office.

Officer decides to PC runaway. 119, § 39H mandates placing the child in the following <u>order of preference</u>:

- **Child's legal custodian or responsible person.** The child may be brought directly home or, if necessary, to the police station in order to facilitate placement with a parent, guardian, agency (like DCF), or "other responsible person known to the child." If the child is brought to the station, a simple notation in the police report should explain why (e.g., "arranged with mother to pick up son at station," or "call for service volume high, brought child to station so chief's secretary could arrange placement").

  A legal custodian or responsible person must promise, in writing, to bring the child to court on the next date.

- **Temporary licensed shelter.** If a child cannot be reunited with his legal custodian or other responsible person, dial 211 and use the Runaway Assistance Program to help place the child.[8]

- **Juvenile court.** Finally, officers may bring the child directly to the juvenile court if they attempted to exercise the above options, but were unable to. There is an affidavit at the juvenile court for officers to sign.

Detention restrictions if brought to station. A child who has to be brought to the station should be held: (1) without handcuffs; (2) in an unlocked, multi-purpose area; (3) under continuous visual supervision; (4) for only the time necessary to get him or her to a legal custodian, responsible person, approved shelter, or court.

No transport in police wagon. Under 119, § 34, children should *only* be transported in a marked or unmarked cruiser, not a police wagon. Also, never transport a juvenile and adult together.

ABANDONED OR AT-RISK CHILD — 119, § 24

POLICE REQUEST DCF ASSISTANCE

Police on-scene intervention reveals emergency. Officers may encounter a child under 18 who is:

- **Abandoned temporarily or permanently.** For example, on a hot day, a parent left his young child unattended in his car at a casino. Other cases have involved children home alone in squalid conditions.

---

8 The 211 call and other placement efforts may occur at the station. 119, § 39H(ii) *only* prohibits bringing a runaway child to the station *after* an officer decides to place the child with a shelter. Prior to a shelter placement, officers may justify going to the station to figure out how best to help the child.

- **At risk due to an intoxicated or abusive adult.** *Comm. v. Hurd,* 29 Mass. App. Ct. 929 (1990) (police received 911 call that a drunk man was getting into a car with three small children).

- **At risk due to any other circumstance.**

Police action:

- **Remove child from situation and notify DCF.** Police may remove the child and notify DCF to respond to the station, hospital, or some other suitable location; or

- **Keep child at location and notify DCF for removal decision.** Police may call DCF and allow it to decide whether to remove the child.

- **File 51A.** Even if DCF responds, this legal obligation typically applies.

DCF procedure. DCF petitions the court that there exists:

- **Reasonable cause that the child is suffering from or in immediate danger of serious abuse or neglect;** and

- **Immediate removal is necessary to protect the child.** *Care and Protection of Lillian,* 445 Mass. 333 (2005).

Court may order transfer of the child to DCF custody for up to 72 hours. At the follow-up hearing the court decides if temporary custody should continue. The standard of proof is preponderance of the evidence.

DCF REQUESTS POLICE ASSISTANCE

Officers should accompany DCF employees, enter, keep the peace, and ensure the child is removed safely. DCF is authorized to seek police help to remove a child. 110 CMR 4.26.

Police entry with DCF does not justify a search for evidence. Comm. v. Cunningham, 2009 WL 614460 (Superior Court): DCF requested assistance from Worcester police in removing a neglected child from a second-floor apartment. Officer Brace knocked on the door, but there was no response. He heard things being moved around. He knocked again, and the door opened. Brace smelled burnt marijuana and saw a crying baby inside.

Brace asked the man if anyone else was in the apartment. Oliver Cunningham came forward and identified himself as "Samuels." The man who opened the door identified himself as "Main." When Brace asked for identification, Cunningham pulled out a Jamaican driver's license in a name other than Samuels, and a large amount of cash. He said he worked in a factory. Neither man had a weapon, and the child was not in danger. Officer Brace and his partner conducted a sweep and found no one else in the apartment.

Brace called the Worcester Vice Squad. Detective Noone saw Cunningham looking at a bed repeatedly, so he moved the mattress and found cocaine.

The officers properly entered the apartment without a warrant, identified the occupants, and determined that the child was safe. Once DCF removed the child, the officers should have left. On the other hand, if officers believed that their observations created probable cause to search for drug evidence, they should have secured the apartment and applied for a search warrant.[9] Since they did not do that, the cocaine was suppressed.

ANIMAL PROTECTION

Protective custody for animal cruelty & fighting. 272, § 104 provides guidelines for law enforcement. If an animal is impounded for cruelty (272, § 77) or fighting (272, § 94), the law enforcement agency or the prosecutor may file a petition with the court requesting that the owner, or any person claiming an interest in the animal, post a security payment for care costs. 272, § 91 enables a district court to order the forfeiture of fighting animals and their humane destruction.

140, § 174F prohibits confining an animal in a vehicle in a manner that threatens its health due to extreme heat or cold. A police officer, animal control officer, or firefighter:[10]

- Must first make a reasonable effort to locate the vehicle owner.
- May enter the vehicle by any reasonable means to protect the animal (e.g., breaking a window).
- May not search or seize items unless otherwise permitted by law.
- Must leave written notice in a secure and conspicuous location on or in the vehicle bearing name, title, and address where the animal may be retrieved (owner must pay for care).
- Will be immune from criminal or civil liability for removing the animal.

---

9 It is doubtful that officers had sufficient probable cause to obtain a search warrant. The odor of burnt marijuana, plus an occupant with cash who stares at a bed, is hardly a strong case.
10 A citizen also has the authority under § 174F to enter a vehicle to rescue an animal. The difference is that a citizen must call 911 before forcing entry.

10 *Post-Arrest Procedures*

PROPER BOOKING PROCEDURES

When the arrestee arrives at the station, he must be properly booked. This includes the inventory procedure discussed in *Chapter 18*. It also includes fingerprints and photographs. 263, § 1A. *Comm. v. Shipps*, 399 Mass. 820 (1987).

The primary purpose is to identify the arrestee. Police may then learn whether there are outstanding warrants or restraining orders. This information is important to the magistrate in deciding whether to impose bail. The booking procedure is also important to the defendant because it creates a public record of his arrest, which allows his family, friends, and attorney to determine his whereabouts.

Booking may be videotaped, even if the defendant is not told he is being recorded. *Comm. v. Gordon*, 422 Mass. 816 (1996).

REASON FOR ARREST

The arrestee must be accurately informed why he was arrested. The police must also provide a copy of an arrest warrant on request. 263, § 1.

TELEPHONE ACCESS

If arrested in the field, the arrestee must be allowed to use the telephone within 1 hour of his arrival at the station. 276, § 33A.

If he came to the station prior to being arrested, the arrestee's telephone rights are triggered by a formal arrest. *Comm. v. Dagley*, 442 Mass. 713 (2004) (murder suspect voluntarily accompanied officers to the station and received *Miranda* warnings at 1:55 a.m.; the interview lasted two hours; the defendant was then formally arrested, booked and advised of his right to a telephone call; he called his parents at around 4:00 a.m.; this sequence of events was proper police procedure).

While officers may wait until the formal arrest to advise a suspect of his right to a phone call, they may not deliberately delay an arrest to take advantage of a suspect. *Comm. v. Melo*, 472 Mass. 278 (2015).

- **Right to phone call does not apply when suspect already incarcerated on another matter.** *Comm. v. Perry*, 432 Mass. 214 (2000) involved the brutal murder of a disabled adult. The defendant was in custody on an unrelated matter when police arrived at the house of correction to question him. The SJC rejected his suggestion that he was entitled to a phone call prior to this interrogation.

- SJC has not decided whether § 33A applies to arrests made out-of-state or initially by federal authorities. *Comm. v. Haith*, 452 Mass. 409 (2008).

Any evidence gained from intentionally withholding an arrestee's phone call is suppressed. The defendant has the burden of proving an intentional violation. *Comm. v. Walker*, 466 Mass. 268 (2013).

Always write down the number called by the arrestee. Comm. v. White, 422 Mass. 487 (1996): The booking officer asked the defendant what telephone number he wished to call. The officer wrote the number on the booking sheet and noted that the call went through. The number was linked to an accomplice, and this fact was offered into evidence at trial. Defense counsel argued that recording the number infringed on the defendant's phone call right. The court disagreed. The practice of documenting the phone number serves an administrative, not investigative function. It confirms that an arrestee was afforded this right and protects against the unauthorized use of station telephones.

May use investigator's cell phone. Comm. v. Williams, 456 Mass. 857 (2010): The defendant was arrested for murder. While in the gang unit office, the defendant was told that he could make several calls from a trooper's cell phone. He telephoned three family members.

The only difference between using a land line and a cell phone is that the number dialed is automatically recorded on the cell. Given that the police are already permitted to write down the phone number (see discussion of *White* above), this difference is insignificant.

Never record arrestee's call unless he is notified. If officers direct the suspect to a phone that records outgoing calls, they must let him know that in advance. *Comm. v. Yacobian*, 393 Mass. 1005 (1984).

There is no requirement that a defendant be permitted to make a private phone call. If nearby officers overhear what he says, they may testify about it. *Comm. v. Dixon*, 79 Mass. App. Ct. 701 (2011) (while on the station phone, police heard murder defendant's comment to his girlfriend: "I fucked up. I fucked up").

SAFE CUSTODY

Examine for injury

The Officer in Charge (OIC) of a police lockup shall immediately examine a prisoner for injuries. 276, § 33 mandates this examination and demands that the OIC — upon finding any bruises, cuts or other injuries — write a report to the chief of the department. The police are liable for their "deliberate indifference" to the medical needs of any individual in custody. *Johnson v. Summers*, 411 Mass. 82 (1991).

No removal of clothing. 276, § 33 limits the extent of the evaluation: "The requirement that the prisoner be examined shall not be deemed to compel the removal of clothing."

Only applies to first lockup after arrest. § 33 states: "When a person is transferred from one place of confinement to another . . . , the requirement that he shall be examined appl[ies] only to the place [where] he is first taken after his arrest."

Prevent suicide

Police obligations when confronted by threat or actual suicide. Under 40, § 36A, whenever a person in police custody commits suicide or dies, the OIC must write a report and send it to the medical examiner within 7 days.

If a person in lockup threatens or attempts suicide, the OIC must describe the event in CJIS within 24 hours. The OIC must also provide a written report to any lockup the subject is transferred to. This ensures the next agency or court is aware of the subject's history.

Requirements for police lockups. 40, § 36B mandates that one cell contain an electronic audio system so that the desk officer can *hear* what is going on inside; and that an officer check each cell at reasonable intervals (recommend no longer than 30 minutes).

Police must receive training in suicide prevention. 40, § 36C. Detainees present a high risk of suicide. Take *any* verbal threats and physical gestures seriously. *Richardson v. Dailey*, 424 Mass. 258 (1997).

Prevent sexual abuse

Detainees must be protected from sexual abuse. This is mandated by a federal law known as the Prison Rape Elimination Act (PREA), 42 U.S.C. Ch. 147, § 15601. Basically, all police agencies must screen detainees to determine whether they are vulnerable to sexual abuse and take steps to protect them. Detainees must have multiple ways to report abuse, including to an entity outside the police agency. A full investigation is required in response to any allegation against staff or other detainees. This includes collecting physical evidence and providing victims with proper medical and mental health treatment. For detailed reporting, investigating, and training guidelines, go to prearesourcecenter.org.

MENTAL HEALTH TREATMENT OPTIONS

Involuntary transfer of prisoner to secure treatment. Under 123, § 18(a), the OIC may arrange for psychiatric hospitalization for a prisoner who is not eligible for bail or unlikely to be released. The OIC should notify a hospital that receives emergency psychiatric patients. The OIC can arrange for a clinician to see the prisoner at the lockup or transport the prisoner to the hospital. The clinician reports his or her recommendation to the judge (the on-call judge if court is closed). The judge may commit the prisoner to a state hospital until the next court day. The police are responsible for transporting the prisoner to the hospital and to court.

Voluntary release of prisoner for treatment. Under 123, § 18(b), the OIC may decide to release a prisoner who agrees to obtain voluntary mental health treatment (perhaps with support from his or her family, friends, or caseworker). This is perfect for the prisoner accused of a minor crime who poses little safety risk and needs treatment. The decision to release belongs solely to the OIC. At the same time, the OIC should inform the bail commissioner and, if necessary, adjust the arraignment date to accommodate treatment. The OIC may transport a prisoner to a treatment facility or arrange for a family member or caseworker to take over.

6 HOUR RULE

The police have 6 hours from the time of arrest to interview a defendant.[1] The clock runs regardless of the topics discussed. *Comm. v. Obershaw*, 435 Mass. 794 (2002).

6 exceptions to this rule: (1) the arrestee needs medical attention; (2) the arrestee is incapacitated from drugs or alcohol; (3) a police emergency delays the interview; (4) police request consent to search; (5) the arrestee signs a written waiver of prompt arraignment; and (6) the arrest occurs outside of Massachusetts. *Comm. v. Fortunato*, 466 Mass. 500 (2013).

24 HOUR PROBABLE CAUSE HEARING

Unless released from lockup, an arrestee must be afforded a probable cause determination by a magistrate within 24 hours of his warrantless arrest. *Jenkins v. Chief Justice of the District Court*, 416 Mass. 221 (1993).[2] This rule was established because the SJC felt that arrestees should have their cases reviewed promptly, since prolonged detention might affect their job and family relationships.

Hearing procedures. The magistrate may simply review the arresting officer's incident report, which must include sufficient facts for probable cause. The review may occur over the telephone, and the arrestee is not entitled to be present or to receive the assistance of counsel. The probable cause determination is not subject to review at arraignment.

The 24 hour limit is not absolute, but the police bear the burden of demonstrating that an extraordinary circumstance caused the delay, such as a major snowstorm or the defendant's hospitalization. For violations of this rule, dismissal is not automatic, but it may be appropriate in cases of misconduct. *Comm. v. Viverito*, 422 Mass. 228 (1996).

ADMISSION TO BAIL

No bail until booking procedures completed. If a defendant refuses to answer booking questions, the police may properly place him in a cell without a phone call or bail hearing until he is ready to cooperate. *Comm. v. Maylott*, 43 Mass. App. Ct. 516 (1997).

Warrant Management System (WMS) must be checked before release. No person may be released from custody until WMS has been reviewed.

SPECIAL BOOKING ISSUES

OUI ARRESTEES

Advise defendant of right to independent examination. Under 263, § 5A, a police officer must inform a person under arrest for OUI alcohol of his "right, . . . at his expense, to be examined immediately by a physician selected by him." Failure to advise a defendant will often result in the case being dismissed.

---

1 The more detailed discussion of the 6 hour rule appears in *Chapter 22*, including a waiver form.
2 The Massachusetts rule is more stringent than the 48 hour limit established by the Supreme Court in *Gerstein v. Pugh*, 420 U.S. 103 (1975).

Beyond notification, police have no obligation to assist the defendant in obtaining an exam. *Comm. v. Rosewarne*, 410 Mass. 53 (1991) (police justified in refusing to transport defendant to a hospital even though he had arranged over the telephone for a blood test there).

Notify the bail commissioner. A defendant who wishes to exercise his § 5A rights must be given a prompt hearing. The bail commissioner may grant bail or decide that the defendant is too intoxicated to release. *Comm. v. King*, 429 Mass. 169 (1999).

JUVENILES

Secure detention: Delinquents 14, 15, 16, & 17 years old

Notification requirements. Under 119, § 67, when booking a juvenile charged with a crime, police must immediately notify a parent or legal guardian.

Police must typically release the juvenile and may only hold him if:

- **The child is at least 14 and the OIC agrees with the arresting officer that he be held;** or

- **The arrest warrant explicitly orders that the youth be detained.**

In either case, police must always notify the bail commissioner.

Key detention restrictions. Proper procedures for detaining juvenile criminals appear in state and federal law. 42 U.S.C. 5601. 119, § 67.

- **No juvenile may be detained in an adult lockup at *any* time.**

- **Juveniles under 14: Not eligible for secure detention.** Officers must hold the child in non-secure custody (see discussion below).

- **Juveniles 14 and over: Eligible for secure detention for 6 hours.** The 6 hour period begins when the juvenile is confined in a locked room or cell, or is cuffed to a stationary object. Police must follow these other guidelines too:

  - *Department of Youth Services (DYS) approved.* Juvenile cells must receive the written approval of DYS.

  - *Separate from adults.* The juvenile must be "sight and sound separate" from adult prisoners. Sound separation means that no conversation is possible.

  - *Documented cell checks.* Similar to adult prisoners, juvenile detainees must be properly monitored to prevent suicide or injury. At least check every 30 minutes.

  - *Juvenile Lockup Dockets.* The Executive Office of Public Safety and Security (EOPSS) requires that police departments maintain a Juvenile Lockup Docket to record instances of secure detention. These records are inspected by EOPSS.

  - *Transfer rules.* Before the 6 hour period ends, the juvenile must be released to a parent/guardian; transported to court; or referred to the Overnight Arrest Program.

Non-secure detention: Delinquents age 12 and 13

Five requirements. Under 42 U.S.C. 5601, there are five requirements for non-secure custody:

- **Unlocked area.** The juvenile must be held in an unlocked, multi-purpose area, such as an office. If a noncompliant juvenile leaves the area, EOPSS guidelines state that "the juvenile can be brought back into the station and placed in a locked area . . . The apprehension order should relate to being unwilling to follow the instructions of an officer, not to being a runaway." Be sure to record the reasons for this action.

- **No residential area.** The space must not be designed for residential use (e.g., no bunks or toilets).

- **No handcuffing to any stationary object.** At no time is the juvenile to be handcuffed to any stationary object. If necessary, some departments may leave a delinquent in cuffs.

- **Hold long enough to process and transfer.** The juvenile should be held long enough to complete identification and processing, then be released to a parent/guardian; or transferred to an alternative juvenile facility or court.

- **Continuous visual supervision.** The juvenile must be under continuous visual supervision until released from the station.

No transport in wagon. 119, § 34 forbids bringing any child to court in a police wagon.

No detention: All CRA children under age 18

Best strategy for Children Requiring Assistance (CRA). For a warrant of protective custody, the police must bring the child to the juvenile court before 4:30 p.m. For a runaway, officers must:

- **Home or station.** Immediately bring the CRA child home or to the station and attempt to re-unite him with his legal custodian or other responsible adult. While at the station, any CRA child should be <u>uncuffed</u> — unlike delinquent children who may be in handcuffs. The other requirements of non-secure detention apply. Do *not* fingerprint or photograph CRA children, or submit their information to CJIS.

- **Shelter.** If the child cannot be reunited with his legal custodian or other responsible person, arrange to have him transported to a shelter.[3] Call 211 for placement help 24 hours a day.

FOREIGN NATIONALS & DIPLOMATS

Definition. A foreign national is *anyone* who is not a United States citizen. This includes any foreign visitors, whether they are here legally or illegally. It also includes anyone with a "green card" (a permanent resident from another country who is not a citizen yet).

Notify consulate. The Vienna Convention is a treaty between nations. Article 36 states that if a foreign national is arrested,[4] authorities shall inform the subject of his right to have

---

3 Bringing a CRA child to the police station is only prohibited *after* an officer in the field decides to place the child with a shelter. See 119, § 39H(ii).
4 Notification is not required during the typical brief detention, such as a *Terry* stop.

his consulate notified. The notification process should not delay the suspect's booking or interrogation. This procedure applies to all Massachusetts police officers. *Comm. v. Gautreaux*, 458 Mass. 741 (2011).

Important information & contacts. Some countries insist on mandatory notification; others leave it up to the foreign suspect to decide. To find out whether the particular country requires mandatory notification, or to obtain a translation of the rights notification form, visit the U.S. Department of State website at travel.state.gov/content/travel/en/consularnotification/QuarantinedForeignNationals/countries-and-jurisdictions-with-mandatory-notifications.html. The phone number for the State Department is 202-647-4000.

Dealing with diplomats.[5] When officers encounter a foreign national they reasonably suspect is committing a crime, they need to determine whether the suspect has diplomatic immunity. The suspect should have diplomatic documents from our State Department. Police can call the State Department's Command Center at 571-345-3146 to verify information.

Officers should:

- Detain the diplomat until they verify his or her status. They are not permitted to arrest or charge the individual, no matter how serious the crime.

- *Not* handcuff the diplomat, unless he or she poses an immediate safety threat.

- *Not* search or frisk the diplomat's person, vehicle, or personal belongings unless it is necessary for officer safety.

- Document exactly what happened. This protects officers. Records of police encounters are reviewed by the State Department if questions ever arise about the incident.

- Stop and cite diplomats for traffic violations. This is not considered a detention or arrest. However, a diplomat may not be compelled to pay the citation.

FEDERAL IMMIGRATION DETAINERS

State and local police officers do not have the authority to detain suspects based solely on a federal civil immigration detainer. *Lunn v. Comm.*, 477 Mass. 517 (2017): Sreynuon Lunn was arraigned in Boston Municipal Court for unarmed robbery. The day before the arraignment, the Department of Homeland Security issued a civil immigration detainer against him. The unarmed robbery charge was dismissed, but at the request of a federal immigration officer, Massachusetts court officers continued to hold Lunn in his cell because of the detainer. Several hours later, federal officials arrived at the courthouse and took Lunn into custody.

Lunn's detention qualified as an arrest. There is currently no federal or state statute that gives state officers the authority to make a civil immigration arrest. State officers may only keep an individual in custody if there is: (1) a judicial warrant (not an administrative detainer); or (2) probable cause of an arrestable state or federal crime.

---

5 This section is derived from a summary by Henry W. McGowen, Office of Chief Counsel, Federal Law Enforcement Training Centers (FLETC).

Part IV

SEARCHES

Chapters 11 – 20

The Constitutional Definition of a Search

FUNDAMENTAL PRINCIPLES

Authority to search is regulated by the Fourth Amendment to the United States Constitution and Article 14 of the Massachusetts Declaration of Rights. These constitutional provisions fundamentally insist that law enforcement base their searches on probable cause and perform them in a reasonable manner. Probable cause ensures that officers invade the privacy of a citizen only when they have adequate justification.

In addition to the probable cause mandate, the process of obtaining a warrant protects citizens. For this reason, a search conducted without a warrant is assumed to be unreasonable unless it falls within one of the limited exceptions to the warrant requirement. *Comm. v. Anderson,* 406 Mass. 343 (1989) (burden of proof always on the government to show that a warrantless search was reasonable).

Foundation for constitutional regulation. Searches are *not* subject to constitutional regulation unless three conditions are met:

- **State action.** The search must be undertaken by a state actor, either a law enforcement official or an agent of the government.

- **Reasonable expectation of privacy.** The search must intrude on the suspect's reasonable expectation of privacy. *Katz v. U.S.,* 389 U.S. 347 (1967).

- **Standing.** The person who is implicated by the search must have a legal right to challenge the police conduct that produced the evidence against him. *Comm. v. Amendola,* 406 Mass. 592 (1990).

STATE ACTION

In order for a search to be constitutionally regulated, it must be carried out by the government. *Burdeau v. McDowell,* 256 U.S. 465 (1921) ("origin and history [of the Constitution] clearly shows that it was intended to be a limitation [only] upon governmental agencies").

LAW ENFORCEMENT PERSONNEL

Obviously, state action exists when law enforcement officers search and seize evidence in their official capacity. The vast majority of cases fall within this category.

AGENTS

A more difficult question involves search activity undertaken by individuals who are not sworn officers. Sometimes their actions are regulated by the constitution when they are connected to law enforcement. *U.S. v. Keith*, 2013 WL 5918524 (U.S. District Court) (no state action when America Online monitored email traffic for child pornography, but state action began when the National Center for Missing & Exploited Children examined the files, since it works in partnership with the government to detect and prosecute pornographers).

PRIVATE CITIZENS

Instigation, direction, or encouragement of police. Private individuals do not become "police agents" just because they decide to conduct a search and turn over the evidence to law enforcement. Private parties become agents only when they conduct a search at the direction, encouragement, or instigation of officers. In *Comm. v. Brandwein*, 435 Mass. 623 (2002), a psychiatric nurse, on her own initiative, disclosed to the police that her patient told her that he robbed a bank. She also turned over a gun he had given her. Since the police did not instigate the nurse's conduct, the evidence was admissible.[1]

While police may not arrange private searches, they are under no obligation to discourage them. *Comm. v. Richmond*, 379 Mass. 557 (1980) focused on a letter addressed to the defendant's former girlfriend (then 16 years old) at her parents' residence. The girl's mother called the local police chief to ask if she could open the letter. The chief, who knew that the defendant was a prime murder suspect, told the mother that she could open the letter if *she decided* that it was in her daughter's best interest. The letter contained highly incriminating statements, and the mother delivered it to the chief.

The police may take advantage of a citizen's desire to help them, so long as they do not direct the effort. This is true even if authorities later reward the person for obtaining evidence. In *Comm. v. Rancourt*, 399 Mass. 269 (1987), an inmate convinced the defendant to write about his involvement in a rape. The written confession was featured at the defendant's trial. The inmate was later rewarded with a reduced sentence. The SJC approved, saying that "an unencouraged hope to curry favor" does not turn one into a government agent.

MEDICAL PERSONNEL

In the process of providing routine treatment or tests, medical personnel may discover evidence. These clinicians are not considered police agents if their procedures were undertaken for *treatment* and not to benefit police. *Comm. v. Storella*, 6 Mass. App. Ct. 310 (1978) (surgeon removed a bullet from the defendant and turned it over to police; he was not acting as their agent because it was medically necessary). *Comm. v. Sargent*, 24 Mass. App. Ct. 657 (1987) (hospital blood test proved defendant's intoxication at his OUI trial; the motivation for the test was medical necessity, not the discovery of evidence).

---

1 Interestingly, the nurse engaged in professional misconduct by violating psychotherapist–patient privilege when she notified police.

PRIVATE SECURITY OFFICERS

Private security typically unregulated by constitution. *Comm. v. Leone*, 386 Mass. 329 (1982): A General Electric security guard stopped the defendant at the plant gate to determine whether his cargo was authorized to leave. The guard searched a bag in the truck and found a gun, which had been stolen from a police officer! Charged with unlawful possession, the defendant argued that the guard, who was a "special police officer" in Lynn, conducted an unlawful search. The SJC disagreed. While privately employed officers must comply with the Fourth Amendment when performing outside investigations, they are less restricted when performing private duties for the protection of their employer's property, which was the case in *Leone*.

Still, a police intrusion must comply with the Constitution if based on information from private security. *Comm. v. Bair,* 2012 WL 2888837 (Appeals Court) (a student allowed campus security to enter his room; his permission to them did not automatically extend to police officers, who were called to the scene when security found drugs; the officers wisely obtained separate consent to enter the student's room).

GOVERNMENT EMPLOYEES

GOVERNMENT EMPLOYEE NOT INVOLVED IN ENFORCEMENT

A person conducting a search is not automatically a "state actor" just because he is employed by the government. State action was meant to apply to government employees whose duties involve enforcing the law or administering a local code, where a violation might subject the offender to punishment. *Comm. v. Cote*, 15 Mass. App. Ct. 229 (1983) (meter reader for a municipal electric department was not a government agent; he had no law enforcement function whatsoever).

In cases where a municipal worker uncovers evidence, officers should limit themselves to examining evidence already discovered. Officers should not search further without obtaining a warrant.

PUBLIC SCHOOL ADMINISTRATORS

Public school administrators must follow some constitutional guidelines. There is no warrant requirement, but school officials must have reasonable suspicion in order to search. And their method must be appropriate given the objectives of the search (what are they looking for?), the nature of the offense (gun on campus or smoking in the boys' room?), and the student's age and sex (17 year old football player or 8 year old special needs child?). *New Jersey v. T.L.O.*, 469 U.S. 325 (1985).[2]

---

2 The most comprehensive discussion of school search and seizure appears in *LED's Juvenile Law, Chapters 18 and 19.* Also, the Constitution does not regulate the searching activities of private school officials.

REASONABLE EXPECTATION OF PRIVACY
PRINCIPLE DEFINED

Private areas protected. The Fourth Amendment and Article 14 are clear about what is protected from unreasonable police intrusion:

A citizen's body, home, and possessions.[3]

These areas merit constitutional protection because they are the zones where citizens have a "reasonable expectation of privacy." Law enforcement officers may not search for and seize evidence in these areas unless they have legal justification.

There are four constitutional justifications to enter private areas:

1. *Search warrant*
2. *Consent*
3. *Exigent circumstances*
4. *Another exception to the warrant requirement*

No constitutional justification needed to enter non-private areas. Should officers perform a search outside a protected zone, they need no advance justification.

Street mindset. So how does the officer on the street, called upon to make split second decisions, decide whether or not she is infringing on the suspect's reasonable expectation of privacy? She should ask:

"Am I entering an area or doing something that a member of the public might reasonably do?"

*   **If the answer is "yes," the suspect has no right to expect that an officer will not immediately engage in the conduct.** After all, it is something members of the public do.

*   **On the other hand, a "no" response puts the officer on notice that she will need constitutional permission to go beyond where citizens normally go.** That permission must involve a warrant, consent, exigent circumstances, or some other recognized exception to the warrant requirement.

This commonsense understanding helps frame the rest of this chapter, which discusses a reasonable expectation of privacy in relation to persons, houses, and possessions.

The defendant must show that, at the time of the police intrusion, he had: (1) a subjective expectation of privacy in the place searched or the item seized, that (2) society accepts as reasonable. *U.S. v. Karo*, 468 U.S. 805 (1991). *Comm. v. Ortega*, 59 Mass. App. Ct. 217 (2003).

Most defendants have a subjective desire for privacy in the area searched (although this might not be true if the facts show the defendant routinely allowed unmonitored access).

---

3 The exact language of the Fourth Amendment is: "The right of the people to be secure in their persons, houses, papers, and effects, against unreasonable searches and seizures, shall not be violated . . ." Article 14, its Massachusetts counterpart, offers nearly identical coverage.

The second part of the test — whether their expectation of privacy was *objectively reasonable* — is typically the main issue.

PERSONS

CITIZENS IN THE COMMUNITY

Citizens always have a reasonable expectation of privacy in their body. This means officers must have probable cause or consent to search a person for evidence. Officers need reasonable suspicion to frisk for their own protection.

Clothing and footwear depend on the situation.

- **Footwear.** The physical characteristics of a person's shoes, like one's face, are constantly exposed to the public. Footprints on the ground are visible for all to see. People display the soles of their shoes when they cross their legs, climb stairs, or put their feet up on furniture. Thus, viewing a person's shoes does not not constitute a search. *Comm. v. Cherry*, 2019 WL 3824236 (Appeals Court) (officer believed the suspect's shoes matched footprints at the victim's house; it was not a search when officer asked the suspect to hold his foot up for an additional inspection; at that point, the officer decided the shoeprints matched, so he had probable cause to seize the shoes as evidence).

- **Clothing removed by hospital for treatment vs. safekeeping.** *Comm. v. Fortuna*, 80 Mass. App. Ct. 45 (2011): A Boston detective responded to the hospital to interview Patrick Fortuna, who said he had been shot in the leg while walking home. He did not know how it happened because the shooter was far away. At this point, hospital staff had already cut off Fortuna's clothing to render aid. The detective took the clothing. When the detective saw gunshot residue on these items, he knew the shooter had been close or the wound self-inflicted. There was no search because Fortuna had *no expectation of privacy* in clothing that had been ripped off him as he received medical attention.

  Compare *Comm. v. Williams*, 76 Mass. App. Ct. 489 (2010): Williams' clothes were not yanked from his body during treatment. His clothes were taken and stored for safekeeping by hospital staff in preparation for treatment. Williams, unlike Fortuna, retained an expectation of privacy in his belongings, which would be returned to him before his discharge. This meant police had to have a legal basis to seize his clothes as evidence: either a warrant, consent, or exigent circumstances.

CITIZENS IN AREAS OF HEIGHTENED SECURITY

Heightened security permitted in areas where citizens should expect reduced privacy. Classic examples include metal detectors at airports, schools and government buildings, and border searches by federal officials. *Comm. v. Rodriguez*, 430 Mass. 577 (2000).

Attempt to avoid an administrative search that has begun provides reasonable suspicion to detain and frisk. Comm. v. Roland R., 448 Mass. 278 (2007): Roland put his bag through the x-ray machine on his way into court. When told his bag was going to be checked manually, he said he did not want anyone to search it. Roland ran. The officer put out an alert on his radio.

Other officers began to chase Roland, not knowing the reason. Roland was handcuffed. He admitted to running "because of what's in the bag" (19 packets of marijuana).

The SJC endorsed Roland's capture because he had effectively consented to an administrative search once he stepped into the metal detector. Roland was not entitled to change his mind. Requiring someone to complete security screening is entirely reasonable. The alternative — allowing people to walk away once they learn their bags will be searched — would jeopardize safety by encouraging "a deadly waiting game [where] people are free to make multiple attempts to smuggle weapons or contraband."

The fact that the pursuing officers did not know the circumstances was irrelevant, since the collective knowledge doctrine treats "the knowledge of each officer . . . as the common knowledge of all officers."[4] Finally, the SJC mentioned that this case would have been different if Roland had left "*before* placing his bag on the table near the x-ray device and stepping through the metal detector."

When allowed anywhere on the property, administrative searches must be regulated by a policy, not just permitted by a sign. *Comm. v. Garcia*, 90 Mass. App. Ct. 753 (2016): An officer at the Plymouth County Correctional Facility saw two vehicles, a BMW and a Volvo, enter the visitor's lot. It was after visiting hours, but the men went inside to post bail for a person being held there. The officer walked around each of the vehicles and conducted a visual inspection. He saw a prescription pill bottle on the driver's side of the BMW. He shined his flashlight inside and saw a small quantity of white pills and a small plastic bag containing blue pills within the bottle.

The officer went into the facility and found the driver, Jason Garcia-German. He instructed him to unlock the vehicle and allow an inspection of its interior. Garcia-German complied. The officer opened the prescription pill bottle and found Oxycodone.

• **Search not justified by probable cause.** The officer's observation of the pills did not provide probable cause to search the vehicle without a warrant. The illegal character of the pills was not apparent until he gained access to the vehicle and examined them.

• **Administrative search invalid too.** At the entrance to the parking lot, a sign advised: "Warning: all vehicles beyond this point are subject to search." However, there was no written policy regulating the conduct of these searches. It was left to officer discretion. Without a written policy (or alternatively, a procedure in which *every* vehicle was searched as it entered the facility), merely posting a sign was inadequate to justify the warrantless search of cars selected by officers patrolling the lot.

PRISONERS & PROBATIONERS

Convicted citizens have a reduced expectation of privacy. *Comm. v. LaFrance*, 402 Mass. 789 (1988) holds:

• **A person on probation may be searched by a probation officer (or a police officer assisting the probation officer) on the basis of a reasonable suspicion.**

---

4 See discussion of the collective knowledge doctrine in *Chapter 2*.

- **If the search will take place inside the probationer's home, then a search warrant is necessary based on reasonable suspicion,** *unless* an exception to the warrant requirement applies (e.g., exigent circumstances).[5] This rule does not affect the traditional authority of probation officers to visit and meet with probationers on a random or scheduled basis at their homes. *LaFrance* explained that each case depends on the conditions of probation, and the extent to which persons other than the probationer will have their privacy invaded. *LaFrance* warned against the police using the probation office as "a subterfuge to conduct a search of a probationer on less than probable cause."

- **Probationer maintains privacy in his cell phone.** *U.S. v. Lara,* 815 F.3d 605 (2016): During a probation search at Paulo Lara's house, police searched his cell phone and discovered texts concerning a gun sale. Given the amount of data contained on his cell phone, Lara had a privacy interest in it despite his probation status. Consequently, probation officers should get consent or obtain a warrant based on reasonable suspicion before examining a cell phone.

- **Parole may conduct warrantless search of home.** Parole is more stringent than probation. Therefore, a parolee's expectation of privacy is lower. As a result, parole officers can always search a parolee's home — without a warrant — if they have reasonable suspicion that there is evidence of a parole violation. *Comm. v. Moore,* 473 Mass. 481 (2016).

Pre-trial detainee's possessions. *Comm. v. Silva,* 471 Mass. 610 (2015): Robert Silva was being held at the Plymouth County Correctional Facility (PCCF) when he became a murder suspect. A trooper wanted to test his sneakers for the victim's DNA. The trooper did not need a warrant to seize Silva's sneakers. He had no expectation of privacy. Although PCCF policy allowed inmates to keep their sneakers, retention was a privilege that could be withdrawn at any time. Silva's signature on the property receipt acknowledged this policy.

DNA database. *Landry v. Attorney General,* 429 Mass. 336 (1999) approved taking DNA samples from every felon upon conviction. See 22E, § 3.

HOMES

THE CURTILAGE

The greatest constitutional protection extends to a home[6] — historically referred to as "the curtilage." Knowing the extent of the curtilage is important for police officers because entry requires a warrant, consent, or exigent circumstances.

Hotel or motel room considered a dwelling.

- **Even though it is only temporary living quarters, hotel or motel guests are entitled to expect privacy in their rooms.** *Comm. v. Hamilton,* 24 Mass. App. Ct. 290 (1987).

---

5 Under the Fourth Amendment, a warrantless search of a probationer's home is permitted based on reasonable suspicion. *U.S. v. Knights,* 534 U.S. 112 (2001).
6 In 1763, William Pitt's remarks in the House of Commons expressed this core principle of our constitutional system: "The poorest man may in his cottage bid defiance to all the forces of the Crown. It may be frail, its roof may shake; the wind may blow through it; the storms may enter, the rain may enter, but the King of England cannot enter; all his forces dare not cross the threshold of the ruined tenement."

- **However, if they are properly evicted, guests lose their right to privacy.** *Comm. v. Molina*, 459 Mass. 819 (2011): Mark Molina reserved a hotel room for three nights. He prepaid and signed a registration card that stated that the hotel could evict a guest for failing to comply with hotel rules, or state or federal law.

  Hotel security told a group that Molina was only allowed to have three guests and no alcohol could be brought in. The visitors became verbally abusive. The manager warned Molina that if he had one more incident, he would be ejected. The next day, guests complained about the odor of marijuana outside Molina's room. After knocking and receiving no response, the manager opened the door with a key. No one was present. He observed a scale and large quantity of marijuana. Security contacted Boston Police. Detectives searched the room and found more marijuana, cocaine, $10,860, and a gun. Molina was arrested upon his return.

  A guest loses his expectation of privacy once his rental period is terminated. Although Molina prepaid, the hotel had legitimate grounds to evict him based on his disruptive visitors and the marijuana in his room.

  Eviction by innkeepers does *not* require advance notice to the guest. By signing the registration card, Molina was notified of the hotel's policies. Also, the manager had warned him that if there was one more complaint, he would be "gone."

College dorm considered a dwelling. *Comm. v. Neilson*, 423 Mass. 75 (1996) held that a dorm room is the equivalent of an apartment or hotel room. It is a student's dwelling that police can only breach with a search warrant, consent, or exigent circumstances.

Oftentimes, backyard considered within the curtilage. *Comm. v. Hurd*, 51 Mass. App. Ct. 12 (2001) (fenced-in backyard was not one that an uninvited visitor would enter without permission).

A side yard of a multi-family home may be in the curtilage. *Comm. v. Leslie*, 477 Mass. 48 (2017): Boston detectives observed four men walking toward a residence that was a known gang location. The property was a three-family home, fenced in on the front and left side. The porch was blocked by a large recycling bin that obstructed its view from the street. The detectives watched the four men, including Bobby Leslie, enter the gate. They met a fifth man, Lacy Price, on the front porch.

Five minutes later, Bobby Leslie walked off a front porch, looked around "in a surveillance-conscious manner," then walked toward the side porch area. The detectives' view was obstructed by the recycling bin, but they saw Leslie crouch down under the porch. Police saw Leslie simulate firing a gun in the air with his hand.

Suspecting that a firearm was hidden under the porch, seven officers walked through the front gate. One detective walked over to the side of the yard and saw a sawed-off shotgun on the ground under the porch.

In ruling that the side yard was within the curtilage, the SJC noted that the front yard was enclosed with a chain link fence, and the left side was enclosed with a large wooden fence and a recycling bin that obstructed the public's view. The porch and side yard were intimately connected to Lacy Price's home.

While officers were entitled to open the front gate and walk onto the porch to speak to Price and his guests, a detective entered a private area when he went into the side yard. He did so without a warrant, consent, or exigent circumstances. The shotgun had to be suppressed.

Mailbox considered part of curtilage. *Comm. v. Garcia,* 34 Mass. App. Ct. 645 (1993) involved officers who arrested drug dealer Garcia in his front hallway. He had a set of keys and cash in his pocket. An officer used Garcia's keys to open the only locked mailbox, finding heroin and cocaine inside. Yet, people expect privacy in their mailbox, especially when it is locked. The officer should have gotten consent from Garcia or a search warrant before unlocking the box.

OPEN FIELDS

"Open fields" is the constitutional term that refers to any area beyond the curtilage. An open field may actually be a field but, more often, it describes a subtle distinction about what area is outside the constitutionally protected home. Once an area is classified as an open field, it may be entered and searched without probable cause or a warrant. *Oliver v. U.S.,* 466 U.S. 170 (1984).

Entranceways. *Comm. v. Pietrass,* 392 Mass. 892 (1984) had to decide whether a screened-in porch at the front of a house was part of the curtilage, since police had entered it without a warrant and made important observations there. The court stated that this porch was one that a visitor would naturally expect to pass through to be able to gain access to the front door. Thus, the porch was not part of the curtilage, and an officer did not engage in an unreasonable search when he saw evidence from this open field area.

The *Pietrass* case would have been decided differently if the porch had been, for example, enclosed in glass and equipped with the real front door of the house rather than a swinging screen door. The key issue was where a visitor would be expected to knock, since that would signal the beginning of the curtilage.

Common areas of a building. Courts have repeatedly stated: "[A]n individual can have only a very limited expectation of privacy with respect to an area used routinely by others." *Sullivan v. District Ct. of Hampshire,* 384 Mass. 736 (1981). That is why common areas of an apartment building are not part of the curtilage.

- *Comm. v. Montanez,* 410 Mass. 290 (1991): The defendant had no privacy expectation in the space above the ceiling over the common hallway outside his apartment. Officers who looked there and found cocaine were not conducting a search regulated by the Constitution.

- *Comm. v. Dora,* 57 Mass. App. Ct. 141 (2003): The case began when John Dora broke into the victim's apartment and sexually assaulted her. He jumped out of a window, leaving his keys behind. The victim gave the keys to police.

  Luckily, a neighbor had seen Dora jump. She saw him again the next morning, apparently searching for something on the lawn. Following her notification, police stopped Dora nearby. He told officers that he had lost his keys several weeks earlier.

  They went to Dora's apartment building. Using the keys found in the victim's bedroom, the police were able to open the door in the main lobby. They took the elevator up to the Dora's fourth-floor apartment. Another key unlocked his door. The police did not open his door after testing the key. Officers simply arrested John Dora in the hall.

- *Warrantless entry into locked common area.* Dora argued that officers needed a warrant to simply enter his locked hallway. However, the fact that the common areas of the building were locked and the general public was excluded did not create an expectation of privacy, since the area was still accessible to 120 tenants and their guests.

- *Fact that police arguably commit a trespass is not significant.* The Appeals Court stated: "While a technical trespass by police officers theoretically may have civil implications, how they gain access to the common hallways of a multi-unit apartment building is of no constitutional consequence."

- Compare the *Dora* case with *Comm. v. Hall*, 366 Mass. 790 (1975): The building at issue contained only three apartments. An unlocked exterior door opened to a vestibule containing two locked doors. Ownership of the building and a buzzer mechanism gave the defendant exclusive control of the interior hallway and stairs. The police could not enter this obviously private area without a warrant, consent, or exigent circumstances.

- *Comm. v. Hanson*, 79 Mass. App. Ct. 233 (2011): Officer Giardini was engaged in surveillance of a multi-family dwelling in Brockton. The officer witnessed Christopher Hanson emerge from the house and engage in three hand-to-hand drug transactions. After the last one, Hanson walked down the rear stairs, pulled back the home's vinyl siding, and shoved a bag behind it. The officer waited, then went over to the siding and retrieved the bag with 47 packets of cocaine. It is hard for a citizen to claim privacy in the exterior of a multi-unit building. As a result, the police did not need a search warrant when they took Hanson's cocaine from that location.

Private driveway and nearby area. A driveway or walkway to a house is not within the curtilage if a visitor would naturally use it to reach the front or back door. *Comm. v. Butterfield*, 44 Mass. App. Ct. 926 (1998).

- *Comm. v. Juvenile (No. 2)*, 411 Mass. 157 (1991): Police officers investigating a motor vehicle homicide properly made a warrantless inspection of the exterior of an automobile parked in the suspect's private driveway. The police inspection revealed hair and fiber in the grill and indentations on the hood consistent with a hit-and-run that claimed the life of a young girl. The juvenile's car was seized as evidence.

  Here, the automobile was parked in a private driveway that was clearly visible from the public street. The driveway was the normal route to the front door. There was a garage at the end of the driveway, but the defendant did not use it.[7]

- Compare *Collins v. Virginia*, 138 S.Ct. 1663 (2018): An officer investigating a stolen motorcycle drove to the defendant's house and saw what appeared to be a motorcycle under a tarp at the top of the driveway. The top section of the driveway was enclosed on two sides by a brick wall about the height of a car and on the third side by the house. To reach the front door of the house, a visitor would have to turn off the driveway before reaching

---

7 In *Comm. v. Simmons*, 392 Mass. 45 (1984), the SJC declared: "In the course of urban life, we have come to expect various members of the public to enter upon [our] driveway . . . If one has a reasonable expectation that various members of society may enter the property in their personal or business pursuits, he should find it equally likely that the police will do so."

the enclosure where the motorcycle was parked. The officer removed the tarp, confirmed that the motorcycle was stolen by running the license plate and VIN, took a photograph, replaced the tarp, and returned to his cruiser. When the defendant came home, the officer arrested him. The court held that the top section of the defendant's driveway was within his curtilage. The initial search required a warrant.

Fields and woods. The concept of open fields actually applies to fields and forests! Any unoccupied or undeveloped area outside of the curtilage qualifies. In *Oliver v. U.S.*, 466 U.S. 170 (1984), Kentucky state troopers bypassed a fence and "no trespassing" signs, walked deeply into the defendant's backyard, and recovered a large crop of marijuana.

The Supreme Court allowed this drug seizure, saying that police properly entered without a warrant despite the fact that they could not see the contraband from the road and had to trespass in order to reach it. The scope of Fourth Amendment protection is not the same as the law governing property rights. Every trespass is not necessarily a constitutional search; it depends on whether the police entry encroached on the curtilage.

POLICE ACTIVITIES AT THE EDGE OF THE CURTILAGE

Overhearing conversations

Officers may overhear private conversations from an area where the suspect has no reasonable expectation of privacy. Basically, a person has no expectation of privacy in conversations which can be overheard by the unaided ear from a common hallway or adjacent apartment. After all, people expect that they will be overheard by neighbors unless they take steps to protect their privacy. *Comm. v. Collins*, 11 Mass. App. Ct. 126 (1981) (police wisely positioned themselves in an adjacent motel room and overheard the defendant discuss his crime).

When officers intrude on a suspect's privacy, they need a warrant or some other legal justification. Consider *Comm. v. Panetti*, 406 Mass. 230 (1990): The Lenox police chief conducted a drug investigation by getting permission from the building owner to place himself in a crawl space, reserved for electrical wires and pipes, that ran underneath the defendant's apartment. From this position, the chief was able to overhear incriminating conversations, which he used to get a search warrant. This activity was impermissible. Overhearing conversations from a position where neither a neighbor nor member of the public would be expected infringed on this suspect's privacy. It was irrelevant that the officer received permission from the building owner. In this situation, a search warrant was necessary in order to eavesdrop from the basement crawl space.

Knocking at door

Police may knock at an entrance so long as they do not insist that an occupant open the door. *Comm. v. Villar*, 40 Mass. App. Ct. 742 (1996): Boston police arrested a drug dealer who left an apartment complex in the rain. They entered the common area and followed his wet footprints to a particular unit. A detective noticed a phone number on the dealer's beeper and instructed dispatch to call it. A telephone rang in the apartment. The detective placed the arrested dealer in front of the peephole and knocked. He did not say anything. Villar opened the door, holding a container of cocaine. Officers arrested Villar and secured the apartment. They obtained a search warrant and found more cocaine. Here, because the police knocked and said nothing, they did not force Villar to open his door. He voluntarily did, which enabled police to see his cocaine.

If police do identify themselves, their "knock and talk" should only occur during normal visiting hours. Otherwise the approach becomes coercive. A knock and talk is typically limited to asking occupants questions. In *U.S. v. Lundin*, 817 F.3d 1151 (2016), officers could not justify their entry and seizure of handguns. Their visit occurred at 4:00 a.m. Unexpected visitors normally knock during the day or early evening. Since the officers had come to arrest Lundin for kidnapping, they needed a warrant or exigent circumstances *before* they knocked at 4:00 a.m.

Shining flashlight in window

Officer standing at a front door may shine his flashlight in the window. *Comm. v. Leblanc*, 2014 WL 2861767 (Appeals Court): Police arrived at Elaine Leblanc's house to investigate a drunk driving incident. When they knocked, they heard a female's voice inside, but no one answered. Through a large window, they could see Leblanc sitting at a table.

One officer knocked on the window and shined his flashlight inside. Leblanc looked over at the officer, who asked her to come to the door. The officer observed that Leblanc was unsteady and had to hold onto the table as she walked. Because any person might have walked up to the window and seen Leblanc, the officer did no more than a citizen might do.

Using binoculars

Using binoculars to observe activities in public is proper. An individual should expect that he might be observed through binoculars entering and exiting his home. *Comm. v. Woods*, 419 Mass. 366 (1995).

Using binoculars to observe activities in a home does infringe on privacy. Although a Massachusetts appellate court has yet to rule on the issue, other jurisdictions have decided that it is improper for officers to use binoculars or other equipment to look into private areas within a dwelling. *U.S. v. Taborda*, 635 F.2d 131 (2nd Cir. 1980) held that visual surveillance of one apartment through a telescope in another apartment violated the suspect's privacy absent a warrant. "The mere fact that telescopic lenses are . . . increasingly common does not mean that, as a society, we must reasonably expect to be watched through them when we are inside our homes unless we pull our drapes or close our shutters." Also see *Vega-Rodriguez v. Puerto Rico Telephone Company*, 110 F.3d 174 (1st Cir. 1997).

This same argument persuaded a Massachusetts judge in a lawsuit brought against a private detective by a woman he was investigating. The judge, in *Digirolamo v. D.P. Anderson & Associates*, 1999 WL 345592, explained that it makes sense to distinguish between the naked eye and a telescopic lens. People understand what can be seen inside their home through the naked eye by those standing beyond their property, and can take appropriate steps to protect their privacy. It is more difficult to gauge what can be seen through a telescopic lens.

Flying overhead

Police do not violate an individual's privacy by engaging in aerial surveillance from a reasonable altitude consistent with FAA regulations. *Comm. v. 1985 Ford Thunderbird*, 416 Mass. 603 (1993): A police helicopter conducted three flights at an altitude of 700 feet over the defendant's property. With the use of binoculars, officers were able to identify marijuana plants. The SJC concluded that the defendant's privacy was not infringed. The helicopter did not fly unreasonably low or violate applicable regulations, and it did not interfere with the defendant's normal use of his backyard. Compare *People v. Snead*, 32 Cal. App. 3d 535 (1973) (helicopter surveillance from an altitude of 25 feet unreasonable and illegal).

Trying key in door lock

Police only need a reasonable suspicion to try a key in the lock of a private home.[8] In *Comm. v. Alvarez*, 422 Mass. 198 (1996), police were on their way to execute a search warrant when they received information that the drugs had been moved to a nearby apartment. Once inside, an officer overheard one of the defendants comment in Spanish that he was not "crazy" enough to keep drugs in this apartment. Other officers found keys in the bedroom which they tried in the lock of the apartment next door. The door opened, and police entered and secured the apartment. They obtained a warrant for this new location and found the massive amount of drugs they had anticipated initially.

While inserting a key into a lock constitutes a warrantless search, the expectation of privacy is minimal. According to the SJC, such an unobtrusive search only requires a reasonable suspicion. Once the key fits, officers should secure the premises and get a warrant before searching inside. Also see *Comm. v. Dora*, 57 Mass. App. Ct. 141 (2003).

K-9 drug detection sniff

K-9 sniff of the curtilage. *Florida v. Jardines*, 569 U.S. 1 (2013): Detective Pedraja received a tip that marijuana was being grown in Joelis Jardines' home. He was unable to verify the tip, so he brought a handler and his drug dog to the house. The dog alerted at the base of the front door, which allowed Pedraja to obtain a warrant and arrest Jardines.

While the officer could walk to the front door like any other visitor, he should not have brought a trained dog to explore what was *inside* the house. The court compared this K-9 sniff to a stranger walking onto someone's front porch with binoculars and peering in the windows. While the stranger would not be trespassing by walking to the door, he would be invading the residents' privacy by using a super-sensitive instrument to detect things he could not otherwise see.

Compare *Comm. v. Welch*, 420 Mass. 646 (1995): Defendant had no reasonable expectation of privacy in sleeping quarters he shared with other firefighters. Consequently, police properly brought a dog into this area to sniff for drugs at the request of a fire department commander. The defendant did have an expectation of privacy in his locked locker, so police wisely got a warrant to open the locker when their dog indicated drugs were inside.

---

8 While we recommend that officers continue to do this, officers should know that if the case ends up in federal court (e.g., drug task force investigation), this type of key check was found unconstitutional in *U.S. v. Bain*, 874 F.3d 1 (1st Cir. 2017).

TECHNOLOGICAL INTRUSION

Police <u>do violate</u> a resident's privacy when they use technology like thermal imaging — not generally available to the public — to learn about activities <u>inside</u> the home. *U.S. v. Kyllo*, 121 S.Ct. 2038 (2001): Narcotics agents used a thermal imaging device to determine that Kyllo was using high-intensity lamps to grow marijuana in his home. The results of the scan enabled police to get a search warrant. The Supreme Court held that the use of technology is a search if, without the technology, the police could only have learned the same information by physically entering the home.

Compare *U.S. v. Stanley*, 753 F.3d 114 (2014): Police discovered child pornography at an IP address. They realized that another person was using this innocent subscriber's internet connection. The subscriber allowed police to use mobile tracking software and a directional antenna. Officers detected a signal coming from Richard Stanley's apartment across the street. They obtained a search warrant and recovered vast quantities of child pornography on Stanley's computer.

Unlike *Kyllo*, Stanley's conduct was not confined to the interior of his home. He shared child pornography with other internet users *outside* his home. He "opened his window and extended an invisible arm to his neighbor's . . . internet connection. In doing so, he deliberately ventured beyond the privacy protections of his home." This was "virtual trespass," and he lost any privacy expectation.

Pole camera surveillance of a home becomes a search when it is extensive. In *Comm. v. Mora*, 485 Mass. 360 (2020), the SJC held that using a pole camera became a search requiring a warrant, even though it was located on a public street. The reason is that the camera created detailed and searchable images — with live notices of activity — for everything that arrived in the driveway of the suspect's dwelling over a two-month period.

GPS technology — even though it monitors a suspect's public activities — may be so intrusive that it constitutes a search. While there is no clear rule about when GPS surveillance is subject to the warrant requirement, the SJC considers the duration and details captured. When using technology to aid an investigation, the police must determine when it is necessary to get a warrant. Consult your prosecutor.[9] *Comm. v. Mora, supra.*

BUSINESSES

Private areas of business premises protected. Business or commercial premises are entitled to constitutional protection in those areas where the business owner has a reasonable expectation of privacy. To illustrate, a supermarket owner expects privacy in the basement of his store designated for "employees only," but not in the public shopping areas. *Comm. v. Lee*, 32 Mass. App. Ct. 85 (1992).

Police officers may enter business premises without a warrant and make whatever observations they can, as long as they limit their entry to areas open to the public. In *Comm. v. Bloom*, 18 Mass. App. Ct. 951 (1984), officers looked through a ventilation duct and saw the defendant expose himself in the urinal area of a public restroom. Had these same officers

---

9 The most complete discussion of these issues appears in *Chapter 20* of this manual.

viewed him inside one of the stalls, a court would have agreed that his privacy had been breached without the requisite constitutional justification of a warrant.

Public and private clubs. Clubs are treated the same as commercial premises. Club members enjoy an expectation of privacy in restricted areas. *Comm. v. Cadoret*, 388 Mass. 148 (1983). *Comm. v. D'Onofrio*, 396 Mass. 711 (1986).

Intensive Care Unit (ICU). *Comm. v. Welch*, 487 Mass. 425 (2021): After being found unconscious in the same apartment with his dead girlfriend, Ryan Welch was treated in the ICU for a serious throat wound. Welch was not under arrest, though police were posted near the room. Welch communicated with medical staff and police by writing notes. These notes were left on a table outside his room. Welch had no privacy interest in the notes, which police later seized.[10] A patient has no privacy in intensive care because of the stream of medical personnel entering the room through an open door. Welch never expressed any privacy concern about his notes until after his arrest.

POSSESSIONS

EXPECTATION OF PRIVACY FOR POSSESSIONS

A citizen's possessions are private. Generally, citizens reasonably expect that their possessions will not be searched unless police have probable cause.

LIMITS OF PRIVACY IN POSSESSIONS

Abandoned property

Property is abandoned when a person <u>voluntarily</u> relinquishes control and gives up his expectation of privacy. The most obvious example is when a suspect gets rid of an item in public. *Comm. v. Nutile*, 31 Mass. App. Ct. 614 (1991) (defendant threw a bag out the window during a police chase; officers properly searched it without a warrant at the side of the highway). *Comm. v. Cabral*, 69 Mass. App. Ct. 68 (2007) (police properly obtained DNA evidence from saliva the defendant spit on a public street).

- **Force.** Since abandonment must be voluntary, it does *not* occur when the police force a suspect to discard property. In *Comm. v. Ferguson,* 41 Mass. 611 (1991), the pursuing officer grabbed the defendant's coat as he "ran out of his jacket" to avoid apprehension. The officer could not search the coat as abandoned property.

- **Trick.** *Comm. v. Ewing*, 67 Mass. App. Ct. 531 (2006): After a woman was raped in her home, Melvin Ewing was questioned and released. Six years later, Ewing was arrested on an unrelated charge. While he was interviewed, police offered him cigarettes. Ewing left the butts in an ash tray. The DNA developed from his cigarettes matched the DNA found on the rape victim. Police may use a trick to get samples, as long as there is no evidence of coercion. Here, Ewing voluntarily abandoned the items as trash.

---

10 Even if these notes were medical records and somehow covered by HIPAA, HIPAA does not include a private right to have evidence suppressed in a criminal case. *U.S. v. Streich*, 560 F.3d 926 (2009).

The dominant factor is the place where the property is found, and the suspect's relationship to that place.

- **Defendant controls location.** *Comm. v. Augello*, 71 Mass. App. Ct. 105 (2008): $775 worth of bottled liquor was stolen from a club. Augello was seen near the club with another man carrying a black suitcase. The police went to Augello's home. Arigoni invited them inside. Officers saw a large black suitcase. Both defendants denied it was theirs. Rather than obtain a warrant, police opened the suitcase on the theory that it was abandoned property. Inside, they found the stolen liquor. Both defendants were charged.

  The prosecutor argued: Since Augello and Arigoni denied owning the suitcase, it was abandoned. The court disagreed. When property is found in a place where suspects have a reasonable expectation of privacy, their verbal disclaimer, by itself, is not abandonment. The dominant factor is the location of the property and the suspect's relation to that place. *Washington v. Evans*, 159 Wash. 2d 402 (2007) (defendant did not abandon a briefcase found in his truck by simply denying that the briefcase was his). *Smith v. Ohio*, 494 U.S. 541 (1990) (the defendant was approached by officers at a YMCA parking lot; he quickly placed a grocery bag on the hood of his car; officers searched it and found drug paraphernalia; protecting his property from inspection was not abandonment).

- **Defendant does <u>not</u> control location.** *Comm. v. Carnes*, 81 Mass. App. Ct. 713 (2012): After a 17 year old was shot to death, Detective Paul Smith spoke to a father and his young son. The son saw a man with a backpack, wearing a white shirt and dark shorts, run behind a shed. He heard a loud noise and saw the suspect reappear without his backpack. The detective found a backpack in the bushes behind the shed. He opened it and saw a gun. He also found an inhaler, which was tested for DNA. Malcolm Carnes lost his expectation of privacy in the backpack he left on property he did not own or control.

Leaving items behind in a dwelling.

- **Voluntary departure.** *Comm. v. Paszko*, 391 Mass 194 (1984) held that the defendant had abandoned a coat and drug paraphernalia found in a hotel room even though he had paid for additional days and retained a key to the room. The defendant's intent to abandon was demonstrated by: (1) his registration at another nearby hotel; (2) his removal of all other personal items; (3) his spending the next night in another state; and (4) his traveling in New York at the time of his arrest, far away from his hotel room. *Comm. v. Mallory*, 56 Mass. App. Ct. 153 (2020).

- **Involuntary departure.** *Comm. v. Netto*, 438 Mass. 686 (2003): Joseph and Nancy Netto, in desperate need of money to buy heroin, robbed and murdered their neighbor. The next day, police arrested the Nettos at a motel. A day later the motel manager asked police to get a trash bag that had been left in the Nettos' room. The police retrieved the bag without a warrant. It contained valuable evidence from the robbery.

  These guests, as a result of their arrest, abandoned their room. It did not matter that their abandonment was involuntary, so long as it was lawful. Consequently, they had lost their expectation of privacy in their room when police returned a day later.

Trash. Sometimes officers search a suspect's trash for evidence. Once garbage becomes accessible to the public, the owner loses any expectation of privacy. *California v. Greenwood*,

486 U.S. 35 (1988) (trash bagged on the curb). Compare *U.S. v. Property at 987 Fisher Road*, 719 F.Supp. 1396 (E.D. Mich. 1989) (privacy expected for trash bags against the wall of a house not visible from the street). *Comm. v. Krisco Corp.*, 421 Mass. 37 (1995) (defendants demonstrated an expectation of privacy in the contents of their dumpster, which was in a fenced and locked area exclusively used by their business; this case would have been different if the dumpster was used by other businesses or located in a publicly accessible lot).

If the person retains a receipt, the police may not consider the property abandoned. *Comm. v. Small*, 28 Mass. App. Ct. 533 (1990): Logan Airport troopers received a tip that Small would be arriving from Los Angeles carrying drugs. As officers approached, Small ran from the airport and could not be found. But officers cheered up: his luggage, which was rotating on the baggage carousel, had been abandoned. They brought his suitcase into an office and opened it. Cocaine was inside. Three hours had elapsed between the time Small ran and the time officers inspected his baggage.

The Appeals Court found the search improper because the suitcase was not abandoned. Small had his baggage claim ticket at the time officers looked inside. The ticket entitled Small to possess the case and preserved his expectation of privacy. Absent a warrant, only exigent circumstances could justify opening the bag, but this reason was lost when officers placed the bag in a secure office prior to opening it. The lesson of *Small*: Officers need to be careful not to consider an item abandoned when the suspect still has a receipt for the property.

Sniffing by trained dog vs. squeezing by officer

Sniffing luggage with a narcotics dog is not a search because the technique is much less invasive than the typical search. The sniff only discloses the presence or absence of contraband and not anything else that might be in the bag. *Comm. v. Truax*, 397 Mass. 174 (1986).

However, need reasonable suspicion to expose U.S. mail to dog. U.S. mail may only be exposed to a drug dog if a reasonable suspicion exists to detain the letter or package. *Comm. v. Pinto*, 45 Mass. App. Ct. 790 (1998) (package was duct-taped, hand-addressed to an individual rather than a business, with a fictitious return address and no named sender; it was sent from an airport used by drug couriers; postal inspectors appropriately subjected it to a dog sniff and turned over the evidence to state officers).

Squeezing luggage is sufficiently invasive to breach an ordinary traveler's expectation of privacy. *U.S. v. Bond*, 120 S.Ct. 1462 (2000): Border Patrol agents boarded a bus in Texas to check the immigration status of its passengers. As an agent walked off the bus, he squeezed a soft-sided piece of luggage, which Bond had placed in the overhead storage space. The agent noticed that it contained a "brick-like" object. The agent found methamphetamine after Bond admitted that he owned the bag and consented to a search.

In rejecting the police activity, the Supreme Court noted that Bond, like any traveler, had an expectation of privacy in the contents of his bag. While a passenger expects that other passengers or bus employees may handle his bag, he does not expect that the bag will be felt in an exploratory manner. Physical inspection is simply more intrusive than visual inspection. The officer breached Bond's privacy when he felt the bag without a warrant, consent, or exigency.

Inspecting and testing impounded crash vehicle

The police may remove a damaged or disabled vehicle from the highway following its involvement in a collision. Testing the vehicle and its parts is not a constitutional search because an individual loses his expectation of privacy under these circumstances. *Comm. v. Mamacos*, 409 Mass. 635 (1991): Following a fatal accident, an officer impounded the defendant's truck and conducted external and internal tests on the truck's braking system, in spite of the defendant's request that the officer return his truck. No reasonable expectation of privacy existed because police have a duty to remove vehicles involved in serious accidents from the street and to examine the mechanical causes.

STANDING

Standing refers to the right of a defendant to object to the police conduct that produced evidence. In order for a defendant to have the right to challenge the validity of a search, his own constitutional rights have to be affected.

FEDERAL STANDARD: REASONABLE EXPECTATION OF PRIVACY

A defendant can only object to government searches in areas where he had a reasonable expectation of privacy. This rule is especially crucial in situations involving third-party premises, since a defendant's Fourth Amendment rights are violated *only* when the challenged search infringes upon *his* privacy. For example, a guest in a hotel room or at a party has no standing to challenge a search of the premises, even though the search produces evidence that will used against him. Similarly, a driver lacks standing to challenge the search of an automobile if it is leased to someone else. *Rawlings v. Kentucky*, 448 U.S. 98 (1980). *U.S. v. Starks*, 769 F.3d 83 (2014).

MASSACHUSETTS RULE: AUTOMATIC STANDING FOR POSSESSION

The Supreme Judicial Court has interpreted our state constitution to provide more protection. *Comm. v. Amendola*, 406 Mass. 592 (1990) confers "automatic standing." This means: "When a defendant is charged with a crime in which possession of the seized evidence . . . is an essential element of guilt, the defendant shall be deemed to have standing to contest the legality of the search . . . [regardless of where it took place]."

The SJC believes the federal standard is an unfair "Catch-22" because, to assert standing, the defendant must show he controlled the area where the contraband was found. But doing that is an admission of guilt. On the other hand, denying any connection to the location causes the defendant to lose his opportunity to challenge the search! In the words of the SJC: "[T]he Government [should not] have the advantage of contradictory positions . . . The Commonwealth, in order to prove possession, aims to show that the defendant was the driver of the Pontiac and in possession of the contraband. But in arguing against standing, the Commonwealth claims that the defendant had no connection with the Pontiac . . . The Commonwealth may not have it both ways."

APPLICATION OF AUTOMATIC STANDING

The automatic standing rule is limited to possession crimes. *Comm. v. Ware,* 75 Mass. App. Ct. 220 (2009) (defendant had automatic standing to challenge the search of his uncle's basement, even though he did not live there, because he was charged with possessing the gun found). *Comm. v. Herring,* 66 Mass. App. Ct. 360 (2006).

Situations beyond the coverage of the automatic standing rule apply the federal rule: reasonable expectation of privacy. *Comm. v. Miller,* 475 Mass. 212 (2016).

- **Conspiracy.** In *Comm. v. Frazier,* 410 Mass. 235 (1991), police seized a woman's handbag filled with cocaine and decided to charge her and Frazier, her partner, with trafficking. Frazier had automatic standing to challenge the search of her purse, even though he had no privacy interest in it. Since the police illegally searched the purse, the court suppressed the evidence against Frazier for trafficking.

  Automatic standing did not apply, however, to Frazier's prosecution for conspiracy. The reason: Cocaine possession is *not* an element of *this* crime. Conspiracy only requires an agreement between two or more people to commit a crime. In short, Frazier had automatic standing for trafficking but not conspiracy — so the same evidence was inadmissible to prove trafficking, but admissible to send Frazier to prison for conspiracy! (For more on conspiracy, see *LED's Criminal Law, Chapters 2* and 20.)

- **Prior possession.** *Comm. v. DeJesus,* 99 Mass. App. Ct. 275 (2021): A Fall River detective saw a Snapchat video in which Christopher DeJesus brandished a large capacity weapon in the presence of Darius Hunt, at Hunt's house, within the past 24 hours. The detective and other officers went to Hunt's house to investigate. DeJesus, Hunt, and others were out front but ran when the police pulled up. A foot chase of Hunt through an unlocked basement door led to finding the firearm on a table. DeJesus was denied automatic standing to contest the seizure in Hunt's basement because DeJesus was charged with possessing the firearm when the video was made *the previous day,* a time different from when the firearm was seized by police.

- **Distribution.** *Comm. v. Negron,* 85 Mass. App. Ct. 904 (2014): After observing a hand-to-hand sale, police arrested and searched the buyer. Based on the drugs found, they then arrested the seller, Anthony Negron. Negron lacked standing to challenge the search of the buyer because he was charged with distribution, rather than possession. He did not have a possessory interest in the drugs found on the buyer's person, which is necessary for automatic standing. Distribution is different from the crime of possession with intent, where the drugs are still with the offenders at the time of arrest.

- **Denying any connection.** The Appeals Court denied standing to a defendant who claimed to have nothing to do with a car or victim he transported to the hospital. He could not later challenge the search. *Comm. v. Page,* 42 Mass. App. Ct. 943 (1997).

INFORMATION OBTAINED UNLAWFULLY FROM THIRD PARTIES

The decision in Amendola does not mean that defendants have standing to contest searches or seizures done to third parties. *Amendola* only applies if a defendant is charged with possessing something found on the premises of a third party, which is an unlikely scenario. *Comm. v. Manning,* 406 Mass. 425 (1990): Police obtained information while making an unlawful arrest of James Walsh. This information became the basis of a search warrant for drugs in Manning's home. Manning did *not* have standing to object to the original unlawful arrest that produced the information contained in his warrant.

The way a defendant challenges the search of a third party is to invoke the doctrine of "target standing." Target standing means the defendant alleges that the police purposefully engaged in illegal conduct "to get" the defendant. This is often argued by organized crime figures. They assert the police violated the rights of lesser criminals — knowing that those cases would be lost — in order to get evidence against "the big fish."

Although routinely argued in federal court, target standing may only be asserted in Massachusetts for blatant police misconduct. *Comm. v. Santiago,* 470 Mass. 574 (2015) (officer's close call on a probable cause drug search was not the type of mistake that warranted target standing).

12 *Plain View*

JUSTIFICATION

Plain view is not a "search." It applies when officers have a lawful reason to be present and see evidence. It makes no sense to require that officers obtain new authorization when they already have a valid reason to be present. *Coolidge v. New Hampshire,* 403 U.S. 443 (1971).

The three-prong test for seizing an item in plain view: (1) lawful presence; (2) inadvertence; and (3) apparent evidence. *Comm. v. Franco,* 419 Mass. 635 (1995).

LAWFUL PRESENCE

The heart of plain view is lawful presence. Their official duties often put officers in a position to view evidence. On the other hand, if they should not have been present in the first place, the evidence they see is suppressed.

VALID REASONS TO BE IN PRIVATE AREAS

Traffic stop. During a lawful traffic stop, officers may seize evidence in plain view if their intrusion is not more extensive than the stop permits. For example, officers could not demand that a motorist open the trunk following a red light violation. On the other hand, if officers saw heroin on the passenger seat, they could seize it. *Comm. v. Moses,* 408 Mass. 136 (1990).

Vehicle inventory. Evidence may be seized if it comes into view during the inventory of a properly impounded automobile. *South Dakota v. Opperman,* 428 U.S. 364 (1976).

Arrest. The same holds true for evidence viewed during a search following a valid arrest. *Comm. v. Walker,* 370 Mass. 548 (1976).

Booking inventory. Evidence is often discovered during a booking inventory following a valid arrest. *Comm. v. Ross,* 361 Mass. 665 (1972) (wallet handed to officer during inventory held bloodstained currency).

Exigent circumstances. *Arizona v. Hicks,* 480 U.S. 321 (1987) found police lawfully entering an apartment because a bullet had been fired from within. An officer, who remained on scene to secure the premises, became curious about stereo equipment that seemed out of place. The officer moved the stereo in order to read the serial numbers. After checking with the station, he learned the equipment was indeed stolen. The Supreme Court suppressed this evidence because the officer could not justify moving the stereo as part of the initial exigency that was his sole purpose for being there.

Execution of search or arrest warrant. Evidence may be seized if officers see it while properly executing an arrest or search warrant. *Comm. v. Beldotti*, 409 Mass. 553 (1991) (police properly seized photographs of nude, female body parts that came into view in a closet where they were legitimately looking for items listed in their search warrant).

INADVERTENCE

The inadvertence rule forces officers who possess probable cause to obtain a warrant. They may not simply choose an opportune moment to see the evidence. *Comm. v. Walker*, 370 Mass. 548 (1976).[1]

At the same time, this rule never applies to contraband, stolen goods, or dangerous objects. Since most evidence falls into one of these categories, the rule rarely affects police activity. *Comm. v. Hason*, 387 Mass. 169 (1982) (although police had plenty of time to get a warrant for the stolen automobile, they could seize it in plain view because the inadvertence rule does not apply to stolen property).

Practically speaking, inadvertence is only an issue if police fail to mention a particular object in their warrant application, even though they had probable cause for it. *Comm. v. LaPlante*, 416 Mass. 433 (1993) dealt with the murder of a mother and her two children. Police obtained a search warrant for Daniel LaPlante's home. Although not listed in their warrant, officers seized items they saw in LaPlante's home because they were related to an earlier break-in at the house where the murders occurred. The inadvertence requirement did not apply to these *stolen items.*

The police also seized clothing from LaPlante's room when his brother identified it as having been worn the day of the murders. In particular, a wet sock proved to be exceptionally valuable because one of the children had been drowned in a bathtub. The SJC said the inadvertence rule did not apply to this plain view seizure either. Police could not have included the sock and other clothing items in their warrant application because they were not identified until the defendant's brother pointed them out! *Comm. v. Chamberlin*, 86 Mass. App. Ct. 705 (2014).

APPARENT EVIDENCE

The incriminating nature of an item must be immediately apparent to officers.

CONTRABAND, FRUITS, OR INSTRUMENTALITIES

Contraband, fruits, or instrumentalities of crime should obviously be seized when observed. *Comm. v. Fuller*, 30 Mass. App. Ct. 927 (1991) (plastic bag with white powder consistent with cocaine). *U.S. v. Folk*, 754 F.3d 905 (2014) (firearms in closet were contraband because investigator knew defendant was a convicted felon).

---

1 Massachusetts courts adhere to the inadvertence requirement, but the U.S. Supreme Court rejected it in *Horton v. California*, 110 S.Ct. 2501 (1990).

OTHER POSSIBLE EVIDENCE

Officers must have probable cause to believe items are "plausibly" related to crime in order to seize them. *Comm. v. Halsey*, 41 Mass. App. Ct. 200 (1996).

- **Sufficient knowledge to seize evidence.** *Comm. v. Sliech-Brodeur*, 457 Mass. 300 (2010): At a murder scene, police properly seized various "post-it notes" affixed to items throughout the house, each bearing the name of one of the defendant's sons. These notes were plausibly related to the murder under investigation since they seemed to indicate the defendant's decisions about her property in the wake of her husband's murder and her own attempted suicide.

  Comm. v. Pierre, 71 Mass. App. Ct. 58 (2008): Police executed a search warrant for Ketty Pierre's apartment based on information that her brother dealt drugs there. Officers discovered storage lockers in the basement. The locker assigned to Pierre held 100s of CDs that appeared to be counterfeit. The CDs had photocopied covers and were organized into groups. Five days later, a recording industry consultant assisted an officer in inventorying the CDs. He confirmed they were counterfeit. This consultation was appropriate because the police had probable cause the CDs were contraband *before* they called in the expert.

- **Insufficient knowledge to seize evidence.** *Comm. v. Cruz*, 53 Mass. App. Ct. 24 (2001): Police had probable cause to believe that there was evidence of drug dealing in the defendant's apartment. While making an initial protective sweep of the apartment, an officer saw what he thought might be equipment used in cell phone fraud. He then obtained a warrant to search the apartment for drugs, but did not mention the cell phone equipment. The officer called in an expert in phone fraud. While the officer searched for drugs, his expert tested a phone and seized other equipment. This was invalid under the plain view doctrine: The incriminating nature of the phone and equipment had not been immediately apparent to the first officer.

Specific knowledge versus "fishing expedition."

- In *Comm. v. Rodriguez*, 378 Mass. 296 (1979), officers were executing a search warrant as part of their rape investigation. While lawfully searching the defendant's apartment, officers seized clothing not listed in the warrant that they thought might be useful. Later, the victim identified certain seized items. Unfortunately, at the time they took clothing from the closet, officers were not aware of its evidentiary value; they only had a hunch.

- Compare *Comm. v. Moynihan*, 381 Mass. 575 (1978): Officers had a description of the specific clothes worn by the defendant during a robbery. They were able to locate his car in a public lot. Officers saw a jacket and coat, lying on the backseat, which matched the victim's description. Immediately knowing its evidentiary value, officers properly took the items.

Officers may rely on their expertise and experience in deciding whether an item is probably evidence. They may also take into account the suspect's implausible explanation about how he obtained the property. *Comm. v. Fudge,* 20 Mass. App. Ct. 382 (1985).

- *Texas v. Brown*, 460 U.S. 730 (1983): Narcotics officer properly seized a tied balloon in plain view during a lawful motor vehicle stop because he saw the driver attempt to conceal the balloon and he knew, based on his training and experience, that heroin was typically transported in this manner.

- *U.S. v. Turner*, 839 F.3d 429 (2016): During a routine traffic stop, the officer saw a plastic bag with 100 gift cards partially hidden under the front passenger seat. The defendant did not have a receipt for the cards and provided a vague story about how he bought them. It is known by police that large numbers of gift cards are often the proceeds of drug dealing, fraud, or theft.

- Compare *Comm. v. Garcia*, 34 Mass. App. Ct. 645 (1993) (trooper's experience not enough to believe that a baggie he saw on the floor of a car was evidence of drug possession — especially given that there were no other suspicious circumstances surrounding his routine traffic stop; the trooper had to bend down, seize the glassine bag, and look at it closely in order to determine that it held some sort of powder residue; this was impermissible; plain view requires that, at the moment the officer sees the item, he knows it is plausible evidence of crime).

Testing allowed on lawfully obtained evidence. The police do not have to obtain a warrant to scientifically test evidence seized in plain view. *Comm. v. Varney*, 391 Mass. 34 (1984) (field testing seized drugs without warrant is proper).

Obtaining Search Warrants

AUTHORITY TO ISSUE SEARCH WARRANTS

Neutral magistrate must issue the warrant. The Fourth Amendment and Article 14 require that a clerk or judge issue a warrant. These magistrates are "neutral and detached," unlike police officers, who are "engaged in the often competitive enterprise of ferreting out crime." *Johnson v. U.S.*, 333 U.S. 10 (1948).

Magistrates authorized to issue search warrants: Justices of the Supreme Judicial Court, superior court, and district court; and clerks, assistant clerks, and temporary clerks of the district court.[1]

Magistrates may issue a warrant authorizing a search for evidence anywhere in the Commonwealth, even if the criminal activity that is the subject of the warrant occurred outside the court's territorial jurisdiction.[2] *Comm. v. Mendes*, 457 Mass. 805 (2010) (Barnstable investigator properly obtained a warrant to search the defendant's home and vehicle in Bourne, concerning drug offenses that occurred in Bourne, despite the fact that the town was outside the territorial jurisdiction of the Barnstable District Court).

THE AFFIDAVIT

PROBABLE CAUSE TO SEARCH

MAGISTRATE CONSIDERATIONS

The officer submitting an affidavit must personally appear before the magistrate. In the rare case where an officer ends up communicating by phone or fax, she must have exhausted all reasonable efforts to personally appear before a magistrate. *Comm. v. Nelson*, 460 Mass. 564 (2011) (holiday weekend insufficient excuse for failing to personally appear).

Magistrates may only base their decision on the written materials submitted. 276, § 2B requires that probable cause exist "within the four corners" of the affidavit.

Magistrates should resolve marginal cases in favor of the police to encourage their use of warrants. "Applications for search warrants . . . are drawn by often overburdened police officers, frequently in haste, and . . . they are not to be subjected to 'hypertechnical' scrutiny, . . . but are to be assessed in a common sense and realistic fashion." *Comm. v. Querubin*, 60 Mass. App. Ct. 695 (2004). If the first affidavit fails, police may resubmit it with additional

---

1 Interestingly, Appeals Court justices and superior court clerks are not empowered to issue warrants.
2 A Massachusetts judge or clerk may not issue a search warrant for evidence outside the territorial boundaries or waters of the Commonwealth, except for computer records. 276, § 1B. See discussion in *Chapter 20*.

information to satisfy the probable cause standard. *Comm. v. Saleh*, 396 Mass. 406 (1985).

Affiants do not have to disclose all steps of their investigation. The police need not provide every detail of an investigation — even those efforts that did not pan out — as long as probable cause supports the warrant *and* the omitted information does not negate probable cause. *Comm. v. Connolly*, 454 Mass. 808 (2009). *Comm. v. Luce*, 34 Mass. App. Ct. 105 (1993) (fact that affiant did not include another agent's unsuccessful effort did not affect warrant's validity).

On the other hand, if officers obtain information that casts doubt on the magistrate's probable cause decision after a warrant is issued, but before they execute it, the officers should return to the magistrate and present the information for a new probable cause determination. *U.S. v. Bowling*, 900 F.2d 926 (6th Cir. 1990).

A clerical error does not nullify a warrant because it does not impact its underlying information. *Comm. v. Pellegrini*, 405 Mass. 86 (1989) (judge's failure to sign warrant was only a clerical error because he clearly intended to do so).

PUBLIC NATURE OF AFFIDAVIT

Affidavit not public until filed. Under 276, § 2B, the judge or clerk who issues the search warrant must deliver the original affidavit within three days to the court where the warrant will be returned. When the police return the warrant, their affidavit is attached to it and filed. At that point, the affidavit becomes a public document.

Impoundment. If officers do not want an affidavit to become public, the prosecutor may petition a judge to impound it. *Newspapers of New England v. Ware District Court*, 403 Mass. 628 (1988) (child abuse investigation).

CONNECTION BETWEEN EVIDENCE & THE PLACE TO BE SEARCHED

An affidavit must explain why evidence is probably located at the place to be searched. This connection need not be proven by direct observation. It may be based on "the type of crime, the nature of the missing items, the extent of the suspect's opportunity for concealment, and normal inferences as to where a criminal would be likely to hide evidence." *Comm. v. Cinelli*, 389 Mass. 197 (1983).

- *Comm. v. Keown*, 478 Mass. 232 (2017): The victim died from ethylene glycol (EG) poisoning. EG is a transparent liquid used in a variety of solvents, including antifreeze. Police suspected her husband, James Keown, of contaminating her food or drink with antifreeze. Keown had falsely told the victim (and his own employer) that they had to move from Missouri to Massachusetts, where he would work remotely, because he had been accepted to Harvard Business School. When the employer learned that Keown had not only forged his Harvard admissions letter, but had also embezzled from the company, he was fired. Keown did not tell the victim he had been fired or that they were in financial ruins. Police suspected he killed the victim to hide these facts and benefit from her life insurance policy.

  Probable cause existed to search Keown's laptop for evidence relating to the victim's death. Keown was a web designer. The forged contracts and documents from Harvard were likely on his computer, and they related to his motive. Finally, the victim died from EG poisoning, which likely would have involved online research by a computer savvy person like Keown.

- *U.S. v. Jenkins*, 680 F.3d 101 (2012): During a traffic stop, the trooper saw the motorist weaving and leaning over several times. His nervous explanation — a dropped cell phone — did not make sense. When the trooper asked for his license and registration, the driver said he left them at home. He produced a postcard with the name "White" on it, claiming he was Joseph White, born in 1966. After the trooper was unable to find a "Joseph White" in the vehicle database, the driver supplied more false information before admitting he did not have a valid license. At the station lockup, the driver identified himself as Jenkins, who was wanted for kidnapping in New Mexico. The trooper obtained a search warrant for the van, where he found a 9 mm pistol and ammunition.

  Probable cause was based on Jenkins' attempts to hide his identity, his refusal to be fingerprinted, and his eventual admission that he was a wanted felon. Transporting contraband "was by far the most likely explanation for his strange behavior," which justified a warrant for illegal weapons and drugs.

- Compare *Comm. v. Mora*, 477 Mass. 399 (2017): A police officer conducting surveillance observed a man engage in what appeared to be a hand-to-hand drug transaction in a parking lot known for numerous drug arrests. 30 minutes later, Steven Mora drove into the lot and approached the suspected dealer. Mora, the drug dealer, and a woman entered Mora's car and left the lot. Police stopped the car and recovered hypodermic needles, drug paraphernalia, and a safe on the floor of the vehicle. Mora was arrested for driving with a suspended license, and the vehicle was inventoried and towed. Police determined that a heavy metal object was inside the safe, and that the safe was designed to secure pistols. They obtained a search warrant for the contents of the safe, and found a handgun, ammunition, pill bottles bearing Mora's name, and hypodermic needles inside.

  The court found that the search warrant lacked probable cause. The affidavit conflated the observations of the suspected drug dealer with observations of Mora, as though they were the same person. There was probable cause to believe that the first male observed was a dealer, but there was no nexus between his activities and the safe inside Mora's car. While Mora was connected to the safe, there was no evidence that he was a drug dealer. There *was* probable cause to believe a firearm was in the safe, but police had no reason to suspect that Mora did not have a license to carry (LTC). The police would have succeeded if they had checked whether Mora had an LTC and put their negative finding in their affidavit.

Permissible to infer that "useful items" in house. The mere fact that a house is the defendant's residence does not establish probable cause for a search warrant. However, where the items sought are "of durable and continuing utility to the defendant," it is likely that they will be found in his home. A defendant is unlikely to dispose of items that are not currently incriminating. *Comm. v. James*, 424 Mass. 770 (1997) (probable cause to search defendant's residence for knives, sneakers, clothing, and face masks).

May not assume the right to search a residence. In *Comm. v. Olivares*, 30 Mass. App. Ct. 596 (1991), probable cause existed to search the defendant's business because of a sale at that location, but not his residence. The police affidavit had no specific information which tied the defendant's residence to illegal drug transactions, other than the fact that he lived there. The defendant was never seen carrying anything from his house or removing anything from his business. Therefore, no inference could be drawn that he was getting cocaine from his home or delivering cocaine there. All activity occurred at his business. The warrant for his business was legal; the one for his home was unconstitutional.

Sometimes police present evidence of a "stash house." *Comm. v. Vargas,* 94 Mass. App. Ct. 1105 (2018): In their affidavit, drug investigators wrote that Jose Vargas had previously used a stash house where heroin, packaging, and other paraphernalia were found. In this case, the investigators focused on a new address where Vargas visited but never stayed. He never parked in front of this apartment building even when there were spaces. Trash from this address contained drug packaging, and Vargas would only meet his "drug runner" here — never at his other apartment where he did sleep, receive mail, and have his car registered. Finally, the investigators noted how high-volume dealers often keep their drug business and their home in separate locations to avoid detection and prosecution. This excellent affidavit presented probable cause for Vargas' stash!

When outside activity is involved, there must be multiple sales in order for police to have probable cause to search the dealer's residence. Compare the following cases:

- **Insufficient connection.** *Comm. v. Pina,* 453 Mass. 438 (2009): Detective Bryan Safioleas of the New Bedford Police Department obtained a search warrant based on information from a confidential informant, who participated in a controlled buy of cocaine from Robert Pina at a pre-arranged location. Police maintained constant surveillance, observing Pina leave his house and drive directly to the deal without stopping.

  Safioleas outlined these activities in his affidavit and concluded that Pina was operating a narcotics delivery service. Drug distributors conduct drug sales away from their principal residence to keep their supply of narcotics concealed. Outside selling also avoids customers constantly visiting on foot and in vehicles, arousing the suspicions of neighbors or police, and the attention of rival dealers.

  Despite this strong information, the SJC held that the Safioleas warrant lacked probable cause that narcotics evidence would be found in Pina's home. Specifically, the defendant was only seen driving to meet the informant *once*, and there were no other facts to indicate that the defendant kept his supply of drugs in his apartment.

- **Sufficient connection.** *Comm. v. Defrancesco,* 99 Mass. App. Ct. 208 (2021): The confidential informant told police about the defendant's drug business. Police followed up by arranging three controlled buys over the course of one month, the defendant arriving in his vehicle for each one. This was probable cause the defendant engaged in ongoing narcotics sales. The defendant used three vehicles (rented in the name of a different person) during the month, but made two sales from a Nissan Rogue. Two days after the last controlled buy, police obtained a search warrant for his apartment and Nissan Rogue. In the Rogue, police seized fentanyl, cocaine, and a gun. The affidavit established that drugs would be found in the defendant's home *and* his Rogue.

- *Comm. v. O'Day,* 440 Mass. 296 (2003): Two times, police saw the defendant leaving his home in his truck, proceeding directly to DJ's Pub and engaging in drug deals inside. The reasonable inference was that the defendant brought a substantial quantity of drugs with him. It was unlikely that the defendant got the drugs inside the bar, as his attorney argued, because he was constantly watched by officers. The drugs were transported in his truck, to which the defendant returned during the evening, presumably to replenish his supply. Given the value of the drugs, the quantity the defendant sold in the pub, and the frequency of visitors to his home, it was unlikely that the defendant would only keep drugs in his truck at home. The warrant to search his home was supported by probable cause.

STALENESS

The affidavit must not be based on stale information. The information must be recent enough to show that the evidence is located at the place to be searched. The affidavit must disclose a clear time frame. *Comm. v. Blake*, 413 Mass. 823 (1992).

Whether information is stale depends on the facts of each case. As eloquently pointed out in *Andresen v. State*, 24 Md. App. 128 (1975): "The likelihood that the evidence sought is still in place is a function not simply of watch and calendar, but of variables that do not punch a clock: the character of the crime (chance encounter in the night or regenerating conspiracy?), of the criminal (nomadic or entrenched?), of the thing to be seized (perishable and easily transferable or of enduring utility to its holder?), of the place to be searched (mere criminal forum of convenience or secure operational base?). The observation of a half-smoked marijuana cigarette in an ashtray at a cocktail party may well be stale the day after the cleaning lady has been in; the observation of the burial of a corpse in a cellar may well not be stale three decades later. The hare and the tortoise do not disappear at the same rate."

- **Durable vs. disposable evidence.** *Comm. v. Burt*, 393 Mass. 703 (1985) (even five months later, stolen coins are likely to be present because they are not easy to transfer). *Comm. v. Huynh*, 2019 WL 7116137 (Appeals Court) (although the warrant was issued three months after the informant last saw a pistol in the defendant's home, the informant had seen this durable item several times over the course of two years). Compare *Comm. v. Malone*, 24 Mass App. Ct. 703 (1987) (a quantity of drugs for personal use is unlikely to remain where it was observed a week earlier).

- **Offender has no reason to get rid of evidence.** *Comm. v. James*, 424 Mass. 770 (1997) (18-day period was not so long that it reduced the likelihood of finding knives in the defendants' homes; there was no reason for them to dispose of these items since they were unaware that they had been identified to the police). *Comm. v. Guastucci*, 482 Mass. 22 (2020) (a person who uploads even one image of child pornography is likely to keep it for a long time; here, a warrant obtained seven months later was not stale).

- **Offender involved in "continuing enterprise,"** so the passage of time becomes less important. In *Comm. v. Rice*, 47 Mass. App. Ct. 586 (1999), police received tips from three informants over a 15-month period about John Rice. Their investigation culminated in a controlled buy of cocaine six weeks before their warrant application. Relying *only* on the buy would have rendered the warrant stale, but the several reports during the prior 15 months convinced the court that Rice was still in business! *Comm. v. Murphy*, 95 Mass. App. Ct. 504 (2019) (sophisticated jewel thieves involved in ongoing criminal enterprise; operations base was the defendant's warehouse; it was likely that equipment and evidence related to these crimes would be at this location even a year later).

- **Possible recovery of deleted computer files.** *Comm. v. Matos*, 2018 WL 4568881 (Appeals Court) (the child pornography on Donny Matos' computer was not stale because the affidavit included Sergeant Cooke's explanation that evidence in computer files can be recovered long after it has been deleted).

ANTICIPATORY WARRANT

Police officers may seek a warrant in advance if they have probable cause that evidence will arrive at a certain location. This "anticipatory warrant" allows police to grab evidence quickly when it arrives. *Comm. v. Soares*, 384 Mass. 139 (1981) (trooper learned that California UPS had opened a parcel containing methamphetamine addressed to the defendant in Massachusetts; trooper obtained an anticipatory warrant to search the defendant's house when the package arrived).

The affidavit must outline explicit conditions for the warrant's execution. This is known as the "triggering event." *Comm. v. Colondres*, 471 Mass. 192 (2015) (when dealer left his house and went to the stash house, probable cause existed to execute a search warrant there; police found 1,700 grams of cocaine).

PARTICULARITY OF PLACES, THINGS, & PERSONS

The warrant must particularly describe the premises to be searched and items to be seized. *Comm. v. Shepard*, 394 Mass. 421 (1985).

PARTICULARITY AS TO PLACES

The description in a warrant is adequate if it is unlikely that the wrong place will be searched. *Comm. v. Hamilton*, 83 Mass. App. Ct. 406 (2013): When he applied for the search warrant, Detective Diliddo believed that there were three apartments at 109 Green Street. He sought a warrant for "109 Green St, Brockton, third-floor apartment." In fact, there were three apartments on the third floor. The warrant could be read as permitting a search of all of them.

However, Diliddo's affidavit included information from an informant that the third-floor apartment was accessed through the side door next to the fire escape, and was at the top of the stairs with a yellow sign on the door "that reads something to the effect of 'Private/Keep Out.'" While Diliddo's description was not accurate in every detail, it sufficiently described the target's apartment. *Comm. v. Walsh*, 409 Mass. 642 (1991).

It is not necessary that the name of the owner/occupant appear in the warrant, so long as the premises are described. *Comm. v. Dinnall*, 366 Mass. 165 (1974) (warrant approved; it described the premises well, but named the owners/suspects as "John and Jane Doe").

Fill-in-the-blank warrant unacceptable in normal cases. In *Comm. v. Douglas*, 399 Mass. 141 (1987), a search warrant was invalid because it described the place to be searched as "premises to be identified by Trooper Sullivan prior to the execution of the warrant." The police wrote the warrant this way because the undercover trooper was planning to wear a wire and track down the illegal possession of narcotics in a weekly high stakes card game. This "floating" poker game occurred at different locations in Hampshire and Franklin counties.

In its decision, the SJC said the constitution does not allow a "fill-in-the-blank warrant" because it replaces a magistrate's judgment with police discretion. The court went on to say: "If we were ever to accept such a broad description of a place to be searched . . . the circumstances would have to be far more pressing." In today's world, one can imagine a situation involving terrorism where a warrant might have to be pursued with this amount of discretion built in.

Building with multiple units. When police know (or should know) that a building contains more than one apartment, they must specify which apartment they have probable cause to search. A description that applies to more than one unit is invalid, *unless:*

- **The suspect has access to all units in the house.** *Comm. v. Dew*, 443 Mass. 620 (2005): The warrant was directed to all areas of a triple decker, even though the defendant mainly lived with his girlfriend on the third floor. Before police got this warrant, the defendant had told officers during an unrelated traffic stop that he had access to the entire house and that his family frequently went into each other's apartments.

- **The police were legitimately unaware of the layout.**

  - *Comm. v. Treadwell*, 402 Mass. 355 (1988): The warrant described the place to be searched as "the front apartment on the 2nd floor above apartment 17 located at 50C Memorial Road . . . having a yellow bumper sticker on it stating 'Make My Day.'" In fact, the apartment searched had the bumper sticker, *but* it was located across the hall from the apartment above unit 17. Since the description applied to two different apartments, it was ambiguous. The lack of clarity was not excused because police *knew* there were multiple apartments. The narcotics were suppressed.

  - Compare *Comm. v. Carrasco*, 405 Mass. 316 (1989): A state trooper obtained a warrant directed to the "second floor" of a three-story, multi-family dwelling on a Lynn street. When troopers arrived to execute the warrant, they found two apartments located on the second floor. They knocked at both doors simultaneously and forced their way in when they heard running footsteps. As soon as troopers realized which apartment belonged to the defendant, they vacated the other, apologizing to the occupants. Despite the trooper's failure to identify which apartment was the object of the search, the SJC upheld the warrant because the trooper legitimately did not know that there was more than one apartment on the floor to be searched.

  - *Comm. v. Dominguez*, 57 Mass. App. Ct. 606 (2003): Salem Police obtained a warrant to search a single family house. During the search, officers discovered an upstairs apartment. They could not have known (without jeopardizing their investigation) that the building had two units. The house had one front entrance, street number, mailbox, doorbell, gas, and water meter. Although Detective Page had been to the assessor's office to check who owned the house, he could not be expected to know that the notation "LU-104" indicated a multi-unit dwelling.

Research about dwelling layout _not_ required. *Comm. v. Carrasco, supra.* held that, while police must properly designate the unit to be searched in a multi-unit dwelling, they do not have to interview the owner of the building or take any other steps which might disclose the reason for their interest in the premises.

PARTICULARITY AS TO THINGS

Clearly defining the evidence sought safeguards the rights of the individual whose property is being searched. 276, § 1 sets out five classifications for evidence:

- **Fruits of crime.** Property stolen or obtained during a crime.

- **Instrumentalities.** Property or articles used to commit a crime.

- **Contraband.** Property or articles that may not be legally possessed (e.g., cocaine).

- **Dead body.** The dead body of a human being.

- **Living person with warrant.** A person with a current arrest warrant.[3]

Proper descriptions

If possible, officers must specifically describe items. This requirement prevents officers from having unlimited discretion about what they seize. In *Comm. v. LaBelle*, 15 Mass. App. Ct. 175 (1983), a warrant authorized a search for "items taken in recent housebreaks in the town of Oakham." This was too vague. When preparing a description of items for a warrant, generic terms such as "stolen jewelry" or "antique coins" are often inadequate.

Sometimes only a general description is possible when police have probable cause but lack information about the specific form evidence will take. For example, officers might reasonably expect that a search of a dealer's apartment will reveal documents that demonstrate drug distribution, but be unable to give a more specific description of them. *Comm. v. Kenneally*, 383 Mass. 269 (1981). *Comm. v. Baldwin*, 11 Mass. App. Ct. 386 (1981) (court upheld search warrant for "stolen vehicles" because the police were able to determine which vehicles on the premises were stolen by a prompt computer check of their VIN numbers).

Special rules: Marijuana cultivation

To obtain a warrant for marijuana cultivation, police must have probable cause that the suspect is engaged in illegal activity. This depends on whether the suspect is growing marijuana under adult use guidelines or the medical marijuana program.

- **Adult use guidelines.** If they are not in the medical marijuana program, and do not have a commercial cultivation license from the Cannabis Control Commission, Massachusetts citizens 21 and over may legally cultivate marijuana for their own personal use. Their cultivation activity must: (1) occur at their primary residence; (2) with a maximum quantity of 12 plants; and (3) with no sales or intended sales. 94G, § 7(a). Without a medical or commercial license, a person who violates *any* of these three conditions is guilty of criminal cultivation under 94C, § 32C.[4] *Comm. v. Canning*, 471 Mass. 341 (2015).[5]

---

3 The authority to search for a living person was added after the U.S. Supreme Court decided *Stegald v. U.S.*, 451 U.S. 204 (1981). See discussion in *Chapter 8*.
4 If the evidence shows the home grower gave marijuana or paraphernalia to someone under 21, who was not his child or grandchild, that is a criminal "social host" violation. 94G, § 13(i).
5 The most detailed breakdown of marijuana laws appears in *LED's Criminal Law, Chapter 21*.

- **Medical program restrictions**. To legally grow medical marijuana, patients or caregivers must: (1) have a hardship cultivation registration; (2) grow up to 10 ounces every 60 days[6]; and (3) not distribute, or intend to distribute, any amount of marijuana. In *Comm. v. Richardson*, 479 Mass. 394 (2018), Joshua Richardson was a medical marijuana patient who had a hardship cultivation registration. Richardson called 911 to report a home invasion. While police checked for intruders, they saw marijuana growing in his basement. Richardson was arrested. Police obtained a warrant and seized 22 plants along with cash and other evidence. Richardson's girlfriend told police he was not a regular marijuana user.

  - *There was insufficient evidence of a marijuana yield in excess of the 60-day supply.* The expert in this case never personally observed Richardson's marijuana grow. In fact, he had a hard time identifying from a photo whether plants were male or female.[7] No evidence confirmed that Richardson intended to cultivate more than 10 ounces of usable marijuana in a 60-day period.

  - *On the other hand, there was overwhelming evidence of his intent to distribute.* Because medical regulations do not contain a plant-based limit for home cultivation, Richardson's intent to distribute could not be based simply on his 22 plants. However, other evidence proved that Richardson was, in reality, a dealer: (1) he had no personal use paraphernalia; (2) his girlfriend said he did not regularly consume marijuana; (3) he reported an armed home invasion in his cultivation area, suggesting others knew he was a dealer and attempted to rob him; and (4) he had over $2,000 cash at the time of his arrest, despite being unemployed.

Special rules: Alcoholic beverages

Mandatory warrant for alcohol in dwellings yields to exigent circumstances. 138, § 46 states: "A . . . police officer . . . who . . . searches for . . . alcoholic beverages in a dwelling [without a search warrant,] shall be punished." While this old statute speaks unequivocally about the need for a warrant, it is largely overlooked today.

- **In typical underage drinking situations, enter based on consent or exigent circumstances.** Officers, as part of their community caretaking role, should attempt to deal with underage drinking the moment they become aware of it, so it does not escalate. *Comm. v. Sueiras*, 72 Mass. App. Ct. 439 (2008) (potential destruction of evidence by underage drinkers in home justifies warrantless police entry). *Howes v. Hitchcock*, 66 F.Supp.2d 203 (D. Mass. 1999) (dangers of allowing unsupervised, underage drinking party).[8]

- **Following warrantless entry, if officers wish to make a more extensive search, they should secure the scene and get a warrant.** 138, § 42 requires that any warrant for alcoholic beverages be based on the complaint of two adults. If the warrant is directed toward a dwelling (including one above a store or tavern), the police have an additional obligation. Under 138, § 43, one complainant must communicate that illegal beverages were kept or sold *within one month* prior to the warrant application.

---

6 Unlike the adult use law, medical marijuana regulations do not specify a maximum number of plants.
7 Female plants produce usable marijuana; male plants do not.
8 For more on the police response, see *Chapter 16*. Also see *LED's Juvenile Law, Chapter 11*.

Third party search warrants

A third party was not involved in the underlying crime. Sometimes police learn that a third party possesses evidence. A court may issue a warrant. *Zurcher v. Stanford Daily*, 436 U.S. 54 (1978) (warrant properly allowed police to search the office of a student newspaper for evidence — specifically news photos of demonstrators who had seriously assaulted officers).

Limitations on searching lawyers, therapists, and clergy. Under 276, § 1, police access to the privileged files of lawyers, therapists and religious officials is severely restricted unless officers can persuade a judge that evidence will be destroyed, or one of these professionals is actually participating in the crime. Be sure to consult with a prosecutor before embarking on this type of search. *In the Matter of a Grand Jury Investigation*, 470 Mass. 399 (2015).

Warrant for client's cell phone. Comm. v. Hernandez, 475 Mass. 267 (2016) (Aaron Hernandez gave his attorney his cell phone; once the attorney downloaded the contents, he no longer needed the phone to represent Hernandez; at that point, investigators properly got a warrant for the phone because they had probable cause it contained evidence of witness intimidation).

Partially defective warrant

A warrant may be partially invalid if the affidavit fails to establish probable cause for certain items. Police may still seize the items supported by probable cause. They may even seize the improperly included items if found in areas where officers were legitimately searching for correctly listed evidence. This legal rule gives the benefit of the doubt to officers who attempt to list all items in their warrant application.[9] *Comm. v. Fernandes*, 30 Mass. App. Ct. 335 (1991).

PARTICULARITY AS TO PERSONS

Named individuals

Massachusetts allows search warrants to be directed at named individuals. Comm. v. Powers, 39 Mass. App. Ct. 911 (1995) (defendant searched as he left his home). In *Comm. v. Santiago*, 410 Mass. 737 (1991), the prosecutor argued that, since the warrant authorized searching Santiago's person as well as his house, the police could search him wherever he was found: on a public street, in a store, in someone's home. The court rejected this argument, commenting that it does not construe a warrant's authorization to search a person so broadly.

Body cavity searches

Because of the intrusive nature of a body cavity search, police officers must satisfy a higher standard than probable cause. The body cavity warrant must be: (1) issued by a judge, and (2) supported by "a strong showing of particularized need and a high degree of probable cause." *Rodriques v. Furtado*, 410 Mass. 878 (1991) (SJC troubled by warrant resulting in a doctor's search of a drug dealer's vagina; "[i]t is difficult to imagine a more intrusive, humiliating and demeaning search than the one conducted inside [her] body").[10]

---

9 In contrast, purposefully omitted items may be suppressed under the inadvertence rule. See *Chapter 12*.
10 See detailed discussion of strip searches and body cavity searches in *Chapter 17*.

All persons present

Searching all persons may be authorized by a warrant if there is probable cause that anyone at the scene is a likely participant in crime. *Comm. v. Griffin,* 45 Mass. App. Ct. 396 (1998). *Comm. v. Smith,* 370 Mass. 335 (1976) emphasizes these factors:

- **The premises to be searched are small, confined and private;**

- **The criminal activity involves shifting participants** so it is practically impossible for police to predict who will be there at a given time;

- **The items targeted are easily concealed;** and

- **Whether persons unconnected with the illegal activity have been on the premises.** This information lets the magistrate assess the risk of innocent people being searched.

The authorization to search "all persons" does <u>not</u> include known occupants. Occupants must be specifically listed in a search warrant. *Comm. v. Brown,* 68 Mass. App. Ct. 261 (2007).

FATAL DEFECTS WITH AFFIDAVITS

An affidavit may not rely on information from an illegal search or interrogation. *Comm. v. Hill,* 51 Mass. App. Ct. 598 (2001).

An affidavit may not rely on false information furnished by police investigators. Two judicial procedures help evaluate these claims.

<u>*Franks*</u> *hearing.* The landmark case of *Franks v. Delaware,* 438 U.S. 154 (1978) allows a defendant to allege that information in the police affidavit is false. Following a hearing, the evidence will be suppressed if the court finds:

- **The police affiant included a false statement — which was made intentionally or with reckless disregard for the truth;** and

- **If the false statement is removed from the affidavit, probable cause no longer exists.** For example, in *Comm. v. Ramos,* 72 Mass. App. Ct. 773 (2008), a detective got a warrant for a storage locker. The detective based his probable cause on a drug dog's alert at Ramos' locker. Unfortunately, the K-9 handler lied about the dog's training and accuracy.

False information does not affect the integrity of the warrant if the <u>affiant</u> did not lie. *Comm. v. Winquist,* 87 Mass. App. Ct. 695 (2015) (detective relied on statement by the neighbor that he had been in the defendant's house and seen letters and other evidence in a wooden box; the detective reasonably believed him since he had heard the same information from other witnesses).

<u>*Amral*</u> *hearing.* *Comm. v. Amral,* 407 Mass. 511 (1990) recognized that a defendant may have well-founded suspicions that the affidavit is false, yet be unable to make a preliminary showing entitling him to a *Franks* hearing. The solution is a procedure that requires a judge to hold an *in camera* (private) hearing. The purpose of this *Amral* hearing is to determine if the defendant deserves a *Franks* hearing.

- **Concrete facts.** The defendant is not entitled to a hearing merely because he suspects an informant does not exist. The defendant must set forth his well-founded suspicion.

- **Hearing.** At the *in camera* hearing, the judge may quiz the affiant or even the informant to learn whether the affidavit contains false information. The judge may conduct the hearing alone or permit the assistant district attorney to participate. Defense counsel may not attend, but may submit questions. If the judge wishes to interview the informant, steps must be taken to protect the informant's identity, including holding the hearing away from the courthouse. A transcript of the hearing must be made to facilitate appellate review. *Comm. v. Alcantara*, 53 Mass. App. Ct. 591 (2002).

SECURING AN AREA PENDING RECEIPT OF WARRANT

DWELLINGS

Requirements. *Comm. v. DeJesus*, 439 Mass. 616 (2003) outlines the strict requirements for properly securing a dwelling pending the issuance of a search warrant:

- **Officers must have <u>probable cause</u> to search the dwelling <u>before</u> they secure it.**

- **Actively seek the warrant before or, at a minimum, while securing the premises.** The preparation of a warrant application safeguards against premature police intrusion into a home. The court in *DeJesus* was dismayed by an investigator's warrantless entry on the basis that he "intended to get a warrant." Tolerating a delayed application encourages officers to enter a home for a "sneak peek" to see whether a warrant is worth the effort.[1]

- **Two ways premises are secured, outside or inside:**

  - *Controlling the outside perimeter.* This method is effective if the dwelling is unoccupied. *DeJesus* insists: "By definition, any evidence located within an unoccupied dwelling can be fully protected by controlling access from the outside."

  - *Entering the dwelling and conducting a physical surveillance inside.* If police secure a dwelling from the inside, they must have "specific information supporting an objectively reasonable belief that evidence will indeed be removed or destroyed unless preventative measures are taken."

    The fact that police lacked information that someone inside the apartment might destroy evidence was the key deficiency in *DeJesus*: "There was no indication whatsoever that the dwelling was occupied at the time — officers had no . . . response to their knocking . . . and . . . heard no sounds coming from within."

    The claim that an accomplice could go to the apartment and destroy evidence was equally unpersuasive to the SJC: "We decline to hold that an arrest on the street, without more, can [automatically justify] a warrantless entry . . . [A]lthough the officers clearly had a right to control the premises from the outside until a search warrant was obtained, they had no basis for believing that immediate entry was necessary to prevent the destruction of evidence." Also see *Comm. v. Owens*, 480 Mass. 1034 (2018).

---

1 The Appeals Court was especially persuasive on this point. *Comm. v. DeJesus*, 56 Mass. App. Ct. 523 (2002).

- **No information acquired while securing the scene may be used for probable cause.** This also prevents officers from simply securing suspicious dwellings and hoping that, in the process, they will see evidence that they can insert into their affidavit. *Comm. v. Watkins*, 425 Mass. 830 (1997).

- **Once a dwelling may be secured from the outside, police may no longer stay inside for that purpose.** *Comm. v. Gray*, 465 Mass. 330 (2013).

- **Officers on scene may prevent individuals from entering or leaving so they will not remove evidence.** *Illinois v. McArthur*, 531 U.S. 326 (2001).

- **Officers must not begin their search until they have the warrant <u>in hand</u> at the scene.** *Comm. v. Guaba*, 417 Mass. 746 (1994).[2]

PERSONS, POSSESSIONS, & VEHICLES

Securing person for warrant. In *Comm. v. Taylor*, 426 Mass. 189 (1997), the police were investigating an arson murder. The police detained the defendant until they had a warrant to seize his clothing and sneakers to test them for traces of accelerant.

Securing possessions. Police may secure possessions pending the issuance of a search warrant. In *Comm. v. Hinds*, 437 Mass. 54 (2002), Sergeant McLean, as part of a murder investigation, received consent to view the defendant's home computer. In the process, he noticed a number of child pornography files. Having discovered illegal files, it was reasonable for McLean to seize the computer prior to obtaining a warrant. *Comm. v. Small*, 28 Mass. App. Ct. 533 (1990) (police secured a suitcase and acquired a warrant for it).

Securing vehicles. In *Comm. v. Gentile*, 437 Mass. 569 (2002), a young woman whose car had broken down accepted a ride with the defendant in his truck. After the young woman called her mother on the defendant's cell phone, she was raped and murdered. The next morning, when he voluntarily came to a state police barracks, the defendant spoke to officers, but then asked to leave. The interviewing officer said he could leave, but that his truck had to stay. Police held the truck until they obtained a warrant. Since police had probable cause for the initial seizure, their approach was legally sound.

TIMING OF EXECUTION

276, § 3A requires that a search warrant be executed as soon as reasonably possible but never more than 7 days after issuance. The 7 day period starts the day after the warrant is signed. This deadline is strictly enforced. *Comm. v. Cromer*, 365 Mass. 519 (1974).

276, § 2 authorizes nighttime searches between 10:00 p.m. and 6:00 a.m. *Comm. v. Grimshaw*, 413 Mass. 73 (1992). The affidavit should state the reasons for a nighttime search. Evidence will be suppressed if nighttime entry was unnecessary. *Comm. v. Yazbeck*, 31 Mass. App. Ct. 769 (1992).

---

2 The *DeJesus* case does not eliminate protective sweeps or warrantless searches based on exigent circumstances. See *Chapter 16* for exigent circumstances and *Chapter 17* for protective sweeps following arrest.

MANNER OF ENTRY

KNOCK AND ANNOUNCE RULE

276, § 2D(b) requires that police officers knock, announce their presence <u>and</u> their purpose before forcibly entering a residence. There are three reasons for this rule:

- **Prevent violence.** Decreasing the potential for violent reactions by surprised occupants;

- **Prevent property damage.** Preventing unnecessary damage to homes caused by forceful police entry; and

- **Protect privacy.** Protecting the privacy of those in their homes.

Unless an occupant opens the door, it is considered a forcible entry. *Comm. v. Gondola*, 28 Mass. App. Ct. 286 (1990) (even though the police commander had a warrant and calmly entered the defendant's apartment through the unlocked front door, he failed to announce his purpose until *after* he crossed the threshold; his entry was *forcible* because no occupant opened the door; the commander's failure to announce caused the court to suppress the evidence found inside). *Comm. v. Rivera*, 429 Mass. 620 (1999).

There are only two situations where police may legally avoid knocking and announcing: (1) they have a no-knock warrant, or (2) they enter to prevent imminent harm. Imminent harm means an immediate risk of death or serious injury. 276, § 2D(c).

Finally, if they do knock and announce properly, officers may, after a suitable time period, forcibly enter to prevent violence or the destruction of evidence.

- **Immediate risk of violence.** *Comm. v. Hamilton*, 83 Mass. App. Ct. 406 (2013) (officers knocked and announced; after five to seven seconds, they forced the door open with a battering ram; the day before, their informant told officers that one occupant possessed a loaded firearm and threatened to make intruders "disappear"; in light of this information, it was reasonable to force entry after a short interval).

- **Immediate and obvious risk of evidence destruction.** *Comm. v. Mullane*, 444 Mass. 702 (2006) (forced entry into massage parlor allowed to prevent destruction of evidence when its employees pretended they did not see or hear the police knocking and demanding entry on the other side of a glass door). *Comm. v. Osorno*, 30 Mass. App. Ct. 327 (1991) (officer did knock and announce, then entered the apartment through an open door in time to see the defendant running toward the bathroom with a bag of cocaine in his hand).

KNOCK AND TRICK

Deception may legally replace the requirement that police announce their identity and purpose. So long as they have a warrant, officers may trick an occupant into letting them enter. Since the trick causes an occupant to open the door, it is not considered "forcible" and, therefore, subject to the knock and announce rule. See, e.g., *Comm. v. Goggin*, 412 Mass. 200 (1992) (officers knocked at the defendant's apartment and claimed they were collecting for

"Pop Warner Football"; Goggin opened the door in response and, after seeing officers with their badges showing, attempted to slam the door shut; police appropriately completed their entry and search).

Given the strict limitations imposed by 276, § 2D, the "knock and trick" has become the preferred strategy to gain entry and prevent the destruction of evidence.

NO-KNOCK

A no-knock warrant is limited to a dangerous situation. Under 276, § 2D(a), police may *only* get a no-knock warrant:

- **Judge.** From a judge (not a clerk magistrate);

- **Probable cause of danger.** If the affidavit in support of the warrant establishes *probable cause* that the lives of police officers and/or others will be endangered if officers announce their presence before entry; and

- **No minor or elder inside** *unless* **possible victim.** The affiant must also include: (1) there is no reason to believe that minor children or adults over the age of 65 are in the home; or (2) there is a credible risk of imminent harm to a minor or adult over 65 on the premises.[3]

A no-knock warrant may no longer be issued on the basis that evidence might be destroyed. 276, § 2D(a). Compare *Comm. v. Ortega*, 441 Mass. 170 (2004) (old rule).

Failure to comply with the rules governing search warrant entry results in suppression of the evidence found inside.[4] 276, § 2D(d).[5] There is no discretion.

Difference between arrest and search warrants. 276, § 2D mandates that an affidavit justify a no-knock warrant issued by a judge. On the other hand, the no-knock rule is less stringent for arrest warrants because there is no governing statute and the standard application does not require that the magistrate specify the manner of entry. It is good practice for officers to explain why they wish to make a no-knock entry, and request that the magistrate indicate on the warrant: "No-Knock." *Comm. v. Scalise*, 387 Mass. 413 (1982).

The bottom line for arrest warrants: Officers may dispense with one or more components of the knock and announce rule if they reasonably fear harm to themselves or others. *Comm. v. Allen*, 28 Mass. App. Ct. 589 (1990) (the defendant and his accomplice were wanted for gun crimes, and police had found a gun on a man who had jumped out of the accomplice's car earlier that day; the police had good reason to anticipate a shoot-out if they announced their intention to arrest these two offenders at the time they executed their arrest warrant).

---

3 Federal law permits no-knock warrants on reasonable suspicion. *Richards v. Wisconsin*, 520 U.S. 385 (1997).
4 The U.S. Supreme Court has held that violations of the Fourth Amendment's "knock and announce" rule do not warrant suppression of seized evidence. *Hudson v. Michigan*, 547 U.S. 586 (2006).
5 Since no-knock warrants are now regulated by statute, 276, § 2D(b), it is probably no longer necessary for police officers to engage in a "doorway reappraisal" at the time they execute a no-knock warrant. See, e.g., *Comm. v. Jimenez*, 438 Mass. 213 (2002) (old rule). *Comm. v. Chamberlin*, 86 Mass. App. Ct. 705 (2014) (old rule).

Other entry tactics are left to officer discretion, but they must be reasonable. *Comm. v. Garner*, 423 Mass. 735 (1996) (police do not need advance judicial authorization to employ a "flash-bang" device or other tactics during the execution of a warrant; however, a judge may later determine that police used excessive force to execute the warrant).

POST-ENTRY CONDUCT

POLICE INTERACTION WITH OCCUPANTS AT THE SCENE

Detaining occupants

A warrant for contraband carries with it the authority to detain occupants while the search occurs. *Comm. v. Catanzaro*, 441 Mass. 46 (2004) held that the term "occupant" does not include visitors. By occupant, the court is referring to the type of person who, as a resident, would ordinarily remain to observe the search of their possessions. It should not be loosely construed to cover anyone present. The warrant justifies detaining occupants because a magistrate found probable cause that someone in the home is committing a crime. Most citizens, unless they intend to flee, would choose to observe the search of their possessions.

On the other hand, a warrant does not allow police to stop occupants in a vehicle away from the scene. *Comm. v. Charros*, 443 Mass. 752 (2005): New Bedford officers obtained a search warrant for the apartment of Michael and Geraldine Charros. Positioned in several cars around the apartment building, officers saw Michael Charros get into a van. They stopped the van after it traveled one mile. Michael was removed and searched. He had cocaine. Geraldine and the couple's eight year old son were also in the van.

Michael was arrested and brought back to the apartment. Geraldine was allowed to arrange for a relative to take her son, then arrested. The home search revealed 250 grams of cocaine and substantial cash.

Here, there were no special circumstances such as those found in *U.S. v. Cochran*, 939 F.2d 337 (1991). Cochran was believed to carry a firearm at all times, and the interior of his residence was protected by a guard dog. Officers decided to stop him as he was driving off his property and have him assist with their entry into his home. In contrast, the *Charros* officers simply decided in advance to stop the defendants away from their home and take them back. To allow officers to make an arrest anywhere in order to execute a warrant would "eliminate any meaningful relation between the place of the seizure and the premises to be searched."

Frisking & handcuffing occupants

Occupants may be frisked and handcuffed when the warrant concerns dangerous activity. *Muehler v. Mena*, 544 U.S. 93 (2005): Executing a warrant for evidence related to a drive-by shooting, SWAT officers secured the premises and handcuffed a woman named Mena, who was initially asleep, and three others found in the home. Officers held all four in the garage for three hours while a search that recovered a gun and other evidence took place. The detainees were allowed to walk around but the cuffs stayed on. Mena sued the police because she was never charged. The Supreme Court ruled: "In such inherently dangerous situations, the use of handcuffs minimizes the risk of harm to both officers and occupants."

Mena's detention for the duration of the search was reasonable because she was an occupant and police had a warrant. Three hours was not unreasonable for a home search.

Searching occupants

A search on scene must be authorized by the warrant or by another legal rule. *Ybarra v. Illinois*, 444 U.S. 85 (1979): Officers brought a warrant that authorized the search of a tavern and its bartenders, but did not authorize police to search the patrons. When officers entered, they detained patrons inside the bar, which the Supreme Court found proper. They frisked patrons, including a man named Ybarra, which the high court also approved. But then an officer insisted that Ybarra empty his pockets, which revealed heroin. This was improper. Ybarra was not named in the warrant, he was not being searched incident to his arrest, and there were no exigent circumstances either (e.g., the searching officer had not seen Ybarra make a sudden move to conceal contraband). The recovered heroin had to be suppressed.

People who arrive after police enter may be detained and searched under the authority of an "all persons present" warrant. *Comm. v. Perez*, 68 Mass. App. Ct. 282 (2007).

ACTUAL SEARCH PROCESS

Present warrant on demand. *Comm. v. Guaba,* 417 Mass. 746 (1994) said the warrant: (1) guides officers about the permissible scope of the search; and (2) notifies the occupant(s) about the officers' authority and reasons for the search. While officers must bring the warrant, they do not have to show or read it to the suspect, unless he specifically requests the information. *Comm. v. Valerio*, 449 Mass. 562 (2007). However, the best practice is to automatically give a copy to the suspect after entry.

Bring affidavit unless it will compromise investigation. Although not required, it is suggested that police attach the affidavit to the warrant. If the warrant later turns out to be defective for some reason, information in the affidavit may rescue it — *but only if* the affidavit was attached to the warrant at the time of execution. *Comm. v. Taylor*, 383 Mass. 272 (1981) (detailed description of evidence in affidavit compensated for vague description in warrant).

There are cases where officers will not want to compromise investigative effectiveness or witness security by allowing the perpetrator to get an immediate look at the affidavit. In those cases, make the defendant's attorney acquire the document through legal channels.

Photograph interior. Officers should photograph the interior of a home or building before and after the execution of a search warrant to prevent false claims about the extent of the damage caused by their police action. *Comm. v. Balicki*, 436 Mass. 1 (2002).

Civilian assistance. Under Article 14 and 276, § 2, the police may be assisted by civilians. Civilians may possess expertise about what to seize and how to retrieve it (especially when technology is involved). Their help may decrease the intrusiveness of a search. However, police must ensure that the judge who issues the warrant includes the name of any civilian who will assist. *Comm. v. Sbordone*, 424 Mass. 802 (1997).

Media representatives may <u>not</u> accompany officers into private homes. In *Wilson v. Layne*, 526 U.S. 603 (1999), the U.S. Supreme Court held that police officers may not permit the media to accompany them while executing a search or arrest warrant in a private residence. The high court warned that officers may be *personally liable* if they blatantly violate a citizen's privacy in this way. This decision applies to private homes. It does not prohibit the police from allowing media representatives to accompany them on ride-alongs or other operations conducted in public places.

SCOPE OF SEARCH

General principles

Under a warrant, police may only search those areas where the objects to be seized could reasonably be found. *Comm. v. Wills*, 398 Mass. 768 (1986) (police properly looked for a knife in a photo album because it could have been hidden in a hollowed out interior). *Comm. v. English*, 2016 WL 320246 (Appeals Court) (police were entitled to search a locked safe because drugs could be found inside).

If all the items listed on the warrant have not been found, police may continue the search until all possible areas for concealment have been inspected. The search must end when all listed items have been found. *Comm. v. Wood*, 389 Mass 552 (1983).

Police do not have to accept the word of the person whose premises are being searched. Officers do not have to begin searching in the location requested by occupants, and they do not have to stop when occupants insist that they have all the evidence. *Comm. v. Wood, supra*. Finally, it is not considered coercive for officers to inform occupants that, if they tell them where the evidence is located, the search will end up being shorter and less disruptive. *Comm. v. Alix*, 2015 WL 7723421 (Appeals Court).

Cellars, gardens, and cars

Probable cause to search a dwelling automatically includes the cellar or attic used by occupants. *U.S. v. Ferreras*, 193 F.3d 5 (1st Cir. 1999): The search of a third-floor attic was upheld under a warrant that listed the place to be searched as the second-floor apartment. A flight of stairs from the second-floor apartment went up to the attic where three bedrooms had recently been constructed. A key from the defendant's key chain opened one of the attic bedrooms containing drugs and other evidence. There were no bathroom or kitchen facilities in the attic or a separate electric meter. The attic search was clearly within the scope of this warrant. Also see *Comm. v. Pierre*, 71 Mass. App. Ct. 58 (2008) (basement storage locker fell within scope of warrant, despite not being specifically listed, because it had the same number as the defendant's apartment).

A search warrant covers a garden or shed within the curtilage.

- **Garden.** *Comm. v. Perez*, 76 Mass. App. Ct. 439 (2010): Investigators obtained a warrant for the first-floor apartment of a two-family home. In anticipation, officers watched the house and saw Perez walk outside and bend down near the front steps. He saw police and ran inside. Officers promptly executed the warrant. Turning their attention to where Perez had been earlier, officers saw freshly disturbed dirt and a nearby spoon. They began digging and found bags of cocaine. Contrary to Perez's argument, the digging occurred three feet from the front stairway. It was within the curtilage.

- **Shed.** *Comm. v. Sanchez*, 89 Mass. App. Ct. 249 (2016): Police executed a search warrant for the defendant's apartment, which was on the third floor. They entered the fenced-in backyard and discovered a locked shed. Police used a key from the defendant to unlock the shed. Inside was a substantial amount of cocaine. The shed was in the curtilage of the defendant's apartment. It was adjacent to his building, and the defendant rented it and restricted access with a lock.

A warrant for a home automatically covers vehicles within the curtilage that are owned or controlled by occupants.

- **Driveway.** *Comm. v. Signorine*, 404 Mass. 400 (1989): Although the warrant did not provide independent probable cause to search Signorine's wife's Corvette, the SJC held that officers properly searched it because it was parked in the driveway. A search warrant automatically covers vehicles owned or controlled by residents when parked within the curtilage, which often includes the driveway. The rule proved tragic for Louis Signorine. His house held no evidence but his wife's Corvette contained a hollowed-out oil can with 112 grams of cocaine!

- **Public street.** For the purpose of searching a vehicle, the curtilage never extends to a public street. In *Comm. v. Santiago*, 410 Mass. 737 (1991), investigators found nothing inside Santiago's apartment, but did find a big stash of cocaine underneath the front seat of his car — which had not been listed in the warrant and which was parked on the public street in front of his building. The SJC refused to extend the *Signorine* decision to cover a vehicle parked on a public road, even though Santiago lived in an apartment with no private driveway or off-street parking.

  The court also rejected alternative justifications for the cocaine seizure: It was not valid under the motor vehicle exception because police lacked probable cause that Santiago had drugs in his car when he pulled up to the building. It was not a search incident to arrest because Santiago was brought inside before officers looked in his car.

- **Semi-public area.** *Comm. v. McCarthy*, 428 Mass. 871 (1999): Detectives obtained a warrant to search McCarthy's condominium. The affidavit indicated that McCarthy sold drugs from his condo and vehicle, but police only requested authority to search his condo. When they arrived at his complex, officers saw McCarthy drive into the parking lot and park in a visitor's space. The officers found drugs in his car, but nothing in his condo! The SJC held that McCarthy's vehicle was *outside* the curtilage, so it was not covered under the warrant for his condo. A shared parking lot, open to visitors, is simply not within the curtilage.

- **Recommendation.** Of course, in all these cases, the situation would have been best handled by listing the specific car in the warrant at the time the affidavit was written. This approach avoids having to rely on where the suspect parks. *Comm. v. Fernandez*, 458 Mass. 137 (2010).

Computers, cell phones, and other devices

There are a number of cases and considerations that govern electronic devices. See discussion in *Chapter 20*.

RETURN OF WARRANT

Written list of items. An officer must make a list of the items seized. This is called a "return." An officer who helped serve the warrant should file the return. *Comm. v. Chandler*, 29 Mass. App. Ct. 571 (1990). The inadvertent omission of an item from the return is not typically a reason to suppress it, although a judge may exclude unlisted evidence that results from police misconduct or prejudices the defense. *Comm. v. Torres*, 45 Mass. App. Ct. 915 (1998).

Police must serve and file the return within 7 days. The 7 day period does not start until the day after the warrant is issued. 276, § 3A. If the warrant is not returned on time, it is not grounds for voiding an otherwise valid search. *Comm. v. Ericson*, 85 Mass. App. Ct. 326 (2014).

Electronic evidence may be examined beyond 7 days. *Comm. v. Kaupp*, 453 Mass. 102 (2009) allows officers to list computers and electronic storage devices they seize on their return. The forensic experts then have a reasonable period of time beyond 7 days to complete their examination. The same is true for cell phones. *Comm. v. Ericson*, 85 Mass. App. Ct. 326 (2014).

If the original warrant lost, its production at suppression hearing may be excused. In *Comm. v. Ocasio*, 434 Mass. 1 (2001), the original search warrant was lost. The court held that other evidence of the contents of a lost warrant (e.g., the application and affidavit) is admissible at a suppression hearing, provided that: (1) the original once existed, and (2) the original was not lost or destroyed in bad faith.

PRESERVATION OF EVIDENCE

Police must properly store and preserve evidence. When evidence is lost or destroyed in a criminal case, the remedy is determined by examining three factors: (1) the culpability of the police and prosecutor; (2) the importance of the evidence; and (3) the potential prejudice to the defendant in preparing his case. After weighing these factors, the court may do nothing or, in the extreme, dismiss the case — especially if the police or prosecutor acted recklessly or in bad faith. *Comm. v. Williams*, 455 Mass. 706 (2010).

If a motion to suppress evidence is granted, police must return any item which the defendant may lawfully possess. Contraband is never returned, even after an illegal search. Under 276, § 1, stolen property must be returned to its rightful owner. Under 276, § 3, property that was not stolen is forfeited "as the public interest requires." *Beldotti v. Comm.*, 41 Mass. App. Ct. 185 (1996) (public interest best served by the forfeiture of a variety of sexual aids directly related to the defendant's gruesome sex crime; court refused the defendant's request to recover these "innocent and legal" items).

The police department holding the evidence is liable for the value of lost property. *Comm. v. Sacco*, 401 Mass. 204 (1987).

15 Consent

JUSTIFICATION

Consent searches are allowed because people may choose to give up their privacy. *Schneckloth v. Bustamonte*, 412 U.S. 218 (1973).[1] For this reason, officers do not have to have probable cause when they ask for consent. This flexibility makes consent a useful investigative tool and, at the same time, a potential instrument for citizen harassment.

REQUIREMENTS

The three essential components:

- **Voluntary & clear.** Consent must be voluntary and clearly communicated.

- **Lawful presence & proper scope.** Officers must be lawfully present at the time they request consent, and the scope or extent of their search must be reasonable.

- **Authority.** The person who consents must control the area or property searched.

VOLUNTARY

STANDARD

Consent cannot be the result of expressed or implied law enforcement direction. *U.S. v. Edmondson*, 791 F.2d 1512 (11th Cir. 1986): Defendant stepped back and put his hands on his head in response to: "FBI, open the door!" This was not consent for agents to enter.

To determine whether the defendant voluntarily consented, courts examine the "totality of circumstances." Judges assess the words and actions of the police as well as the characteristics and experience of the suspect. In other words:

- **How did the police behave?**

- **What were the characteristics of the defendant?**

The police and prosecutor have the burden of proving, by a preponderance of the evidence, that consent was voluntary. Preponderance of the evidence is the same as probable cause. *Comm. v. Ware*, 75 Mass. App. Ct. 220 (2009).

---

1 Like plain view, consent is concerned with the suspect's expectation of privacy. With plain view, the police have a valid reason to intrude on the suspect's privacy when they see the evidence. With consent, it is the suspect's permission that puts officers in a position to find evidence.

POLICE BEHAVIOR

No force

Consent may not follow police force or a show of force. Officers must not resort to intimidation. *U.S. v. Tibbs*, 49 F.Supp.2d 47 (D. Mass. 1999) (ten police officers showed up at the apartment of the defendant's girlfriend at 10:00 p.m. while her six year old son was sleeping; officers spoke to the girlfriend in an intimidating manner prior to her "allowing" them to search). Bear in mind, a person may consent if he was afraid of another person (such as an accomplice), but not the police. *Comm. v. Walker*, 370 Mass. 548 (1976).

Written consent not required

Although persuasive, written consent is <u>not</u> required. *Comm. v. Rivera*, 441 Mass. 358 (2004). If officers do rely on written permission, it must be acquired *before* the search begins. *U.S. v. Tibbs, supra.* (time marked on signed consent form indicated that it was filled in 25 minutes after police arrived to search).

Failing to use an available consent form may indicate a lack of voluntariness. *U.S. v. Forbes*, 181 F.3d 1 (1st Cir. 1999).

Informed consent not required

The police do not have to warn an individual of his right to refuse. *Comm v. Burgess*, 434 Mass. 307 (2001). The landmark case of *Schneckloth v. Bustamonte*, 412 U.S. 218 (1973) explains why:

> "[I]t would be thoroughly impractical to impose on the normal consent search the detailed requirements of an effective warning. Consent searches are part of the standard investigatory techniques of law enforcement agencies. They normally occur on the highway, or in a person's home or office, and under informal and unstructured conditions. The circumstances that prompt the initial request to search may develop quickly or be a logical extension of investigative police questioning . . . While surely a close . . . question, these situations are still . . . far removed from 'custodial interrogation' where, in *Miranda v. Arizona*, we found the Constitution required certain now familiar warnings . . ."

Advising a suspect that he may refuse increases the likelihood that consent is voluntary. *Comm. v. Wallace*, 70 Mass. App. Ct. 757 (2007): Wallace offered to help a 12 year old girl at a hotel carry a suitcase to her mother's car. When they were out of view, he squeezed her breast and told her not to tell anyone.

A week later, police noticed a man, who resembled the composite sketch, illegally parked. Officer York asked Wallace to come to the station to answer questions, and he agreed. York asked Wallace if he would consent to a search of his car. Wallace was reluctant because he did not want his wife to know about the sexual materials he had hidden.

Officer York assured him that he had no intention of revealing the details of any search to his wife. York also told Wallace he could refuse. Wallace consented. Police found photographs of young girls, KY jelly, a camera, condoms, duct tape, and pornographic magazines. The victim and her mother identified Wallace in a lineup. Perfect police work.

Pressure to consent

Officers may not suggest that a citizen's failure to consent will result in adverse legal or family consequences.

- *U.S. v. Tibbs, supra.* Officers told the defendant's girlfriend that, if she did not consent to a search, they would have child services remove her sleeping, six year old child. The threat to take her child forced the girlfriend's consent. The ammunition found in her home was suppressed. Compare *U.S. v. Bey*, 825 F.3d 75 (1st Cir. 2016) (while waiting for a consent form to arrive, an officer asked the defendant's girlfriend about her four year old son and mentioned reporting the incident to DCF; this was not coercive because the officer was a mandated reporter, and his request for information was legitimate and not overbearing under the circumstances).

- *Comm. v. Kipp*, 57 Mass. App. Ct. 629 (2003): At the police station, a Spanish-speaking officer told the defendant that, if the police searched pursuant to a warrant, they would damage the apartment, but if Kipp consented to a search, they would "show a little courtesy." The Appeals Court strongly criticized this type of pressure.

At the same time, consent is voluntary even if it follows an officer's announced intention to apply for a search warrant. Officers must say they will *seek* a warrant and not imply that they have the power to issue one themselves. *Comm. v. Farnsworth*, 76 Mass. App. Ct. 87 (2010) (officer informed the defendant's mother that she had a right to refuse to consent to a search of her house — where drugs had been found during a lawful entry by firefighters — but that he would seek a warrant if she did not permit it; her decision to consent, in response to this message, was voluntary).

This tactic is acceptable only if police have information that amounts to probable cause. *Comm. v. Paul*, 2012 WL 3154545 (Appeals Court) (officer told defendant that if he did not want to consent to a search of his home, she would apply for a warrant; her statement was not deceptive because she had probable cause to get a warrant for evidence of reckless endangerment). Compare *U.S. v. Saafir*, 754 F.3d 262 (4th Cir. 2014) (North Carolina officer told the defendant he had probable cause to search his car due to the presence of a hip flask; this was wrong because the officer had no reason to believe the flask contained alcohol, or that the defendant was driving under the influence; the defendant's consent was invalid).

Promise of leniency

Police may promise not to charge a suspect in order to get consent to search — as long as they keep their promise. *Comm. v. Albert*, 2013 WL 6847724 (Appeals Court) (police properly promised the defendant they would not charge him with drug possession if he let them search his bedroom drawer; they never did charge him with drug possession, just with possession of the ammunition they found there).

SUSPECT CHARACTERISTICS

Education, emotions, & substance abuse

The suspect's educational background, emotional makeup, and intoxication are relevant. For instance, the consent of a 17 year old, inebriated high school student will receive closer scrutiny than the consent of a 40 year old, sober physician. Given the disparity in age, education, and mental awareness, the physician is much less susceptible to police intimidation than the 17 year old. *Comm. v. Alleyne*, 474 Mass. 771 (2016) (male defendant was not too intoxicated to consent to a search of a woman's purse in plain view inside a grocery bag in his hotel room; he conversed with police coherently and changed his baby's diaper at the officer's request).

Reaction to authorities

Prior cooperation often indicates voluntary consent. *Comm. v. Beldotti*, 409 Mass. 553 (1991) (defendant asked police to come to his home; he and his parents agreed to cooperate fully).

Consent is voluntary when the suspect authorizes a search to prove his innocence. *Comm. v. LeBeau*, 451 Mass. 244 (2008) (murder suspect voluntarily accompanied police to the station and told them several times that he was willing to do anything to clear his name; he also knew that he could refuse consent because, before he gave it, he insisted that officers agree not to arrest him if they found drugs in his suitcase).

A suspect's assertive reaction to police helps show voluntary consent. *Comm. v. Hinds*, 437 Mass. 54 (2002) (no indication that the defendant was intimidated by the police since he demanded to see their identification and reviewed their warrant before he let them in; he later consented to a search of his computer, which held child pornography). *Comm. v. Fencher*, 95 Mass. App. Ct. 618 (2019) (defendant refused to allow police to take her fingerprints or search her car; so her later consent for police to examine her phone was voluntary).

Commenting on one's right to refuse indicates voluntary consent. *Comm. v. Charlton*, 81 Mass. App. Ct. 294 (2012) (the defendant led police to a bedroom where a woman lay with a gunshot wound; a detective asked for permission to search the apartment; the defendant gave consent in a way that showed he knew he could refuse).

Consent from more than one person is usually voluntary. *Comm. v. Yehudi Y.*, 56 Mass. App. Ct. 812 (2002) (father and mother agreed to allow police to search their son's room).

Custody

It is more difficult, but still possible, for police to get voluntary consent from a suspect in custody. *Comm. v. Hill*, 57 Mass. App. Ct. 240 (2003): Cambridge detectives investigated two car breaks. They discovered a bag with tools near the scene, and a key in the bag led them to Carl Hill's apartment. The building manager said he let Hill into his apartment the night before because Hill claimed to have lost his key — the same key found in the bag. When detectives knocked, Hill stepped aside and allowed them to enter. Officers noticed several bottles of wine underneath a table, car stereos with wires hanging out, and gloves in a trash bag. They knew Hill had a long record of break-ins.

The detectives asked him to get dressed and come to the station. Told he was not under arrest, Hill agreed to go. Before they left, detectives saw a bicycle lock and asked for permission to insert a second key from the scene into the lock. He agreed, and the key fit.

At the station, Hill waived his *Miranda* rights. He told officers a far-fetched story about finding the stolen items on the road. The police asked Hill for consent to search his apartment. He signed a consent form and was arrested. The detectives, accompanied by Hill, returned and seized the wine, gloves, stereos, and other evidence. The court was satisfied that Hill's consent was voluntary throughout the process.

CLEAR COMMUNICATION

While the suspect may _explicitly_ or _implicitly_ consent, his communication to the police must be clear and unambiguous.

- **Explicit.** *Comm. v. Cantalupo*, 380 Mass. 173 (1980) (defendant consented when he said, "Hey, I'm clean, search me," and opened his jacket for police).

- **Implicit.** *Comm. v. Monteiro*, 2012 WL 2504053 (Appeals Court) (consent was voluntary when motorist said "okay" and released the trunk lid in response to an officer's request to "look inside" during a suspicious traffic stop).

Consent may be nonverbal. Comm. v. Carrion, 2018 WL 503413 (Appeals Court): Jose Carrion fatally stabbed the victim. Police went to Tanya Franklin's apartment, where Carrion was known to stay. Franklin let officers enter, which allowed them to arrest Carrion on a warrant.

Franklin asked what was going on, and an officer responded by asking her if she knew what Carrion wore the previous evening. Franklin walked into the bedroom and retrieved a pair of jeans. The officer saw the jeans were blood-stained. When Franklin noticed the stains, she tried to hide them, but the officer told her they would freeze the scene and apply for a warrant. The jeans, along with other evidence, were later seized under a warrant.

While Franklin did not verbally ask the officer to follow her into the bedroom, her walking there in response to his question was a nonverbal invitation. The fact that she immediately retrieved the pants also proved her consent.

Officers may not take advantage of a suspect's ambiguous comments or gestures.

- *Comm. v. McGrath*, 365 Mass. 631 (1974): One officer called out to McGrath, who he knew from a previous arrest for drug possession. McGrath responded, "I'm clean this time," and spread his hands out. The officer stepped in and patted him down. He found a vial of amphetamines. The court did not think that McGrath's comment — while walking away — was an invitation to search.

- *Comm. v. Rogers*, 444 Mass. 234 (2005): Officer Ellsworth encountered a woman who was crying at approximately 4:40 a.m. She told the officer that, after she paid for drugs, "Danny" and a woman named "Rose" assaulted her and took back the drugs. Ellsworth concluded that "Danny" was Daniel Rogers and that "Rose" was his girlfriend. Ellsworth had been to Rogers' apartment at least ten times during the past year in response to complaints of drug use, fights, and prostitution.

Ellsworth and two other officers, all in uniform, knocked on Rogers' door and Rose answered. Ellsworth asked where he could find Danny. Rose pointed in the direction of the kitchen. The officers walked through the living room to the kitchen where Rogers was seated at a table with a large pile of cocaine.

Here, Officer Ellsworth asked Rose where he could find Rogers. Rose's response of stepping back and pointing was unclear. It could have been construed as either indicating Rogers' location *or* permitting police entry.

For a physical gesture to indicate consent, it must be in response to either: (1) an explicit request to enter (e.g., "Hi Rose, Springfield Police, may we come in?); *or* (2) an explicit statement about the police purpose (e.g., "Rose, we need to speak with Danny about an incident tonight. Where is he now?" Her pointing at the kitchen now becomes a clear invitation to enter).[2]

Voluntary consent may come from a non-English speaker, provided the request and response were properly translated. Be sure to document who helped translate. *Comm. v. Adonsoto*, 475 Mass. 497 (2016) (ideally, translated conversation should be recorded).

LAWFUL PRESENCE

HOME OR OTHER PRIVATE BUILDING

Improper police authority

Unlawful entry invalidates later consent. *Comm. v. Yehudi Y.*, 56 Mass. App. Ct. 812 (2002): A uniformed police sergeant entered a home following an undercover officer's purchase of drugs from a juvenile. The way the sergeant got inside troubled the court. The sergeant did not knock at the front door. Instead, he came into the house on the second floor by a back staircase and entered the parents' living area on the first floor from an interior staircase. The sergeant then asked the parents for consent to search their child's room. The parents signed a consent form. But the court ruled their consent was obtained by exploiting an illegal entry. The evidence was suppressed.

Fraudulent claim of public safety authority is coercive, so it invalidates consent.

- *U.S. v. Giraldo*, 743 F.Supp. 152 (E.D.N.Y. 1990): Police officers posed as gas company employees and falsely warned the defendant of a possible gas leak in order to enter his apartment. Permitting the police to use this type of ruse jeopardizes public safety because it might prompt citizens to bar officials seeking to protect them from a real emergency.

- *Pagán-González v. Moreno*, 919 F.3d 582 (1st Cir. 2019): Ten FBI agents appeared at Pagán-González's door with the alarming news that computers in Washington, D.C. — the heart of the country's political and military operations — were receiving a virus from a computer at Pagán-González's location. This lie convinced Pagán-González to provide the agents with written consent to search his computers. In reality, the agents were looking for child

---

2 The *Rogers* case repeated the longstanding rule that police do not have to remind a homeowner of his or her right to refuse in order to obtain consent to enter. "Informed consent" is not mandated.

pornography, which they found. The report of a virus and show of force by federal agents created a fake emergency that prevented Pagán-González from giving voluntary consent.

- *Comm. v. Ramos,* 430 Mass. 545 (2000): Officers wanted to obtain the defendant's photograph to learn whether she had sold crack to an undercover trooper several days earlier. Investigators devised a plan to lure Ramos from her apartment. After knocking, police told Ramos they had received a report of a disturbance and wanted to be certain she was safe. Her boyfriend told police to leave. An officer said she needed to come outside so he could personally see her, or the Fire Department would be called to break down the door. Eventually, Ramos left and was photographed. Here, threatening to remain outside or break down her front door was police coercion, not consent.

Consent to enter is not consent to search. Permission to enter a building, apartment, or other area — by itself — does not give the officer authority to search. Specific consent *to search* must be obtained separately. *Comm. v. Gray,* 465 Mass. 330 (2013).

Surreptitious police entry

Police may enter a suspect's home secretly because they are not taking advantage of their authority. A suspect does not feel pressure to let an undercover officer into his home. *Comm. v. Yehudi Y., supra.* (undercover officer properly entered a house through an unlocked back door to buy drugs from the defendant; this entry did not rely on a claim of police power; the undercover behaved just like the defendant's other teenage customers, who freely entered and exited his upstairs bedroom).

Scope of consent

The search must happen when consent is given. If the search is delayed, consent becomes stale. A person granting consent may place limits on the police. For example, if the suspect is arrested and removed, a search may be invalid if the court finds that consent was conditioned on the suspect being present. *Comm. v. Gaynor,* 443 Mass. 245 (2005).

Unless explicitly limited, the scope of consent is what is reasonable.

- **Properly within the scope.** *Comm. v. Caputo,* 439 Mass. 153 (2003): Plymouth detectives were investigating a double murder. Caputo invited them into his house. He later argued that police had to leave once he told them he did not wish to speak. But there was no reason for police to believe Caputo had withdrawn his consent. He never asked officers to leave and did not object when detectives went outside to inspect his car, then came back inside.

  U.S. v. Chaney, 647 F.3d 401 (2011): While executing an arrest warrant in a hotel room for someone else, Detective Newcomb frisked Vincent Chaney and asked him for identification. Chaney said it was in his back pocket, but that pocket was empty. Newcomb asked if it was somewhere else. Chaney said Newcomb could check his left front pocket. Newcomb reached in and removed a plastic bag containing cocaine. He then grabbed a social security card. Chaney was arrested.

  Because a pocket is a cramped space, consent to search includes removing items that could be the object of the search or that obstruct access to other items. Here, the detective found the drugs before he found the ID. If it had been the other way around — he found the ID first — the detective would have had to end the search.

- **Beyond the scope.** *Comm. v. Thomas*, 67 Mass. App. Ct. 738 (2006): Based on a report of domestic violence, Eugene Thomas was arrested for A&B. Thomas asked officers to lock the door on the way out. One officer stayed in the house to look for the key. He looked in the kitchen and living room, then the bedroom. He opened a drawer in the nightstand and found a gun. At about the same time, the officer who had gone to the cruiser returned to retrieve the key from the front hall closet, where Thomas said it would be.

  Opening the nightstand went beyond the scope of Thomas' consent to search. Thomas gave consent to search for keys, so it was reasonable to check the front door, a hall table, or a hook near the entrance — but searching his bedroom was unreasonable. The presence of two officers was also a factor. One officer could have radioed the other to learn the location of the key from Thomas in the cruiser.

Consent may be withdrawn at any time. Once withdrawn, the search must stop unless justified on some other legal ground. *Comm. v. O'Laughlin*, 446 Mass. 188 (2006): Annmarie Kotowski was found beaten severely in her apartment. Michael O'Laughlin lived two doors down and became a suspect. Officer Buell asked O'Laughlin for consent to search his apartment. O'Laughlin allowed an officer to take photos. Two technicians found a red stain on the kitchen door. O'Laughlin asked them to leave. Understanding that consent had been withdrawn, investigators decided to secure the apartment and get a search warrant. O'Laughlin then agreed to let them back in. *Comm. v. Stewart*, 469 Mass. 257 (2014).

Scientific testing

Police may test evidence lawfully obtained during a consent search without getting a separate warrant. *Comm. v. Aviles*, 58 Mass. App. Ct. 459 (2003) (upon learning that her husband had been raping her daughter, the wife turned over her husband's undershirts to the police; once police properly obtained the defendant's laundry, they could test the semen found on the shirts for DNA without obtaining a warrant).

VEHICLES

Lawful stop

First, officers must have a valid reason to stop the motorist. *Comm. v. Bartlett*, 41 Mass. App. Ct. 468 (1996).

Proper request

Second, officers must have a <u>reasonable suspicion</u> that evidence of crime will be found inside the vehicle. The leading case, *Comm. v. Torres*, 424 Mass. 153 (1997), decided:

- Officers may <u>not</u> request consent during a routine traffic stop, even if they tell the motorist he is "free to refuse." Eliminating this practice is a welcome restriction, since it was typically employed by officers playing their hunches on the basis of a motorist's age, race, nationality, or ethnic background. Courts and progressive police commanders have long realized: Failing to adopt a legal standard for when officers may ask for consent will encourage some officers to use this tactic arbitrarily.

- **Officers may <u>not</u> request consent at the end of a routine stop, even if they tell the motorist he is "free to leave."** In Massachusetts, once officers return a motorist's paperwork, the stop is over.

- **Reasonable suspicion that there is evidence in a vehicle is <u>required</u> in order to detain a motorist and request consent.**[3] Consider *Comm. v. Robie*, 51 Mass. App. Ct. 494 (2001): There was one reason why the officer stopped Robie. He was speeding. The officer developed reasonable suspicion to ask for consent to search when: (1) Robie retrieved his license from underneath a mat in the rear passenger area; (2) there were three pairs of gloves on the seat; (3) Robie was extremely nervous and gave evasive answers about where he had been; and (4) the officer learned from a colleague in a nearby department that Robie was a suspect in several recent housebreaks.

  Compare *Comm. v. Cordero*, 477 Mass. 237 (2017): The traffic stop for broken tail lights and tinted windows was good. The driver, Gabriel Cordero, had a valid license and no outstanding warrants. At that point, the trooper should have given Cordero a citation and allowed him to leave. Instead, he asked for consent to search. The request was not supported by a reasonable suspicion that Cordero was transporting illegal drugs. It was not enough that Cordero was nervous and had some criminal history; that the stop occurred in "high crime" area; or that Cordero made supposedly evasive comments about going to a fast food restaurant and coming from his cousin's house.

Officers do <u>not</u> have to explain:

- **Why they are asking for consent and what they will look for.** *Comm. v. Egan*, 12 Mass. App. Ct. 658 (1981).

- **The motorist's right to refuse.** *Comm. v. Costa*, 65 Mass. App. Ct. 227 (2005) began when Fall River police requested that Taunton police arrest Edward Costa for domestic violence. Fall River also advised that Costa might have a firearm. When Officer Brady found Costa in Taunton and frisked him, he found no gun. Without telling him he could refuse, Brady asked Costa for consent to search his pickup truck. Costa agreed and produced his keys. A loaded handgun was in the truck. In approving the search, the court acknowledged the value of "informed consent," but noted that Massachusetts has never *required* it.

Officers should:

- **Ask for consent the same way each time.** It is much easier to defend in court. This author suggests the following: "Mr. Jones, will you give me permission to immediately and completely search your vehicle and its contents. I will do it as quickly as I can."

---

3 Consent without suspicion is only permitted in a taxi safety program. *U.S. v. Woodrum*, 202 F.3d 1 (1st Cir. 2000) approved of the Boston Police Department's Taxi Inspection Program for Safety (TIPS), which developed after a rash of cab robberies and two murders. TIPS allows officers to stop any taxi displaying the appropriate decal "to check on the operator's safety." Participation is voluntary, and cab owners affix decals on the outside and inside passenger compartment of their cabs. While a passenger expects privacy after determining the cab's destination and agreeing to pay a fare, the driver ultimately commands the taxi, which allows him to voluntarily participate in TIPS and consent to a police stop.

Notice how the language is concise *and* comprehensive — i.e., the procedure will be "immediate" and "complete"; the activity will be a "search"; the extent or scope of this activity will be the "vehicle and its contents"; and the goal is a reasonably "quick" procedure.

- **Ask one time.** Occasionally there may be a legitimate reason to repeat a consent request — e.g., suspect's inattention, nervousness, confusion, or language difficulty. As a general rule, however, multiple requests to search are coercive. *Comm. v. Cordero, supra.* (officer asked the driver three times for consent, even though he was clearly reluctant).

- **Get verbal instead of written consent.** If challenged, explain that requesting consent is an investigative step that *spontaneously develops* on the side of the road during a traffic stop. In the vast majority of cases, officers do not know whether their stop will stay routine or morph into reasonable suspicion — so it is unrealistic and inefficient to bring a written consent form to the driver's window. Once officers use a consent form, they will be expected to employ it every time. *U.S. v. Forbes*, 181 F.3d 1 (1st Cir. 1999) (trooper admitted he kept vehicle consent forms in his cruiser, but did not use one in this case; he had no reason for the oversight, which suggested consent was involuntary).

- **Get a clear response.** Silence is not a substitute for consent. *Comm. v. Ortiz*, 478 Mass. 820 (2018).

Scope

A person's general consent covers a search of closed and open containers in the glove box, passenger compartment, and trunk. Officers do not need to ask for separate permission to look inside each closed container they encounter in those areas. *U.S. v. Forbes*, 181 F.3d 1 (1st Cir. 1999) (defendant's consent to search covered zipped duffel bags in the trunk). *Florida v. Jimeno*, 500 U.S. 248 (1991) (requiring separate consent for each container would make the consent process overly cumbersome for the motorist and officer).

Officers have some latitude in how they search these areas — as long as they do not damage property. *U.S. v. Torres*, 663 F.2d 1019 (10th Cir. 1981) (driver's consent to search permitted officers to pull out the ash tray in the car door and then, when money was seen inside, to carefully remove the cover to get the cash). *U.S. v. Santurio*, 29 F.3d 550 (10th Cir. 1994) (the officer had consent to search the vehicle and "merely removed a few screws from the strip holding down the carpet" in order to find a false floor; this was proper because the officer "did not 'tear up' the van"). Compare *U.S. v. Strickland*, 902 F.2d 937 (11th Cir. 1990) (consent to search did not enable officers to slash the spare tire with a knife in order to locate contraband; no citizen normally consents to the destruction of their own property).

Officers need separate permission to open a container that is actually locked. *U.S. v. Reeves*, 6 F.3d 660 (9th Cir. 1993) (suspect consented to a search of his car for letters and papers; officer properly opened a briefcase in the trunk by manipulating its combination lock; however, it would have been unreasonable to break open a locked briefcase without additional permission from the suspect).

Officers need separate permission to search beyond the passenger compartment, glove box, and trunk. *Comm. v. Ortiz*, 478 Mass. 820 (2018): Officer Hamel lawfully stopped a vehicle for the violation of a city ordinance and recognized its driver, Anthony Ortiz, from an earlier foot chase. He also knew Ortiz and his passenger had previously been charged with serious drug offenses. Ortiz spoke little English, so when Officer Hamel asked him for his license and registration, his passenger translated. Then Hamel asked Ortiz in English if there was anything dangerous in the vehicle. Without translation, Ortiz quickly responded: "No, you can check." This was voluntary consent.

Hamel asked both men to exit. Other officers searched the front and back seat areas and found nothing. They then opened the hood and, after removing the air filter, discovered a black bag with two guns. Their engine search was unlawful.

Ortiz did not expect the search to extend to his engine. Making a separate request would have helped — e.g., "Mr. Ortiz, we're almost done. You should be on your way soon. There is one more thing. Will you give me permission to search under your hood?"

AUTHORITY

PERSON IN SOLE POSSESSION

When they wish to have permission to search a particular person, police must receive consent from that person only. Similarly, if the property to be searched is owned or used exclusively by one person, then only that person may provide valid consent.

THIRD PARTY: JOINT ACCESS & CONTROL

Where two or more persons have equal rights to use the property, each person may consent to a search. This is an important concept for police because the voluntary consent of *any* joint possessor is valid.

Comm. v. Hernandez, 93 Mass. App. Ct. 172 (2018): Flor Prudencio shared an apartment with Hernandez and their three children. She told a police officer that Hernandez, who was at work, had threatened to shoot her three weeks earlier. She brought the officer to the apartment's only bedroom and opened the closet door. Inside were men's, women's, and children's items. Prudencio pointed to a suitcase on the top shelf. The officer opened the unlocked suitcase and found a loaded revolver inside a "Huggies" container. Hernandez was charged with illegal possession of a firearm, improper storage, and threats. Prudencio clearly had joint access and control over the closet and suitcase.

The test is joint access and control, not actual use. *U.S. v. Duran*, 957 F.2d 499 (7th Cir. 1992): The defendant's wife could consent to a search of a separate building on their farm, which her husband supposedly used as a gym. While the wife did not typically enter the building, she still had the key to go inside. The court noted: "[O]ne can have access to a building or a room but choose not to enter." The wife gave agents valid consent, which resulted in the discovery of a substantial amount of drugs.

Absent exigent circumstances, when one occupant objects and the other consents, police lack consent. *Georgia v. Randolph*, 547 U.S. 103 (2006): Scott Randolph and his wife, Janet, separated when she took their son to Canada. She returned several months later and complained to police that her husband was a cocaine user. Scott explained that he had removed their child to a neighbor's house out of concern that his wife might take his boy again. He denied cocaine use and countered that his wife was the one who abused drugs. There were no allegations of violence.

Sergeant Murray asked Scott for permission to search the house. He adamantly refused. The sergeant turned to Janet for consent, which she readily gave. Murray entered and found cocaine. He secured the scene and applied for a warrant. Officers seized additional evidence under the warrant. Scott Randolph was charged.

- **If a physically present occupant refuses to permit entry, then any warrantless entry and search is invalid against him.** A disputed invitation, without more, gives a police officer no claim to legitimately enter.

- **At the same time, one co-tenant's refusal to consent does <u>not</u> prevent:**

  - *Another co-tenant from delivering evidence to police outside the home*; or

  - *Another co-tenant from telling an officer what he knows*, which police can then use as the basis for securing the premises and getting a warrant; or

  - *A police entry based on exigent circumstances.* This last exception applies to virtually all allegations of domestic violence where one occupant objects and another agrees to police entry. In *Georgia v. Randolph,* there was absolutely no concern about domestic abuse or even possible evidence destruction, since both parties were outside the house when police arrived.

Only a co-tenant who is <u>present and objects</u> can prevent police entry and/or search.

- **Present but no objection.** *Comm. v. Ware,* 75 Mass. App. Ct. 220 (2009): Two juveniles were assaulted with a handgun by the defendant and his uncle, who fled inside 12 York Street prior to police arrival. Initially, the uncle invited officers into the hallway, although he did not allow a search. Police then went to the defendant's second-floor apartment to follow up on information from the uncle. When they returned, the uncle had already closed his door and would not answer. A little while later, his wife allowed officers to enter. The uncle did not protest. Officers decided to secure his office and obtain a search warrant. They found the gun. Notice how this case is different from *Georgia v. Randolph* because the uncle did not object when his wife invited the officers inside.

- **Objection but not present.** *Fernandez v. California,* 134 S.Ct. 1126 (2014): Police responded to a report of a violent robbery. A witness pointed to a building and told the officers, "The guy is in the apartment." A minute later, they heard screaming and fighting. Officers knocked. Roxanne Rojas answered. She was crying and holding a baby. She had a large bump on her nose and blood on her clothes. Fernandez appeared at the door and said, "You don't have any right to come in here." Police arrested him for assaulting Rojas.

The original robbery victim then identified Fernandez as his attacker. Fernandez was taken to the station for booking. One hour later, Detective Clark returned and requested consent to search from Roxanne Rojas. She agreed. Inside, Clark found the clothes worn and sawed-off shotgun used during the robbery.

Rojas's consent was valid despite Fernandez's earlier objection. He had been lawfully arrested so, according to the Supreme Court, he was "in the same shoes as [any] occupant who is absent for any other reason." It makes no sense to allow an occupant's refusal to have legal force after he leaves the premises.

Family relationships

Married and unmarried partners. In the absence of some information which indicates exclusive use — such as the inability to produce the key to a locked cabinet — officers may assume that a spouse or unmarried partner has authority to consent. *Comm. v. Podgurski*, 44 Mass. App. Ct. 929 (1998) (although wife went to a shelter to escape defendant's abuse, she still had access and control to their home and could consent to police entry). *Comm. v. Noonan*, 48 Mass. App. Ct. 356 (2000) (Noonan's girlfriend occupied the apartment with him; she had total access *except* for a bureau that was reserved for Noonan alone; she could lawfully consent to a search of all other portions of the apartment)

Good relations not required. *Comm. v. Martin*, 358 Mass. 282 (1970) began with a husband's armed robbery and ended when his wife allowed police to search their home. Officers found the ski masks worn during the robbery. Martin argued that his wife could not consent because she hated him! The SJC disagreed. The nature of the relationship is irrelevant. The issue is whether the party has joint access and control.

Police may assume that adult family members can allow them to look around. Adult family members typically have "the run of the house." *Comm. v. Albert*, 2013 WL 6847724 (Appeals Court).

Grandparents and parents may consent to a search of their child's property if they have access. This is true whether the child is a minor or adult. *Comm. v. Ortiz*, 422 Mass. 64 (1996).

- **Legitimate access.** *U.S. v. Casey*, 825 F.3d 1 (1st Cir. 2016): The grandparents had the authority to consent to the search of the defendant's bedroom in their house. The grandfather told police that the defendant's room was unlocked and open, that he did not contribute to rent or food, and that they could enter his room at will.[4]

- **No established access.** *Comm. v. Santos*, 97 Mass. App. Ct. 719 (2020): Mother and father owned a two-family house and lived in the upstairs apartment. Their adult daughter lived in the downstairs apartment. The mother gave permission to a Holyoke police officer to search the downstairs apartment, which resulted in the officer finding her son's illegal handgun and ammunition. The fact that the mother had allowed her son to sleep on the couch in her daughter's apartment on several occasions did not prove her authority to consent to a police search there. The officer had a duty to explore the facts further by asking whether there was a landlord–tenant relationship. Because the officer did not know, the mother's consent was invalid and the gun was suppressed. Also see *U.S. v. Robinson*, 999 F.Supp 155 (D. Mass. 1998) (a mother did not have authority to consent to a police search of her son's pants pockets or closed bag, but she *did* have authority to allow police to search above the ceiling tiles in her son's room).

---

4 Their consent search produced a firearm used to murder an undercover police officer.

Children who are routinely left alone may consent to police entry and a limited search.
U.S. v. Clutter, 914 F.2d 775 (6ᵗʰ Cir. 1990): Three children (ages 14, 12, and 8) lived with their mother and her boyfriend, who both worked nights and left the kids alone. The two older boys observed large quantities of marijuana in the house and spoke to police with the help of their biological father. The father told the police that he feared the boys would be in danger if they helped officers prepare an affidavit for a search warrant. He suggested that an officer visit the apartment so the boys could let him in. The court found the search consensual.

Until this issue is squarely addressed by a Massachusetts appellate court, the safest course of action is for officers to either: (1) wait for the parents to return and seek consent from them; or ideally (2) secure the premises and obtain a warrant.

Property relationships

Third parties may only consent to police entry and/or search if they are co-inhabitants or in possession of an explicit contract. *Comm. v. Porter*, 456 Mass. 254 (2010): 16 year old Porter and his mother were staying at a shelter that required all occupants to obey strict rules. The manager and staff had keys to each unit. All residents signed a zero tolerance policy for drugs and weapons.

The manager learned that Porter told several individuals he had a gun in his room. She contacted Boston Police. Officers arrived the next day. They went to Porter's room and had him step out into the hallway. They found a loaded Glock .40 in the closet. The prosecutor argued that the shelter manager's consent had been sufficient.

- **Third party consent.** The SJC used the *Porter* case to announce a strict rule. A third party may legally consent to a police search *only if* she:

  - *Is a co-inhabitant with joint access and control* — such as a spouse, intimate partner, family member, roommate, or established overnight guest; *or*

  - *Has a signed contract allowing her to permit a police search.* This second requirement applies to landlords, propety managers, and hotel/motel clerks. After all, the SJC reasoned, Porter and his mother never gave *written permission* for the shelter manager to allow a *police* search. They only gave written permission for the manager and staff to search.[5]

- **Police lesson.** Before they can enter and/or search based on consent, officers must ask questions to determine whether the third party is a true co-inhabitant *or* in possession of a contract authorizing her to permit a police search (which officers will rarely, if ever, encounter). Again, in *Porter*, the manager did not live with mother and son, and the manager did not have a signed document from the mother saying she could permit a police search of their unit. Consequently, the gun and ammo were suppressed.

---

5 Ironically, if the manager had searched Porter's room on her own and turned his gun over to police, Porter would have had no legal basis to object, since he and his mother had already given permission to the staff to conduct room inspections!

- *Porter* **rule does <u>not</u> apply to exigent circumstances.** The decision does not limit, in any way, the authority of police to enter in response to exigent circumstances.[6] However, there was no exigency in *Porter,* where officers delayed their response for a day after receiving the manager's report about the gun. In contrast, *Boston Housing Authority v. Guirola*, 410 Mass. 820 (1991) involved an exterminator who lawfully entered an apartment and saw a sawed-off shotgun. When he notified police, officers immediately responded, secured the weapon, and applied for a search warrant.

Third parties may allow police to enter and/or search a common area or abandoned unit.[7] *Comm. v. Ploude*, 44 Mass. App. Ct. 137 (1998) (owner had authority to allow a fire chief and ATF agents to enter the building and conduct an arson investigation outside the defendant's locked office). *Comm. v. Sandler*, 368 Mass. 729 (1975) (landlord may consent to a police search once the tenant clearly abandons the premises or comes to the end of the lease term).

Tenants and roommates. A tenant or roommate may consent to a police search, except in areas where the suspect maintains exclusive control. *Comm. v. Rodriguez*, 364 Mass. 87 (1973) (co-tenant lawfully gave consent for a police search of the bathroom, which he and the defendant used, and where the officer found a revolver).

Hosts. A host may consent to a police search of any jointly used property or area. This may happen without the guest's knowledge. A host may not consent where his guest maintains exclusive control over a room, suitcase, dresser drawer, or other item that the guest reasonably believes the host will not intrude upon. *Comm. v. Magri*, 462 Mass. 360 (2012).

Bailees and bailors. A *bailee* receives property from a *bailor*. The bailee may typically consent to a search while he controls the property. In *Comm. v. Campbell*, 352 Mass. 387 (1967), a vehicle owner gave permission to a friend to use his car to go on a date. Police approached the friend (the bailee) and asked him if he would drive to the police station because the car contained evidence related to a young girl's murder. The bailee agreed, which was within the scope of his authority over the vehicle at that time. Police recovered evidence once they got a search warrant for the car. The SJC rejected the owner's (bailor's) later legal challenge.

A bailee may *not* consent to a search beyond the scope of his limited authority. For example, a coat check attendant at an event could not consent to a search of a closed package left by a patron. *Comm. v. Weiss*, 370 Mass. 416 (1976).

Finally, a bailor may *not* consent to a search of property that is under the control of a bailee.

Motorists.

- **The owner, who is typically the driver, has the primary authority to consent to a vehicle search.** If the owner is not present, the driver may consent to a police search; a passenger typically does not have that authority. *Comm. v. Santiago*, 30 Mass. App. Ct. 207 (1991) (passenger, after arrest, asked trooper to retrieve his guitar from the trunk; the trooper obtained keys consensually from the driver; in the trunk, the trooper saw cocaine in plain view; court said this was a valid consent search).

---

6 See *Chapter 16* for a detailed discussion of exigent circumstances.
7 What constitutes a "common area" or "abandoned property" was addressed in *Chapter 11.*

- **Police may not use consent from one occupant to search items that obviously belong to another.**[8] *U.S. v. Infante-Ruiz*, 13 F.3d 498 (1st Cir. 1994) (the driver consented to a search of the trunk, but his consent did not cover an unlocked briefcase because he identified it as belonging to a passenger). Compare *U.S. v. Barber*, 777 F.3d 1303 (11th Cir. 2015) (police stopped a car in which Tyrone Barber was a passenger; the driver, Geofrey Robinson, had a suspended license; Robinson consented to a search; officers found a bag on the passenger-side floor containing a gun and Barber's business cards; Barber was charged and argued that police should have asked him for consent to search his bag, but the court held that police reasonably believed the bag was covered by Robinson's consent; drivers do not usually place their bags on the driver-side floor near the pedals, they use the passenger-side more often; plus, Barber said nothing about the bag when police initially removed it).

Employers. An employer may consent to a search of his business premises or property except for areas under the exclusive control of an employee. *Comm. v. Wahlstrom*, 375 Mass. 115 (1978).

APPARENT AUTHORITY

Officers may rely on individuals who act as though they have the authority to allow police to enter and/or search. *Comm. v. Dejarnette*, 75 Mass. App. Ct. 88 (2009): Jennifer Chicklis did not have the authority to permit officers to search a "Dr. Seuss" backpack owned by defendant Nickolas Dejarnette. However, Jennifer rented the apartment, consented to a police search, and mentioned that one of her children lived there. It was reasonable for officers to believe that the "Dr. Seuss" backpack on the kitchen floor belonged to her daughter. Since searching this backpack appeared to be covered by Jennifer's consent, the police lawfully seized Dejarnette's drugs and ammunition inside. They knew these items belonged to him when they saw his name written inside the backpack! See *Illinois v. Rodriguez*, 497 U.S. 177 (1990) (landmark case on apparent authority).

If officers should doubt the person's authority, they must ask further questions. *Comm. v. Lopez*, 458 Mass. 383 (2010): Victor, a motel manager, talked to Officer Desimone about removing a discarded hypodermic needle (a service the police regularly provided). Later on, Officer Desimone went to the room where he thought Victor lived with a container for the needle. He knocked, announced himself, and stated, "Hello, Victor." A woman opened the door. The officer asked for Victor. The woman looked "like a deer in the headlights," then responded, "I don't know." Desimone showed her the container. He asked, "Can I come in?" She responded, "Yeah, sure." The woman appeared nervous and possibly high on drugs.

Through an open bedroom door, Desimone observed three men then heard a "thump." He saw José Lopez standing next to a metal trash can. He arrested Lopez when he saw a revolver at the bottom of the can. That night, Victor told Desimone that he had rented the room to Lopez and his family.

In its decision to suppress the gun, the SJC found that Officer Desimone improperly entered. The court held that Desimone should have asked more questions when an unknown woman opened the door — e.g., Who are you? Whose room is this? The answers would have told him whether the woman at the door had the authority to let him enter.

---

8 This is different from a motor vehicle search based on probable cause, where *any* object that may hold evidence is subject to a search. See *Chapter 16* discussion of *Wyoming v. Houghton.*

Police do _not_ have to ask questions when it seems obvious that the person has the authority to let them in. *Comm. v. Fernando Santos*, 465 Mass. 680 (2013): The young victim lived in a second-floor apartment with his mother. His grandmother lived in the first-floor apartment with her boyfriend, Fernando Santos.

One night, the victim was sleeping downstairs on his grandmother's couch when Santos came home drunk and raped him. The boy told his grandmother, who called his mother. The mother dialed 911.

Arriving officers found Fernando Santos walking on the street. After they placed him in the cruiser, they approached the house. The victim had walked back into the grandmother's apartment and was waiting in the living room. The victim's mother led police into the grandmother's apartment. Officers noticed a stain on the couch that appeared to be semen. They asked the grandmother if they could take the cushion as evidence. She agreed.

Here, the police reasonably believed that the victim's mother had the authority to let them enter the first-floor apartment even though, as they would later find out, she did not live there. After all, officers were responding to a 911 call concerning rape, and the caller gave a street address, not an apartment number. The officers were met on the porch by a woman who identified herself as the 911 caller and led them through two open doors into the grandmother's apartment.

16 Exigent Circumstances

"Exigent" means calling for immediate action. Exigent circumstances are present when there is a compelling need to act. Two situations qualify:

- **Motor vehicle exception.** Police are usually excused from the warrant requirement when they develop probable cause that evidence is located in a vehicle.

- **Exigency in the home.** Police may also enter a home or other private building, without a warrant, if they are concerned that violence, injury, destruction of evidence, escape, or a significant disturbance will occur if they delay.

MOTOR VEHICLE EXCEPTION

JUSTIFICATION

The motor vehicle exception is a longstanding exception to the Fourth Amendment and Article 14 warrant requirement. It is allowed for two reasons:

- **Mobility.** The inherent mobility of a vehicle makes it impossible in most situations to obtain a warrant without risking the loss of evidence. *Comm. v. Markou*, 391 Mass. 27 (1984).

- **Reduced privacy.** The rule also recognizes that a suspect has a lesser expectation of privacy in a vehicle. *Rakas v. Illinois*, 439 U.S. 128 (1978).

The motor vehicle exception applies to other vehicles which are mobile and regulated, such as airplanes and boats. *Rakas v. Illinois*, 439 U.S. 128 (1978).

Mobile homes. A more difficult question is whether a motor home should be regarded as a motor vehicle or as a dwelling subject to the warrant requirement. The answer depends on whether the vehicle is operational and being used for transportation, as opposed to functioning as a fixed place of residence. *California v. Carney*, 471 U.S. 386 (1985).

REQUIREMENTS

The motor vehicle exception applies when:

- **Probable cause.** The police have probable cause to believe a vehicle contains evidence at the time they begin their search; and

- **Public area.** The vehicle is lawfully stopped on a public way or parked in an area of potential public or perpetrator access.

PROBABLE CAUSE

Probable cause to search may be more general under the motor vehicle exception than under a warrant. *Comm. v. Markou*, 391 Mass. 27 (1984) started with a call coming to Pittsfield 911 from a citizen, who said the defendant just helped himself to some stereo equipment and made off in a yellow Mustang. Officers knew the defendant and stopped his car. They found some equipment under a cover in the back seat and arrested him. A more extensive search of his vehicle produced other evidence. Interestingly, describing evidence as "stolen stereo equipment" in a search warrant affidavit would have been too vague.[1] Yet, the SJC approved. General probable cause based on a spontaneous report justifies a vehicle search in public.

Probable cause *after* stop

Officers may develop probable cause through their lawful contact with motorists.

- **Sufficient.** *Comm. v. Ciaramitaro*, 51 Mass. App. Ct. 638 (2001): After an illegal turn, the defendant was stopped. He repeatedly got out and appeared nervous. He said he was lost even though he claimed to live in town. When he kept putting his hands in his pockets, officers frisked him and discovered a digital scale. Using their flashlights from outside the vehicle, officers saw illegal weapons — a dirk knife and switch knife — in the car. Seeing these weapons gave police probable cause to arrest the defendant and search the vehicle.

- **Insufficient.** *U.S. v. Gemma*, 2014 WL 1654133 (Massachusetts District Court): Trooper Morris stopped Michael Gemma for speeding. A.L., a young female, was in the passenger seat. She was not wearing a seatbelt and had no ID. When Morris asked her date of birth, she said "December 23 . . . 1992?" in a question-like manner.

  Morris asked A.L. to get out so he could speak to her. A.L. said she had moved to Boston from Puerto Rico and had known Gemma for two years. Morris did not believe her. He placed her in his cruiser to keep her safe from passing cars. Morris then spoke to Gemma, who only knew A.L.'s first name and said he had known her for a month. Morris searched the vehicle, including the trunk. He found women's lingerie, high heeled shoes, condoms, and a laptop. A registry check showed Gemma had a suspended license. He was arrested.

  At the barracks, A.L. revealed that she and Gemma were returning from New York, where he had posted internet advertisements offering sex with her. Morris now obtained a warrant for the laptop and Gemma's cell phone. The evidence resulted in a federal indictment for interstate transportation of a minor for prostitution, 18 U.S.C. 2423.

  While a teenage female driving with an older male and their inconsistent statements was enough for further investigation, it did not amount to probable cause *at the time* the trooper searched the car. The information he received later at the barracks did tip the scale for probable cause, but it came too late.[2]

---

1 See discussion in *Chapter 13*.
2 No one conducted an inventory on the vehicle before it was towed, which was another oversight.

The odor of marijuana, along with another distribution factor, provides probable cause to search. Chapter 4 fully discusses the limited police authority to remove occupants and search for marijuana.

Presence of hidden compartment is probable cause to search for contraband or a weapon. In *Comm. v. Rosario-Santiago,* 96 Mass. App. Ct. 166 (2019), Trooper Reynolds had probable cause there was a·hidden compartment in Rosario-Santiago's car: (1) his driving had been fast and erratic (leading to the stop); (2) he seemed to make up answers in response to the trooper's basic questions about the origin of his trip; (3) he secretly (by faking a yawn) reached toward a bag in the back seat and then denied doing so; (4) the bag contained a heat-sealed package of the sort used to transport drugs; (5) he had urinated in a cup found in the console (which drug couriers do so they can keep driving and meet their delivery deadline); (6) elastic bands of the sort used to bind cash and drugs were in the front seat area; and (7) the trooper saw, on the carpet near the console, a "wear mark" probably made from the repeated opening of a compartment.

Armed with probable cause, Trooper Reynolds looked under the dashboard and found an installed wire. With the help of an experienced colleague, the trooper manipulated the wire causing a mechanical door to open and reveal packets of oxycodone.

Also see *Comm. v. Haynes,* 83 Mass. App. Ct. 903 (2013) (trooper, who used to sell cars, noticed that the radio panel of a new rental vehicle was slightly ajar; he removed it to reveal a handgun in a hidden compartment).

Evidence on occupant as basis to search the vehicle. When police discover contraband or other evidence on an occupant, the question becomes whether they now have probable cause to search the vehicle for additional evidence. The answer depends on the type of evidence and what else they know about the situation. *Comm. v. Ierardi,* 17 Mass. App. Ct. 297 (1983) (seven bullets and a packet of cocaine found on a person removed from the vehicle gave police probable cause to believe that there might be a gun and other drugs in the car).

Probable cause _before_ stop

Police sometimes have probable cause before they stop a vehicle. Comm. v. Gouse, 461 Mass. 787 (2012): Officers had probable cause that an illegal firearm was in the car based on reports from a bystander, the victim's father, and an anonymous informant. The nervous behavior of the defendant's two female companions corroborated the tips. When they did not find a gun on the defendant's person, officers wisely concluded that it must be in the car.

No probable cause without a connection between the crime and the suspect's vehicle. Comm. v. Dame, 473 Mass. 524 (2016): A woman was found murdered in her bedroom, naked from the waist down. The door had been forced open, and there were pieces of paper towel on the floor. The next day, police interviewed Ronald Dame, whom the victim had previously dated. Dame had several scratches on his cheek. During the interview, police went outside Dame's house and retrieved a paper towel from his car. Sperm on the towel was evidence.

Unfortunately, police lacked probable cause to search the car. Police had no information linking the crime to Dame's vehicle. Officers had no proof he drove his car the night of the murder or had used it during the crime.

Time gap between crime and stop does not necessarily eliminate probable cause. *Comm. v. Hernandez*, 473 Mass. 379 (2015): Officer Hanson received a report of an armed robbery at 8:30 p.m. The victims provided the license plate number of a green Honda Civic, and said there was a Dominican flag hanging from the rear view mirror. The two suspects were Hispanic. At 1:33 a.m., Hanson learned an armed home invasion occurred 50 yards from the earlier robbery. At 2:20 a.m., dispatch alerted him to another home invasion involving the same green Honda. The dispatcher noted that the owner lived on Phillips Street.

Officer Hanson drove toward Phillips Street and saw the vehicle. He called for backup and pulled the car over after it failed to stop at a stop sign. The officers searched and found a gun in the trunk. The 6-hour gap between the robbery and stop did not negate probable cause. It was really unlikely that someone new was driving.

If police have <u>pre-stop</u> probable cause, they must execute their search without "unreasonable delay" or seek a warrant. In *Comm. v. Eggleston*, 453 Mass. 554 (2009), a Berkshire County task force investigated the defendant, William Eggleston, who worked at a tire store.[3] Multiple informants told police that Eggleston usually sold crack cocaine at work and supplied Joseph Pini, a known dealer.

One day in January, two informants told police that Eggleston was scheduled to receive a large shipment and sell it to Pini after 5:00 p.m. At 4:15 p.m., police began surveillance of the tire store, intending to arrest Eggleston and Pini after their transaction. At 4:20 p.m., Pini drove past the tire store.

The supervisor decided that the traffic conditions and unpredictability of these suspects presented too great a risk of high-speed pursuit.[4] He felt it would be wiser to arrest Eggleston the minute he left the store, which officers did. They recovered 379 grams of crack in his SUV.

- **Warrantless vehicle searches must be "reasonably prompt."** The SJC did not want officers exploiting the motor vehicle exception to avoid getting a warrant. In *Eggleston*, probable cause for a search warrant existed long before officers arrived at the tire store, *but* their delayed search was designed to: (1) corroborate the tips received (i.e., that Eggleston would leave work when Pini showed up); (2) enable Eggleston to place additional evidence into his vehicle (i.e., he often carried cocaine on his person); and (3) confirm anticipated criminal conduct (i.e., that Eggleston and Pini would exchange drugs and money). These were defensible reasons to postpone their search decision until the last possible moment.

- **Practical implications.** In most cases, the police spontaneously develop probable cause to search a vehicle during a traffic stop, so *Eggleston* is irrelevant. On the other hand, if police develop probable cause before they stop and search a vehicle, they must be able to point to some aspect of their investigation that was strengthened by *not* getting a warrant in advance. Typically, if police want additional corroboration of their tip (e.g., allowing their suspect to meet an accomplice), that will be a good enough reason. The bottom line: Since any delay between probable cause and the warrantless search will be scrutinized by the court, the best practice is to get a search warrant when there is time.

---

3 How about this for a classic drug dealer nickname: "Goodyear Bill."
4 On the stand, Sergeant Foley described Pini as "a nut" who might be tempted to flee like a wild man!

LOCATION OF SEARCH

The search may occur on the street, at a police facility, or in both locations. Police typically complete their search on scene, but it is not required. Sometimes safety, traffic, or a lack of manpower makes towing the vehicle to a police facility the better option. This is acceptable if the search is completed within a reasonable period of time. *Comm. v. Lara*, 39 Mass. App. Ct. 546 (1995) (detective saw a drug transaction involving the defendant; detective quickly searched the vehicle on the street and found nothing; it was then towed to the station where another detective found a cache of 40 bags of cocaine behind a radio speaker cover).[5]

A parked vehicle may be searched if the public or a perpetrator has potential access.

*   **Driveway search.** *Comm. v. Harris*, 47 Mass App. Ct. 481 (1999): The police witnessed two dealers openly transacting drug sales from the trunk of a Cadillac. Other officers chased a buyer. With people yelling "police" in this Springfield neighborhood, the officers became apprehensive that the defendants would be alerted to their presence. They converged on the driveway and found cocaine and a small scale in the trunk.

    The defendants later demonstrated that, at the time of the search, the Cadillac was parked in the driveway with a flat tire and a blown engine! Even so, the court approved the warrantless search on the theory that perpetrators or members of the public might get quick access to the evidence in the car.

*   **Towed from driveway.** *Robinson v. Cook*, 706 F.3d 25 (2013): Two 13 year old boys were riding their bicycles when a car pulled up next to them. The passenger engaged one of the boys in a swearing match about a recent fight. Before driving away, the car struck the boy, flipping him over the handlebars.

    Police located a vehicle matching the boys' description in Robert Robinson's driveway, one mile from the hit and run. The passenger door was ajar, and the engine was warm. Police spoke to Robinson, who gave an inconsistent account of when he and his son last used the car. The officers properly towed the vehicle to the station, so Robinson and his son could not move or meddle with this important piece of evidence.

Officers should complete their search within 2 hours or get a warrant. Substantial delays may cause the suppression of evidence on the grounds that a warrant should have been obtained. *Comm. v. Bell*, 78 Mass. App. Ct. 135 (2010).

Consider the excellent police work in *Comm. v. Holness*, 2018 WL 2729448 (Appeals Court). At 4:10 a.m., police were dispatched to the intersection of Talbot Avenue and Aspinwall Road in Dorchester in response to a ShotSpotter activation. On arrival, officers saw broken glass in the street. The defendant's motor vehicle was approximately 320 feet from the intersection, and it had been in a recent collision. It was Christmas morning when few other vehicles were on the road. Police seized the car.

The next day, detectives got a warrant for the vehicle supported by additional evidence from a video recording of the intersection at the time of the crash. The search produced two shell

---

5 The same is true for a warrant. *Comm. v. Lugo*, 64 Mass. App. Ct. 12 (2005) allows police to search a vehicle with a warrant at the scene of the stop or following a tow to the police station.

casings. When the officers originally denied the defendant access to his motor vehicle, which was inoperable due to the recent crash, they had probable cause to seize it without a warrant. They wisely got a warrant when they knew their search would be delayed.

SCOPE OF SEARCH

A lawful search extends to all areas and containers — open, closed, or locked — that might hold evidence, including the trunk. *Comm. v. Bakoian,* 412 Mass. 295 (1992) (because he was looking for drugs, detective could remove air filter from engine and discover contraband).

- **Locked container.** In *Comm. v. Moses,* 408 Mass. 136 (1990), a vehicle caught an officer's attention because it was idling at a bus stop and its occupants seemed to be engaging in a drug sale. The officer saw the front seat passenger duck down. Meanwhile, the possible buyers scurried into a nearby building.

  The officer stopped and ordered the driver to turn off the ignition and hand over the keys. The driver and passengers were ordered out. The officer found cocaine on the front seat and a gun underneath. This discovery gave police probable cause to search the rest of the car for additional drugs and weapons. The SJC allowed officers to pry open a locked suitcase, viewing the intrusion as consistent with the evidence-gathering purpose of the motor vehicle exception.

- **Specific container.** Sometimes probable cause relates solely to a particular container in the vehicle. For example, an informant reports that the drug dealer stores his cocaine "in a blue Coleman cooler on the front seat." *Comm. v. Wunder,* 407 Mass. 909 (1990). With such focused probable cause, police may conduct a warrantless search of the identified item, but *not* the entire vehicle. *California v. Acevedo,* 500 U.S. 665 (1991) (officer saw defendant place a paper bag with drugs in the trunk; officer stopped defendant and, without a warrant, retrieved the bag and opened it; officer limited his search to the bag).

When police have probable cause to search a vehicle, they may also search any passenger's belongings that might hold evidence. This is true even though the police lack probable cause to believe that the passenger is guilty of any wrongdoing. Once officers have probable cause to search a vehicle, the passenger's expectation of privacy is reduced. To rule otherwise would provide an incentive for criminals to hide evidence in their passenger's belongings.

Wyoming v. Houghton, 526 U.S. 295 (1999): Highway Patrol stopped a vehicle for speeding. An officer observed a hypodermic syringe in the driver's shirt pocket. The driver admitted that he used it for illegal drugs. The officer began to search the vehicle. He found a purse. The defendant, who had been sitting in the front passenger seat, admitted it was hers. Inside the purse, officers discovered drug paraphernalia and a syringe with methamphetamine.[6]

---

6 Until the SJC or Appeals Court rules differently, *Houghton* guides Massachusetts officers.

HOME EXIGENCY

Exigent circumstances in a home have two major limitations. First, the emergency cannot be one that should have been anticipated by police. Second, officers must obtain a warrant when the emergency ends. The emergency is typically over if:

- **The suspect has been arrested or removed from the scene.**

- **There is no longer any risk that evidence will be destroyed or removed.** *Mincey v. Arizona,* 437 U.S. 385 (1978).

- **All occupants of the premises have been removed and the police can post a guard** to prevent others from entering until a warrant is obtained. *Comm. v. Lewin,* 407 Mass. 617 (1990).

In *Comm. v. Taylor,* 2014 WL 3953081 (Appeals Court), the victim reported that the defendant hit him in the head with a handgun in their front yard, took the gun to the backyard, and returned to the front without it. Although there was probable cause to believe the gun was in the backyard, exigent circumstances did not justify a warrantless search of that area. Officers had already secured the scene. They should have gotten a warrant before searching the recycling bin in the yard.

HOT PURSUIT

Officers in hot pursuit of a felony suspect may enter a home. In *Comm. v. McCollum,* 79 Mass. App. Ct. 239 (2011), officers saw Steven Williams get into a stolen car. Williams smashed into a cruiser and escaped on foot. An officer saw him tossing bags of cocaine in a field. Williams ran into an apartment building.

Officers waited for the building manager. They searched several apartments with the occupants' consent, then knocked on apartment 12. When no one responded, the manager opened the door with a key. Williams was on a bed pretending to be asleep. Alan McCollum was sitting next to him with his young daughter. Police arrested Williams. While securing the apartment, officers found an empty holster in a closet. McCollum then admitted to having an illegal gun nearby. Its discovery led to his arrest, after which police secured the apartment and obtained a search warrant for additional evidence.

Notice how police entered the apartment in hot pursuit of Williams, but once they had secured him and McCollum, they knew the emergency was over. Officers wisely secured the premises and obtained a warrant. *Warden v. Hayden,* 387 U.S. 294 (1967).

Unlike a felony, misdemeanors may be quite minor. This is why hot pursuit into a home is not always permitted. Only an additional emergency — such as potential violence, destruction of evidence, or escape from the home — justifies warrantless entry. The Supreme Court stated: "On many occasions, the officer will have good reason to enter," but the officer must stop to get a warrant if it is not truly an exigent situation. *Lange v. California,* 141 S.Ct 2011 (2021).

- **Most of the time, flight itself brings on exigencies.** First, the suspect generally knows the officer is there — that is why he is fleeing! Second, the officer often will not know who the suspect is or if the suspect entered his own home or a stranger's. Third, the officer will probably not know if the suspect has gone into one door with intent to run out another.

- **That is why it makes more sense to spell out the factors that call for an officer to stop and get a warrant or criminal complaint.** As a result, do <u>not</u> enter a dwelling in hot pursuit of a misdemeanor suspect if you:

    - *Know the suspect fled into his own home,* and

    - *Do not believe the suspect will destroy evidence* of a crime you have probable cause to arrest for, and

    - *Have no information the suspect poses a risk of violence.*

- **Other factors that eliminate hot pursuit:**

    - *The offense is civil. Comm. v. Martin*, 91 Mass. App. Ct. 733 (2017): Two officers approached a legally parked vehicle with three men inside. The vehicle was full of marijuana smoke. The officers began work on issuing civil infractions. Dequan Martin got out and ran into a nearby home. The officers tackled him inside and found a gun in his pocket.

        At the time of the chase, the officers had probable cause only to cite Martin for a civil marijuana offense. This civil infraction was not a jailable misdemeanor and provided no basis for entering a dwelling in hot pursuit.

        When officers argued that they believed Martin committed a breaking and entering during his flight, the court countered that there was no reason to believe that Martin entered unlawfully. The home was close to where the car was parked; he entered without force; no one inside showed alarm about Martin's sudden entry; and officers had just talked with his mother on the sidewalk nearby.

    - *The only crime is a non-jailable misdemeanor, Comm. v. Jewett*, 471 Mass. 624 (2015). — for example, refusal to stop for a police officer, 90 § 25.

Seeking breath or blood test evidence will not justify entry either. *Comm. v. DiGeronimo*, 38 Mass. App. Ct. 714 (1995). If the crime is OUI alcohol, entering a home will not be justified to obtain a breath or blood sample, since these forms of evidence may not be compelled from a suspect even with a warrant. See *Comm. v. Bohigian*, 486 Mass. 209 (2020).

The pursuit may be short. In *U.S. v. Santana*, 427 U.S. 38 (1976), police confronted a suspect on the doorstep to her apartment. She quickly ran inside (where she could easily destroy evidence or grab a weapon). Officers properly entered in hot pursuit to arrest her.

Police should warn potentially innocent occupants before entering. *Trent v. Wade*, 776 F.3d 368 (2015): At 2:00 a.m., Texas police officer Wade saw two ATVs racing on the highway. He tried to stop the ATVs, but they fled. Wade pursued one driver, Richard Trent, to his house. Trent ran inside. Wade opened the unlocked door and entered without knocking or announcing his presence. Trent's father, mother, and brother were inside, sleeping. While the hot pursuit entry made sense, the officer should have warned the occupants before he entered.

POTENTIAL CRIME SCENE

Officers may enter to investigate a possible crime in progress. Sometimes officers discover an open door or other suspicious signs. They may enter without a warrant to determine if any intruders are present and to secure the premises. *Comm. v. Young,* 382 Mass. 448 (1981).

As long as officers behave reasonably, they are not liable to the homeowner. *Macdonald v. Town of Eastham,* 946 F.Supp.2d 235 (D. Mass. 2013):[7] Philip Macdonald had intentionally left the side door of his house open so that his cat could roam freely, and police did not know this when they received a call from a neighbor that no one was home and the door was open. Two officers arrived at Macdonald's house and announced their presence. When no one answered, they walked through the open door into the kitchen. They conducted a protective sweep of the house and saw illegal drugs. At this point, they wisely secured the home, obtained a warrant, and collected the evidence.

DOMESTIC VIOLENCE

REASONS FOR ENTRY

Serve restraining order

Officers may enter private property to serve a restraining order. *Comm. v. Mulvey,* 57 Mass. App. Ct. 579 (2003).

Determine whether abuse occurring

Officers may enter a home to determine whether someone has been abused. The police response to domestic violence must be "evaluated in relation to the scene as it [appeared] to the officers at the time, and not . . . with the benefit of leisured retrospective analysis." *Comm. v. Rexach,* 20 Mass. App. Ct. 919 (1985).

- *Comm. v. Gordon,* 87 Mass. App. Ct. 322 (2015): Police received a 911 call for a disturbance in apartment 1 of a building attached to a bar. A tenant from apartment 2 let them in. She did not call 911, but had heard an argument and crashing sounds coming from apartment 1. She said a male tenant lived there with his girlfriend. Police knocked on the door and received no response. Dispatch then told them the call came from the bar.

  While police maintained surveillance on apartment 1, Officer Coup went downstairs to the bar. A bartender told Coup: (1) a woman named Kay had asked her to call police; (2) when the bartender asked if she was all right, Kay said, "no"; (3) Kay's hair was wet, her shirt looked like it had been pulled, and she was carrying her dog; and (4) Kay had walked toward the entrance to her apartment when she left.

---

7 On appeal, this decision was upheld — *MacDonald v. Town of Eastham,* 745 F.3d 8 (2014) — but on a much more technical basis. We cite the earlier decision because it is more relevant to police officers.

Coup returned upstairs and relayed the information. Fifteen minutes had passed. The building owner arrived. He said the tenant was James Gordon, his girlfriend Kay often stayed there, and Gordon's car was still in the driveway. He let the officers in.

Police conducted a brief search to see if someone inside needed help. No one was there. In plain sight, they saw illegal drugs for sale. Police secured the scene and obtained a warrant for the evidence. Given the dangerous nature of many domestic violence incidents, the police had no choice. They had to enter to make sure Kay was safe.

- *Comm. v. Qadir*, 93 Mass. App. Ct. 1111 (2018): Springfield police officers were dispatched to a residence based on a report of a fight. When they arrived, officers saw seven or eight people running into the house. One officer found a woman outside bleeding from the mouth. She said, "They beat me up," and pointed at the house. The officers knocked on the front door. When it was opened, they stated their intention to enter and conduct a protective sweep. Upstairs, behind a locked bedroom door, officers heard footsteps and something being dragged across the floor. They demanded access. After some delay, the defendant opened the door. Officers entered and opened the closet door. They saw an open cooler filled with handguns and ammunition. Like *Gordon*, this case was a measured response to ensure there were no victims on the premises.

Reasonable belief subject of order present

Potential victim's objection has no bearing on the reasonableness of police entry. *Comm. v. Morrison*, 429 Mass. 511 (1999) found Amherst police responding in the aftermath of a shouting match between Joe Morrison and Jamie Daniels. The officers knocked at Daniels' door and received no response. They had dispatch contact the apartment manager to arrange a well-being entry. The manager opened the door with his key, but the door was chained from the inside. Daniels appeared but hesitated to let officers in. They tried to persuade her, but Daniels commented that she was going to court "to get rid of the order anyway." Officers ordered her to unlock the chain. She complied. They found Morrison hiding under her bed. He was arrested. In supporting the officers' decision to enter, the SJC explained:

> "Battered women tend to minimize and deny the severity and extent of the abuse . . . [Officers] should not be put in the position of second-guessing the continuing need for protection under an order in the confused and hectic circumstances of a heated encounter. They might rightly be concerned that the assurances she gave them at the door were the result of intimidation by the defendant . . . If they had accepted her statements at face value and turned away, and she had been harmed a short time later, the police might have been criticized for not affording a potential victim the full measure of protection a protective order provide[s]."

Also see *U.S. v. Bartelho*, 71 F.3d 436 (1st Cir. 1995) (police entered despite a woman's objection; they found her boyfriend hiding with a rifle).

LIMIT ON ENTRY

A potential victim must be at risk in order to justify an exigent entry. In *Comm. v. Midi*, 46 Mass. App. Ct. 591 (1999), an officer took a complaint from Carla Andrade that her boyfriend, Daris Pierce, had beaten her up. At the time she gave her report, Andrade had left the dwelling and was safe with her family. Pierce was not aware that she had notified police, so there was no risk that evidence would be destroyed. Exigent circumstances were lacking.

Although officers had ample time to get an arrest warrant, they went directly to Pierce's apartment. Officers found drugs and a gun. Since their discovery was the product of the unlawful entry, the evidence was suppressed.

DISTURBANCE

LOUD PARTY

41, § 98 authorizes police entry into any home or building to restore peace.

- **No entry if disturbance over.** *Comm. v. Kirschner*, 67 Mass. App. Ct. 836 (2006): At 3:00 a.m. on July 4th, Hamilton police arrived at James Kirschner's house based on a neighbor's complaint about fireworks. Kirschner explained that the "unwanted guests" had run away. He asked police not to enter, but agreed to go inside and get his ID. Police confirmed that he and his guests were over 21.

  Officers Walsh and Foley decided to check the perimeter. Kirschner did not say anything. They observed illegal drugs on the back deck. Kirschner was arrested, and the officers decided to remove the remaining guests from his father's house. Each guest was patted down, questioned, and breath tested for alcohol. Two were arrested with drugs and two found themselves in protective custody.

  Officer Weston walked into the house looking for more people. He entered Kirschner's bedroom and saw two counterfeit driver's licenses in an open desk drawer. Kirschner and several others were charged with possessing counterfeit licenses and conspiracy.

  - *Insufficient emergency.* The yard and deck were in the curtilage, and the search of these private areas could not be justified. By the time police arrived, the fireworks had ended, and the unwanted guests were gone.

  - *Insufficient consent.* The court rejected the argument that police had implied consent to enter the backyard because Kirschner did not object. Consent must be clearly communicated. Seeing drugs resulted from the improper entry.

  - *Insufficient basis to enter house.* Officers had no reason to believe anyone in the house was at risk. Even if officers were concerned about the guests once the host was arrested, they had other options besides warrantless entry. Officers could have asked Kirschner whether he wanted their assistance in arranging for his guests to leave; they could have contacted Kirschner's father to find out what his wishes were; or they could have attempted to speak with the guests by knocking on the door or calling them on the telephone.

- **No entry if occupant agrees to cooperate.** Loud music did not justify a warrantless entry in *Comm. v. Kiser*, 48 Mass. App. Ct. 647 (2000). After 3:00 a.m., four officers were returning to their cars from another call when a woman approached to complain about a noisy party. Derrick Kiser answered his door in response to police knocking and agreed to turn down the music. Police recognized him as a local gang member and saw an unidentified male run across the room. The officers forcibly entered and ordered partygoers to leave. They accompanied the defendant to his room where they saw cocaine in plain view. The court ruled that loud music did not amount to a breach of the peace in view of Kiser's cooperation. Since the entry was improper, the resulting evidence had to be suppressed.

- **Entry justified for persistent disturbance.** *Comm. v. Mullins*, 31 Mass. App. Ct. 954 (1991): Officers were dispatched to the defendant's residence due to complaints of loud music. As officers walked to the house on their second visit, they saw and heard the defendant yelling obscenities from her window. Neighbors had gathered outside. The officers' initial efforts to quiet the defendant were unsuccessful, so they entered the house through the partially open front door. The defendant had barricaded herself in the bedroom. Their final request to end the disturbance was met with verbal abuse. Officers forced their way in and placed her under arrest for disturbing the peace.

   Note how *Mullins* differs from *Kiser*, where officers received immediate cooperation. Here, the officers only entered when their efforts to defuse the situation failed.

- **Entry justified by violence.** *Brigham City v. Stuart*, 126 S.Ct. 1943 (2006): The police responded at 3:00 a.m. to complaints about a loud party. As they approached the house, officers heard a loud fight. The noise seemed to be coming from the back. Officers went into the backyard and saw a brawl through the kitchen window. A juvenile was being held back by several adults. He broke free and punched one of the adults in the face, sending him to the sink spitting blood. At this point, officers opened the screen door and announced their presence. Arrests followed. The Supreme Court approved: "Nothing in the Constitution requires that officers stay put and watch until someone is rendered unconscious or worse."

UNDERAGE DRINKING OR MARIJUANA USE

The safety risks — along with the potential destruction of evidence — justify police entry to deal with an unsupervised party or one where an adult is illegally providing alcohol or marijuana. *Comm. v. Sueiras*, 72 Mass. App. Ct. 439 (2008): Melissa Sueiras, a teacher at Hoosac Valley High School, had a reputation for hosting underage drinking parties. Based on a 911 call, Officer Keith Erdeski arrived and questioned intoxicated juveniles leaving Sueiras' house. Through the window, Erdeski could see Budweiser and Smirnoff bottles on a shelf near some juveniles. He spoke with Sueiras at her front door and told her that he had probable cause to enter. Sueiras said she had been upstairs and did not know what was going on. Inside, Erdeski found juveniles in possession of alcohol and a group of kids hiding.

- **Potential destruction of evidence.** Erdeski testified that posting an officer at the door while a warrant was sought would have stopped minors from leaving, but would not have prevented them from consuming or destroying the evidence! The court agreed: The potential loss of evidence justified immediate entry.

- **Health and safety risks.** Aside from lost evidence, there are a variety of health and safety risks at stake. *Howes v. Hitchcock*, 66 F.Supp.2d 203 (D. Mass. 1999) lists the dangers of youth drinking — e.g., alcohol poisoning, fights, sexual assaults, property destruction, impaired driving, and physical injury.

These concerns apply with equal force to marijuana. Although marijuana has been legalized in small quantities for adults 21 and over, it is still illegal for anyone under 21 to possess or consume it. Just like alcohol [138, § 34], there is a "social host" law [94G, § 13(i)] that forbids transferring marijuana to minors, or allowing minors to consume marijuana on private property.[8]

EMERGENCY AID

The police play an important safety role unrelated to law enforcement. To justify a search under the emergency aid exception, *Comm. v. Arias,* 481 Mass. 604 (2019) requires that:

• **Officers have a <u>reasonable suspicion</u> that emergency assistance is needed to prevent physical harm, protect life, or provide assistance to someone injured**; and

• **They conduct a protective sweep designed to deal with the emergency.**

Because the entry is made to prevent harm — not to investigate — our courts require reasonable suspicion (not probable cause). The officers' conduct after entry must respond to the emergency and not become an excuse to search for evidence of crime.

E-911 HANG UP

All police departments know the dilemma posed by an E-911 hang up call. It could be a malfunction, a child playing with the phone, or a domestic violence victim dazed on the floor. Most of the time it is nothing, but it has to be checked out.

E-911 regulations require that police call back any unanswered or silent 911 call, and they recommend that a cruiser respond if dispatch receives no response to a call back. 560 CMR 2.01. Officers dispatched to a silent E-911 call should attempt to gain entry normally by knocking or ringing the bell. Typically, an occupant will reassure the officer that nothing is wrong. When confronted with no answer, officers should:

• **Check with dispatch about any past problems at the particular address.**

• **Walk around the perimeter.** Look and listen for any indication that people are inside (e.g., cars in the driveway, lights or television on).

• **Try to gather information from neighbors.**

• **If concerned after a preliminary inspection, consult with a supervisor to determine whether to force entry.** *Gradisher v. City of Akron*, 794 F.3d 574 (2015). Use the least intrusive method to enter the home (e.g., fire department assistance, neighbor with a key).

---

8 Like alcohol, <u>only</u> parents or grandparents may provide it to their children and grandchildren on their property. See *LED's Criminal Law, Chapters 21 and 22.*

INJURY RISK

A vulnerable person inside a dwelling may need immediate assistance.

- **Elder.** *Comm. v. Lindsey,* 72 Mass. App. Ct. 485 (2008): A man who did not speak English saw an elderly woman who appeared to be asking for help and pointing to a house. The man told a neighbor, who knew the elderly woman was in poor health. She called police. When police arrived, the elderly woman had disappeared.

  Officer Nelson concluded that the woman had probably gone back into her house and might need medical assistance. No one responded to his loud knock and announcement, so he called the fire department, who gained entry with a hydraulic tool.

  While searching for the woman, officers entered an unlocked bedroom where they saw handguns, a silencer, and ammunition. There were drums of fuel in the kitchen, some only two feet from the stove. The officers did not move any evidence and secured the scene. When Jack Lindsey arrived home from the hospital with the elderly woman (his mother), he cooperated with police. He admitted having no license and turned over the weapons. The home entry and warrantless search for the woman were totally reasonable.

- **Physically abused child.** *U.S. v. Tepiew,* 859 F.3d 452 (7th Cir. 2017): In Wisconsin, a seven year old child gave her school counselor a drawing. Underneath, she had written that she was sad because her mom "got hit in the ribs and has a black eye" and is "hurting." The student told the counselor her mother's boyfriend beat her mom up and that he also hurt her one year old brother, who had sustained a head injury.

  The counselor contacted police, who went to the child's home to conduct a welfare check. No one answered the door, although the officer heard the television and saw someone moving inside. Another officer went to the back door and heard someone lock it from inside. Concerned that the mother and one year old child were inside, seriously hurt, and possibly being prevented from seeking medical attention, the officer knocked again and warned that he was going to knock down the door. He waited 15 seconds, then kicked down the door and entered. The mother, boyfriend, and child were inside. The child had numerous injuries, including a fractured skull.

- **Sexually abused child.** *Comm. v. Gomes,* 2020 WL 2507582 (Appeals Court): Police were called at 4:00 a.m. by a mother. Her 15 year old daughter had climbed out the window and went with Virginio Gomes, a 24 year old man, into his home.[9]

  Police knocked and entered Gomes' unlocked apartment and heard music in a bedroom. That door was locked. Officers knocked again and demanded entry. The music stopped, and voices were heard inside. Officers announced they would kick the door unless it was opened. When there was no response, they did. Gomes and the girl were inside.

  The Appeals Court noted that "rape . . . poses a threat of 'serious injury' to a child." This emergency justified entry. The officers limited their actions to arresting Gomes and returning the girl to her mother.

---

9 The mother had obtained a 209A order against Gomes on behalf of her daughter, which police wisely confirmed. However, even without an order in effect, the court would have approved the police entry here.

Multiple entries may be justified when occupants — whose whereabouts are unknown — are possibly still inside. *Comm. v. Entwistle*, 463 Mass 205 (2012): On January 21, Neil Entwistle's mother-in-law called police because she had not heard from her daughter since January 19. No one had answered the door when she arrived for a planned lunch. Another friend had arranged to have dinner at the Entwistles' home that night, but no one answered. The mother-in-law said it was unlike her daughter not to call.

Sergeant Sutton and Officer O'Neil went to the house. Some of the Entwistles' friends were waiting in the driveway. The lights were on and a dog was barking inside. One friend said the Entwistles would never go away without making arrangements for their dog.

Believing the Entwistles might be inside, officers entered. Sutton noticed a bill from BMW and noted the VIN number. O'Neil picked up a digital camera and turned it on to see when it had been used last. The police put out a BOLO and checked with local hospitals.

On January 22, the mother-in-law filed a missing persons report. Police had not located the Entwistles' vehicle or gathered any more information. Officers made a second entry and smelled an unpleasant odor. They followed it to the master bedroom and found Entwistle's wife and baby dead under a comforter.

- **First entry.** When police entered on January 21, there was reasonable suspicion to fear for the Entwistles' safety. Any injury to an adult would have jeopardized the baby. O'Neil justified examining the camera as a legitimate step in a missing persons investigation.

- **Second entry.** On January 22, there was even more reason to fear for the Entwistles. 24 hours had passed, and police had been unable to track down their vehicle. Although Sergeant Sutton did not believe anyone was in the house based on his earlier search, he had only taken two steps into the bedroom and had not gone into the bathroom. The first search did not eliminate the risk that a missing person was still inside. Encountering the foul odor, officers wisely went to its source.

SUICIDE RISK

Any legitimate suicide risk will justify police intervention. *Comm. v. C.M.D.*, 2017 WL 958462 (Appeals Court): Sergeant May learned the victim was being harassed on Facebook by the defendant. The posts also indicated that the defendant intended to commit suicide soon. May knew the defendant had a history of being unstable. Officers went to his home and knocked repeatedly. After receiving no response, they properly entered.[10]

Suicide risk may be heightened by a gun in the home. Police officers should assess the following:

- **If the gun is not legally possessed, officers may seize it with consent or a search warrant** (after police secure the scene); or

- **If the gun is legally possessed, pursue an administrative remedy.** When the holder of an LTC or FID poses a credible risk of danger, the investigating police officer should notify

---

10 For a discussion of involuntary mental health commitment, see *Chapter 9.*

the licensing authority and ask that the LTC or FID be suspended for unsuitability.[11] If the licensing authority does this and demands immediate surrender of all guns, then their continued possession is unlawful. An officer may enter a home to seize them with consent or secure the premises and apply for a search warrant. See *Comm. v. Adams*, 482 Mass. 514 (2019).[12]

GAS LEAK

A gas leak or other fumes typically provide a reason to enter for emergency aid. *Comm. v. Cantelli*, 83 Mass. App. Ct. 156 (2013): A maintenance employee was called to Peter Cantelli's apartment to locate the source of a gas leak. Cantelli refused to answer the door. A technician from National Grid arrived and told Cantelli that it was an emergency. Cantelli still refused. When police officers threatened to break down his door, Cantelli opened it two inches. The technician could detect explosive levels of gas!

Police forced entry to shut off the stove and open windows. Cantelli said he must have hit the burner by accident. The police left, but the manager of the complex obtained an emergency court order to disconnect his stove. The next day, the manager asked the police to help a constable serve the order because Cantelli owned weapons. Officers encountered another wild scene, and subdued Cantelli in a room with numerous guns.

This obvious emergency justified warrantless entry on both occasions. It was also reasonable for police to handcuff Cantelli until maintenance turned off the gas.

Not all odors justify entry. *Comm. v. Tuschall*, 476 Mass. 581 (2017): On June 11, police received a report from a neighbor that a "smell like drugs" was coming from Kyle Tuschall's apartment. On June 12, police spoke to the neighbor by phone, who said that the fumes were giving her headaches and bothering her dog.

On June 13, officers knocked on Tuschall's door, but no one answered. They smelled a strong chemical odor. The neighbor said Tuschall and his girlfriend lived there, and the two usually left together in the morning, but only Tuschall had left that day. The detectives got the girlfriend's cell number and called, but could not reach her.

The detectives decided to enter the apartment to look for the girlfriend. The building owner let them in. The detectives went room to room, calling the girlfriend by name. They saw items consistent with small-scale methamphetamine production. They contacted the fire department, and obtained a search warrant based on what they saw. Tuschall arrived while the police were executing the warrant. He was arrested for various drug offenses.

---

11 Unlike an LTC, when a licensing authority seeks to suspend or revoke an FID because the holder is unsuitable, the authority must petition the district court. Filing the petition temporarily suspends the FID pending a hearing, 140, § 129B 1½(c). The statute does not say what happens when court is not open. It would be consistent with a need for prompt action for police to consider the suspension effective when the licensing authority *decides* to seek suspension, so long as the petition is filed the next business day.

12 As a third option, a private person with concerns about the lawful owner of a weapon may be referred to the district court to obtain an Extreme Risk Protection Order (ERPO) seeking suspension of a person's LTC or FID and surrender of the weapons. Upon receiving an ERPO, police are empowered to enter a home to seize the weapons with consent, a warrant, or exigent circumstances.

The SJC rejected the police decision to enter and suppressed the evidence. Prior to entry, police had no reasonable belief that residents faced an imminent threat of injury. Two days had passed since police were notified. While the odor was unpleasant, the neighbor had seen Tuschall leave the apartment in fine health. The smell had not increased. Police did not reasonably believe the girlfriend was injured either. They made no effort to contact her employer or family, and made only a few attempts to call her cell before entering her home.

ANIMAL SAFETY

Police may enter to protect the health and safety of an animal. In *Comm. v. Duncan*, 467 Mass. 746 (2014), Heather Duncan called police to her house to serve a restraining order on her husband. Officers noticed dogs, "in bad shape," in the fenced-in yard. Duncan assured officers she was taking care of them.

Six days later, Duncan's neighbor reported two dead dogs on the property and a third "emaciated" one. Upon arrival, officers saw dogs leashed to a fence with no food or water. One was whimpering. Two were dead. They could not get to the front door because of a padlocked gate, so officers sounded their siren and air horn. No response. They directed dispatch to use the local water and sewer directory to reach the property owner. No results. They then had the fire department remove the padlock. The SJC approved. Society has a deep concern for animals.

SCOPE OF EMERGENCY AID

In all cases, officers must deal with the emergency — not use it as an excuse to search for evidence. Consider *Comm. v. Kaeppeler*, 473 Mass. 396 (2015): David Kaeppeler spent the evening drinking at a club. When it closed, he invited his friends to his home. Kaeppeler only let John Smith and Elana Thomas spend the night. The three drank tequila.

The next morning, friends stopped by to pick up Smith and Thomas. No one answered the door, so they let themselves in. Both Smith and Thomas were asleep on sofas. The friends managed to wake Smith, but not Thomas. They took her to the hospital. Later that evening, Smith became ill and went to the hospital. Physicians concluded the victims had ingested GHB and alcohol.

At 9:15 p.m., hospital staff requested that police perform a well-being check on Kaeppeler. Police knocked repeatedly before he answered. After being told of the two individuals in the hospital, Kaeppeler invited the officers inside. He told police he was not feeling well. The officers asked whether he had any GHB. He said "no." Kaeppeler agreed to go to the hospital. The officers asked where the tequila bottle was, and Kaeppeler told him they had been drinking from the bottle on the kitchen counter, and there was another one in the garage.

After Kaeppeler was transported to the hospital, an officer remained at the house. He arranged for an evidence collection officer to photograph and collect the bottles. Several months later, the bottle on the counter tested positive for GHB. Kaeppeler was charged.

- **Emergency entry justified.** The request from hospital staff presented an emergency. The police conduct at Kaeppeler's home — prior to seizing the tequila bottles — was focused entirely on his well-being.

- **Tequila seizure improper.** If police had seized the bottles immediately to determine whether they contained a contaminant that had made people ill, it would have been justified as emergency aid. Instead, police had custody of the bottles for four months before having them tested!

    In reality, the seizure was for an investigative purpose — so police had to either: (1) obtain Kaeppeler's consent; or (2) secure his home and get a search warrant to remove the bottles. While Kaeppeler consented to police entry, he did <u>not</u> consent for officers to stay and seize the tequila. Also see *Comm. v. Sondrini*, 48 Mass. App. Ct. 704 (2000).

FIRE SCENE

WARRANTLESS ENTRY

To remove occupants. Comm. v. Ringgard, 71 Mass. App. Ct. 197 (2008): When police responded, they saw a hallway filled with smoke and Donald Ringgard standing near a flaming stove. The officers repeatedly told him to get out, and asked if anyone else was inside. Ringgard did not respond, so officers forced the door open. Ringgard began screaming obscenities, telling officers to get out. They escorted him to the porch and told him to stay there. They checked the house for other people.

Ringgard came back inside and screamed, "Get the fuck out of my house!" Officers took him outside again. When firefighters arrived, Ringgard tried once more to come in and pushed an officer. In the course of subduing him, officers observed a gun on the floor.

The officers were not required to permit Ringgard to remain inside (even if he was the owner) because it would have endangered him and given firefighters the extra task of safeguarding him. Since officers were lawfully in the house, they properly seized the pistol when it came into view.

To check for cause and origin. Firefighters may be joined by other investigators for this purpose while firefighters and their equipment are still engaged at the scene. *Comm. v. Zhan Tang Huang*, 87 Mass. App. Ct. 65 (2015) (trooper from the Fire Marshal's Office arrived at the scene of a deadly fire at 5:15 a.m.; firefighters were still inside attending to "fire extensions,"[13] and he was not permitted to enter until 7:00 a.m. to investigate the cause and origin; at that time, smoke was still emanating from burning debris and the bodies of the deceased were present).

In contrast, *Michigan v. Clifford*, 464 U.S. 287 (1984) rejected a warrantless entry by fire officials six hours after the fire had been completely extinguished and no apparatus remained at the scene. At that point, an administrative warrant was necessary.

---

13 Fire extensions are areas where fire can spread through walls and other conduits.

ADMINISTRATIVE WARRANT

An administrative warrant permits entry into a fire-damaged building after the exigency is over. Under 148, § 2, the "heads of fire departments in cities, towns or fire districts shall investigate the cause and circumstances of every fire or explosion . . . to ascertain whether it was caused by carelessness or design." This statute authorizes an administrative warrant for this purpose. To obtain one, officials must show that a fire of undetermined origin occurred and that they "will not intrude unnecessarily on the fire victim's privacy [because their search will occur] at a reasonable and convenient time."

SEARCH WARRANT

Investigating beyond cause and origin. Although investigators may be suspicious of arson, they only need an administrative warrant as long as the exact origin and cause of the fire remain unknown. However, as soon as investigators develop probable cause of crime *and* wish to expand their search into other areas of the structure, they must immediately secure the scene and obtain a search warrant. *Comm. v. Jung,* 420 Mass. 675 (1995).

DANGER OF VIOLENCE, DESTRUCTION OF EVIDENCE, OR ESCAPE

Officers must have probable cause <u>and</u> a real threat that violence will occur, evidence will be destroyed, or the suspect will escape. *Comm. v. Arias,* 481 Mass. 604 (2019).

These factors create exigent circumstances. Of course, all of them do not need to be present in every case. *Comm. v. Paniaqua,* 413 Mass. 796 (1992).

- **Felony and present.** Probable cause exists that the suspect committed a felony, and there is strong reason to believe he is inside the building;

- **Violence.** The underlying crime involved violence;

- **Armed.** The suspect is known, or believed to be, armed;

- **Dangerous to delay.** Entering immediately offers a better chance of a peaceful outcome;

- **Awareness of police.** If a suspect is actually *or potentially* aware of police involvement, he often has an incentive to be violent, destroy evidence, or escape;

- **Destruction of evidence.** Delay to get a warrant might result in the destruction of evidence;

- **Nighttime.** Magistrates are less available, so getting a timely warrant is more difficult;

- **Escape.** There is a likelihood that the suspect might escape if not apprehended immediately.

IMPROPER TO CREATE EXIGENCY

Police cannot create exigent circumstances to justify their decision to enter without a warrant.[14] *Comm. v. Alexis*, 481 Mass. 91 (2018): Police responded to a home invasion where a man was duct taped at gunpoint and his baby hit in the face. The victim told police that he recognized one of the three violent thieves as Jean Alexis. The detective wrote an incident report and filled out an arrest warrant application. Because it was late in the afternoon and his shift had ended, he decided not to seek an after-hours warrant.

The next morning, this detective informed his sergeant that Alexis had been identified and that he was in the process of getting a warrant. The sergeant was familiar with Alexis from a recent incident and knew where he lived. Instead of waiting for the warrant, the sergeant and four other officers planned to knock on Alexis' door to see if he was home and, if the opportunity arose, arrest him.

As officers approached, Alexis saw them through the glass front door. He ran toward the back of the house and tried to climb out a window. When officers shouted at him to show his hands, he retreated into the house. The officers forced entry and made the arrest. They conducted a protective sweep and saw jewelry from the home invasion. They then obtained a search warrant and found more evidence.

Here, police created the exigency because they knew that Alexis would probably attempt to flee when he saw officers. While officers had probable cause to arrest, and were lawfully present outside his home, they could have obtained a warrant the day before or the morning of the arrest.

The crime occurred the previous day, and there was nothing suggesting that Alexis even knew he was a suspect. Police could have set up surveillance while they waited for the warrant and arrested Alexis if he left his house. The exigent circumstances that emerged during the arrest were created by the officers' premature attempt to enter. Since the evidence was discovered after this flawed entry, it had to be suppressed.

Police also may not justify their decision to enter based on what happened once they got inside. *Comm. v. Molina*, 439 Mass. 206 (2003): Officers entered an apartment without a warrant to arrest the defendant for rape. A woman who lived there became angry and screamed at them. The officers grabbed a knife (the victim had been raped at knifepoint) and heard the defendant offer several excuses about what happened.

In *Molina*, the investigators had undeniable probable cause, *but* they lacked exigent circumstances for their warrantless entry. They had no evidence that the defendant might flee or destroy evidence, or that he even knew his crime had been reported. The only exigency — an altercation between the female inhabitant and officers — was the direct result of the improper entry. Molina's knife and statements were suppressed.

---

14 This rule is established under Article 14 of the Massachusetts Constitution. In contrast, the U.S. Supreme Court, in *Kentucky v. King*, 131 S.Ct. 1849 (2011), decided that police do not create exigent circumstances by knocking on the door of a home to see whether an occupant will deal with them. Under their view of the Fourth Amendment, police may knock on any citizen's door and, if someone inside tries to destroy evidence or flee, the police may respond without a warrant to deal with this emerging exigency.

VIOLENT CRIME

Dangerous situations often demand an immediate response.

- *Comm. v. McDermott*, 448 Mass. 750 (2007): Michael McDermott arrived at work the day after Christmas and shot his coworkers because "God" told him to. He killed seven people. Once Detective Foley learned what happened, he thought McDermott might have killed others before work. This concern was based on his experience in multiple homicide cases. Foley sent officers to secure McDermott's residence and check for additional victims.

  After receiving no response to their knocking, officers entered with a key from the building manager. They found no victims, but saw ammunition, a firearms manual, and a box with the word "danger" on it. They secured the apartment and obtained a warrant.

  Exigent circumstances justified entry. Seven people had been killed with multiple weapons. The police did not know whether McDermott had a wife, children, or anyone staying with him for Christmas. The officers acted reasonably: staying in the apartment for five minutes, looking only where people could be found, and not removing any items pending the issuance of a search warrant.

- *Comm. v. Figueroa*, 468 Mass. 204 (2014): Police responded to a murder at a restaurant. Witnesses gave a general description of the shooter. Police located a cab driver who had dropped off a man fitting the description and picked him up in the same area a few minutes later. The cab went to 59 Salem Street.

  There, officers described their suspect to the first-floor tenant, who said it matched the man staying with the woman upstairs, Nancy Alon.

  Alon told officers she was alone with her sleeping children, but then a door slammed. They pushed past her and found Richard Figueroa hiding under a bed. Officers cuffed Figueroa and seized a duffel bag with ammunition. Alon now consented to a search of the rest of the apartment. This was good police work from start to finish.

AWARENESS OF POLICE

A suspect's awareness about an investigation is a compelling reason for police to act. Once a suspect knows police are involved, he is motivated to destroy evidence, engage in violence, or try to escape. *Comm. v. Martinez*, 47 Mass. App. Ct. 839 (1999): The undercover officer was going to make a controlled buy. The surveillance team was surprised by an accomplice, who unexpectedly came out of the motel room and saw the officers. Police arrested her immediately. Officers then were concerned that the remaining drug dealers might think she had fallen into police hands if she failed to return. This would have placed the undercover, as the court wrote, "in deadly peril." Officers had no choice. They entered the room without a warrant and arrested the other offenders. See *Comm. v. Arias*, 481 Mass. 604 (2019).

On the other hand, exigent circumstances do not exist simply because police locate a felon or see a crime indoors.

- *U.S. v. Adams*, 621 F.2d 41 (1st Cir. 1980): A warrantless arrest in the defendant's apartment was unlawful even though he was an escaped felon. The police were not in hot pursuit. There was no threat that evidence was about to be destroyed, and no reason to believe the defendant was armed or about to flee. The police simply knew that the defendant was in a particular apartment. The court noted that the police should have staked out the apartment while an arrest warrant was obtained.

- *Comm. v. Huffman*, 385 Mass. 122 (1982): A warrantless search of an apartment was invalid even though the police could plainly see through an open window that the occupants were packaging drugs for sale. The police had time to get a warrant because there was no indication that the occupants were aware they had been seen by police. As a result, the offenders had no motive to flee or destroy evidence.

UNANTICIPATED OFFENDER BEHAVIOR

An unanticipated move by a suspect may justify immediate entry. *Comm. v. Collazo*, 34 Mass. App. Ct. 79 (1993): Collazo arranged to sell cocaine to an undercover officer, Dennis Brooks, at an outdoor location. All their prior dealings took place in a vacant lot. At the last moment, Collazo wanted the deal to happen in his apartment. Seeing the cocaine for the first time and fearing that his surveillance team was out of range, Brooks signaled for a warrantless entry and the arrest of all four defendants.

The situation in *Collazo* was very different from *Comm. v. Wigfall*, 32 Mass. App. Ct. 582 (1992). In *Wigfall*, officers had three hours to obtain a warrant, and no place other than a basement apartment had ever been mentioned for the drug sale. They had time to get a search warrant for that location.

Problems that should have been anticipated do not create exigent circumstances. *Comm. v. Forde*, 367 Mass. 798 (1975): During a narcotics investigation, four persons were taken into custody. After the arrests, police discontinued their surveillance and transported them to the station. Three hours later, an officer in the booking area overheard a conversation. One arrestee commented that, when released, he would immediately return to the house and warn the others. Fearing the destruction of evidence, police made an immediate warrantless entry there. The SJC held that the possibility that an arrestee may return is obvious. Officers had no excuse for not securing the house and applying for a warrant after the initial arrests.

DESTRUCTION OR LOSS OF EVIDENCE

The possible destruction or loss of evidence calls for immediate action.

- **Feeling engine.** *U.S. v. Owens*, 917 F.3d 26 (1st Cir. 2019): Shortly after a home invasion and double-homicide, an officer arrived at Gregory Owens' home and placed his hand on a vehicle to see if the engine was warm; given the cold weather, the officer would have lost the evidence of operation if he had taken the time to obtain a warrant.

- **Chop shop.** *Comm. v. Ramos*, 470 Mass. 740 (2015): Two officers used LoJack to identify a garage as the probable location of a stolen vehicle. They knew the garage was suspected of being a "chop shop," where stolen vehicles were dismantled and their VIN numbers destroyed. Officer Avery heard ratchets and wrenches being used inside the garage, and when he knocked and announced his presence, he heard tools being dropped and people yelling. A number of men ran. The officers did not know who was still inside. They did know the defendant lived at this address and had been previously arrested for vehicle theft. With this in mind, officers properly entered without a warrant to prevent any further destruction of the vehicle and its parts by anyone who remained on scene.

- **Blood on hands.** *Comm. v. Ferreira*, 481 Mass. 641 (2019): Police had substantial evidence that the defendant fatally stabbed his ex-girlfriend. When he came to the station the next day, he had cuts on his hands. There was probable cause to swab his hands, and it was necessary to do so immediately without a warrant. Visible and nonvisible blood evidence might have been lost if the defendant had been allowed to leave the station and wash his hands.

Exigent circumstances to secure evidence may extend to a person not under arrest. *Comm. v. Skea*, 18 Mass. App. Ct. 685 (1984): Police found the defendant in possession of an envelope with four diamonds. He claimed he bought them, but had no bill of sale and could not remember the name of the salesperson. The officers confiscated the diamonds to determine whether they had been stolen. At the time, officers declined to arrest the defendant for the drugs they had found earlier in his possession. He was released and later arrested when the police investigation determined that the diamonds were stolen.

Skea is an excellent example of how probable cause to search may not always correlate with probable cause to arrest. What if a shoplifter or pickpocket, suspecting he is under surveillance, stashes his loot in an innocent person's pocket, or a child is thought to possess narcotics by accident? In both of these cases, the police lack probable cause to arrest, but have probable cause to search. Also see *Cupp v. Murphy*, 412 U.S. 291 (1973).

Dangerous objects in public. Objects found in a public place — such as weapons or contraband — may be seized without a warrant. The risk that the item will disappear or be unlawfully used amounts to exigent circumstances. *Comm. v. Figueroa*, 412 Mass. 745 (1992).

Search Incident to Arrest

INCIDENT TO PROBABLE CAUSE OR THE ACTUAL ARREST

When officers develop probable cause to arrest, they may search. *Comm. v. Vargas*, 2014 WL 3953080 (Appeals Court) (officer had probable cause to arrest passenger for receiving a stolen vehicle; as a result, he properly searched him and found a gun).

The officers' belief that their search might lead to evidence of another crime will not, by itself, invalidate their original decision to arrest. *Comm. v. Petrillo*, 399 Mass. 487 (1987) (police arrested the defendant for trespass on school property after he lied that he was late for class; the fact that an officer had heard the defendant was a drug dealer did not, without more, prove that the trespass arrest was a pretext to search).

On the other hand, if an arrest is purely driven by a desire to search, a court may suppress the evidence. *Amador-Gonzalez v. U.S.*, 391 F.2d 308 (1968) (police waited more than an hour after his traffic offense to arrest the defendant for it; once they found drugs, officers never bothered to book him for the traffic offense).

AT TIME OF PROBABLE CAUSE

No need for a formal arrest, as long as probable cause exists before the search.

- *Comm. v. Skea*, 18 Mass. App. Ct. 685 (1984): Holyoke officers saw an illegal drug on the console of a parked Camaro. When the vehicle owner, Stephen Skea, returned to the car, police searched him and found an envelope with four diamonds in his jacket pocket. Skea asserted that he had purchased them two weeks before for fifty dollars, yet he had no bill of sale and did not know the seller's name. The police kept the diamonds.

  The officers decided not to arrest Skea for drug possession. This was consistent with their informal policy not to arrest for a small amount of drugs unless their search revealed more. When further investigation confirmed that the diamonds were stolen, Skea was arrested several weeks later with a warrant.

  Skea objected to the original search on the grounds that no arrest followed. The court responded that it makes no sense to require a greater restriction on a suspect's liberty — formal arrest — in order to justify the lesser intrusion of a search. Thus, probable cause to arrest is the minimum requirement for a search incident to arrest, and whether the officers choose to follow through with an actual arrest is left to their sound discretion.

- *Comm. v. Moscat*, 49 Mass. App. Ct. 622 (2000): Officers responded to a call and saw six youths standing next to beer bottles. One officer told the kids to leave. One youth, Moscat, rode away on his bike. He was bent over, holding his left hand close to his body as if to conceal something. The officer followed in his cruiser and asked him what he was holding. Suspecting a bottle of beer, the officer began to reach his hand toward the left side of Moscat's shirt. To his surprise, a revolver fell to the ground. Moscat was arrested and convicted of unlawful possession of a firearm.

  Although the officer tried to portray his actions as a frisk for safety, it was really a search incident to arrest. The officer had probable cause that Moscat was a minor in possession. He searched to recover the beer he thought Moscat was hiding. Discovering the gun was a valid result of this search for evidence.

- *Comm. v. Kotlyarevskiy*, 59 Mass. App. Ct. 240 (2003): While booking a shoplifter, Officer Aziz found a note with a name and phone number. Aziz called the number to see if he could arrange "a drug buy." A male voice answered and identified himself as "Tsezar." Aziz arranged to purchase $100 worth of marijuana. Tsezar said to meet at Dunkin' Donuts. He would be in a red van with a friend. Tsezar showed up and refused to sell marijuana to Aziz (acting undercover) because he was nervous. Tsezar demanded payment first. Aziz refused. Then other officers moved in, searched Tsezar, and retrieved a .357 magnum pistol. He was arrested. No drugs were found on his person or in his car.

  Since police had probable cause to arrest Tsezar for possession of marijuana with intent to distribute, they could search him at the scene. Tsezar's decision to cancel the deal did not defeat probable cause.

SITUATIONS WHERE SEARCH INCIDENT TO ARREST DELAYED

Searches at the station

A search may be delayed in order to seize a suspect's clothing and shoes. *Comm. v. Gliniewicz*, 398 Mass. 744 (1986) (proper to seize boots worn at time of arrest once officer noticed blood stains and the similarity of the tread to the one at the crime scene).

Testing lawfully obtained evidence automatically follows. *Comm. v. Robles*, 423 Mass. 62 (1996) (police lawfully acquired defendant's coat incident to arrest; they had the coat chemically analyzed and learned that blood stains were present, which helped convict him of murder; court rejected claim that officers needed separate warrant for testing).

Once police lawfully obtain credit cards, they may retrieve information from the magnetic strip without a warrant. *U.S. v. Bah*, 794 F.3d 617 (2015): Following an arrest, officers found 68 gift cards hidden by the defendants. By using a skimmer, officers learned the vast majority of cards were encoded with stolen account numbers. The police did not need a warrant. Cardholders do not have a reasonable expectation of privacy in the magnetic strips which are routinely read by third parties — such as gas stations, restaurants, and stores — to facilitate financial transactions.

5555

Strip searches

Intrusions defined. *Comm. v. Thomas*, 429 Mass. 403 (1999).

- **Strip search** is an inspection of private areas without any scrutiny of body cavities.

- **Visual body cavity search** extends to a visual inspection of the anal and genital areas.

- **Manual body cavity search** is the most intrusive because it involves touching a body cavity. For this reason, it may only be done with a warrant issued by a judge and supported by a high degree of probable cause. *Rodriques v. Furtado*, 410 Mass. 878 (1991).

In order to conduct a strip or visual body cavity search, police must have <u>probable cause</u> their suspect possesses contraband or a weapon that might not be discovered during a manual search.[1] Strip searches are necessary because "controlled substances [and weapons] may be . . . concealed on the body so as to be virtually undetectable during the manual probing of . . . a fully clothed person." *U.S. v. Cofield*, 391 F.3d 334 (1st Cir. 2004). *Comm. v. Prophete*, 443 Mass. 548 (2005).

These searches must <u>always</u> be conducted in a non-humiliating, professional manner. Recommended safeguards include:

- **Same gender.** Strip searches, especially those conducted at the station, should be observed only by officers or police personnel of the same gender as the offender.

- **Private room.** Police should conduct strip searches in a private room whenever possible.

- **Only investigating officer(s).** A strip search should be done where no one, other than the searching officers, can see the person being inspected.

- **Full nudity unnecessary.** Effective strip searches may be accomplished without having the offender completely disrobe. Have the individual remove clothing from the upper half of his body, allow him to replace his clothing, then have him remove clothing covering his lower body (including his shoes), and allow him to get dressed once the job is finished.

- **Emergency circumstances.** Officers may need to inspect a suspect in the field to recover contraband or weapons. Do this in the least intrusive manner possible.

- **Videotape.** *Comm. v. Cruz*, 2014 WL 2514562 (Appeals Court) (best documentation of professional procedures; it is not always possible).

Example of probable cause and professional procedures. *Comm. v. Vick*, 90 Mass. App. Ct. 622 (2016): Officer Cazeau issued Vick a parking citation. While placing it on the windshield, he saw that Vick's pants were down around his knees. Cazeau, intending to arrest Vick and his passenger for this behavior, ordered them not to move their hands. He ordered the passenger out and searched him. He had a "crack pipe" in his pocket.

---

1 Somewhat controversially, the U.S. Supreme Court allows automatic strip searches of *all* pre-trial detainees under the Fourth Amendment. *Florence v. County of Burlington*, 132 S.Ct. 1510 (2012).

Cazeau called for backup and Officer Green arrived. Green searched Vick and felt a hard object in the cleft of his buttocks. Vick tightened his muscles and pulled away. He violently resisted. Police transported him to the station. During the ride, he tried to get his cuffed hands down the back of his pants. A drug-sniffing dog alerted to Vick's vehicle at the scene.

At the station, Green obtained permission for a strip search from his supervisor. Vick refused to remove the object voluntarily, so two officers attempted to remove his pants. Vick resisted, so three more officers entered the cell to assist. They removed his pants. They could see a plastic bag of crack cocaine in his buttocks. Without touching Vick's body, Green grabbed the bag and flicked it on the ground.

The search at the station was a strip search, not a manual body cavity search. There was no touching, probing, or manipulating of Vick's anal cavity. The drugs were easily removed without endangering his health or safety. The police had probable cause.

The search preserved, as much as possible, Vick's privacy and dignity. Officer Green gave Vick the opportunity to remove the bag himself. The search was conducted in a private cell. There were no more officers than necessary given his resistance. All were male. The struggle lasted only a minute.

Example of no probable cause for strip search. *Comm. v. Agogo*, 481 Mass. 633 (2019): Chelsea officers saw Donne Agogo engage in street-level drug deals with several people. Based on their training and experience, they believed that street dealers often conceal drugs in their crotch. When officers approached, Agogo took a "bladed" stance and displayed an animated demeanor. He also pulled away before officers started to frisk him.

After the frisk, officers discovered $20 in his pocket. This amount was consistent with the street value of the cocaine they had found on the suspected buyer. At the station, Agogo loudly protested when police announced his strip search.

On these facts, officers had, at best, a reasonable suspicion that Agogo might be concealing drugs. Officers never saw Agogo place anything in his crotch or walk as if he had a hidden object there. Agogo did not attempt, at any point, to block officers from reaching or viewing his groin area.

Example of probable cause, but unprofessional procedures. *Comm. v. Morales*, 462 Mass. 334 (2012): Detective Daniel Desmarais received information from an informant that Carlos Morales was selling heroin out of his Ford Explorer. Police observed Morales conduct a deal.

When Morales was searched following a chase, he clenched his buttocks. Desmarais felt a lump that was not a weapon. Desmarais walked Morales to a more secluded area by a house and pulled back his waistband. A plastic bag containing powder was protruding from his buttocks. When Desmarais told another officer, "He's hiding it in his ass," Morales attempted to run. The scuffle ended with Morales in handcuffs, lying face down on the sidewalk with his buttocks exposed to public view. Onlookers, including Morales's father, saw him there. The decision to strip search Morales was excellent. The manner in which it was done became unprofessional and humiliating. The evidence had to be suppressed.

For object in anal or genital opening, officers should either transport the arrestee to a hospital, have him voluntarily remove it, or obtain a warrant. Comm. v. Jeannis, 482 Mass. 355 (2019): At the Revere station after his arrest, Stanley Jeannis complained to Lt. Callahan that he did not feel well because he had swallowed drugs. Callahan did not believe him because he showed no signs of overdose, but the lieutenant wisely followed protocol and requested medical assistance.

Jeannis said he might throw up, so Callahan and Officer Singer led him to a cell with a toilet. They noticed Jeannis was walking abnormally and "clenching his buttocks." Callahan ordered Jeannis to remove his pants. Jeannis argued, then pulled down his waistband and said, "I don't have anything." Officer Singer had taken hold of Jeannis' arms and could see a plastic bag protruding from his buttocks. Singer helped Jeannis easily remove the bag. It contained packets of heroin and cocaine.

Because there was no "touching or probing of the defendant's anal cavity, and the bag of drugs was easily removed without endangering [his] health or safety in any way," the SJC concluded that Officer Singer did *not* conduct a manual body cavity search.

In the future, when officers encounter an object (typically drugs) inside a person's anal or genital opening, the best approach is:

- **Option 1: Transport arrestee to the hospital and have a medical clinician remove the object**. This should be done in situations where officers are concerned that the object might cause serious injury if not removed by medical personnel (e.g., the bag of drugs might rupture; the concealed weapon might cut the area).

- **Option 2: Request that the arrestee voluntarily remove the object.** Consent removal eliminates the need to obtain a warrant. Calmly explain that if the arrestee does not remove the object himself, police must monitor him, apply for a search warrant from a judge (which typically takes two to three hours) and, if the warrant is issued, transport him to a medical facility where a clinician will remove the object. When an arrestee understands that police must engage in this cumbersome, invasive procedure, he will often decide to remove the object himself. Problem solved. But, if he refuses. . .

- **Option 3: Obtain a search warrant from a judge.** This is not difficult since, at this point, officers will have seen the object in the anal or genital opening. Direct observation provides the "high degree of probable cause" required for a manual body cavity search warrant. Explain in the affidavit how officers gave the subject the chance to remove the item, but he refused. This proves the "particularized need" also required by the judge in order to sign the warrant.[2]

---

2 In *Jeannis*, Chief Justice Gants, who wrote the opinion for the court, recommended that officers "gently flick" the object protruding from the anal opening. He opined that if the object (in this case, a bag of drugs) dislodged and came out, then police could recover it without having to apply for a warrant. If the object remained stuck in the anal opening after being "flicked," police could apply for a warrant. On balance, this author, in consultation with other law enforcement practitioners, does not recommend the "gentle flick" technique because it risks injury, assault, humiliation, sexual touching, or other lawsuit-worthy allegations from defendants.

SCOPE OF SEARCH INCIDENT TO ARREST

276, § 1 RESTRICTIONS

During a search incident to arrest, 276, § 1 states that officers may:

- Always search for weapons regardless of the reason for the arrest.

- Only search for evidence related to the crime for which the arrest was made.

- Seize any other evidence found during a search for weapons or evidence related to arrest.

276, § 1 only regulates search incident to arrest. If a search can be justified on another legal ground, the limitations do not apply.

A search must be objectively and subjectively reasonable under 276, § 1. The objective test is whether the search related to the reason for the arrest. The subjective test is whether the officer was really looking for arrest-related evidence.

- **Objective failure.** *Comm. v. Holloway*, 81 Mass. App. Ct. 910 (2012): Michael Holloway was arrested at a residential housing complex for trespassing. Upon making the arrest, the officer seized two mountain bikes located near Holloway, although Holloway said only one of them was his. Holloway was charged with trespass and receiving stolen property.

  Seizing the bicycles went beyond the scope of a search incident to arrest for trespass. A warrantless seizure of property unrelated to an arrest must be supported by probable cause. The officer had no reason to believe, at the time of the arrest, that the bicycles were stolen. There had been no reported theft. The fact that Holloway did not know the brand or cost of the bicycle did not create probable cause.

- **Subjective failure.** In *Comm. v. Rose*, 25 Mass. App. Ct. 905 (1987), a trooper arrested Rose for operating under the influence. After placing Rose in handcuffs in the cruiser, the trooper searched his vehicle and found empty beer cans and a liquor bottle on the floor. He also found a red nylon bag, which he opened. The bag held drug paraphernalia. A black suitcase under the driver's seat had a scale with drug residue. Even though it was theoretically possible for evidence of OUI to be hidden in the bag or suitcase, the court believed that the trooper was really looking for any evidence he could find. Therefore, the subjective test of 276, § 1 was violated. Evidence from the bag and suitcase was suppressed.

- **Objective and subjective success.** *Comm. v. Kegler*, 65 Mass. App. Ct. 907 (2006): Police were entitled to search Bennie Kegler's wallet incident to his arrest and to unfold a piece of paper inside, because fruits of the robbery could have been concealed inside both. The police had probable cause that cash had been stolen and that Kegler might hide it in a folded paper inside his wallet (which turned out to contain heroin).

PEOPLE

Body of the arrestee

Of course officers may search the person arrested. *Chimel v. California*, 395 U.S. 752 (1969).

"Grabbing area" even when handcuffed

The search extends to the area within an arrestee's reach to prevent his ability to access a weapon _or_ destroy evidence. The fact that the defendant is handcuffed does not eliminate the officer's right to check the grabbing area.

- **Motivation: Preservation of evidence.** *Comm. v. Elizondo*, 428 Mass. 322 (1998): An undercover officer bought drugs from the defendant at his apartment. The defendant had retrieved cocaine from the bathroom. When police entered and made the arrest, he was handcuffed within five feet of the bathroom. The door was open. An officer quickly checked the grabbing area and seized a deodorant can next to the sink. It had a false bottom which, when removed, contained cocaine.

- **Motivation: Officer safety.** Courts permit a larger grabbing area when the officer's motivation is protection. In *Comm. v. Quilter*, 81 Mass. App. Ct. 808 (2012), a squad of officers from a youth violence strike force went to Paris Quilter's home to execute an arrest warrant for trespass. Quilter answered the door in his underwear. He asked if he could get dressed. Officers escorted him to his bedroom.

  They knew Quilter had prior arrests for gun possession. Quilter wanted to go to the closet to get pants. The officers told him that, for safety reasons, they would get his clothes. Quilter sat down on the far end of the bed away from his closet. An officer thought this was strange and asked Quilter to stand up. When he did, the officer lifted the mattress and discovered a firearm. The search was within Quilter's grabbing area.

Grabbing area established at time of arrest, not search. *Comm. v. Figueroa*, 468 Mass. 204 (2014) (even though Figueroa was handcuffed and no longer in the same room as his duffel, the bag had been in his grabbing area at the time of his arrest; therefore, it was properly searched incident to his arrest).

Searching outside the grabbing area improper. *Vale v. Louisiana*, 399 U.S. 30 (1979) (Donald Vale was arrested on the front steps of his home; a search of his dwelling was not justified).

Minimal impact of 276, § 1

Weapons access always a justification. 276, § 1 has little impact on the search of a person because § 1 *always* allows a search for weapons regardless of the underlying crime. In *Comm. v. Dessources*, 74 Mass. App. Ct. 232 (2009), Detective John Boyle observed four individuals walking in the Cambridge Common. One of them, John Dessources, was drinking a can of beer — an arrestable violation of a city ordinance.

Dessources admitted to having a box cutter in his pocket, which Boyle recovered along with several bags of marijuana for sale. Once Boyle had probable cause to arrest Dessources, even for the typically nonviolent crime of public drinking, he could search for weapons.

Seizure of any "hard object" justifiable. *Comm. v. Barillas*, 485 Mass. 250 (2020) declared: "[A]ny hard object left in the possession of a suspect who is being arrested . . . may be used as a weapon." That is why Trooper Wilson properly seized Barillas' cell phone and kept it in his pocket during transport to the station. At the station, however, the phone needed to go to the booking officer and be documented as seized property.

Container discovered while looking for weapons may yield probable cause of a _new_ offense. Its search may follow. *Comm. v. White*, 469 Mass. 96 (2014): Officers Bikofsky and Hussey learned that William White had outstanding warrants for 209A and drug violations. They stopped White's car and arrested him.

Bikofsky searched White and found a prescription pill container in his pocket. White said it was his blood pressure medication. Bikofsky saw the label with White's name and one pill inside. From another pocket, Bikofsky removed a "One Touch" container that would normally hold small, thin strips for diabetic blood testing. When Bikofsky shook the container, it sounded like pills were inside. He opened it and saw more pills identical to the one in the prescription bottle.

At White's request, Officer Hussey retrieved White's keys from the ignition so he could lock the car. He saw on the front passenger seat another prescription pill bottle with no label and identical pills inside.

At the station, Bikofsky used a medical website to identify the pills as methadone. White did not have a prescription. He was charged for illegal drug possession.

- **Search incident to arrest.** The crimes under the warrant — 209A and drugs — were committed at an unknown time in the past. Therefore, White could not be searched incident to arrest for evidence *related to those crimes* under 276, § 1.[3]

   276, § 1 allowed Officer Bikofsky to search White for *weapons*. When he felt a hard object, Bikofsky could make sure it was not a weapon. After he shook the "One Touch" container and heard the sound of pills, he knew that it did not hold a weapon. At this point, the SJC felt that he was not authorized to open the container.

- **Commentary.** What the SJC failed to recognize was its prior decision in *Comm. v. Clermy*, 421 Mass. 325 (1995). In that case, troopers arrested Carlo Clermy on an outstanding warrant in front of a "crack house." One trooper quickly searched him, finding a beeper and some cash. A more thorough search followed after Clermy had been handcuffed. The trooper felt a hard object in Clermy's groin area. He removed a plastic bottle for prescription medicine. The trooper opened it to find crack cocaine.

   An initial search may be followed by a thorough search incident to arrest, even if the subject is handcuffed. The trooper reasonably believed that the hard object might be a weapon, but that safety concern did not justify opening the bottle once the trooper took it from Clermy. That is why the trooper wisely explained that his reason for looking inside the bottle was *not* protection. It was his *new* probable cause that Clermy possessed illegal drugs. After all, most people do not store legitimate medication in their underwear!

---

3 Drugs seized at the time of the defendant's arrest on an outstanding warrant would not be evidence of his possession, sale, or distribution of drugs at the time of his earlier drug offense. This was especially true in this case, since the arrest warrant was for a post-disposition default.

The same logic applies to the *White* case. Once Officer Bikofsky knew that a different medicine should be in the container, he had probable cause to believe that, at a minimum, a Class E controlled substance was probably inside. This is the argument that officers and prosecutors should use in the future to avoid a repeat of the *White* decision.

Keys

Seizure of keys justified if potential evidence or weapon, but <u>not</u> to determine identity.

- **Improper.** *Comm. v. Blevines*, 438 Mass. 604 (2003): Three state troopers approached Charles Blevines at the entrance to a bar. He was drinking beer. Trooper Brian Moore asked for his name and date of birth. Blevines, who was not carrying ID, said "Charlie Jackson." Because his date of birth did not match his stated age, Trooper Moore believed Blevines had given a false name, so he arrested him for public drinking. Moore searched Blevines and recovered a key chain. One key was for a GM car.

  Trooper Calaso checked to see if the key fit any GM cars in the parking lot, in order to establish Blevines' identity. He tried the key in the trunk of a Chevy Celebrity and it opened. Trooper Walls, using a flashlight, observed a plastic bag containing what appeared to be cocaine under the front seat. Trooper Calaso retrieved the cocaine. Back at the Brockton police station, an officer knew Blevines by name.

  - *No seizure as evidence.* Under 276, § 1, an arrest search is limited to the seizure of evidence related to the particular arrest and/or weapons. It is clear that these keys were not evidence of public drinking!

  - *No claim that keys dangerous.* While the SJC said that the police may take keys on the basis that they pose a safety threat, these officers did not make that claim in court. This author strongly recommends: Routinely seize key chains incident to arrest as a potential weapon. They can be used to injure; some people keep small knives or other dangerous items on them; some hardcore offenders even have a handcuff key on their chain. Officers may testify to these risks.

  - *No authorization for identity check.* In this case, troopers argued that they could seize Blevines' keys in order to identify him by locating his car. The SJC countered that "questions of identity" must be resolved by "less intrusive means." Specifically, booking allows police to fingerprint, photograph, and question a suspect; or, as happened here, for another officer to recognize him. If these methods fail, then identity must "be resolved . . . [at] arraignment, . . . not by questionable police actions at the scene of the arrest which trench upon an individual's right to be free from . . . unjustified inquiries and intrusions."

  - *No motor vehicle exception or plain view.* The motor vehicle exception did not support looking into Blevines' car either, since police had no probable cause to believe the vehicle contained evidence when they approached it. Although Trooper Walls observed cocaine through the car window, "plain view" did not apply since the trooper only was present because of the initial, improper seizure of the keys.

- **Proper.** *Comm. v. Kipp*, 57 Mass. App. Ct. 629 (2003): Carmen Rosario told the Lowell police that a man she knew was keeping a duffel bag containing drugs and guns at her apartment. The police came over, inspected the duffel, and showed her a photo array from which she identified Angel Kipp as the bag's owner. The police then went to Kipp's apartment. Kipp and his wife were outside. The police arrested him and removed a loop of keys, which included a key to Rosario's apartment.

  Seizing Angel Kipp's keys was clearly permissible under 276, § 1. Since Kipp's arrest involved the possession of narcotics and guns in another person's apartment, police wisely believed that one of his keys might open the apartment and link him to the stash.

Cell phones

Police may _not_ search a cell phone incident to arrest. They need consent or a warrant. Based on *Riley v. California*, 134 S.Ct. 2473 (2014), the author recommends the following:[4]

- **Check phone to assess whether it is a weapon.** Never assume a phone is a phone! There have been cases where a phone turned out to be a disguised weapon (e.g., a knife, derringer, taser, or OC spray container).

- **View any texts or other marking on the phone's exterior.** It is not a search to view the outside of the phone. *Comm. v. Alvarez*, 400 Mass. 1015 (2018) (after lawfully seizing the defendant's cell phone during his arrest, the officer saw a text "pop up" asking to buy drugs; there was no need to get a warrant or ask for consent to retain this evidence).

- **Consider whether exigent circumstances justify answering the phone and/or conducting a warrantless search.** For example, officers might answer an offender's phone during a drug distribution, sexual enticement, or kidnapping investigation to avoid losing evidence. If the caller implicates the defendant, record his statements in the police report. *Comm. v. Barrett*, 97 Mass. App. Ct. 437 (2020) mandates that an investigator testify why getting a search warrant was impractical before he answered or searched the suspect's cell phone.

- **Secure the phone only if there is *probable cause* that it contains evidence.** Efforts to secure the phone and prevent the loss of potential evidence include turning off the device, removing its battery, or placing it in a secure container (e.g., a Faraday bag).

- **Inform the defendant of his search options — either consent or a warrant.** An officer might say, for example: "Mr. Smith, I have your cell phone. You may allow me to search it. I will download any relevant information onto a department computer and return your phone as soon as possible. If you do not want to consent, that is fine. You have the right to refuse. But, if you do, I will apply for a search warrant. This will probably take a couple of hours. If I am granted the warrant, I will submit your phone for forensic analysis within seven days. If the court does not give me a warrant, I will give the phone back to you. What would you like me to do?" Many offenders will consent when given this choice. *Comm. v. Farnsworth*, 76 Mass. App. Ct. 87 (2010) (voluntary consent may follow an officer's statement that, if the suspect refuses, he will seek a warrant). *Comm. v. Wangnoon*, 2018 WL 894026 (Appeals Court) (police must have probable cause to ask for consent on the basis that otherwise they will apply for a cell phone search warrant).

---

4 A more detailed discussion of cell phone searches appears in *Chapter 20*.

- **Conduct consent search or apply for a warrant.** In cases where a phone is locked, officers should ask the defendant to unlock it or provide a password. If he refuses, *Comm. v. Gelfgatt*, 468 Mass. 512 (2014) empowers a judge to order the defendant to enter a cell phone passcode or otherwise provide police access.

Moving arrestee and securing area

Police may move an arrested person for a <u>legitimate purpose</u> and secure the area.

- **Outside arrest to inside dwelling.** *Comm. v. Gonzalez*, 60 Mass. App. Ct. 903 (2003): The police went to execute an arrest warrant for Rosa Ortiz, the defendant's mother. Ortiz occupied a first-floor apartment. When she answered the door, Trooper Coppenrath advised her that he had a warrant. Coppenrath also suggested that Ortiz leave her jewelry and bring some form of ID and a jacket to court. Coppenrath asked if he could accompany Ortiz into her apartment while she removed her jewelry and got a coat. Ortiz agreed. Once inside, she entered the bedroom and closed the door. Coppenrath came in and saw the defendant on the bed. Coppenrath instructed Gonzalez to "show his hands." The trooper grabbed his right hand, which was holding small packages of heroin.

  Ortiz consented to the entry.[5] Once inside, an officer was entitled to escort Ortiz into other rooms, unless he orchestrated her movement as a way to search. There was no suggestion that Coppenrath did this.

- **Inside arrest to other room.** *Comm. v. Lee*, 383 Mass. 507 (1981) (the seizure of a weapon was proper when an officer escorted the defendant to his bedroom so that he could dress himself). *Comm. v. Franco*, 419 Mass. 635 (1995) (an officer moved the defendant from the dining room to an area with increased ventilation because he appeared to be suffering an adverse reaction to the odor of drug processing material in the kitchen sink; in the new room, the officer saw a gun barrel protruding from under a shelf).

PROTECTIVE SWEEP

A "protective sweep" is a quick inspection of those places where a person might be hiding. *Comm. v. Bui*, 419 Mass. 392 (1995). *U.S. v. Hernandez-Mieses*, 931 F.3d 134 (1st Cir. 2019) (protective sweep must be quick; here, the 22-minute sweep concerned the court as a possible evidence-gathering effort).

Automatic sweep of immediate area

Following an arrest inside a building, officers may sweep the immediately adjoining area. *Maryland v. Buie*, 495 U.S. 325 (1990).

Beyond immediate area, reasonable suspicion of danger

To go beyond the immediate area, officers must have a reasonable suspicion that there may be someone who poses a danger. The type of fugitive being apprehended may, by

---

5 The court rejected the Commonwealth's argument that the police are always entitled to enter an apartment to execute an arrest warrant. Ortiz was initially arrested in the hallway outside, so an entry incident to arrest was not automatically proper.

itself, create reasonable suspicion to sweep the whole premises. Unlike an encounter on the street, officers are at a serious disadvantage in their adversary's home. They risk being ambushed. *Comm. v. DeJesus,* 70 Mass. App. Ct. 114 (2007).

Courts assess:

- The violent nature of the crime and the defendant's criminal history.
- The location of the arrest in relation to the area swept.
- The defendant's resistance or cooperation at the time of arrest.
- The presence of other individuals or at least suspicion of their presence.

Consider *Comm. v. Matos,* 78 Mass. App. Ct. 156 (2010): Springfield's tactical response team came to Matos' house with an arrest warrant. Knowing his history with firearms, the team planned to enter and fan out to all floors. They knew Matos, his mother, and his seven year old niece were present. The police knocked and the mother answered. Officers saw Matos run into a second-floor room. They kicked open the door and secured him. Even after Matos was handcuffed, police acted reasonably by continuing their sweep to see whether other confederates were present. Two officers went into the basement. Two officers found the niece in her bed, and others went into the attic where they saw cocaine and a safe. The on-scene supervisor wisely secured the house and got a warrant for the evidence.

Protective sweep may continue as long as there is potential danger. *Comm. v. Jones,* 98 Mass. App. Ct. 120 (2020): A man called 911 saying he was hiding in a closet in a Salem apartment. His girlfriend was also in the apartment, perhaps being held against her will by four men who might be armed.

Salem police set up a perimeter around the four-story house. The reporting party came out the back door and repeated his story.

Salem officers knocked and announced. There was no answer. They entered. In the kitchen, they found three people. All were frisked and handcuffed for safety. The girlfriend came into the kitchen. Although she appeared "out of it," she said she was "okay."

One officer saw a man through the back door window and ordered him not to move, but he retreated into the stairwell. Arn Jones was captured on the fourth floor landing. A protective sweep of that floor followed to make sure no one else was hiding, which led to the discovery of evidence in a bedroom and drug distribution charges against Jones after officers secured the evidence and obtained a warrant to collect it.

The emergency sweep after Jones' capture was proper. Just because the reporting person mentioned four men did not mean police were limited to worrying about just four men. While the victim had said she was "okay," police could not ignore the possibility that she was under duress and some additional suspects beyond Jones were still inside the building.

Once the scene is secure, any search for evidence, including guns, requires a warrant. *Comm. v. Thach,* 2017 WL 4364472 (Appeals Court): Police received a 911 call that an individual had fired multiple shots at another person near a dwelling. When police arrived minutes later, witnesses told them what home the armed shooter entered. The officers knocked. No answer. They pushed an air conditioning unit out of a window and climbed inside. They conducted a protective sweep, looking for the shooter and any victims. They found the shooter on the third floor with no weapons. After escorting him in handcuffs to the second floor, they returned to the third floor and found two firearms.

A warrantless entry and protective sweep were justified because police were dealing with an "active shooter" scenario. However, their sweep should have been limited to finding the shooter and any potential victims. When police returned to the third floor after their sweep ended and looked for weapons, they needed a search warrant.

Insufficient basis for sweep.

- **Arrestee clearly alone.** *Comm. v. Nova*, 50 Mass. App. Ct. 633 (2000): Officers knocked with an arrest warrant, then heard Nova's voice and the sound of running. They broke down the door and caught Nova attempting to run out the back. Five minutes later, officers went back inside to secure the apartment, since they had broken the door. Before stationing a guard to wait for the landlord, officers walked through and saw evidence of drug dealing.

  While their initial entry was lawful, police lacked authority to enter Nova's apartment again. Officers had no reason to believe that someone was present because they had not seen anyone the first time. Consequently, evidence viewed during the second sweep was suppressed.

- **Arrestee cooperates.** *Comm. v. Saywahn*, 91 Mass. App. Ct. 706 (2017): Benjamin Saywahn was wanted by police because he was present during a marijuana sale when someone was shot. Police went to his home to execute an arrest warrant. When he answered the door, police immediately recognized him. They handcuffed him just inside the door. He did not attempt to resist or flee. When officers asked whether anyone else was in the home, Saywahn did not make eye contact and mumbled something inaudible. Asked again, he hesitated and said "no." Police conducted a protective sweep and saw a firearm protruding from under a mattress in an upstairs bedroom.

  The fact that Saywahn was being arrested in connection with a shooting warranted caution. But once he was cuffed at the door, his arrest was over. Officers should have left at that point.

- **Presence of person, but police unconcerned with danger.** *Comm. v. DuBois*, 44 Mass. App. Ct. 294 (1998): Officers lawfully entered a garage to arrest a cocaine dealer who had run inside. They heard a voice from an adjacent garage call, "Charlie, is that you?" The officers did not respond, but walked through an open door. The voice was coming from a camper. Officers entered and saw the defendant lying on a bed next to cocaine packages. He was arrested.

  While hot pursuit supported their initial entry and arrest, officers lacked justification to conduct a protective sweep when they heard a voice from the adjacent garage. For a protective sweep, officers must have a reasonable suspicion that the area harbors a potentially dangerous individual. The mere presence of someone is not enough. Here, the officers clearly were not worried about their safety because, as the court pointed out, they did not draw their weapons or take other precautions when they entered the camper.

MOTOR VEHICLES

Officers may search a vehicle incident to arrest if the arrestee was just in it. *Thornton v. U.S.*, 541 U.S. 615 (2004): The defendant parked his car. He was arrested nearby for drug possession. The officer found a gun underneath the front seat. It made no difference that the defendant had already gotten out of his car. "The stress . . . is not diminished because the arrestee exited his car before the officer initiated contact, nor is an arrestee less likely to destroy evidence if he is outside of — but still in control of — the vehicle. In either case, the officer faces a substantially similar, volatile situation, so it makes sense for the same rule to govern."

Passenger compartment & containers

The scope of a search incident to arrest extends only to the passenger compartment, never the trunk. Realistically, the passenger area is the only place where an arrestee might quickly obtain a weapon or destroy evidence. *Comm. v. Bongarzone*, 390 Mass. 326 (1983) (rear portion of a Ford Bronco behind the last passenger seat was considered part of the passenger compartment; therefore, police properly opened the tailgate to inspect this area following an arrest).

Impact of 276, § 1

Two cases show the impact of 276, § 1 on vehicle searches. Consider *Comm. v. Toole*, 389 Mass. 159 (1983) and *Comm. v. Perkins*, 465 Mass. 600 (2013).

- **Facts of** *Toole*. A trooper stopped the defendant in his truck and arrested him on an outstanding warrant for assault and battery. The defendant was handcuffed and moved to the rear of his truck. A trooper observed an empty holster on the defendant's belt. With two other troopers on scene, he searched the truck cab and found a gun. He asked the defendant whether he was properly licensed to carry a firearm. The defendant said "no."

- **Facts of** *Perkins*. At 10:30 p.m., Officer Lavin saw a vehicle disobey a stop sign. He activated his lights. The vehicle traveled less than one block before stopping in the parking lot of an apartment building. Two passengers left the vehicle and started walking away. When Lavin ordered them to get back in the car, both men jogged into the building. The driver, Fabian Perkins, remained and identified himself. Perkins produced a learner's permit and claimed that he did not know his passengers. He was arrested for operating unlicensed. Lavin and another officer searched the interior of the vehicle and found a firearm, marijuana, and cocaine. Six officers then entered the building to find and arrest both passengers.

- **Analysis.** *Toole* and *Perkins* decided that the searches violated 276, § 1.

  - *Weapons.* At the time of the searches, both defendants were in custody. Once a suspect is cuffed and in the cruiser, searching the passenger compartment can no longer be justified for safety.

    The fact that two passengers remained at large in *Perkins* did not justify a protective search either. The passengers had already left, so officers did not need to secure the car for their safety.

- *Evidence.* The second justification under § 1 failed as well: The searches were not likely to produce evidence of the crimes *for which the defendants were arrested*. Toole was arrested for simple A&B; Perkins for operating without a license.[6] Both crimes are not realistically linked to any physical evidence.

- *Other legal reason.* Finally, 276, § 1 has an "escape clause" if the search can be justified under another legal theory. In both *Toole* and *Perkins*, the searches did not fall within the motor vehicle exception. The *Toole* officer did not have probable cause to believe there was an illegal firearm because he asked Toole if he had a license to carry *after* searching the truck! As for *Perkins*, officers never had any basis to believe there were weapons or drugs in the car. Finally, the search in *Toole* was not a valid inventory because the department did not have an inventory policy! Impounding the vehicle and conducting an inventory would have worked in *Perkins*, but officers had already searched for evidence so the court never considered this reason.[7]

- *Summary.* Once occupants are removed, officers cannot justify a search incident to arrest of the passenger compartment for weapons. However, officers may search the compartment, regardless of the arrestee's custody status, if they are looking for evidence associated with the arrest. *Comm. v. DaRosa*, 94 Mass. App. Ct. 635 (2019).

Vehicle search for evidence depends on the crime being investigated. *Comm. v. Lelos*, 61 Mass. App. Ct. 626 (2004): A 911 caller saw a car "with a kid in a baseball hat" pass her house four times at 7:30 a.m. The car had license plate 441YFP. A check revealed that its owner, Michael Lava, had an extensive record involving house breaks.

Approximately an hour later, Officer Bruno responded to a house alarm. He saw the suspect vehicle with Gregory Lelos in the front passenger seat. Suddenly, Michael Lava ran from a side yard and jumped in. With lights and siren, Bruno stopped the car and frisked both men for weapons. Searching underneath the passenger seat, he found gloves, a cap, and a baggie containing gold chains (later linked to a burglarized home). Bruno's vehicle search was supported by probable cause. Also see *Comm. v. Starkweather*, 79 Mass. App. Ct. 791 (2011).[8]

SEARCH OF LUGGAGE OR OTHER CONTAINERS

Police may _immediately_ open a container to discover weapons an arrestee might access. *Comm. v. George*, 35 Mass. App. Ct. 551 (1993) involved the arrest of a motorist for operating without a license. Clifford George initially lied to the officer about having a New York license (he gave a false SSN), then unexpectedly passed a canvas gym bag to his passenger. The officer grabbed it, finding a substantial quantity of cocaine inside.

Clearly, the officer did not search the gym bag to secure evidence of unlicensed operation. He was motivated by the other recognized purpose of 276, § 1 — safety. The gym bag was large enough to contain a weapon, and neither George nor his companion were handcuffed at the time. See *Comm. v. Pierre*, 72 Mass. App. Ct. 580 (2008).

6 See 90, § 8B. For more information, review *LED's Motor Vehicle, Chapter 4*.
7 Although the passengers left the contraband behind, the court rejected the prosecutor's "abandonment" claim. The items were stored in a closed vehicle. There was no evidence that the passengers intended to permanently relinquish control over their property. For more on abandonment, see *Chapter 11*.
8 Interestingly, the Massachusetts rule in 276, § 1 was adopted by the U.S. Supreme Court for the nation in *Arizona v. Gant*, 129 S.Ct. 1710 (2009).

Police may also open a container if they have probable cause that it might contain evidence related to the arrest.

- *Comm. v. Madera*, 402 Mass. 156 (1988): The police had probable cause to believe that the defendant would carry heroin back from New York. They arrested him when he arrived by bus. They removed a gym bag from his shoulder and discovered numerous bags of heroin inside. The SJC allowed the warrantless search because requiring a warrant in this kind of case places an unnecessary burden on law enforcement.

- *Comm. v. Netto*, 438 Mass. 686 (2003): Joseph and Nancy Netto, in desperate need of money to buy heroin, robbed and murdered their neighbor, Robert Levesque. The next day police found the Nettos at a motel. Police entered their room with a warrant and removed them in handcuffs. Officers then seized a leather bag, pocketbook, and some clothes from the room.

  The police had probable cause these items were linked to the Nettos' crimes. The fact that the suspects were handcuffed and removed did not end the officers' authority to immediately return to the room and seize evidence. The court quoted the *Madera* case: "The police are entitled to a bright line rule that permits them, even in the absence of exigent circumstances, to search a bag carried by a person whom they lawfully arrest . . . where there is also probable cause to believe that the bag contains evidence of the crime for which the arrest was made."

Suggested strategy. In the final analysis, when encountering an arrestee in possession of luggage or other containers, the safest course of action is to take custody of the items and wait until the booking inventory to inspect them. *Illinois v. Lafayette*, 462 U.S. 640 (1983) (proper to secure shoulder bag of arrestee and conduct an inventory at the station). At the same time, if officers feel there is a dangerous object inside or evidence related to the underlying arrest, they may search the container at the scene.

18   *Inventories*

There are two types of inventories:

- **The booking inventory,** which involves individuals in police custody (detainees); and

- **The vehicle inventory,** which involves lawfully impounded vehicles.

An inventory is <u>not</u> a search for evidence. It is an administrative procedure. While evidence is sometimes revealed, a desire to find it is *not* an acceptable reason for the procedure. That is why officers should not refer to an "inventory search" in their reports or testimony. Simply call it an "inventory" or "administrative procedure."

BOOKING INVENTORY
JUSTIFICATION

Constitutional authority for the procedure appears in *Illinois v. Lafayette*, 462 U.S. 640 (1983). The reasons to inventory a detainee's belongings are:

- **Preserve his property while he is held at the station;**

- **Protect the police from disputes over lost, stolen, or returned property;**

- **Prevent escape, self-injury, or harm to others in the station.**

REQUIREMENTS

Article 14 and the Fourth Amendment require that a booking inventory involve:

- **Lawful custody.** The detainee must be lawfully in police custody.

- **Written procedures.** Booking procedures must be in writing.

- **Inspection conforms to policy.** The inspection must conform to the policy. It must not become a cover to search for evidence.

DETAINEE LAWFULLY IN POLICE CUSTODY

Arrests. A routine inventory is justified whenever a detainee is booked for *any* crime. *Illinois v. Lafayette, supra.* (defendant arrested for minor offense of disturbing the peace; police inventory justified once he came to station).

Protective custody. Although the cases speak about the inventory as a pre-incarceration safeguard, the reasons for it justify an inventory any time a person is held at the station. Since a Massachusetts appellate court has yet to rule on the matter, departments are advised to include language in their booking policy to cover protective custody situations.

If police arrange for a third party to take possession of a suspect's belongings, there is no need for a booking inventory. *Comm. v. Abdallah*, 475 Mass. 47 (2016): After a disturbance outside his hotel room, police arrested Jared Abdallah on an outstanding warrant for larceny. Police took possession of a small backpack Abdallah had been wearing and transported it to the station with him. There, they inventoried the contents of the bag, finding several thousand dollars in cash, bags of cocaine, and several hundred Percocet pills.

The police could have left the bag in the custody of the hotel clerk, who had agreed to secure the rest of Abdallah's possessions. The clerk was already securing expensive items, such as a computer and video game system. If the officers believed it was reasonable to leave the other items at the hotel, there was no reason to single out the backpack and take it to the station.

STANDARD POLICY

Police departments must have a booking policy. 127, § 3 (police must keep a record of all money and property in the possession of a prisoner). *Comm. v. Rostad,* 410 Mass. 618 (1991).

Apply the booking policy of the place of detention. *Comm. v. Barillas*, 484 Mass. 250 (2020) (if an arrest involves multiple agencies, officers are obligated to follow the booking policy of the agency that controls the lockup).

Locked containers

The policy should allow officers to open locked containers when: (1) they have the key or combination at the time they conduct the procedure; or (2) they reasonably believe the contents pose an imminent danger to the police or public. Otherwise, officers must record the locked container as an item without opening it, *or* obtain a search warrant if they have probable cause it contains evidence. *Comm. v. Vanya V.,* 75 Mass. App. Ct. 370 (2009).

Medication

Title II of the Americans with Disabilities Act (ADA) requires that departments provide medication to individuals in their custody who request and need it. Upon request, detainees should be permitted to take identified medication that has been prescribed by a licensed medical provider.[1] A detainee should be given only the dosage noted on the label, and the supervising officer must witness the detainee take the medication and note it in the booking record.[2,3]

---

1 The only exception is medical marijuana. 94I, § 7(D) (no accommodation must be made in a correctional facility for medical marijuana; this rule applies in a police lockup).
2 While 94C, § 9 prohibits the administration of a controlled substance by a non-licensed person, this recommended policy simply affords a detainee the opportunity to self-administer prescribed medication in accordance with label directions.
3 These recommendations are based on an article by Attorney Eric Atstupenas, who is General Counsel to the Massachusetts Chiefs of Police Association (MCOPA).

If there is any question concerning the administration of medication, the OIC may confer by telephone with a qualified medical professional, arrange for an evaluation of the detainee at the station, or have the detainee transported to the hospital.

The policy should require that any medication be identified. Here is recommended language:

> When possessed by a person in department custody, medication of any kind must be identified and handled with care. Identification may be accomplished by asking the person in custody; inspecting the package or bottle, its contents or labeling; accessing a reliable website; contacting a knowledgeable pharmacist or other health care professional; or some other method.
>
> Once identified, the medication must be documented on the booking form and held in a secure location. In consultation with the booking officer and, if necessary, a health care professional, the OIC will decide whether the medication will be provided to the subject in police custody. The OIC will document his or her decision. Each dose or administration will be documented by the officer who supervises it.
>
> Any purported medication possessed by a subject that, in fact, is identified as contraband shall be reported immediately to the OIC. The contraband will be entered into evidence.

Comm. v. White, 469 Mass. 96 (2014) (court rejected the practice of identifying drugs on a website during booking; a clear and consistent policy would have changed the outcome).

SCOPE OF BOOKING INVENTORY

The inventory must conform to department policy. *Comm. v. Wilson*, 389 Mass. 115 (1983).

The inventory must not be a pretext for an investigatory search. A lawful inventory is not "a calculated means of discovering evidence." *Colorado v. Bertine*, 479 U.S. 367 (1987).

Comm. v. Seng, 436 Mass. 537 (2002): The SJC decided that no valid inventory purpose was served by recording the multi-digit account numbers written on the back of a bank card found in the defendant's wallet. Furthermore, the account numbers were not obviously incriminating at the time, so recording them could not be justified as a valid plain view seizure by the booking officer.

The *Seng* decision acknowledges that it is always proper to inspect the contents of a wallet during booking, to record the cash and credit cards within, and to review proper identification. The police need not "blind themselves" to information visible during an inventory search; what they may not do is investigate the information in the wallet without obtaining a search warrant. Also see *Comm. v. Murphy*, 63 Mass. App. Ct. 11 (2005).

The policy must be submitted in court. *Comm. v. Brinson*, 440 Mass. 609 (2004) requires that prosecutors produce the written policy when an inventory is challenged. This enables a court to assess whether officers performed in a manner consistent with their department policy.

THIRD-PARTY CLAIMS TO PROPERTY

Follow inventory policy to resolve claims to detainee's property. *Comm. v. Barillas*, 484 Mass. 250 (2020): During the arrest of a murder suspect, Tomas Barillas, on unrelated warrants, Trooper Wilson properly took Barillas' cell phone as a potential weapon during his search incident to arrest. Barillas was booked into the Lynn police lockup. Trooper Wilson still had the phone in his pocket when he interviewed Barillas' younger brother, James, 20 minutes later. The trooper was surprised when James said that the cell phone was his, though Barillas often used it. James signed a consent search form. Among the evidence found on his phone was video of Barillas confessing to murder.

Trooper Wilson should have promptly turned the phone over to the booking officer for inventory with Barillas' belongings. Under these circumstances, Wilson's effort — outside the normal booking procedure — to identify the cell phone's owner was investigatory rather than administrative. As a result, James' consent to search was improper.

INVENTORY OF MOTOR VEHICLES

JUSTIFICATION

A vehicle inventory is conducted for essentially the same reasons as a booking inventory. *South Dakota v. Opperman*, 428 U.S. 364 (1976).

• **Protect the vehicle and its contents;**

• **Protect the police and tow company from false claims;**

• **Protect the public and police from dangerous items that might be left in the vehicle.**

REQUIREMENTS

Article 14 and the Fourth Amendment require:

• **Lawfully impounded vehicle.** The vehicle must be lawfully impounded by police.

• **Written procedures.** Inventory procedures must be in writing.

• **Inspection conforms to policy.** The inventory procedure must conform to policy. It must not become a pretext for an investigative search.

VEHICLE LAWFULLY IMPOUNDED

The inventory must be conducted when officers on scene <u>decide</u> to tow the vehicle. When the owner or someone in lawful control of the vehicle makes the decision, police should not conduct an inventory. For example, the owner decides to tow her disabled vehicle and notifies AAA.

On the other hand, if officers decide to tow a vehicle improperly parked on private property (266, § 121A), they must conduct an inventory. The issue is who makes the final *decision* to tow, not who selects or pays the tow company. *Comm. v. Daley,* 423 Mass. 747 (1996). *U.S. v. Dunn,* 928 F.3d 688 (8th Cir. 2019) (officers ignored the fact that Dunn arranged for a private tow; department policy allowed them to decide to tow his vehicle because it was impeding traffic; their inventory revealed guns and illegal drugs; this was valid).

Impoundment does not occur unless police are present. For example, the department is notified about a private tow from a posted area (266, § 120D), but officers are not dispatched.

Police may not delay their impoundment decision pending the results of their inventory. *Comm. v. Lek,* 99 Mass. App. Ct. 199 (2021): Detective Sandoval patrolled Lowell in plainclothes "to focus on gang suppression through motor vehicle stops." He saw Lang Lek's car fail to fully stop at a stop sign. He initiated the car stop on Elm Street, which he testified was a safer area with better lighting. Unlike the initial street where Lek committed the violation, Elm Street had no legal parking.

Detective Sandoval noticed that Lek was dressed all in red, the color of the Bloods gang. Lek provided another person's driver's license. The detective ordered Lek to exit, frisked him, and told him to sit on the curb. He did <u>not</u> handcuff Lek, arrest him, or tell him that his car would be towed. He began searching the car and found a pistol in the glove box. Lek was then arrested.

The Appeals Court believed that the detective's decision to impound, in reality, depended on the results of his investigatory search, which "infected the inventory."

- **Officers should communicate their decision to impound <u>before</u> the inventory** — e.g., "Mr. Motorist, I have not decided whether to arrest you, but I have decided to tow your vehicle."

- **As long as the police legitimately must tow the vehicle, the inventory is proper — regardless of the officers' expectation that their inventory will reveal evidence.** *Comm. v. Ubilez,* 88 Mass. App. Ct. 814 (2016). *Comm. v. Lopez-Rosario,* 2017 WL 1423593 (Appeals Court): Police were performing surveillance of a suspected stash house, and their target was Ariel Lopez-Rosario. They observed Lopez-Rosario drive his Saturn into a private parking lot. Officers arrested him for operating after suspension. They performed an inventory of the Saturn and found cocaine. The officers testified that they expected to find drugs, but department policy required that they tow the Saturn, which was unlawfully parked. Lopez-Rosario could not have been asked to move it because he did not have a valid license, and no other person was present.

Inventory proper even if driver allowed to leave in the tow truck. *U.S. v. Rivera,* 988 F.3d 579 (1st Cir. 2021): The vehicle's driver and only occupant, Pablo Rivera, was unlicensed. The trooper decided he would not arrest Rivera, but policy required that his vehicle be towed from the highway. Trooper Vladimir Louissaint told Rivera that he could ride with the tow truck to the impound lot but, during the inventory, heroin and a gun were found in the trunk. Rivera was arrested.

The fact that Rivera was planning to go with the tow truck did not eliminate the need for an inventory. Rivera was unlicensed and the car would not be returned to him at the tow lot, so concerns about theft and false claims still existed, as did the possibility of dangerous items in the vehicle.

REASONABLE ALTERNATIVES

The police must consider "reasonable alternatives" before impounding and towing a vehicle.[4] Reasonable alternatives include: (1) allowing a competent, alternative operator to legally drive the vehicle from the scene; *or* (2) leaving a vehicle lawfully parked at the location where police encountered it. Whether a reasonable alternative exists depends on the circumstances. *Comm. v. Caceres*, 413 Mass. 749 (1992).

Alternative operator

A competent, alternative operator must be:

- **Present at the scene before officers notify the tow company;**

- **In possession of a valid driver's license;** and

- **Approved by the owner, or someone clearly authorized by the owner, to take custody of the vehicle.**

Officers do not have to wait for an alternative operator once the towing process is initiated. *Comm. v. Ellerbe*, 430 Mass. 769 (2000) (lone driver under arrest for operating after suspension; car illegally parked in store lot; police not obligated to wait for a friend to remove it). *Comm. v. Delvalle*, 2016 WL 4426380 (Appeals Court) (no obligation to allow arriving friends to take a vehicle that was already in the process of being towed).

An alternative operator without his license in possession is disqualified, and no further investigation should take place into his license status. *Comm. v. Bettencourt*, 447 Mass. 631 (2006). Operators who provide a license should have their status checked through CJIS.

An alternative operator must be authorized by the owner or by someone clearly connected with the owner. In *Comm. v. Nicholas*, 93 Mass. App. Ct. 1123 (2018), Nicholas was arrested for operating after suspension at 1:14 a.m. Cooper, his passenger, had a valid license but incorrectly claimed the vehicle was registered to Nicholas' mother. The police were appropriately concerned that they might be accused of misappropriation if they turned over the car without any evidence that Cooper even knew the owner. Their inventory, which uncovered illegal drugs, was proper.

Officers must ask the driver if he wishes for a competent, alternative operator to take the vehicle. *Comm. v. Goncalves-Mendez*, 484 Mass. 80 (2020): The driver was arrested for an outstanding warrant. His passenger possessed a valid license, had no warrants, and was not impaired. The police officer should have asked the driver if he wanted his passenger to take custody of the vehicle before conducting an inventory and towing the car. It is the duty of the officer, not the driver to bring up a reasonable alternative to towing.

---

4 Article 14 requires the consideration of "reasonable alternatives"; the Fourth Amendment does not. *Colorado v. Bertine*, 479 U.S. 367 (1987).

Lawfully parked

Lawfully parked means that the vehicle is secure and legally parked in a public or private location. Secure means that the vehicle is locked with the windows closed. *Comm. v. Lugg,* 2014 WL 6847704 (Appeals Court) (open windows needed to be secured by officer).

Vehicle lawfully parked after police stop and risk of theft. If the vehicle is lawfully parked following a police stop, and there is no alternative operator, the vehicle should still be towed if officers determine there is a risk of theft or vandalism at that location. *Comm. v. Eddington,* 459 Mass. 102 (2011): At 4:15 a.m., officers saw two people leave a "problem house" carrying beer bottles. They got into a car and drove away.

Officers activated their blue lights because the occupants possessed open containers of alcohol. The driver pulled over and parked legally on a side street. The driver, Gerald Eddington, admitted that his license was suspended. He was arrested. Officers learned that the car was not registered to either Eddington or his passenger. Since it was 4:30 a.m., the officers decided not to contact the vehicle owner. Their pre-tow inventory resulted in the discovery of a firearm under the seat. Both driver and passenger were charged.

The decision to impound the vehicle made sense: (1) the car was owned by a third party not present at the scene; (2) the driver had a suspended license so, even if he was released promptly, he would not have been able to get the car; and (3) the location presented a significant risk of theft or vandalism to vehicles.[5]

Do not tow if vehicle lawfully parked before police stop — even if risk of theft. *Comm. v. Oliveira,* 474 Mass. 10 (2016): At 4:30 p.m., Mitchell Violet and Jemaul Oliveira were arrested for shoplifting. Police verified the car was registered to Violet's girlfriend. Police told them that the vehicle would be inventoried and towed. Both became upset, and Violet stated that he wanted his girlfriend to get her car. The police did not honor his request. The officers also said the store manager asked them to tow the vehicle. Their inventory revealed a loaded firearm inside the glove compartment. On appeal, the SJC ruled:

- **The officers' decision to impound was unreasonable.** Violet requested that the police leave the vehicle where it was parked until his girlfriend — the owner — could retrieve it. Violet had only been arrested for shoplifting. He would likely be released and could get the car himself. Even if not released on bail, he could call his girlfriend from the station.

- **The officers could not rely on the manager's tow request because they did not learn whether the store owned or controlled the lot.** There was some indication that police spoke with the manager *after* they began their inventory.

- **Finally, police could not rely on a risk of theft or vandalism to the car.** Violet lawfully parked *before* any police contact. When a driver chooses a lawful parking space — on the street, in a driveway, or in a parking lot — officers should typically allow it to stay since there is no liability risk. After all, the driver picked the parking spot, so he becomes responsible for any damage or theft that occurs as a result of his choice.

---

5 The SJC was adamant in *Eddington:* A "high crime" location may never, by itself, justify a decision to impound.

Authorized impoundment

Officers are authorized to impound a vehicle in the following situations.

- **Driver arrested for operating under the influence (OUI).** "Melanie's Law" mandates a 12 hour impoundment when any arrested motorist refuses the breathalyzer (BT) or blood test. 90, § 24(f)(iii). Since officers do not know, at the time of arrest, whether the defendant will refuse a test, they must always tow the vehicle pending that post-arrest decision — even if it is lawfully parked or there is someone at the scene who would normally qualify as an alternative operator.

  Departments should explicitly state in their policy that mandatory towing applies to OUI alcohol <u>and</u> drug arrests. *Comm. v. Kry*, 2017 WL 35535 (Appeals Court) (Northampton police have a mandatory tow policy for all OUI arrestees, including those impaired by drugs; this policy justified inventory and discovery of a sawed-off shotgun in the defendant's car, even though another driver was available after his OUI drug arrest).

- **Vehicle abandoned or trespassing on private property.** Officers should know the status of the property where a vehicle is parked *before* they call for a tow and conduct an inventory. See *Comm. v. Oliveira, supra.* 90, § 22C (removal of vehicle abandoned for more than 72 hours on public or private property). 266, § 121A (vehicle on another person's property without permission may be towed, whether or not the property is posted "no trespassing").

- **Vehicle illegally parked.** *Comm. v. Tisserand*, 5 Mass. App. Ct. 383 (1977) (double parking). *Comm. v. Wallace,* 70 Mass. App. Ct. 757 (2007) (handicap parking). *U.S. v. Exume*, 2013 WL 3494427 (U.S. District Court) (tow zone). 90, § 20A (tow or boot permitted if five unpaid parking tickets).

  In *U.S. v. Hardy*, 395 F.Supp.3d 191 (D. Mass. 2019), Wellesley police pulled over Hardy, who parked at a meter. Officers arrested him on a warrant and for his suspended license. During the inventory, officers found a gun. Hardy was alone and, although his car was in a metered parking spot, the officers did not know when he would be released from custody. Nor did they know whether his car would be ticketed and eventually towed by the city if it remained there. They reasonably impounded his car.

- **Vehicle disabled and/or unsafe.** Police may impound and tow a vehicle involved in a significant collision [*Comm. v. Mamacos, 409* Mass. 635 (1991)] or with a safety defect that would cause it to fail inspection [*Comm. v. Elwell*, 2015 WL 4633768 (Appeals Court)].

- **Vehicle may not be lawfully operated.** For example, it is unregistered, uninsured, or has attached plates. *Comm. v. Daley*, 423 Mass. 747 (1996). *Comm. v. Ubilez, supra.*

Officers are authorized to impound a vehicle in other situations where the driver can no longer operate — and there is no alternative operator or the vehicle is not lawfully parked. Comm. v. Sanchez, 40 Mass. App. Ct. 411 (1996) (following traffic stop, driver arrested on outstanding warrant; two passengers did not have any ID; third passenger had a valid license but said she did not want to drive and was just getting a ride; the vehicle owner could not be identified; police could not leave this car parked by the highway; they had to tow it; their inventory properly revealed cocaine in the trunk). *Comm. v. Bienvenu*, 63 Mass. App. Ct. 632 (2005).

Rental vehicles

Rental vehicles may <u>not</u> be impounded solely on the basis of an unauthorized operator. A renter's decision to let an unlisted person drive, *without more*, may violate the rental agreement, but it does not justify impoundment.[6] It is not the crime of use without authority either. *Comm. v. Campbell*, 475 Mass. 611 (2016).[7]

In certain situations, police may notify a rental company and impound their vehicle at the direction of their representative. Upon encountering an unauthorized operator, officers should notify the rental company and impound the vehicle at the company's request if one of the following applies:

- **The rental agreement has expired.** *Comm. v. Watts*, 74 Mass. App. Ct. 514 (2009) (trooper had the right to contact Enterprise; even though the defendant was an authorized driver, the rental agreement itself had expired the day before).

- **The unauthorized operator does not have a valid license.** *U.S. v. Lyle*, 919 F.3d 716 (2019): Lyle was arrested with a suspended license. He had been driving a rental car and was not authorized on the agreement. The inventory produced methamphetamine and $40,000 in the trunk. Lyle should not have been driving any car because his license was suspended, and a rental company with knowledge of the relevant facts certainly would not have given him permission nor allowed a renter to do so. Lyle's possession of the car was unlawful the moment he started driving.

- **The driver is arrested and an authorized operator is not at the scene to take custody of the vehicle.** *U.S. v. Williams*, 930 F.3d 44 (2019)(defendant arrested for reckless driving and authorized rental operator not at the scene; police properly towed vehicle).

- **Officers are unable to determine whether the *authorized* operator gave permission to the current driver.** If the rental agreement is active and the unauthorized driver has a license, officers may still investigate whether the individual listed on the agreement did, in fact, allow the current driver. If unable to confirm, officers should notify the rental company and follow its disposition decision. *Comm. v. Campbell, supra.*

SCOPE OF VEHICLE INVENTORY

Location

The inventory must take place at the scene before the car is towed <u>or</u> right after the car arrives at the tow lot. Delay undermines the reasons behind the inventory. *Comm. v. Woodman*, 11 Mass. App. Ct. 969 (1981) (inventory invalid because the van had already sat for two days in the tow lot).

---

6 The U.S. Supreme Court held that an unauthorized driver of a rental car still maintains an expectation of privacy. *Byrd v. U.S.*, 138 S.Ct. 1518 (2018) (police needed consent from an unauthorized rental car driver because, although he was not listed on the agreement, he had been given permission by the renter to drive at the time he was stopped by police).
7 For more on use without authority under 90, § 24, see *LED's Motor Vehicle Law, Chapter 12.*

Conform to policy

The inventory must be conducted in accordance with a written policy. "Standard procedures reduce the discretion of police to search at will, and so lessen the possibility that police will use inventory procedures as investigative searches." *Comm. v. Garcia*, 409 Mass. 675 (1991). *Comm. v. Brinson*, 440 Mass. 609 (2004) (if challenged in court, officers should provide the prosecutor with a copy of the policy).

Since it is an administrative procedure, the best practice is to conduct an inventory the same way every time. *Comm. v. Rosario-Santiago*, 96 Mass. App. Ct. 166 (2019) (it risks evidence suppression if a police officer conducts a targeted inventory procedure that begins in the location where he expects to find evidence).

During a typical inventory, officers should inspect:

- The exterior of the vehicle for signs of damage.

- The passenger compartment, including the glove box.

- The trunk.

Officers must examine any place where personal property might be kept — including "hides." *Comm. v. Mitchell*, 2016 WL 1391097 (Appeals Court): The initial stop was for illegally tinted windows. The driver had a suspended license. The passenger was unlicensed too. Officer Femino properly impounded the vehicle. While conducting an inventory, Femino noticed that the carpet lining in the center console area was pulled away from the frame. He recognized the opening as a potential "hide" where someone might store money, jewelry, narcotics, or firearms. He put his finger into the opening and pulled the carpet lining down, revealing a loaded gun. The department's inventory policy directed officers to examine "any place" in the car where valuables might be kept. Because valuables might be in a hide, its inspection was *required* under this policy.

Officers must examine the contents of any closed or open containers that might hold personal property.

- *Comm. v. Allen*, 76 Mass. App. Ct. 21 (2009) (department policy mandated opening containers, so the officer properly discovered an illegal gun when he inspected a shoe box inside a closed book bag in the trunk; police may inspect a closed container inside another closed container to fulfill their inventory obligations).

- *Comm. v. Valle*, 2013 WL 6725763 (Appeals Court) (by policy, the inventory extended to all storage areas and compartments; this included a jacket left on the back seat; once the officer lifted the jacket and determined it contained a heavy object, that object had to be inventoried as well; it turned out to be an illegal firearm).

Locked containers. The best practice is for department policy to direct officers to open and inventory locked containers if they lawfully obtain the key or combination from the motorist and/or vehicle owner. Officers should open the container by force only in an emergency.

Absent a key or combination, or an emergency, officers should obtain a search warrant to open a locked container. *Comm. v. DiFalco,* 73 Mass. App. Ct. 401 (2009).[8]

Document the inventory on a department-issued form. Failing to document an inventory results in the suppression of evidence and may subject the department to liability. *Comm. v. Torres,* 85 Mass. App. Ct. 51 (2014).

Recommendation: When multiple vehicles are towed at events or during snow emergencies, department policy should authorize an alternative procedure. The typical inventory is too cumbersome, so department policy should allow officers to fulfill their responsibility by looking into the passenger compartment from outside and noting any obviously expensive items on a supplemental report.

No pretext for investigative search

There is no need to conduct an inventory once items are turned over to a third party. *Comm. v. Nicoleau,* 90 Mass. App. Ct. 518 (2016): Police attempted to stop Jahliel Nicoleau because one of his headlights was out and his registration and license plates were invalid. Nicoleau continued to drive to his grandmother's house, where he lived. Officers arrested him outside the house for failure to stop. They arranged to have the unregistered vehicle towed.

Nicoleau's grandmother emerged from the house. Officers searched the vehicle and gave her a music player and the keys. The police also removed a backpack from the backseat, but instead of handing it to the grandmother, they searched it. An illegal knife was inside.

Having made the decision to give the music player to the grandmother, the police did not have discretion to inventory the backpack, which also could have been turned over to her.[9]

An inventory should not involve areas where a motorist is <u>unlikely</u> to store personal property.

- *Michigan v. Thomas,* 458 U.S. 259 (1982) (searching vehicle air vents was not within the scope of a lawful inventory; air vents are not places where people normally put personal items).

- *Comm. v. Lara,* 39 Mass. App. Ct. 546 (1995) (prying the cover off the dashboard inconsistent with inventory).

- *Comm. v. Muckle,* 61 Mass. App. Ct. 678 (2004) (looking inside a crumpled Dunkin' Donuts bag in the cargo area of a van was inconsistent with the main purpose of an inventory — safeguarding an owner's property; therefore, drugs in bag had to be suppressed).

Using a drug sniffing K-9 inconsistent with inventory. *Comm. v. Alvarado,* 420 Mass. 542 (1995) (use of a drug sniffing K-9 was totally inconsistent with the purpose of an inventory; so was dismantling a coffee maker found in the backseat area).

---

8 The warrant requirement does *not* apply to locked containers under the motor vehicle exception. *Comm. v. Moses,* 408 Mass. 136 (1990). See *Chapter 16.*
9 This case is similar to *Comm. v. Abdallah,* 475 Mass. 47 (2016), discussed previously in the booking section.

Finally, a properly performed inventory may transform into a search for evidence under the motor vehicle exception. *Comm. v. Baptiste*, 65 Mass. App. Ct. 511 (2006): At 3:00 a.m., Trooper Pagliaroni saw a Cadillac traveling at 87 mph. While speaking with the driver, Pagliaroni saw white powder on the console. The driver had a suspended license and outstanding warrant. Pagliaroni also learned that the passenger's license was suspended. The passenger accepted a ride off the highway from another trooper.

Pagliaroni conducted an inventory while waiting for a tow truck. He examined the console and found a cup holder that could be released by pushing a button. Pagliaroni pressed the button, but it was jammed. He then used a flashlight to look underneath the holder and saw cocaine in a plastic bag. He later filled out an inventory form, but did not mention the cocaine. He did record it in his incident report.

- **Inventory and investigation are different.** The investigative search is designed to gather evidence; an inventory is conducted to safeguard the vehicle and its contents.

- **Impound decision.** Here, the driver and passenger could not drive. Trooper Pagliaroni had to conduct an inventory and tow.

- **Scope of inventory.** Since the inventory policy requires the inspection of all areas "where property is likely to be kept," the trooper had to look inside the console. The console is a storage area comparable to the glove box. Still, the court ruled that attempting to release the cup holder and looking underneath it could not be justified as an inventory procedure. This is not an area where people typically store personal items.

- **Motor vehicle exception.** At the same time, Pagliaroni's decision to look under the cup holder was permissible under the motor vehicle exception. After all, the trooper had already observed cocaine on the console. This gave him probable cause to look further. Because the cocaine was seized pursuant to this investigative search, it did not have to be listed on Pagliaroni's inventory report.

- **Best practice.** Officers should include any evidence discovered during an inventory on the form as well as in their incident report. *Comm. v. Nicholson*, 58 Mass. App. Ct. 601 (2003).

19 Administrative Inspections & Searches

The Fourth Amendment and Article 14 allow warrantless administrative searches of "closely regulated" industries. The reason is that owners understand they must accept reduced privacy if they conduct certain types of business. *New York v. Burger*, 482 U.S. 691 (1987). *Thurlow v. Crossman*, 336 Mass. 248 (1957).[1]

Administrative inspections must comply with statutory guidelines. *Comm. v. Tart*, 408 Mass. 249 (1990).

A business owner or agent's failure to cooperate with an administrative inspection can be a crime — provided the police conduct their inspection within statutory guidelines. *Comm. v. Eagleton*, 402 Mass. 199 (1988) (used car salesman convicted of failing to cooperate with authorized police inspection under 140, § 67).

Officers may engage in an administrative inspection even if they are suspicious that criminal activity is occurring on the premises.

- *U.S. v. Villamonte-Marquez*, 462 US 579 (1983): The warrantless boarding of a vessel by Customs officers was proper even though they were motivated by a tip that the vessel held marijuana. As the Supreme Court remarked: "We . . . see little logic in sanctioning examinations of ordinary, unsuspecting vessels but forbidding them in the case of suspected smugglers."

- *Comm. v. Tremblay*, 48 Mass App. Ct. 454 (2000): The Governor's Auto Theft Strike Force received an anonymous tip that the defendant was managing an auto salvage company with three stolen cars on his lot. Under 140, §§ 57–69, troopers assigned to the strike force decided to conduct an administrative inspection, allowing them to examine all second-hand motor vehicles, parts, and records. Their protocol was: (1) determine who is in charge; (2) give that person a copy of the inspection law; (3) complete an inspection form; (4) ask to inspect records; and (5) ask permission to inspect vehicles and parts.

  Two troopers spotted a stolen vehicle and, at the direction of their supervisor, secured the lot. Another trooper obtained a warrant. The ensuing search revealed two additional stolen cars. The protocol employed was perfect.

---

1 Examples of inspection authority in Massachusetts: 94, §§ 35, 60 (milk); 111, § 9 (food and drugs); 148, §§ 4, 5 (fire hazards); 129, § 7 (animals); 159, § 27 (premises of a common carrier); 138, § 63 (premises licensed to sell alcohol); 140, § 201 (restaurants).

On the other hand, officers may <u>not</u> use their administrative power to seek evidence unrelated to their administrative authority. *Comm. v. Krisco Corporation*, 421 Mass. 37 (1995): An environmental investigator with the Attorney General's Office conducted an administrative inspection of an auto body shop as a way to gain entrance to the business and seize hazardous materials from its dumpster. She adopted this strategy because she had not been able to develop probable cause for a search warrant. The SJC rejected her approach because the authority to inspect auto body shops was unrelated to her real purpose for administrative entry — conducting an environmental crimes investigation. Also see *Comm. v. Rosenthal*, 52 Mass. App. Ct. 707 (2001).

Once an inspection reveals evidence of crime, authorities must stop and obtain a search warrant. While officers may be motivated to pursue an administrative inspection based on their suspicions of related criminal conduct, once their inspection reveals evidence of crime, they must obtain a warrant to seize the evidence they found. *Comm. v. Tremblay, supra.*

In *Comm. v. O'Donnell*, 92 Mass. App. Ct. 262 (2017), an administrative warrant only permitted the town to inspect the property for violations of the sanitary code. When the police engaged the services of electrical inspectors and began searching for evidence of the criminal theft of electricity, they went beyond the scope of the administrative warrant. They should have ended the administrative inspection, secured the premises, and obtained a search warrant.

APPLICATION TO MASSACHUSETTS BUSINESSES

DEALERS IN CONTROLLED SUBSTANCES

Pharmacies are part of the heavily regulated controlled substances industry. Under 94C, § 30, police officers may inspect premises dealing in controlled substances with an administrative warrant or, sometimes, without a warrant.

Administrative warrants. *Comm. v. Frodyma*, 386 Mass. 434 (1982) outlined four justifications for a warrant: (1) inspections are desirable for a given area; (2) the particular premises have never been inspected; (3) complaints have been lodged; or (4) a pharmacist or physician has recently made unusually large purchases of controlled substances.

Frodyma also held that administrative warrants must designate the type of records and items inspectors will review. Officers may acquire records, containers, and samples. However, they may *not* inspect financial or sales data (other than shipping data) *unless* the owner or agent in charge consents in writing. The warrant must be served during normal business hours and returned within 10 days of issuance. 94C, § 30.

Warrantless inspections apply to anyone who manufactures or dispenses controlled substances, including hospitals, clinics, pharmacies and doctors' offices. They are permitted if the owner or agent in charge consents, an imminent threat to health or safety exists, or a "conveyance" (vehicle of some sort) is inspected. The scope of this inspection is identical to an administrative warrant.

MOTOR VEHICLE DEALERS

Warrantless inspections are permitted at dealer locations. 140, § 58 establishes three licenses. Class 1 is for any person who is a recognized agent of a motor vehicle manufacturer and whose principal business is the sale of new motor vehicles. Class 2 dealers are in the business of buying or selling second hand motor vehicles. Class 3 dealers buy second hand motor vehicles for the purpose of remodeling and selling them, or buying or selling parts.

Inspections. Under 140, § 66, the attorney general, State Police colonel, Boston Police commissioner, chief of police of any city, selectmen of any town, or any officer authorized by one of them, may enter licensed premises to examine vehicles, parts, and records. Inspections must occur during normal business hours. *Comm. v. Eagleton*, 402 Mass. 199 (1988).

It is a crime under 140, § 67 if the licensee or person in charge refuses to admit an *authorized* officer, or refuses to exhibit all vehicles, parts, and books. Penalty: HC NMT 1 year; and/or Fine NMT $200. While investigators have the authority to inspect these businesses, they may *not* seize any parts or records without a search warrant. *Comm. v. Tremblay, supra.*

COMMERCIAL VEHICLE OPERATORS

Random inspection by qualified FMCSA officers. *Comm. v. LeBoeuf*, 78 Mass. App. Ct. 45 (2010): Police officers certified by the Federal Motor Carrier Safety Administration (FMCSA), a division of the U.S. Department of Transportation, may randomly stop commercial vehicles and conduct safety inspections. To be certified, officers must attend a two week school at the State Police Academy, pass two federal examinations, and participate in field training. In *LeBoeuf*, a Framingham officer, certified as an inspector, stopped a dump truck and discovered that the driver had a revoked commercial license. He was arrested.

Commercial trucking is closely regulated and the applicable guidelines appropriately limit who may perform the inspections (certified FMCSA agents), which vehicles may be inspected (commercial trucks), when they may be inspected (vehicles in operation), and what items may be inspected (license, registration, medical certificate, log, and vehicle components).

DEALERS IN FIREARMS

Ledger must be open at all times to inspection. 140, § 123 insists that the ledger that records all gun sales, rentals, leases, and gunsmithing activities "must be open at all times" to police inspection. In addition, § 123 directs "[t]he licensing authority [to] enter, one time per calendar year, during regular business hours, the commercial premises owned or leased by any licensee, . . . and inspect, in a reasonable manner, [its] records and inventory."

This statute authorizes police inspectors to copy records. In order to seize physical evidence (e.g., guns, ammunition, etc.), officers must obtain written consent or a search warrant.

INNKEEPERS

Any hotel or motel must maintain a guest register. 140, § 27 requires that all motel and hotel managers maintain a register that includes the name, address, and room number of each guest. If the room is occupied by five or more members of a group, one person's information can be entered on their behalf. No one may be allowed to enter a room until the proper register entry has been made.[2]

Records must be kept for one year *and* provided on demand for inspection to licensing authorities, their agents, and the police. Penalty for noncompliance: HC NMT 3 months; and/or Fine NLT $100, NMT $500.

Police may no longer demand records and charge an innkeeper for noncompliance — unless they first obtain legal process. Based on the U.S. Supreme Court's decision in *City of Los Angeles v. Patel*, 135 S.Ct. 2443 (2015), if detectives or officers want to obtain records from a motel or hotel, they should: (1) ask the manager for consent; (2) obtain a search warrant; or (3) persuade a prosecutor to issue an administrative subpoena. Only after obtaining a warrant or subpoena may an owner or agent be charged for failure to comply under 140, § 27.

PAWNBROKERS

Entry authorized at any time to inspect business. Under 140, § 73, the chief of police of a city, the selectman of a town, any officer authorized by them, or any state trooper may enter, at any time, the premises used by a licensed pawnbroker. They may also examine all articles and records. Under 140, § 74, it is a crime for a licensed pawnbroker or other person in charge to refuse to admit an officer or to fail to exhibit articles and books on demand. Penalty: HC NMT 1 year; and/or Fine NMT $200. Also see 140, § 79 (pawnbrokers must keep records and pictures of *any* person pawning articles).

---

2 There is even a companion statute, 140, § 29, that prohibits a guest from registering with a false name, or an innkeeper from knowingly letting that happen. Penalty: Fine NLT $10, NMT $25. *Comm. v. DeBrosky,* 363 Mass. 718 (1973). This law is still constitutional, though not very helpful!

20 | *Electronic Evidence*

DIGITAL DEVICES
CELL PHONES

INTERCEPTING CALLS

The police may not intercept cell phone communications without a warrant. Federal law, 18 U.S.C. § 2515, prohibits the unlawful interception of conversations over cell phones. Citizens, as well as the police, are covered. *Comm. v. Damiano*, 444 Mass. 444 (2005) (a citizen testified that she knew how to scan away from personal telephone calls intercepted by her scanner; yet, when she heard the conversation between the defendant and his drug customer, she listened for five minutes and called police; the exclusionary rule applied because she did it on purpose).

ABANDONED OR LOST PHONES

Police may immediately search an abandoned cell phone. *Comm. v. Martin*, 467 Mass. 291 (2014) (defendant placed cell phone on an outdoor window sill and told detectives he did not want it anymore).

Police may immediately search a lost or misplaced cell phone to the extent necessary to determine its owner. Steps might involve looking in frequent contacts and calling someone to learn who owns the phone. Once officers learn the identity of the owner, they should obtain consent from that person or a warrant before further exploration of the phone's contents. *Comm. v. Driscoll*, 2012 WL 1970381 (Appeals Court) (officer at scene of drug store break-in found a cell phone in a snow bank; the officer properly searched it to locate the owner's photo which, he realized, matched the man he had seen earlier).

PHONES SEIZED BY POLICE

Police may <u>not</u> search a cell phone incident to arrest. They need separate consent or a warrant because citizens have a significant expectation of privacy.[1] Based on *Riley v. California*, 134 S.Ct. 2473 (2014), the author recommends the following:

Check for weapon

Never assume a phone is a phone! There have been instances where a suspect's phone turned out to be a disguised weapon (e.g., a knife, derringer, taser, or OC spray container).

---

1 Even probationers maintain a privacy interest in their cell phones. *U.S. v. Lara*, 815 F.3d 605 (2016). See discussion in *Chapter 11*.

Comm. v. Barillas, 484 Mass. 250 (2020) (any hard object may be seized as a weapon during a search incident to arrest, and the physical characteristics of a cell phone may be checked to determine whether it conceals a weapon).

View phone exterior

It is not a search to view the outside of a suspect's phone for texts or other information. *Comm. v. Alvarez*, 400 Mass. 1015 (2018): The defendant was arrested for selling cocaine in a grocery store parking lot. His cell phone was lawfully seized during a search incident to arrest. When the cell phone rang at the station, the officer glanced at the phone and saw a text message on its outer screen. It read, "N word, I need some shit." The officer did not open or manipulate the phone to view the text. His observation was not a search.

It is not a search to text a suspect's phone. *U.S. v. Brixen*, 908 F.3d 276 (7th Cir. 2018): An individual with the Snapchat username "Snappyschrader" held himself out to be 31 years old and agreed to assist a 14 year old female in purchasing undergarments. He did not realize he was communicating with a police detective. When "Snappy" showed up for a supermarket rendezvous, police arrested him and seized his phone. To illustrate to Snappy that he had been communicating with police, the detective sent a message to his phone from an undercover Snapchat account. Snappy then confessed.

This was not a search. The detective did not manipulate the phone or access its contents. The notification appeared on the screen, just like a ringtone is heard by anyone present.

Answer or search if exigent circumstances

Exigent circumstances may justify answering a phone and/or conducting a warrantless search. Police may need to immediately locate evidence on a cell phone to respond to a bomb threat or child abduction. Or, a more common situation, officers may answer an offender's phone during a drug distribution or sexual enticement investigation to avoid losing evidence. If the caller implicates the defendant, record his statements in the police report (e.g., "The female caller immediately said, 'Darren, meet me at the park in 10. I need another big 50.' The next three callers also placed orders for various quantities of cocaine."). *Comm. v. Barrett*, 97 Mass. App. Ct. 437 (2020) (an investigator must testify why getting a warrant was impractical before answering a suspect's cell phone).

Example of no exigency. *Comm. v. Dyette*, 87 Mass. App. Ct. 548 (2015): Police approached a park at night and saw Darren Dyette and another man run. Police found two loaded guns where they had been.

Dyette was caught nearby, but claimed he had not been in the park. When asked why he was breathing heavily, Dyette said he was arguing with his girlfriend on his cell phone. The officer took Dyette's phone, looked at the call log, and saw an array of disjointed numbers and symbols that had been typed in. Dyette was arrested.

At the station, Dyette continued to claim that he had been arguing with his girlfriend. The booking sergeant was concerned that incoming calls would "push out" previous calls if they waited for a warrant. His examination occurred five hours after the arrest. The log showed that Dyette had not been talking with his girlfriend.

The SJC rejected the claim of exigent circumstances. The phone was not locked or password-protected. The problem of losing call records could have been easily averted by turning off the phone and seeking a warrant.

Secure if probable cause

Absent exigent circumstances, police may seize a phone only if they have probable cause that it contains evidence. At this point, officers may take steps to prevent the loss of evidence — such as turning off the device, removing its battery, or placing it in a secure container (e.g., a Faraday bag).

Seizure justified if cell phones, by themselves, can help prove accomplice connection. In *Comm. v. Arthur*, 94 Mass. App. Ct. 161 (2018), three men in two cars were observed parking on a street. Two men left one car to walk around the block. The third got out and peered through backyards, acting as a lookout. Then the original two men fired shots at a house. All three ran back to their cars, but were stopped by police and arrested. Police seized the vehicles and, three days later, applied for a warrant to take custody of two cell phones found in one vehicle and three in the other.

The mere presence of the phones in two cars helped prove the three men coordinated this attack, even if the contents of the phones were never reviewed.

Seizure also justified if cell phones likely used during the crime. In *Comm. v. Snow*, 486 Mass. 582 (2021), shortly after a shooting, Boston Police were alerted to a parked vehicle with three occupants changing clothes. The arriving officers saw that the front seat passenger matched the description of the shooter. The driver, Dondre Snow, was talking on his cell phone just before police confronted him. Police seized Snow's cell phone and those belonging to the other occupants, Daquan Peters and Dwayne Diggs.

The cell phone of the deceased victim contained recent text threats from a contact labeled "Slime Buttah." Police knew Dwayne Diggs had the street names "Butta" and "Butta Bear."

While an investigator's opinion that crime participants often use cell phones to communicate is never enough to support searching a phone [see *Comm. v. White*, 475 Mass. 583 (2016)], there were additional facts in the affidavit for Snow's phone that did provide probable cause for a warrant:

* A cell phone was used to text a threat to the victim;

* Shortly after the shooting, the defendant was using a cell phone to talk to the person who rented the car used in the murder; and

* Renting a car and changing clothes after the crime demonstrated pre-crime planning.

Obtain consent or a warrant

Once the phone is secure, officers should inform the defendant of his two options — consent to a search or insist on a warrant. An officer might say, for example: "Mr. Smith, I have your phone. You may allow me to search it. With your consent, I will download any relevant information onto a department computer and return your phone as soon as possible.

If you do not want to consent, that is fine. You have the right to refuse. But, if you do, I will apply for a search warrant. This will probably take a couple of hours. If I am granted the warrant, I will submit your phone for forensic analysis within seven days. If the court does not give me a warrant, I will give the phone back to you. What would you like me to do?"

Many offenders, eager to get their phone back, will consent when given the choice. *Comm. v. Farnsworth*, 76 Mass. App. Ct. 87 (2010) (voluntary consent may follow an officer's statement that, if the suspect refuses, he will seek a warrant).

In order to ask for consent on the basis that police will otherwise apply for a warrant, police must have probable cause for a warrant to begin with. *Comm. v. Wangnoon*, 2018 WL 894026 (Appeals Court): Wangnoon only agreed to sign the consent form after police told him that if he did not, they would seize his phone as evidence and "break through it." At the time, police may have suspected that Wangnoon knew more about a murder than he was saying, but that was not enough. Because police lacked probable cause to support their statement that they could seize the phone as evidence, Wangnoon's consent was not voluntary and could not justify the search.

Example of proper consent for cell phone search. *Comm. v. Fencher*, 95 Mass. App. Ct. 618 (2019): The victim told police that he suspected his niece, Alexa Fencher. The niece agreed to a recorded interview at the police station and waived her *Miranda* rights.

- **First, officers had probable cause to seize Fencher's cell phone.**

  - The victim had been badly beaten by multiple assailants during a home invasion approximately six hours earlier;
  - The victim had a restraining order against Alexa Fencher.
  - Fencher's white Hyundai Sonata was seen in the area of the victim's residence less than two hours before the assault;
  - Fencher had a key to the victim's residence and there was no forced entry;
  - There were possible blood stains on the exterior of the Hyundai Sonata when Alexa Fencher arrived at the station the next morning; and
  - Fencher told detectives she had cell phone videos of herself at a bar during the time of the attack. Such evidence could establish or dispute her alibi.

- **Second, Fencher voluntarily consented to a search of her phone.** She signed a form and provided her passwords. [*Note:* If a suspect consents clearly during a recorded interview, there is no need to have him or her sign a form. The recording is positive proof.]

Consent to search ends when the officer returns the phone. *U.S. v. Escamilla*, 852 F.3d 474 (5th Cir. 2017): Miguel Escamilla was stopped by Border Patrol agents for avoiding their checkpoints. They became suspicious he was smuggling drugs. One agent asked: "Do you mind if I look through your phone?" Escamilla silently handed it over. It was a "burner" phone containing only three numbers. Two were saved under a single letter rather than a name. The agent handed the phone back to Escamilla saying "I'm done with it."

Escamilla was then arrested based on his connection to a recovered stash of heroin. Agents drove him to a nearby Border Patrol station and seized his personal property. Agents searched his phone a second time, and used the contact numbers to obtain records from AT&T.

Escamilla consented to the original search of his phone by handing it to the agent. When the agent gave the phone back, his consent ended. The second search at the station required its own consent or warrant.

WARRANT ISSUES

Only one warrant is necessary to seize _and_ search a cell phone. *Comm. v. Arthur,* 94 Mass. App. Ct. 161 (2018) (only one warrant needed to seize and search cell phones possibly containing evidence of a shooting).

The affidavit should state a date range for the relevant events. *Comm. v. Snow,* 486 Mass. 582 (2021) (affidavit must mention a beginning and ending date for potential evidence).

The affidavit should also specify the type of files that will contain evidence relating to the crime under investigation. *Comm. v. Fulgian,* 477 Mass. 20 (2017).

- *Comm. v. Dorelas,* 473 Mass. 496 (2016) (search warrant affidavit provided probable cause to search the defendant's iPhone for text messages and photographs attached to text messages relevant to the shooting under investigation; it was appropriate for police to search stored picture files on the iPhone because they could have contained threatening communications, even after being deleted from the text history).

- *Comm. v. Keplin,* 2018 WL 1659688 (Appeals Court) (search warrant affidavit established probable cause to believe that Ronald Keplin used his cell phone to advertise and communicate with customers of his prostitution enterprise, and to record the financial aspects of his business; therefore, officers properly sought permission to seize customer contact information, sales, money owed, and transactions concerning internet advertising).

The best practice is to incorporate a "minimization protocol" into the warrant application or, at least, document the one used during the warrant's execution. A minimization protocol describes the manner in which technicians intend to limit their inspection to potentially relevant information. It often includes the software and "search terms." Describing how investigators plan to limit their electronic search is important to courts.[2]

A warrant for a phone with an assigned number permits police to conduct a quick search to confirm its number. *Comm. v. Perkins,* 478 Mass. 97 (2017) (police seized nine cell phones from a residence pursuant to a search warrant; they had probable cause to search the call logs of each phone to determine which, if any, was the phone they were looking for).

Compare *Comm. v. Hernandez,* 2014 WL 6092216 (Superior Court): Police went to Aaron Hernandez's house to execute a search warrant for a cell phone with the number 203-606-8969. Hernandez said the phone was with his attorney, so police got it from the lawyer right away, but did not power it on to check the number. Instead, officers took two more cell phones from the house — even though they already knew that a white iPhone did not belong to Hernandez and the other phone was unlocked. They could have turned both on and verified their numbers. They also could have called 203-606-8969 to see if either phone rang. Instead, they improperly seized both phones.

---

2 P. Hanley and W. Charles,"Should State Law Enforcement Officials Be Required to Develop and Implement Minimization Protocols to Govern the Execution of Digital Search Warrants?" *Mass. Law R.* Vol. 100, No. 1, pg. 5.

Electronic evidence, including cell phones, may be examined beyond 7 days. Officers simply need to list the seized phone(s) on their warrant return. The forensic experts then have a reasonable period of time beyond 7 days to complete their examination. *Comm. v. Ericson*, 85 Mass. App. Ct. 326 (2014). *Comm. v. Arthur*, 94 Mass. App. Ct. 161 (2018).

COURT ORDER FOR ACCESS

Under Article 12, there must be proof beyond a reasonable doubt that a defendant can access the device in order to obtain a court order directing him to decrypt computer files, enter his passcode, or apply his finger to a scanner.[3] *Comm. v. Gelfgatt*, 468 Mass. 512 (2014). In *Comm. v. Jones*, 481 Mass. 540 (2019), police responded to a report of a stolen purse at a hotel. The victim, Sara, identified Dennis Jones, whom she had been dating, as the thief. She eventually disclosed that Jones had induced her to work as a prostitute in exchange for housing. Jones used an LG brand cell phone to communicate with her and a female associate about prostitution.

Police arrested Jones and obtained a warrant for the LG phone, which could not be unlocked without a password. The Commonwealth filed a motion and showed, beyond a reasonable doubt, that Jones used the LG phone regularly based on: (1) Sara's statements; (2) the phone was found in Jones' pants pocket; and (3) cell site location information (CSLI) records placed the LG next to another phone registered to Jones. The fact that multiple people used the phone was irrelevant. Exclusive control is not required.

Police tip. When officers seize a phone, they should ask their suspect if it belongs to him. He will usually admit it. If officers later need a court order under *Jones* to gain access, they will have proof beyond a reasonable doubt from the mouth of their suspect.

If the suspect's attorney has the phone, get a warrant. Police must obtain a warrant — not a subpoena — to search a lawyer's office for evidence because there is a risk that they will observe materials protected by the attorney–client privilege. Consult with a prosecutor before doing this. *Grand Jury Investigation*, 470 Mass. 399 (2015).

DIGITAL CAMERAS

Search of digital camera images requires a warrant. Digital cameras, like cell phones, have the capacity to store enormous quantities of photo and video recordings that can reveal intimate details about a person's life. *Comm. v. Mauricio*, 477 Mass. 588 (2017). While there is some concern that cell phones will be remotely wiped or data encrypted, there is less risk with digital cameras, which are not usually connected to the internet.

Digital camera images likely document the nature of a relationship, which provides probable cause for a warrant following a domestic violence murder. *Comm. v. Fernandes*, 485 Mass. 172 (2020): The defendant confessed to police that he killed his girlfriend. Pursuant to a search warrant, a digital camera was seized in the residence. Because the crime involved killing a domestic partner inside the home, evidence explaining the nature of the relationship between defendant and victim was relevant to show motive. Probable cause did not need to rely on the narrow basis that perpetrators sometimes photograph their victims' bodies.

---

3 Under the Fifth Amendment, the lesser standard of proof by clear and convincing evidence applies.

PHONE & COMPUTER RECORDS

Administrative subpoena for phone or computer records. Under 271, § 17B, the Attorney General, a district attorney, or one of their assistants may obtain certain records from a telephone or computer service company based on reasonable suspicion that the records "are relevant and material to an ongoing criminal investigation." The demand must come from a prosecutor, not police officer. *Comm. v. Feodoroff*, 43 Mass. App. Ct. 725 (1997) (ten demands for telephone records by police lieutenant invalid). The company must deliver records within 14 days (unless reduced or increased by court order).

These records — e.g., a subscriber's name and address and a log of calls — require no judicial authorization because customers have a limited expectation of privacy in the phone and computer records they know a commercial carrier keeps. *Comm. v. Vinnie*, 428 Mass. 16 (1998). However, no content-based information (e.g., emails, texts, websites accessed) may be disclosed under an administrative subpoena.

No subpoena necessary if voluntary disclosure based on exigent circumstances. *Comm. v. Chamberlin*, 473 Mass. 653 (2016): A detective asked T-Mobile for call records associated with a number being used to communicate serious threats to the victim and his family. T-Mobile produced the records without a subpoena, although one was sent the following day. A § 17B subpoena is not required unless there is a *demand* for records. Here, T-Mobile believed, in good faith, that exigent circumstances warranted producing the documents.

Out-of-state records by warrant. 276, § 1B provides that: (1) a Massachusetts court may issue a search warrant to an out-of-state corporation for records of electronic communications and computer services; (2) the corporation must respond within 14 days (unless the court orders otherwise); and (3) the corporation must provide an affidavit of authenticity for the records.[4] This law also requires that Massachusetts corporations respond to out-of-state subpoenas in the same manner.

COMPUTERS

Police may typically search a computer associated with an IP address. *Comm. v. Molina*, 476 Mass. 388 (2017): A State Police trooper conducted a search for child pornography by accessing the Roundup Ares program.[5] The search indicated the IP address of a computer that might be sharing child pornography. The trooper connected directly to the computer and viewed its shared files. The trooper recognized terms commonly associated with child pornography and downloaded two videos containing pornography.

The district attorney sent an administrative subpoena to Verizon and obtained the name of the subscriber, Hermes Declid, and the physical address associated with the IP address. Police conducted surveillance and confirmed it was Declid's apartment. They also learned that four other people lived there, including Josue Molina. They executed a search warrant and discovered that the Ares program was not on Declid's computer. It was on Molina's.

---

4 Same rule applies to grand jury, trial, or administrative subpoenas.
5 The Roundup Ares program is another version of the Ares file-sharing program, which allows users to directly connect to other users' computers to search and download files. While the Ares program is freely available to the general public, the Roundup Ares program is only available to law enforcement.

The search warrant for the entire apartment was proper because anyone in the apartment could have been using the IP address for child pornography. Since files could have easily been transferred between devices at the same location, all devices present could be searched.[6]

Police do not always have to determine who was using the IP address. *Comm. v. Martinez*, 476 Mass. 410 (2017): Police discovered a computer with a Comcast IP address that was sharing child pornography. The district attorney issued an administrative subpoena to Comcast and learned that the IP address was assigned to a subscriber named Angel Martinez at a certain address in Fall River. Police could not verify that Martinez currently lived there, but they still obtained a valid search warrant. The fact that someone other than the subscriber could be using the same IP address did not defeat probable cause. The issue was whether the *address* contained evidence. The name of the account holder was incidental.

Electronic evidence may be examined beyond 7 days. *Comm. v. Kaupp*, 453 Mass. 102 (2009) allows officers to list computers and electronic storage devices on their warrant return. The forensic experts then have a reasonable period of time beyond seven days to complete their examination.

MISCELLANEOUS ISSUES WITH ELECTRONIC EVIDENCE

LINKING COMMUNICATION TO DEFENDANT

Confirmation is necessary to prove that the defendant wrote an email, instant message, text, Facebook post, or other electronic communication. Evidence that a defendant's name appears as the author, or that the communication originated from his account, is *insufficient* proof that he was the author. There must be additional "confirming circumstances." *Comm. v. Purdy*, 459 Mass. 442 (2011).

- **Sufficient proof.** *Comm. v. Gilman*, 89 Mass. App. Ct. 752 (2016): David Gilman was the 12 year old victim's middle school music teacher. While on a field trip, Gilman gave the victim his cell phone number. They exchanged messages frequently, and eventually engaged in sexual contact. Police obtained Gilman's school-issued laptop. Officers were able to view many chat logs containing the victim's and Gilman's declarations of love and descriptions of sexual encounters. There was strong evidence that Gilman wrote the messages: they came from an account bearing his name and picture; they were located on the hard drive of his password-protected laptop; and the conversations were full of personal references, such as pet names for each other. *Comm. v. Gonsalves*, 99 Mass. App. Ct. 638 (2021) (victim received a barrage of text messages from her ex-boyfriend after a 209A order was issued; the messages contained recurring spelling errors typical of his texts).

- **Insufficient proof.** *Comm. v. McMann*, 97 Mass. App. Ct. 558 (2020): The victim had a "no contact" 209A against the defendant. She received a message from his Instagram account saying, "Yoooo." An officer interviewed the defendant, who denied sending the message and showed great surprise when he opened his Instagram account in front of the officer. This was not enough proof he sent it. Nothing in the message conveyed facts about their relationship. The writing was not his style either.

---

6 The SJC noted that it may develop a digital search protocol that would minimize unnecessary intrusion when multiple people live within a residence.

If relevant, timing of communication must be proven. *Comm. v. Dembowski*, 94 Mass. App. Ct. 1114 (2018) (no proof about whether the defendant communicated before or after probation was imposed — so his message could not be used as the basis to revoke his probation).

SOCIAL MEDIA INVESTIGATIONS

Defendant's possession of firearm in a Snapchat video supported a search warrant. *Comm. v. Watkins*, 98 Mass. App. Ct. 419 (2020): Boston police officers monitoring the Snapchat account of the defendant, Josiah Watkins, watched a "selfie" style video posted on May 8 in which Watkins brandished a distinctive TEC-9 firearm with the magazine detached. A subsequent video showed Watkins in the company of Luis Santos. Santos was sitting on a bed loading a magazine into a TEC-9 and then aiming the weapon at the camera.

Santos had been released from DYS custody, but was subject to GPS monitoring. On request from Boston Police, DYS provided location information showing Santos was at his home all day on May 8. The Snapchat account for Santos showed posts for May 7 (Santos assembling a TEC-9 firearm with ammunition laid out on the bed), May 8 (Santos holding a loaded magazine), and May 14 (a picture of a TEC-9 captioned with "Shyt change on my block . . . I got put all my trust in semi autos").

A search warrant for Santos' home was executed on May 16. A TEC-9 firearm loaded with a magazine containing 23 rounds of ammunition was recovered. The information used to get the warrant was not stale. Though videos or pictures posted to Snapchat may be created prior to the day they are posted, Santos's May 14 post was a present tense statement about his need for semi-automatic weapons.

Based upon the eight-to-ten second Snapchat video depicting Watkins holding a TEC-9 in Santos' home, Watkins was also convicted of unlawful possession of a large capacity weapon.

Defendants may investigate alleged bias in police monitoring of social media. *Comm. v. Dilworth*, 485 Mass. 1001 (2020): Acting in an undercover capacity, Boston police officers became "friends" with Richard Dilworth on Snapchat. There, they viewed videos of Dilworth with a firearm. In January, officers arrested Dilworth and seized a loaded firearm from his waistband. After Dilworth's release on bail, officers saw him again on Snapchat with another gun. Another arrest followed for gun possession.

Dilworth alleged that "the department was using Snapchat as an investigatory tool almost exclusively against black males," which is known as selective prosecution. He sought records to support his claim. A superior court judge properly required Boston Police to turn over one year's worth of Snapchat surveillance reports resulting in criminal complaints.

THIRD-PARTY EVIDENCE

While police do not need a warrant to view evidence already observed by a private party, they do need a warrant to expand their search of the device.

- *Comm. v. Cormier*, 2011 WL 3450643 (Superior Court): Matthew Cormier brought his computer hard drive to a data recovery technician. Cormier signed a "Data Recovery

Agreement," which stated that all information on the drive would be kept private. John Trask, the technician, randomly opened files to ensure the processing was proceeding properly. Discovering several images of underage, nude girls, Trask called police.

Sergeant Thomas Neff met with Trask and viewed the child pornography. Some of the files referred to a different software brand, which indicated that they were backed up on another hard drive, probably in Cormier's residence. Sergeant Neff obtained a search warrant. When police executed it, they found a large safe containing a thumb drive filled with child pornography.

Sergeant Neff could properly examine materials initially discovered by a private party who was not acting as his agent. Neff wisely got a warrant when he wanted to go further. *U.S. v. Rivera-Morales*, 961 F.3d 1 (1st Cir. 2020).

- Compare *U.S. v. Lichtenberger*, 748 F.3d 478 (2015): While it was permissible for Holmes to conduct a private search and show police what she had viewed, the police could not exceed the scope of her initial search. Because she opened more files for Officer Huston, his warrant and resulting evidence had to be suppressed.

No standing to complain when police get suspect's email, texts, or other information by lawfully accessing another person's account. *U.S. v. Johnson*, 2019 WL 917175 (D. Mass): A Rhode Island detective began investigating a Craigslist user who posted to a site entitled "Perv on your daughter." The detective emailed Richard Woodhead, the Craigslist user who made the post, then served a warrant on Yahoo, Woodhead's email provider. In response to the warrant, Yahoo provided emails to Woodhead from various Craigslist users, including Johnson.

Johnson was eventually arrested for child pornography. He tried to suppress the original emails discovered from Woodhead's Yahoo account. However, Johnson did not have a reasonable expectation of privacy in the contents of Woodhead's account. If a letter, email, or text is sent to another, the sender's expectation of privacy ends on delivery.

VIDEO SURVEILLANCE

POLICE BODY WORN CAMERAS (BWC)

When done for a new investigation, police must get a search warrant to review a BWC recording made inside a home. *Comm. v. Yusuf*, 488 Mass. 379 (2021): The sister of the defendant, Abdirahaman Yusuf, called Boston Police about a domestic disturbance in her home, seeking the removal of the defendant's girlfriend. An officer equipped with a body worn camera (BWC) entered.

This officer walked past Yusuf's sister, who was yelling up the stairs at Yusuf and his girlfriend. Through an open bedroom door the bodycam captured video of a woman zipping on her coat. In the background hung floral print curtains. Yusuf told the officer that his girlfriend would leave shortly.

Once the couple was ready to go, the officer halted the two at the top of the stairs while officers downstairs cleared the way, moving the sister into the living room. The officer escorted the defendant and his girlfriend out and shut off his camera. He later downloaded a copy of the video on a DVD. He notified a detective in the youth violence strike force who had been investigating Yusuf for firearms offenses.

Two weeks later, Yusuf posted on social media a live video of himself holding a firearm in a bedroom. In the background were floral print curtains. The detective saw this post and viewed the DVD from the domestic, confirming the floral print curtains in Yusuf's bedroom.

The detective obtained a search warrant by noting the link between the curtains in the social media post and the bodycam video. A firearm, ammunition, and narcotics were seized. Yusuf and his brother were arrested.

- **Purpose of BWC recordings.** According to the SJC, there are three reasons to record police encounters with citizens:

    - Protect police officers from false allegations of misconduct;
    - Ensure police accountability; and
    - Preserve a record of a police-civilian interaction.

- **The BWC recording during the domestic response was not a search.** At the express invitation of Yusuf's sister, the officer with the bodycam was in the home to render assistance. With the camera mounted on his chest, the recording showed only what the officer could see in plain view. The camera provided no enhancements. Once inside, the officer only moved where he needed to go to resolve this call for service. That is why his BWC recording, in areas where he was lawfully present, was not a search. This is consistent with earlier cases approving police photographs to document a search scene or evidence following a legal entry.

- **However, a warrant was required to review bodycam video for an unrelated investigation.** A citizen might not expect that a video created during a lawful police visit would be accessed without restriction and reviewed for reasons unrelated to that visit.

The SJC listed proper purposes for reviewing bodycam recordings without a warrant:

- **An officer writing a report of an incident may review his BWC video in order to write accurately;**

- **A supervisor may access the video to review a citizen complaint or officer performance.**

Whatever the initial justification, if review of video from inside a home leads to suspicion of an additional, unrelated crime, the review should stop and a warrant should be sought. Police department policy should restrict access to video and protect the privacy of the recorded view inside a home.[7, 8]

---

7 The SJC noted, "The home is not a place to which the public has access." This statement might justify withholding bodycam video of the inside of a home from release following a public record request.
8 The police reform law created a BWC task force to make recommendations for law enforcement agencies. See Chapter 253 of the Acts of 2020, Section 104. Other states like California, New Jersey, and Washington have enacted statutes based on best practices to regulate BWCs. The goal is to get the benefits of BWCs while avoiding the erosion of privacy in a manner inconsistent with society's reasonable expectations.

NON-TARGETED SURVEILLANCE

Non-targeted surveillance cameras view or record activity in public and private spaces constantly. They are installed by private or public property owners. The SJC notes that "[l]aw enforcement officers appropriately have relied on . . . non-targeted video surveillance, to identify and apprehend suspects." *Comm. v. Mora*, 485 Mass. 360 (2020). In fact, obtaining surveillance footage from cameras installed by property owners has emerged as one of the most helpful and common types of evidence relied on in Massachusetts courts.

Witnesses may testify to observations made while viewing a video monitor. *Comm. v. Capeles*, 2011 WL 2682631 (Appeals Court): The police saw Juan Capeles — on a hidden video feed — attack and rob their informant in a hotel room. The video feed was not recording. Their oral testimony could be based on what they saw at the time.

Witnesses, including police officers, may testify based on observations of video surveillance. The video has to be available or, if lost, the officer has to be able to describe how he or she knew it pertained to the defendant's criminal case. *Comm. v. Connolly*, 91 Mass. App. Ct. 580 (2017) (surveillance video of defendant's assault of an elderly woman was accidentally erased by the building manager after the officer saw it, but before the defense attorney could).

TARGETED SURVEILLANCE

Article 14 requires a warrant for a pole camera that closely monitors a dwelling. *Comm. v. Mora*, 485 Mass. 360 (2020): A seven-month drug investigation used five cameras on utility poles. One monitored the front of Nelson Mora's home for five months; another monitored the front of Ricky Suarez's home for two months. Controlled buys and wiretaps were also employed. Investigators then used this information to obtain warrants and seize a lot of heroin, cocaine, and $415,000.

These camera systems resulted in surveillance so "extensive that . . . it exposed otherwise unknowable details of a person's life" — including every visit from every person to the residence and every other activity out front. There is a marked contrast between the capability of pole cameras and human surveillance. This is why a warrant was required for the cameras. Less pervasive coverage would not have necessitated a warrant.

Whether police need a warrant for targeted video surveillance depends on:

- Its **duration;**

- Whether it is **continuous or intermittent;**

- Whether it may be **monitored live** by a user;

- Whether it can **gather information in quantities** that would be difficult for a human to compile and analyze; and

- The level of **visual detail** captured. *Comm. v. Mora, supra.*

FACIAL RECOGNITION

Under 6, § 220, officers shall only request a facial recognition search in writing, and have it performed by the Registry of Motor Vehicles (RMV), State Police, or FBI. Officers need:

- **A court order supported by reasonable suspicion that a facial recognition search is relevant and material** (i.e., important):

  - To an ongoing criminal investigation; or

  - To mitigate a substantial risk of harm to any individual or group of people; or

- **If <u>no</u> court order:**

  - To identify a deceased person; or

  - To prevent a substantial risk of harm to any individual or group, provided the written request to the agency performing the search presents reasonable suspicion of an emergency.

- **Exemptions.** Under § 220(e), these requirements do <u>not</u> apply to:

  - Law enforcement electronic devices that use facial recognition for the sole purpose of user authentication;

  - Automated video or image redaction software that does not have facial or biometric recognition capabilities; or

  - Evidence from a biometric surveillance system that was not intentionally solicited by or obtained with the assistance of a public agency or official.

- **State Police exemption.** The State Police do not have to obtain a court order or provide a written request when "performing investigatory functions related to the issuance of identification documents by the [RMV]." At present, State Police assigned to the RMV are able to assist law enforcement officers with proper requests for facial recognition.[9]

Law enforcement agencies must document each facial recognition search and provide information quarterly to the Executive Office of Public Safety & Security (EOPSS) — including the date and time of the request, number of matches returned, databases searched, names and positions of the requesting individuals, reasons for the request, searching agencies, and data detailing individual characteristics in the request. This information is not a public record.

---

9 For more details, see *LED's Motor Vehicle Manual, Chapter 4.*

LOCATION MONITORING
AUTOMATED LICENSE PLATE READER (ALPR)

Limited use of Automated License Plate Readers is <u>not</u> a search requiring a warrant. *Comm. v. McCarthy*, 484 Mass. 493 (2020): The Barnstable Police Department developed evidence about a suspect dealing heroin from his residence. During surveillance of the suspect's home, Jason McCarthy's black Hyundai was seen briefly. Police suspected McCarthy of supplying heroin to their suspect.

- **The State Police operate Automated License Plate Readers (ALPRs) on the Bourne and Sagamore Bridges leading to Cape Cod.** These cameras photograph every vehicle registration plate that crosses the bridges in either direction, and record the date, time, and direction of travel for each vehicle. The records are preserved for one year and available for law enforcement use. The ALPR system permits investigators to add registration numbers to a "hot list" so that they will get a live notification when the plate crosses the bridge.

  Barnstable officers added McCarthy's plate to the hot list on February 1. They received a notice that McCarthy's vehicle crossed onto Cape Cod on February 8. Officers followed McCarthy, who met the original suspect on a quiet residential street for 30 seconds before both men drove away.

  Police obtained a record from the ALPR system showing McCarthy made 48 trips over the bridges between December 1 and February 12. This was consistent with the police suspicion that McCarthy was supplying their original suspect.

  On February 22, the ALPR system notified officers that McCarthy's vehicle crossed onto the Cape. Again, officers followed both men to the same residential street. Believing that a drug transaction occurred, police stopped them. The original suspect had heroin and made incriminating statements after waiving *Miranda*. McCarthy waived *Miranda* and incriminated himself too.

- **The use of ALPR information by police was not a search requiring a warrant.** A person's specific location in public is not private. That is why police may follow a person anywhere in public. However, modern surveillance far exceeds what could have been accomplished by government agents in the 1700s. The possibility of watching and tracking a person was limited in that era to the ability of an investigator to observe and follow a suspect day and night. The inability of the government back then to provide this level of scrutiny for days or weeks created a degree of privacy that should be somewhat reflected in our contemporary rules.

  The SJC remarked in *McCarthy*: "With enough cameras in enough locations, the historic location data from an ALPR system in Massachusetts would invade a reasonable expectation of privacy and would constitute a search for constitutional purposes."

  Here, four ALPRs at only two fixed points was <u>not</u> a search under the Fourth Amendment or Article 14. The ALPRs showed only that the defendant traveled on or off Cape Cod. The cameras did not allow the police to monitor all his public movements.

PUBLIC TRANSPORTATION RECORDS

No warrant required for limited search of CharlieCard data. *Comm. v. Henley*, 488 Mass. 95 (2021): When Josiah Zachery was arrested for murdering a rival gang member and shooting at an officer, a CharlieCard was seized from him. A Boston detective contacted the Transit Police and provided the number on Zachery's CharlieCard and requested a travel history with corresponding surveillance video.

The CharlieCard was capable of recording 14 months of information. Had the MBTA provided such an extensive record of Zachery's travel, this would have been a constitutional search. Instead, the MBTA provided two days of records. This was not a search because there is no reasonable expectation of privacy in such limited records. The card provides far less data than other forms of tracking, such as a cell phone. Moreover, the surveillance cameras are plainly visible at each location where the CharlieCard is used.[10]

The surveillance recordings showed that Zachery traveled from his Hyde Park neighborhood directly to the Jamaica Plain location of the shooting while wearing clothing he later stripped off. This evidence was properly obtained without a warrant.

CELL PHONE LOCATION

SEARCH WARRANT REQUIRED FOR CSLI

To acquire historical cell site location information (CSLI), officers must obtain a search warrant. According to *Carpenter v. U.S.*, 138 S.Ct. 2206 (2018), nearly everyone carries a cell phone, which means they can be tracked at all times. While callers understand that their service provider records the numbers they dial, most are not aware that their *location* is also recorded.

Obtaining historical CSLI to prove a suspect's location through his phone is an incredibly useful investigative technique that demands a warrant. *Comm. v. Balboni*, 89 Mass. App. Ct. 651 (2016): Lexington police discovered a burning truck late at night with a gas can and baseball cap nearby. Police suspected that Samuel Doxsey and Scott Balboni deliberately set the fire. Doxsey had a motive. The truck belonged to a person who he had just been told sexually assaulted his sister. Doxsey used his credit card to purchase gas for a cannister one hour before the fire in Lexington, even though he lived in New Hampshire. The warrant affidavit established probable cause that CSLI would reveal whether the defendant traveled from New Hampshire to Lexington at the time of the fire. In fact, CSLI did implicate Doxsey and Balboni.

A police request to a company for CSLI may not take the place of a search warrant. *Comm. v. Gumkowski*, 487 Mass. 314 (2021) (even though 18 U.S.C. § 2703 allows a company to voluntarily provide CSLI, a police request for CSLI will always require a search warrant or exigent circumstances).

---

10 The MBTA also posts on its website its policy of cooperating with police requests for information about card use.

The scope of the data request depends on the crime being investigated, but it must be for no more than two weeks. *Comm. v. Augustine*, 467 Mass. 230 (2014).[11]

Warrant also required to use cell phone tracker. A StingRay cell site simulator is a device that tricks cell phones into sending their location information. To use the simulator, police obtain the subscriber's mobile identification number from their phone company and program it into the device. Once the device catches the phone signal, it begins reporting general location information and signal strength, which can be used to determine the phone's exact location. Because a cell site simulator discovers a person's location at will, a search warrant is required before the device is turned on. *Jones v. U.S.*, 168 A.3d 703 (D.C. Court of Appeals 2017).

PINGING CELL PHONE IN EMERGENCY

Officers use the term "pinging" to describe the ability of a cell phone service provider to determine the location of a phone in real time. This is authorized without a warrant if police confront an emergency.

- **Emergency aid.** This rule covers people who are at risk for serious injury or death — e.g., a missing college student, a suicidal neighbor. Consider *Comm. v. Lugo*, 482 Mass. 94 (2019): The defendant and three friends — Deshowitz, Thames, and Moulton — developed a plan to rob the victim of marijuana. Deshowitz contacted him under the guise that she was buying weed. The group met the victim, drove him to his house, and shot him there.

  Police learned that the victim was last seen alive with Deshowitz. Through RMV records, police learned that Deshowitz lived in Stoughton. A Stoughton Police detective, Michael Tuitt, was familiar with both Deshowitz and her sister. He went to their residence where he learned that Deshowitz was not home, but her sister offered to call her cell phone. Tuitt recognized Deshowitz's voice but was concerned that she was speaking in a whisper and pausing a lot. Tuitt said to Deshowitz, if she could not speak because people were with her, to say "Seven." Deshowitz responded "Seven." He then asked her, if she could not get away, to say "Four." She responded "Four." Finally, the detective told her that if she was not really in Abington (where she claimed to be with friends), to say "Seven." She responded "Seven." After this conversation, Tuitt believed Deshowitz was in danger and persuaded her phone company to ping her phone's current location. Police went to the location and ended up arresting the murderers.

- **Exigent circumstances**. This rule covers locating a dangerous criminal. *Comm. v. Almonor,* 482 Mass. 35 (2019): The police knew Jerome Almonor murdered the victim with a sawed-off shotgun. They learned his cell number four hours after the shooting. Almonor's service provider pinged his phone at a Brockton address. Police entered the house and arrested him, then obtained a search warrant so investigators could seize a sawed-off shotgun and bulletproof vest.

---

11 Also see *Comm. v. Augustine II*, 472 Mass. 448 (2015) (police had probable cause to obtain a search warrant for the defendant's CSLI records for the two-week period from August 24th to September 6th; the murder victim was last seen on August 24th and the defendant's location could show whether he was with her when she disappeared; her body was not discovered until September 19th, so the entire two-week period of CSLI was necessary because he could have deposited her body at any point during that period).

Almonor was aware the police would be looking for him, since the shooting occurred in the daytime in front of witnesses. He had already fled the scene. Police knew that Almonor had brutally murdered a person for no apparent reason. This was not a case in which the threat posed by their suspect was limited to the specific victim.

Once the emergency is over, police should still obtain a warrant to take formal custody of records related to the ping. This is the best practice if the ping led to an arrest and/or seizure of evidence.[12] The phone service may require this step in order to release a copy of its records to law enforcement for later use in court. On the other hand, if the ping did not lead to a criminal case (e.g., a missing person was found and returned home safely), then officers may want to simply send a brief report to the service provider for its records.

Court presentation of historical CSLI or pinging results.

- **Defendant may not typically challenge CSLI or the ping of another's phone.** *Comm. v. Lugo*, 482 Mass. 94 (2019) (defendant did not have standing to contest the collection of CSLI associated with someone else's cell phone; there was no reasonable expectation of privacy in another person's cell phone when it was tracked for a brief period of time — two hours — and the defendant was not the intended target of the decision to track).

- **CSLI admissible as a business record with expert testimony.** *Comm. v. Bin*, 480 Mass. 665 (2018) (CSLI admissible as business records in this murder trial because a trooper from the electronic evidence unit explained how they were collected and what they meant).

USING CELL PHONE APP TO TRACK

Cell phone applications (apps) can be used to locate a stolen cell phone. No need for search warrant or expert testimony in court. *Comm. v. Wilson*, 2016 WL 1728900 (Appeals Court): After a robbery, Sergeant Michael Harrington used the "Find My iPhone" app to learn that the victim's stolen phone was inside a home in Boston. A Nissan Altima matching the description of the one used in the robbery was parked nearby.

Police entered the residence. The first floor was unoccupied, and the occupant on the second floor claimed to have no knowledge about the robbery. When they knocked at the third-floor apartment, officers heard noise and things being moved around. A woman eventually came to the door, denied anyone else was inside, and refused consent to enter.

Twenty-five minutes later, police observed two men leave the building and enter the Altima. A stop and search of the Altima revealed the victim's bank card. Police secured the third-floor apartment pending a search warrant. The woman tried to leave with her baby. When police searched her bag, they found the iPhone in a container of baby wipes.

Sergeant Harrington testified in court that he had used the iPhone app successfully on previous occasions. This adequately explained to the jury how the app works. Expert testimony was unnecessary.

---

12 This excellent recommendation comes from Jeremy Bucci of the Northwestern District Attorney's Office.

GPS TRACKING DEVICE

A GPS tracking system monitors and records the location of a vehicle without the owner's knowledge. *Comm. v. Thissell*, 74 Mass. App. Ct. 773 (2009).

POLICE-INITIATED INVESTIGATION

Police must obtain a warrant in order to install and monitor a GPS tracking device. *Comm. v. Connolly*, 454 Mass. 808 (2009) states the reasons why a warrant is necessary: (1) using a citizen's vehicle to conduct GPS monitoring interferes with his property; and (2) the absence of a warrant requirement would allow law enforcement to track any individual indefinitely and without suspicion by simply attaching a transmitter to his vehicle. Also see *U.S. v. Jones*, 565 U.S. 946 (2012).

- **The affidavit for a GPS warrant must establish probable cause** that an offense has been, is being, or is about to be committed, and that GPS monitoring of the vehicle will produce evidence *or* aid in the apprehension of an offender.

- **The GPS warrant may authorize monitoring for no more than 15 days from the date the warrant issues.** The warrant return must indicate the date the device was installed.

- **Police may renew GPS warrants in additional 15-day increments.** *Comm. v. Rousseau*, 465 Mass. 372 (2013) (excellent affidavit provided probable cause for GPS monitoring of a suspect involved in multiple incidents of arson and impersonating a police officer).

Vehicle passenger (in addition to the owner and operator) has standing to challenge GPS monitoring because he has a reasonable expectation that his movements will not be subjected to extended government surveillance. For this reason, police should obtain a warrant even when they install a GPS unit in their informant's car during their investigation. *Comm. v. Rousseau, supra.*

Massachusetts will probably allow police to track a vehicle's pre-equipped GPS system without a warrant. *State v. Clifton*, 580 S.E.2d 40 (N.C. App. Ct. 2003) (police used GPS without a warrant to locate the victim's truck, which the defendant had purchased with a counterfeit check).

POLICE ACCESS TO PROBATION GPS RECORDS

Police may obtain post-conviction, historical GPS data from probation without a warrant. GPS data is archived in the probation department's Electronic Monitoring Center, affectionately known as ELMO. In *Comm. v. Johnson*, 481 Mass. 710 (2019), Jamie Johnson was on probation and agreed to wear a GPS monitoring device on his ankle. When he was arrested near the scene of a break-in a year after his probation ended, detectives checked with probation for GPS records of his location during several, unsolved break-ins during the prior year. The locations and times matched perfectly, and Johnson was convicted. The SJC held that Johnson had no reasonable expectation of privacy in GPS data because he had agreed to wear the device at all times for the *purpose* of tracking his location!

It was irrelevant that police accessed this data *after* Johnson's probation ended. Finally, the police investigation was targeted toward several unsolved crimes and not designed to expose all aspects of Johnson's personal life in the hopes of finding something damning.[13]

Police probably can obtain <u>pre-trial</u>, GPS data without a warrant. *Comm. v. Norman*, 484 Mass. 330 (2020): Eric Norman was charged with drug dealing and, as a condition of pre-trial release, placed on GPS monitoring. A later search of GPS data, requested by the Medford Police, linked Norman to a home invasion. The SJC ruled the judge did not have a legitimate reason to impose GPS monitoring initially, so the information about Norman's location at the time of the home invasion had to be suppressed. The SJC never addressed whether, had GPS monitoring been proper, the police would have had access to this data without a warrant. Until the court specifically decides, officers should continue to seek data from probation without a warrant based on the reasoning in *Johnson, supra.*

GPS movement data requires expert testimony to prove its accuracy. *Comm. v. Davis*, 487 Mass. 488 (2021): After shots were fired at a motor vehicle, an eyewitness gave a description of the race, hair, and clothing of a man who fled the area. A poor quality surveillance video showed the shooting itself. Police investigators checked whether any defendants wearing GPS bracelets were in the area. Matthew Davis was assigned a bracelet, and his location matched the streets and times associated with the shooting. Measurements of the speed at which his GPS bracelet moved also matched the movement of the shooter seen on surveillance video.

The technology used to track the bracelet's *location* was tested by the company that monitored the bracelet, and was admissible. The different technology used for tracking the *speed* of the bracelet had never been tested. It was inadmissible.

PRIVATE-INITIATED INVESTIGATION

At present, it is not a crime in Massachusetts for a private person to electronically monitor the movements of another private person. Other states have made it a crime regardless of the offender's motivation. *Comm. v. Brennan*, 481 Mass. 146 (2018) (provides list of state statutes).

At the same time, electronically monitoring a citizen secretly may constitute criminal harassment. *Comm. v. Brennan, supra.* (SJC determined there was sufficient evidence to charge Francis Brennan with 265, § 43A, criminal harassment, based on his installation and monitoring of GPS devices; he placed them on a married couple's cars because of his strange suspicions that the husband was being unfaithful; Brennan had never met either spouse; needless to say, when police solved the mystery, the couple experienced substantial emotional distress from these bizarre revelations).

---

13 The SJC also noted that 276, § 90 provides "an apparently unlimited, authorization for law enforcement to review probation records, including the historical GPS location data recorded from a probationer's GPS device."

MOSAIC ANALYSIS

As new technology increases the information police can assemble, the SJC limits how much publicly available information police can obtain without a warrant. The court uses the analogy of a mosaic: Though meaningless when looked at individually, many pieces of tile when placed together form a picture. In the same way, when the collection of many tiny bits of information allows police to form a complete picture of some part of a person's life (travel, associations, finances, home life, etc.), it triggers a constitutional concern for privacy. A warrant will be required before police may gather that much data about a person.

In McCarthy (ALPRs), Mora (pole cameras), and Henley (MBTA records), the issue is whether the data generated became "pieces of tile in a mosaic." In *McCarthy,* using registration plate hits from a set of four publicly-operated ALPR cameras on bridges was not a search because even several month's worth of this data provided only a limited picture. Would that have been different if Barnstable added dozens of ALPRs to its streets, and if the surveillance went on for a year? What if the suspect was on public assistance and police sought his record of EBT transactions in addition to the ALPR data? Would the court's social justice concerns about privacy and wealth affect its legal analysis?

In *Mora*, video recordings of Suspect B's occasional appearance at the home of Suspect A would need no warrant, but police should have gotten a warrant to record months of highly detailed 24-hour surveillance of the front of Suspect A's home. The extensive collection of video gave a full picture of Suspect A's home life.

In *Henley*, it was legal for police to obtain without a warrant video of the suspect's use of a CharlieCard to get onto the subway on two occasions, but 14 months' worth of the same government records would have required a warrant.

As you can see, the problem with "mosaic analysis" is that determining at what point police need a warrant for public information relies on case-by-case analysis. To avoid this legal unpredictability, we recommend the following strategic approach.

When accessing public information without a warrant, take the smallest bites possible to develop probable cause, then get a search warrant for more. This approach is the safest course of action. For example, Barnstable investigators first asked the State Police to provide a live notice if McCarthy's car crossed onto the Cape. Police used this information to track McCarthy to a 30-second meeting with a known drug dealer. Having confirmed suspicious activity, police could have sought, by warrant, a historic record of McCarthy's crossings to the Cape for three months. Setting a date range for the requested information is important.

Consider another example: If investigators are looking to establish whether a known suspect visits the home of a potential suspect, a pole camera might be set up to provide a live alert to an investigator only when a particular registration plate is detected. Investigators would not look at any other video. If those snippets provided probable cause that the potential suspect is involved, a search warrant could be obtained to enable investigators to review prior video and continue broader surveillance with their pole camera.

SECRET RECORDING

PURPOSE OF WIRETAP STATUTE

Technology facilitates secret recording, which places privacy at risk. When the wiretap statute, 272, § 99, was enacted, lawmakers were concerned about the availability of recording devices. The threat to privacy came from both law enforcement *and* citizens, who were increasingly recording others. At the same time, legislators recognized the critical importance of electronic surveillance as a law enforcement tool, especially to combat organized crime. For this reason, lawmakers outlawed most secret recording by private citizens and insisted on judicial supervision for law enforcement operations. 272, § 99(A) (Preamble).

There are civil and criminal prohibitions against unauthorized recording. *Birbiglia v. Saint Vincent Hospital*, 427 Mass. 80 (1998) (doctor successfully sued hospital for using secret recordings of him in a meeting as the basis for revoking his staff privileges). 272, § 99(C) punishes any person who willfully and secretly records, or attempts to record, oral communication.[14]

The law only covers oral communication. In *Comm. v. Wright*, 61 Mass. App. Ct. 790 (2004), the defendant, an assistant manager at a print shop, installed a video camera in the store bathroom. A female employee, who the defendant was sexually interested in, discovered it. She called 911. After he admitted owning the camera, police arrested the manager because the recording contained snippets of voices and a few words. The words, not the video, made the recording a felony under 272, § 99.[15]

TYPES OF SECRET INTERCEPTIONS

Nonconsensual interceptions occur when none of the parties to the conversation know they are being recorded.

- Private parties are <u>never</u> authorized to do this.

- Law enforcement officers may <u>only</u> do this with a wiretap warrant.

On the other hand, <u>one-party consensual</u> interceptions occur when at least one party knows the conversation is recorded and consents to that fact. Most secret recordings fall into this category.

Private citizens may <u>not</u> secretly record other people. *Comm. v. Hanedanian*, 51 Mass. App. Ct. 64 (2001) (disgruntled client was properly convicted of secretly recording his attorneys; this was illegal regardless of the attorney–client privilege).

While a ban on private secret recording makes sense, the Constitution does not permit a ban on secret information-gathering directed at police officers. *ACLU of Illinois v. Alvarez*, 679 F.3d

---

14 Offenders can get up to 5 years in State Prison. The most detailed breakdown of this criminal statute appears in *LED's Criminal Law, Chapter 15.*
15 Because the *Wright* decision exposed the lack of privacy protection against secret videographers, the legislature passed 272, § 105, which does prohibit secret, naked pictures of others. For a breakdown of this law, see *LED's Criminal Law, Chapter 10.*

583 (7th Cir. 2012). In Massachusetts, *Project Veritas v. Rollins*, 2020 WL 7350243 (1ˢᵗ Cir.) decided that officers can no longer bring criminal charges under 272, § 99 against citizens, including members of the media, who secretly record them in the public performance of their duties.[16]

Of course, citizens may also openly record officers in public, as long as they do not interfere with police operations. In *Glik v. Cunniffe*, 655 F.3d 78 (2011), Simon Glik used his cell phone camera to film officers arresting a young man in a park. After handcuffing the offender, an officer said: "You've taken enough pictures." Another officer arrested Glik for secret recording and disturbing the peace. Glik successfully sued them for false arrest.

- **The First Amendment gives citizens the right to document police activities.** Filming officers holds them accountable. It also frequently helps officers. For example, a citizen's recording might exonerate an officer charged with wrongdoing.

- **There are limits.** *Glik* held that "the right to film . . . may be subject to reasonable time, place, and manner restrictions."

  - *Interference.* Officers may prevent recording activity that interferes with the police operation. *Gericke v. Begin*, 753. F.3d 1 (2014) (New Hampshire officers, during a nighttime traffic stop, had the right to order Carla Gericke to get back in her car and move away from the scene; but, when she immediately complied, officers could not order her to turn off her camera and surrender it to them).

    Do *not* order citizens to turn off their cameras. Instead, give them verbal direction: e.g., "Sir, you're too close. Go over to the sidewalk." Since recording is legal, focus on the improper behavior — not the act of recording itself.

  - *Need for privacy. Project Veritas v. Rollins, supra.* suggests that officers should move to a private location to preserve the conversational privacy of a victim or witness.

  - *Evidence.* In deciding whether to seize a phone with video footage of a crime be careful. If the arrest was problematic, it may be alleged that the device was seized as a cover-up. In short, video evidence often invites more scrutiny than it may be worth. That is why supervisory input is important. The decision to seize a citizen's device as evidence should be made in good faith.[17]

    Officers should explain to the citizen that he may consent to having *only* the video of the incident copied and preserved, and that the phone will be returned as soon as possible. If the citizen agrees, provide a receipt.[18] If the citizen refuses, secure the device and obtain a search warrant for its contents.

Investigative detention is a proper response to filming police in suspicious circumstances. *Turner v. Driver*, 848 F.3d 678 (2017): In Texas, Phillip Turner was videotaping the Fort Worth Police Station from a public sidewalk across the street. Two officers approached him and asked if he had identification, but Turner continued videotaping.

---

16 The federal court's decision effectively overrules two prior Massachusetts appellate decisions. *Comm. v. Hyde*, 434 Mass. 594 (2001). *Comm. v. Manzelli*, 68 Mass. App. Ct. 691 (2007).
17 *Glik* did not discuss how to seize a phone as evidence.
18 Simply taking the phone and dropping it into the evidence room until the trial is over, absent consent or a warrant, will be viewed by a court as unconstitutional and punitive.

The court held that the officers' initial questioning and detention of Turner — before he was handcuffed and placed in the patrol car — was reasonable. Turner might have been casing the station for an attack or stalking an officer. Turner's videotaping of the station was suspicious enough to warrant a brief detention. However, handcuffing and placing Turner in the patrol car constituted an unlawful arrest. At that point, the officer's actions were disproportionate to the potential threat.

OTHER EXCEPTIONS TO BAN ON SECRET RECORDING

Accidents. An illegal interception must be on purpose. *Comm. v. Ennis*, 439 Mass. 64 (2003): Steven Knight, an inmate at the Plymouth House of Correction, placed a telephone call to Jaear Williams. Williams added Ennis, bypassing the facility's telephone system. At the beginning of the call, Knight and Williams had heard a pre-recorded announcement that the call was being recorded. Ennis missed it and bragged on tape about committing a murder.

Telephone equipment. The wiretap statute prohibits the use of an "intercepting device." The definition of a device does not include "any telephone equipment [installed] . . . in the ordinary course of business." 272, § 99(B)(3). *Dillon v. MBTA*, 49 Mass. App. Ct. 309 (2000).

Phone company investigation. Phone company investigators may intercept calls to prevent violations of 269, § 14 (annoying phone calls). They do not need judicial authorization and may turn over their results to police. *District Attorney v. Coffey*, 386 Mass. 218 (1982).

Office intercom. Also exempt from coverage is "an office intercommunication system used in the ordinary course of business." 272, § 99(D). In *Comm. v. Pierce*, 66 Mass. App. Ct. 283 (2006), through the audio-visual system that monitored the cells, Officer Fisher overheard Joseph Pierce admit that he owned the gun that had been found in the car. Maintaining safety is a legitimate business practice of a police station, so the intercom system is outside the coverage of the wiretap law. *Comm. v. Look*, 379 Mass. 893 (1980) (murder suspect made incriminating statements to an investigator that were heard over the intercom by two desk officers; the officers had turned it on for safety reasons; the interrogating officer was old and the suspect had been violent earlier).

Booking video. An audiovisual recording of booking does not violate the wiretap statute, even when a prisoner has no idea he is being recorded. Booking is an administrative procedure, not the kind of secret investigation the wiretap law was designed to regulate. *Comm. v. Gordon*, 422 Mass. 816 (1996).

Eavesdropping.

- **On a phone extension with no recording.** No violation occurs when a person listens in on a standard extension phone and does not record the conversation. *Comm. v. Vieux*, 41 Mass. 526 (1996) (the victim's sister secretly picked up the extension phone; after the victim hung up and the defendant thought no one was on the line, the sister heard him admit to rape).

  This is even true when police eavesdrop as an investigative tactic! *Comm. v. Eason*, 427 Mass. 595 (1998) (state troopers persuaded a witness to make two calls to the defendant;

the troopers properly listened in on an extension as the defendant admitted to committing a home invasion; their testimony about the overheard conversation was admissible).[19]

- **In person with silent video.** *Comm. v. Camilli*, 2012 WL 1284387 (Appeals Court): James MacDonald, a real estate developer, made an audiovisual recording of a corrupt cash payment to Paul Camilli, the supervisor of public works for the Town of Maynard. MacDonald gave the video to Sergeant Brian Connors, who told him not to record again.

  MacDonald told Sergeant Connors that he was scheduled to make another payment. Connors provided MacDonald with $500 in marked bills and listened through the bathroom wall. He made a silent video of the exchange.

  The first recording was audiovisual, so it *did* violate the wiretap statute. However, it was admissible in evidence because MacDonald acted on his own without police direction. The second video and Connors' eavesdropping were proper. This video did not capture any sound, and Camilli did not have a legitimate expectation of privacy in MacDonald's office. Camilli ran the risk that their conversation would be overheard or observed by someone with MacDonald's permission.

NONCONSENSUAL INTERCEPTION BY LAW ENFORCEMENT

For the nonconsensual interception of conversations, investigators must comply with the strict requirements of 272, § 99 and obtain a wiretap warrant. Only specially designated prosecutors may apply after receiving written authorization from a District Attorney or the Attorney General. *Comm. v. Vitello*, 367 Mass. 224 (1975).

Warrant application must be presented to a superior court judge in the county where the interception will take place or the applicant is located. *Comm. v. Assad*, 393 Mass. 418 (1984).

The investigation must involve a "designated offense." The various offenses in 272, § 99(B)(7) include violence, gaming, prostitution, judicial integrity, narcotics, extortion, and bribery.

The affidavit must present a reasonable suspicion that the underlying offense involved organized crime. Organized crime is a "continuing conspiracy among . . . disciplined groups . . . to engage in supplying illegal goods and services." 272, § 99(A). At the same time, organized crime encompasses more than full-time professional criminals.

- **Sufficient.** *Comm. v. D'Amour*, 428 Mass. 725 (1999) (murder involving the deceased's wife and her boyfriend, and perhaps others organizing an alibi in Florida, was organized crime). *Comm. v. Terzian*, 61 Mass. App. Ct. 739 (2004) (scheme organized by defendant, a practicing attorney, to persuade another person to commit perjury and intimidate a witness). *Comm. v. Lykus*, 406 Mass. 135 (1989) (ransom note referred to the kidnappers as "we").

- **Insufficient.** *Comm. v. Jarabek*, 384 Mass. 293 (1981) (no reasonable suspicion of organized crime; only one school committee member and an assistant superintendent were trying to get a $2,000 "kickback" from a fence installer). *Comm. v. Long*, 454 Mass. 542 (2009).

---

19 The *Eason* case did not involve a *Blood* warrant (see later discussion) because police did not use equipment to record a conversation in a private home. They simply listened in on the extension.

Since a wiretap is an extraordinary investigative method, the burden is on law enforcement to demonstrate why less intrusive methods are inadequate. *Comm. v. Hernandez,* 2018 WL 560747 (Appeals Court) (affidavit submitted in support of wiretap application showed investigators attempted a number of other techniques — such as physical surveillance, GPS tracking, trash analysis, financial records analysis, cell phone toll record analysis, and confidential informant interviews — that failed to produce evidence against the top level of individuals controlling the sex trafficking operation; to entirely dismantle the operation, investigators needed wiretap evidence against its principals). *Comm. v. Westerman,* 414 Mass. 688 (1993).

Police are not required to recruit an informant to avoid the need for a wiretap. *Comm. v. Quezada,* 2018 WL 894087 (Appeals Court) (state police refused to try to enlist federal informant).

The affidavit must identify the particular individuals and phone lines to be monitored. Police may record unidentified parties having conversations with their named targets about the crimes under investigation. *Comm. v. Ricci,* 57 Mass. App. Ct. 155 (2003).

A wiretap warrant may permit the interception of cell phone calls and text messages. *Comm. v. Moody,* 466 Mass. 196 (2013) (drug trafficking conspiracy).

The prosecutor may apply for broader coverage if they learn about new kinds of criminal activity. *Comm. v. Westerman, supra.* (it started as a "loan sharking" investigation, but intercepted conversations discussed drug dealing as well; the prosecutor petitioned the court to expand the investigation).

Secret entry. A warrant may authorize secret entry to install the listening device.

Listening time. A wiretap warrant must be executed within 30 days of equipment installation. The actual listening time is limited to 15 consecutive days within the 30-day period. The court may grant 15-day extensions upon application. *Comm. v. Wallace,* 22 Mass. App. Ct. 247 (1986).

Tape return within 7 days. 272, § 99(M) states that surveillance tapes must be returned within seven days after the warrant ends. The return goes to the judge who issued the warrant. *Comm. v. Ricci,* 57 Mass. App. Ct. 155 (2003). *Comm. v. Rankins,* 429 Mass. 470 (1999) (prosecutor may present recordings to grand jury even before judicial review).

Warrant service. An attested copy of the warrant must be served on the targets and phone line subscribers. How quickly depends on what is written in the original affidavit. If the affiant alleges "exigent circumstances," the warrant must be served within 30 days after it expires. If the affiant alleges "important special facts concerning the need for secrecy," service must occur within three years of expiration. 272, § 99(L)(1).

Records for trial. 272, § 99(O)(1) mandates that the defendant receive records of the interceptions at least 30 days before trial. If police fail to turn over records, any recording is suppressed. This rule is strictly enforced. *Comm. v. Picardi,* 401 Mass. 1008 (1988).

PEN REGISTERS & CROSS FRAME TRAPS

Devices record numbers, not conversations. While a wiretap enables one to listen and record phone conversations, a pen register notes the numbers dialed from a particular phone. A cross frame trap does the opposite, noting incoming calls. *Comm. v. Valdez*, 402 Mass. 65 (1988).

Wiretap warrant required. Even though pen registers and cross traps are not as intrusive as a wiretap, Massachusetts still requires a wiretap warrant under 272, § 99.[20] However, police never need separate authorization if they already have a wiretap in place. *Comm. v. Westerman, supra.* A judge may order that the phone company help install these devices. *District Attorney v. New England Telephone,* 379 Mass. 586 (1980).

ONE-PARTY INTERCEPTION BY LAW ENFORCEMENT

272, § 99 authorizes the <u>warrantless</u> interception of oral communication:

- **Under the supervision of a law enforcement officer;**

- **Investigating a designated offense;**

- **When at least one participant in the conversation consents to its interception;** and

- **The officer has a reasonable suspicion that the offense involved organized crime.**

  - *Sufficient proof. Comm. v. Remedor,* 52 Mass. App. Ct. 694 (2001) ("any retail street sales of cocaine, even if small in quantity, [most likely] have a nexus to organized crime"). *Comm. v. Hearns,* 467 Mass. 707 (2014) (defendant involved in a gang in which senior members directed junior members to sell drugs and weapons, and carry out violent "missions"). *Comm. v. Mitchell,* 468 Mass. 417 (2014).

  - *Insufficient proof. Comm. v. Tavares,* 459 Mass. 289 (2011): A police informant secretly recorded the defendant admitting to a drive-by shooting. In a controversial decision, the SJC suppressed these tapes because there had been no organized plan to kill the victim, and no evidence that Tavares or any other party was involved in an enterprise like drug trafficking. The fact that Tavares met with people *afterwards* to conceal the killing was insufficient to prove an organized crime connection.

No other requirements. All the other warrant requirements — e.g., establishing investigative necessity, returning the tapes within seven days — do not come into play during warrantless, one-party consent recording. *Comm. v. Thorpe,* 384 Mass. 271 (1981). *Comm. v. Davis,* 83 Mass. App. Ct. 484 (2013).

---

20 The federal wiretap law only applies to the interception of voices. Therefore, pen registers and cross traps may be installed without a warrant. The devices may be authorized by court order for a maximum of 60 days, with the possibility of a 60-day extension. 18 U.S.C., § 3122.

INSIDE DWELLING: *BLOOD* WARRANT

Article 14 prohibits secretly recording conversations inside a suspect's dwelling without a warrant. *Comm. v. Blood*, 400 Mass. 61 (1987) involved a police informant who wore a wire to record conspirators planning a gold theft. Many conversations took place in the perpetrators' homes. At the time, Massachusetts and federal law authorized one-party consent recordings anywhere, but the SJC felt that conversations in a home should be protected.[21] Rather than insist on a full-blown wiretap warrant, however, the SJC authorized the less cumbersome procedure of a regular search warrant under 276, § 1. The SJC reasoned that a regular warrant would still uphold Article 14, by subjecting police information to the scrutiny of a neutral magistrate.

As a result, when law enforcement officers want to record in a suspect's home, they must obtain a search warrant, nicknamed a "*Blood* warrant" after the case that created it. The *Blood* warrant is different because, instead of seizing tangible evidence (such as drugs or stolen property), it authorizes the collection of oral communication.

FOUR EXCEPTIONS TO *BLOOD* WARRANT

1. Federal investigation. The wiretap statute and Article 14 do not apply to federal officers conducting a federal investigation. 272, § 99(D)(1). The reason is that state law may not unduly restrict federal law enforcement. As a result, when local officers participate in a federally run investigation, the *Blood* warrant standard does not apply. In contrast, when state involvement creates at least a "combined enterprise," participating federal officers are held to the Massachusetts standard if the case ends up in state court. *Comm. v. Gonzalez*, 426 Mass. 313 (1997).

2. Officer safety. 272, § 99(D) permits police officers, "who [are] acting in an undercover capacity," to *always* wear a wire for safety. However, the recorded interceptions may not be used *as evidence* unless they comply, when necessary, with the *Blood* decision. *Comm. v. Collazo*, 34 Mass. App. Ct. 79 (1993).

3. Outside of suspect's dwelling. The *Blood* rule protects a suspect in his home and, probably, in other clearly private areas, such as an office. Beyond the four walls of a dwelling or other private place, *Blood* does not apply. This means that an undercover investigator or informant does not need a warrant to record suspects in less private places, such as their vehicles.

- *Comm. v. Remedor*, 52 Mass. App. Ct. 694 (2001): Paid informant and police undercover officer both wore body wires during cocaine buys with dealers in vehicles. The Appeals Court noted that the *Blood* warrant "seems to have been limited to intercepts of conversations occurring entirely within a private home."

- *Comm. v. Abdul-Kareem*, 56 Mass. App. Ct. 78 (2002): The defendant hired a police informant to shoot a business rival in the knees. On the way to a meeting in the defendant's car, the informant wore a wire. The tape of their conversation was played for the jury at the defendant's trial for conspiracy to commit mayhem. No warrant was necessary.

---

21 Federal law still permits consensual recording without a warrant, even in homes.

4. *Exigent circumstances.* *Comm. v. Rodriguez,* 450 Mass. 302 (2007) held that an exigent situation will allow police to proceed without a *Blood* warrant. In this case, Joel Rodriguez paid Pedro Tirado $400 to accept a package with cocaine. U.S. Customs intercepted it, and an undercover officer delivered it to Tirado, who admitted to being paid but claimed he did not know what was inside.

The police persuaded Tirado to call Rodriguez, who agreed to pick up the package. They placed a listening device inside Tirado's shirt. Rodriguez arrived, paid Tirado only $200 and took the package. When police converged, Rodriguez claimed the package was Tirado's and the money was a loan. But his story disintegrated because Trooper Colon heard Rodriguez counting cash and telling Tirado he would get the rest later. Tirado never asked for a loan.

Rodriguez argued that the *Blood* decision afforded him privacy in another person's home. In a strange twist, the SJC ignored previous cases and commented that a suspect *might* have an expectation of privacy in an *associate's* dwelling.[22] Even so, any privacy claim by Rodriguez could not affect the outcome of this case. The reason: The investigators had exigent circumstances that nullified any *Blood* obligations. They were faced with a large shipment of cocaine and needed to quickly substantiate Tirado's story by recording a meeting with the alleged mastermind. There was no time to get a warrant.

CONSEQUENCES OF UNLAWFUL INTERCEPTIONS

Unlawful recordings by government officials or their agents are suppressed, and so is the testimony of any individuals who listened to the unlawful recording, either while it was being made or later.

Still, the testimony of anyone personally involved in the recorded conversations is admissible. The reason is that actual participants may testify normally. A wiretap transgression should only exclude evidence that was obtained as a result of the illegal activity. *Comm. v. Ortiz,* 431 Mass. 134 (2000) (secret recording of an undercover drug deal with the defendant was suppressed as a violation of *Blood,* but the undercover agent was still allowed to testify because his testimony was not derived from the illegal recordings).

Recording by a private party (not acting as a government agent) is admissible. In *Comm. v. Crowley,* 43 Mass. App. Ct. 919 (1997), a boarder in Crowley's home secretly recorded Crowley beating his seven year old daughter. The tenant made the recordings while inside his private room. He gave them to police. It makes no sense to exclude evidence that the police had no part in creating. *Comm. v. Rivera,* 445 Mass. 119 (2005).

On the other hand, police have an obligation to tell a private party to stop secretly recording others. *Comm. v. Barboza,* 54 Mass. App. 99 (2002): A father, concerned that his 15 year old son was being sexually exploited by 57 year old George Barboza, placed a recording device on the family telephone. He secretly recorded two conversations between his son and Barboza that confirmed the existence of a sexual relationship. The father went to the Wilmington Police. The police did not ask him to stop recording, so he made two more tapes. In this case, the first two recordings were admissible. However, the last two recordings had to be suppressed. Although the father was not explicitly told by the police to continue, their silence made him their unwitting agent.

---

22 See *Comm. v. Rodriguez,* 67 Mass. App. Ct. 636 (2006) and *Comm. v. Price,* 408 Mass. 668 (1990) (no *Blood* warrant necessary to videotape drug transaction in a motel room where defendant had been invited).

Part V

INTERROGATIONS

Chapters 21 – 23

21

Voluntary Statements
Under the Fourteenth Amendment

INTRODUCTION

The most decisive evidence in a criminal case often comes from the mouth of the accused. There are two types of incriminating statements.

- **The spoken admission is the most frequent.** It occurs when the suspect speaks to another person — a civilian or police officer — and provides information implicating himself in a crime.

- **An adoptive admission** is any statement made in the presence of the suspect, where the suspect's response — whether orally, by gesture, or by revealing silence — indicates his acceptance. Since a person's silence may mean something other than his acknowledging guilt (it may mean inattention or confusion, for instance), evidence of an adoptive admission must be carefully received.[1] To justify its use, investigators must prove that: (1) the suspect heard and understood the statement; (2) he had an opportunity to respond; and (3) the context was one in which he would have been expected to respond.

  Consider *Comm. v. Ferreira*, 481 Mass. 641 (2019): When she learned of her sister's death from her other sister, Ana called the defendant and asked him, "Where is my sister?" The defendant answered, "I don't know." Ana then said, "You killed my sister. You can run. I'm gonna kill you." Even though the defendant heard Ana's accusation, he hung up the phone without saying a word. This was a classic adoptive admission.

The law governing police interaction stems from three constitutional principles:

- **Voluntary statements.** Only voluntary statements may be used. [Origin: Due process clause of the Fourteenth Amendment and Article 12.]

- **Warnings during custodial interrogation.** During custodial interrogation, a suspect must be warned of his right to remain silent and to have a lawyer present. [Origin: Fifth Amendment and Article 12.]

- **No interference with the attorney–client relationship** once a defendant has been arraigned or indicted. [Origin: Sixth Amendment and Article 12.]

---

1 No adoptive admission may be inferred if the statement is made after the accused has been placed under arrest, after the police have read him his *Miranda* rights, or after he has been significantly deprived of his freedom by the police. *Comm. v. Ferrara*, 31 Mass. App. Ct. 648 (1991).

OVERVIEW OF INTERROGATION ISSUES

Fourteenth Amendment Voluntary *Subject of Chapter 21*	• **Is the statement voluntary?** All statements (even to private citizens) must be voluntary. The court considers whether: • The interaction was coercive. • The characteristics of the suspect made him susceptible to coercion. • **Consequences.** • An involuntary statement may not be introduced at trial. • If it was voluntary, the next consideration is whether *Miranda* applies.
Fifth Amendment & *Miranda* Issues *Subject of Chapter 22*	• **State Action:** Who obtained the statement? • *Miranda* does not cover communications by a private individual, unless he is a police agent. • *Miranda* does cover communications to a police officer, quasi-law enforcement official, or agent. • **Applicability of Miranda Warnings.** *Miranda* warnings are required to protect the suspect's privilege against self-incrimination when an official: • Has the accused in a "custodial" situation; and • "Interrogates" him; • To obtain "testimonial evidence." If any of these three requirements is missing, then the officer does not have to advise the accused of his *Miranda* rights. If all three are present, the officer must consider: • **Proper Administration of Rights.** Were the *Miranda* rights properly: • Administered by the officer; and • Waived (i.e., given up) by the accused; or • Invoked (i.e., used) and then waived by the accused.
Article 12 Right to Counsel *Subject of Chapter 23*	• **Pending Charges:** The Article 12 right to counsel may apply if: • The accused has been arraigned or indicted on a charge; and • Police questioning relates to that pending offense without a lawyer present or an adequate waiver.

FOURTEENTH AMENDMENT REQUIRES VOLUNTARY STATEMENTS

A defendant's statements must be voluntary. "A conviction founded in whole or in part on statements which are the product of physical or psychological coercion deprives the defendant of . . . due process . . . and is invalid." *Comm. v. Mahnke*, 368 Mass. 662 (1975). To be voluntary in Massachusetts, a statement must satisfy the two-prong analysis mentioned in *Comm. v. Callahan*, 401 Mass. 627 (1988):

- First, the speaker must have been rational.

- Second, the speaker must not have been coerced into making a statement.

RATIONAL SPEAKER

A statement is involuntary if made by an irrational speaker with severe mental illness, intoxication, injury, or other condition. *Comm. v. Larregui,* 2019 WL 4071972 (Appeals Court) (the defendant made irrational statements to the arson investigator; she was under the influence of PCP; she exhibited delusional behavior both before and after questioning — she proclaimed she was God, she claimed she was giving birth, etc.).

If a suspect appears extremely high, extremely emotional, and detached from reality, he should not be interviewed. On the other hand, if a suspect is capable of understanding questions and responding coherently, officers need not delay. The vast majority of interviewed suspects are rational. The main dispute usually centers on whether their statements were coerced. *Comm. v. Davis*, 403 Mass. 575 (1988).

LACK OF COERCION

Totality of circumstances. There is no clear test to determine whether a suspect was coerced into making a statement. A court will scrutinize all of the surrounding circumstances.

Two major considerations lie at the heart of a court's assessment:

- First, how did the police behave?

- Second, what are the characteristics of the suspect?

The same considerations that determine whether a suspect's statement is voluntary also determine whether he validly waived his Miranda rights — a topic discussed in the next chapter. *Comm. v. Bousquet*, 407 Mass. 854 (1990).

POLICE BEHAVIOR

How police communicate with a suspect determines whether his statement is voluntary.

Physical coercion

Flagrant mistreatment is unacceptable. "Certain interrogation techniques . . . are . . . offensive to a civilized system of justice." *Miller v. Fenton*, 474 U.S. 104 (1985). *Haynes v. Washington*, 373 U.S. 503 (1963) (defendant beaten). *Comm. v. Collins,* 11 Mass. App. Ct. 126 (1981) (defendant forced to lie naked and handcuffed on the bathroom floor with a gun pointed at his face during questioning).

Threats

Coercion is not limited to physical force. Direct <u>and</u> indirect threats are coercive too. *Arizona v. Fulminante*, 499 U.S. 279 (1991) presents an indirect threat. Oreste Fulminante confessed to a fellow inmate, who was acting as a government informant. The plan was for the informant to offer "protection" to Fulminante from rough treatment by other inmates, but only if he told the informant "everything he did." Exploiting the defendant's fear of being raped in prison was conceived by government officials.

In *Comm. v. Monroe*, 472 Mass. 461 (2015), police interviewed Charles Monroe after a victim identified him as the person who forced her into a building at knifepoint and sexually assaulted her. Monroe waived his *Miranda* rights. Detective Brissette turned the conversation toward Monroe's daughter. Monroe said he did not want to live a day without seeing his daughter. Brissette repeatedly told Monroe that he would be the reason his girlfriend lost custody. Detective O'Rourke added that the baby would be raised by strangers. Monroe implored them: "Please don't take my daughter." He sobbed. He then made incriminating statements.

This was coercion. The detectives threatened Monroe by repeatedly and falsely claiming that if he did not tell them what happened, his child would be taken away. Monroe was only 18 years old, had emigrated from Africa, and had a poor educational background. The tone of the interview was hostile, and Monroe was handcuffed the entire time. Compare *Comm. v. Hammond*, 477 Mass. 499 (2017) (when defendant mentioned her concern for her children, the detective said, "I understand, but you're not doing yourself any good lying to us." This was far from the barrage of references to the suspect's daughter in *Monroe*).

Legitimate pressure. *Comm. v. Berg*, 37 Mass. App. Ct. 200 (1994): The defendant's written confession to the police, after he received *Miranda* warnings, stated that he was the owner of controlled substances in his home. His confession was voluntary because the police *truthfully* explained to him that both he and his mother would be charged with narcotics offenses unless he took responsibility. The police did have probable cause to arrest the defendant's mother, who lived in the apartment. Officers used no false information. A true statement about a relative's criminal exposure is a legitimate tactic to obtain an incriminating statement. *Comm. v. Montoya*, 464 Mass. 566 (2013).

Withholding or promising medical or mental health treatment

The police may not delay medical or mental health treatment.

- **Proper.** *Comm. v. Garcia*, 443 Mass. 824 (2005): When police learned for the first time that the defendant was diabetic, they arranged for him to be brought to a nearby medical center for an insulin injection. Since the defendant did not exhibit any signs of medical distress before or after the injection, his incriminating statements were voluntary.

- **Improper.** *Comm. v. Magee*, 423 Mass. 381 (1996): On July 4th at 4:00 a.m., Joyce Magee went to the station with her boyfriend to commit herself to a mental health facility. She had told her boyfriend that she was upset about the way her baby son had died six years prior. At the time, his death had been attributed to Sudden Infant Death Syndrome (SIDS). On this night, she eventually confessed to suffocating her child.

  The SJC suppressed her verbal and written confession as involuntary. Magee was interviewed in a closed room by a succession of three officers for seven hours. She repeatedly asked "to be committed," but was told she would not get help until she answered questions. Magee shook uncontrollably and suffered sleep deprivation. The police should not have withheld treatment until their suspect made statements.

The police may not promise mental health treatment in a misleading way. In *Comm. v. Felice*, 44 Mass. App. Ct. 709 (1998), a trooper did not promise psychiatric help to an arson suspect in exchange for a confession. The trooper merely told Felice that he believed setting a fire was a cry for help, and that he would try to get treatment arranged. Although a close case, the court found the officer's promise of help was not overly manipulative. While Felice was depressed and agitated during the interview, the trooper responded honestly when Felice questioned whether he was going to jail. The trooper simply remarked that he could not tell Felice what the judge would do. The key: The trooper never said that Felice would not be prosecuted or go to jail. He merely promised to do his best to "get help."

Tricks, tactics, & misrepresentations

If the suspect decides to speak, providing false information may be permissible if it is the only questionable police tactic. *Comm. v. Tremblay*, 460 Mass. 199 (2011).

- **Proper.** *Comm. v. MacKenzie*, 413 Mass. 498 (1992): Officers walked MacKenzie by his co-defendant in the station, then later pretended that this person had implicated him. The ploy worked, and MacKenzie confessed to murdering an elderly woman. The SJC approved because MacKenzie waived his rights *before* these tactics were used.

  Comm. v. Neves, 474 Mass. 355 (2016): Police interviewed Adilson Neves in connection with the robbery and murder of a taxicab driver. The officers falsely told Neves that they had "terrific" surveillance video of his Honda near the location of the shooting, and that his fingerprint had been found on the taxicab. They also encouraged him to "come clean" in order to protect his girlfriend, who had called for the cab, and to prevent his 11 year old brother from thinking he was a "monster." These tactics were not overly coercive. Neves was unshaken by the officers' questioning. He initially told officers he did not believe them and gave a detailed alibi.

- **Improper.** *Comm. v. Rosario*, 477 Mass. 69 (2017): The defendant ultimately admitted that he threw Molotov cocktails into a building, starting a deadly fire. Two psychiatric experts testified that, at the time of the defendant's interrogation, he suffered delirium tremens (DTs) from alcohol withdrawal. The court found his interview involuntary due to a combination of the DTs and objectionable interview tactics: (1) although the defendant originally said he stopped at the location because he observed the fire and wanted to help, the officers falsely told him a witness placed him at the scene before the fire began; (2) the officers told him that if his friends caused the fire, they might blame him and he would be left "holding the bag"; and (3) the officers engaged in "formatting," which means that they told the defendant details about the crime, which he then adopted as part of his confession.

Police may <u>never</u> trick a suspect into waiving his Miranda rights. *U.S. v. Giddins*, 858 F.3d 870 (4th Cir. 2017): Police arrested three women for bank robbery and seized their getaway car, which belonged to Master Giddins. One of the women said Giddins was involved. Officers obtained an arrest warrant for him. They then contacted him and said his car had been used in a bank robbery. When Giddins went to the station, Detective Morano gave him a *Miranda* waiver. Giddins asked, "Is this the procedure for me to get my car back?" Detective Taylor told him it was. Giddins asked, "But do I still get my car?" Taylor replied, "Before I release the car, I would like to know some answers." Giddins asked if he was in trouble, and Taylor said he was not. He signed the waiver.

Giddins' *Miranda* waiver and statements were coerced. The detectives made it appear that if he did not answer questions, he would not get his car back. The detectives also lied to Giddins about whether he was "in trouble." There was no doubt he was, because a warrant for his arrest already existed. *Comm. v. Jackson*, 377 Mass. 319 (1979).

False information or "minimization" should <u>never</u> be combined with an offer of leniency. *Comm. v. DiGiambattista*, 442 Mass. 423 (2004). Offering a false version of the evidence may be an acceptable strategy — e.g., "John, is there any reason that two people saw you leave the warehouse at 2:00 a.m. on Saturday?" However, combining this with an offer of leniency may pressure an innocent suspect to confess — e.g., "John, we have your prints at the murder scene. Admit it now and you're looking at manslaughter. Stay quiet and you'll spend the rest of your life in prison."

The danger in promising a lenient outcome is that "an innocent defendant, confronted with apparently irrefutable (but false) evidence of his guilt, might rationally conclude that he [is] about to be wrongfully convicted and give a false confession in an effort to salvage the situation." *Comm. v. Scoggins*, 439 Mass. 571 (2003).

Minimization is defined as a "soft-sell" technique. The police interrogator tries to lull the suspect into a false sense of security by offering sympathy, face-saving excuses, and even moral justification — by blaming the victim or an accomplice, citing extenuating circumstances, or playing down the seriousness of the charges. *Comm. v. DiGiambattista*, 83 Mass. App. Ct. 180 (2013).

Minimizing a crime also becomes toxic when officers blatantly misrepresent the defendant's legal predicament. *Comm. v. Baye*, 462 Mass. 246 (2012) (defendant set numerous fires one night in Northampton; two people died; his confession was suppressed mainly because the lead investigator misrepresented, multiple times, that deaths caused by arson do not qualify as murder if the person did not intend to kill anybody).

Example of an improper interview. *Comm. v. Ortiz*, 84 Mass. App. Ct. 258 (2013): The 19 year old defendant was being interrogated during a murder investigation. He had some experience with law enforcement, but had never been interrogated before. Prior to going to the station, he smoked marijuana. The three hour interview was not overly long, but was conducted without a break or water, leaving the defendant exhausted. The detectives used several improper techniques. They:

- Falsely told Ortiz that five witnesses placed him in the hallway before the gunshots, and one witness gave her statement under oath.

- Told him it was his "last chance" to tell his story, misstating his right to present a defense.

- Minimized Ortiz's involvement — saying they knew he did not intend for the shooter to kill someone when he gave him the gun, and suggesting there was a difference between giving someone a gun to "scare" versus "kill."

- Wrongly insisted that Ortiz would be "in this for capital murder" if he gave the gun to the shooter to kill, while only being seen as a "screw up" if he gave the gun to the shooter to scare someone. Young and impressionable, Ortiz believed that he would get the death penalty unless he admitted some involvement. The detectives assured Ortiz that if he only gave the gun to the shooter for protection, he would be "out of the picture." It is no wonder that Ortiz confessed.

Example of a proper interview. *Comm. v. Johnson*, 463 Mass. 95 (2012): Shortly after a restaurant was robbed and the owner shot in the face, police found Gary Johnson hiding in a nearby backyard. He was escorted to the scene and identified by witnesses.

At the station, Detective Brian Black administered *Miranda* warnings and obtained a waiver. The interview was recorded. For the first 50 minutes, Johnson claimed he had gotten into an argument with his parents and went to his friend's house, then ended up falling asleep in the backyard. He claimed he did not hear any sirens, police radios, or gunshots.

Detective Black informed Johnson of the potential charges. Johnson covered his face and hung his head. He continued to stick with his story. Black equated the interview to a report card, telling Johnson that people were going to listen to the interview and either give him an "A" or an "F." Moments later, Johnson said, "You know what, sir? You're good. I'm going to give you a handshake. You know what? I did do it." He then confessed in detail.

The interview lasted only an hour. The tone was not hostile. Johnson's handcuffs were removed. Detective Black questioned Johnson about additional evidence the investigation might yield (such as Johnson's fingerprints in the building), but he did not say that the police had this evidence.

The detective's statements — "This is kind of a bad situation"; "If for some reason you went into the restaurant to do a robbery and somehow a gun went off, I don't know how, today is the day to tell me that"; and "I want to give you an opportunity today to get out in front of all this" — all fell within the general rule that an officer may suggest that it would be better for the suspect to tell the truth. They did not imply that Johnson's cooperation would result in a lesser sentence.

Promises and pressure

Promising a specific legal outcome forbidden. Officers may say to a suspect that his cooperation will be brought to the prosecutor's attention. They may even say that cooperation has been considered favorably by courts in the past. However, officers may not promise *a specific outcome*, since only a prosecutor or court has the final authority to drop charges or impose a lesser sentence.[2]

- **Improper.** *Comm. v. Rivers*, 93 Mass. App. Ct. 120 (2018): Police were aware that Matthew Rivers was involved in a violent fight. Officer Johnson, who was familiar with Rivers, called and told him that if he came forward and gave a detailed account, he would "very likely avoid being charged with a felony." Rivers agreed to come in for an interview and ultimately made incriminating statements. Officer Johnson's conversation with Rivers amounted to a prohibited assurance that it would lessen his sentence if he cooperated.

- **Acceptable.** *Comm. v. Mandile*, 397 Mass. 410 (1986): The officer presented the "slight" conditional promise to the defendant that, "if he demonstrated good faith by revealing the location of the weapon, the district attorney would *discuss* leniency."

Reasonable psychological or religious appeals are permissible. *Comm. v. Cunningham*, 405 Mass. 646 (1989) (the detective told the defendant, when he insisted upon his innocence, "If you had nothing to do with [the crime], you don't have anything to worry about if you tell the truth"). *Comm. v. Barry*, 2014 WL 561651 (Appeals Court) (the detective advised the defendant to admit what he did so the *victim* could get psychological help and heal from the abuse). *Comm. v. Mazariego*, 474 Mass. 42 (2016)(the detective asked the defendant if he was religious and, when the defendant answered affirmatively, said: "You can hide from us, but you can't hide from God"). *Comm. v. Cartright*, 478 Mass. 273 (2017) (police mentioned several times that the victim could not "rest in peace" unless the defendant admitted what happened).

Legal advice

Before questioning, officers are not obligated to inform a person that he is a suspect. However, if police do inform an individual of their suspicions, a court is more likely to conclude that the suspect spoke voluntarily because he understood the consequences of cooperation. *Comm. v. Raymond*, 424 Mass. 382 (1997).

Officers are not obligated to provide legal advice either. *Comm. v. Cunningham*, 405 Mass. 646 (1989) (defendant admitted he was present at a murder because he did not understand that he could be charged as an accomplice even though he did not stab the victim; officers had no duty to tell him about the law relating to accomplices).

Of course, if investigators respond to a suspect's legal question, they must provide accurate information. *Comm. v. Mitchell*, 89 Mass. App. Ct. 13 (2016) (18 year old Terrance Pabon waived his *Miranda* rights and claimed he had nothing to do with a murder; in response to Pabon's question, the investigator said that being an accomplice was like playing

---

2 Technically, when officers act as if they have authority to determine a sentence, they are engaged in "plea negotiations," which are inadmissible as evidence. See *Comm. v. Wilson*, 430 Mass. 440 (1999), which discusses Mass. Rule of Crim. Pro. 12(f).

in a football game — where the players all act toward a common purpose; the court found that the detective's football analogy was accurate and did not mislead Pabon).

In all cases, officers must <u>never</u>:

- **Mislead a suspect about the need for a lawyer.** In *Comm. v. Groome*, 435 Mass. 201 (2001), investigators told Groome his girlfriend was dead. Groome then asked if he needed a lawyer. The police replied that he was not under arrest, was not charged with any crime and, therefore, did not need a lawyer. The SJC was very concerned about this misleading statement because, at the point when investigators said this, a high degree of suspicion had already fallen on the defendant. The court warned: "Police deception can [destroy] the voluntariness of any subsequent statement."[3]

- **Tell a suspect that if he calls an attorney, "all deals are off the table."** *Comm. v. O'Brian*, 445 Mass. 720 (2006).

- **Tell a suspect that police are legally obligated to tell the truth.** *Comm. v. Mazariego*, 474 Mass. 42 (2016): The detective told Mazariego, a murder suspect, that because their conversation was being recorded, the detective could not lie to him. This was misleading, since the law permits officers to, at times, misrepresent the strength of their evidence.[4]

- **Suggest that their interview is the only opportunity to speak with police.** *Comm. v. Thomas*, 469 Mass. 531 (2014): Chiteara Thomas was suspected of setting fire to a three-family house, which resulted in the death of a third-floor resident. A detective told Thomas that if she ended the interview, she would lose her one chance to talk about the fire. His message was misleading. There is no situation in which a suspect would not have the chance to talk with police at a later time.

- **Imply that a statement to police is the only way a defendant will be able to present his side to a jury.** *Comm. v. Novo*, 442 Mass. 262 (2004): Rui Novo was accused of beating his girlfriend's son to death. During his videotaped interview, the officers repeatedly claimed that Novo could not testify unless he spoke to them first — e.g., "If you don't give us a reason . . . a jury's never going to hear a reason!" Misrepresenting a defendant's right to testify is unacceptable.

  Compare *Comm. v. Newson*, 471 Mass. 222 (2015) (although the detective indicated the defendant's failure to explain his involvement in the shooting would make him "look like a cold-blooded killer," he never expressly stated that his silence would be used against him or that he would lose his right to testify at trial).

Police may promise not to arrest their suspect at the end of the interview. *U.S. v. Thunderhawk*, 799 F.3d 1203 (2015): Federal agents approached George Thunderhawk after receiving a report that he had sexually abused a child. They said he could leave at any time, and that he would not be arrested at the end of the interview, regardless of what he said. Thunderhawk agreed to speak. He denied the allegations, but admitted that he got into bed with the victim. At the end of the interview, the agents let him go home. He was arrested one month later.

---

3 See detailed discussion of the *Groome* case in *Chapter 22*.
4 See earlier discussion in this chapter about acceptable versus unacceptable police deception.

Thunderhawk's statements were voluntary. The agent truthfully told him that he would not be arrested at the end of the interview — not that he would never be arrested or prosecuted.

Police may implicate another agency's informant if they do not mislead him. A confidential informant's statements are voluntary and may be used against him — if investigators do not say anything to imply that they will be kept confidential. In *Comm. v. Doe*, 37 Mass. App. Ct. 30 (1994), the defendant served as a confidential informant for a Salem detective, who contacted Beverly investigators when he suspected that his informant had been involved in a Beverly bank robbery. The informant agreed to meet with Beverly detectives and, without receiving *Miranda* warnings, made highly incriminating admissions during a relaxed conversation in his home. The defendant even allowed officers to photograph him for an array later shown to bank employees. They did not mislead him. He knew, at the outset, that officers from another department were going to question him about a robbery.

Setting & style of interrogation

Physical setting. A court will consider the setting for the interrogation. The police station is an inherently more coercive environment than an accused's home or business. No doubt a windowless room in the basement of the police station with the door closed will present a more coercive environment than an open room next to the lobby.

Number of officers. The number of officers present during questioning has an impact. Two plainclothes detectives conversing with the accused outside his home will be less intimidating than an interaction with four uniformed officers encircling him inside the station.

Length of the interrogation. Detention for an extended period of time supports a defendant's claim that he confessed because his will was broken. In *Comm. v. Beland*, 436 Mass. 273 (2002), the defendant had been given an opportunity to sleep, but was awakened for a 3:00 a.m. interview. Typically, the SJC strongly disapproves of the practice of off-hours interrogation, especially when there is no apparent necessity to interrupt a suspect's sleep in the middle of the night. However, in this case, since the defendant had an opportunity to rest prior to the early morning questioning, new information (the death of the victim) made re-interrogation appropriate. Further, the defendant was reasonably alert during the interview.

Providing food, drink, and bathroom privileges. *Comm. v. Tolan*, 453 Mass. 634 (2009): Peggy Tolan murdered her husband and then called 911. Tolan was at the house when paramedics and officers arrived. She appeared upset, but said she was willing to speak with police. Tolan remained at the police station for eleven hours, speaking with investigators periodically for a total of 5½ hours. At the end of the interview, she was arrested. Although eleven hours may seem extreme, officers allowed her to take breaks throughout the day. They also reminded her that she was free to leave and request an attorney. Tolan later argued that her failure to use the restroom and her minimal food intake made her statements involuntary. The SJC disagreed. Officers repeatedly offered her food, drinks, and use of the restroom.

Arranging child care. *Comm. v. Cruz*, 442 Mass. 299 (2004): After being unable to locate a substitute caretaker, officers purchased a McDonald's Happy Meal for the suspect's daughter and a soda for the suspect. At the station, arrangements were made for a family member to pick up the child. The suspect, meanwhile, sat with his daughter while she watched television and ate. There were no officers in the room, and the suspect was not questioned until after the child left.

SUSPECT'S CHARACTERISTICS

Age

Age is a major factor because younger people are more prone to suggestion and police coercion. Courts carefully scrutinize the circumstances surrounding their statements. *Comm. v. Davis*, 403 Mass. 575 (1988).[5]

Education

An accused person with minimal education may be susceptible to coercion. In contrast, well-educated suspects are generally found to be less vulnerable. *Comm. v. Corriveau*, 396 Mass. 319 (1985) (defendant was "an experienced and well-educated businessman").

Intelligence

Someone with low intelligence may be susceptible. Officers should question this type of suspect carefully. *Comm. v. Wallen*, 35 Mass. App. Ct. 915 (1993) (police took special care in speaking with the suspect and communicating his rights; while he had a low IQ and only read at a fourth-grade level, he answered questions coherently).

Mental illness

A mentally ill person is vulnerable. Police must be careful. *Comm. v. Harris*, 468 Mass. 429 (2014): After recovering a dead body, police telephoned 21 year old Laurence Harris because he was the last person to speak to the victim by cell phone. Harris agreed to come to the station. He was given *Miranda* warnings and interviewed for three hours. He had no prior police involvement, and suffered from poor physical and mental health (anorexia and depression). He made incriminating statements and was overheard on the station phone telling his sister, "I killed my boyfriend."

His statements were voluntary. Although young, Harris went to the station, received *Miranda* warnings, and understood the officers' questions. The officers were kind to him and offered food. Also see *Comm. v. Walters*, 485 Mass. App. Ct. 271 (2020) (the defendant said officers should kill him and that he wanted to die, but otherwise provided a coherent murder confession; when he vomited and fell on the floor, officers offered to call EMS and provided water and a break for the defendant to compose himself; his confession was voluntary).

Consider the need for medication. *Comm. v. Sanchez*, 476 Mass. 725 (2017) (once the defendant alluded to his medications for mental illness, it would have been better if officers asked about his specific needs; still, Sanchez was coherent and able to understand the questions; his demeanor indicated that he was not impaired by alcohol, heroin, or lack of medication).

---

5 The specific *Miranda* precautions that apply to juveniles are discussed in *Chapter 22*.

Disability

Officers must be sensitive to any disability that may affect whether the accused can comprehend or communicate. Specifically, 221, § 92A requires that the arresting officer get an interpreter for any deaf or hearing-impaired person. Statements are inadmissible without this safeguard. *Comm. v. Kelley*, 404 Mass. 465 (1990). Also see *Comm. v. Sanchez*, 476 Mass. 725 (2017) (officers simplified their questions to accommodate the defendant's learning disability.) *U.S. v. Sweeney*, 887 F.3d 529 (1st Cir. 2018) (investigator offered to get the defendant's eyeglasses so he could read the *Miranda* form).

Avoid rushing Miranda or a suspect's answers. *Comm. v. Dowds*, 483 Mass. 498 (2019): While walking home to Lawrence, Dowds came across a vehicle in Danvers with keys in it. As he drove from the lot, the owner ran up and grabbed onto the car. Dowds drove erratically to dislodge the owner, causing a crash and killing him. Dowds was arrested quickly. Although he had a history of brain injuries, Dowds spoke voluntarily in response to reasonable and patient police questioning.

Language proficiency

Police must ensure that the suspect can adequately speak English or provide translation services. The law does not require independent interpreters. Police officers who are fluent may interpret. *Comm. v. Bins*, 465 Mass. 348 (2013) (defendant spoke Brazilian Portuguese but understood *Miranda* warnings given in continental Portuguese; any minor variations in translation did not prevent his understanding). *Comm. v. Vasquez*, 482 Mass. 850 (2019).

Any interview using an interpreter should be recorded, unless it is impractical at the time. *Comm. v. AdonSoto*, 475 Mass. 497 (2016).

Experience with justice system

A person's history with the criminal justice system is relevant. Someone with a criminal background is familiar with police practices and, consequently, less likely to feel intimidated. *Comm. v. Jackson*, 432 Mass. 82 (2000) (defendant's experience with police — he had been incarcerated in state prison twice — indicated that he voluntarily waived his *Miranda* rights; it was also persuasive that he gave an innocent explanation at the outset and, after being confronted with physical evidence, gave a plausible explanation while still denying responsibility for the murder).

Self-protection

If the accused has the presence of mind to refuse to answer certain questions, or to assert himself in other ways, he is probably not intimidated. *Comm. v. Durand*, 457 Mass. 574 (2010) (defendant identified the officers' interrogation tactics and stated that he was not fooled — "I'm not stupid. Don't play me like an idiot. It's not going to work because I didn't hurt that kid"). *Comm. v. Walker*, 466 Mass. 268 (2013) (Walker's ability to give self-serving facts about his lack of memory showed that all of his statements were voluntary).

Physical condition

An injured or ill suspect is more vulnerable. *Muncey v. Arizona*, 437 U.S. 385 (1978) (defendant could not speak freely in the hospital while suffering unbearable pain). Compare *Comm. v. Sneed*, 440 Mass. 216 (2003) (although she was a 70 year old asthmatic, Maxine Sneed's statements were not coerced; investigators calmly interviewed her at home). *Comm. v. Bell*, 473 Mass. 131 (2015) (defendant's admission on the street that he started the deadly fire was voluntary despite his pain from burn injuries).

Alcohol or drug intoxication. The fact that a suspect consumed alcohol and/or drugs is important in evaluating whether he spoke freely. *Comm. v. Knowles*, 92 Mass. App. Ct. 617 (2018).

- **Officers may rely on outward signs of sobriety** when interrogating a person who may be under the influence of drugs or alcohol. *Comm. v. LeBeau*, 451 Mass. 244 (2008): Lt. Smith encountered suspect LeBeau carrying a beer can at 11:20 p.m. He asked how much LeBeau had been drinking. Although he said five to eight beers since 5:00 p.m., LeBeau did not smell of alcohol, appeared sober, spoke clearly, and easily navigated a steep gravel slope leading to his friend's house.

- **Officers may also rely on their prior experience with the suspect.** *Comm. v. LeBlanc*, 433 Mass. 549 (2001) (officer had known defendant for approximately fifteen years and had observed him under the influence to varying degrees; the officer could authoritatively testify that the defendant was not impaired when he spoke about the crime).

ALL STATEMENTS AGAINST ACCUSED MUST BE VOLUNTARY

Massachusetts has a strict screening process known as the "humane practice" rule. First, the judge must conclude that the defendant's statements were voluntary beyond a reasonable doubt. Second, the jury is instructed that it must be satisfied, beyond a reasonable doubt, that the accused spoke voluntarily in order to consider any of his statements.[6] *Comm. v. Miller*, 68 Mass. App. Ct. 835 (2007).

Massachusetts prohibits _any_ involuntary statement, even one to a private citizen. Consider *Comm. v. Mahnke*, 368 Mass. 662 (1975): Police had been stymied in their investigation of George Mahnke. A father decided to conduct his own investigation into the whereabouts of his missing daughter, who was Mahnke's girlfriend. The father and several family members abducted Mahnke and drove him to a cabin in the woods. There, they extracted his murder confession by subjecting him to prolonged questioning and violent threats. Mahnke was turned over to police after he confessed and showed them where he hid the body. The SJC ruled that Mahnke's statements were inadmissible even though they were made to private citizens not acting as agents of law enforcement.[7]

---

6 Federal due process requires only that a defendant's confession be proved voluntary by a preponderance of the evidence.
7 Interestingly, this Massachusetts interpretation contradicts the U.S. Supreme Court's decision in *Colorado v. Connelly*, 479 U.S. 157 (1986). *Connelly* held that the Fourteenth Amendment applies only to statements obtained by law enforcement, *not* private citizens.

As an additional legal protection, a conviction may not be based solely on a defendant's uncorroborated confession. "There must be some evidence, besides the confession, that the criminal act was committed by someone . . . and not imaginary." *Comm. v. Landenburg*, 41 Mass. App. Ct. 23 (1996).

In *Comm. v. Villalta-Duarte*, 55 Mass. App. Ct. 821 (2002), the defendant sexually assaulted an infant for whom his wife provided daycare. Later he experienced a religious conversion and confessed to police. The law does not require corroboration for each element of the crime, it simply requires evidence that a crime was committed. Here, the victim began to cry hysterically whenever she was brought to the defendant's apartment, she developed an intractable diaper rash in her vaginal area, and had scratches on her face. Moreover, there was evidence that these symptoms disappeared after the victim was placed in a different daycare setting. Thus, sufficient evidence existed that the defendant committed this crime.

Custodial Interrogation
22
Under the Fifth Amendment & Miranda

THE *MIRANDA* WARNINGS

In the landmark decision of Miranda v. Arizona, 384 U.S. 436 (1966), the Supreme Court adopted rules designed to protect an accused's Fifth Amendment rights. The rights at stake are communicated in the form of warnings, which have become familiar to every citizen through television! *U.S. v. Dickerson*, 120 S.Ct. 2326 (2000). The *Miranda* warnings inform the suspect that:

- He has the right to remain silent;
- His statements can be used as evidence against him;
- He has the right to counsel;
- If he is indigent, counsel will be furnished to him at the government's expense; and
- He may stop questioning at any time for any reason.[1]

WHEN MUST THE *MIRANDA* WARNINGS BE GIVEN?

The Supreme Court did not intend for Miranda warnings to govern every police interaction. The vast majority of police/citizen discussions do <u>not</u> fall under *Miranda's* protective umbrella. *Comm. v. Bryant*, 390 Mass. 729 (1984).

Properly distinguishing when *Miranda* applies is essential. If officers fail to provide warnings when necessary, a court will suppress the defendant's statements. On the other hand, if officers provide warnings in a situation where they are not required, they may hinder their ability to obtain information from a suspect who has been prematurely alerted to their suspicions.

Miranda warnings are only required when a person is in custody and subjected to interrogation. Custodial interrogation means "questioning initiated by law enforcement officers after a person has been taken into custody or otherwise deprived of his freedom of action in any significant way." *Comm. v. Haas*, 373 Mass. 545 (1977).

Custody exists when the suspect is either:

- **Under arrest;** *or*

- **Significantly detained.**

---

1 This last warning was not required by the original *Miranda* decision, but has become the standard over time in Massachusetts. *Comm. v. Wadlington*, 467 Mass. 192 (2014).

Interrogation occurs if:

- **A law enforcement officer;**

- **Communicates with the suspect** by either:

    - *Express questioning;* or

    - The *functional equivalent* of express questioning;

    - In an effort to obtain *testimonial evidence.*

If one of these elements is absent, *Miranda* warnings are not required and the admissibility of a statement depends solely on whether it was voluntary. See *Chapter 21* on voluntariness.

CUSTODY

It is important for officers to know when a suspect is in custody because, at this moment, they may not question him without Miranda warnings. In court, the defendant must prove that he was in custody at the time police interviewed him. The police then "bear the heavy burden" to prove the defendant waived his rights. *Comm. v. Almonte*, 444 Mass. 511 (2005).

ARREST

When officers arrest a suspect, that person is always entitled to Miranda protection.

SIGNIFICANT DETENTION

Custody also occurs when a suspect is significantly detained. This occurs when a seizure has the qualities of an arrest — without actually being one. *Comm. v. Groome*, 435 Mass. 201 (2001) provided the four factors that courts use to determine whether an unarrested suspect was in *Miranda* custody. (*Hint*: think "LIFF".)

- **Location.** Does the interrogation take place in a police-dominated atmosphere?

- **Interview style.** Is the style of the interview aggressive?

- **Focus.** Do officers accuse the suspect of a crime?

- **Freedom to leave.** Is the suspect free to end the interview by leaving the place of interrogation or by asking officers to leave?

Location of the interrogation

Police station often custodial. When the Supreme Court decided *Miranda v. Arizona*, they were mainly concerned about interrogations at the station since, "within that atmosphere," the investigator "possessed all the advantages." Courts continue to recognize the station as the prime location for physical and psychological pressure.

The best way to avoid custody: (1) have the suspect voluntarily accompany officers to the station; and (2) inform the suspect that he is free to leave at any time.

- **Case where police avoided custody.** *Comm. v. Groome*, 435 Mass. 201 (2001): Peter Groome murdered his girlfriend with a chisel in the driveway of their Hyannis home. He hid her body underneath his car and took her car to work the next day. When officers arrived at the school where he taught, they told Groome they were investigating a stolen car, and he agreed to accompany them back to the Cape. Police told him that he was not under arrest. During the 45 minute drive, there was no interrogation.

  They arrived at the Yarmouth state police barracks at 2:30 p.m. Groome was interviewed by two detectives and permitted unescorted bathroom breaks. When Groome asked whether he "had to stay here," a detective replied that they wanted to ask him questions, but he was free to go. Groome chose to stay.

  When informed that his girlfriend was dead, Groome asked if he needed a lawyer. The police replied that he was not under arrest or charged with a crime, so he did not need a lawyer. At 4:00 p.m., after officers learned that the victim's blood had been found on her car, Groome was given *Miranda* warnings and arrested for murder. All of Groome's pre-*Miranda* statements were admissible because he was not in custody.

  - *On the ride to the Cape.* Although the location (a police vehicle) was not neutral, Groome was told, before he got in, that he was not under arrest. Nothing was said by the officers to suggest that he was a suspect in any crime, and they asked no questions.

  - *At the station.* Groome was not in custody from the time he arrived at the barracks until police confronted him about blood on the car: (1) he was repeatedly allowed to leave the interview room unescorted; (2) no officer said anything to suggest that he was a suspect; (3) the interview was informal and included small talk about unrelated matters; and (4) Groome was told he could leave.

  - *Right to counsel.* Groome argued that police interfered with his right to counsel, but the SJC found that Groome was not in custody when he asked about his need for a lawyer. Therefore, the *Miranda* safeguards — including the right to counsel — had not yet attached. At the same time, the SJC held that officers should not have misleadingly downplayed Groome's need for a lawyer.

- **Case where suspect was in custody at the station.** *Comm. v. Haas*, 373 Mass. 545 (1977): Haas' wife and children were found murdered in their home The investigation immediately focused on him. Police called Haas at his office and directed him to return home without explanation. Upon arrival, officers prevented Haas from entering his house. They transported him to the station and refused to answer his questions on the way. Once there, they asked Haas one question without informing him of his rights. His answer placed him at the scene at the time of the murders. These circumstances — especially the way officers withheld information until he was inside the station — led the SJC to conclude that Haas was in custody and deserved *Miranda* protection.

In the back of the cruiser typically custodial. *Comm. v. Jones*, 42 Mass. App. Ct. 378 (1997): Two women were assaulted and robbed during the day. They identified the defendant to a nearby officer. The officer asked defendant Jones to sit in the back of his cruiser. With the victims repeating their accusations and Jones denying them, the officer began asking him questions. Jones attempted to leave, but the officer shut the door (which could not be opened from the inside). Although the officer's tone was conversational, the overall circumstances created a custodial situation. The officer should have provided *Miranda* warnings. Also see *Comm. v. Damiano*, 422 Mass. 10 (1996).

Home usually noncustodial.

- **Cases with no custody at home.** *Comm. v. Sneed*, 440 Mass. 216 (2003): 70 year old Maxine Sneed was a suspect in the theft of $24,000 from the Lottery Commission where she worked. A state trooper and civilian investigator from the Attorney General's Office visited her home on a day that she called in sick. The investigators never advised her of her *Miranda* rights and she made incriminating statements. However, she was not in custody. She let the investigators enter her home. They did not raise their voices or sound intimidating. At one point, Ms. Sneed left the room to speak with her daughter by phone. Sneed was not placed under arrest at the end of the interview, even though her statements provided probable cause. A reasonable person in her position would have felt free to ask the men to leave.

- *Comm. v. Mitchell*, 89 Mass. App. Ct. 13 (2016): 16 year old Markeese Mitchell was a suspect in a murder. His grandfather returned a phone call from police and agreed to an interview at his home. Detectives arrived at 9:05 p.m. and met with Mitchell, his grandfather, and his father. They told the three that they could end the conversation at any time. They sat at the kitchen table. When asked if the detectives could record the interview, all three refused. Mitchell denied any knowledge of the incident at first, but when the detectives showed him surveillance photographs, he admitted being present. Still, he continued to deny being involved in the stabbing. The interview ended at 10:25 p.m. The interview was noncustodial because: (1) the officers made an appointment to come to the house; and (2) Mitchell asserted himself by refusing to be recorded, and the officers honored his refusal.

- **Case with custody at home.** *U.S. v. Rogers*, 659 F.3d 74 (2011): An individual notified police when he found child pornography on a personal computer he bought from Brian Rogers. Local police enlisted the help of the state police and, because Rogers was a noncommissioned officer, the Naval Criminal Investigative Service (NCIS).

  NCIS requested that Rogers' commander order him to return home. Upon arrival, Rogers found three officers questioning his pregnant wife. Although he was told he would not be arrested, Rogers was under a military order to be at home. Any member of the armed forces would have felt that he lacked the freedom to leave and was compelled to answer questions. Rogers was in custody for *Miranda*, and his statements were obtained illegally because he never received the proper warnings.

Business premises not necessarily custodial. A suspect is not in custody merely because police officers search his business premises with a warrant. As long as police do not curtail the suspect's movement or use threatening language, their search of the business does not make the encounter custodial. *Comm. v. Ferrara*, 31 Mass. App. Ct. 648 (1991).

Prison or jail not necessarily custodial. For an inmate to be in custody for *Miranda*, there must be some additional restraint on his freedom that prevents him from leaving the scene of the questioning. In other words, the prisoner must be in custody beyond the confines of ordinary prison life. *Comm. v. Smith*, 456 Mass. 476 (2010). *Comm. v. Girouard*, 436 Mass. 657 (2002) (defendant was incarcerated on an unrelated charge when he was interrogated about a murder; when he was confronted with DNA evidence, he broke down and confessed; still, the SJC found "no custody" because the defendant had not been forced to meet with officers and had the ability to end the interview).

Interview style

The police interview style affects whether Miranda custody exists.

- **Conversational and nonaggressive.** *Comm. v. Kirwan*, 448 Mass. 304 (2007): Scott Kirwan stabbed and killed a man during a bar fight. After speaking with witnesses, Officer Hurley went to Kirwan's house and was let in by his father. Hurley asked Kirwan to tell him about the fight. He responded: "A kid pushed me and I pushed him back." He shrugged his shoulders and looked down. Hurley asked: "How did the kid get a hole in his chest?" This was not custodial interrogation. Kirwan's father invited him in. Hurley was the only officer present and spoke in a conversational tone.

- **Aggressive and accusatory.** *Comm. v. Hall*, 2012 WL 5364574 (Appeals Court): Police pressured Hall by telling him they would "go out and find him" if he did not come to the station for an interview. During the interview, the police repeatedly accused him of lying. The officers threatened to charge Hall with filing a false police report if he did not tell the truth about his "stolen car." This was clearly custody for *Miranda*.

Custody does <u>not</u> automatically exist when a suspect confesses. Rather than "freeze" the encounter at the moment of confession, courts assess whether there was "a fundamental transformation in the atmosphere." *Comm. v. Bryant*, 390 Mass. 729 (1984).

Consider *Comm. v. Hilton*, 443 Mass. 597 (2005): Initially the defendant's son was the suspect in an arson that killed five people. Kathleen Hilton, his mother, voluntarily accompanied police to the station and was calmly questioned. The SJC insisted that she was still *not* in custody when she confessed, because the investigator wisely continued his nonconfrontational approach ("Tell me more . . . You sound upset . . . What else do you want to say?").

The setting *did* become custodial when a detective from the Fire Marshal's office entered the room. His accusatory, rapid fire questions transformed the interview. This detective made a mistake by not providing *Miranda* warnings. Hilton's statements during this portion of the interview were suppressed.

Focus of investigation

Uncommunicated suspicion is *never* a factor. *Comm. v. Becla,* 74 Mass. App. Ct. 142 (2009): Responding to a report of an accident, Officer Steven Cecchini saw Janusz Becla pulling his car into a driveway. The officer asked Becla what happened and he responded, "Isn't it obvious, I hit a pole?" Becla's speech was slurred and there was alcohol on his breath.

Officer Cecchini later testified that he had probable cause at that moment to arrest Becla, but he did not communicate his view or provide *Miranda* warnings. Instead, he asked Becla to perform field sobriety tests, then arrested him afterwards.

A district court judge ruled that Cecchini should have provided *Miranda* warnings at the point he "made up his mind" to arrest Becla. The Appeals Court said the judge was wrong. An officer's "unarticulated thoughts" cannot create the type of coercive environment that *Miranda* was designed to address.[2]

A *clear* accusation typically creates custody. As soon as police interviewers obviously accuse their suspect, officers must administer *Miranda* warnings. *Comm. v. Molina,* 467 Mass. 65 (2014) (custody began when detective changed his conversational style and accused Molina of lying about a shooting).

Compare *Comm. v. Amaral,* 482 Mass. 496 (2019): Jeremy Amaral was interviewed about a murder the previous day. Even after confronting Amaral about his dishonesty, investigators did not tell him that he was a suspect, or that they had evidence against him. The officers only communicated that they wanted to know more about the events leading up to the victim's death. The interview was conducted in a calm and cordial manner. Amaral felt comfortable enough to make dinner plans with his mother during a phone conversation at the station.

Freedom to leave

The best way for officers to avoid custody: Tell the suspect he is free to leave.

- **No custody.** *Comm. v. Bermudez,* 83 Mass. App. Ct. 46 (2013): Jose Bermudez was possibly involved in a shooting. Bermudez's interrogation was noncustodial even though it took place at the station. Bermudez had gone there voluntarily with his mother. The questioning was conversational and nonthreatening. Bermudez was not restrained, and he was told he would be allowed to leave with his mother — which he did. Police later brought charges.

- **Custody.** *Comm. v. Coleman,* 49 Mass. App. Ct. 150 (2000): Three officers went to Coleman's house and interviewed him about a shooting. Coleman sat on the edge of his bed with an officer. Two other officers blocked the door. Coleman was 19 years old. An officer told Coleman that he was the prime suspect and lied that his fingerprints had been found on the gun. Coleman responded to this false statement by admitting he had touched the gun but not fired it. The officer threatened to tell rival gang members if he did not confess. Coleman began to cry and confess. This was obvious custodial interrogation requiring *Miranda*.

---

2 The other features of the interaction, field sobriety tests and brief conversation, did not rise to the level of *Miranda* custody either. See later discussion in this chapter.

At the same time, being detained, without more, is not typically Miranda custody. *Comm. v. Tejada,* 484 Mass. 1 (2020): At 2:00 a.m., Jose Tejada approached a stranger in his neighborhood and asked to be taken to the police station because he killed three people. The neighbor called police instead.

Tejada repeated what he told his neighbor, and added that he tried to kill himself. He was asked about the location of the shooting and what he did with the weapon. He seemed anxious but cooperative.

The officers frisked and handcuffed Tejada, then took him to the address he provided. Receiving no answer when they knocked, officers broke down the door to see if anyone needed assistance. Tejada's wife and two children were found shot to death upstairs.

Certain statements after Tejada was handcuffed and placed in the cruiser were suppressed, but officers were not required to give *Miranda* when they first spoke with him. In reviewing the *Groome* factors (LIFF), the SJC found the police questioning was non-custodial.

- **The location was non-coercive.** Officers spoke to Tejada while he sat on a curb in a public parking lot.

- **The interview questions were open.** The officers asked Tejada straight-forward, open questions that were influenced by his statements: What happened? Who did you kill? Where do you live? Why did you do it? Where is the gun?

- **The focus was not on Tejada as a suspect.** The officers did not accuse him.

- **Free to leave.** Tejada was detained because a reasonable person would not believe he was free to leave after admitting to killing someone. However, this one factor is typically not enough for *Miranda* custody. Tejada's possible intoxication and suicidal thoughts did not make his admissions involuntary either. Tejada had no difficulty understanding or speaking.

NONCUSTODY SITUATIONS WHERE *MIRANDA* NOT REQUIRED

General on-scene questions

When they arrive on scene, officers need not provide blanket warnings to citizens. *Comm. v. Callahan,* 401 Mass. 627 (1988): Officers entered a house in response to a radio call. A man at the door, later identified as Joseph Callahan, said: "Follow me." While climbing the stairs, Callahan said: "She's been shot, better get an ambulance." Viewing a dead woman in the apartment, an officer asked: "What happened?" Callahan replied: "She was going to throw me out, so I shot her." Such preliminary conversations do not come inside *Miranda's* tent. *Comm. v. Zhan Tang Huang,* 87 Mass. App. Ct. 65 (2015).

Investigative detentions

An investigative detention is a seizure, but Miranda custody requires a significant detention or arrest. As a result, officers may detain suspects and avoid *Miranda* warnings when they:

- Ask a reasonable number of questions to learn the suspect's identity and confirm or dispel their suspicions;

- Understand that the suspect is not obligated to answer; and

- Release him after a reasonable amount of time if probable cause has not developed.[3]

Consider *Comm. v. Cawthron*, 479 Mass. 612 (2018): As Detective Donovan was walking toward a convenience store, he overheard Keith Cawthron on his cell phone. Donovan suspected that Cawthron was arranging a drug deal. When Cawthron left in his car, Donovan followed him to a steakhouse parking lot. He parked and called for backup.

Five minutes later, a black vehicle parked next to Cawthron. Craig Flodstrom got out. He shook hands with Cawthron, exchanging an item that Donovan could not see. Donovan got out and identified himself as a police officer. Flodstrom said, "This is how I feed my family."

Detective Columbus arrived. The detectives separated the two men and questioned them. Foldstrom told Donovan he sold 300 Oxycodone pills to his uncle, Keith Cawthron, for $2 per pill. He pulled $600 from his pocket. He was arrested.

Meanwhile, Columbus asked Cawthron what he purchased. Cawthron said pills for $2 each, which he put under the seat in his car. Columbus found the bottle and arrested Cawthron.

The detectives were not required to initially give the defendants *Miranda* warnings. An investigative stop, without more, is not custodial. The defendants were not told they were suspected of a crime, and their discussions were one-on-one in an open, public space. The fact that they were arrested at the end of the interview did not mean they had been in custody.

When an investigative detention involves arrest-like restraint — e.g., handcuffs, drawn weapon, or prone positioning — the interaction becomes custodial. *Miranda* safeguards apply as soon as a suspect's freedom is "curtailed to a degree associated with a formal arrest." *Comm. v. Gordon*, 47 Mass. App. Ct. 825 (1999): Sheryl Gordon ran from the bushes next to a convenience store that had just been robbed. She matched the suspect's description. She resisted police by "thrashing and squirming," so she was cuffed and put in a cruiser. An officer, while trying to calm her down, asked what she was doing in the area. She said, "I didn't want to do it; he made me do it." *Miranda* warnings did not precede her confession. Handcuffed in a cruiser, Gordon was in custody. Furthermore, this was not a preliminary question because, by that time, substantial suspicion had fallen on Gordon.[4]

Traffic stops, accidents, & sobriety tests

Officers should rarely advise motorists of their Miranda rights because most traffic stops are brief and public. The same rules for investigative detentions apply roadside. Officers may ask a reasonable number of questions. For example, in *Comm. v. Calderon*, 2011 WL

---

3 What constitutes a reasonable amount of time for an investigative detention is discussed in *Chapter 4*.
4 *Comm. v. Velluci*, 96 Mass. App. Ct. 274 (2020) is the rare case where pre-arrest handcuffing did <u>not</u> create *Miranda* custody. During a traffic stop, the defendant approached the officer — in an agitated state — despite directions to get back in his car. The officer handcuffed the defendant, telling him it was for the officer's safety and asking, "What's happening? "This general question, despite the handcuffs, was not custodial interrogation under these circumstances.

2270411 (Appeals Court), Myriam Calderon was picking up her son. Trooper Gifford saw Calderon get out. She smelled of alcohol and was off balance. Gifford asked if she had been drinking. Calderon admitted to having a beer while cooking dinner. Gifford administered sobriety tests, then said, "It's clear to me that you've had more than one beer." Calderon admitted, "I had two tequila nips." While Gifford's statement was accusatory, it did not create a custodial interrogation. "It was," the Appeals Court remarked, "typical for a routine stop of this nature." Also see *Comm. v. D'Agostino*, 38 Mass. App. Ct. 206 (1995).

Officers should not give Miranda rights to motorists before directing them to perform sobriety tests, including reciting the alphabet. *Vanhouton v. Comm.*, 424 Mass. 327 (1997).

Restraint for medical treatment is not custody for Miranda. *Comm. v. LaFleur*, 58 Mass. App. Ct. 546 (2003): At an accident scene, the defendant said, "I had too much to drink" when an EMT asked what happened. The EMT told an officer, who approached the defendant as he was being loaded into an ambulance strapped to a gurney. The defendant admitted to the officer that alcohol had affected his driving. No *Miranda* warnings were provided. Since the physical restraint was not applied by law enforcement, a reasonable person in the defendant's position would have understood that he was being detained due to his medical condition. The questioning was brief and occurred in public with EMTs present, which lessened the possibility of police domination. The officer also did not tell the defendant that he was a suspect.

Telephone conversations

A telephone conversation between an officer and suspect is _never_ custodial. The suspect's freedom is not affected because he can always hang up! *Miranda* does not come into play during phone calls — even if the officer has obtained an arrest warrant for the offender. *Comm. v. Ryan*, 11 Mass. App. Ct. 906 (1981) (police had arrest warrant for larceny; defendant learned of the warrant and made a series of calls to the investigator during which he implicated himself and another person). *Comm. v. Clark C.*, 59 Mass. App. Ct. 542 (2003) (juvenile who phoned lieutenant investigating a home invasion was not in custody; his statement, "I didn't do all that the lady said I did, I just hit her," was admissible).

Undercover work

Undercover officers do not need to provide Miranda warnings because their targets experience the opposite of police coercion. In *Illinois v. Perkins*, 496 U.S. 292 (1990), an undercover officer posed as a fellow inmate and, by proposing an escape plan, lured the defendant into bragging about committing a murder that authorities had been investigating for years. In ruling that *Miranda* did not apply, the *Perkins* court reasoned that *Miranda's* essential ingredient — a police-dominated atmosphere — was absent. Perkins spoke freely to someone he believed was a like-minded criminal. This is the essence of undercover work!

INTERROGATION

Interrogation exists when officers engage in questioning (or its functional equivalent) to get testimonial evidence.

QUESTIONING

Express questions

Express questions directly ask for information about a crime. *Comm. v. Acosta*, 416 Mass. 279 (1993) (question at scene — "Where do you live?" — should have been preceded by *Miranda* because police were trying to link Acosta to drugs in the apartment).

On the other hand, when a suspect speaks without being questioned, his statement is <u>not</u> the product of interrogation.

- **Unsolicited.** *Comm. v. Ferrer*, 68 Mass. App. Ct. 544 (2007): Eliud Ferrer was with a group standing in a closed gas station underneath a "no trespassing" sign. When police drove over, the men ran. Ferrer was caught and arrested. Ferrer said to Officer Celester: "Your boys are dumb. They could have me for seven or eight years instead of this trespassing bullshit." Officer Celester responded: "They are pretty smart and they are good at what they do." Ferrer then said: "They'll never find it. You're just wasting my time." His comment made officers search the area and find a gun.

  The exchange between Ferrer and Officer Celester was not custodial interrogation. Ferrer started it. The officer's reply was a "natural reflex" not intended to get Ferrer to incriminate himself. As a result, Ferrer's statement was admissible at trial to prove that he had possessed the recovered gun.

- **Overheard.** Comments that police are lawfully in a position to overhear are <u>not</u> prompted by questioning. Therefore, they do not have to be preceded by *Miranda* warnings. *Comm. v. Garcia*, 409 Mass. 675 (1991) (troopers, helping the defendant make a phone call after booking him for drug distribution, overheard him say to his wife: "I got busted. They got most of it").

Functional equivalent

The "functional equivalent" of interrogation covers words or actions that the police know are likely to produce an incriminating response. *Rhode Island v. Innis*, 446 U.S. 291 (1980).

Staged police conversation. When officers purposefully speak to each other so that the suspect will talk, they engage in a type of interrogation.

- **Improper tactic.** *Brewer v. Williams*, 430 U.S. 387 (1977): Brewer was arrested in Davenport, Iowa for abducting a ten year old girl in Des Moines. Officers transporting Brewer agreed with his attorney not to question him. However, one officer, knowing that Brewer was deeply religious, began a conversation with his partner that he knew would be overheard. The officer emotionally stated that he hoped they could locate the little girl's body so that she could "go to heaven" because her parents were entitled to a "Christian burial." The defendant blurted out where officers could find the body and led them to the dead girl.

Although the officer never questioned Brewer, the Supreme Court held that his "Christian burial speech" was the functional equivalent. In other words, the officer's comments had the same effect as direct questioning because they were designed to elicit an incriminating response. The court suppressed Brewer's statements.[5]

- **Not induced by police.** Compare the emotional appeal in *Brewer* with *Rhode Island v. Innis*, 446 U.S. 291 (1980). Thomas Innis initially exercised his right to remain silent. The arresting officer later mentioned to his partner that he was afraid a child might find the murder weapon if officers could not locate it. Overhearing this comment, Innis led officers to the shotgun. The Supreme Court found that this brief exchange did not amount to interrogation because the officers did not intend to trigger Innis' conscience.

  Comm. v. Mitchell, 35 Mass. App. Ct. 909 (1993) also illustrates this principle. In *Mitchell*, with the defendant in custody for a minor offense, officers discussed whether he resembled the suspect in another crime. The defendant overheard them and spontaneously (and ironically) incriminated himself in yet another offense — the rape of a 13 year old girl on her way to school — by describing the "pink pants" he wore in an effort to show his innocence.

  Here, the police did not directly question the defendant since they never asked him to describe his clothing. Was the police conversation "the functional equivalent" of direct questioning? The court said "no." The conversation in the booking area was not deceptively undertaken to make the defendant incriminate himself. At the time, the officers had not connected the defendant to the rape and were not aware of the significance of his pink pants. *Comm. v. Caputo*, 439 Mass. 153 (2003).

Provocative police comments that entice a suspect to incriminate himself are interrogation.

- **Interrogation tactic.** *Comm. v. Martin*, 467 Mass. 291 (2014): While in a holding cell, Cleveland Martin made statements about the victim to a detainee several cells away. Court Officer Crowley informed Detective Doogan, who went to the lockup, but remained out of sight. Crowley warned Martin to remain silent, but Martin instead told Crowley that "the bitch" had stabbed the cab driver, not him. Crowley said, "You mean to tell me that there was two dudes in the car and the girl did the stabbing?" Martin responded, "Yeah, why not? What, just because she's a girl? Are you saying a girl can't stab someone?"

  Martin's statement — "the bitch did it" — was spontaneous. On the other hand, Crowley's statement — "You mean to tell me . . . the girl did the stabbing?" — crossed the line into interrogation. An officer in Crowley's position should know that this type of statement will *provoke* an incriminating response. *Comm. v. Sanchez*, 476 Mass. 725 (2017).

- **No interrogation.** *Comm. v. Foley*, 445 Mass. 1001 (2005): Foley was arrested for beating his wife. While in handcuffs in the cruiser, he was screaming. An officer commented, "Are you having a rough day, man?" In response, Foley yelled, "I choked her out, but she deserved it." The officer's question was designed to calm Foley, not incriminate him.

  Comm. v. Rodriguez, 75 Mass. App. Ct. 235 (2009): Rodriguez sold cocaine from his home. After his arrest, his wife told their neighbor, Detective DiLiddo, that she was worried

---

5 Fortunately, there was still sufficient evidence to convict him.

about not having enough money. DiLiddo approached Rodriguez, who was handcuffed. Without advising him of his *Miranda* rights, DiLiddo asked if he had any money for his children. Rodriguez apologized for conducting business across the street and said, "I meant no disrespect." He gave DiLiddo $100 for his wife. Since the detective's comment was not designed to incriminate, Rodriguez's "guilty apology" was spontaneous.

Displaying object.

- **Interrogation tactic.** In *Comm. v. Rubio*, 27 Mass. App. Ct. 506 (1989), police executed a search warrant at Rubio's apartment. Officers arrested Rubio and, without saying anything, held an open female purse filled with cocaine in front of Rubio's face as they were leading him out of the apartment. Rubio immediately said the drugs belonged to him and not his girlfriend. This display was the equivalent of an accusatory police question —"How do you explain this?" — so it needed to be preceded by *Miranda* warnings.

- **No interrogation.** In *Comm. v. Harkness*, 35 Mass. App. Ct. 626 (1993), an officer chased Harkness onto a roof and, after handcuffing him, found a gun nearby. One officer escorted him down the stairs while another followed with the gun. As Harkness was being put into the cruiser, he said, "That gun isn't mine, but I know whose it is." No questions had been asked, yet Harkness later insisted that he should have received *Miranda* warnings before his statement. The court disagreed. The officer had not thrust the pistol toward Harkness in a way that demanded an explanation (like the cocaine in *Rubio*). The gun was simply being held, and it was Harkness who chose to comment.

Forcing a meeting between co-defendants.
In *Comm. v. Brant*, 380 Mass. 876 (1980), defendant Brant refused to speak with police, so officers told Brant that his co-defendant had just implicated him. They then put him in a room with his accomplice. Afterwards, Brant confessed. The court disapproved because investigators had used an indirect form of interrogation as an "end run" around Brant's right to silence.

TESTIMONIAL EVIDENCE

Miranda **upholds the privilege against self-incrimination, which only applies to testimonial evidence.** When a suspect reveals his knowledge, thoughts or beliefs, it is considered testimonial evidence. "Testimonial" means speech or conduct (such as a gesture) that communicates an idea. *Comm. v. Fernandes*, 427 Mass. 90 (1998).

Miranda **does not cover police action designed to obtain <u>non</u>testimonial evidence.** This includes: (1) physical evidence; and/or (2) statements by the accused that do not assert facts or beliefs.

Physical nontestimonial evidence

Obtaining physical evidence is nontestimonial because it does not force the suspect to reveal his thoughts. *Schmerber v. California*, 384 U.S. 757 (1966).

- **DNA samples.** *Comm. v. Letkowski*, 83 Mass. App. Ct. 847 (2013): Accused of rape, Letkowski claimed that the officer had no right to gather DNA with an oral swab after Letkowski had invoked his right to remain silent. The court disagreed. Collecting physical evidence does not require that a suspect convey his inner thoughts.

- **Field sobriety tests.** Suspects may be asked to *physically* perform. *Comm. v. Ayre*, 31 Mass. App. Ct. 17 (1991).

- **Voice and handwriting exemplars.** Providing a voice exemplar — a recording of the sound and quality of a suspect's voice — is nontestimonial. The same is true for a handwriting exemplar that can be compared with a written document (e.g., a bank robbery note). *Comm. v. Buckley*, 410 Mass. 209 (1991).

- **Gun license.** Ordering a suspect to produce his gun license is nontestimonial. *Comm. v. Haskell*, 438 Mass. 790 (2003): Arriving on scene, Lt. David Reilly found officers detaining Haskell for unlawful gun possession. Reilly asked Haskell whether he had a license to carry (LTC) without giving him *Miranda* warnings. Haskell said he did not and was arrested.

  The privilege against self-incrimination does not permit a suspect to refuse to produce *physical evidence* (such as a license) when lawfully ordered to do so. Police did not have to give *Miranda* warnings before demanding that their suspect produce his LTC.

  The problem in this case: Lt. Reilly asked Haskell if he had an LTC instead of simply demanding that he produce one. Since Reilly requested that Haskell reveal his knowledge, Haskell was entitled to *Miranda* warnings.[6]

  Compare *Comm. v. Pok*, 2014 WL 5461492 (Appeals Court) (officer just demanded that the three occupants produce an LTC for the gun he found in their car; *Miranda* did not apply when Pok spontaneously admitted, in response, that he owned the gun).

Important point: Police may use reasonable force to <u>perform nonintrusive tests</u> over an arrestee's objection — as long as they do not later testify to his refusal. *Comm. v. Lydon*, 413 Mass. 309 (1992) ruled that police may *force* an arrestee to submit to nonintrusive tests that produce physical evidence. Here, James Lydon was arrested for murder. Following booking, a technician arrived to swab Lydon's hands for gunshot residue. Lydon refused to allow the test and said he wanted his attorney. The police stopped the test, but they did not need to.

The SJC pointed out that officers could have used *reasonable force* on Lydon to complete the "swab test." The Fifth Amendment and Article 12 do not protect against the production of physical evidence — e.g., firearms residue, fingerprints, DNA, handwriting samples, etc. — where the goal of the test is to obtain evidence independent of the suspect's thoughts.

However, the Fifth Amendment and Article 12 do prevent officers from testifying at trial that the defendant refused to cooperate with police — since non-cooperation *does reveal* the defendant's inner thoughts about his ability to pass an evidence gathering test. See, e.g., *Comm. v. McGrail*, 419 Mass. 774 (1995) (testifying about defendant's refusal to take a breathalyzer and/or perform sobriety tests improper). *Comm. v. Hinckley*, 422 Mass. 261 (1996) (testifying about defendant's refusal to provide sneakers to police for comparison with footprints at crime scene improper). *Comm. v. Conkey*, 430 Mass. 139 (1999) (testifying that the defendant refused to provide his fingerprints, even though he said he would, violated the defendant's constitutional right against self-incrimination).

---

6 See discussion about how to avoid the *Haskell* problem in *Chapter 3* concerning field investigations into gun possession.

Verbal nontestimonial evidence

When an officer's questions are not designed to produce testimonial evidence, Miranda warnings are unnecessary.

- **Consent.** Requesting consent to search is not interrogation. *Comm. v. Wallace*, 70 Mass. App. Ct. 757 (2007).

- **Alphabet sobriety test.** *Vanhouton v. Comm.*, 424 Mass. 327 (1997) held: "The fact that the motorist must use his or her voice to perform the test does not necessarily make the response testimonial . . . The alphabet [is] a set of generic linguistic symbols that the average person masters early in life . . . [T]he recitation determines only whether the . . . motorist has sufficient mental coordination [to drive]." *Miranda* does not apply.

- **Post-arrest identification.** *Comm. v. Ramirez*, 55 Mass. App. Ct. 224 (2002): When defendant Ramirez was arrested for dealing cocaine, an officer asked him his name. The defendant answered, "George Lassu." The officer knew he was lying. This exchange took place before Ramirez was given *Miranda* warnings. Still, the court held that *Miranda* was unnecessary. The officer testified that he recognized Ramirez from a previous encounter where he had given a false name. The fact that the officer knew that Ramirez had lied on a prior occasion did not mean that he expected him to do it again. He had asked a question that the police routinely ask anyone under arrest. Ramirez's prior false response did not immunize him from similar requests in the future.

Routine booking questions about one's identity — e.g., address, social security number, date of birth — seek nontestimonial information, so Miranda does not apply.

- **Booking question about address — nontestimonial.** *Comm. v. Kacavich*, 28 Mass. App. Ct. 941 (1990): Police executed a search warrant for drugs at an apartment. During booking, the defendant answered questions concerning his residence without the benefit of *Miranda* warnings. His statement about living in the apartment was admitted at trial. The questions were meant to identify the defendant, not to develop incriminating evidence. The fact that nontestimonial evidence is ultimately used to a defendant's detriment does not change the analysis.

- **Booking question about employment — possibly testimonial.** Where an arrestee's employment status may incriminate him, police must give *Miranda* warnings before asking about it. In *Comm. v. Woods*, 419 Mass. 366 (1995), the defendant was arrested for dealing cocaine. He was carrying a lot of cash. During booking, *Miranda* warnings were not provided before the defendant was asked about his job. He acknowledged being unemployed. Routine booking questions may be asked without *Miranda* because they are designed to identify the defendant for court. Learning about an arrestee's employment is unrelated to this goal.

- **Physical and verbal responses to administrative requests — usually nontestimonial.** *Comm. v. Guy*, 441 Mass. 96 (2004): During booking, the defendant was asked a routine question, "Are you injured?" He only said that he had been hit on the side of the head. This statement was important evidence at trial because he tried to justify stabbing the victim by claiming severe injuries. Since his booking response produced incriminating information, the defendant insisted that he should have been given *Miranda* warnings. However, this question was clearly nontestimonial. The defendant's physical well-being is important to the police in all arrests because they are liable for a prisoner's medical condition.

PUBLIC SAFETY EXCEPTION TO MIRANDA

When public safety is at stake, officers may briefly interrogate a suspect in custody without administering Miranda warnings.[7] *New York v. Quarles*, 467 U.S. 649 (1984).

- **Proper.** *Comm. v. Kitchings*, 40 Mass. App. Ct. 591 (1996): An officer properly decided to search a parked van for drugs. He placed the driver and a passenger in the back of his cruiser. During his search, he discovered a loaded ammunition clip and called for backup. He promptly placed the two additional passengers in his cruiser uncuffed. Outnumbered four to one and concerned for his safety, the officer turned to the men and shouted, "Where's the gun?" One of them answered, "It's on the back seat." The officer found two handguns. His need to avoid immediate danger excused his failure to give *Miranda* warnings.

  Comm. v. Richardi, 2013 WL 1435155 (Appeals Court): Officer Burchell heard a loud bang and saw John Richardi and another man running toward him. He overheard Richardi say, "How did the cops get here so quickly?" Richardi, who smelled of alcohol, was angry as Officer Burchell spoke to him, so Burchell handcuffed him and placed him in the cruiser. Burchell simultaneously received a dispatch about a vehicle involved in an accident. He saw a heavily damaged truck off the road. A handgun was on the ground near the driver's door. It was 2:40 a.m. Officer Burchell properly asked Richardi if he had been driving, if there were more weapons, and if anyone else was involved or injured in the accident.

- **Improper.** *Comm. v. Martin*, 444 Mass. 213 (2005): Based on the report of a victim who had been threatened at gunpoint, Boston police surrounded the defendant's apartment and coaxed him out. He was handcuffed. A detective convinced him to disclose the location of his firearm inside the apartment. No *Miranda* warnings were provided. The public safety exception did not apply. The defendant and his apartment had been secured by police. They could have gotten a *Miranda* waiver without risking further danger.

The public safety exception also covers:

- **Learning about the risk posed by drug paraphernalia.** *U.S. v. Noonan*, 745 F.3d 934 (2014) (officer properly avoided *Miranda* to ask about the possibility of explosive chemicals to make methamphetamine in the defendant's car).

- **Learning whether a suspect of the opposite sex is armed.** *Comm. v. White*, 74 Mass. App. Ct. 342 (2009): At the time of the stop, Officer Fitzgerald ordered the female operator to get

---

7 The SJC might be open to applying the public safety exception even after the suspect invokes his right to counsel. In *Comm. v. Castano*, 478 Mass. 75 (2017), police arrested the defendant for murder. After he invoked his right to an attorney at the station, officers asked him where his gun was. Because they were concerned that he had disposed of it an area where children were present, they asked him to describe the gun and even brought him to the scene to try to locate it. The motion judge allowed the evidence based on the public safety exception. On appeal, the SJC noted there were good arguments on both sides. However, the SJC ended up affirming the conviction on other grounds, without deciding whether the exception applied.

out of the car and place her hands on the roof. While waiting for a female officer to frisk her, Fitzgerald said, "You better tell us if you have anything because we're going to find it." The operator admitted that she carried a gun in her waistband. This exchange did not need to be preceded by *Miranda* warnings. Fitzgerald's comment was, according to the Appeals Court, "sensitive and sensible" because he wanted to stay safe *and* avoid putting his hands on a woman while waiting for a female officer.

- **Learning whether an armed accomplice left the scene.** *Comm. v. Clark*, 432 Mass. 1 (2000): Trooper Charbonnier radioed that he had been shot during a traffic stop. Another trooper arrived and found the defendant, David Clark, crawling alongside the road. Clark was handcuffed at gunpoint. Officer Frost arrived to assist. Frost remained with Clark while the trooper checked on his wounded comrade (who later died). Officer Frost asked Clark, "Is there anybody else with you?" Clark replied, "Nobody's with me. I'm by myself." Officer Frost responded, "Don't lie." Clark said again, "I'm by myself."

  Clark later challenged the admission of his statements because he had not been provided with his *Miranda* rights even though he was obviously in custody and interrogated.[8] Officer Frost's questions were clearly designed to discover whether there were other dangerous individuals nearby. The shooting took place near a residential neighborhood and it was dark. A weapon had not yet been found. In these circumstances, Officer Frost needed answers to prevent further danger. See *Comm. v. Pinney*, 484 Mass. 1003 (2020).

The public safety exception applies with equal force to juveniles. *Comm. v. Alan A.*, 47 Mass. App. Ct. 271 (1999).

OTHER GOVERNMENT OFFICIALS & MIRANDA

***Miranda* never covers questions from private citizens.** The warnings only protect the accused in a police-dominated situation. *Comm. v. LaFleur*, 58 Mass. App. Ct. 546 (2003).

***Miranda* does not cover interrogations in foreign countries by foreign officials.** *Comm. v. Wright*, 479 Mass. 124 (2018) (defendant killed his mother and grandmother and fled to Canada; his statements to Canadian police were voluntary; *Miranda* was not an issue).

Beyond the police, *Miranda* applies to other government investigators whose questions may lead to criminal punishment. *U.S. v. Diaz*, 427 F.2d 636 (1st Cir. 1970) (defendant entitled to warnings from draft board secretary concerning his selective service compliance because his answers might lead to prosecution). *Comm. v. Juvenile*, 402 Mass. 275 (1988) (juvenile corrections officials, even for private agencies, must give *Miranda* warnings when investigating crime).

Public school officials should <u>not</u> give Miranda warnings prior to questioning a student about a school incident. *Comm. v. Ira I.*, 439 Mass. 805 (2003).[9]

---

8 These statements were critical because they eviscerated Clark's defense. He wanted to convince the jury that another person, who he had picked up in his vehicle, actually shot the police officer.
9 See detailed discussion in *LED's Juvenile Law, Chapter 24*.

HOW MUST *MIRANDA* WARNINGS BE WAIVED?
ELEMENTS OF A VALID WAIVER

A valid waiver has three components:

- **Proper communication.** Police properly communicate the rights;

- **Voluntary & knowing.** The suspect understands his rights to silence and counsel; and

- **Willing to speak.** The suspect indicates that he will talk with police.

PROPER COMMUNICATION OF WARNINGS

In the field, read the Miranda warnings from the laminated card included with this manual.[10] Officers should speak clearly and slowly so that the rights are understood. Briefly pausing after each bullet point helps. *Comm. v. Holley*, 79 Mass. App. Ct. 542 (2011) (officer's quick recitation of *Miranda* — captured on videotape — was too difficult to understand; defendant's incriminating remarks were suppressed).

Miranda Warnings
• You have the right to remain silent.
• If you choose to speak, anything you say can be used against you in court.
• You have the right to consult with a lawyer before answering any questions, and you can have him or her with you during questioning.
• If you cannot afford a lawyer and want one, a lawyer will be provided by the Commonwealth before questioning, at no cost to you.
• You may answer questions now and waive (that means, give up) your right to counsel and your right to remain silent.
• If you decide to talk to me, you still have the right to stop at any time and for any reason.
• Do you understand what I have told you? Will you talk to me now?

Attach photocopy of LED Miranda card to incident report so it can be offered into evidence. *Comm. v. Mitchell*, 47 Mass. App. Ct. 178 (1999) (best practice to respond to legal challenges).

In the station, use the proper Miranda form. An adult waiver form appears on page 22-36. The juvenile form appears on page 22-37.

*Do **not** recite the Miranda warnings from memory.*

- *Comm. v. Dagraca*, 447 Mass. 546 (2006): Sergeant Trudel arrested Gregory Dagraca on his porch with money, drugs, and a sales ledger. Trudel informed Dagraca of his *Miranda* rights — from memory — and asked who lived in the house. Dagraca responded that he

---

10 The Law Enforcement Dimensions' card has been approved in numerous hearings before district and superior courts. The other side contains witness instructions for showups and field views. See *Chapter 25*.

lived there, but was not the owner. Other officers arrived with a search warrant and found large amounts of cocaine inside.

Sergeant Trudel performed excellent police work by getting Dagraca to admit that he lived there. Without that statement, there was insufficient proof that Dagraca possessed the drugs inside.[11] Unfortunately, Trudel forgot to say, "If you choose to speak, anything you say can be used against you." The mistake invalidated Dagraca's waiver, which ended the case.

- *Comm. v. Ayala*, 29 Mass. App. Ct. 592 (1990): Eduardo Ayala was arrested for raping a child on the beach. An officer, who was fluent in Spanish, recited *Miranda* warnings. Instead of giving the warning that "any statement could be used against him," the officer told Ayala "if he wished to make a statement, he could do so." This mistake was especially problematic because, instead of warning Ayala, it encouraged him to speak.

***Miranda* warnings must be conveyed in a language the defendant understands.** *Comm. v. Bins*, 456 Mass. 348 (2013). *Comm. v. Rosario*, 2021 WL 1263892 (Appeals Court): The detective's oral recitation of the *Miranda* rights in Spanish did not properly convey the right to a lawyer without cost.[12] Though the defendant also signed a Spanish language *Miranda* waiver form, the Commonwealth did not present a translation of this form to the court.[13]

Do *not* minimize Miranda. *Comm. v. Gaboriault*, 439 Mass. 84 (2003): The defendant stabbed his girlfriend and son. At the station, a detective referred to *Miranda* as "just a formality" before reading the rights. The defendant signed a waiver and confessed. The court warned officers to avoid words that minimize *Miranda's* importance.

VOLUNTARY & KNOWING WAIVER

A waiver must be voluntary and knowing beyond a reasonable doubt. The identical standard determines whether an accused spoke voluntarily. See *Chapter 21. Comm. v. Medeiros*, 395 Mass. 336 (1985).[14]

However, police are not obligated to:

- **Inform a suspect about the subject of the interrogation.** *Comm. v. Hensley*, 454 Mass. 721 (2009) ("our cases do not require that a defendant have information regarding the crime about which he will be questioned"). *Colorado v. Spring*, 479 U.S. 564 (1987) ("we have never read the Constitution to require that the police supply a suspect with a flow of information to help him calibrate his self-interest in deciding whether to speak"). *Comm. v. Cartright*, 478 Mass. 273 (2017) (police properly arrested the defendant for a minor offense and then interrogated him about a murder without telling him that he was a murder suspect).

---

11 The house was under renovation, and Dagraca was still receiving mail at his girlfriend's house. Thus, the cocaine could have belonged to a worker performing renovations or a past tenant. For more on "constructive possession," see *LED's Criminal Law, Chapter 20.*
12 Rights should be read from a card. Spanish language *Miranda* rights cards are available from LED.
13 This was an error by the prosecutor.
14 *Colorado v. Connelly*, 479 U.S. 157 (1986) (under federal law, waiver need only be voluntary by a preponderance of the evidence).

- **Provide legal advice.** Police should not help suspects decide whether to waive their rights. At the same time, they may not mislead the accused about the meaning of a particular right. *Comm. v. Grenier*, 415 Mass. 680 (1993) (defendant asked the investigator to explain the phrase, "Anything I might say can be used against me"; the officer truthfully responded that the defendant's comments "would be recorded and might later be stated in court").

- **Inform a suspect that he has already been charged.** *Comm. v. Robinson*, 78 Mass. App. Ct. 714 (2011): A fire in an apartment building killed two residents. Kevin Robinson was in the vicinity when the fire broke out. He had an ongoing feud with the landlord, and gasoline residue was found on his clothes. Several days later, Robinson voluntarily accompanied investigators to the station. Robinson signed a *Miranda* waiver. After several hours of questioning, Robinson asked if he could leave. The officers had obtained a warrant for his arrest before the interview began, but had not told him. Now they arrested him.

  Robinson's *Miranda* waiver was voluntary. He had a long history of police involvement. Although he initially complained that his stomach hurt, he refused medical assistance. He was given many opportunities to stretch, smoke, drink water, and take antacid. After being informed that he was under arrest, he spoke to officers for another 40 minutes.

The best practice is to obtain an explicit statement that the suspect understands his rights and waives them. It is also acceptable when the suspect's *conduct* — e.g., he starts answering questions — shows he willingly gave up his rights. *Comm. v. Aarhus*, 387 Mass. 735 (1982).

Refusing to sign a written waiver does not nullify a suspect's verbal waiver. *Comm. v. Jules*, 464 Mass. 478 (2013) (although he did not sign the waiver form, the defendant agreed to speak to officers about his girlfriend's death; this was a totally acceptable waiver).

Officers must describe their waiver interaction in their report. *Comm. v. Alcala*, 54 Mass. App. Ct. 49 (2002).

- **Sample 1:** "Mr. Jones was handcuffed and seated alone in the back seat of my cruiser. He was alert and showed no signs of intoxication. The arrest involved no physical confrontation, and Mr. Jones complained of no injuries.

  I advised Mr. Jones of his *Miranda* rights by reading them from a card. A copy of the card is attached. Jones responded in a calm voice: 'Yeah, I understand. I still don't know why you'd arrest me for pushing my wife.'"

- **Sample 2:** "Ms. Lawrence was handcuffed and seated on the curb in front of the Quik Mart on 33 Prospect Street. I advised her of her *Miranda* rights by reading them from a card. A copy of the card is attached. Lawrence said: 'I watch TV. I got it. I'll talk to you.'

  Since I smelled an odor of alcohol on her breath, I asked her how much she had been drinking. She said she had three beers earlier and was 'a little buzzed.' She denied taking any other drugs. Her speech was clear, and her responses were coherent."

In particular, note any signs of intoxication or withdrawal. Typically, a suspect's waiver is valid even though he is under the influence or experiencing drug withdrawal. In *Comm. v. LeClair*, 68 Mass. App. Ct. 482 (2007), LeClair drove Campanale to a Burger King parking lot for the purpose of robbing a customer. Campanale shot the victim and then was killed by police following a wild chase. LeClair lived.

At the station, LeClair was asked whether he had consumed drugs or alcohol. He said "no." *Miranda* followed, and LeClair signed a waiver. At the end of the interview, he said he actually had ingested a Fentanyl patch, which provides a "high" similar to heroin, but he showed no signs of sickness or withdrawal. LeClair's confession was admitted into evidence because police did a good job of documenting that his drug ingestion had not affected his ability to speak.

Officers should not say, or even imply, that a suspect's statement will remain confidential. *Comm. v. Santana*, 477 Mass. 610 (2017) (the defendant agreed to be recorded if his statement was "confidential"; the investigator properly said he could not agree to that and then read the *Miranda* warnings).

Suspect's belief that he will get "a deal" — absent a government promise — does not nullify his waiver. *Comm. v. Luce*, 34 Mass. App. Ct. 105 (1993) (defendant waived his rights and mentioned that he was considering cooperating in exchange for a deal; he then described his cocaine business; since police never promised him anything for his information, his confession could be used against him at trial).

SPECIAL PROTECTIONS FOR JUVENILES

Courts recognize the vulnerability of children.[15] Juveniles, like adults, are only entitled to *Miranda* warnings before custodial interrogation. However, courts must consider a child's age in determining whether custody existed. In *J.D.B. v. North Carolina*, 564 U.S. 261 (2011), a detective questioned a 13 year old break-in suspect at his school. The child was not told that he could call his grandmother, whom he lived with. The detective also talked about the possibility of pre-trial detention in an intimidating way. The Supreme Court noted that "a frighteningly high percentage of adults confess to crimes they never committed." Children are more susceptible. *Miranda* warnings should have been given to J.D.B.

Courts must also consider a child's age in assessing whether an interrogation happened. *Comm. v. Quinones*, 95 Mass. App. Ct. 156 (2019).

Parent or interested adult

Failure to have a parent or interested adult present to assist a child <u>age 12 or 13</u> will invalidate <u>any</u> Miranda waiver. *Comm. v. MacNeil*, 399 Mass. 71 (1987). See form on 22-37.

A waiver for a child <u>14, 15, 16, or 17</u> requires adult assistance, unless the youth is "highly sophisticated." This standard is difficult to satisfy. *Comm. v. Guyton*, 405 Mass. 497 (1989) (juvenile had extensive contact with police and juvenile court but he was "naïve"). There is no right to adult consultation once a person turns 18. At that age, an individual is considered an adult offender. *Comm. v. Smith*, 471 Mass. 161 (2015).

Parent preferred. Police should first try to locate a parent, then seek an interested adult. Deliberately avoiding a parent is improper, but there is "no minimum search requirement" before police may seek another adult. *Comm. v. Hogan*, 426 Mass. 424 (1998) (because the 14 year old's mother was out of town and his father was incarcerated, investigators properly called his grandmother to act as an interested adult).

---

15 The most comprehensive discussion of juvenile *Miranda* appears in *LED's Juvenile Law*, Chapter 24.

At least 18 years old. In *Comm. v. Guyton*, 405 Mass. 497 (1989), the juvenile's sister, who was 17, was presumed to lack the maturity to properly advise her brother. His statement was suppressed because she was legally incapable of helping him waive his rights.

Not incapacitated. The interested adult must not be physically or mentally incapacitated, or under the influence of alcohol or drugs. *Comm. v. Leon L.*, 52 Mass. App. Ct. 823 (2001).

Likely advocate. The interested adult must be likely to act in the best interest of the juvenile. However, the adult does not have to be completely free of conflicting loyalties. In *Comm. v. Berry*, 410 Mass. 31 (1991), although the father had argued with his son and called police, he still could serve as an advocate. The police did not observe "continuing animosity" between father and son prior to the boy's murder confession.

A parent or adult does not become disinterested or antagonistic because he encourages the juvenile to tell the truth. *Comm. v. Phillip S.*, 414 Mass. 804 (1993).

Rights belong to juvenile. A parent or other adult may not waive rights on behalf of a child. Ultimately, the child must decide. *Comm. v. Phillip S.*, 32 Mass. App. Ct. 720 (1992).

Mandated interaction

Until the parent or adult arrives, police must avoid talking with the juvenile. Investigators should tell the parent/interested adult that she is getting the opportunity to confer with the child about his rights. The best practice is to offer private consultation. Moreover, police *must* honor any request by a juvenile or adult to meet privately, even in the middle of an interview. *Comm. v. Pacheco*, 87 Mass. App. Ct. 286 (2015).

The juvenile <u>and</u> parent or adult must understand the warnings. *Comm. v. Wade W.*, 2012 WL 1398617 (Appeals Court) (mother obviously did not understand the concept of a "waiver").

Age 14, 15, 16, or 17: "Meaningful opportunity" to consult. The juvenile does not have to actually seek the adult's advice. Police must give the juvenile an *opportunity* to consult.

- **Sufficient.** *Comm. v. Ward*, 412 Mass. 395 (1992): A 16 year old gave an incriminating statement linking him to a brutal murder of a homeless man. Prior to his confession, police asked his mother if she wanted to talk with her son about the rights. The son told her that it was "ok" and began to speak. This waiver was valid.

- **Insufficient — parent not at the scene.** *Comm. v. Alfonso*, 438 Mass. 372 (2003): Alfonso, who was 15 years old, was detained at his friend's house in connection with the theft of firearms. A detective read *Miranda* rights, then asked Alfonso if he wanted to have his mother present. Alfonso said "no." He confessed. His waiver was inadequate. A juvenile in trouble may be too embarrassed to request help. This is why police must get a parent/adult on scene *before* seeking a waiver.

Age 12 or 13: "Actual opportunity" required. Young juveniles must actually discuss their rights with an adult. In other words, officers are expected to actively promote an interaction between adults and young juveniles. *Comm. v. Phillip S.*, 414 Mass. 804 (1993).

WILLING TO SPEAK

Length of time waiver lasts

A Miranda waiver lasts for a reasonable amount of time, and the police are not required to repeat Miranda whenever a defendant implicates himself. Comm. v. Martinez, 458 Mass. 684 (2011) (Martinez waived his *Miranda* rights voluntarily at 9:15 p.m. When he gave his second statement at 3:00 a.m., the waiver was still valid). Compare *Comm. v. Sousa*, 350 Mass. 591 (1996) (18 hour time lapse between interviews too long to rely on initial waiver).

Officers are not required to re-administer the rights before asking questions about different offenses. Comm. v. Marquetty, 28 Mass. App. Ct. 690 (1990).

Polygraph

Following a valid Miranda waiver, a suspect may consent to a polygraph examination. The examiner may offer his opinion that the suspect is not telling the truth, but may not intimidate him. *Comm. v. Auclair*, 444 Mass. 348 (2005) (defendant agreed to polygraph; when told he was probably lying, he cried and admitted killing his girlfriend's baby).

OTHER SAFEGUARDS

6 HOUR RULE

Post-arrest, the police have 6 hours to interview the defendant about any subject. The rule is designed "to standardize the treatment of all suspects regardless of whether they [are] arrested while court [is] in session or not." *Comm. v. Siny Van Tran*, 460 Mass. 535 (2011).

The clock starts at the moment of arrest. Comm. v. Martinez, 458 Mass. 684 (2011).

The 6 hour rule covers:

- **Discussions about any offense.** *Comm. v. Powell*, 468 Mass. 272 (2014): Police arrested Errol Powell for larceny of a motor vehicle, even though they had probable cause for murder. Powell was put in a cell at 2:45 p.m. and not interviewed until 11:45 p.m. The interview focused almost exclusively on the murder. The SJC declared: The manipulative approach of these investigators is exactly what this rule prevents. Evidence suppressed.

- **Discussions initiated by the defendant.** *Comm. v. Fortunato*, 466 Mass. 500 (2013): It was irrelevant that Fortunato asked to talk about his robbery. The detective needed to get a valid waiver for a discussion more than 6 hours after Fortunato's arrest. His statement was suppressed. Compare *Comm. v. McWilliams*, 473 Mass. 606 (2016) (McWilliams did *not* discuss his bank robbery with Detective Crowley beyond the 6 hour period; he later asked Crowley to get his glasses from his backpack on his bike in a parking garage; when Crowley did "the favor," it led him to discover surveillance video placing McWilliams near the bank just after the robbery).

There are 6 exceptions to the 6 hour rule:

- **Medical attention.** The time required to treat the defendant's injuries does not count. *Comm. v. Vaida*, 2012 WL 516157 (Appeals Court).

- **Incapacitation.** If the arrestee is incapacitated due to drugs or alcohol, the 6 hour period commences at the point of sobriety. *Comm. v. Rosario*, 422 Mass. 48 (1996).

- **Emergency.** The time that officers spend away from the defendant during an unanticipated emergency (e.g., a natural disaster) does not count. *Comm. v. Powell*, 468 Mass. 272 (2014).

- **Consent search.** A police request for consent to search is outside this rule because it is not considered part of an interview. *Comm. v. Simpson*, 2011 WL 4581508 (Appeals Court).

- **Waiver.** The waiver is separate from *Miranda*. It must include the time when the defendant can be brought to court. *Comm. v. Morgan*, 460 Mass. 277 (2011). See model form page 22-38.

- **Out-of-state arrest.** *Comm. v. Morganti*, 455 Mass. 388 (2009) (murder arrest in California not covered by this rule when a trooper flew out to bring him back to Massachusetts).

MANDATORY RECORDING

All custodial interrogations _and_ any interrogation at the station must be recorded. This rule comes from *Comm. v. DiGiambattista*, 442 Mass. 423 (2004), which involved an arsonist who police tricked into confessing. In assessing whether his confession was voluntary, the SJC decided that most interrogations should be recorded: "Given the fine line between proper and improper interrogation techniques, the ability to reproduce the exact statements made during an interrogation is of the utmost benefit."

Here is how the *DiGiambattista Rule* works:

- **Stationhouse.** Most departments have a recording system for stationhouse interrogations. *DiGiambattista* is clear that any incriminating conversations at the station — even those where the suspect is not issued *Miranda* warnings — must be preserved.

- **Field custody.** *DiGiambattista* goes further by insisting that all custodial interrogations be recorded — regardless of where they take place. Unless officers are equipped with body-worn cameras (BWCs), compliance is challenging in the field.

  If a suspect is not in custody or interviewed at the station, police do *not* have to record. *Comm. v. Jones*, 75 Mass. App. Ct. 38 (2009) (defendant not in custody when interviewed about a murder at his workplace in the employees' lounge; no recording necessary).

- **Consequence.** The failure to comply with *DiGiambattista* results in the judge telling jurors that police testimony about an unrecorded statement should be "considered with great care." This cautionary instruction, while certainly not helpful, is less harmful than suppressing the defendant's statement altogether.[16]

---

16 The SJC remarked in support of its position: "Law enforcement officials who have chosen not . . . to preserve this critical evidence cannot complain that we have decided to highlight to juries the potential significance of that choice."

- **Explanation.** Officers should always try to record custodial and stationhouse interrogations, but they should not avoid interviewing just because they do not have a recording device available. *DiGiambattista* held that prosecutors may "address any reasons . . . why no recording was made." However, the jury instruction is mandated *regardless* of the reason — even if the defendant refused to be recorded! *Comm. v. Tavares*, 81 Mass. App. Ct. 71 (2012).

When practical, record any interrogation involving an interpreter. This will allow the court to fairly assess whether the accused received an accurate translation of police questions. *Comm. v. AdonSoto*, 475 Mass. 497 (2016).

As long as there is a conspicuous sign, officers do not have to inform a suspect that he is being recorded at the station. The reason why, according to *Comm. v. Ashley,* 82 Mass. App. Ct. 748 (2012), is that people today expect their statements will be recorded for court. The author recommends placing a sign on the entrance to the interview room and on the wall across from the door. Make each sign visible with letters at least 2" high. Suggested text:

> ## Attention
> **Any communication in this room is being video and audio recorded.**
> By order of the Chief of Police

Do not ask for permission to record. The best practice is to turn on the device and tell suspects they are being recorded. There is no need to ask for permission. *Comm. v. Alleyne*, 474 Mass. 771 (2016).

In the event that a suspect objects to being recorded, investigators should:

- **Emphasize that the recording is for protection.** Explain that a recording preserves this suspect's exact words and prevents investigators from later misinterpreting his comments. The vast majority of suspects will agree to continue. If a suspect still objects, then:

- **Agree to turn off the recorder after the suspect completes a *Miranda* waiver.** When officers record a suspect's adamant demand that they turn off the recording device — along with his *Miranda* waiver — they have proof that *he* chose to make an unrecorded statement. Officers may then document the suspect's statement in their report. *Comm. v. DaSilva*, 471 Mass. 71 (2015) (recording of refusal admissible so jury knows police followed proper procedures).

Record entire interview. "[T]here is a potential for abuse if the recorder is started and stopped . . . The [best] practice is to record the entire interview, including the defendant's silences and emotional outbursts." *Comm. v. Fernette*, 398 Mass. 658 (1986). This means investigators should not conduct unrecorded pre-interviews. The danger was highlighted in the Central Park jogger case. Four defendants, after long hours of unrecorded pre-interviews, falsely confessed to rape on videotape. We now know: The only way to learn if officers are employing suggestive techniques is to record the entire interview. Leo, R., *Bringing Reliability Back*, 2006 Wisconsin L. Rev. 479. *Comm. v. DiGiambattista*, 83 Mass. App. Ct. 180 (2013).

Explain <u>any time</u> the recorder is shut off. For example: "Okay, Detective Smith is going to shut off the recorder so that John Defendant may use the bathroom and eat lunch. It is 12:24 p.m. by my watch. [Tape is shut off . . . then turned on] We are now resuming the interview with John Defendant, who had a drink and sandwich for lunch. It is 1:15 p.m. and we are still located in the first-floor interview room of the Smalltown Police Department. So, John, we were talking about your visit to Andy Accomplice's house on October 10th . . . ."

Officers do <u>not</u> have to record certain interviews.

- **Nonsuspects** — especially when police have not yet decided that a crime occurred. *Comm. v. Issa*, 466 Mass. 1 (2013) (defendant showed up at the police station to talk to police about the victim's death two hours after her body was found; the police had not asked him to come and had not yet determined that her death was a homicide; no reason to record).

- **Intelligence gathering.** *DiGiambattista* intended for police to record statements that might be used in court against the accused. Sometimes officers seek information from criminals solely for intelligence or investigative purposes. A common example is the drug dealer who may implicate his supplier in exchange for leniency. In these situations, it is counterproductive and legally unnecessary to record.

HOW SUSPECTS INVOKE THEIR RIGHTS & OFFICERS MUST RESPOND
INVOCATION OF RIGHTS

Any reasonable expression of a suspect's wish to remain silent or be represented by counsel <u>invokes</u> his rights. The term "invoke" means "to use or apply."[17]

RIGHT TO REMAIN SILENT

A suspect may verbally or nonverbally invoke his right to silence. *Comm. v. Hearns*, 467 Mass. 707 (2014) (after *Miranda* warnings, Hearns said, "Well then, I don't want to talk, I haven't got nothing to say"). *Comm. v. Clarke*, 461 Mass. 336 (2012) (negative head shake invoked Clarke's right to silence).

In an investigation, when the suspect hears Miranda warnings for the <u>first time</u>, the police should not require that he invoke silence with "the utmost clarity." *Comm. v. Clarke, supra.*: After reading the *Miranda* rights from a form, a detective asked Brandon Clarke whether he wanted to talk about an indecent assault on the subway. Clarke, who was upset and nervous, "shook his head back and forth in a negative fashion." Another detective chimed in: "If you don't want to speak, we're going to end this and put you back in the cell." Clarke eventually confessed.

The interview should have stopped because Clarke's gesture asserted his right to silence. Instead, police told him the consequences of not speaking (back in the cell) which jarred him into talking.

---

17 *American Heritage Dictionary* (Houghton Mifflin, 4th Office Edition).

In these situations, Article 14 requires that police give the accused the benefit of the doubt and stop the interview.[18] Even if detectives believed that the meaning behind the head shake was unclear, they could only ask one follow up question, such as: "Mr. Clarke, I saw you shake your head, does that mean you do not want to talk to us?"

On the other hand, "heightened clarity" is expected when a suspect wants to stop his interrogation _after_ he already waived his rights and answered questions.

- **Expressing reluctance.** *Comm. v. Costa,* 414 Mass. 618 (1993): Toward the end of a three hour interrogation, in which Costa flip-flopped about his whereabouts during a murder, he said: "I don't want to be a canary . . . I won't squeal on my friends." He then confessed. While Costa might have been reluctant to talk, he never invoked his right to silence. *Comm. v. Durand,* 475 Mass. 657 (2016) (defendant's statements — "I can't take any more of this" and "I want to go home and go to bed" — were too ambiguous to show his unwillingness to continue with the interrogation).

  Compare *Comm. v. Neves,* 474 Mass. 355 (2016): One hour into his interview, Adilson Neves said, "I don't feel like talking, man. I just, I just want to see my mom, dog." Rather than seek to clarify the statement, the officers asked if he told his mom what happened. After several more requests to see his mother, Neves said, "I'm done, I'm done talking now." The officers continued to question him. Neves' first statement, "I don't feel like talking," might not have been sufficiently clear to invoke his right to silence. But his later statements were crystal clear. Police should have stopped questioning at least when Neves said that he was "done talking now."

- **Selectively answering questions.** In *Comm. v. Roberts,* 407 Mass. 731 (1990) the defendant would say, for example, "I don't wish to comment on that one," but then answer other questions posed by the police. This was not a request to remain silent after his initial waiver.

  Compare *Comm. v. Howard,* 469 Mass. 721 (2014): Clyde Howard was read his *Miranda* rights in connection with a murder. He signed a waiver. But once the conversation focused on his prior relationship with the victim, Howard said: "I would like to stop at this point because it becomes intricate now and who knows what's going to happen." The detective improperly continued. Nothing suggested Howard was limiting his silence to any particular topic.

- **Staying silent.** Silence may indicate that a suspect has decided to invoke his right, *or* that he wishes to collect his thoughts. That is why, when a suspect is silent in response to a question after already agreeing to talk, the investigator should ask a follow-up question, such as: "Do you need more time to think?" or "Did you understand my question?" Typically, the suspect will respond in a way that indicates he is still willing to talk.

---

18 This is not to say that the police may never use their judgment and proceed. For example, in *Comm. v. Rodriguez,* 67 Mass. App. Ct. 636 (2006), Rodriguez was arrested for drug trafficking and, after hearing his *Miranda* rights, he said: "If you think I am going to cooperate, don't waste your time. You chose to be a cop, that's your job. I chose my job, I will do my time." While his statement implied that Rodriguez would not help the police implicate his suppliers or accomplices, it was certainly not an invocation of his right to silence. After this "opening statement," he quickly waived his rights and incriminated himself. The Appeals Court approved.

- *Comm. v. Sicari*, 434 Mass. 732 (2001): The defendant waived his *Miranda* rights. In the middle of the interview, he was confronted with evidence. He did not answer questions for 30 minutes. After this period of silence, the defendant talked about his involvement in the kidnapping and murder. The delay did not constitute a request to remain silent; it reflected the defendant's emotional realization that he had been caught.

- *Comm. v. Leahy*, 445 Mass. 481 (2005): Paul Leahy stabbed a woman to death in a bathroom at a highway rest stop. Arrested on scene, he was twice informed of his *Miranda* rights. At the station, when the officer asked Leahy if he wanted to speak, he replied, "Not right now, in a minute. I need to figure some things out." This response was not an assertion of his right to silence. After waiting for twenty minutes, the trooper said: "When you need to figure things out, it's good to talk to somebody else." Leahy agreed, then confessed. The trooper's statement about the value of talking was permissible.

RIGHT TO COUNSEL

Police never have to seek a waiver from a suspect who appears with his attorney. *Comm. v. Simon*, 456 Mass. 280 (2010) (it makes little sense to warn someone about his legal rights in front of his attorney).

Pre-custodial request

Police do not have to honor, but should clarify, a suspect's <u>pre-custody</u> request for a lawyer. *Comm. v. Molina*, 467 Mass. 65 (2014): After a shooting, police asked Alex Molina if he would come to the station. Trooper Serrano interviewed him in a small, windowless room. The interview was conducted mostly in Spanish and videotaped.

Serrano provided *Miranda* warnings. When asked if he would talk, Molina said, "Whatever you say" and signed the waiver form.[19] Serrano asked general questions. Molina started to get nervous when the questions got more targeted. He said: "[I]f I had known [it] would be like this, I would have brought an attorney because I truly don't even know what happened." Serrano told Molina they already knew about the shooting, so if he lied, he would look suspicious. Molina continued to talk and was eventually charged.

When Molina mentioned counsel, he clearly was not in custody for *Miranda*. The fact that Serrano read Molina his rights did *not* mean he was in custody. After all, Molina had voluntarily come to the station, and the questioning was conversational, not aggressive. At the point he mentioned a lawyer, the SJC held that Molina did not have a *right* to counsel.[20]

---

19 Serrano should have followed this comment with a statement like: "No, it's not what I think. It is totally up to you to decide whether to give up your rights." The court still found the waiver was voluntary.
20 The SJC did leave the door open that it might require, in a future case, that police honor a defendant's pre-custodial request for a lawyer, in the same way that *Miranda* now requires that they honor a post-custodial request for counsel.

The lessons of *Molina* are that officers should:

- **Never downplay a citizen's need for counsel** *unless* there is *no* probability that the person will become a suspect; and

- **Clarify any ambiguous, pre-custodial requests for counsel.** In *Molina*, the ideal dialogue between investigator and suspect would have been:

  Molina: "Hey, you asked me to come down here and I'm answering your questions. But I honestly would have brought my attorney if I'd known it would be like this."

  Serrano: "You are free to call an attorney or to leave our interview. I'm just asking you some questions. Why does it bother you that I'd want to know about the shooting yesterday? You work near there, don't you?"

  Notice how an investigator has much more latitude to *encourage* a pre-custodial suspect to keep talking after he mentions the possibility of counsel. Compare *Molina* with the strict limitation in *Comm. v. Santos*, 463 Mass. 273 (2012), discussed in the next section.

Post-custodial request

To get a valid waiver, officers do not have to explicitly ask a suspect if he wants a lawyer. *Comm. v. Bui*, 419 Mass. 392 (1995) (defendant understood *Miranda* warnings provided in English and Vietnamese; while officers did not specifically ask if he wanted a lawyer, the defendant understood that he was entitled to one, which was sufficient).

A suspect's <u>attempt to contact his attorney</u> invokes his right to counsel. *Comm. v. Russell*, 2013 WL 373861 (Appeals Court): Joshua Russell hit the victim with a golf club. At the station, he signed a *Miranda* waiver and told Officer Botelho that he wanted to call his lawyer. Russell made several unsuccessful calls. Trooper Clements then brought Russell into an interview room and gave him another *Miranda* waiver. Russell told Clements he was trying to get in touch with his lawyer. Clements asked, "Having all your rights in mind, do you want to talk to us now?" Russell made a statement.

The problem: Russell had already invoked his right to counsel when he asked to call his attorney. He did not have to also request that his interview be delayed until he spoke with her.[21]

A suspect's <u>reasonable expression</u> of his desire for counsel works too.

- **Current desire sufficient.** *Comm. v. Hooks*, 38 Mass. App. Ct. 301 (1995): The defendant requested a lawyer when he inquired, "Didn't you just tell me that I have the right to have a lawyer present?" The detective responded, "Absolutely. Positively." To which the defendant said, "Well, let's get a lawyer, 'cause I don't understand exactly . . . ." Since this was a clear statement of his desire for a lawyer, continued questioning was improper.

---

21 One could argue that *Comm. v. DiMuro*, 28 Mass. App. Ct. 223 (1990) supports what the officers did in the *Russell* case. That said, officers should abide by the conservative approach demanded by *Russell*.

Comm. v. Segovia, 53 Mass. App. Ct. 184 (2001): The defendant, whose English proficiency was limited, received *Miranda* warnings. He told the officer that he needed a translator and asked to consult with a friend "who was an American and a paralegal." The court held that the officer should have understood this as a request for counsel.

- **Future desire insufficient.** In *Comm. v. Durand*, 475 Mass. 657 (2016), the defendant told police: "I am going to have to get a lawyer. Everything is going to come down on me!" The police properly continued to question him. An accused who says he *might* seek counsel is not the same as one who says he *wants* counsel.

Even a suspect's concern about affording a lawyer invokes his right to counsel.

- **Improper.** *Comm. v. Hoyt*, 461 Mass. 143 (2011): At the station, one detective asked Hoyt if he would speak. Hoyt said, "I'd like an attorney . . . but I can't afford one. So I guess I'll just speak to you." The detective said, "We don't get you an attorney, we can let you use the phone, but it's up to you." Hoyt said, "I'll just talk to you." He signed the waiver.

  Hoyt's statement, "I'd like an attorney," was unambiguous. His difficulty was paying for one. When a suspect invokes his right to counsel but says he cannot afford counsel, this does not make the request unclear. The officers should have stopped.

- **Proper.** *Comm. v. Jones*, 439 Mass. 249 (2003): After waiving his *Miranda* rights, Paul Jones denied his involvement in a murder. When the detective told him that two accomplices had implicated him, Jones said that he was "going to need a lawyer sometime." The detective responded that Jones was entitled to a lawyer and that there was an assistant district attorney down the hall who could get him one. Jones said that he had no money and could not afford one. The detective told him that he did not need any money because the state would provide counsel. Jones looked at the detective and "shook his head in the negative." He then confessed. This dialogue was completely adequate to learn whether the defendant really wanted counsel.

While an ambiguous statement may invoke the right to counsel, police should typically ask one follow-up question to clarify the request. *Comm. v. Santos,* 463 Mass. 273 (2012): Police decided to interview William Santos about a shooting near a pharmacy. They arrested him on an unrelated warrant and brought him to the station. Santos signed a *Miranda* waiver. After being questioned for 45 minutes, mostly about whether a man named Lou had borrowed a certain vehicle, Santos said: "You ask Lou that. I'm not going on with this conversation. I want a lawyer, because — ask Lou that."

The detective left the room and returned in three minutes. He said: "Earlier . . . you said you wanted a lawyer . . . it's the car that was bothering you." Santos replied: "No, I'm willing to talk to you, but you keep pushing this on me." The detective added: "You do not have to talk to us, okay. I don't know if it was a situation where you just got confused and you were upset with that line of questioning." Santos then agreed to answer questions about other topics without an attorney. He was given another round of *Miranda* warnings and signed a waiver.

The problem — from the SJC's perspective — was that the detective's questions were not designed to clarify Santos' rights. They were *really designed* to keep him talking by promising not to discuss the car. His statements were suppressed. The important lesson for officers:

- **When uncertain about whether a suspect invoked his rights, ask *one question* to clarify his intent.** For example, a detective should ask: "Are you requesting to speak with an attorney right now?" If a suspect says, "Yeah," the conversation is over. Period. If a suspect, like Santos, adds, "Well, if you keep talking about the car," only then may a detective respond, "I won't mention the car anymore; do you still want a lawyer?"

- **A suspect *never* has to give a reason for requesting silence or an attorney.** *Comm. v. Thomas*, 469 Mass. 531 (2014) (detective should not have challenged arson defendant's request for counsel — "Things are gonna get hotter . . . you already lawyered up"). Also see *Comm. v. Vargas*, 475 Mass. 388 (2016).

Police may get a waiver from a suspect who only requests counsel for the limited purpose of making a written statement. *Comm. v. Santana*, 465 Mass. 270 (2013): Ramon Santana was arrested in New Jersey in connection with a double murder. Trooper Beaupre read *Miranda* warnings. When Beaupre asked if he would speak, Santana said, "I'll talk, but I'm not signing anything without a lawyer." Beaupre asked Santana to sign the waiver. Santana remarked, "I'm not signing anything else." He answered questions for several hours. This was proper.

Police response to attorney contact

The police must immediately tell a suspect that his attorney is trying to contact him _and_ recommends that he not talk to police. *Comm. v. McNulty*, 458 Mass. 305 (2010).[22]

- **This rule only applies to an attorney.** The police have no obligation to inform a suspect that a third party intends to retain legal counsel. *Comm. v. Nelson*, 55 Mass. App. Ct. 911 (2002) (defendant's uncle told arresting officer that defendant's mother was arranging for a lawyer for her son; officer did not have to relay this information to the defendant).

- **Attorney may contact police in person or over the telephone.** The duty to inform applies whether the attorney telephones or arrives at the station.

- **Police should verify that the individual is an attorney.** Here is a suggested protocol: "Counsel, I must verify some information. Where is your office located? What is your BBO number?" The last question is essential because any attorney in Massachusetts will know that BBO stands for "Board of Bar Overseers," the agency that registers attorneys and provides ID numbers. When attorneys arrive at the station, insist on seeing their "bar card." Attorneys get a new one each year from the SJC. This is a reasonable screening process. Attorneys cannot later claim it was designed to delay their client contact.

- **Notification must be immediate.** *Comm. v. McNulty, supra.* (police must inform suspect immediately; here, the booking officer did not tell the attorney his client was at the station and sent his call into voicemail; when the attorney called back, he was referred to another officer, who gave counsel yet another number for a sergeant).

- **Suspect decides whether to speak with attorney.** If the suspect wants help, police must suspend questioning until a meeting occurs or until a *reasonable* amount of time passes.

---

22 *McNulty* conflicts with federal law, which holds that police are not required to notify a suspect of his attorney's request to communicate. *Moran v. Burbine*, 475 U.S. 412 (1986).

- **Burden on police to prove defendant refused to consult with counsel.** Since the police will already be recording the interview (remember the *DiGiambattista* rule), the suspect's response should be on tape.

The defendant decides whether to speak with his attorney. *Comm. v. Vao Sok*, 435 Mass. 743 (2002): Vao Sok murdered a five year old girl. His appointed attorney spoke with the officer administering a polygraph. The attorney requested that the polygraph and all questioning cease. The officer honestly informed Vao Sok of his attorney's wishes but said that it was his choice. The defendant agreed to continue and ultimately confessed. The SJC affirmed Vao Sok's conviction and commended the professionalism of the investigator.

The defendant may still choose to speak after he meets with counsel. *Comm. v. Hoose*, 467 Mass. 395 (2014): Robin Hoose stabbed two people after a night of cocaine use. Three days later he voluntarily went to the station. At one point, counsel arrived. A detective told Hoose, and he met privately with his lawyer.

While leaving, the attorney told police that Hoose had been instructed not to answer any questions. Afterwards, a detective asked Hoose how he wanted to proceed. Hoose said he wanted to talk with Detective Laster, whom he trusted. Laster read Hoose his rights, but Hoose was concerned that his attorney might be angry. Another detective said: "Well, ultimately, you're your own boss." Hoose waived his rights and confessed. Once his lawyer left, the detective did nothing wrong by asking Hoose how he wanted to proceed.

The rule concerning attorney contact does not apply in certain situations.

- **Officers need not inform a suspect about past conversations.** *Comm. v. Collins*, 440 Mass. 475 (2003): Once Collins learned he was the target of a sexual abuse investigation, he retained counsel. The lawyer said he wanted to be present at any interview. Scheduling difficulties with this attorney prompted the detective to go out and arrest Collins. The detective did not need to tell Collins about his lawyer's wishes in order to obtain a valid *Miranda* waiver. It was the attorney's obligation to speak with his client about that.

- **Officers do not have to report that an attorney ordered them to be silent.** An attorney can expect that police will communicate his recommendation that his client stay silent, but not that police will abide by his directive! The former is legal advice; the latter attempts to invoke the client's right to silence. *Comm. v. Martin*, 467 Mass. 291 (2014) (detectives were not bound by an attorney's instructions in a letter; they properly informed the defendant about his attorney's desire to be present; the defendant properly decided to sign a waiver).

- **Officers are not expected to volunteer information.** *Comm. v. Phinney*, 416 Mass. 364 (1993): Phinney voluntarily accompanied detectives to the station. He was repeatedly told that he could leave. He waived his *Miranda* rights. During the interview, Phinney's attorney called. The detectives did not mention that Phinney was being interviewed because the attorney only asked about whether the police were thinking of searching his client's home. Investigators did not tell Phinney about his lawyer's call before he confessed to murder. Because the lawyer did not specifically ask about Phinney's whereabouts or whether he was being interrogated, the police had no obligation to volunteer this information.

PROPER RESPONSE TO INVOCATION OF RIGHTS

Once a suspect invokes his right to silence and/or counsel, authorities must immediately terminate any interrogation. *Comm. v. Smith*, 473 Mass. 798 (2016).

A defendant's post-arrest decision to stay silent or talk with an attorney is inadmissible at trial. *Comm. v. DePace*, 433 Mass. 379 (2001) declared: "The right to counsel would be of little value if the price for its exercise was the risk of an inference of guilt." There are three exceptions to this rule: (1) the defendant, at trial, claims to have told police, at the time of his arrest, the story he is testifying to; (2) evidence of the defendant's request to speak with an attorney is needed to explain why the police interview ended abruptly because, at trial, the defendant suggests that his statement ended because of police incompetence or misconduct; and (3) the defendant is relying on an insanity defense, where evidence of his post-arrest silence is being introduced as part of his trial strategy. *Comm. v. Letkowski*, 469 Mass. 603 (2014).

Once a suspect validly waives his Miranda rights, the police may question him until he expressly states that he wants an attorney or does not wish to talk anymore. *Comm. v. Pennellatore*, 392 Mass. 382 (1984).

POTENTIAL TO RESUME QUESTIONING

RIGHT TO SILENCE

When a suspect invokes his right to remain silent, police are not automatically prohibited from later questioning. In *Michigan v. Mosley*, 423 U.S. 96 (1975), the defendant was arrested for robbery and exercised his right to remain silent. The interrogation stopped. Over two hours later, another officer re-advised the defendant of his rights and questioned him about a different crime.[23] The defendant confessed. The Supreme Court held that the second interrogation was lawful because the police:

* "Scrupulously honored" the suspect's right to remain silent when first exercised;

* Began the second interrogation after a significant time lapse; and

* Properly advised the suspect of his *Miranda* warnings before both interrogations.

Police must honor the suspect's initial silence. *Comm. v. Rankins*, 429 Mass. 470 (1999): State Police detectives interviewed Alex Rankins about a murder. Rankins became upset and said he did not want to talk any longer. Rankins said that his mind was "blown," and he would let investigators know the next day if he would continue. Questioning stopped. The next evening, investigators returned and provided *Miranda* warnings. Rankins made incriminating statements. The police properly honored his silence each time.

---

23 While the investigators in *Mosley* discussed a different crime when they re-approached the defendant, this was not central to the Supreme Court's decision and does not seem to be required in Massachusetts. *Comm. v. Santo*, 375 Mass. 299 (1978): The Springfield police honored the defendant's decision not to discuss his involvement in a murder. At the time he invoked his right to silence, he was being held in Connecticut. The next day, officers re-advised him of his rights in Springfield. Santo waived his rights and talked about the murder (the *same offense* that had been the subject of his earlier refusal). The SJC approved.

Only re-approach defendant after a 2 hour interval. The SJC has never specified a minimum time period, although a two hour interval was approved in *Michigan v. Mosley.* 35 minutes was far too short in *Comm. v. Callender*, 81 Mass. App. Ct. 153 (2012).

The suspect must be properly advised of his rights each time. *Comm. v. Fortunato*, 466 Mass. 500 (2013). *Comm. v. Jordan*, 2018 WL 1770243 (Appeals Court) (police did it right: Jordan invoked silence with original detective, but said he would talk to one he knew and liked; that detective arrived three hours later; Jordan was re-advised of his rights, signed a waiver, and spoke freely).

Once suspect released, officers may immediately try to question him. The waiting period only applies while a suspect remains in custody. *Comm. v. Lopes*, 455 Mass. 147 (2009) (defendant exercised his right to silence at the police station; when officers removed his handcuffs and told him that he was not under arrest and free to leave, they properly conversed with him; the defendant's voluntary responses were admissible).

RIGHT TO COUNSEL

Stop interrogation until counsel available. *Edwards v. Arizona*, 451 U.S. 477 (1981) created a clear rule for law enforcement. Once a suspect invokes his right to counsel under *Miranda*:

- **Stop interrogation.** The current interrogation must stop; and

- **Make counsel available.** The suspect may not be approached for further interrogation until counsel has been made available to him.

The Supreme Court adopted this rule "to prevent police from badgering a defendant into waiving his previously asserted *Miranda* rights."[24]

The Edwards rule is <u>not</u> offense specific. Once a suspect invokes his right to counsel regarding one offense, he may not be re-approached regarding any other offense unless counsel is present. *Minnick v. Mississippi*, 498 U.S. 146 (1990).

The Edwards rule applies as long as the suspect remains in custody. *Comm. v. Perez*, 411 Mass. 249 (1991): Norman Perez was arrested in Puerto Rico for a murder he committed in Lowell. Interviewed by a state trooper in Puerto Rico, Perez invoked his right to counsel. Questioning stopped. Six months later he returned to Lowell. Detectives there re-advised him of his rights and obtained an incriminating statement following his waiver. His remarks were inadmissible because Perez did not have the chance to see a lawyer. Since Perez was still in custody, the passage of time did not alter his right to counsel. It did not matter that he was approached by two separate police departments six months apart.

Only three exceptions to Edwards.

- **First, a defendant's statement is admissible in response to notification about a police procedure.** *U.S. v. Zephier*, 989 F.3d 629 (8th Cir. 2021): An FBI agent and a tribal investigator sought to interview Xavier Zephier in jail about an allegation of sexual assault. After hearing *Miranda* warnings, Zephier said he would not make a statement until after he had

---

24 The *Edwards* rule is different from the rule governing a subject who invokes his right to remain silent, because that person may be re-interrogated following a suitable interval. *Michigan v. Mosley, supra.*

seen a lawyer. The investigators accepted his response and moved on to the second piece of business. They served a search warrant for a DNA sample from Zephier's cheek. As Special Agent Mertz explained the warrant and its procedure, Zephier insisted on making a statement. Zephier chose to explain his relationship to the victim and comment that he had previously been accused of rape.

- **Second, if a defendant *initiates* conversation, police may resume questioning following a new waiver.** Asking about routine matters (e.g., requesting a meal or phone call) does not qualify. *Comm. v. Sanchez*, 476 Mass. 725 (2017) (day after invoking his right to counsel, Sanchez told an officer performing a routine cell check that he wanted to speak to detectives without a lawyer; there was no violation because he initiated the contact and waived his *Miranda* rights again). *Comm. v. Gonzalez*, 487 Mass. 661 (2021).

  In *Comm. v. D'Entremont*, 36 Mass. App. Ct. 474 (1994), the investigator informed a rape suspect, who had invoked his right to counsel, that she was willing to speak with him if he changed his mind. The defendant later said that he wanted to tell his side of the story and admitted to engaging in intercourse with the victim. The detective's statement of her availability was proper. It was simple and nonconfrontational. The detective re-advised him of his rights, secured a waiver, and interviewed him without a lawyer present.

- **Third, at least 14 days after the defendant is freed from custody, the police may approach him and seek a new waiver.** Requiring that police observe a 14 day buffer ensures "plenty of time for the suspect to get reacclimated to his normal life, to consult with his friends and counsel, and to shake off any residual coercive effects of his prior custody." *Comm. v. Thomas*, 469 Mass. 531 (2014) adopting the rule in *Maryland v. Shatzer*, 559 U.S. 98 (2010).

CONSEQUENCES OF A *MIRANDA* VIOLATION

Any statement or physical evidence obtained in violation of Miranda will be suppressed. *Comm. v. Martin*, 444 Mass. 213 (2005). However, even though police violate a suspect's *Miranda* rights, they may still be able to offer a later, properly obtained statement if:

- **There was a break in the stream of events.** This means there was a break in time that insulated the second statement from the tainted original; or

- **The cat was not out of the bag.** This means the initial statement did not incriminate the defendant, so at the time of the later statement, any incriminating information was new.

"Break in stream of events" case. *Comm. v. Prater*, 420 Mass. 569 (1995): 19 year old Charles Prater admitted to ax murdering his friend while very drunk and high. The court found he did not voluntarily waive his *Miranda* warnings before his initial confession. Prater was so intoxicated, he even misspelled his name on the waiver.

The court did rule that a second, videotaped confession was admissible. It was not tainted by the first one because: (1) almost three hours passed so the effect of the drugs and alcohol had worn off; (2) Prater got to telephone his mother; (3) in the video, Prater calmly and clearly described what he did; (4) this confession was motivated by his guilty conscience, not police pressure; and (5) Prater spelled his name correctly on the second waiver form. In short, Prater's second confession came after a significant break in the stream of events.

"Cat not out of the bag" case. *Comm. v. Larkin,* 429 Mass. 426 (1999): Police issued *Miranda* warnings 10 minutes too late because Larkin was already in custody. However, Larkin admitted nothing in the initial 10 minutes. In fact, he spent most of the time asking questions, and the troopers gave accurate answers that enhanced his understanding of his situation. Although he technically should have received warnings earlier, Larkin was not prejudiced by the oversight since he did not implicate himself — i.e., the cat was not out of the bag. His later *Miranda* waiver and confession were proper for this reason.

_____ **Police Department**

I, _____ (full name), am _____ (age) years

old. I was born on _____ (date of birth). Officer

_____ (full name) is advising me of my constitutional

rights. I understand that:

- I have the right to remain silent.

- If I choose to speak, anything I say may be used against me in court.

- I have the right to consult with a lawyer before answering any questions, and I can have him or her with me during questioning.

- If I cannot afford a lawyer and want one, a lawyer will be provided by the Commonwealth before questioning — at no cost to me.

- I may answer questions now and waive (that means, give up) my right to counsel and my right to remain silent.

- If I decide to talk to the police, I still have the right to stop talking at any time and for any reason.

Please check one:

I ____ am willing to speak with the police officer now.

I ____ am **not** willing to speak with the police officer now.

_____   _____   _____
Signature of Citizen   Time   Date

_____   _____   _____
Signature of Police Officer   Time   Date

_____ **Police Department**

I, _____ (full name), am _____ (age) years

old. I was born on _____ (date of birth). Officer

_____ (full name) is advising me of my constitutional

rights. I understand that:

- **I have the right to remain silent.**

- **If I choose to speak, anything I say may be used against me in court.**

- **I have the right to consult with a lawyer before answering any questions, and I can have him or her with me during questioning.**

- **If I cannot afford a lawyer and want one, a lawyer will be provided by the Commonwealth before questioning — at no cost to me.**

- **I may answer questions now and waive (that means, give up) my right to counsel and my right to remain silent.**

- **If I decide to talk to the police, I still have the right to stop talking at any time and for any reason.**

_____ (name of adult), who is my

_____ (relationship to you), is present and will

help me decide whether to waive my rights and speak with the police.

Please check one:

        I ____ **am willing to speak with the police officer now.**

        I ____ **am not willing to speak with the police officer now.**

Signature of Juvenile	Time	Date

My signature indicates that I also understand these rights completely:

Signature of Interested Adult	Time	Date

Signature of Police Officer	Time	Date

_____ **Police Department**

I, _____ (full name), am _____ (age) years old.   I   was   born   on   _____ (date of birth).   Officer _____ (full name) is advising me of my right to limit the length of my interview.

I understand that the law prohibits a police officer from interviewing me for longer than 6 hours after I am arrested. The purpose of this rule is to prevent the police from delaying my appearance in court. This rule takes effect after any arrest at any time of day or night.

I   also   understand   that   the   earliest   I   can   be   brought   by   the   police   to   the _____ (name of court) for arraignment is _____ a.m./p.m. (circle one) on _____ (date).

Now that I have this information, I have chosen to allow the police to speak with me beyond the 6 hour time limit. The police did not pressure me to continue this interview.

_____   _____   _____
Signature of Citizen   Time   Date

_____   _____   _____
Signature of Police Officer   Time   Date

Right to Counsel
Under Article 12

RIGHT TO COUNSEL EXISTS UPON INDICTMENT OR ARRAIGNMENT

The Fifth Amendment right to counsel applies whenever a suspect is subjected to custodial interrogation — whether or not he has been formally charged with a crime. The application of the Fifth Amendment and *Miranda* was the subject of the previous chapter.

In contrast, the Article 12 right to counsel prevents police interference with an accused's legal defense — whether or not the defendant is in custody. That is why, in Massachusetts, the protection of Article 12 springs into existence "at and after arraignment or indictment by the grand jury." *Comm. v. Smallwood*, 379 Mass. 878 (1980) (only arraignment or indictment qualifies; the fact that the defendant is the subject of a complaint or arrest warrant does not trigger Article 12 rights).[1]

SCOPE OF RIGHT TO COUNSEL

A violation of Article 12 occurs when the police, by themselves or through an agent, deliberately obtain incriminating remarks about a defendant's <u>pending</u> charges.

STATE ACTION

The right to counsel may only be breached by law enforcement officials or their agents. When the defendant makes incriminating statements to someone with no police connection, Article 12 does not apply. *Comm. v. Silanskas*, 433 Mass. 678 (2001): Newspaper reporter could not breach the defendant's right to counsel when he interviewed him at the Plymouth House of Correction awaiting trial. The reporter had no connection to law enforcement.

OFFENSE SPECIFIC

Article 12 only offers "offense specific" protection. This means the prohibition against questioning *only extends* to offenses for which the defendant has been arraigned or indicted. A suspect may still be interrogated about unrelated offenses. *Comm. v. Chase*, 42 Mass. App. Ct. 749 (1997) (while the defendant was being held for armed robbery, police interrogated him concerning an unrelated truck larceny; with respect to the uncharged truck incident, the defendant lacked an Article 12 right to counsel, so his *Miranda* waiver at the jail was valid).

---

1 The Sixth Amendment right to counsel used to afford the same protection as Article 12, but the U.S. Supreme Court greatly restricted its scope in *Montejo v. Louisiana*, 129 S.Ct. 2079 (2009). At the time, the Massachusetts Appeals Court hinted that it might jettison Article 12 and adopt the Supreme Court's position someday. *Comm. v. Tlasek (No. 1)*, 77 Mass. App. Ct. 298 (2010).

In *Comm. v. Rainwater*, 425 Mass. 540 (1997), Arthur Rainwater was arrested for a stolen car. Following his arraignment, Rainwater was approached at the jail by a detective. Rainwater waived his *Miranda* rights and proceeded to tell the detective about other car thefts he had perpetrated. The confessions were properly obtained, even without his attorney present, because they did not deal with the pending stolen car case. However, the SJC warned officers not to discuss topics that are "inextricably intertwined" with pending charges. In other words, if uncharged and pending offenses stem from the same event, then a police-initiated discussion is out of bounds without the defendant's lawyer present.

POTENTIAL VIOLATIONS OF THE RIGHT TO COUNSEL

IMPROPER POLICE CONDUCT

Direct communication

In Massachusetts, once the accused asserts his right to counsel, all interrogation concerning charged offenses must stop. Although it has been rejected by the U.S. Supreme Court,[2] Massachusetts retains a "bright line" rule to protect defendants:

- **Arraignment.** If a defendant asserts his right to an attorney at his arraignment;

- **Absolute bar.** The police are absolutely barred from initiating an interrogation;

- **Unless counsel present.** Unless counsel is made available;

- **Automatic suppression.** A waiver of counsel that violates this rule is invalid, and the resulting statement will be suppressed.

Police should never listen to attorney/client communication in the lockup. Sight monitoring is permissible, but listening is illegal and unethical. *Comm. v. Fontaine*, 402 Mass. 491 (1988) (charges pending against the defendant were dismissed because the police electronically intercepted privileged communications between him and his lawyer).

Police should not "bad mouth" a defense attorney. In *Comm. v. Manning*, 373 Mass. 438 (1977), the police knew that the defendant had legal representation, but spoke to him about his pending drug case. They criticized his attorney and encouraged the defendant to become an informant. This misconduct was so blatant, all charges were dismissed.

Police should not offer to intervene in a pending case. Police may not offer to help a defendant resolve *pending charges* without consulting defense counsel or receiving a valid waiver of counsel. This is true even in situations where the police are offering a deal that is clearly in the defendant's interest. *Comm. v. Carlson*, 17 Mass. App. Ct. 52 (1983) (police would resolve the defendant's gun case with no jail for information concerning their arson case).

---

2 In *Montejo v. Louisiana*, 556 U.S. 778 (2009), the Supreme Court overruled *Michigan v. Jackson*, 475 U.S. 625 (1986), declaring that *Miranda* warnings adequately protect both the Fifth and Sixth Amendment rights to counsel. It no longer prohibited all post-arraignment interviews about pending charges.

Use of an informant

For an informant to become an agent, the government must <u>solicit</u> his cooperation. The fact that an individual initiates contact with police, chooses to cooperate, and is later rewarded, does *not* make him an agent — so long as he was initially promised nothing for his assistance. *Comm. v. Harmon*, 410 Mass. 425 (1991) (inmate volunteered to provide information to a detective he knew; the detective simply said: "Keep your ears open"; this comment expressed the investigator's willingness to listen in the future, but it did not turn the prisoner into his agent; it was irrelevant that the prisoner later received a reduction in sentence because the benefit had not been promised or even implied up front).

An investigator or prosecutor violates Article 12 by recruiting a jailhouse informant — even if the informant is not told to target any particular individual. *Comm. v. Murphy*, 448 Mass. 452 (2007): Frederick Murphy was in jail awaiting trial. An inmate did favors for him (hid his "shank" and tried to bribe a witness in his case). The inmate was actually an informant who got Murphy to admit his role in the murder ("I was angry, so I licked that drug dealer"). The SJC found Murphy's right to counsel was violated because the informant had an agreement with the U.S. Attorney that he would receive a lesser sentence for information. Such open-ended deals risk encouraging a jailhouse snitch to seek out, and even fabricate, confessions.

The fact that an informant served as a government agent in the past does not mean that he remains one in the future. *Comm. v. Caruso*, 476 Mass. 275 (2017) (jailhouse informant was not an agent in this case, even though he had provided information in two prior murder cases; there was no evidence the government asked for his help or put him and defendant Caruso in the same cell in order to elicit information; as a result, the informant could testify that Caruso admitted he sent the pipe bomb that killed the waitress).

PROPER POLICE CONDUCT

If the accused <u>independently</u> decides to speak with police, officers may obtain an Article 12 waiver. *Comm. v. Torres*, 442 Mass. 554 (2004) involved a mother of three children and her boyfriend. Over several months, her boyfriend (defendant Torres) beat the children, eventually killing the baby. Torres was held at the house of correction on an unrelated matter.

The prosecutor dispatched troopers to the jail with instructions to serve the murder indictment *without* questioning Torres. Upon arrival, troopers told Torres he had been indicted. Torres interrupted, saying that he had not hit the kids. A trooper read Torres his *Miranda* warnings and told him that he knew Torres had a lawyer. The trooper suggested that Torres not say anything. Torres said he wanted to speak. The trooper reminded him that he had a lawyer, but Torres insisted. The trooper read the *Miranda* rights a second time. Torres gave a statement — at one point crying about what happened to the baby. When asked to reduce his statement to writing, Torres refused because his attorney had directed him not to sign anything.

- **Article 12 in play.** Torres' indictment triggered his Article 12 right to counsel.

- **Waiver possible.** The SJC found Torres' waiver valid: "Nothing . . . prevents a suspect charged with a crime and represented by counsel from voluntarily choosing, on his own, to speak with police in the absence of an attorney. . . Although a defendant may later regret his decision, [Article 12] does not disable a criminal defendant from exercising his free will." *Miranda* warnings, although devised to inform suspects of their Fifth Amendment rights, are sufficient for this purpose.

- **This was defendant-initiated, not police-initiated.** In *Torres,* the troopers did not tell the defendant that they came to discuss his case. On the contrary, officers advised him not to speak and gave *Miranda* warnings twice. *Comm. v. Anderson,* 448 Mass. 548 (2007) (at the defendant's request, a detective visited him in a Maine prison to hear his confession about a Massachusetts murder; the detective showed him a letter from his newly appointed attorney advising him not to speak with police; even so, he confessed; this was acceptable).

IMPROPER CONDUCT BY OTHER OFFICIALS

Other government officials, not just police officers, are prohibited from speaking with the accused about a pending case.

- *Comm. v. Hilton,* 443 Mass. 597 (2005): After Kathleen Hilton's arraignment, a court officer asked her whether she really burned down the building and killed five people. She admitted it. Court officers are considered law enforcement agents and may not talk to prisoners about their cases. This rule is essential, since court officers regularly interact with defendants without counsel present. The right to counsel will be seriously diluted if court officers can, on their own initiative, question defendants and turn over incriminating responses to the prosecutor.

  On the other hand, if a court officer makes a casual remark to a prisoner without intending to incriminate, and the prisoner responds with an admission, the response does not violate Article 12. *Comm. v. Bandy,* 38 Mass. App. Ct. 329 (1995).

- *Comm. v. Howard,* 446 Mass. 563 (2006): Richard Howard raped his 14 year old niece. He threatened to kill her if she told anyone. A few months later, the victim found out she was pregnant. Brenda Mozdzierz, a DCF investigator, and Walter Dacyczyn, a state police trooper, met as part of a team to interview the victim. Afterwards, Dacyczyn told Mozdzierz not to make contact with Howard until further notice.

  Howard was arrested and arraigned, yet Mozdzierz went to the courthouse to talk with him. Since Mozdzierz was a government official, her incriminating interview was considered the same as police interrogation. She violated Howard's Article 12 rights, and his comments to her were suppressed.[3]

---

3 Fortunately, Howard was still found guilty based on DNA evidence.

Part VI

IDENTIFICATIONS

Chapters 24 – 25

State Action & Right to Counsel

PRINCIPLES

A crucial function of police work involves accurately identifying offenders. Officers must be well-versed in the applicable procedures because "the identification of the perpetrator is the most frequently litigated issue of criminal trials in the superior court."[1]

Officers must carefully conduct identifications to avoid unjust results. Mistaken identification remains the primary cause of wrongful convictions. *Comm. v. Johnson*, 420 Mass. 458 (1995).

The procedures which officers use to identify an offender must satisfy two constitutional requirements:

- **Right to Counsel.** The Sixth Amendment requires that those subjected to certain identification procedures receive the assistance of counsel.

- **Fundamental Fairness.** The due process clause of the Fourteenth Amendment demands that officers use a fair process to identify an offender. An unfair process is unnecessarily suggestive in a way that risks misidentifying the accused.

STATE ACTION

State action exists whenever an identification process is initiated by law enforcement. State action also involves *contrived encounters*, which consist of calculated moves by the police to bring about the observation of a suspect by a witness. *Comm. v. Redmond*, 357 Mass. 333 (1970) (a witness was purposefully asked by investigators to come to the station 47 days after a robbery to view their suspect before his lawyer arrived).

Accidental encounters that lead to an identification are typically admissible because they are not the result of state action. *Comm. v. McWilliams*, 473 Mass. 606 (2016): A witness to a bank robbery recognized the defendant as he walked down the street. He took a picture of him with his cell phone, went into the bank, showed it to the teller, and asked her if it depicted the robber. The witness did nothing to pressure the teller into confirming his own suspicion. He wanted to learn whether the robber was outside the bank and police should be called.

---

1 J.W. Carney, "Issues in Eyewitness ID Cases" in Blumenson, ed., *Massachusetts Criminal Defense*.

Comm. v. Calhoun, 28 Mass. App. Ct. 949 (1990): In almost comic fashion, the victim was being interviewed when the suspect happened to arrive at the station to retrieve his towed car. The victim spontaneously identified him as the getaway driver from the armed robbery she had experienced. This happened even though investigators tried to shield her in another room when they realized their suspect was in the building. But she saw him because the custodian had just removed the door for repair!

However, accidental identifications are no longer automatically admissible.

- *Comm. v. Jones*, 423 Mass. 99 (1996) featured a key witness who had two highly suggestive encounters with the defendant. While the police played no part in arranging them, their suggestive nature troubled the SJC.

  The encounters occurred months after the crime. On two separate occasions, the main witness saw Jones, an African American, in court shackled to the Vietnamese man whom she had definitely seen at the motel the night of the crime. She claimed that Jones was the black man involved. However, the police had not recorded her original description of the man she had seen quickly in the lobby. Without this information, the jury had no way of comparing Jones' appearance with the witness' prior description *before* the suggestive encounters. The SJC felt justice required suppressing the ID.

- Compare *Comm. v. Horton*, 434 Mass. 823 (2001): The victim of a shooting was initially unable to identify Horton's picture in an array. The victim then saw a newspaper article concerning the defendant's arrest for the shooting. The victim was in Florida at the time and his father had sent him the article. Since the police were not involved in transmitting the newspaper article, the identification was not improper. Unlike *Jones*, this case involved the witness' exposure to a single newspaper photograph. As a general rule, if the police do not manipulate the press reports, media exposure is not a reason to invalidate an identification. Moreover, in *Horton*, the victim had been with the defendant during the evening before the shooting, so there was a solid foundation for the identification.

RIGHT TO COUNSEL

Identification procedures may be characterized as either "corporeal" or "noncorporeal."

- **Corporeal identifications involve a live witness viewing the suspect in person.** Police techniques include showups, field views, live lineups, and live voice identifications.

- **Noncorporeal identifications involve a witness viewing a representation of a suspect.** Police techniques in this category include single photograph displays, photo lineups, composite drawings, and the identification of objects.

NONCORPOREAL PROCEDURES: NO RIGHT TO COUNSEL

There is _never_ any right to counsel during noncorporeal identifications. It makes no difference when the procedure is conducted. For example, officers may show a witness a photo lineup with the defendant's picture long after he has been arraigned or indicted. Officers need not concern themselves with notifying defense counsel prior to such procedures. *U.S. v. Ash*, 413 U.S. 300 (1973). *Comm. v. Ross*, 361 Mass. 665 (1972).

CORPOREAL PROCEDURES: UPON INDICTMENT OR ARRAIGNMENT

The right to counsel for a corporeal identification attaches at the moment the defendant is indicted or arraigned. This means that only a post-indictment or arraignment exhibition of the accused will trigger his right to counsel. *Comm. v. Tempesta*, 361 Mass. 191 (1972).

To illustrate how rigorously this rule is applied, consider *Comm. v. Key*, 19 Mass. App. Ct. 234 (1985). Charles Key was arrested on a warrant for armed robbery and taken to Roxbury district court. Police brought the victim into the courtroom and asked if she "recognized anyone." She identified Key. A minute later, Key was arraigned and counsel appointed to represent him. The defendant claimed his right to counsel had been violated when police caused the victim to view him "in the dock" awaiting arraignment. The court firmly held: The fact that an arrest warrant and complaint existed did not trigger his right to counsel. This right only exists at or after arraignment or indictment.

Before a corporeal procedure may occur without counsel, the defendant must waive the presence of his attorney. It should be in writing, and a defendant's *Miranda* waiver does not operate as a waiver of counsel for a post-arraignment or indictment procedure. *Comm. v. Cooper*, 356 Mass. 74 (1969) (without his knowledge and without counsel present, the defendant was viewed by a witness through a two-way mirror as he walked among police officers and others in a large room; this ID was invalid even though he had waived his right to counsel under *Miranda*). *Comm. v. Mendes*, 361 Mass. 507 (1972).

Cooperation with counsel. Police have been strongly advised by the SJC to provide defense counsel with the facts of the case and to consider their suggestions about the identification process. *Comm. v. Clifford*, 374 Mass. 293 (1978) (counsel should have been given more than 30 seconds to consult with his client prior to the police lineup). *Comm. v. Tanso*, 411 Mass. 640 (1992) (police defused any potential claim of suggestiveness by letting the defense attorney position his client in the lineup; court commended the investigators' professionalism).

Police control procedure. Defense counsel has *no* authority whatsoever to control or alter the way police conduct an identification procedure. *Comm. v. Tanso*, 477 Mass. 640 (1992) (defense counsel had no right to be present at a post-lineup interview with the witness).

25 *Fundamental Fairness*

Although eyewitnesses are tremendously helpful in identifying criminals, they are not infallible. Even honest, well-meaning witnesses make errors.[1] That is why the police have an obligation to minimize the chance of mistaken identification.

The Constitution commands that officers use fair methods to identify criminals. In other words, they may never employ an "unnecessarily suggestive" procedure that risks implicating an innocent person. *Simmons v. U.S.*, 390 U.S. 377 (1968).

The best practices presented here incorporate the Supreme Judicial Court guidelines. See SJC Study Group on Eyewitness Evidence.[2] Failing to follow the SJC protocol may result in suppression of the identification. *Comm. v. Thomas*, 476 Mass. 451 (2017).

FIELD INVESTIGATION

INTERVIEWS

Officers should obtain a <u>detailed description</u> of the offender(s) before an identification procedure. It allows them to focus on the right suspects. Also, by recording the witness' description in their field notes, officers prevent a defense attorney from suggesting that they or the witness tailored their description, after-the-fact, to correspond to the suspect selected. *Comm. v. Laaman*, 25 Mass. App. Ct. 354 (1988).

The witness' <u>opportunity to view</u> the offender at the time of the crime is a crucial factor. *Comm. v. Navarro*, 86 Mass. App. Ct. 780 (2014). *Comm. v. Boiselle,* 16 Mass. App. Ct. 393 (1983) (although the assailant wore a ski mask with eye and mouth openings, the witness focused on him for four minutes, from a distance of two feet, in good light; she remembered his "unique" dark brown eyes). Compare *Comm. v. Moon*, 8 Mass. App. Ct. 375 (1979) (witness had a short time to observe the assailant in weak lighting and provided a minimal description).

---

1 Research demonstrates that eyewitness testimony "causes more miscarriages of justice than any other method of proof." Donigan, *The Evidence Handbook*, 4th ed. (Traffic Institute, Northwestern Univ., 1980).
2 Report of July 25, 2013 at mass.gov/files/documents/2016/08/ql/eyewitness-evidence-report-2013.pdf. The Study Group insists that every law enforcement agency should have a written policy on eyewitness identification. Pages 85 to 109 of the SJC Report are the most applicable to police officers. Any specific reference to the guidelines in this chapter appears as "SJC Report at ____."

Officers get the most accurate information when they use a "cognitive interview" style.[3] The basic sequence is:

- **Minimize anxiety.** A witness is more likely to respond to an empathetic officer. A calm witness is more likely to accurately recall what happened.

- **Encourage the witness to take an active role.** Remember, the witness has the information. Officers who adopt a controlling tone inhibit people. The witness needs to feel free to share what memories he can access.

- **Ask the witness to mentally recreate the situation.** Recall is enhanced when officers have the witness place himself back at the scene and picture the event unfolding.

- **Request a narrative description.** Ask open-ended questions (e.g., "What happened?") and try not to interrupt. Some officers employ rapid-fire questions. This interview style *greatly* reduces the amount and accuracy of information.

- **Ask questions to get additional information.** Close-ended questions really help the witness provide more detail (e.g., "Did you see the license plate?" "What else do you remember about his clothing?"). On the other hand, leading questions distort memory and must be avoided (e.g., "Was he wearing a black stocking cap?" "Did the car have a Mass. plate beginning with RTJ?").

- **"Is there anything else I should have asked?"** This one question often prompts the witness to recall a unique fact about the offender's appearance or behavior.

- **Sincerely thank the witness and provide contact information.**

Hypnotically aided testimony inadmissible because it is not generally accepted by experts as a reliable method of enhancing a witness' memory. *Comm. v. Kater III*, 409 Mass. 433 (1991).

Officers may dispense with an ID procedure when a witness is personally familiar with the suspect. Comm. v. Adams, 458 Mass. 766 (2011) (during a police interview, Adams' 12 year old brother, Josiah, identified him as one of the shooters; there was no need for police to have him go through the motions of an identification procedure).

*Officers should **never** communicate to a witness their belief that the suspect committed the crime.* It then becomes impossible to determine whether the identification is the product of the witness' true recollection or police assurances that "they have their man." *Comm. v. Nadeau*, 2012 WL 5503344 (Appeals Court) (an intruder broke into the victim's home; before police arrived, the 911 dispatcher told the victim, "We may even have him"; this prejudice was magnified when police showed the victim the stolen goods from her house prior to her viewing the defendant alone).

Investigators should tell witnesses not to research photos of suspects on the web. Instead, suggest that witnesses only provide new information to police, who can then structure further investigation. *Comm. v. Barros*, 2020 WL 2516861 (Appeals Court): On October 29,

---

3 The original and best description of the cognitive interview appears in Fisher, R. and Geiselman, R., *Memory-Enhancing Techniques for Investigative Interviewing (The Cognitive Interview)* (Charles Thomas Publisher, Springfield, Illinois, 1992). The SJC Report mentions the cognitive interview at page 91.

Detective Brewster investigated an A&B at the Candy Bar on Tremont Street. The victim described the suspect as a short, Cape Verdean male in his late 20s. The club manager told the detective that the suspect was a regular patron and drove a blue Nissan.

Weeks later, the victim provided Detective Brewster with a photograph from Facebook dated November 19. She stated that this was her assailant. She provided the suspect's name as well.

Detective Brewster used the information to construct a photo lineup. The victim selected the defendant's photo and said she was 100 percent sure of her identification. This was unnecessarily suggestive, and the prosecutor could not use it at trial. The victim, also a regular at the Candy Bar, had obtained the defendant's name and photograph from staff at the club. Yet, at the time of the crime, the victim provided a limited description to police. Her viewing the defendant's Facebook photo happened after others told her he was the perpetrator. This was highly suggestive.

CORROBORATION

Reasonably detailed description creates reasonable suspicion <u>and</u> avoids claims of police bias. *Comm. v. Staley*, 98 Mass. App. Ct. 189 (2020): When the Citizen's Bank in Harvard Square was robbed, dispatch broadcast the description of the suspect as a tall, thin black male, aged 50 to 70, wearing a hat, sunglasses, and a black jacket.

Cambridge Officer McNeely knew that crime suspects fleeing busy Harvard Square often use public transit to escape, so he entered the MBTA subway at Central Square, the next inbound station. He commanded an inbound train to stop, knowing other trains had been halted at Harvard Square. Joined by Officer Norton, Officer McNeely walked the crowded train from front to back and saw a number of black passengers who did not match the description. In the last car, the officers found a tall, thin black male, between 50 and 70 years old. He had a black jacket draped across his lap.

Officer McNeely saw this man had a thin mustache and goatee. He checked by radio on whether the suspect description included facial hair. He learned the suspect might have had a thin mustache.

Officer McNeely asked Robert Staley to exit the train. He agreed. Speaking calmly throughout, Officer McNeely explained that a bank robbery had occurred nearby and Staley matched the description of the suspect. "If everything is okay, I will release you immediately and you will be on the next train," he said. Staley had packets of cash from the robbery in his pockets. This was outstanding police work.

Officers should seek physical evidence linking their suspect to the crime. Ideally, convictions are not based solely on eyewitness testimony. Here are two more examples of excellent police work:

- *Comm. v. Pickens*, 57 Mass. App. Ct. 926 (2003): Two women were raped in their apartment; while one woman was able to identify the defendant from a nonsuggestive photo array, the investigators added a piece of evidence that confirmed the accuracy of her ID — they lifted the defendant's fingerprint from a lottery ticket left in the apartment.

- *Comm. v. Miles*, 420 Mass. 67 (1995): The victim had been raped while blindfolded. Even so, the defendant fit the victim's detailed description of the man she had seen at the reservoir riding a bicycle. The victim later identified the defendant's bicycle. In addition, the defendant developed poison ivy on his entire body, similar to the victim. Poison ivy grew at the site of the rape. The defendant's former girlfriend corroborated much of the information told to the victim by her assailant, including that the defendant had lost a lot of weight and his seven year relationship with her had ended.

Officers may testify to the results of a field identification, provided the defendant has an opportunity to cross examine the original witness.

- *Comm. v. Cong Duc Le*, 444 Mass. 481 (2005) approved the testimony of a detective describing the witness identifying the defendant as the perpetrator of a vicious beating — even though the witness denied it in court. Allowing officers to testify about an earlier identification is a safeguard against the witness who later recants out of fear, pressure, or forgetfulness.

- *Comm. v. Machorro*, 72 Mass. App. Ct. 377 (2008): Jane and Mary were walking to a friend's home when an assailant ran up behind them and grabbed their crotches. Both women turned to face him as he walked away. Then Jane saw a police cruiser and got the attention of a trooper. She pointed at the assailant, and the trooper ordered him to the ground at gunpoint. Jane and Mary identified the man in handcuffs, Teodoro Machorro.

  At trial, neither Jane nor Mary remembered Machorro. However, Jane testified that she had never lost sight of her assailant and was 100% confident that "the man in cuffs" grabbed her. The trooper testified that Mary also identified the defendant at the scene. Since both witnesses were subject to cross examination, the police could testify about the field identifications.

The critical lesson for officers: Carefully document the circumstances and statements that occur during any ID procedure. If a witness later develops cold feet or does not remember, police testimony about the field identification may be enough for conviction.

TYPES OF EYEWITNESS EVIDENCE

Showups require the prompt display of a single suspect or a photograph to a witness.

Field Views occur when police arrange for a witness to observe a group of individuals in a public place.

Lineups are a display of photos or persons consisting of one suspect and ideally seven fillers.

Digital Imaging Systems (also called "Mug Books") are collections of photos of previously arrested persons which may be used when a suspect has not been determined, and other reliable sources have been exhausted.

Composites are sketches based on a witness' description.

PROCEDURES
SHOWUPS

The showup is the most frequent police ID method. It is quick and, if done properly, fair.

BENEFITS

Witness recollection fresh. In the immediate aftermath of a crime, a showup allows a witness to view a suspect while the witness' recollection is fresh, which minimizes the chance of mistaken identification. *Comm. v. Crowley*, 29 Mass. App. Ct. 1 (1990).

Efficient procedure. The showup also has the benefit of being easy to arrange, which promotes efficient police work by enabling officers to quickly determine whether they have detained the perpetrator or an innocent person. *Simmons v. U.S.*, 390 U.S. 377 (1968).

STEPS IN THE FIELD

Reasonable suspicion is the minimum amount of information officers must have in order to detain a suspect for a showup.[4] At the same time, the police are not obligated to arrange a showup just because the victim is available. The police may opt for another identification procedure. The police should *never* repeat a showup with a witness who already identified the suspect. *Comm. v. Santos*, 402 Mass. 775 (1988).

Officers should arrange a showup <u>within 2 hours</u> following a crime.[5] *Comm. v. Phillips*, 452 Mass. 617 (2008): Responding to a shooting, Detective Dankers learned that the victim's body had been dropped out of a window followed by three men running from the house. Shawn Echols gave a description of the men. One was wearing a green jacket.

Three men were stopped at a liquor store, and Officer Danker brought Echols there. He said they were not the men who fled from the house. Soon after, Officer Holder saw Parrish Phillips in a green jacket hiding behind a tree. Phillips started to run, then stopped. The victim's wallet was found during a frisk. Echols came to the scene and identified Phillips.

The showup occurred within one hour of the crime. Echols did not hesitate. Since the ID took place in the dark, police properly used their cruiser "takedown" lights to illuminate Phillips for the witness. Also see *Comm. v. Meas*, 467 Mass. 434 (2014).

---

4 It is possible to have a suspect participate in a showup with his consent, but it is legally risky. Officers who lack a reasonable suspicion to detain a suspect should, if possible, use another ID procedure that does not require a detention, such as a field view or photo lineup.
5 SJC Report at 88 establishes the value of the 2-hour time limit.

Acceptable reasons for a delayed showup.

- **Very strong case.** *Comm. v. Hill*, 64 Mass. App. Ct. 131 (2005): The victim observed an individual in her bedroom looking through her jewelry box. The victim had an unobstructed view of his face and reported her observations to Officer Moody. Later that day, a witness told Moody that he had seen a man fitting that description exit a car parked near the building. He described the unique vehicle: blue body with a white top, square headlights, a white bumper sticker with black lettering, and a large dent in the rear passenger door on the driver's side.

  The next morning, Officer Moody observed a similar-looking car drive through a red light. He pulled it over and radioed for other officers to bring the victim to the scene. She arrived and identified the defendant immediately.

  Although 24 hours is a long time, this showup was not unnecessarily suggestive. Officer Moody had originally investigated the break and heard the victim and witness describe the intruder and his vehicle. He pulled over the defendant within a mile of the crime scene. It only took an additional fifteen minutes to conduct the showup.

- **Part of a series.** *Comm. v. Martin*, 447 Mass. 274 (2006): On a July morning, a 15 year old girl left the beach in Yarmouth. A man grabbed her from behind and threw her to the ground. She screamed. Another person approached, and the man fled.

  The victim told Officer White that she had a front view of her attacker — a white male, about forty years old, tall and thin, wearing a light blue shirt with a green alligator logo. She also believed he was wearing shorts because she could see his legs. Her assailant wore a yellow hat, and had a tan and brown hair.

  During the next four days, the police brought the victim to different areas in Yarmouth and Hyannis. Detectives and the victim stopped at least six times to view individuals who fit the general description. She did not identify anyone.

  Five days after the attack, Yarmouth police learned that Barnstable police had stopped a man who had been called to their attention by the victim's father. (Her father had been searching the area on his own.) At the time, the victim was at the Yarmouth police station. A detective told her: "There is a suspect on the beach." Upon arrival, the victim saw her father and realized he had alerted police. The defendant was standing with two uniformed officers. She identified him, specifically mentioning a mark on his head. The SJC held that this mature young girl was not overly influenced by her father or police.

  - *Series of showups similar to a lineup.* If the victim had assisted the police on the day of the attack and not been contacted until five days later, the showup would have been fatally flawed. Instead, the victim had looked at people in the community at least six times. At least two of these people had been flanked by uniformed officers. The final showup with the defendant was part of a series. It was the equivalent of a nonsuggestive lineup.

- *Other options.* The police could have used other strategies to identify the defendant. They could have: (1) attempted to obtain the defendant's cooperation to appear in a lineup; or (2) attempted to get his permission to take his photograph; or (3) photographed him without his permission during their threshold inquiry; or (4) placed him under surveillance. While other options may have been less suggestive, the one investigators chose was fair.

- **Confirmation of victim's chance encounter.** *Comm. v. Pearson*, 87 Mass. App. Ct. 720 (2015): On July 2nd, Stephanie Smith told police that she had been raped the previous week. On August 18th, Smith's boyfriend flagged down a police officer to report that Smith had just seen the man who raped her. The officer stopped Peter Pearson's vehicle, ordered him out, and handcuffed him. When backup arrived, the officer retrieved Stephanie Smith, who said she was 100% sure. The showup was proper even though it occurred 53 days after the crime. It was a chance encounter in "the world at large," so there was no suggestiveness.

- **Emergency situation.** *Comm. v. Cox*, 6 Mass. App. Ct. 968 (1979) (victim was in hospital intensive care unit, so showup was permitted thirty hours after the shooting).

- **Multiple witnesses.** This strategy employs a showup with one witness to supply probable cause to arrest, then officers do photo lineups with the other witnesses. Any suggestiveness associated with the delayed showup will not infect the photo lineups. *Comm. v. Astacio*, 2014 WL 738153 (Appeals Court) (good police procedure to conduct a showup with one victim 2½ hours after the robbery, and a photo array later with another victim).

Officers must prepare their witnesses:

- **Get a detailed description of the suspect from each witness before the showup.**

- **Keep witnesses separate.** The police must keep witnesses separate and tell them not to talk to each other. When witnesses interact, it is obviously suggestive because they tend to influence each other. *Comm. v. Marks*, 12 Mass. App. Ct. 511 (1981). However, if an officer makes a good faith effort to separate witnesses, joint viewing may be necessary in a highly tense situation. *Comm. v. German*, 483 Mass. 553 (2019) (after being shot at during a robbery, two terrified women refused to be separated for a showup; other witnesses had left the area, so police had to rely on these women for an immediate showup).

- **Read pre-selection instructions to each witness on the laminated card included with this manual.**[6] When using the card, officers should briefly pause after each "bullet point." This greatly aids the witness in comprehending how the procedure will happen. *Comm. v. German*, *supra*.

---

6 The Law Enforcement Dimensions' card was favorably referenced in the report of the SJC Study Group. The card contains the exact language in the SJC report. See pages 99 and 106.

Showup & Field View Witness Instructions

- You are going to be asked to view some people.*
- The person you saw may or may not be among the people you are about to view.**
- It is just as important to clear innocent persons from suspicion as it is to identify the guilty.
- Regardless of whether you identify someone, we will continue to investigate the incident.***
- If you identify someone, I will ask you to state, in your own words, how certain you are.
- If you do select someone, please do not ask us questions about the person you have selected, because we cannot share that information with you at this time.
- Regardless of whether you select a person, please do not discuss the procedure with any other witnesses in the case or the media.
- Do you have any questions before we begin?

* The SJC wants officers to say, "some people," even if the witness is engaged in a showup. SJC Report at 106. This is helpful because the same instructions may be used for "field views" (discussed in the next section).

** Whether it is a showup, field view, or lineup, this witness instruction is the *most important* in ensuring a fair process! When given, there is a 42% reduction in wrong choices. Equally important, the instruction has little effect on correct identification rates — only a 2% reduction.[7]

*** This instruction helps take the pressure off the witness — who may be afraid that the police will abandon their investigation if he does not pick a perpetrator.

Officers must present suspect fairly.

- **Ideally, transport the witness to the place where the suspect is being detained.** It is less suggestive to ride with the witness and have him look at someone, than to have a person exit the cruiser for viewing. Try to prevent the witness from hearing radio transmissions or other conversations related to the investigation.

  - *Alternative strategy:* It is permissible, based on a reasonable suspicion, to restrain and transport the suspect to a nearby location for a showup. This approach may be necessary with an injured and/or traumatized party. *Comm. v. Crowley,* 29 Mass. App. Ct. 1 (1990).

  - *Important caution:* Never bring the suspect back to the actual crime scene because his presence may contaminate physical evidence. He might argue, for example, that his fingerprints or DNA were left during the ID procedure. To avoid this, perform the ID near, but not at, the crime scene — e.g., an adjacent parking lot to the convenience store where the robbery took place.

---

7 Steblay, N.M., Social Influence in Eyewitness Recall. *Law & Human Behavior* 21, 283–298 (1997).

- **Do not tell the witness where the suspect was found, whether he said or did anything suspicious, or whether he might have evidence related to the crime.**

- **Present each suspect separately to each witness.** In multiple offender and/or witness cases, officers should take pains to present each suspect separately to each witness. This precaution ensures that witnesses will not influence each other and, equally important, will not be influenced to pick a suspect simply because he appears with another suspect.

    Key optional strategy: Once a witness identifies a suspect during a showup, consider having other witnesses view photo lineups instead. Should the initial showup be suppressed, the photo lineups will likely survive any legal challenge.

- **Remove suspect from cruiser.** Officers should *always* remove a suspect from their cruiser. It is highly suggestive to keep an individual in the back — an area universally associated with guilty perpetrators. In addition, the cruiser shields much of the suspect's body, making an ID less convincing than if the witness sees the suspect's whole body and face.

- **Position suspect so witness does not see cuffs.** Police will often use handcuffs to detain a dangerous suspect. Officers can simply turn the suspect so that the eyewitness does not observe the cuffs. This step helps to avoid sending the message that the police know they have caught the perpetrator. *Comm. v. Escobar,* 2014 WL 2006715 (Appeals Court).

- **If safe to do so, avoid having officers surround or hold the suspect when he is presented to the witness.** *Comm. v. Perretti,* 20 Mass. App. Ct. 36 (1985). Positioning *plainclothes* officers on either side of the defendant does not change the identification procedure from a showup to a lineup. *Comm. v. Delmore D.,* 2017 WL 1829787 (Appeals Court).

- **If necessary, use a flashlight or cruiser takedown lights to illuminate suspect.** *Comm. v. Drane,* 47 Mass. App. Ct. 913 (1999).

- **Present suspect as you find him; do not remove or add clothing.** For example, if the offender was described as wearing a red coat, and officers find a coat nearby, they should not have him put it on. There are two reasons: (1) officers risk contaminating the coat, which affects the reliability of DNA or other forensic testing; and (2) it adds to the suggestiveness of the procedure.

On the other hand, if officers detain a suspect wearing a red jacket, they should not have him remove it. Simply present the suspect as is. *Comm. v. Powell,* 72 Mass. App. Ct. 22 (2008) (man seen climbing out of a car dealership window at night; witnesses called 911 with a description, including a white hat and teal jacket; minutes later, Officer Randall detained Roderick Powell; witnesses identified him; the fact that Powell was wearing the hat and jacket was not a suggestive influence created by Officer Randall).

When a suspect changes his own appearance after police find him, officers may correct this. *Comm. v. Harrigan,* 2019 WL 4806158 (Appeals Court) (police found Troy Harrigan based on a witness' description of an armed robber wearing a certain color baseball cap with a logo; when officers told Harrigan he would be viewed by a witness, he turned the brim of his cap backwards; Harrigan did this twice, but an officer properly turned his hat forward each time).

- **As soon as an identification occurs, ask the witness: "Without using a numerical scale, how certain are you?"** Because certainty can be artificially inflated by positive feedback, the officer should ask for the witness' reaction immediately. Officers must avoid providing any feedback or encouragement.[8] In addition, numerical scales are discouraged because they tend to automatically imply doubt when there may be none on the part of the witness. It is most useful to hear the witness' verbal reaction, not their attempt to "quantify" certainty.

- **Sincerely thank the witness, remind him not to talk with other witnesses or the media, and provide contact information** (so he can call "when" he remembers anything else).

- **File a police report.** See last section in this chapter.

FIELD VIEWS

BENEFITS

Equivalent of a lineup. Because the witness looks at more than one person, a field view is more like a lineup than a showup. *Comm. v. Dyous*, 79 Mass. App. Ct. 508 (2011).

No time constraint. Unlike showups, field views may occur well after the commission of a crime. In *Comm. v. Levasseur*, 32 Mass. App. Ct. 629 (1992), a detective began to take the rape victim on trips to the factory where the defendant worked. She observed "thousands of people and vehicles." The detective never directed her to look at any particular person.[9] After nine trips spread out over a five-month period, the victim saw the defendant drive by and immediately began sobbing ("That's him! That's him!").

Reasonable suspicion unnecessary. Officers simply bring the witness to a location where the suspect has chosen to be, so there is no need to detain the suspect based on a reasonable suspicion. *Comm. v. Walker*, 14 Mass. App. Ct. 544 (1982) (police had witness walk through Boston Common without directing her toward any particular area).

---

8 SJC Report at 97. This precaution ensures that witnesses state their confidence level immediately without any confirming influences to contaminate their choice (e.g., the officer says: "Good choice, we thought he was our man" or "Don't worry, the other witness picked him out too") Wells & Seelau. "Eyewitness ID: Psychological and Legal Policy on Lineups," 1 *Psychology, Public Policy & Law* 765 (1995).
9 There is an aspect of this case that would be scrutinized more carefully today. The victim initially selected Lavasseur's picture from a collection of 60 photos. The field view followed because she told the detective: "I do not want to positively identify him as the man who raped me until I see him in person." Having a witness engage in two identification procedures with the same suspect is highly disfavored but, at the time, the Appeals Court approved because *the victim* (not the police) asked to see her selection in person, and the detective never made any comments about the photograph. See SJC Report at 100 discussing the danger of "unconscious transference" when witnesses see the same suspect in successive photo or in-person displays.

STEPS IN THE FIELD

Prepare witnesses:

- Get a detailed description of the suspect from each witness before the field view.

- Keep witnesses separate.

- Read pre-selection instructions to each witness from the enclosed LED card.

Go to an area with at least several individuals who look like the suspect. If the witness described the assailant as a 30 year old white male with a muscular build, and officers have her look at a little league coach surrounded by ten year olds, they are really performing a showup. On the other hand, if they bring her to a restaurant with 20 white males of various sizes and hair styles, and she picks out a waiter — that is a strong ID! *Comm. v. Chase,* 372 Mass. 736 (1977) (witness brought to lounge with twenty-five people).

- **Avoid courthouse.** It is hard to imagine a more suggestive setting. As a result, whenever the police intend to have a witness from an unrelated case view a defendant in court, they must receive *prior* permission from a prosecutor. *Comm. v. Napolitano,* 378 Mass. 599 (1979).

  A courthouse view is not always suggestive. The suspect should appear in an unsuspicious area (not the "prisoner dock"). *Comm. v. Lieu,* 50 Mass. App. Ct. 162 (2000) (victim picked out Lieu in court when he attended his friends' probable cause hearing; this was not suggestive because Lieu was in the middle of a group of other Asian males).

- **If possible, pick location where only one suspect will be present.** Ideally, in multiple offender cases, officers should take pains to allow each suspect to be viewed separately by each witness. This precaution ensures that witnesses will not be influenced to pick a suspect simply on the basis that he appears in the company of another suspect.

- **Effective strategy for multiple witnesses.** Once a witness identifies a suspect during a field view, consider having other witnesses view photo or live lineups. Should the initial field view be suppressed by a court, the photo/live lineups will survive.

Post-selection procedures:

- **As soon as an identification occurs, ask the witness: "Without using a numerical scale, how certain are you?"** This post-selection question appears on the LED card.

- **Sincerely thank the witness, remind him not to talk with other witnesses or the media, and provide contact information** (so he can call "when" he remembers anything else).

- **File a police report.** See last section in this chapter.

PHOTO & LIVE LINEUPS

COMPOSING LINEUPS

Photo or live lineups are composed in exactly the same way. Investigators should:

- **Get a detailed description of the suspect from each witness <u>before</u> the lineup.**

- **Include only one suspect in each procedure.** With a single-suspect lineup, if the witness picks a filler (a nonsuspect), it is an error that will not result in charges against the person picked. But if more than one person is a suspect, even a random guess by the witness has a chance of being a "hit" on a suspect. *Comm. v. Walker,* 460 Mass. 590 (2011).

- **Select fillers (nonsuspects) who generally fit the witness' description of the perpetrator.** When there is a limited or inadequate description of the perpetrator, or when the description of the perpetrator differs a lot from the appearance of the suspect, fillers should resemble the suspect in significant features. Do not use police personnel as fillers if there is a possibility that the witness saw them previously. Above all, investigators must ensure that their suspect does not unfairly stand out.[10]

- **Complete uniformity of features is not required.** A lineup in which all people look very similar actually reduces the chance of an accurate identification by a witness with a good memory. Avoid using fillers who so closely resemble the suspect that a person familiar with the suspect might find it difficult to distinguish him from the fillers. *Comm. v. Jones,* 375 Mass. 349 (1978).

Create a consistent appearance between the suspect and fillers with respect to any unique feature (e.g., scars, tattoos) by artificially adding or concealing that feature.

- **A distinguishing feature is only acceptable when it has *no* influence on the witness.** *Comm. v. Arzola,* 470 Mass. 809 (2015) (the victim told police that the assailant wore a gray shirt; the defendant was the only person in the photo lineup wearing a gray shirt, however, the witness mentioned his hair, complexion, and eyes — not shirt color — as the reason for her identification). *Comm. v. Holland,* 410 Mass. 248 (1991) (only defendant's photo depicted long hair, but this was not suggestive because the victim had described her attacker as having short hair; therefore, her choice of the defendant's photo, in spite of his long hair, was even more reliable).

- **Mug shots imply the existence of a prior record and are suggestive.** Police must minimize prejudice by masking the signs that the photos are mug shots (severing front and profile views; removing height scales and chest plates with a name or number). *Comm. v. Gee,* 36 Mass. App. Ct. 154 (1994).

---

10 Wells, G. "The Selection of Distracters for Eyewitness Lineups." *Journal of Applied Psychology* 78, 835–844.

Lineups must have a total of 8 photos, unless exigent circumstances justify presenting a reduced number. Comm. v. Pina, 481 Mass. 413 (2019).

- **Select a photo that resembles the suspect's appearance at the time of the incident.**

- **Position the suspect randomly in each lineup, both across cases and with multiple witnesses in the same case.** For example, do not have the suspect always positioned in the number five slot if there will be three witnesses that view the lineup.

- **When showing a new suspect, avoid reusing all the fillers in lineups previously shown to the same witness.** It is good to re-use a few fillers.

- **Ensure that no writing concerning a previous arrest is visible to the witness.** *Comm. v. Vardinski,* 438 Mass. 444 (2003) (highly prejudicial for the back of the suspect's photo to contain the notation "Boston Police Department Mug Shot Form").

- **Do a last check of the photos or individuals in the lineup.** Make sure a distinctive feature of the suspect does not stand out. *Comm. v. Thornley,* 406 Mass. 96 (1989) (only defendant was pictured with eyeglasses, which was the major reason why witnesses selected his photo).

CONDUCTING SEQUENTIAL LINEUPS

Police should use the <u>sequential</u> method[11] *and, if practical, video or audio record the entire procedure.*[12] A recording is the best evidence of police professionalism *and* the reactions of the witness during the process.

- **No joint viewing.** There are obvious pitfalls in having multiple witnesses jointly observe a lineup. In *Comm. v. Marks*, 12 Mass. App. Ct. 511 (1981), a mother and daughter, both victims of an assault, viewed the suspect. After hearing her mother identify Marks as the perpetrator, the 14 year old daughter also identified him. The court decided that the daughter's selection most likely had been influenced by her mother's choice.

- **Two-way mirrors permissible.** Standing behind a two-way mirror often makes a witness less afraid. A suspect who is shielded by a mirror may be less nervous as well. *Comm. v. Clifford,* 374 Mass. 293 (1978).

---

11 SJC Report at 88. When pictures or individuals are presented one-at-a-time in the sequential approach, it discourages the witness from simply deciding who looks most like the perpetrator, a phenomenon known as "relative judgment." Rather than relative judgment, the witness is forced to use an absolute judgment strategy: "Is Number 1 the person I saw? Yes or no. Is Number 2 the person I saw? Yes or no." False identification rates are lower with the sequential approach than with the simultaneous approach (where all of the pictures or people are shown at the same time to the witness). Lindsay and Wells, *Journal of Applied Psychology* 70, 556–564 (1985).
12 SJC Report at 88 and 102.

The lineup administrator must not know when the witness is viewing the suspect. A "blind" procedure eliminates the possibility that a witness will be unintentionally influenced.[13] There are two ways to implement this safeguard:

- **The lead investigator may put together a photo or live lineup, then hand it off to another officer who does not know the identity of the suspect.** This neutral or "blind" officer cannot possibly influence the witness during the lineup.

- **The "folder shuffle" is another strategy that works with photo lineups.** The investigator places each photograph into a folder and shuffles their order. The witness opens each folder so that the investigator cannot see which photo appears. The investigator does not know when the witness views the suspect. This technique is especially useful for smaller departments that may not always have a second officer available.

The administrator must read pre-selection instructions to the witness.

- <u>Always</u> **use the appropriate form.** See page 25-22 (photo) or 25-23 (live). Be sure it is signed and kept in the case folder.[14]

- **In addition to the form, officers may occasionally have to address other issues.**

  - *"Mug shot" comment.* If a witness says that he knows he will be looking at mug shots, officers should respond: "There are many reasons why our department has someone's picture on file. Do not assume the people shown are criminals, they may be in our files because they applied for a driver's license or gun, hackney, or liquor license. We also mix in pictures of officers not in their uniforms." *Comm. v. Lamont L.*, 54 Mass. App. Ct. 748 (2002) (advisable for police to instruct witness to draw no adverse inference simply because the police have an available photo of a suspect).

  - *Different types of photos.* If there are different styles of pictures or markings on some of the photos, provide the following instruction: "Please pay no attention to any markings on the photographs or any other differences in the types of photographs." Officers should try to avoid differences, but some deviation will not make a lineup unnecessarily suggestive. *Comm. v. Chase*, 372 Mass. 736 (1977).

  - *Protection.* It is entirely appropriate to agree to provide protection if a witness is apprehensive about viewing a lineup. *Comm. v. Watson*, 393 Mass. 297 (1984) (prior to the identification procedure, police properly promised to assist their witness in moving from the housing project where the crime took place).

The administrator must properly present the photographs or individuals to the witness.

- **Present one at a time.** Do not show photos side-by-side. This display erodes the effectiveness of the sequential approach by turning it into a simultaneous lineup.[15]

- **If a witness asks to look at a photo or participant again, show him the <u>entire</u> lineup one**

---

13 SJC Report at 88 and 93–94.
14 The language conforms to the SJC's recommendations. SJC Report at 106–108.
15 Lindsay, R., et al., "Sequential Line-Up Presentation: Technique Matters." *Journal of Applied Psychology* 76, 796–802 (1991).

more time. To avoid a request for a third showing, be sure to say, "I can only show you the entire group one more time." Change the presentation order before the second showing.[16]

- **As soon as an identification occurs:**

  - *Ask the witness: "Without using a numerical scale, how certain are you?"*

  - *Have the witness sign and date the photo chosen, and preserve all the other photos in the lineup for court.*

  - *Avoid reporting any information about the individual selected.*[17]

- **Sincerely thank the witness, remind him not to talk with other witnesses or the media, and provide contact information** (so he can call when he remembers anything else).

SPECIAL ISSUES

Children as witnesses. With a young child, the best practice is to present three photo lineups. The first has no suspect included to see if the child will make no choice. The second has a picture of a nonsuspect known to the child (e.g., "Oh, that's a picture of Uncle Marty"). The third should contain a photo of the suspect along with appropriate fillers.

The police must have a very good reason to present a suspect's photo twice to the same witness. In *Comm. v. Watson*, 455 Mass. 246 (2009), the first photo display occurred when the gunshot victim was in the hospital and heavily medicated. The second viewing occurred several days later when the victim was out of the hospital. This was acceptable under the circumstances, especially since the defendant's photo was in a different position each time.

This practice may also be approved when the second lineup contains a *substantially different* photo of the suspect. *Comm. v. Carter*, 475 Mass. 512 (2016).

Grand jury order based on reasonable suspicion. Police may attempt to identify a suspect by having the prosecutor seek an order for a lineup from the grand jury. The grand jury may order a lineup based on reasonable suspicion linking the suspect to the crime under investigation. The reasonable suspicion standard makes sense since, if police had probable cause, the prosecutor could already obtain an indictment. *Comm. v. Doe*, 408 Mass. 764 (1990).

Deliberate alteration of appearance. Sometimes a defendant will deliberately change his appearance to thwart a witness from making an identification. To combat this tactic, the prosecutor may request that a court order the defendant to change his appearance for a

---

16 SJC Report at 88 and 97.
17 *Comm. v. Bonnoyer*, 25 Mass. App. Ct. 444 (1988): An eyewitness recognized the voice of one of the robbers. She also noticed that the second offender had a large nose and light brown hair, but a mask covered his eyes and he did not speak. Police learned that the distinctive voice belonged to William Jensen, so they placed Jensen's photo in an array along with some pictures of others he was known to hang out with, including a man named Bonnoyer. The witness immediately selected Jensen's photo and, "feeling under pressure to make another selection," identified Bonnoyer as the second robber. A month later the witness told a detective that she had significant doubts about her earlier selection of Bonnoyer. The detective told her not to worry; Jensen had confessed and named Bonnoyer as his accomplice. Fueled by this information, the previously tentative witness identified Bonnoyer in court with supreme confidence. Suppressing her ID was necessary because it had been tainted by the detective's comment. Also see *Comm. v. Ayles*, 31 Mass. App. Ct. 514 (1991).

lineup (e.g., to shave or grow his beard, cut his hair, or wear glasses). *Comm. v. Cinelli*, 389 Mass. 197 (1983) (based on the witness' statement that the perpetrator had a slight beard, the defendant was properly ordered not to shave his beard for several days prior to the lineup).

USE OF SINGLE PHOTO IN THE FIELD

Photographic showups are more suggestive than in-person showups. *Comm. v. Moon*, 380 Mass 751 (1980).

Even so, a single photo ID may occur in exigent circumstances.

- *Comm. v. Leary*, 2014 WL 6676906 (Appeals Court): Michael Leary drove around a crowded parking lot, exposing himself masturbating. Many children were present. Police displayed a registry photo on a computer in their cruiser. This was proper even though the witness knew it came from a computer query based on the plate number provided. The procedure was not overly suggestive because the witnesses had already provided a description of the suspect (white male; in his twenties; with a white, ribbed tank top), and the officer gave them proper pre-selection instructions.

  Only 30 minutes had passed between the initial radio call and witness contact. There was a public safety concern (even though the crime was nonviolent), and police needed to rule this suspect in or out. The later showups with the other two witnesses were also well done.

- *Comm. v. LeBlanc*, 2017 WL 3862480 (Appeals Court): Police responded to the scene of a stabbing and learned that the victim had been in a fight with two men. The victim told police that the one who stabbed him was tattooed and had a "Mohawk" haircut. The officer recognized the description as matching Darrin LeBlanc, who lived in the area. The officer pulled up LeBlanc's most recent booking photograph on the screen in his police cruiser and read the victim showup instructions from the LED card. The victim immediately identified LeBlanc. The photo showup was fair. It occurred close in time to a serious attack.

Photo showup not justified days after larceny. *Comm. v. Carlson*, 92 Mass. App. Ct. 710 (2018): The victim hired professional movers to transport her belongings to her new residence. The day after the move, she reported that $30,000 worth of jewelry had been stolen. Police spoke to one of the movers, who said that Jason Carlson, who had just been employed as a mover for that day, had asked to be dropped off at a pawn shop on his way home. The next day, a detective went to the pawn shop and spoke to the owner, Euidong Do, who asked whether the detective had a picture of the suspect. The detective produced a photo of Carlson. Do positively identified him. Do gave the detective the jewelry.

The single photo showup was not justified: (1) This was a property crime; (2) there were no immediate safety concerns; (3) the identification did not occur immediately after the crime; (4) there was no risk the evidence would be lost or destroyed since the detective knew the jewelry was at the pawn shop.

A single photo may also be used in these situations.

- **Confirm suspect known by victim.** *Comm. v. Watkins*, 473 Mass. 222 (2015). *Comm. v. Bennett*, 2018 WL 4558138 (Appeals Court): Dymphana Jeffers was standing with her boyfriend, her brother, Timothy Barnett, and the defendant. An argument broke out during which Jeffers' boyfriend was shot. Shortly after the shooting, while the police were present, Jeffers hysterically stated several times that the shooter's name was "James Bennett." At the police station, Jeffers viewed a single photo of the defendant and confirmed he was the shooter. The police had good reason to show a single photo. The shooter had not been found, and police concluded that Jeffers already knew the assailant.

- **Learn whether witness recognizes person.** Police may show a witness a single photo if the officer "simply asks whether the individual recognizes the person." *Comm. v. Vardinski*, 438 Mass. 444 (2003) (police showed defendant's photo to a Veteran's Administration [VA] police officer and a VA patient; both confirmed that they had seen him in the area).

- **Confirm suspect who sold drugs to undercover officer.** *Comm. v. Sylvia*, 57 Mass. App. Ct. 66 (2003): Marcus Lawrence was working undercover. Cory Sylvia sold him cocaine. After leaving the park, Officer Lawrence drove away and reported to other officers that Sylvia was wearing blue and gray camouflage with a full beard and dreadlocks. Lawrence made another purchase of drugs from a light-skinned Hispanic male. He arrived at the station 40 minutes later. An officer showed him two booking photographs, one of a Hispanic male and another of Sylvia. Lawrence could not identify the Hispanic male, but he did say that Sylvia had sold him drugs.

  Cory Sylvia objected, but the court felt Officer Lawrence had been fair. Lawrence provided a detailed description of Sylvia *before* the showup. The streamlined procedure actually decreased the danger that "other images would crowd in" from other cases that Officer Lawrence had been involved in that day. Also, Lawrence did not identify the Hispanic person in the other photo. This suggested that Lawrence was not pressured to automatically identify everyone as a dealer.

- **Confirm suspect who escaped.** *Comm. v. Pierre*, 2017 WL 1907215 (Appeals Court): Trooper Ledin observed a vehicle speeding. It revved its engine, then made a quick turn and almost hit his cruiser. Ledin attempted to stop the car. Eventually, it skidded to a stop and the occupants fled. Ledin chased the driver, who was holding his waistband tightly. The driver jumped over a fence, and Ledin discontinued his chase. A firearm was located in the yard near the fence. Ledin searched the abandoned car and found a medical bill with a name on it. He entered the name into his mobile data terminal (MDT) and obtained the person's registry photograph. Ledin identified the person immediately as the driver and told dispatch he was 100% sure.

A video showup may be conducted in exigent circumstances. *Comm. v. Vasquez* 482 Mass. 850 (2019) (police had no direct witnesses to the shooting of a woman in a car, so they showed surveillance video separately to three relatives of the victim; the relatives recognized the defendant, who was the victim's boyfriend). *Comm. v. Pleas*, 49 Mass. App. Ct. 321 (2000) (quality of video was so poor that a police officer was allowed to testify that he could identify defendant Pleas because he had known him socially for years; it would have been misleading to require the jurors to rely on their own comparison of Pleas' court appearance and the video image — since he had changed his appearance for trial).

VOICE IDENTIFICATIONS

A witness may identify a suspect by voice. Comm. v. Cruz, 445 Mass. 589 (2005) (a store clerk was able to identify a masked armed robber based on his distinctive voice because he had been a frequent customer). The following precautions are recommended:

- **Witness should typically request procedure.** Unless he mentions it, a witness should not be asked to make a voice identification.

- **Close in time to the crime.** The voice recognition procedure should be conducted as close as possible to the crime.

- **Witness should not see speaker.** Preferably, the witness should not view the speaker.

- **Do not have suspect repeat crime phrase.** Hearing the same harsh words may make the victim or witness pick the suspect on that basis alone, not on the sound of his voice. *Comm. v. Marini*, 375 Mass. 510 (1978) (highly prejudicial to have the victim looking at the suspect as he repeated the vulgar words used during the offense).

Voice showup. In *Comm. v. Burgos*, 36 Mass. App. Ct. 903 (1993), 45 minutes after the crime, the victim identified the defendant as the man who stole jewelry from her at knife point. First, the victim made a visual identification, then the defendant said something. On hearing him speak, the victim declared she was absolutely sure he was her assailant.

Lineup procedure.

- **The best practice is to change the order of the lineup following the witness' sight identification.** Then there is no risk that it will impact the voice process. *Comm. v. DeMaria*, 46 Mass. App. Ct. 114 (1999).

- **Use the appropriate form.** See page 25-25. Be sure it is signed and kept in the case folder.

Court-ordered procedure. Comm. v. Miles, 420 Mass. 67 (1995) involved a victim who had the presence of mind to talk with her attacker following a rape in which she had been blindfolded. The police did an excellent job obtaining a court order for voice identification. The victim heard five individuals read the same passage from a fifth grade text book. The victim sat in one room, while the readers were in an adjoining room. The victim could not see the readers, nor could they see her. Defense counsel attended and selected when his client would read. The identification of the defendant produced a conviction.

DIGITAL IMAGING SYSTEMS ("MUG BOOKS")

The digital imaging system is composed of pictures contained within a department's database. To prepare for witness viewing, ensure that the images of the suspect are contemporary; attempt to show only one image of each individual; and select images by specific physical characteristics relevant to the suspect (e.g., race, age, sex).

Witness instructions. Instruct the witness without other persons present.

- **Describe the system only as a "collection of images."**

- **The person who committed the crime may or may not be in the system.**

- **The individuals depicted may not appear exactly as they did on the date of the incident because features such as head and facial hair are subject to change.**

- **Assure the witness that regardless of whether he makes an identification, the police will continue to investigate.**

- **Ask the witness to state, in his own words, how certain he is of any identification.**

- **Do not discuss the procedure with other witnesses or the media.**

COMPOSITE SKETCHES

A composite drawing should never be completed by more than one witness at a time. The police artist should explain the process. *Comm. v. Orton*, 58 Mass. App. Ct. 209 (2003).

While it is a very helpful investigative tool, a composite sketch may not, by itself, provide probable cause to charge a suspect. The composite may be the source of leads, but each lead must be "fairly tested" by another identification method. *Comm. v. Poggi*, 53 Mass. App. 685 (2002) (aside from composite sketch, proper photo lineup necessary to confirm that this defendant committed the armed robbery).

IDENTIFYING OBJECTS

Police may have a witness identify a particular object used during a crime. The stringent constitutional standards for identifying individuals do not apply to objects. Still, the police must conduct a fair procedure. *Comm. v. Thomas*, 476 Mass. 451 (2017) suggests the following:

- **Have the witness describe the object before it (or a photograph) is shown.**

- **Tell the witness the object shown/pictured may or may not be the one the witness saw.**

- **If an ID occurs, ask the witness to state how certain he is of the identification.** Clarify whether the object is the actual one seen by the witness, or simply looks like the object.

- **Document the procedure** — preferably by a video or audio recording but, at a minimum, in the incident report.

Examples of good procedures.

- *Comm. v. Berisilla*, 470 Mass. 422 (2015) (parking lot identification of a jacket after a shooting was critical to the police effort to apprehend the murderer; it would not have made sense in this situation to arrange a jacket lineup).

- *Robinson v. Cook*, 706 F.3d 25 (1st Cir. 2013) (officers took each witness separately to the station parking lot, where there was a row of cars; the victim recognized Robinson's car by the dangling rubber trim piece and a red warning sticker he had noticed during the incident; the other witness recognized the color, the rubber strip, and the fact that it was a Honda).

- *Comm. v. Smith*, 2012 WL 4936620 (Appeals Court) (photo lineup of guns admissible to prove defendant's possession of a particular type of firearm during the robbery).

DOCUMENTING IDENTIFICATION PROCEDURES

Officers must thoroughly document any ID process in their report. They should include:[18]

- **Any pre-selection description** of the offender by the witness.

- **The witness' opportunity to view** the perpetrator during the crime.

- **The date, time, and location** of any ID procedure.

- **Who was present.**

- **The witness instructions.** Just attach a copy of the card or form to the report.

- **The ID procedure** (e.g., showup, field view, sequential photo or live lineup, etc.).

- **The results of the procedure**, including the witness' own words regarding how certain he is. Results include anytime a witness makes an identification, fails to identify the suspect, or identifies the wrong person. Be precise. Do not write summary statements, e.g., "The witness could not make a positive ID of the suspect." Such a statement is uninformative and possibly misleading if, for example, the witness really said, "The person I saw is not in this lineup."

Comprehensive reports increase the likelihood of success in court. The legal assessment of a defendant's identification has two phases:

- **Initially, the defendant bears the burden of demonstrating, by a preponderance of the evidence, that the police ID procedure was unnecessarily suggestive.** If the court is not persuaded, then the identification process is admissible. On the other hand, if the accused meets this burden, then evidence of the field identification is excluded from the trial.

- **At this point, the prosecution's only recourse is to prove, by clear and convincing evidence, that the witness' ability to identify the defendant has an independent source.** If the court agrees, the witness is allowed to identify the defendant during the trial. If not, the case is typically dismissed. Whether an independent source exists depends on the court's evaluation of six factors spelled out in *Comm. v. Botelho*, 369 Mass. 860 (1976):

---

18 See SJC Report at 86.

- *Opportunity.* The witness' opportunity to view the perpetrator during the crime;

- *Accuracy.* The accuracy of the witness' description prior to the identification;

- *Time.* The amount of time between the crime and the police-arranged procedure;

- *Certainty.* The witness' certainty in making the identification;

- *Suggestive influence.* The magnitude of suggestive police conduct;

- *Mistake.* Any mistaken choices or inability to choose the defendant previously.

- **To convict, the jury must be persuaded — beyond a reasonable doubt — that the defendant was correctly identified as the perpetrator.** *Comm. v. Franklin*, 465 Mass. 895 (2013).[19]

The SJC now limits in-court identifications. Police officers and witnesses are no longer automatically allowed to identify the defendant during their testimony. *Comm. v. Collins*, 470 Mass. 255 (2014). Officers need not worry about the particulars of this rule. It simply reinforces the main message of this chapter: Sound field procedures are increasingly important and scrutinized when it comes to identifying perpetrators. *Comm. v. Gomes*, 470 Mass. 352 (2015) (high court promulgates detailed jury instructions on how to evaluate eyewitness identification evidence).

---

19 *Comm. v. Johnson*, 473 Mass. 594 (2016) ruled: If an out-of-court identification is excluded as inherently unreliable under *Commonwealth v. Jones*, 423 Mass. 99 (1996), then the in-court identification is automatically excluded. The "independent source" rule never applies to these cases, unlike those where police procedures were the reason that the field identification was excluded.

Photograph Lineup Instruction Form

- You are being asked to view a set of photographs.

  - You will be viewing the photographs one at a time.
  - Please look at all of them.
  - They are in random order.
  - Please make a decision about each photograph before moving on to the next one.
  - I am required to show you the entire series.

- The person you saw may or may not be in this set of photographs.

- The officer showing the photographs does not know whether any of the people in the array are the person you saw.

- The individuals in the photographs may not appear exactly as they did on the date of the incident because features such as head and facial hair are subject to change.

- You should remember that it is just as important to clear innocent persons from suspicion as it is to identify guilty parties.

- Regardless of whether or not you select a photograph, our police department will continue to investigate the incident.

- If you do select a photograph, I will ask you to tell me, in your own words, how certain you are of your identification.

- And, if you do select a photograph, please do not ask me questions about the person shown. The law prevents me from sharing information with you at this stage of our investigation.

- Regardless of whether you select a photograph, please do not discuss this procedure with any other witnesses or the media.

- Do you have any questions before we begin?

Witness' Signature _____ Date _____

Investigator's Signature _____ Date _____

Administrator's Signature _____ Date _____

Lineup Instruction Form

- You are being asked to view a group of people.

    - You will be viewing them one at a time.
    - Please look at all of them.
    - They are presented in random order.
    - Please make a decision about each person before moving on to the next one.
    - I am required to show you the entire group.

- The individuals may not appear exactly as they did on the date of the incident because features such as head and facial hair are subject to change.

- The person you saw may or may not be in this group of people.

- You should remember that it is just as important to clear innocent persons from suspicion as it is to identify guilty parties.

- The officer who will be administering the lineup does *not* know whether any of the people in the lineup are the person you saw.

- Regardless of whether or not you select someone, our police department will continue to investigate the incident.

- If you do select a person, I will ask you to tell me, in your own words, how certain you are of your identification.

- And, if you select someone, please do not ask me questions about the person. The law prevents me from sharing information with you at this stage of our investigation.

- Regardless of whether you select someone, please do not discuss this procedure with any other witnesses or the media.

- Do you have any questions before we begin?

Witness' Signature _____ Date _____

Investigator's Signature _____ Date _____

Administrator's Signature _____ Date _____

Voice Lineup Instruction Form

- **You are being asked to hear a group of people speak.**

    - You will hear them one at a time.
    - Please listen to all of them.
    - They are presented in random order.
    - Please make a decision about each person before moving on to the next one.
    - I am required to have you listen to each person.

- **The person — whose voice you heard during the incident — may or may not be in this group.**

- **Please pay no attention to the content of the words spoken. They have been chosen at random.**

- **The officer administering the procedure does not know whether any of the voices belong to the person you heard.**

- **You should remember that it is just as important to clear innocent persons from suspicion as it is to identify guilty parties.**

- **Regardless of whether or not you select someone, our police department will continue to investigate.**

- **If you do select a person, I will ask you to tell me, in your own words, how certain you are of your identification.**

- **And, if you select someone, please do not ask me questions about the person. The law prevents me from sharing information with you at this stage of our investigation.**

- **Regardless of whether you select someone, please do not discuss this procedure with any other witnesses or the media.**

- **Do you have any questions before we begin?**

Witness' Signature _____ Date _____

Investigator's Signature _____ Date _____

Administrator's Signature _____ Date _____

Subject Index

This subject index is in alphabetical order and designed to help you locate a topic easily.

A

Abandoned Property 11-15
Administrative Searches 19-1
Admission of Crime 3-6
Affidavit, search warrant 13-1
Agent of Police 11-2
Alcohol Warrants 13-9
Amral **Hearing** 13-11
Animals, protection 16-17
Anticipatory Warrant 13-6
Apparent Authority, consent 15-16
Arrays, photo 25-12
Arrest
- booking 10-1
- definition of 7-3
- jurisdiction inside MA 8-3
- jurisdiction outside MA 8-3
- post-arrest procedures 10-1
  - juveniles 10-5
  - OUI 10-4
- pre-arrest handcuffing 4-15
- probable cause 2-3
- right of 7-6
- warrant 7-1
Article 12 Right to Counsel 1-3, 23-1
Attenuation Doctrine 1-4
Attorney (see Counsel)
Automated License Plate Reader 20-14
Automobile Exception (see Motor Vehicle Exception)

B

Basis of Knowledge 3-7
Bail 7-9

Blood **Warrant** 20-27
Booking 10-1
- inventory 18-1
Body-Worn Cameras (BWC) 20-10

C

Canine Use (see K-9)
Cell Phone Searches 17-10, 20-1
Chokeholds 6-7
Clerk's Hearing (see Complaint)
Commercial Vehicle Inspections 19-3
Community Caretaking 2-22, 4-32
Complaint 7-10
Computer Records 13-1, 14-8, 20-7
Consent Search 15-1
- adult family member 15-13
- houses 15-6
- vehicles 15-8
- voluntary 15-1
Consequences, of unlawful acts
(see Exclusionary Rule)
Constitutional Amendments 1-2
Controlled Buy 3-21
Corroboration 3-11
Counsel, right to
- attorney notification 22-27
- Article 12 and Sixth Amendment 23-1, 24-1
- under *Miranda* 22-1
- waiver 22-17
Curtilage 11-7
Custody under *Miranda* 22-2

D

Declaration against Penal Interest 3-6
De-escalation 6-2
Detention (see Investigative Detentions)
Domestic Violence, entry 16-9
Duty to Intervene 6-8

E

E-911
- confirming caller identity 3-2
- silent call response 16-13

Electronic Evidence 20-1
Emergency Aid 16-13, 20-17
Encounter
- field 2-2
- difference from seizure 4-5
- initial frisk 5-1

Entrapment 3-23
Evidence
- preservation of 14-9
- types of 13-8

Exclusionary Rule 1-3
- exceptions to 1-4

Exculpatory Evidence 1-10
Execution of Warrant
- arrest 8-9
- search 14-1

Exigent Circumstances 16-1
- create exigency 16-20
- domestic violence 16-9
- emergency aid 16-13
- factors for entry in home 16-19
- fires 16-18
- homes 16-7
- hot pursuit 16-7
- house parties 16-11
- motor vehicle exception 16-1

Exit Orders, from vehicles 4-22
Evidence, care of/loss of 14-9
Eyewitness Evidence 25-4
- SJC guidelines 25-1

F

Fire Scene, searches 16-18
Flashlight, officer use of 4-19, 11-12
Force, use of 6-1
- deadly 6-6
- de-escalating 6-2
- demonstrations 6-5
- non-deadly 6-2
- proportionate 6-3

Foreign National 10-6
Franks **Hearing** 13-11
Fresh Pursuit
- in Massachusetts 8-5
- interstate 8-3

Frisks 5-1
- packages or containers 5-12
- persons 5-9
- reasonable suspicion for 5-1
- vehicles 5-13

Fruit of the Poisonous Tree 1-4
Functional Equivalent 22-10

G

GPS Tracking 20-18
Guns, report of possession 3-15

H

Handcuffing, pre-arrest 4-15
Hot Pursuit 16-7
House under Fourth Amendment 11-7
House Parties 16-11
Humane Practice Rule 21-13

I

Identifications 24-1, 25-1
- composites 25-19
- counsel, right to 24-2
- fair procedures 25-5
- field views 25-10
- lineups 25-12
- one-on-one showups 25-5
- photo arrays 25-12

Inadvertence Requirement 12-2
Incident to Arrest, search 17-1
- G.L. c. 276, § 1 17-6
- home (see Protective Sweep)
- packages or containers 17-14
- person 17-7
- vehicle 17-14
Independent Source 1-5
Inevitable Discovery 1-6
Informants
- basis of knowledge 3-7
- corroboration 3-11
- types 3-1
- veracity or reliability 3-4
Interrogation (see *Miranda*)
- mandatory recording 22-23
Inventory 18-1
- booking 18-1
- motor vehicle 18-4
Investigative Detentions 4-1
- activities 4-16
- duration 4-16
- movement 4-18

J

Joint Access & Control
(see Third Party, Consent)
Jurisdiction, for arrests 8-1

K

K-9 4-33
Knock & Announce 14-3
- knock and trick 14-3
- no-knock warrant 14-4
- rule itself 14-3

L

Lineups 25-12

M

Mental Health Seizure 9-8
Miranda 22-1
- custody 22-2
- interrogation 22-10

- juveniles 22-20
- public safety exception 22-15
- resuming questioning 22-32
- waiver 22-17
Motor Vehicle Exception 16-1
- probable cause 16-2
- scope of search 16-6
Motor Vehicle Stops
- conducting 4-19
- dealing with driver 4-19
- dealing with passengers 4-20, 4-23, 4-31
- exit orders 4-22
- factors to initiate
  (see generally, *Chapters 2 & 3*)
- inventory 18-4
- motor vehicle exception 16-1
- search incident to arrest 17-14
Mutual Aid 8-4

N

Names
- checking identities in field 4-16
- vehicle stops 4-21, 4-27
Narcan 9-5
Neutral and Detached Magistrate 13-1
Nexus, betw. place & items searched 13-2
Nighttime, warrant 14-2

O

One-Party Consensual Interception 20-21

P

Particularity, search requirement 13-6
Party
- loud 16-11
- under-age drinking/marijuana 16-12
Peace Officer Standards & Training Commission (POST) 6-9
Phone Call, right to 10-1
Pinging Cell Phone 20-14
Plain View 12-1
Plain Feel 5-11
Pole Camera Monitoring 20-12
PREA (Prison Rape Elimination Act) 10-3
Probable Cause 2-3

Promises, resulting in confession 21-8
Protective Custody 9-1
Protective Sweep 17-11
Public Safety
• entries in homes 16-13
• exception to *Miranda* (see *Miranda*)
• motor vehicle stops 2-22, 4-30
Pursuit, as a seizure 4-6

Q

Questioning (see *Miranda*)

R

Racial Profiling 2-15
Reasonable Expectation of Privacy 11-4
Reasonable Suspicion
• defined 2-2
• factors 2-3
Reliability (see Veracity)
Rental Vehicles 18-9
Right of Arrest (see Arrest)

S

Search Warrants (see Warrants)
Seizure, definition of 4-5
Show of Authority 4-5
Show Cause Hearing (see Complaint)
Sixth Amendment, right to counsel
• identifications 24-1
• interrogations 23-1
Staleness 13-5
Standing 11-18
State Action 11-1, 23-1
Stop & Frisk (see Threshold Inquiry, Frisks)
Strip Search 17-3
Suicide 10-3
Summons (see Complaint)

T

Testimonial Evidence 22-12
Third Party
• consent 15-11
• warrant to search 13-10
• warrant to search and arrest 8-12
Threats, impact on voluntariness 21-4
Threshold Inquiry (see Investigative Detentions)
Tracking Device (see GPS)
Traffic Stop (see Motor Vehicle Stop)

U

Underage Drinking & Marijuana Parties 16-12
Use of Force (UOF) 6-1

V

Vehicles, shooting at 6-7
Veracity 3-4
Voluntariness of
• any statement by accused 21-1
• consent 15-1
• *Miranda* waiver 22-18

W

Warrants
• arrest 7-1
• execution of 14-1
• search 13-1
Wiretaps 20-21

X, Y, Z (no entries)